13 – Lucky For Some

The History of the 13th (Lancashire) Parachute Battalion

Andrew Woolhouse
2013

First published in 2013 by Amazon Createspace

First Edition

ISBN-13:
978-1482029161

ISBN-10:
1482029162

The author welcomes and encourages comments and corrections to the material
appearing in this work. Please email them to woolhouse3@googlemail.com

Cover © designed by Joseph Woolhouse

PREFACE

Watching Major John Howard's glider force take Pegasus Bridge in the epic film 'The Longest Day' made Richard Todd one of my childhood heroes. There were no video recorders or DVD players in the 70's and the early 80's and I would only get to see the film once every few years. Nevertheless, the scenes of the D-Day landings were etched into my mind. I could never forget the film's dialogue either, "His boots are on the wrong feet", "Hold until relieved" and "John has a long moustache."

I grew up intently listening to my Grandad's war stories and running around wearing his father's Great War medals. I always wanted to know "Grandad, did you kill any Germans?" I'm sure every veteran of the Second World War has been asked that question at some point and in my younger years he would never give me a positive answer, but as I got older he admitted to me that he 'probably' did. With age I began to understand what he meant, he carried and fired the mortar for his platoon of the 4th Battalion Lincolnshire Regiment and had gone to Normandy a few days after D-Day. He fought in the Falaise Gap and from there to the outskirts of Le Havre, where he was blown up – by a mortar bomb on 3rd September (the anniversary of the beginning of the war and also my wife's birthday!). Evacuated home to spend over a year in hospital, his war was over. He often spoke about the friends that he had lost and from time to time, he mentioned his brother Walter. Walter was a paratrooper and was killed in Normandy, that's all he knew.

My Grandad passed away in 2003 and I felt lots of regret regarding his wartime experiences, there was so much more I wanted to know but never asked, especially because I was older (29) and better informed. Over the following years I learned more about the D-Day landings and decided that I needed to see the beaches and battlefields of Normandy for myself. I visited the usual places: the landing beaches, Pointe du Hoc, Pegasus Bridge, the Merville Battery, the Hillman and the harder to find Morris strongpoint's, Longue Sur Mer, Gainneville (where my Grandad was wounded) and of course the cemeteries (British, American and German). The one other place I visited was Uncle Walter's grave.

No-one really knew anything about Walter – other than he was a paratrooper and was killed near the Seine? I decided to find out about him. A quick internet search later and I found that he had been a member of the 13th Battalion (Lancashire) The Parachute Regiment, 6th Airborne Division, killed 26th August 1944 and was buried in St Desir Cemetery, the only man of his unit there.

I researched his unit, their tasks and their objectives. Dropping on D-Day and fighting across Normandy in the 'Pursuit to the Seine'. The war diaries showed me where they had fought and the area where Walter must have fallen. I came across a brief 13 Para history, written by a Major Ellis Dean and in it he wrote:

"And that was virtually the end of the campaign in Normandy, as far as the 13th were concerned. Other Battalions now led the advance and the Goal move towards the Seine occurred on 26th when in a desperate attempt to reach Pont Audemer before the bridge over the River Risle was destroyed, the Battalion set off on an early morning 'road walk – run'. To no avail, the bridge was blown and as a farewell gesture perhaps, the retreating enemy fired a last salvo, killing a member of the Mortar Platoon."

Walter was the only man of 13 Para killed that day, it had to be him. I managed to trace Major Dean and decided to make a phone call. "I was hoping to find out about my uncle, he was in the mortar's and was the last man killed in Normandy." I asked. "Yes, that's right. I was about 30 yards away." What a result! I couldn't believe it. Major Dean explained to me the whole situation, telling me that 13 Para were pulled out of the frontline straight after so Walter's body was taken to a nearby church and left for the unit taking over the area to deal with, the 49th Division – My Grandad's Division! He must have only been a couple of miles away from his brother.

By this time, I had begun researching 13 Para and soon collected various documents, photographs, accounts, letters and veteran stories, and in a few years I had amassed quite a collection, not only on Normandy but throughout the war. I consulted Major Dean and decided the best thing I could do with the large plastic box and a computer hard-drive full of information, was to write this book – documenting the whole history of the 13th Parachute Battalion from start to finish, attempting to honour each of their fallen ranks.

Researching this proud and gallant battalion has been very hard at times, especially when veterans I have been in regular contact with, passed away. Many passed away during the making of this book. Like before with my Grandad, I wish I had started many years before.

This is not an in-depth, flawless, military strategic situation book, but an easy reading perspective from the veterans themselves. A good knowledge of WW2 and the campaigns involved is not necessary but will no doubt help. To communicate the whole of the complex situations involved would be impossible and impractical; there are hundreds of other books available for the reader to refer to themselves.

I have tried to keep the book as factual as possible, cross-referencing war diaries with reports, eye-witness accounts and various documents. Spending time on the battlefields has helped me create maps and diagrams, coupled with some 'Then, Now and Ghost' photographs in order to aid the reader to visualise or to perhaps use the book as a simple battlefield guide. I do not profess to be an author, I have merely pieced the story together for the veterans, tried to fill in the blanks and correct a few errors made by 90 year old minds, trying to remember in detail, 70 years back. There will undoubtedly be slight mistakes and conflict of opinion, but these events did not happen yesterday.

Many thanks to:

Ellis "Dixie" Dean, David Tibbs, David Robinson, Ray Walker, Jack Watson, Dennis Boardman, Sir Peter Downward, Ray Batten, Alf Williams, Bill Sanders, Don Jones, Fred Wilcock, Fred Smith, Norman Skeates, Ken Oldham, John Wallace, Carl Rymen, Pieter Stolte, IWM Airborne Assault archives (Duxford), the National Archives and Lee Richards, the members of ww2talk.com and many others.

And finally to Diane and Joe – for putting up with the "boring" husband, father and holidays!

Andrew Woolhouse

TRIBUTE - ELLIS "DIXIE" DEAN

One man served with the 13th Battalion (Lancashire) The Parachute Regiment longer than any other and no-one was a more proud a member than "Dixie". Finishing the War in Europe as Lieutenant, he rose to Captain in the Far East and ended up as a Company Commander and held the rank of Major. In the New Year's Honours List for 1963 he was awarded an MBE for his services. His citation submitted by Lieutenant-Colonel G.W. Hawkes, MC, then Commander of 12/13 Battalion (TA), explains perfectly the kind of man he was:

RECOMMENDATION FOR HONOURS OR AWARDS

MAJOR ELLIS DEAN, MC, TD[1]

Award: Member of the British Empire

REMARKS OF BRIGADE COMMANDER
Most strongly recommended.

Signed: *A.J. Deane-Drummond*

Major DEAN joined the Parachute Regiment in September 1943 and served with distinction in the invasion of NORMANDY, where he won the Military Cross. He later saw active service in the FAR EAST before demobilising in 1946.[2]

When the Territorial Army was reformed in May 1947, he was one of the first volunteers. In 1954 he became Second-in- Command of 13th Battalion The Parachute Regiment and is now Second-in-Command of 12/13 Battalion The Parachute Regiment.

He is a first-class leader and a most accomplished and experienced officer. Despite a back injury in 1955, which now prevents him from parachuting, he has continued to work hard and loyally for the good of the battalion. It is only his inability to parachute which has prevented him being recommended to command the battalion.

On the amalgamation of the 12th and 13th Battalions in 1956 he was faced with the lack of administering the old 13th battalion detachment at LIVERPOOL – 80 miles distant from Battalion Headquarters. Since the difficult days of the amalgamation he has contrived by sheer hard work and unfailing interest in the affairs of the unit, not only to hold this detachment together, but to increase the recruiting to such a high level that it is today the strongest link in the Battalion structure.

His drive, experience and great sense of purpose have contributed enormously to the progress of the Battalion in this period.

---

[1] Territorial Decoration awarded for long service.
[2] He actually joined the Para Regt in 1942 when his parent unit 70th Royal Welch became 6th (Royal Welsh) Para Bn. It was Sept 1943 when he joined 13th Para Bn. The citation does not mention the Ardennes and Germany campaigns. His MC was for all 3 campaigns.

He has recently announced, with regret, his intention to retire from the T.A. active list at the end of this year due to increased pressure of work in his business and a desire to make way for others.

This submission is the third successive recommendation for an award in recognition of his outstanding and prolonged service to the Territorial Army.

After his Army service, "Dixie", as he was affectionately known, continued his love affair with his unit and comrades. He became the historian of the 13th (Lancashire) Parachute Battalion, wrote unpublished accounts of his wartime experiences (much of which are included in this book) and also wrote and issued the 13th Bn Newsletters.

But for a chance phone call looking for help tracing the circumstances of my Great-uncle's death, this book would never have happened. From there it was "Dixie" who helped me fill in the blanks, correct the errors I made and most importantly, he gave me access to the memory of a man who remembered events in great detail.

My heart sank on the 7th August 2012, the day I received the email from Fay & Bern Robins that I never wanted to read:

Dear Friends

It is with very great sadness that we have to report that Major "Dixie" Dean MBE. MC died in hospital on Sunday 5th August at the age of 90.

Major "Dixie" had recently suffered a stroke, the final straw after a long illness.

Our Major was one of the originals from the 2/4th Battalion The South Lancashire Regiment later to become a Veteran of the 13th Battalion The Parachute Regiment who fought from Normandy and went all through the war and was the last surviving officer to have done so. Afterwards Major "Dixie" was a founder member of the local TA.

The 13th Battalion was one of the Major's great passions and loves. Major "Dixie" kept in touch with many Veterans and was considered the 13th Battalions historian with his immense knowledge and produced a newsletter twice a year, even sending out his final one earlier this year while receiving "care" due to his immobility.

Major "Dixie" is survived by his loving family, wife Jean, a daughter and two sons.

Like many, we are honoured and privileged to have known Major "Dixie", Officer, Gentleman, One of the Best ! ! !

We will send round details of the funeral as soon as we have them, hopefully in the next couple of days.

Kind Regards
Bern & Fay

"Dixie" helped me every step of the way, but passed away before I finished.

Thank you "Dixie".
RIP Major Ellis "Dixie" Dean MC. TD. MBE.

CONTENTS

ABBREVIATIONS

105745	Map Reference	Est	Establish / Estimated
12/857	12 Komp, 857 Gren Regt	Excl	Excluding
2 i/c	Second-in-Command	Fd	Field
A/C	Aircraft	FDL	Forward Defence Line
A/L	Airlanding	Fm	Farm
A/Tk	Anti-Tank	Fmn	Formation
AA	Anti-Aircraft	FOO	Forward Observe Officer
Adjt	Adjutant	Fwd	Forward
Adm	Administrative	Gp	Group
Adv	Advance	GR	Grenadier Regiment
Airldg	Airlanding	Gren	Grenadier
Amn	Ammunition	Grn	Garrison
Appt	Appointment	HD	Highland Division
Armd	Armoured	How	Howitzer
Arty	Artillery	Hvy / Hy	Heavy
Att	Attached	I	Intelligence
Bde	Brigade	IC	in-command
Bks	Barracks	Incl	Including
BM	Brigade Major	Ind / Indep	Independent
Bn	Battalion	Inf	Infantry / Information
Br	Bridge / British	Inf	Infantry
Brhead	Bridgehead	Infm	Information
Bty	Battery	Instr	Instruction
Cas	Casualties	Int	Intelligence
CB	Counter-battery	IO	Intelligence Officer
Cdn	Canadian	Junc	Junction
Cdo	Commando	LAA	Light Anti-Aircraft
C-in-C	Commander in Chief	Ldg	Landing
CO	Commanding Officer	LMG	Light Machine Gun
Comd	Command	LO	Liaison Officer
Conc	Concentration	LST	Landing Ship Tank
Constr	Construction	Lt	Light
Co-ord	Co-ordinate	LZ	Landing Zone
Coy	Company	M	Mortar
Def	Defence	m/c	Motorcycle
Det	Detachment	MDS	Main Dressing Station
DF	Defensive Fire	Med	Medium/Medical
Disposn	Disposition	MG	Machine Gun
Div	Division / Divisional	Minefd	Minefield
DR	Despatch Rider	MMG	Medium Machine Gun
DZ	Drop Zone	Mor	Mortar

Mov	Movement	Rds	Rounds
MT	Motor Transport	RE	Royal Engineers
O Group	Orders Group	Ref	Reference
OC	Officer Commanding	Regt	Regiment
Offr	Officer	Res	Reserve
OO	Operation Order	Rly	Railway
Op	Operation	RM	Royal Marines
OP	Observation Post	RQMS	Regt Quartermaster Sgt
OR	Other Ranks	RUR	Royal Ulster Rifles
Ord	Ordnance	RV	Rendezvous
Paratp	Paratroop	Sec	Section
Pdr	Pounder	Sig	Signals
Ph	Photograph	Sig	Signal
Pk	Park	Sitrep	Situation Report
Pl	Platoon	SP	Self-Propelled
Posn	Position	Sqn	Squadron
Pro	Provost	SS	Special Service
Pt	Point	Str	Strength
PT	Physical Training	Sup	Support
PW	Prisoners of War	Tk	Tank
Pz	Panzer	Tkd	Tracked
Pz Gren	Panzer Grenadier	Tp	Troop
QM	Quartermaster	Tpt	Transport
R Sigs	Royal Signals	Trg	Training
RA	Royal Artillery	U/S	Unserviceable
RAMC	Royal Army Medical Corps	Veh	Vehicle
RASC	Royal Army Service Corps	Wef	With Effect
Rd	Road	X-rds	Crossroads

13 - LUCKY FOR SOME

The History of the 13ᵗʰ (Lancashire) Parachute Battalion

"Where is the prince who can afford so to cover his country with troops for its defence, so that ten thousand men descending from the clouds might not, in many places, do an infinite deal of mischief before a force could be brought together to repel them?"

Benjamin Franklin, 1784

1.   BACKGROUND TO AIRBORNE FORCES

Lieutenant General Sir Michael Gray KCB OBE the Colonel Commandant of The Parachute Regiment between 1990 and 1993 made the following statement:

Supreme fitness is required to build up the body and mind, in order to create total self confidence and to overcome the initial fear of leaping into the unknown.

Stamina is needed to carry the tortuously heavy loads of equipment and ammunition into battle. Above all, parachutists need the spirit of the warrior and to be imbued with the will to overcome the opposition; even when faced with vastly superior odds; and the endurance to carry on and continue to fight to the bitter end when that is necessary.

It is the mixture of these qualities and skills, together with parachuting, which creates a thinking soldier who, in the process, forms a close bond with his comrades. He knows the capabilities of the men around him, they know and respect him. He is mentally and physically robust and is therefore able to handle stress in all its forms. He believes that nothing can stop him, His morale is high, he is self-disciplined and totally motivated to win!

Such is the AIRBORNE Soldier!

The airborne soldier did not exist until the 1920's. The Russians experimented and developed a force capable of descending from the sky. They liked the idea of airborne infantry, and what they could achieve and were very proud of their methods, so much so, that they invited many officers from many countries to observe their exercises. Among the observers was Kurt Student, a German Colonel and an ex-fighter pilot veteran of the Great War.

Student became excited about airborne operations, but was powerless to create his own equivalent because at this time the 'Treaty of Versailles' was in full effect. But what he could do was to create a pool of skilled glider pilots, so German men were encouraged to take up gliding (a German air force was out of the question). During the 1930's the Germans became very skilled in the piloting of light gliders, many of whom became the hub of the Luftwaffe.

Also present at one of the Russian 'Locust Warriors' (as they liked to call them) manoeuvres was General Wavell, who in a 1936 War Office report, wrote *"If I had not witnessed the descents, I could not have believed such an operation possible."* He had just witnessed 1,200 men, 150 machine guns and 18 field guns dropped by parachute and assembled into a fighting force, without mishap.

In January of 1936 the Fallschirmjager (German paratroopers force) was formed and Kurt Student was selected as their commander. A single battalion quickly became a division, complete with gliderborne troops in 2 years. Each was a volunteer and trained in advance tactics that looked at assaulting and capturing strategic positions behind enemy lines. For 2 more years they trained hard and developed many new techniques in parachuting and gliding into battle. The men got massive urges to use their elite methods and did not have to wait very long. The Germans launched the first airborne assault on March 12th 1938, when German paratroopers seized and captured an airfield at Wagram, during the take-over of Austria. April 1940 saw further airborne attacks on airfields in Norway and Denmark.

A month later the Fallschirmjager's biggest impact was felt at the Belgian fortress of Eben Emael, reckoned to be impregnable and designed to prevent an attack by Germans over the Albert Canal. This did not deter the Fallschirmjager and with just 78 troops landing on top, in 10 gliders, they overcame the defences made up of steel and concrete cupolas with hollow charges. A little over a day later and the entire fortress and 1,000 Belgium prisoners were in their hands - all for the loss of 6 killed and 19 wounded. A further 2,500 paratroopers were dropped across Holland and Belgium and succeeded in their various tasks, mainly consisting of capturing key airfields and bridges. The elite troopers held on with grit and determination until relieved by the armoured units using Germany's new 'Blitzkrieg' tactics.

The very same day, 10th May 1944, saw the resignation of Neville Chamberlain and Winston Churchill became his successor. Very impressed by the dare, bravery and attack mindedness of the Fallschirmjager, Churchill quickly realised the potential and need for Britain to possess such a force. On the 22nd June 1940 he sent out a letter to General Ismay, it read:

"We ought to have a corps of at least 5,000 parachute troops, including a proportion of Australians, New Zealanders and Canadians, together with some trustworthy people from Norway and France. I see more difficulty in selecting and employing Danes, Dutch and Belgians. I hear something is being done already to form such a corps but only I believe on a very small scale. Advantage must be taken of the summer to train three forces, who can, none the less, play their part meanwhile as shock troops in home defences. Prey let me have a note from the War Office on the subject."

Ringway Airport near Manchester was chosen to be the home of the 'Central Landing School', later to become the 'Parachute Training School' (PTS). Major John Rock of the Royal Engineers took charge of the organisation. When he did he had nothing, no planes, no men, nothing. He brought in 6 Whitley MkII bomber aircraft, parachute instructors and packers from RAF Henlow. The first men to become paratroopers were those of No.2 Commando (originally from the South Lancashire Regiment) and they arrived at Ringway on the 8th July.

After the intensive training No.2 Commando become 11 SAS battalion and higher authorities were anxious to see what they capable of. In an 'experimental' raid, the battalion was to assault the Tragino aqueduct in Italy.

Operation 'Colossus' was the assault and destruction of an aqueduct over a small stream in the 'heel' of Italy. The aqueduct was the water supply for 2 million Italians and it was considered that by cutting off this supply it would create panic and alarm in southern Italy. A small raiding party known as 'X Troop' consisting of 7 officers and 28 men from the newly formed 11 Special Air Service Battalion under the command of Major T.A.G. Pritchard was dropped on the Tragino Aqueduct, under the cover of a diversionary bombing raid on Foggia. 5 of the 6 Whitley bombers dropped the men within 250m from the target; the sixth dropped its men 2 miles north due to navigational problems.

The main aqueduct structure was blown and now all the commandos had to do was to march 50 miles to the mouth of the River Sele. Here the British submarine HMS Triumph was to rendezvous the raiders 5 days later and extract them to safety. Unfortunately one of the Whitley's had crash landed after experiencing engine trouble at this very spot. HMS Triumph was ordered not to risk being spotted. It simply could not attempt to extricate the commandos, leaving the men of X-Troop stranded. They had split into smaller parties for the march, but all were eventually caught before they could reach the coast.

Expanding further, 31st October 1941 saw the formation of the 1st Airborne Division, consisting of the 1st Parachute Brigade and the 1st Airlanding Brigade (Gliders). The commanding officer was Guards officer Brigadier F.A.M. "Boy" Browning (left). A raid was planned by Combined Operations to test their capability and was passed as feasible by Lord Louis Mountbatten. Operation "Biting" (or the Bruneval Raid) was the plan to assault and capture a radar installation near the French coastal village of Bruneval.

After the poor extraction attempt of X-Troop in Italy, it was decided that the paratroopers must be given a realistic hope of a safe return to Britain. The Royal Navy with No.12 Commando providing covering fire would attempt to evacuate the paratroopers from the beach after the raid was completed.

'C' Company, 2nd Battalion of the 1st Parachute Brigade under the now famous Major John Frost (Arnhem fame) were the unit chosen for the task. During the night of 27th February 1942 Whitley bombers dropped the paratroops and within a few hours all objectives were completed without much trouble.

The raid was a resounding success although they lost 2 killed and 6 missing. A report by German authorities investigating the event stated that *"The operation of the British Commandos was well planned and executed with great discipline. Although attacked by German soldiers they concentrated on their primary task."* The radar had been stripped of components and 2 prisoners were taken one of which was the operator. The information gained by the 'stealing' of the installation played a crucial role in the RAF's fight against the Nazi regime.

By July 1942 the 1st Airborne Division had grown in size by another brigade, the 2nd, and was now a full division. On 1st August 1942 they officially became the Parachute Regiment. The headgear was chosen after an orderly was paraded in various colours and the choice came down to two, maroon or blue. No decision could be agreed on so the orderly was asked for his opinion "I rather like the red one" was his reply. The emblem was selected (designed by Edward Seago, camouflage officer of Southern Command) and the colours claret and blue (Browning's pre-war racing colours; they were not chosen, as has been suggested, by his wife, the novelist Daphne du Maurier).

The North African campaign began and a 3rd Brigade was formed, mainly as a pool of reserves. The campaign was a success and was followed by the Sicily and Italy campaigns. Many a bloody battle was won and British Airborne came away with the nickname 'Die Rote Teufeln' or 'The Red Devils'.

The Parachute Regiment soldiers can quite easily be summed up by words of Field Marshal the Viscount Montgomery of Alamein.

"What manner of men are these who wear the maroon red beret? They are firstly all volunteers, and are then toughened by hard physical training. As a result they have that infectious optimism and that offensive eagerness which comes from physical well being. They have jumped from the air and by doing so have conquered fear. Their duty lies in the van of the battle: they are proud of this honour and have never failed in any task. They have the highest standards in all things, whether it be skill in battle or smartness in the execution of all peace time duties. They have shown themselves to be as tenacious and determined in defence as they are courageous in attack. They are, in fact, men apart – every man an Emperor."

Churchill wanted *"to have a corps of at least 5,000 parachute troops"*. So on 23rd April 1943 the British War Office ordered a second airborne division was to be raised. The 6th Airborne Division was born. It was to be called the *6th Airborne* to give German Intelligence the impression that the British had a larger number of paratroopers than they actually had.

With the 1st Airborne Division away, Syrencot House was left quiet. This beautiful Georgian house near Figheldon once home to the 1st Airborne was now the same to the 6th Airborne. Major General Richard Nelson Gale was tasked with the formation of the new unit, having once been the commander of the 1st Parachute Brigade and fresh from his previous post, Deputy Director of Air in the War Office, he knew all about the problems and solutions involved with building an elite band of paratroopers. It was agreed that the divisional emblem should continue as the 'Bellerophon astride the winged horse Pegasus' as used by the 1st Airborne Division. A sign that was now famous, to friend or foe alike. It is a very fitting emblem as it illustrates the 'first ever' airborne warrior. Next, he decided that the divisional motto should be something that every one of his men could draw something from. *"GO TO IT!"* was chosen after being seen on one of the first Divisional Routine Orders. Gale explains this himself in his book 'With the 6th Airborne Division in Normandy'. *"This motto will be adopted by the 6th Airborne Division and as such should be remembered by all ranks in action against the enemy, in training and during the day to day routine duties."*

He already had the 3rd Brigade (although sadly under strength due to reinforcing the 1st Airborne). A Canadian parachute battalion was given to him, but he still needed two more battalions for the division. 2 infantry battalions were chosen to be converted into paratroopers. The men who's lives were to be changed for ever belonged to the 10th Green Howards (to become 12th Battalion - Yorkshire) and the 2nd/4th South Lancashire Regiment (13th Battalion - Lancashire).

After lots of hard work amassing troops for tasks ranging from engineers to military police, the final line up of the 6th Airborne Division thus became:

3rd Parachute Brigade

Brigadier General James Hill

8th (Midland Counties) Parachute Battalion
9th (Home Counties) Parachute Battalion
1st Canadian Parachute Battalion
3rd Airlanding Anti-Tank Battery, RA
3rd Parachute Squadron, RE

5th Parachute Brigade

Brigadier General Nigel Poett

7th (Somerset Light Infantry) Parachute Battalion
12th (10th Bn Green Howards) Para Battalion
13th (2nd/4th Bn South Lancashire) Para Battalion
4th Airlanding Anti-Tank Battery, RA
591st Parachute Squadron, RE

6th Airlanding Brigade

Brigadier General Edwin Flavell

1st Battalion the Royal Ulster Rifles
2nd Bn the 'Ox & Bucks' Light Infantry
12th Bn the Devonshire Regiment
249th (Airborne) Field Company, RE

Divisional Troops

53rd (Worcestershire Yeomanry) Airlanding Lt Regt, RA
2nd Forward (Airborne) Observation Unit, RA
2nd Airlanding Light Anti-Aircraft Battery, RA
22nd Independent Parachute Company
6th Airborne Armoured Reconnaissance Regiment
286th (Airborne) Field Park Company, RE
6th Airborne Divisional Signals
63rd Composite Company, RASC
398th Composite Company, RASC
716th Light Composite Company, RASC
6th (Airborne) Divisional Ordnance Field Park, RAOC
6th (Airborne) Divisional Workshops, REME
10th Airlanding Light Aid Detachment, REME
12th Airlanding Light Aid Detachment, REME
6th (Airborne) Divisional Provost Company, CMP
317th (Airborne) Field Security Section, Intelligence Corps
6th Airborne Divisional Postal Unit

Units Attached to the Division

The Glider Pilot Regiment
HQ, 245th Provost Company, CMP

The Parachute Battalion, circa 1944 to 1945

Battalion Headquarters (5 Officers, 22 men)
Commanding Officer (Lieutenant-Colonel)
Second-in-Command (Major)
Adjutant (Captain)
Assistant Adjutant (Lieutenant)
Quartermaster (Captain)

Headquarter Company (9 Officers, 226 men)

Company Headquarters (1 Officer, 10 men)
Intelligence Section (1 Officer, 8 men)
Signals Platoon (1 Officer, 27 men)
Mortar/Medium Machine Gun Platoon Platoons (1 Officer, 40 men)[1]
Anti-tank Platoon (1 Officer, 30 men)
Administrative Platoon (3 Officers, 62 men)

Three Rifle Companies (5 Officers, 112 men)

Company HQ (2 Officers, 13 men)
Three Rifle Platoons *each* comprised of;
Platoon HQ (1 Officer, 3 men)
Three Sections, *each* comprised of 10 men

Total Strength: 613 all ranks (29 Officers and 584 men)

The Elements of the Battalion

Battalion Headquarters

Like the standard infantry battalion there was a Lieutenant-Colonel, Major, Captain and Lieutenant, plus the attached Medical Officer. The remainder of the strength was provided by NCO's, Regimental Police and the batmen/orderlies.

Intelligence Section

The Intelligence Section was equipped with 8 sniper rifles, which were selected Lee-Enfield models fitted with telescopic sights. They were to be deployed as snipers, observers and intelligence gathering.

Signals Platoon

As well as carrying radio sets the Signal Platoon was also equipped with airborne bicycles and motorcycles to aid their message carrying duties.

Anti-tank Platoon

Equipped with 9 PIAT's, the platoon could defend the battalion from minimal armoured attack until the arrival of the heavier anti-tank guns in the glider elements. They also fielded 3 Bren guns for their defence.

---

[1] There were 2 Platoons, each with 4 weapons. The mortar tubes could be replaced by Vickers Medium Machine Guns; it was at the discretion of the battalion commander how many of each weapon he wanted (e.g. 4 mortars and 4 Vickers).

Administrative Platoon

The Admin Platoon collected the various tradesmen and attached personnel needed to support the unit in non-combat areas.

The Rifle Company

The Platoon had 3 Sections, plus a small Headquarters element consisting of a Lieutenant, Sergeant, Batman and runner. The Officer was provided with a pistol and Sten, the Sergeant a Sten, the 2 men each a rifle.

Each Section was commanded by a Sergeant; with a Corporal as his 2i/c each Section carried 2 Sten guns (carried by Sgt and Cpl) and 7 rifles (One fitted with telescopic sights). There was a Bren gunner.

The 3 Rifle Platoons served under a small Company HQ, commanded by a Major with a Captain as his second-in-command. Added to the usual NCO's and runners, were 3 medics.

"The order was given - Those not wishing to volunteer take three paces forward. I stood still and so became a parachutist by not stepping forward."

Colour Sergeant Harry Watkins 1943

2.   THE 2nd/4th BATTALION SOUTH LANCASHIRE REGIMENT

The 2nd & 4th Battalion of the South Lancashire Regiment's 'war' began on 1st May 1940 when they moved into the Walberswick area. They were part of the Costal Defences of Britain.

The Germans invaded Norway, Denmark, the Low Countries and France, using high tempo operations involving fast moving formations of tanks and armoured vehicles supported by paratroopers, artillery and aircraft. The BEF was finally defeated at Dunkirk and ousted from the continent and the threat that the Germans might invade Britain increased.

Coastal defences were built up especially in the Suffolk region as the beaches in the area offered excellent provision for the landing of tanks and related vehicles required for an amphibious attack. On top of this, large areas of flat land offered the Germans perfect paratrooper drop zones and Walberswick was such a place. The 2nd/4th set about building, reinforcing and manning defences. Wire was laid, marshes were flooded and bridges over dykes were removed or destroyed. The entrance to the River Blyth was blocked with block-ships. At the end of June 1940 the 2nd/4th area was visited by Winston Churchill who gave the defences his seal of approval. The Battle of Britain came and went, and along with it, the threat of German invasion.

By 1943 the 2nd/4th South Lancs found themselves stationed at Dover in another costal defence role. Most of the days and nights in early 1943 around Dover had the same story, a 2 hour barrage from the German long range guns at Calais over 22 miles away. Enemy aircraft would also strafe and drop HE bombs from time to time on the Citadel and Dover area. In between the shelling and bombing, various training exercises based on enemy attempts to land by parachute or by beach assaults were carried out.

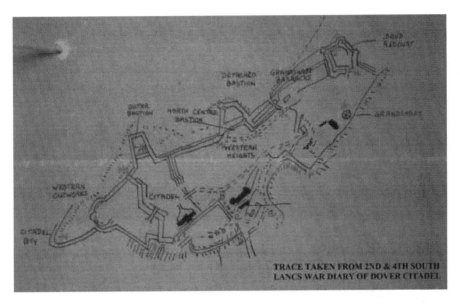

TRACE TAKEN FROM 2ND & 4TH SOUTH LANCS WAR DIARY OF DOVER CITADEL

John Cork (Dover Civilian)

"My Mother and I lived at 92 High Street. There were no warnings, just the screaming of a shell passing overhead or the sound of large banging. You knew you were in for a shelling, which could go on for a long time or a short period. On Dover sea front there is a large plaque from one of the German gun sites in France. 2,226 shells were listed as fired at Dover. The shelling started at 10:11 on Monday August 12th 1940. The first German shells landed on Dover and no warning or sirens went off — just loud explosions. The last shells landed on Tuesday September 26th 1944 at 02:00. Over 50 were fired and the last landed at 19:15. September was the worst experience for those in the Dover area.

"The saddest day of my young life was on Wednesday September 13th 1944, my best friend was returning from London, having spent a few days on holiday and getting away from the shelling. He was standing, beside his sister, on one of the platforms of Dover Priory Station having just stepped off the train. At that moment (16:03) a shell landed on the station. He was blown to bits and his sister was totally unmarked. His age was 9. His name was Fredrick Ernest George Spinner. To me he was just 'Freddy', my best schoolmate. And all my life, not a week goes by and I remember him — 60 years plus."

Lieutenant Jack Watson

"In July 1942 I was commissioned into the South Lancashire Regiment to the 2nd/4th Battalion. We moved from Otley to Folkestone and then onto the Citadel at Dover, all in coastal defence duties. We were shelled quite a bit in Dover, but the shells landed mainly in the town itself. From our positions in the Citadel we could see the flash of the guns over in Calais. We were quite safe in the Citadel, it was very cosy and warm and the soldiers lived in casemates."

After 3 years of defensive duties the 2nd/4th Battalion was about to be disbanded. On the 1st July 1943 the 5th Parachute Brigade was officially formed at Bulford and attached to the 6th Airborne Division.

Two months previously in May 1943, had brought further changes to the career of Brigadier Joseph Howard Nigel Poett as he was selected to raise and command the 5th Parachute Brigade. Coming from a military family background; he had attended Sandhurst and later joined the Durham Light Infantry. Further postings saw him join the War Office and there he served in several capacities, including being in attendance at a diplomatic meeting between Churchill and Roosevelt after the Pearl Harbour attacks. It was on returning home from these meetings he possessed the desire to take command of a Battalion again. The 11th Battalion the Durham Light Infantry became his next post until he was tasked with the raising of the 5th Parachute Brigade.

Brigadier J.H.N. Poett (5th Para Brigade)

"At Llanelli one morning early in May, 1943, I went into my office and found waiting for me a letter from the Military Secretary at the War Office telling me that I had been selected to command a Parachute Brigade and asking whether I was prepared to parachute. It was a complete surprise. Parachuting had never entered my mind.

"Of course it needed no thought by me. The Airborne Forces were *corps d'elite*. Every parachutist was a volunteer. The tests for selection were strict. When the airborne soldier won his red beret and wings he was a proud man. My reply to the Military Secretary went back within the hour. In no time joining instructions reached me. I was to form the 5th Parachute Brigade at Bulford, which would be part of the 6th Airborne Division which was being raised at the same time."

The 7th (Somerset Light Infantry) Parachute Battalion then part of the 3rd Brigade was transferred to the 5th Brigade to add experience and also to form the bench mark for the standard required. To build the new 5th Brigade up to full strength it required two more full battalions of approximately 600 men. A different recruiting system was taken for the formation of the two further battalions. Instead of selecting volunteers from every corner of the army, complete battalions were chosen by the War Office for parachute training. On 12th May 1943 the South Lancashire Regiment received notification from the War Office informing them that the 2nd/4th Battalion was to become a Parachute Battalion. No-one was forced to become a parachutist, the principle remained the same – each man would still be offered the choice, he still had to volunteer. Along with the 10th Green Howards, the men from 2nd/4th South Lancashire was chosen to be part of the newly formed brigade.

The Lancashire men were asked to parade in the other ranks mess hall at the Citadel and in walked Brigadier "Ted" Flavell dressed very elegantly, wearing his airborne patches on his highly decorated uniform. He was the owner of the DSO and MC with 2 bars, a veteran of the Great War; earning 3 MC's and had recently returned from North Africa where he had been commanding 1st Parachute Brigade for which he was

awarded the DSO. Inspiring and impressive he spoke about airborne troops and he explained that the 2nd/4th Battalion had been selected to become the 13th (Lancashire) Parachute Battalion and that every man would be given his chance to volunteer or could remain in the South Lancashire's and be transferred to another battalion as the 2nd/4th would be disbanded. There was a demonstration involving a parachute and the chance to earn an extra 2 shillings a day parachute pay. After the speech the men were told to form up into their companies and Major M.F. Hussey de Burgh repeated the information given by Flavell (left) and then gave the order, "Those not wishing to volunteer take 3 paces forward."

Colour Sergeant Harry Watkins

"We had no opportunity to discuss it with our friends but I had been serving with most of the Company for 5 years and had come to know and respect them, besides there always was a good spirit in the 2nd/4th and I suppose what I volunteered to do was to continue serving with my friends."

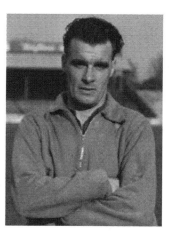

Stan Pearson the Manchester United and England inside-forward (left) served with the 2nd/4th's but was not allowed to train as a parachutist at the request of Manchester United for fear of a serious injury. He did, however, continue for a while in the Signal Platoon.

In al,l 13 Officers and 317 other ranks volunteered for parachute training. No-one seems to be able to come up with an answer as to why was the 2nd /4th's were chosen. I asked all the veterans that I interviewed the question and none had any idea. Back in June/July 1940 No.4 Troop No.2 Commando was formed from volunteers of 2nd/4th Battalion of the South Lancashire regiment. They were chosen for the Norway expeditions as they had received some training above the standard infantry training. Because of their already high level, they did not have to undertake the basic Commando training that other units did. The men of No.4 Troop fought in many key battles in World War 2, distinguishing themselves in the process. Look no further than the 'Greatest Raid of All' the attack on St. Nazaire. No.2 Commando provided the fighting troops for the operation. Many of the casualties and men mentioned in despatches were from the

Lancashire area. Major Copland was also a former South Lancs and earned himself the DSO for his part in 'Operation Chariot' as second-in-command.

John Wall, a pre-war territorial with the South Lancs, also states that his understanding was: "because the $2^{nd}/4^{th}$'s had already shown a keenness to undertake the parachute training, in particular that they had tried unsuccessfully to volunteer for an earlier formed battalion."

Major Ellis "Dixie" Dean

"Asking why the $2^{nd}/4^{th}$ after the war, I was told by a senior officer that the General Officer Commanding the Lancashire TA Division would have been instructed by the War Office, to nominate a battalion from his Division for parachuting. If he wanted to impress the authorities of how well he had trained his men, he would have detailed what he considered the best under his command. On the other hand, if he had a battalion which was a constant source of trouble, he might be pleased to see the back of it… So it' still a mystery, with a total of 18 battalions perhaps he put all the names in a hat and picked one out."

By the 25th May the Battalion was installed at Larkhill and on 18th June the Advance Party under Captain F.A.N. Elliston set of for Hardwick Hall to prepare the billets for the remainder of the volunteers who would all be travelling by rail on the 22nd June.

"Beside the lakes west of Hardwick Hall there was an army camp where in 1941 early pioneers of the British Airborne forces formed the 1st Parachute Brigade."

The Airborne plaque at Hardwick

3.   HARDWICK HALL

Hardwick Hall was the next stop for the volunteers. Located in the Derbyshire countryside and situated beside two lakes. Hardwick Hall was the Depot and School for Airborne Forces. It contained the Parachute and Air-landing Training elements together with a Battle School, and here men were selected to be trained as airborne troops. By the end of the war, some 17 Parachute Battalions had passed through the Hardwick Camp.

Once at Hardwick, the volunteers were given stringent medicals in order to meet the criteria required to be a parachutist. The basic outlines of which were:

1. Personnel will not be below 19 years and not more than 32 years
2. Without clothes must not exceed 182 lbs
3. Below the height of 6' 2"
4. Visual acuity must not be below 6/12 in each eye, with normal colour vision
5. Hearing must comply with hearing standards
6. Must be dentally fit with no full upper or lower dentures
7. Generally fit into army medical category A1

Brigadier J.H.N. Poett (5th Parachute Brigade Commander)

"I was pretty fit when I went to Hardwick but soon realized that the standard of fitness required in the Parachute Regiment was well above anything I had experienced. This unfortunately tested my damaged knee more than it would stand. I had had to be careful at my preliminary medical examination, before joining the Brigade, that the MO did not discover this weakness."

The training at Hardwick was heavily based on fitness and endurance; it really put the men through their paces. Every movement was performed 'at the double' even in leisure time proceeding to the NAAFI, or in the evening to the camp cinema, would be performed in this manner. Each new volunteer was given a leaflet in which explained exactly was expected of them as an Airborne Soldier.

Lance Corporal George O'Connor

"The first words of welcome I heard were, "the house is out of bounds, but there's a huge roller in the grounds if you have any energy left. By the time we have finished with you, you will be able to pull that across the lawn. By the time we have trained you, you'll be able to carry it." The training might have only been for a fortnight but, the day lasted from 6am until 10pm and it was all spent training, except for meal times and Sunday church parade."

AIRBORNE FORCES

You are joining the Airborne Forces. They are something new, different and specialized. They are composed of picked troops.

Show by your turn out, saluting, soldierly bearing and efficiency that you belong to a Corps d'Elite. The credit and reputation of the Airborne Forces are in your hands at much as in mine.

Whether you are dropped by parachute or landed by glider, you will normally go into battle by air. That is the difference between your new task and any other you have done in the Army. That is what makes your new work different and intensely interesting.

But do not think that you will be landed in the centre of Germany as a "suicide force." You will not. Airborne Forces will be used in close co-operation with land or air or naval forces. They will always be followed up and reinforced as quickly as possible.

The sort of tasks you may have to do are :—

(i) Capture a line or a particular point in the rear of the enemy, cut his communications, isolate him from reinforcements.

(ii) Attack the enemy in his rear, while our main forces attack his front.

(iii) Capture airfields in enemy country.

(iv) Assist seaborne landings by attacking coast guns and beach defences in rear.

(v) Be landed close behind our own Armoured Divisions, who have broken through, so providing the infantry, guns and co-operation they require.

(vi) Raid special objectives.

(vii) Assist, by landing with arms, friendly inhabitants of occupied countries in the event of invasion.

Occasions may arise when Airborne Forces will be used in a normal ground role. They are armed and equipped to do so.

In almost every case Airborne Forces will lead the way and be the advanced guard of the attack.

As this advanced guard, the Airborne Forces must be first-class in every way. Every member must be more efficient, more alert and resourceful, and above all more highly disciplined than any other troops in the world.

The following principles are essentials in war and the highest standards in them must be achieved and maintained.

1. Discipline.—With this introduction to your membership of the Airborne forces is given you my views on Discipline. Read them carefully. They are the result of experience on the battlefield and if you take them to heart and practise them, neither the Airborne Forces nor you yourself will fail in battle.

2. Speed.—In thought and action.—This is the prior requirement in war and all risks will be taken to achieve it.

3. Alertness and the power to observe.—Without extreme alertness the soldier is doomed. The man who is alert and sees his enemy first is the one who survives, not only to kill his immediate opponent, but to fight and kill again.

The British are naturally an unobservant people, and it is only by constant training in alertness and the power of observation that these become a habit. It is this habit gained by what you do in training that you will practise in war.

Saluting, especially the flags on Commanders' cars, is one of the best tests of the alertness and discipline of the man or unit. I judge the alertness and discipline, and therefore the efficiency of a unit very largely on its saluting. The test of war invariably confirms this judgment.

4. Initiative.—Not by leaders alone but by all ranks.—To do nothing when faced with a situation through lack of orders is little short of criminal. To have a go and do something, even if it is now proves wrong, is infinitely better, morally, mentally and physically. I will never drop on anyone who has a go, even if he is wrong.

5. Fitness.—You will be expected to travel by air, to land by parachute or glider, to fight immediately on landing, and to look after yourself on the ground, on compact rations, perhaps for as long as six days at a time. To do this you must be fit. The Airborne Forces may accept all fighting men, but you must be the best of the A1 class. Concentrate on building up your staying power, so that you can undergo hardships and think quickly all through. Train also to be capable of short spells of high-speed marching and fighting. If you are not fit you are a drag on your comrades and you will not survive in battle.

6. Marksmanship.—All weapons.—Airborne troops cannot afford to waste one round of ammunition. All

ranks must be expert shots, with all the weapons they are armed with, since the success or failure of any operation will largely depend on the marksmanship of each individual.

7. Supporting fire.—Both automatic and over-whelming.—No troops, however well trained and dashing, can advance against even minor opposition unsupported by fire. Further, a weapon that is neither shooting nor in a position to shoot is not fulfilling its function. It is essential, therefore, for the majority of weapons to be actually firing, or prepared to give, supporting fire, only those weapons essential to its success being carried to the assault. Therefore, every movement or offensive action will be heartily supported by every weapon available. This principle must become second nature and be automatic.

8. Security.—Airborne troops will invariably be given the fullest available details on maps, air photographs, and models of any operation they are called on to carry out. This means that at least 24 hours before the operation every soldier taking part will be in full possession of all the details of the operation. This demands a very high standard in security. In plain words —Keep your mouth shut. The success of the whole operation, your own life and equally, if not more, important the lives of your comrades, will be jeopardised, if one word is given away.

Now you know what sort of thing you will be required to do; and you know the qualities you will need to take your place worthily in Airborne Forces and to uphold the very high reputation they have already earned.

From now on you will be training hard. Your training will be sound, but you alone can get full value from it. Put all you know into your work.

Never forget that you will be the advanced guard, doing a vital task on which the success of a major attack may depend. Airborne Forces lead the way in battle; so must they lead the way in the whole Army and the world in spirit, bearing, efficiency and discipline.

[signature]

Lieut.-General
Comd. Airborne Troops.

1944.

THE AIRBORNE FORCES SIGN

The Airborne Forces Sign is Bellerophon mounted on the winged horse Pegasus, the first recorded instance of an Airborne Warrior.

His exploits are recounted in Greek mythology.

He is chiefly famous for his slaying of the fire-breathing monster the Chimæra. Mounted on Pegasus, with spear in hand, Bellerophon rode into the air, swooped down upon the monster and destroyed it.

Many stories have been written of the origin of Pegasus. The winged horse may symbolise the clouds, and the fight with the monster represent a thunderstorm in which the heavenly rider destroyed the evil elements of the storm.

The origin of the monster Chimæra is probably to be found in the eruptions of the volcano of this name in Greece.

Though Bellerophon is sometimes represented as an armed warrior, he most commonly appears in art when mounted on Pegasus, as depicted in the Airborne Forces Sign.

(50/4856) Wt. 55366 35m 3/44 H.& S. Ltd.
Gp. 393

Lieutenant Peter Downward

"The training was far tougher than anything I had yet undergone. A lot of time was spent in the gymnasium, climbing ropes, chest heaves, unarmed combat, vaulting over the horse and every day a workout around the surrounding countryside gradually working up to 10 miles in 2 hours on run-marches with full kit. You had to pass these tests plus a session in the boxing ring before you could go forward for jump training. If you failed you were RTU [returned to unit]. By the end of each training day one was too tired even to go down the local pub and simply flopped into bed straight after dinner. On getting up in the morning one felt muscles you had no idea ever existed, particularly in the stomach and back!

"An essential part of the training was over the assault course below the park area surrounding Hardwick Hall and across the end of the dammed up lake. At one point, we had to dash over a narrow bridge with explosive charges being detonated in the water below, throwing up plumes of water."

Private Geoffrey Read

"Beginning with a 20ft high obstacle constructed with wooden scaffold poles lashed into 4ft squares that had to be scaled, then dropping into the first of the lakes, being assailed at all times with thunder flashes hurled by enthusiastic and sadistic instructors, and while actually crossing the lake, being subjected to slabs of guncotton being detonated all around, and shouts from our tormentors "Get a move on!". On reaching the far side one encountered the first culvert approx. 2ft square, and about 20ft long, through which we had to crawl, it was very claustrophobic, made worse by having your face close to the heels of the bloke in front of you, at the end there was a drop of about 4ft directly into the next lake taking a miracle contortion to contrive somehow to keep your rifle dry. Once again whilst crossing lake number two subjected to the same torment, this time however exiting by way of clambering up the bank running down the slope, over an area criss-crossed with tripwires to an 10ft wall which had to be overcome, this being accomplished section by section, the first man arriving at the wall, leaning back to the wall, cupping his hands in front of himself thus forming a stepping stone, i.e. the rest of the section climbing by means of hands, shoulders, and over, the stepping stone then being pulled up by means of his rifle, continuing downhill to an area I can best describe as a slurry pit, to facilitate crossing this, there were 4 inch rails perched on top of posts clear of the mud requiring confidence and a keen sense of balance to run over, otherwise wading through and being faced with a big scrub-up. Clearing this, continuing on, trip-wires and other obstacles on the way, such as a 9ft ditch which had to be jumped, and just to make sure that we put in the required effort, coils of barbed wire were spread all over the bottom, moving on, two 10ft walls about 15ft apart had to be crossed by means of two cables, shoulder width apart stretched between them to be crawled over, again using one man as a stepping stone to reach top of first wall. Having navigated this obstacle, running on to encounter what was known as triple Danart, an obstruction which consisted of three large coils of barbed wire, one placed on top of two, to be crossed, with the first man of the section (taskman) literally throwing himself onto the obstacle holding his rifle in two hands across in front of his face for protection, this to allow the rest of the section to pass over, the last man over was to peel the taskman from the obstacle, sometimes being very painful. Carrying on we would arrive at the far side of the lake which had to be crossed using two cables about 4ft apart, one above the other stretched over the lake, resulting in a few soakings. Continuing on, back up the slope to encounter a wire mesh fence to negotiate, then being immediately faced with a drop of about 30ft, to be descended by means of abseiling to what turned out to be the target end of a 50 yard rifle range, across which we had to crawl whist live MG fire was directed on fixed lines overhead, then double to the firing point, where the armourer was waiting to make sure your rifle barrel was clear by application of a clearing rod and pull-through. Then, being issued with 5 rounds to be fired from the prone position at the now exposed targets, bearing in mind that this whole operation had been carried out in the fastest possible time, it was surprising that any of us could even hit the flipping target. Next, double back to cleaning area to get off the worst of the accumulated mud and slush before collecting some dry clothing and proceeding to the ablutions hut for a shower, then taking your denims to the drying room, then back to wash out the rest of your clothing."

Lance Corporal Don Jones

"My army career began after being conscripted in July 1943. After 8 weeks of basic training we were all sent to different regiments for further training. I ended up in Chester, joining the 22nd Foot of the Cheshire Regiment. With these I learned every aspect of the Vickers machine gun. It was during this training that I volunteered for parachuting, my reasons being that I did not fancy landing into battle on some foreign beach and secondly, I had a friend in the 6th Welsh Parachute Battalion.

"Next, I ended up at Clay Cross in Derbyshire; here we were tested to see if we were daft enough to be paratroopers. I obviously was. From Clay Cross my next destination was Hardwick Hall in the Derbyshire hills. Here we did what was called a 'Toughening up Course', this included rock climbing, endurance schemes and route marches as platoons for 10 miles, running and walking with full kit and rifle, all in 2 hours!" This was known as 'The Bash'."

Private Peter Fraggetter

"My group of 32 set off in the seventh slot. At long last the expected sweating agony had begun. We knew from experience that many would fall by the way, and by the second mile the odd man was already squatting at the roadside verge as 'holding' became out of the question. Sweat was already irritating maddeningly as it exuded from every pore, while the first blister points, the heels and soles, were making themselves known yet again. The full water bottle bouncing against your hip, the never used gas-mask incessantly chafing the small of one's back and the full ammo pouches niggling the rib and on top of all this there was the rifle sling in its customary, never ending groove.

"By the end of the 3rd mile some men had already called it a day. Perhaps they were already teetering on the brink of 'chucking' the whole para business, or even beyond their peak of fitness; too tired before they even started out. You easily recognised them for they lay resting on a comfortable grassy bank or sitting on a convenient kerbstone. Those who were genuinely unwell lay flat-out.

"Most felt the blisters burst before or during the 4th mile, a testing time for many of us. Sweat had turned to slush in your socks, and your shirt clung wetly to every stinking part of you not covered by sticking khaki denim trousers. More sweat stung your eyes and dripped off ears and nose, while your thumping head and heart threatened to burst. Your chest heaved and sank rapidly as it searched for ever bigger demands of oxygen, and again you asked "is all this worthwhile?"

"Towards the end of the 5th mile the trailing 'blood wagon' was picking up casualties and damaged men - those who had collapsed and hurt themselves on the unyielding road. Others were merely rolled aside to recover their senses, in which case they could either lay there moaning or, according to their frame of mind, clamber with left-over strength onto a following pick-up lorry. These chaps would have probably failed the Para entry test unless some mitigating factor of health prevented a better performance. Even a common cold could prove too big a handicap. Others might look despondently tearful, and some, utterly clapped-out wouldn't care less - they were beyond caring. The two prior weeks hardships were already too much; they'd had enough: it would mean going into a different regiment where such stringent fitness wasn't needed or necessary. My chest was in full heaving thump, for there was little worthwhile air about and I had really to work my lungs into finding the vital oxygen. On the run stages it became a continuous process of gasp, blow, gasp, blow that lasted for 10 minutes, before the march short periods gave respite. Then the heart pounding and blood bursting run of gasping for air had to be tolerated all over again. Some Hardwick bashes had taken place in rain, or in the wintertime. How I envied them on that humid, awful, hot and airless day.

"By the finish my feet were a mess of blisters, while my back was rasped badly. I alternately swapped my rifle from one shoulder to the other and cursed it twice every minute. In fact I cursed everything, including myself. My body was mechanical rubber when the 8th mile was behind us. Medics already punctuating the route ahead of us in anticipation were fully occupied as we slogged past them. We were virtually dried out; and even my shirt didn't now stick disgustingly to every part of my upper body. And like the others still loudly cursing the bouncing water bottles, I was very tempted to guzzle the contents, regardless. But I'd have to fall down first - and then get permission; then stay hors de combat. The army rules regarding drinking were stupidly strict. The stifling atmosphere was causing much difficulty in breathing, as I could well feel. Gasping was hardly the word for it. And through my boggled mind the possibility of self-destruction from exertion was now giving me dreadful thoughts. How I managed to put the 9th mile behind me I'll never know.

"Within yards of the point where the 9th became the 10th and last mile, the tall punctuated chap in front of me suddenly went down heavily in complete collapse. 'Crash' went the metal parts and rifle. Unable to slow my running legs I went sprawling full length over his instantly inert body, banging my knuckles and rifle onto the ground. Already crying, I was content to stay down, but Len and David wouldn't hear of it and dragged me upwards and onwards. How they found enough strength to lift me I can't imagine, for my sagging heap couldn't have been any help. Every bone now ached, made worse by the unhelpful fall: the few moments of inactivity had given a taste of bliss. But it didn't pay to stop; not even for a moment. The last mile was a tearful stagger home for what I remember of it.

"What was somewhat galling about our 'bash' though was the fact that those chaps who'd fallen out in the last few miles passed the test too! Not that I minded that in itself; I was glad for them. But it's that I could have done the same thing! I could have remained stretched out on that spotty faced chap and still departed for Ringway!"

Private Geoff Condliffe (better known as Count Bartelli, famous wrestler)

"In November 1943 just when I had worked my way up to a plum job as despatch rider to the Colonel, my transfer to the Paratroops came through and I found myself back in England at Hardwick Hall, training to become a member of that most elite corps, The Parachute Regiment.

"At Hardwick Hall I found the true meaning of two words: training and exhaustion. The course was designed to weed out the weak from the strong, and it did, as the Army obviously didn't intend to waste time and money in teaching men to parachute, which after all was only a means of transport, if they were not able to cope with the tasks and hardship they would meet once they were on the ground in enemy territory.

"The training was to prepare for a series of tests culminating in a 10 mile run, walk, run in battle order. The idea being that we ran until we were exhausted then walk a short distance and then run again. This had to be practiced and practiced so that quite often by lunchtime I staggered into our billets and lay spread-eagled on the bed with all my equipment on, thinking "to hell with my lunch, I'm going to lie here". There were times when I felt I didn't even have the energy to remove my equipment. But I was not alone; everyone else in the room was in the same state of fatigue. The instructors who were obviously very much aware of how we all felt, gave us a few minutes to regain our breath before they barged into the billets shouting "Come on lets be having you, get your gear off, it's lunchtime." That was the sort of encouragement our exhausted bodies needed, for it was very important that we didn't skip meals, we needed to keep up our strength to enable us to cope with the rest of the course. It was an intensive and condensed course due to wartime conditions and the urgent need for trained men; no one from the Commanding Officer downwards seemed to be still for a moment, walking was not allowed outside the buildings, everything had to be done at the double whether going to the cook house, toilet or whatever. It was a very arduous and testing tine."

Private Ray "Geordie" Walker

"After being told by my Platoon Sergeant "I don't want to see you back here with your papers franked RTU." I set off on my journey full of hope. Along with other hopefuls at Chesterfield Station we were met by a driver with his truck to escort us to Hardwick Hall which was some 7 miles distant. The men on my course were drawn from every branch of the army. One man had served in the Jersey Militia prior to the occupation of the Channel Islands by the Germans. Another was a deserter from Eire; he wanted to fight instead of being idle in a neutral country.

"Our task was to gain 100% physical fitness. From dawn to dusk we would always run and never walk. Within our group we had five men who found the training arduous. These men were Royal Navy Telegraphists and their mentor was a Captain in the Royal Artillery (some 8 months later, this 'exclusive' band of men played an important role during the D-Day landings in Normandy 1944).

"We spent some time in a lecture room dismantling and re-assembling items or domestic and military equipment. This exercise was to assess our hand-eye coordination. After which it was back to the assault course for some back breaking work. Soon our stamina and strength surprised us and we developed enormous appetites to replace our expended energies.

"In our free time we participated in sport. On one occasion our Sergeant ordered my pals and I to play hockey against a combined team of ATS and VAD nurses. Needless to relate the girls won. During the match one of our team was accidently hit in the mouth by a nurse wielding her hockey stick. For some considerable time Private McCrudden spat blood. Thereafter he was given the nickname 'Spit'.

"Saturday night was usually spent relaxing in the taverns of Chesterfield or Mansfield. Men missing the last 'Liberty' truck back to camp would 'acquire' bicycles and these were later dumped in the lakes at Hardwick Hall."[2]

At the end of 2 grueling weeks in Hardwick, those who survived were told that they had passed and now were entitled to wear the Parachute Regiment badge on their arms along with the Pegasus sign, but the wings (the most coveted item of all) would only follow after they were through the next stage, the jump course at Ringway.

---

[2] Many years later when the National Trust took over the Hall and the Park they dredged from the two lakes over 600 bicycles and 4 motorcycles!

"First I went to PTS my CO he advised
Bring lots and lots of underwear you will need them I surmise
But I replied by god sir no matter what befalls
I'll always keep my trousers clean when jumping through the hole"

First Verse 'Jumping Through The Hole'.

4.   RINGWAY

12th July 1943 was the day 335 men gathered at Ringway (above, IWM, Duxford), now Manchester Airport, for parachute course No.72. Of these, 253 were the Officers and men of the South Lancs that had stood up to everything that Hardwick could offer. The remainder were various other volunteers from all corners of the British Army.

Lieutenant Peter Downward

"There was an assortment of cartoon pictures around the mess by a wartime officer in the Regiment, I believe these still exist. One in particular I recall was of a chap hurtling earthwards with his parachute still packed on his back. The title, which might have little impact on present day youth, was "Hanging around waiting for opening time." There were others which were only an introduction to the sick humour that a parachute might not open!

"We were given an introductory lecture with pictures, and items of harness and canopy. It seemed that we would be using the new Irvine canopy, 32ft circumference, made of nylon and with one panel removed to allow easier spillage of air upwards rather than around the periphery; this would reduce any violent oscillation. There were 28 shroud lines, or cords, attached to the four lift-webs which stretched upward from one's shoulders – front left, front right, rear left, rear right. After explaining the

development of the 'chute' we were then shown the packing shed (left, IWM Duxford) where the parachutes were brought back for inspection and repacking in readiness for the next jump. Over the long packing tables on which the canopies and lines were stretched, were large notices for the benefit of the WAAF packers; "Remember, a man's life hangs on the job you do." It was always a bit of a joke not to get involved too closely with a packer as she had the means of bringing any affair to a quick close. Actually, if there were a parachute failure no girl knew who was the packer responsible; the serial number and record card relating to each chute remained confidential."

Private Ray "Geordie" Walker

"The journey from Chesterfield to Ringway was about 50 miles and I was able to appreciate seeing scenery which up to now was unknown to me. On arrival we were met by our RAF Sergeant Instructor who would guide us through every aspect of our training. After our briefing we were shown to our billets, nissen huts on the airfield perimeter. We dropped our kit off and went straight round to the cookhouse for a meal. Much to our surprise the food was superior to that of which we normally received from our own Army cooks. "Any complaints?" was never asked.

"Next day we marched over to a nearby hangar to commence training. Its interior resembled a gigantic gymnasium with all manners of equipment that I had never seen during my service with the infantry. We learned the art of falling without sustaining injury. Fortunately our falls were protected with thick mats. One item of equipment thrilled me. This was a steel rope stretching from the ceiling to the floor at an angle of 45 degrees. On climbing to the ceiling I held a wooden handgrip attached to a pulley on the wire, and then launched myself into space. The descent was rapid and on approach to floor level, I had to let go, hit a mat, roll over and come to attention in front of a vaulting horse. Any misjudgement resulted in a badly bruised body. After mastering the basics we progressed to using a special platform erected in the roof of the hangar. This was a mechanically controlled jumping platform."

Lance Corporal George O'Connor

"We were attached to a parachute harness that was suspended on a wire, which in turn was fixed to a revolving drum, with a fan on the end of it, to control the speed of descent when we jumped. The fan whirred like mad as you descended and did not stop until you landed with a thump on a mat."

Lance Corporal Don Jones

"Next was the greatest thrill of all. Draw a parachute, get on a bus and taken to Tatton Park 5 miles south west of Ringway. Here we did our first jump, from a gondola hung from a barrage balloon. You went up as five trainees with the RAF instructor to 700ft. Then the balloon stopped, the instructor called out "Action stations." pause then "Go!" and all members of the stick jumped, one at a time. From the balloon you fell for 120ft before your chute opened, you then looked around to see which way you were drifting. You then had to get your feet and knees together before you hit the ground and do a roll when you did. Then the chute had to be collapsed, get out of your harness and roll up the chute. After all this was done all that was left to do was to take your chute to a recovery wagon and go to the small wooden hut for a cup of tea and some cake."

Private Geoff Condliffe

"An unforgettable day for us all! We drew parachutes from the stores and heard words that were to be repeated each time we went for a chute. "If it doesn't work, bring it back!" This was the RAF store man's idea of a joke which was never found to be amusing as the paratroopers were uptight with pre-jump nerves. I was soon sitting cramped in the little basket suspended beneath a huge silver barrage balloon with an instructor and 4 other men. The great torpedo shaped monster made of silver nylon panels, looked like a gigantic whale complete with a tail. It was tethered to about 1,000ft of steel cable on a winch, mounted on a Fordson Lorry and operated by men of the Royal Air Force. The same type of balloons were used to protect London and other big cities from air attacks, in fact my home town of Crewe had been surrounded by them due to the strategic importance of the Rolls Royce factory which at that time was making aeroplane engines.

"The Fordson lorry was shackled to the ground with chains attached to rings set in concrete, to prevent it becoming airborne if the massive fish-like object was caught in the strong winds. The square passenger, basket underneath the balloon had a large hole in the floor and the sides were only about 3 ft deep, the rest was open to the elements. Being an open basket had its advantages, you could see everything that was going on and this to some extent took our minds off the ordeal that lay ahead."

Private Ray "Geordie" Walker

"The instructor shouted to the winchman sat at the controls on the back of his truck "Up 700ft and five to go." We sat on the floor with our legs protruding through a large hole. On the command, "GO!" I launched myself through the hole and out into space. At breakneck speed I fell 120ft before my chute opened. Now to prepare for a safe landing and follow the instructions shouted to me by the ground controller using his megaphone. Safely on the ground I felt exhilarated and looked forward to a welcome cup of tea at the nearby mobile canteen. Soon I was joined by my pals and we had much to talk about before collecting our parachutes and returned to Ringway, joking and singing."

Lance Corporal George O'Connor

"I was told fearful stories about the balloon jumps, but I ignored them, no-one could frighten me now. I had to admit, it was more frightening jumping from a balloon everything seemed so quiet while waiting to jump. The thing I disliked the most, was that the parachute took a lot longer to open, because there was no slipstream as there was from a plane, the chute seemed to take so long to open, it seemed as if it wasn't going to open before you hit the ground at about 120 mph."

Lieutenant Peter Downward

"I think I was last in the stick and I made it clear that I needed no 'pushing'. I gave the order to myself "Green on, Go!" and jumped. It seemed to be a long time (actually it was about 3 seconds) before I felt the jerk on my shoulders and realised I was no longer falling.

"Looking up into the canopy was the most wonderful sight, almost like an orgasm as one instructor described it. "Feet together, feet together, side left!" the instructor bellowed from his loudspeaker below and crump you were on the ground in a heap, and it was all over! A quick roll up of the chute and then over to the instructor who would tell you what you did wrong, or even what you did right.

"Back on the bus, everyone was recounting their own experiences, not listening to anyone else's, followed by singing parachute songs like "Jumping Through The Hole."

"Jumping Through The Hole"

First I went to PTS my CO he advised
Bring lots and lots of underwear you will need them I surmise
But I replied by god sir no matter what befalls
I'll always keep my trousers clean when jumping through the hole

Chorus: Jumping through the hole jumping through the hole
I'll always keep my trousers clean when jumping through the hole

I went into a hanger an instructor by my side
And on Ken Cardners circus had many a glorious ride
On these ingenuous gadgets said he you will learn to fall
To keep your feet together when jumping through the hole

Chorus

They swung me on the swing boys they shot me down a chute
They took me to a high aperture I though it rather cute
Said he this apparatus will teach you I recall to keep your feet together
When you are jumping through the hole

Chorus

They took me out one morning it was cold and damp and dark
They took me in a so-called bus bound for Tatton Park
In keeping with the weather I said to one and all
I take a dim and misty view of jumping though the hole

Chorus

They fitted me with parachute a helmet for my head
The sergeant looked with expert eye it fits you fine he said
I'll introduce you now to Bess for that is what we call
The big balloon from which you will soon be jumping through the hole

Chorus

Up six hundred five to drop said he
Five to drop good god I cried one of them is me
So clinging very grimly to the handles on the floor
I cursed the day I volunteered for jumping through the hole

Chorus

I hit my pack I rung the bell I twisted twenty times
Feet hung up in the rigging lines
I didn't care at all
For I had kept my trousers clean when jumping through the hole

Chorus

There's a moral to this story and it's one that should be told. It's the keeping of the trousers clean when jumping through the hole.

Private Ray "Geordie" Walker

"After completing the 3 balloon jumps we had our first flight in an aircraft. This was a 23 minute flight over the North Cheshire Plain in a twin-engine Whitley bomber. Our pilot was a South African and was badly scarred from a crash which left half his face blue from burns; he had the nickname "Bluey". We boarded his plane and prepared for takeoff and taxied out to the runway. Soon the engines were given full power, brakes released and we were charging down the runway and up into the sky. This flight enabled our instructors to see if anyone was prone to airsickness. The next time we wore parachutes."

Two day and one night jump completed, all that stood in the way of the trainee parachutist was the 5 jumps from a plane. Once inside the old Whitley the men sat (as there was no room to stand) 5 either side of the hole in the floor that was once the entrance for the lower gunner turret. Inside the plane was dark draughty and had a smell of the high octane aviation fuel. The instructors would check each man, and then would explain to them all that No.1 would jump from his side, then No.2 from the other and so on. Everyone knew this, it had been practiced enough. Parachutes were clipped up to the static line and then checked.

Lieutenant Peter Downward

"You went out in quick succession, each man shuffling forward on his bottom to jump in sequence as numbered. An essential part of the drill was to remember that 2 large cylindrical containers, each about 7ft long, would also come hurtling back in the slipstream in the middle of the stick. No.5 when he took up his position on the floor had to clip onto his static line a cord which in turn was connected to a pull switch; this was the release mechanism for the containers. As soon as No.5 jumped, No.6 would shout "container, container, container" and then jump. Failure to observe this timed delay could result in No.6 colliding with the containers as they flashed past under the fuselage.

"I jumped No.1 and was amazed at the difference in contrast with the exit from the balloon. One was aware of the immediate buffeting of the slipstream, the fuselage hurtling over you and the sight of the tail wheel as it flashed past, but what was fascinating (and consoling) was to see the rapid developing of the chute. We all agreed it was much easier than going out in cold blood from the balloon."

Brigadier J.H.N. Poett (5th Parachute Brigade Commander)

"A well-trained parachutist should be able to control the direction of his flight by pulling on the lift webs of his parachute and land into the wind with a roll. He should descend with his feet and knees together so as to help with this roll. During his descent he should be looking out for landmarks, so that on landing he knows where he is. I regret to say that I was seldom able to do any of these things."

Lance Corporal George O'Connor

"I swung my legs over the hole and the lad behind me shoved me with his boot and I was through the hole, in a flash. I'm not ashamed to say it; my eyes were tightly closed as I passed down the hole. I felt a rush of air as my parachute hit the slip stream, my parachute opened with a crack; I opened my eyes and looked skywards, that great big 28 feet diameter lump of nylon was floating gently above my head. I looked down to earth and it seemed to be rushing up towards me, I didn't appear to be descending, but I was now swinging, backwards and forwards, like a pendulum. It wasn't until I was about 30ft from the ground that it felt as if I was descending. My feet were about to touch the ground, I was caught by a gust of wind and I was swung up into the air again. I landed on my back, instead of my feet, so I did a backward roll, as my instructor had taught me. Released my harness, collapsed my chute, before it could drag me along, like a sail. The rest of the lads, followed. All except one, he had broken his leg, by the time I found that out, he had been whisked off to the hospital. The rest of us gathered around the instructor, all babbling at the same time, that we would like to do another jump, I noticed that one of them had blood dripping, it appeared he hadn't jumped, cleanly through the hole, the slip stream caught him and his head had bounced from side to side, as He went through the 'dustbin'."

Lieutenant Peter Downward

"There were various snags you had to be aware of, particularly going through the hole in the floor. If you didn't propel yourself far enough forward, your parachute pack was likely to catch on the edge of the hole and tip you forward, but to be too vigorous in leaping forward you were likely to hit the other side of the hole and suffer a bloody nose. This was known as 'Ringing the Bell', many paratroops suffered in this way."

All 13 (of the new 13th Parachute Battalion) officers passed the jump course. Lt-Col Russell (whose report stated - A good show! Has done well in all phases of parachuting) the Commanding Officer of the 2nd/4th knew that because of his age, he could not command the new 13th Parachute Battalion and would have to be replaced. A further 211 other ranks of the 2nd/4th passed leaving 29 failures, refusals and injuries, one of which was fatal.

Lieutenant Jack Watson

"It was my turn to do a night jump from a balloon at about 1am in the morning. I had been woken up by Claude Milman who said to me "Come on it's your turn; we've just had a fatal." A man called Charlesworth had jumped out of the balloon and had what was known as a 'Roman Candle', this was the term used to describe a parachute not opening properly and flailing uselessly above the parachutist as they plummeted to earth."

The 13th (Lancashire) Parachute Battalion had acquired their first entry on the Roll of Honour. Private Douglas Charlesworth on his last jump (a night balloon drop) was killed on the 22nd July 1943. The 'Roman Candle' was and still is every parachutist's worst fear. Save this one incident, the course went well and the course report stated: "Fairly good at first, early stick jumping poor. After hard work raised standard on final two jumps."

"Jumping through the hole" (IWM, Duxford).

"WE WIN OR DIE WHO WEAR THE ROSE OF LANCASTER."

From a poem by Leonard Wall

5. 13th (LANCASHIRE) PARACHUTE BATTALION

On completion of course 72 a final parade was attended in 'The Hangar' and the successful parachutists were told "that on accepting their 'Wings', refusal to jump in future would be severely punished by a long sentence of detention." The new men of the Parachute Regiment wasted no time at all sewing the converted blue and white wings onto the right shoulder of their tunics (pictured, left). They donned their red berets complete with the Parachute Regiment cap badge. The instructor also gave each man a small winged badge, a present from the makers of the parachutes, Irvings. On top of all this, they each received the best present of all, 10 days leave in which they could report back to their families and friends and inform them of their new superhuman powers.

Throughout July, 251 of the 'non-jumpers' were sent to various other units leaving the 13th Battalion massively under strength, therefore the next priority was to draft in more volunteers. Various officers arrived as did Padre Foy who had earlier in the year become part of the 2nd/4th South Lancashire's, he took over from Reverend Briscoe who went to 5th Brigade HQ. Over the coming months more men came from all corners of Britain and in some cases the World. Each had his own reason, "for the extra 2 bob a day…", "to make this girl proud of me", "to try and make something of myself and be a good soldier" or simply, "to get in the war!"

Others were desperate to join the Parachute Regiment, but had a harder time trying to get transferred. Many Commanding Officers did not want to loose their best soldiers to the Army's newest regiment and this itself shows the quality of man that the Army Air Corps had amongst their ranks.

Private Ken Oldham

"I'd joined the South Lancashire Regiment back in 1940 after working as an apprentice electrician and boot-maker. When we had the chance to volunteer for parachuting I had done so along with most of my mates. I remember being gathered in the gym at Larkhill and listening as the Commanding Officer gave us the news that we were no longer the South Lancs, but the 13th (Lancashire) Parachute Battalion."

Corporal Bill Webster

"In the summer of 1943 I was a REME fitter attached to the Durham Light Infantry and had several times volunteered for parachuting, only for the CO refusing my application on the grounds that I was a skilled tradesman. The next time a recruiting team came to the barracks, I was hanging around outside the gymnasium where interviews were being conducted, when one of the team's Officers asked me if I was interested in volunteering. I told him of my eagerness and how my ambitions were continually thwarted by the CO. It was then arranged that my name should be added to the list of successful applicants after the CO had approved and signed it. Naturally he was furious when he learnt of my posting to Hardwick and swore that he would have me back with the Durham's on completion of my Para course. And he did, but it wasn't long before I was sent to HQ 6th Airborne REME and from there it was only a short step to the 13th, but before my posting, I was asked if I was at all superstitious."

Captain David Tibbs (RAMC)

"1939 onwards I was a medical student at Guy's Hospital and present during many of the major air-raids as a fire watcher on the roof tops, transporter of casualties in the hospital or assistant in the operating theatre 1942. Wartime regulations allowed me to qualify 6 months early. In 1943 I felt unhappy at not playing a more active role. There were no vacancies for medical officers in the Royal Navy (top preference amongst young doctors) at that time, so, on entering the Army in the Royal Army Medical Corps (RAMC) I applied to join the newly formed 6th Airborne Division as a parachutist.

"I was assigned to the 225 Parachute Field Ambulance, put in charge of a section of 20 RAMC men and together with them took the parachute course. Throughout late 1943 and early 1944 energetic training continued in the care and transport of the wounded, in field craft (such as map reading) and in attaining a high standard of general physical fitness. There were 8 further parachute jumps with several at night and, later on, from Dakota aircraft which had a large side exit and incomparably better than the old Whitley. I was fortunate in having a section of 20 really first class men in my charge and we trained together no doubt learning a lot from each other. In the role of Duty medical officer I attended many parachute drops and saw a number of accidents, some fatal, such as those caused by a 'roman candle'; when the parachute fails to open. Rather daunting if you are to jump the next day."

When the 6th Airborne Division was being formed is was noted that there was an urgent need for medical orderlies, especially those that would be prepared to parachute in with the fighting troops, and there was a shortage of men that met this requirement. Colonel McEwan RAMC found out that around 150 Conscientious Objectors had become available around this very same time. Although these men would not fight, as they were not prepared to kill others, but they were fully prepared to follow troops into battle in order to care for the wounded. Before 1943 they were not permitted to join the RAMC, so they worked in dangerous jobs such as bomb disposal. A quick revision and a meeting with the Conscientious Objectors brought about the opportunity to volunteer for parachuting and join the RAMC, but on account of their non-combatant nature they could not rise above the position of Private. They were all given army service numbers beginning with '9700'.

The 75th course of parachute training saw Lt-Col Harvey along with Lieutenants Wagstaff, Wilson and Tibbs pass, along with 87 Conscientious Objectors. They all secured postings to 224 and 225 Parachute Field Ambulance Brigade attached to the 6th Airborne Division.

Captain David Tibbs (RAMC)

"Many Conscientious Objectors were in the 6th Airborne Division. They were excellent men but not allowed any rank above private. They had previously been on bomb disposal but when the bombs on London ceased to fall they had willingly volunteered to join the RAMC as parachuting medical orderlies. It was agreed that they would not be required to carry weapons and could, treat German wounded equally with our own, conditions which were the RAMC code anyway. Most were well educated and with deep Christian convictions such as Quakers or Plymouth Brethren. Six of these men were in my section."

Private Graham Corbett (RAMC)

"I was one of 100 or so Conscientious Objectors that joined the 6th Airborne Division. Further more, all these men had previously served for up to 2 years as volunteers in bomb disposal units! I was one of them.

"When I was called up I joined what was known as the Non Combatant Corps, a unit which could not handle weapons or ammunition. Sometime later I volunteered for bomb disposal. This was very hazardous as we basically dug up hundreds of unexploded bombs that had littered the areas that had suffered from the Luftwaffe 'Blitz' bombings. When most of the bombs had been removed we were given 3 options – return to the Non Combatant Corps, join the Labour Battalion of the NCC down coalmines and the like, or do what I did and volunteer for parachuting as a Medical Orderly.

"Parachute training done, we spread out across the 6th Airborne Division, I ended up being posted to the 13th Battalion along with Privates Bert Roe, Ernie Barnes, Tom Backshell and John McCruden (below)."

Others wanted to be in the Airborne, but got there in a different way to what they had originally expected.

Corporal Gordon Simpson

"When war broke out I thought it would be exciting to fly a Spitfire, so I applied to be trained, only to be turned down for medical reasons, a result of recent surgery to remove my appendix. I then had difficulty in joining the army, since as an engineering apprentice; I was in a reserved occupation. But in 1941 the authorities relented, and I was allowed to join the Ordnance Corps. I was selected and trained as an NCO Instructor, and posted to the RAOC Training Regiment at Chilwell. It was a soul less place, and I wasn't satisfied with my employment, so in late 1943 I applied to join the Parachute Regiment, and when qualified joined the Depot at Clay Cross."

Private Dennis Boardman

"I signed up because I had heard so much on the radio and read a lot in the newspapers about Hitler and Germany and I just felt it was my duty to participate. I felt that we were fighting for a legitimate cause against the evil and tyranny of the Nazis, and there was no doubt in my mind that something had to be done. I did my basic army training at Saighton Camp outside Chester in England for 9 weeks and then I was posted to the Royal Artillery to train as a radio operator in October 1942, taking an 8 week course, this included learning the Morse Code. You had to be able to receive at the rate of 18 words a minute and send out at 24.

"Getting a bit bored with the Artillery I volunteered for the Glider Pilots. However, I failed because my right eye was weaker than my left eye and in those days you were not allowed to wear glasses. At this point I decided to volunteer for the parachute regiment and I found my calling. The Commandos and the Parachute Regiment were, and are still, known as the toughest men in the army and I quickly realised it was for me. I went to take part in the selection process in Chesterfield in September 1943 and after passing, was posted to the 13th Battalion signals platoon."

Another parachuting accident occurred on the 4th September 1943 when on Exercise 'Luard' a descent by 'B' and 'C' Companies resulted in Corporal Edward Sighe being killed on landing. Corporal Sighe, described as "an asset to the section", was an original ex-South Lancs volunteer who had passed on course 72 just 6 weeks earlier. The battalion lost another man just 5 days later when Private Wilfred Deakin (left) tragically died at home.

Officers and men continued to join the unit, slowly bringing the Battalion up to strength. Major John Cramphorn was one such officer posted to the Battalion.

Major John Cramphorn

"On the outbreak of war I was embodied into the army with the rest of my Territorial Army unit, 6th Battalion the Essex Regiment. I was commanding a Company at the time and in November, in accordance with a recent War Office decision to exchange all ranks between regular and Territorial Battalions; I was posted to 2nd Battalion of my Regiment, part of the British Expeditionary Force in France.

"We came home via Dunkirk, and for the next 3 years I helped to train a succession of reinforcements for overseas, but was always refused permission to accompany the troops I had trained. As a consequence I was very frustrated.

"In the summer of 1943 the Battalion moved to South Wales for a pre-invasion assault landing exercise, and quite by chance I fell into conversation with Lt-Col Peter Luard, who was a complete stranger to me. During the course of our talk together, I learnt that he was about to take command of a newly raised Parachute Battalion, and there was a vacancy for a Company Commander. Would I be interested in joining his Battalion, he asked. He questioned me about my Army service to date. My answers must have satisfied him because he then told me to apply for a parachute course, adding that a CO could no longer refuse permission to anyone wishing to volunteer for parachuting.

"Immediately on our return to the Isle of Wight after the exercise, I sent my application for a transfer to the War Office, and was soon on my way to Hardwick where I met Major Gerald Ford and was surprised to learn from him that he was training to fill the very vacancy in the 13th that I was expecting to do. He completed the course before I did and when I reported to Newcombe Lines, Larkhill, Gerald who was a regular army Officer, commissioned into the South Lancashire Regiment and also senior to me, was already occupying the Company Commander's chair. However, Lt-Col Luard arranged a temporary appointment for me at Divisional HQ."

3 days later, on 10th September, Lieutenant-Colonel Peter Luard (Left, WO 171 1246), originally from the Oxfordshire and Buckinghamshire Light Infantry and more recently the 2i/c of the 4th Para Bn, officially assumed command of the 13th (Lancashire) Parachute Battalion. Lieutenant-Colonel G.D.B. Russell, as he always knew he would be due to his age, was posted to the 5th Battalion of the West Yorkshire Regiment.

Lieutenant Ellis "Dixie" Dean

"I reported to begin my Army career on 29th August 1940. 2 years later I was serving as a Sergeant in the 70th (Young Soldiers) Battalion of the Royal Welch when we were appointed to become the 6th (Royal Welch) Parachute Battalion and I would estimate that over 200 young soldiers accompanied Major C.H.V. Pritchard to his new command, myself among them.

"A little over 6 months later, he was to recommend me for a commission, which I received in August 1943. At the beginning of September 1943 I was serving in 'Depot Company', Hardwick, and had been taken off a draft for 1st Division on account of my inexperience as an Officer. When I heard that the CO [Luard] of the 13th Battalion was here, interviewing recruits for his battalion, and I arranged to see him. Again I thought my inexperience had resulted in being turned down, and even stressing that I had served as a Sergeant in the 6th Parachute Battalion for 8 months, didn't seem to impress him. The Colonel explained that there would be little enough time to train his battalion, so he was looking for experienced Officers only. 3 weeks later [29th Sept] I was posted to the 13th (Lancashire) Battalion, my own county and I was a very proud man. I travelled down to Larkhill with Lieutenants Fred Skeate who was to be the Mortar Officer and Stan Jeavons who like myself, joined 'B' Company.

"The battalion was housed in wooden 'Belisha' barracks of Newcombe Lines, Larkhill, vacated by the 6th Battalion on their move to North Africa."

All through September 1943 the strength continued to build up and by the end of the month the Battalion was a mere 380, 90 of which were Officers and NCO's (not including L/Cpl's). Men and equipment continued to pour in and by the end of October the unit strength was up to 560.

Private Len Cox

"In July 1943, I was stationed in Hollywood Barracks, Belfast, having been embodied with the rest of my TA Yeomanry unit on the outbreak of war. I was the No.1 of a 25 Pounder gun team. I had already tried both in 1941 and again in 1942 to transfer into the Parachute Regiment, only for the CO to block my application. But it was a case of third time lucky, and I was posted to Hardwick, where I had no difficulty completing the pre-jump course. I did my jumps in September on Ringway Course No.87, and was posted to the 13th immediately afterwards."

Lance Corporal George O'Connor

"I was a member of 'C' Company and we were sorted out into platoons and then into sections, as more men arrived. The Barracks was a collection of 7 huts laid out in the form of a spider, the seventh hut was in the centre and the other 6 were connected to the centre, like spiders legs to the body, the centre hut contained showers and toilets, the 6 legs were our sleeping quarters. Looking from the window, I could see Stonehenge, I soon got to know it very well, as there were no visitors to it in those days except for us Para's."

Private Peter Maynard

"I joined the army at the age of 17 in 1938 in the London Yeomanry as a Bren Gun Carrier driver. In 1939 I went to France with the BEF and got out at Dunkirk off the big pier that was used before it was closed because of the bombing.

"I dumped the Bren Carrier on the side of a road about 3-4 miles from the beach. My mates and I in the carrier smashed the controls and radio then started walking. We had been walking for a while when we saw a 3 tonne truck on its side with squaddies climbing all over it. So we ran over to see what was going on. When I got there I then knew why the squaddies were swarming the truck like wasps... It was full of cigarettes! I dived in there and shoved all the packs I could into my battle dress. When we got to the beach, we were lined up on the pier with a Naval officer standing there with a revolver in his had threatening to shoot any man that would not keep order! While I was stood there waiting to get on a ship, on the pier there was a sailor manning a mounted twin Lewis guns with his Naval cap perched on the back of his head. Every time a Stuka came over he'd have a pop at it, but the recoil of the guns made his hat shake so much it was a miracle it never fell off!

"A few years later when I heard about the Airborne I volunteered and after my training I became a Bren gunner."

Lieutenant Harry Pollak (Jewish Austrian refugee)

"I immediately volunteered to serve in the British army and at first was not accepted because of my Austrian origin. Nevertheless I was soon called up. To my disappointment I was posted to the Pioneer Corps, which is the labour corps of the British Army. All recruits of foreign nationality, particularly those originating from enemy territory were initially enrolled there.

"We were told we would have a week's recruit's training followed by a week's embarkation leave and then go abroad to join the BEF in France. This was early 1940 and on arrival in France nobody knew what to do with us. So they found us a job filling sandbags and building machine gun posts which we knew to be useless and unwanted. What is the good of a machine gun post if you have no machine guns? My big chance came when I was made a corporal and told to take my section to a shop on a crossroad and build a machine gun post on the flat roof. I decided to make a really good job of it and we piled on the sandbags which we had to carry up a very rickety ladder. Hard work it was. By the afternoon of day two we stood in the road, admired our handiwork and then returned to camp intending to return next day to tidy up. When we arrived next morning the house and our machine gun post had vanished. All we found was a heap of rubble. The house had collapsed under the weight of our machine gun post. Nobody seemed to care a lot; it was considered a misfortune of war. Nevertheless I did not get promotion for the quality of our work.

"After evacuation from St Malo, I was finally posted back to the Pioneer Corps as an officer, however not for long. I was asked whether I would accept a posting of a secret nature. I agreed and so began one of the more interesting periods of my army life. It was all very peculiar. I was asked to go to Regents Park in London and sit on a well-designated park bench. I would then be joined by a middle-aged lady in civilian clothes who would suggest a walk in the park during which she would tell me as much as I needed to know. In fact she told me very little and I discovered soon enough that they never told you more than the absolute minimum required to do the job. The less you knew, the less you could give away either carelessly or for any other reason, such as for instance capture. All she told me was that I would be sent to an STS (Special Training School) where I would be taught a great many skills and as part of my progress I would discover for myself what it was all about. At the end of the course I could decide whether to go ahead and they would tell me whether I was suitable. At the end of the interview she added that the personal risks were greater than would normally be expected of a soldier.

"Not long after I met with a group of 5 people one of whom was a girl. It did not take long to work out that we were meant to form a group to liaise with resistance organisations, train them in the use of weapons and explosives and other subversive activities. The training was most exciting and our instructors were quite a colourful bunch of people some of whom were released from prison to teach skills like pick-pocketing, safe cracking, entering a building without leaving a trace and many more. We became crack shots, were taught to drive anything from a motor bike to a railway engine and beyond all became demolition experts. In short there were few aspects of subversive work we were not involved in. Finally there was a course on radio communication, coding and decoding of messages.

"Finally we discovered there were only two ways to get abroad, either by submarine or by parachuting into the area in which we were supposed to work. Hence we were sent to Ringway Airport to learn parachuting, air to ground and ground to air radio communications and a few more tricks of the trade.

"At the end of all this I was told my French was not good enough to be part of a group of agents moving freely about the area in which we were to work. It was suggested I should go in on my own, do a job and return immediately. This meant parachuting in and being snatched out again by a Lysander aircraft landing in a field. I was all for this.

"After my operation had been cancelled the fourth time because of bad weather over the target area I was thoroughly fed up, a fact which was not lost on my superiors. Hence it was suggested that I should have further training as an Intelligence Officer and then be posted to the Parachute Regiment [5th October 1943]. I first did ordinary regimental duties, then was sent to the Army School of Military Intelligence at Matlock and ended up an Intelligence Officer."

Private David "Robbie" Robinson

"I served in the 70th (Young Soldiers) Battalion of the Royal Leicestershire Regiment until it was disbanded in 1942 and I was transferred to the RASC and taught to drive. Later I was sent to a unit of 49th Division, but I wasn't happy. Most units didn't seem to be very combative, so I volunteered for parachuting, reporting to Hardwick in September 1943. Around this time the Army Air Corps had just been changed to the Parachute Regiment as I earned my wings at Ringway.

"On joining the 13th in October, along with about 100 others including future Sergeants Bradley of 'A' Company (left), Hollis and Longden of 'B', also Privates B. Chitty and D. Burgess, I was posted to the Anti-Tank Platoon who was equipped with PIAT's. The men of the 13th were a very mixed bunch. There was the large group from the 2nd/4th South Lancs, professional footballers, a number from Borstal, a pickpocket, veterans of North Africa and also a group of European Jews, who had escaped to this country and changed their names to English sounding ones.

"Over the next weeks and months we trained hard in many different locations, Salisbury Plain, Brecon Beacons, Oxfordshire, Devon etc. Usually for 2 weeks at a time followed by 2 weeks back at Larkhill studying weapons and the like. Colin Longden became my best mate and we spent time going out together and we visited each others relatives as we travelled around England during our training.

"My mother knitted me a small 10" doll of a para in uniform, complete with red beret. We fitted him out with his own parachute (a mortar flare parachute). I carried him in my uniform inside pocket everywhere, until I was demobbed. (Of course this doll did extra jumps, from the cookhouse roof when the lads had had a few! I still have him."

Another one of the Jewish 'Enemy Aliens' was Peter Dreyfuss who came to England in 1935 from Frankfurt, Germany where he was born. His father had the foresight to see what was coming in Germany for the Jews and sent Peter to Mill Hill Public School where he stayed until he left in 1939.

On the day the war broke out Peter went to the Army recruiting office to volunteer but he was refused because he had not been 6 years in England and was considered to be an 'Enemy Alien'. After the invasion of France and all 'Enemy Aliens' were interned in camps in England. In 1941 a recruitment officer came to the camp, so he entered the Pioneer Corps (the only regiment they were allowed to join). He was asked to take the name of Denby whilst in the Army because if he was captured with the name of Dreyfuss he would have been given the 'special treatment', before he was put to death by the Germans.

He was offered to apply for a Commission but refused as he was keen to get frontline contact with the enemy which he felt an officer could never achieve. He felt furious at what the Germans had done to the Jews and his family and wanted to "fight them back". He eventually volunteered and joined the Parachute Regiment and was asked to join the Intelligence Corps because of his fluent knowledge of German as well as his knowledge of French.

Lieutenant Ellis "Dixie" Dean

"A little over a week later [after arriving at Larkhill], I was back at Hardwick, a student at the Divisional Battle School. The course lasted 4 weeks and then, myself and the 3 sergeants who had accompanied me on the course, went home on 10 days leave, so it was late November when I reported back to Larkhill. But not much had changed; priority had gone to reinforcing 1st Airborne in Italy.

"During my absence, Terry Bibby, a former 'B' Company subaltern had rejoined the Battalion and expressed a wish to serve in his old company and had in fact already assumed command of 6 Platoon. I now moved to 'C' Company as Officer in Command of 9 Platoon, but within days was attached to the Mortars. Stan Jeavons and myself were to attend a short course of 3" mortar training at the Netheravon Small Arms School. Two Mortar Platoons were being trained, with No.2 Platoon having an alternative role as Vickers Machine Gunners. There was a school of thought in the Army that the days of the Vickers gun were over, they were right to a certain extent, but the Bren had neither the range nor the fire power of the German Spandau's, so the old tripod mounted Vickers had been brought back. It was explained to us that we were being trained to take over the Mortars, should either of the regular officers become casualties.

"The course only lasted 10 days, but on our return, we found the Battalion fully up to strength in all ranks."

Private Ray "Geordie" Walker

"My family home in Chirton, North Shields had been destroyed by a German bomber during the night of the 12th April 1942. Fortunately members of my family were not killed and I celebrated my 17th birthday 4 days later.

"I was vengeful and decided as soon as possible to join the Army. I enlisted with my local regiment the Royal Northumberland Fusiliers. As a Voluntary Enlistment I was given the 'King's Shilling'. After completion of training at Upton I was posted to the 7th Bn Royal Northumberland Fusiliers based at Tilshead, Salisbury Plain. As the Latin motto of this regiment was "Quo Fata Vocait" (Where Fate Calls), what was to be my fate? My destiny was soon to be realised in a most unexpected development. Whilst at Tilshead a party of officers and men from the Parachute Regiment visited us to recruit volunteers for their Regiment. As 'extra' pay was on offer I volunteered.

"After several weeks of enjoying good companionship (on training course 92, Geordie passed with the comments - Quiet and hard working, good performer, confident, cheerful), it was with sadness that we had to say "Cheerio" and perhaps never see each other again. The Army dictated that we were to be posted to different battalions of the 6th Airborne Division. I arrived at Larkhill on the 5th December 1943. Our camp bore the name 'Newcombe Lines' and was located on the southern slope of Larkhill and about 1 mile from Stonehenge. The 12th (Yorkshire) Battalion were our neighbours and they occupied barracks on the eastern edge of a shared barrack square.

This arrangement enabled us to foster good relations with the men of 12 Para. Much to my surprise the Regimental Flag flying above the 13th Battalion Regimental HQ was all black with a red rose centrepiece. As the Battalion motto was "Win or Die".[3] I wondered what my fate may have in store for me."

When Princes fought for England's Crown
The House that won the most reknown
And trod the sullen Yorkist down.
Was Lancaster.
Her blood red emblem, stricken sore
Yet steeped her pallid foe in gore
Still stands for England evermore
And Lancashire.
Now England's blood like water flows
Full many a lusty German knows
WE WIN OR DIE WHO WEAR THE ROSE
OF LANCASTER.

---

[3] Win or Die" was taken from the poem by Leonard Wall written in 1917 from his trench shortly before he was killed in action.

"I well remember with what mixed feelings on 17th February 1944 I heard of the proposals for the part we were to play in 'Operation Overlord'... Our great moment had arrived."

Major-General Richard Gale

6. GETTING READY FOR THE REAL THING.

1943 saw the war turn positively in the Allies favour. January had seen Hitler's armies heavily defeated in Stalingrad, eventually surrendering there on 2nd February. The North African campaign ended with the German and Italian surrender in May, leading to the invasion of Sicily in July and the Germans evacuating Sicily in August. Bomber Command stepped up the pressure, sending constant night raids over Germany and the American Air Force hit Germany with daylight raids. 8th September saw the Italian surrender to Allies, followed the next day by Allied landings at Salerno and Taranto. Italy then declared war on Germany on October 13th and the Russians pressed hard on, and recaptured Kiev. Following these successes Churchill, Roosevelt and Stalin met in Teheran, and top of the agenda was no doubt the opening up of the 'Second, Western Front'.

In late 1943 and up to February 1944 Major General Gale himself did not even know the extent as to what the 6th Airborne's future would be. He had heard a lot of talk about the 'Second Front', it was widely known that the invasion of Hitler's armies in Europe was imminent. Would the 6th Airborne be dropped over the 'Atlantic Wall' or would they play second fiddle to the expected arrival back from Italy of 1st Airborne Division? Would they be used on specialised targets or as a diversion? The only option was to train for every possible eventuality.

Gale looked at Allied and Axis airborne assaults from the past. He studied the *Coupe de Main* attacks used by the Germans to seize the Belgian fortress Eben Emael. The Germans successfully took the 'Impregnable' fortress with great ease using co-ordinated glider and paratrooper tactics. He examined the mass paratrooper attacks on Crete, most notably the high casualty rates the Germans suffered, which was enough to make Hitler suspend further drains on his elite Fallschirmjager. Great lessons had also been learned from the Allied airborne assaults of Operations 'Colossus', 'Biting' and 'Freshman'.

Lt-Col Luard had the 13th (Lancashire) Parachute Battalion train in every aspect of what might be required of them. From August 1943 the Battalion was extremely low in numbers, the Officers and NCO's were almost up to strength, but the actual fighting men were not. Whilst the reinforcements were arriving each week as they passed their jump courses, the Officers attended many training courses. The specialist platoons (Signals and Mortars) were soon up to strength and priority was given to their advancement. Rifle Companies in the early stages were very small, but had sufficient numbers of NCO's, so navigation work and training in the positioning of defensive positions was given priority.

As more men arrived, so did the number of planes available. The Albemarle squadrons used in the Middle East came home in November 1943 and thus enabled the men to do more practice jumps and exercises as a Battalion rather than the previous Company strength ones. The Albemarle was not much of an improvement on the Whitley and was pretty much the same method. The four engine Halifax was also brought into service with the transport squadrons of the RAF but it was chiefly used as a tug for the giant Hamilcar glider. For the parachuting role, only a stick of 10 was carried, and the exit was exactly the same as from the Whitley.

December 1943 was another busy month for the 13th as they built up their manpower strength and intensified their training. Officers and men took turns in attending field firing courses, booby trap courses and enemy document courses; they also kept up their proficiency in parachuting with a series of refresher jumps.

Lance Corporal Don "Taff" Jones

"I qualified in December 1943 and I was posted to the 13th (Lancashire) Parachute Battalion. They were stationed at Larkhill on Salisbury Plain. At the time they had no MMG's so I was put into the Mortar Platoon. I was familiar with the sights on the mortar as they were similar to those of the Vickers machine gun. After a number of weeks a MMG Platoon was formed from one of the Mortars and I became part of the MMG's."

Lieutenant Ellis "Dixie" Dean

"In the middle of December, a sizeable draft reached Larkhill from Hardwick, and at last the Battalion were up to strength, and serious training could begin. For the remainder of the month the emphasis was on physical fitness, and I imagine that most, like myself, were stretched to our limits of endurance during the next fortnight. The series of tests through which the entire Battalion were put applied to all the units of 6th Airborne.

"Every volunteer for parachuting was vigorously screened at Hardwick before he even started his training, but now our stamina, strength and resolve, were submitted to an even sterner examination. In rapid succession tests of 10 miles in 2 hours, dressed as for battle and carrying full scale arms and ammunition. Next of 20 miles in 3 hours wearing full G1098 kit and carrying full scale ammunition was followed by the big one. The Battalion now faced a march of 50 miles in 24 hours, again dressed and equipped as for battle. We all had our own particular 'Bogey' with many the 10 miles in 2 hours being the severest test. Come the turn of the year, confident in our physical abilities and stamina, thought could be given to more advanced formation training. I was now instructed to take over No.2 Mortar Platoon."

On the 16th and 17th December the men and officers took Physical Efficiency Tests No.1 & 2 (the first test was 10 miles in 2 hours in battle order and the second being 15 miles in 3 hours wearing PT kit). Less than a week's recovery time later, on the 23rd the dreaded Physical Efficiency Test No.3 arrived - a grueling 35 mile march in full battle order, this was completed in 10 ½ hours.

Lance Corporal George O'Connor

"One of our exercises, I think it's called 'yomping' now, we had to 'run-walk' great distances, wearing our full equipment and carrying our weapons, taking it in turn to carry the heavier weapons. Some of the poor sods, finished with blisters on their blisters, it was a matter of pride, that we all finished the run, even if we had to carry a few, some of the way. One Para we nicknamed 'Muscles' used to finish the run, then carry on doing his weight lifting exercises. Me, I used to have a shower, massage my legs, and then cycle to Southampton, to be with my Fiancée."

Private Ray "Geordie" Walker

"My first full day at Larkill was hectic with visits to the Medical Officer the Quartermaster and the Barber. Former regimental flashes were removed from my tunic and replaced with Airborne Insignia. We were now paraded in front of our new OC, Captain Ellison. We took an immediate liking to him; he was an officer and a gentleman, he made us feel completely at ease whilst explaining our new role. Briefly 'R' Company was a reserve from which men were eventually posted to companies within the Battalion. Those of us that were fleet of foot would join a Rifle Company, whilst men with the most muscle power would go where their strength was required, the Mortar Platoons.

"Captain Ellison gave a brief history of the Battalion. My draught had brought the Battalion up to full operational strength. Captain Ellison duly dismissed us and suggested we relax in the canteen with a few beers.

"Life in 'R' Company was most enjoyable despite the rigors of a strenuous training programme. We became extremely fit and we developed keen appetites. Spare cash was often spent on extra meals in the NAFFI or Salvation Army canteens. Money reserved for 'beer' was for weekend revelries in the pubs of Amesbury or Salisbury. These drinking sessions had in their wake the usual crop of 'incidents'. Fortunately the ever tolerant Captain Ellison invariably turned a blind eye to our misdemeanours."

Dennis Edwards (7th Battalion)

"One of the outstanding features that made the British airborne soldier amongst the finest and most feared of fighting men during the Second World War was 'Esprit de Corps' - the loyalty and devotion uniting those members of the armed forces who felt themselves to be highly privileged to wear the Red Beret. Feats of outstanding valour in battles across the world have already been written into the history books, yet it was in non-battle situations that this great spirit can best be demonstrated.

"Those American and British soldiers who were stationed in many camps across barren Salisbury Plain managed to get in a good deal of practice in the art of street fighting and unarmed hand-to-hand combat, although the method employed will not be found in any Military manual, nor did it have the approval of the Mayor, Aldermen, Councillors or citizens of the City of Salisbury where most of the battles occurred on Friday, Saturday and Sunday nights - that was assuming that the Airborne soldiers meagre pay had not run out, or the taverns of the city had not been drunk dry. It was not unusual for the public houses to have sold their quotas of beer by Friday night - in which case the long suffering people of Salisbury enjoyed a comparatively peaceful weekend.

"If we were outnumbered we would immediately yell out our airborne battle cry which had been originated by our 1st Airborne Division in North Africa and adopted by all airborne men thereafter. Up would go the cry "Waho Mohammed". The effect of that cry was truly amazing. Within minutes, and from all directions, Red Berets would appear and a pitched battle would commence.

"Our unwritten airborne law was clearly understood by every Red Devil - at least amongst the lower ranks - and regardless of which airborne unit they served in; if an airborne man was in trouble and called out our battle cry, it didn't matter what you were doing, you immediately responded to the call.

"Many a lass, out walking with an airborne lad, would be dumbfounded as her escort, on hearing the battle cry, would say "Sorry – I've got to go" and would rush off to join in the battle.

"If it dragged on it often meant a long walk back to camp with a black eye or bleeding nose and/or mouth because the last lorry transport would have left in order to return the troops before midnight. The long walk also meant that we would not arrive back in camp until well after midnight, which forced us to find a way of getting inside without entering the guarded entrance gate."

Lance Corporal George O'Connor

"There were Americans stationed nearby and I met quite a few of them and we swapped yarns, but the majority of the lads couldn't stand them. I think the main reasons were that they had smart uniforms, they were much better paid than us and they threw their money around. They were not used to strong British beer and they gave off the impression they were showing off, even though it wasn't intentional. The local girls favoured them, which didn't go down very well with our lads.

"One morning, Red Cap Military Police accompanied by civilian Police, visited the barracks. "What men had visited Salisbury, the previous evening?" they demanded to know. We were all paraded in front of the Police; it was obvious who had been in Salisbury that evening. The battle scars and the collection of multi-coloured eyes, some of the paras, were displaying, spoke for themselves. The police took the most badly damaged paras away, but they were soon released, the Police couldn't prove any of them had been in Salisbury the evening in question. They soon arrived back at the barracks, grinning all over their badly damaged faces.

"We were taught unarmed combat. We also kept our hand in parachuting, by jumping from balloons when no planes were available. We did night jumps – a different kettle of fish, especially when you landed in a tree. I think some of the men finished up with squeaky voices."

Christmas Eve came and with it, the arrival of a photographer for the Battalion photograph. Later in the day 5 more visitors arrived. They were American officers from the "Screaming Eagles", the US 101st Airborne Division and they joined the 13th Battalion as guests for Christmas leaving on Boxing Day taking with them several of their British counterparts to pay a return visit.

Brigadier J.H.N. Poett (5th Parachute Brigade Commander)

"The 101st US Airborne Division had come to the Newbury area. We were twinned with them and got to know them well. Colonel Robert Sink was my opposite number and when I went to call on him, he suggested that I should do a jump with his Regiment.

"On my return to Bulford, I looked in on a balloon jump by the 13th Battalion. Just as I reached them, one of the very rare parachuting accidents occurred, a fault known as a 'Roman Candle'. The poor man [L/Cpl Stanley] was killed. A parachute failure can be unsettling to others present. It was the custom for the Senior Officer present to go up immediately and do a jump. I had done a jump with my Brigade HQ in the early morning, and then came my jump with the Americans, so this was my third that day."

Private David "Robbie" Robinson

"We kept up the parachute training and I remember Lance Corporal Stanley died after a refresher balloon jump on New Years Eve at Netheravon, his chute didn't open properly and he was killed instantly. The jumping resumed shortly after and I was in the next set of 5 to jump [Stanley had been one of the original drafts and is now buried in his home town of Warrington].

"After all the intensive training I was very pleased and proud of myself. Wearing my Red Beret whilst on leave, I felt that I could hold my head up high. At school I had been considered as a small wimp of no consequence, I was only 5ft 2in, weighing 111 lbs, but now I was a para!"

That same day, New Years Eve 1943, Private Charles Hewitt also lost his life, in another accident. 'B' Company had not been involved in the 146 person balloon descents because they were on a field firing exercise at Cranbourne Chase. Pte Hewitt died in Shaftesbury Hospital "as a result of a mishap whilst firing a 2" mortar."

Stores kept coming in and the Battalion received a number of upgraded binoculars and also wrist watches for distribution to the Officers. These were to replace the cumbersome pocket watches that they currently used. More importantly, the further personnel that arrived during the month had swelled the Battalions manpower to 657.

Private Geoff Condliffe

"On arrival at Larkhill I received the black shoulder flashes and lanyard of the 13th (Lancashire) Battalion. As it was a Lancashire Battalion I felt quite at home although there were men from all parts of the country. The next few months were marvellous, there was all the physical training you could wish for and regular games of rugby too. I got on extremely well with the physical training Instructor CSM Parish. I was assigned to the Mortar platoon and was to carry the mortar barrel weighing 44 lbs. It really was a great time, as I was doing what I was cut out for.

"Being a lover of tradition and of the history of our country, I took the opportunity to visit Stonehenge and also to explore the historic City of Bath and sometimes take a swim in the old Roman Baths. One week was spent on the shooting range at Sennybridge in Wales where we were able to practise our prowess with rifles and Bren guns and, of course, 3" mortars. It could have been most enjoyable if the rain had not come down in torrents during the whole of the visit."

Brigadier James Hill (3rd Parachute Brigade Commander)

"From January 1943 until D-Day in June 1944, we had to keep the chaps interested and on top form. One of the things I introduced in order to do that was parachuting dogs. A team of paratroops were trained in handling Alsatian messenger dogs. The dogs were given bicycle parachutes, as they were roughly the same weight as bicycles. The first time we took one of the dogs up he didn't want to jump, so we shoved him out. It turns out he enjoyed himself so much that the next time he couldn't wait to go! The dogs were trained to be messengers, but they were really just a sideshow to keep the men amused."

Lance Corporal Ken Bailey

"In January I received instructions from the CO to investigate the possibility of parachuting war dogs into action together with the parachute troops. The dogs were required to be already trained patrol dogs supplied by the War Dog Training School and I went there to select suitable dogs. The Commandant and Chief Instructor gave me a free hand to select those I thought most suitable, and after a fortnight's testing, 4 dogs were selected as possible and journeyed back to Larkhill with me. Training began from the moment of kennelling. 2 months later all the theoretical work was ready for practical testing."

One of the dogs selected from the training school in Hertfordshire was 'Bing' a 2 year old Alsatian-Collie cross. Bing had been called Brian by his civilian owner Betty Fetch and was the smallest of his litter and due to wartime rationing he was given up. After selection the dogs were gradually made accustomed to loud noises typical of battle as well as smells such as cordite. Men would run off and hide whilst the dogs kept watch, and then take their owners to the hiding places. Next the same 'game' was played again, only this time the dogs would not see where the men had hidden and had to find them by scent. They were trained to freeze to a standstill when ever they heard a noise in quiet locations. Essentially they were trained to become extra eyes and ears.

Private Ray "Geordie" Walker

"I joined 'A' Company under the command of Major Harris MC[4]. My new No.2 Platoon Commander was 2nd Lieutenant "Joe" Hodgson, a tough and cheerful North

---

[4] Major William "Bill" Harris was a formidable character had been awarded an immediate MC in 1941 while serving in Abyssinia. He had led his company forward under heavy Italian machine gun fire, and personally directed the operations of his mortar platoon with complete disregard for his own safety. The fighting went on for several days, until the Italians finally fell back. At one point during an enemy counter-attack, a shell set fire to the grass and Harris' position was attacked by cavalry, cheering madly

countryman from Cumberland. By a quirk of fate, we had both previously served with the Royal Northumberland Fusiliers.

"One night whilst in the Guard Room enjoying a cup of tea and a cigarette, 2 Glider Pilots came in and requested the use of our telephone. Our Sergeant asked "What's the problem?" They replied "We have landed our glider behind your barracks instead of at Netheravon airfield." The next day the glider was dismantled and taken away on a low-loader by the RAF.

"As winter gave way to Spring the tempo of our training increased. We could now complete a forced march of 50 miles in a day and without too many blistered feet. Our skills in the use of a variety of weapons met with the approval of our officers. One week it would be a mock battle in the Brecon Beacons the next week could find us street fighting in the ruins of Southampton's docklands."

Pte David "Robbie" Robinson (A-Tk Pl)

"The Anti-Tank Platoon only consisted of 30 men, a Sergeant and an Officer, The men were organised into 3 sections, each consisting of; 3 men with PIAT's, 6 ammo carriers and a Corporal. When in action one section was to go with each of the 3 Companies (A, B & C), meaning that each Platoon had a PIAT and 2 ammo carriers.

"We went on normal training exercises and practice drops mostly on Salisbury Plain but we did travel to various parts of the country to do different aspects of training. I can remember going to Yeovil for swimming, to Wales for field training and explosives, to Newton Abbott to run up and down hills playing soldiers and with plenty of time on Salisbury Plain learning weapons techniques etc. We handled all kinds of weapons, our own and German, we even used German tanks! I did lorry driving course as well."

Private Len Cox

"I was posted to 4 Platoon of 'B' Company but had to drop down to Private. During the training that winter I was sent to the Royal Engineers School at Ripon on a 'Mines and Demolition' course. On my return I joined 9 Platoon in 'C' Company."

Lieutenant Ellis "Dixie" Dean

"Salisbury Plain in the winter months was not the most welcoming of training areas and every effort was made to move around to more interesting locations, provide variety and so keep us happy and fully occupied. We all realised that the "Second Front" operation was to start in the spring of 1944 and somehow or other we were to play a part in it. Foremost in all our minds in January was the thought of leave, but immediately prior to travelling to our homes, the Battalion moved by rail to Manchester and on the following morning (29th Jan) marched through the city. There were no drums beating or Colours flying but bayonets were fixed. On the saluting base in addition to the Lord Mayor and Garrison Commander, was His Majesty's Lord Lieutenant Lord Derby, known throughout the county as the "Uncrowned King

---

and firing as they came. Firing a Bren gun from the hip and directing the fire of his rifle sections, Harris halted the charge at 40 yards, and emptied 20 saddles.

of Lancashire" (below: the march past, WO 171 1246. "Dixie" is fourth left, with holstered pistol). After the march past, Company groups dispersed to Liverpool, Warrington and Preston where the next day demonstrations were given to local Home Guard units, before the Battalion concentrated in Warrington and went on leave from there."

By the 31st of January the Battalion was fully up to strength boasting 743 men, most of which enjoyed the 10 days leave.

Private Peter Denby-Dreyfuss (Intelligence Section)

"At the end of my leave at home, during a bad German air-raid, I decided to leave a day early to meet someone. That night there was another bad raid and an unexploded anti-aircraft shell came through the house roof, through the ceiling in the room where I should have been and straight through my pillow, where my head would have been! The shell then proceeded into our sitting room and bounced through the French window and into the garden."

It was during this phase that Major-General Gale had received his instructions as to what role his newly formed 6th Airborne Division was being lined up for. General "Boy" Browning arrived at Gale's HQ at 11am on 17th February. Using the map of Northern France spread out on Gale's large, tilted map table; Browning outlined the plan of "Operation Overlord".

Pointing to the Normandy area and in particular the beach areas, Gale's task was to seize the two bridges over the Orne Canal and River in between the villages of Benouville and Ranville.

The Allied plan was to assault the Normandy coast between Cherbourg and the River Orne, the American paratroopers were to take and secure the Western area and the British the Eastern. The Seaborne elements were to arrive on the 5 beaches in between the two airborne elements. The 6th Airborne Division was to operate on the East flank, protecting the beaches from German armour and reinforcements. By denying the Germans the two bridges (at Benouville and Ranville), the Panzer units held in reserve by Hitler himself, could not sweep westwards and ultimately on to the beaches where they could possibly thwart the whole invasion.

Major-General Richard "Windy" Gale (Commander, 6th Airborne Division)

"I had never envisaged what I was told this day. I hope I had the good grace not to show what I really felt. I was, in fact to place one parachute brigade and one anti-tank battery under the command of one of the sea assault divisions, the 3rd British Infantry Division. I was told that, regrettably, the size of the force had to be limited by the number of aircraft that could be made available for this part of the overall plan.

"I feared that so small a force would be inadequate for the take, not of seizing, but of holding the bridgehead, it is a terrible thing for a commander to feel that his formation is being committed piecemeal to battle and even then not under his command. Great, therefore was my relief when a few days later, I was told that the whole of 38 and 46 Groups RAF would be available and that a divisional operation would be possible.

"Our first task in order of priority was to seize intact the bridges at Benouville and Ranville; and to secure a bridgehead of sufficient depth to ensure that these could be held.

"Secondly, in the North of the area in which we were to be landed there was an important costal battery. This was located on the high ground at Merville. It was so situated that it could fire on the beaches, as well as on the sea approaches. Our task was to seize and silence this battery before the assault craft came within its range.

"Thirdly, the road approaches from Le Havre and the River Seine crossed the River Dives some 5-7 miles to the East of the River Orne. Could the bridges over the River Dives be destroyed a certain delay would be imposed on any German reinforcements coming from this direction. The third task allotted to the division was, therefore the destruction of the bridges over the River Dives at Varaville, Robenhomme, Bures and Troarn.

"Next, but without prejudice to the other tasks, we were instructed to interfere with, and delay as much as possible, the movement of any enemy reinforcements from the East towards Caen.

"Complete photographs of the whole area was available and from this we could glean as much information as possible. These investigations showed very clearly that two excellent dropping or landing zones existed within our area in which we were to fight."

Brigadier Poett's 5th Brigade was given the task of seizing the two crossings over the Orne River and Canal de Caen and securing the area against any kind of infantry or armoured assault.

The bridges had to be seized intact for use in further operations should the Normandy landings be successful and they were expected to be ready for demolition, therefore a swift and powerful assault was needed. The only possible way was to assault them by a *coup de main* party landing in gliders as close to the objectives as possible (marked 'X' & 'Y'). Landing in gliders would give the element of surprise and then aggressive forces would be needed to overrun the defences as quickly as possible. 'D' Company of the Oxfordshire and Buckinghamshire Light Infantry were chosen to spearhead the operation.

The 7th, 12th and 13th Parachute Battalions would then land (on DZ 'N') in order to reinforce the Ox & Bucks at the bridges, take and secure the villages of Le Bas de Ranville and Ranville respectively.

Brigadier James Hill and his 3rd Brigade would have the responsibility of taking and holding the ridge that stretched from Le Plein in the north to Le Bois de Bavent, a thick impassable wood to the east. The 9th Battalion would drop (on DZ 'V') in order to take the Merville Battery, a 4 gun position over looking and threatening the landing beaches and the approaches. 8 Para (DZ 'K') and the Canadian Battalion (DZ 'V') were allotted key bridges to destroy over the River Dives to the East, thus slowing the movements of German reinforcements towards the 6th Airborne Division's positions. Airlanding units would come in later in the day to further reinforce the bridgehead, they were to land on LZ 'N' (formerly DZ 'N') and LZ 'W' across the Orne.

A number of 'Pathfinders' from the 22nd Independent Parachute Company would be jumping first in order to mark out the various drop zones with Eureka Beacons. These beacons would be picked up by the main body of aircraft following soon after.

Brigadier J.H.N. Poett (5th Parachute Brigade Commander)

"The simultaneous landing of the *coup de main* force and the Pathfinders was an important feature of the plan. Both these groups needed surprise. This was obviously necessary for the *coup de main* and it was equally important for the Pathfinders, whose flight plan was directly over the Atlantic Wall. They would be flying at a low altitude to come in under the radar screen.

"The contingency plan included an assault crossing of the two waterways by the 7th Para Battalion. Detailed orders were issued to the Battalion for this operation. They carried 30 inflatable dinghies and 12 recce boats in large kit bags attached to the legs of the paratroopers and released on a cord before landing.

"I decided to drop with a small command post at the same time as the Pathfinders, so that, if the *coup de main* did miscarry, I could control the contingency plan and adjust the deployment of the Brigade."

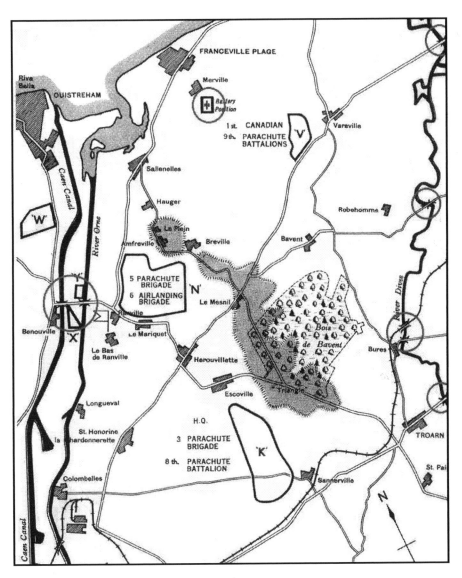

The Primary Targets of the 6th Airborne Division (circled)

*"The newspapers keep calling it the Second Front; I don't know why they call it the Second Front. I myself have been fighting the Germans on a number of fronts, and I expect a good few of you have too. They should call it Front Number 6 or Front Number 7. As long as they didn't want us to fight on Front Number **13**...*

General Montgomery (Commander, 21ˢᵗ Army Group)

7.   ALMOST READY FOR THE REAL THING

Lieutenant Ellis "Dixie" Dean

"At the end of February another rail journey carried us to Sennybridge in South Wales, where the weather was even colder than at Larkhill. But the change of scene was welcome and the several days of field firing which followed proved of great value, particularly for the mortars and machine guns as we were firing in support of the Rifle Companies for the first time.

"On the 3ʳᵈ March Corporal Ernest Lyons was killed on the field firing ranges at Sennybridge. He was engaged in a house clearing exercise, using live ammunition. Following the accepted drill, he opened a room door, threw in a 3 lb grenade, but didn't wait for it to explode, before dashing in to 'spray' the room with his sten and was killed in the blast."

Major General Richard "Windy" Gale (Commander, 6ᵗʰ Airborne Division)

"By now all the troops knew that General Montgomery was to command the Allied invasion of North-West Europe; the so called 'Second Front.' It was thus a great day when we heard that he was to visit us (above: Monty inspects 13 Para with Lt-Col Luard, IWM Duxford). To us all this inspection meant a great deal: for we knew we were to be scrutinised by a practiced and very relentless eye.

"The day of his inspection was very cold and the troops had to stand about for some time. The Commander-in-Chief walked round; as he passed a man with an Africa Star he would stop and talk with him; of course he talked with others. The men looked splendid.

"After walking round the troops the C-in-C talked to each brigade group. For this he stood on a Jeep and the troops crowded round him. He told them of the impending invasion and of his confidence in them, the Army, in our allies the Americans; he spoke of the impressive air forces and he impressed them with the need for confidence in themselves, their leaders, their equipment, their allies and their cause."

Alan Moorehead (War Correspondent)

"I travelled with him [Montgomery] one week. He would talk to each of the Officers and with the troops turned inward, he walked the ranks. He walked slowly, peering sharply at the men, face to face. At the end of the inspection Monty would get on his Jeep in front of a loudspeaker and tell the soldiers to break rank and gather round him.

"This was always an astonishing moment. Men in heavy boots would charge towards the Jeep. It caused a heavy rumbling in the earth and then they would sit on the grass. Nothing else was of any interest any longer, nothing except this simple proposition: the assault. To run, to shoot, to kill. And not to be killed. All the usual decoration of life was stripped away: the normal life of playing football and going out with girls and visiting the movies.

"No mention of God. No mention of England. Not a single eternal verity. No hate. No question of revenge. The words were the least of it. The whole performance succeeded because it was the expression of a wanted emotion. Without their consciously knowing it, the speech adopted an attitude which the soldiers wanted to have."

Private Donald Lord (Anti-Tank Platoon)

"[In a letter home] I did a parachute jump on Thursday [7th March] morning at 7am and I landed in the trees, you should have seen me dangling on the end of my parachute which was hanging on a branch.

"Last Wednesday I saw General Montgomery and he gave us quite an interesting talk."

General Montgomery (Commander, 21st Army Group)

"I wanted to come here today so that we could get to know one another; so that I could have a look at you and you could have a look at me – if you think that's worth doing. We have got to go off and do a job together very soon now, you and I, and we must have confidence in one another. And now that I have seen you I have complete confidence... complete confidence... absolute complete confidence. And you must have confidence in me.

"We have been fighting the Germans a long time now, a very long time, a very long time... a good deal too long. I expect like me you are beginning to get a bit tired of it... beginning to feel it's about time we finished the thing off. And we can do it. We can do it. No doubt about that. No doubt about that whatsoever. The well trained British soldier will beat the German every time. We saw it in Africa. We chased him into the sea in Tunisia... then we went over to Sicily and chased him into the sea again.

"The newspapers keep calling it the Second Front; I don't know why they call it the Second Front. I myself have been fighting the Germans on a number of fronts, and I expect a good few of you have too. They should call it Front Number 6 or Front Number 7. As long as they didn't want us to fight on Front Number **13**...

"We don't want to forget the German is a good soldier... a very good soldier indeed. But when I look around this morning and see the magnificent soldiers here... some of the finest soldiers I have ever seen in my lifetime... I have no doubt in my mind about the outcome... no doubt whatever. No doubt at all that you and I will see this thing through, together.

"Now I can't stay any longer. I just want to say goodbye and very good luck to each one of you."

March 1944 had brought better weather and better aircraft. The arrival of the American Dakota transport aeroplane made parachuting a much easier task. The Dakota allowed a 20 strong stick of parachutists to walk up to and step out of the side door. No more 'ringing the bell'. Sticks could clear the plane much quicker, thus enabling a better concentration of troops on the ground, which in turn shortened the time taken to rally the men together. Leg kit bags were also introduced and practiced with. For the first time a Battalion drop was attempted and was a complete success, except for one incident.

Lieutenant Ellis "Dixie" Dean

"A couple of days later when one of the other battalions carried out their identical exercise, one mans chute became caught in the tail wheel and for over an hour the plane flew round and round with the poor unfortunate man spinning in the slip stream. I don't suppose the pilot realised it, but his route took him over Newcombe lines, all training came to a halt as we all gazed skywards, hoping and praying that somehow a rescue could be achieved. Eventually, with a motor-launch close at hand, the aircraft flew at wave top height over Studland Bay, and the man's static line was severed. There was no happy ending to the story: but we had volunteered knowing full well the risks, and our morale was not affected in any way."

There was also another fatal accident for the 13th. Private Victor Llewellyn on 16th March was the victim of another 'Roman Candle'. This was during Exercise 'Fath', a Battalion jump from C47's.

Due to high winds, the planned Brigade drop for Exercise 'Bizz' was cancelled after two failed attempts, the drop was simulated and the exercise began (21-23rd March). The 13th Battalion's task was to seize the bridge at Farringdon. Several days later the 13th changed roles for Exercise 'Bizz II' and had to defend the bridge (25-28th March).

During the night whilst the men of 13 Para were taking their turn at defending the bridge, several trucks drove up to the bridge, there was a short fire fight (using blank ammunition) and the umpires deemed the attacking force the victors, claiming to have landed in gliders and taken the bridges by *coup de main*. The attackers in the 'trucks' were none other than, 'D' Company, the Ox & Bucks Light Infantry. General Gale and Brigadier Poett observed this very significant fight with great intensity.[5]

During the month the Battalion received 528 of the better made Mark V Airborne Sten guns to replace the old Mark II versions. The Sten V (below) featured wooden grips and stock, and a Lee Enfield sight fitted on the barrel.

Elsewhere, the 'war dogs' had completed 2 months of their own training and by now had acclimatised themselves somewhat by jumping from stationary aircraft (with engines running) and had had flights in aircraft, so now it was time for the real thing.

The aircraft most suitable for parachuting dogs was the Albemarle as there was less danger of the static lines becoming entangled. Jumping from the 3 by 8 foot hole at the rear, their eyes and ears were protected from the air stream and they did not tend to somersault.

Lance Corporal Ken Bailey (Dog Handler)

"Around midday on 2nd April, the Met people forecast ideal conditions for the next 2 days. The jump was therefore arranged for late the following afternoon. My dog (Alsatian bitch "Ranee") was given minimal water and was not fed before the drop. I carried with me the dogs feed, consisting of a 2lb piece of meat, and the dog was readily aware of this. We took off from Netheravon and headed for the Divisional drop zone 2 miles away. I was to jump at No.9 and the dog would be No.10, the first 8 to jump were other parachutists who included my CO, Colonel Luard and our Medical Officer, Captain Whitley, who had also acted as my 'vet'. Everyone was to turn and observe the dog after leaving the aircraft and a team of RAF experts would wait and observe from the landing area.

"The Albemarle first made a 'dummy' run over the DZ during which the chute was fitted to the harness, the moment the aircraft throttled back on the run in for the live drop the dog became excited. When the red light came on the dog followed me down to the 'action stations' position. As the green light came on, she eagerly watched the

---

[5] This was a direct dress rehearsal for Major John Howard's *Coup de Main* force which had been selected to spearhead the invasion of Europe.

stick disappear through the hole, though still keeping the place he had been taught behind my heels.

"After my chute developed, I turned to face the line of flight; the dog was 30 yards away and slightly above. The chute had opened and was oscillating slightly. She looked somewhat bewildered but showed no sign of fear. I called out and she immediately turned in my direction and wagged his tail vigorously. The dog touched down 80ft before I landed. She was completely relaxed, making no attempt to anticipate or resist the landing, rolled over once, scrambled to her feet and stood looking round. I landed 40ft from her and immediately ran to her, released her and gave her the feed; she was then left to play.

"Whilst the dog played we discussed the drop. It was decided that the chute was too small as she landed in 14 seconds. The next trial drops were postponed for 2 weeks until a new chute could be designed and made. During this time the bitch was monitored for any side effects from the drop.

"The new chutes arrived (24ft diameter compared to the previous 18ft) and the same dog and procedure was adopted with great success. I landed before my dog this time and got to the area she was going to land before she touched down, again she showed no fear. Each of the other dogs then made 4 descents, after which they resumed a normal existence."

5 paradogs – "Ranee" is in the centre (apologies for poor copy, courtesy Ken Bailey)

Major General Richard "Windy" Gale (Commander, 6th Airborne Division)

"In these final exercises I, therefore stressed not only the importance of capturing and seizing ground, but the even greater importance of holding it. What the airborne soldier has gained by surprise and by skill he must hold with guts and determination. Immediate counter attacks must be expected and these would be heralded by intense mortar fire covering the move of self-propelled guns and tanks with determined, well trained infantry.

"One thing perhaps more than any other struck me during all this period. It was the behaviour of the troops. We had practically no military crime to contend with. All seemed to be imbued with the seriousness of the task in hand; all had a real and deep sense of their responsibilities; and all seemed impressed with the sacredness and justice of the cause for which they were training and eventually going to fight."

One final Divisional exercise ("Mush") was carried out 19th - 23rd April. The 1st Airborne Division parachuted in, as the 6th Airborne Division acted as defensive ground troops. The hearts of the 6th Airborne Division men sank; they believed that they had been overlooked and that the more battle hardened and experienced 1st Airborne Division had been chosen to participate in the expected invasion.

Lieutenant Ellis "Dixie" Dean

"Colonel Luard addressed all the officers in secret and told us not to be disappointed, as our time would surely come. Exercise 'Mush' was one of the few occasions when the Platoon was used in the machine gun role (left: The Vickers MMG .303). The Colonel accompanied by Brigadier Poett came along and the Brigadier asked how the training was coming along. "As well as could be expected, as we only use the guns one day a week." He seemed a little surprised "This will never do" and guided the CO away. In next to no time the Platoon was on their way back to Larkhill, with a Small Arms School trained instructor from 7 Para with orders that from now on we were to train as machine gunners only.

"At the end of April the complete Platoon spent a week at Netheravon and benefitted tremendously from the instruction of the staff there, and at the end of that week, I stayed on. A call went out for experienced machine gunners and Sergeant George Kelly and Private Jack Carr were posted to us."

Brigadier J.H.N. Poett (5th Parachute Brigade Commander)

"On 2nd May I issued written orders to [Major John] Howard for the *coup de main* operation and briefed him in detail. I then gave him a pass permitting entry to Brigmaston House where the divisional planning was done and access to all the 'Secret Intelligence' material.

"During the study and planning period, security was of top importance. The 6th Airborne Division planning was done in a specially protected small house, known as Brigmaston Farm House. Each brigade was allotted a room in the house. Here intelligence summaries, maps and air photographs were kept under conditions of maximum security. An accurate scale model of the whole of the divisional area was maintained, and also detailed large-scale models of the bridges over the river and the canal, their surroundings and defences. The Intelligence material was constantly kept up-to-date."

Private Geoff Condliffe

"In rotation we were sent home for weekend leave and it was to be the last time that many saw their loved ones. Naturally, I took advantage of being at home to engage in a wrestling match at Warrington under my stage name of "Jeff Condor". My opponent was a Welshman who was also a sergeant in the Army, Taffy Jones (well, he was a

Welshman). I was 100% fit but a little out of practice, I took a terrible fall on my head and was rushed unconscious to the hospital, which was a bit ironic considering all the bumps I'd taken during the previous few months as a paratrooper.

"I soon recovered, but was suffering from loss of memory so I was kept in hospital for a further few days before being despatched back to the 13th very late from my leave, but with a note from the hospital explaining my absence. I arrived back at Larkhill with a little help from fellow travellers but unfortunately all was not well. I kept getting memory loss, a condition that persisted for the next few months."

Steven Dreyfuss, brother of Pte Peter Denby-Dreyfuss (Intelligence Section)

"He loved to shock my rather nervous Mother. Shortly after he joined the Parachute Regiment, when he was on leave, he jumped out of the first floor window of our suburban house in Hendon to give my mother a fright!

"The last time I saw him was when I was in Cumberland and he was on his last leave and specially come all the way up there to see me for 2 days. The school gave me time off and we both had bikes and hiked there. I remember clearly how he told me then that this would be his last leave before he dropped in France and that he

would not come back and how I should not be upset. I thought at the time that this was just hero talk but learned later he'd carefully met all the people he knew to say goodbye to them, including his old teacher, my aunt (but not my parents!) with the same message."

Photo: Peter Denby-Dreyfuss (as a corporal before dropping to private on joining the Parachute Regiment) with younger brother Steven.

Lieutenant Harry Pollak (Intelligence Officer)

"By the early spring of 1944 I was briefed as to the area of operation of my battalion. I was ordered to assemble all information required to plan our part of the plan in the greatest detail, both logistically and tactically. Much of my time was taken interpreting aerial photos provided by RAF Marlow, the HQ for aerial reconnaissance. Finally the day came to prepare briefing material first at brigade and later at battalion level. We had to build models of the target area not only as seen from the air but also from the ground by individuals once they have landed. The basis of this was the most detailed and skilful aerial reconnaissance providing not merely vertical photos but also oblique ones taken from various angles, allowing us to calculate the exact size of objects, so that the models were exactly to scale.

"All preparations went according to plan and the briefing material was available the day it was required. All this was not allowed to interfere with training by way of parachuting. Small and slow though aircraft were in those days, we jumped when they flew at a rate of 3 miles per minute. 30 men had to get out of the plane and unless they were to be strung out over miles of countryside the exit had to be done in a matter of seconds. This took infinite practise. Equally vital was the speed of assembly as a fighting force after landing. Parachutists are extremely vulnerable from the point of landing until assembly is complete. We had a drill for this and rehearsed it over and over again against a stopwatch. All this had to be done under cover of darkness, making it clear we were rehearsing for a night assault. All officers used hunting horns, which were an invaluable aid to orientation. I have kept mine as a souvenir."

Even though the final plans were all but completed, the Germans still kept the planners busy. They never let up fortifying the Atlantic Wall. They were adding on daily basis new pillboxes, blockhouses and anti-invasion defences, such as "Rommel's Asparagus" intended to prevent parachute and glider landings.

Major General Richard "Windy" Gale (Commander, 6th Airborne Division)

"It was not until fairly late in our planning that the 'stakes' appeared. One day Lacoste came to me with an anxious look on his face and an enormous bunch of photographs. The Germans had started putting in enormous stakes, cut down tree trunks, all over the country. We had information that the poles were mined and connected by wires. The first thing that worried me was, was this general all over Northern France or was it local? Had they in fact guessed or gleaned the area of the assault? Would they be waiting for us? These doubts were quickly dispelled because on examination of other areas showed that the plan was general. That was an enormous relief. But how to deal with this new aspect?"

Lieutenant-Colonel Frank Harrington Lowman MBE (Royal Engineers)

"There remained the problem of dropping the poles and then removing them. Permission was obtained to fell some 100 trees in the New Forest, something unheard of in peacetime, and these were then transported to Bulford Fields on Salisbury Plain where they were erected according to the pattern in the air photographs. Following trials of various possible methods a standard drill was evolved as follows:

(a)   The ground around the base of each pole was excavated to a depth of 6" and about 12" out from the pole.

(b)   A 5lb sausage of plastic explosive was attached round the base of the pole to be fired by safety fuse and igniter. These sausages were made up in bicycle inner tubes and carried down by parachute engineers as bandoliers.

(c)   Each pole was then removed by human porterage provided by an infantry working party and the shallow crater filled in and stamped down. Demolished poles were carried away to the side of the (landing) strip and laid at the base of a standing boundary pole and at 45° to the axis of the strip to allow gliders to turn off. 6 infantry teams of 12 men were required for each strip and they were headed by a RE NCO to ensure a safe separation from the demolition parties."

Maj-Gen Gale: "*Have you seen these air photos, Frank? Do you realise what they mean and what do you propose to do about them?*"

Lt-Col Harrington Lowman: "*Yes Sir. They are anti-Airlanding poles and we shall have to blow them down and carry them away.*"

Brigadier J.H.N. Poett (5th Parachute Brigade Commander)

"I selected Lieutenant-Colonel Pine-Coffin's 7th Para Battalion to be responsible for relieving Howard's force at the bridges. Lieutenant-Colonel Johnson's 12th Para Battalion would be responsible for securing the bridgehead south and south-east of the Orne River Bridge. Lieutenant-Colonel Luard's 13th Battalion was to secure the village of Ranville and also clear as much as was necessary of the poles on the landing ground, in readiness for the glider force due to land at 3:30am. This glider force would include General Gale's Tactical HQ and an urgently needed anti-tank Gun Battery."

Private Ray "Geordie" Walker ('A' Company)

"On one exercise we teamed up with some Sappers and went to a field full of mini telegraph poles, they were obstacles designed to hinder glider landings. The Sappers ran down the rows of poles and blasted them out of the ground with high explosives and the men of 'A' Company removed them so that 'imaginary' gliders could land safely. It was back-breaking work but the task was completed on time.

"Around this time Major Bill Harris MC was promoted to Second-in-Command of the Battalion. His replacement was Major John Cramphorn, formerly of the Essex Regiment. The month of May was hectic. We completed a successful night parachute drop from Stirling bombers based at Tarrant Rushton, Dorset. Sadly the Battalion suffered another fatality on this exercise."

Lieutenant Ellis "Dixie" Dean (MMG Platoon)

"Private John Wills was a young member of my Platoon and was killed on 10th May, on a night Stirling jump. He had already left the plane and his chute developed normally. Another aircraft flying in low collapsed his chute and he fell 400 ft to his death."

Corporal George Simpson (Anti-Tank Platoon)

"In the spring of 1944 I was still at Clay Cross but towards the end of April, along with a number of other NCO's. I was posted to the 13th and arrived at Larkhill in the dark. We were found beds in one of HQ Company's barrack rooms and on looking out of the window next morning, the first thing I saw, half a mile across the fields, was Stonehenge. Major Tarrant interviewed me and asked about my previous service, when I said I had instructed in mines, explosives and enemy AFV recognition, he said my training made me ideal for the Anti-Platoon. I reported to Lieutenant Lagergren, who put me in charge of No.3 Section.

"In the 13th I found the comradeship and pride in the Regiment which up to now had been missing in my other units. There was a terrific spirit among us all, and the discipline was different, one of trust and confidence, much more relaxed, not the rigid adherence to strict rules and regulations."

Lieutenant Ellis "Dixie" Dean (MMG Platoon)

"May also saw the arrival of the experienced Sergeants Jack Brady and "Taffy" Lawley. Lawley, an ex-miner, joined the 'Special Services' in 1940 at 35 years old. He was accepted for service in No.2 Commando, and kept his rank of Sergeant. Taffy qualified as one of the first parachutists at RAF Ringway. Towards the end of 1940, he had taken part in the first ever British airborne operation, Colossus."

Sergeant Albert "Taffy" Lawley

"I was stick commander for Operation 'Colossus'. We blew the aqueduct and inspected our handwork and found that we had made a good job if it! To hear the water rushing down the mountainside like a raging torrent was music to our ears; we had achieved what had been allotted us, thus laying the foundation of what was to be a great force. How proud I was to be one of this party.

"On route to the RV we were surrounded by dogs, men, women and children then armed troops and police. We had no choice but to surrender. I ended up in Campo Concentramento PG 78 Sulmona. A prison camp is a good testing ground for friendship, but the friendship of Sgt P.P. Clements and myself weathered it to the very end. We kept as fit as possible and were always on the alert for a way of escape, and were able to send much valuable information home by the code we were taught at Mildenhall. From the same source we got in return, maps, money and messages hidden in parcels we received. We helped Lt Deane-Drummond attempt to escape twice [he was captured along with Lawley during Op Colossus, later in the war he was captured again at Arnhem and he escaped again after hiding in a cupboard for over 14 days!].

"On 27th August 1943 a prisoners dream came true. A fleet of American bombers flew up the valley and bombed Sulmona station. We were cheering, better than any football crowd. On 3rd September, a week later Sulmona got its second bombing and on the 8th, Italy asked for peace. For 4 days after everyone was free to do what they liked, but we were ordered by the senior British officer that we were not to try and get back to our own troops, if we did so, it was at the risk of court martial. If it had not been for this order, many more would have escaped instead of being recaptured and taken to Germany. After seeing a German reconnaissance plane Clem and I decided to head off into the mountains and find our way to our own lines. We stayed in a village high in the mountains and stayed with a good hearted Italian called Giovanni.

"On the 13th October we witnessed the withdrawal of the enemy and we went through him to contact the Green Howards in the village of Casacalenda, on the main road to Termoli. What a day one of the happiest in my life and I have ever since looked upon 13 as my lucky number. After imparting our information on the enemy etc. we were soon on our way home.

"On arrival in England we were sent home on a couple of months leave. Later, and after being pushed around Army Selection Training units and finding much difficulty in getting back into Airborne because of my age (39), I found myself at Hardwick on a refresher course; then on to Ringway. It was grand to meet some old pals still there I thoroughly enjoyed this course; I got very fit and felt at least 10 years younger. After Ringway on to Cray Cross, and soon I was posted to the 13th Battalion 6th Division; a posting with which I was very disgusted, as I claimed to belong to the 1st Battalion. But although I protested very vigorously, it was of no avail and I soon found myself at Larkhill with the 13th Battalion. My regrets were soon dispelled, as I found the 13th a jolly crowd, well trained and well disciplined."

The 13th (Lancashire) Parachute Battalion had not yet met the enemy, but in less than a years training, proving the toughness and dangers of becoming paratroopers, they had accumulated 8 names on their Roll of Honour.

ROLL OF HONOUR – UK TRAINING PERIOD

Pte	CHARLESWORTH Douglas	3656064	22/07/1943	Manchester South Cemetery
Cpl	SIGHE Edward	3660933	04/09/1943	Salford (Weaste) Cemetery
Pte	DEAKIN Wilfred F.	7973434	09/09/1943	Manchester Gorton Cem
Pte	HEWITT Charles	3663335	31/12/1943	Liverpool Kirkdale Cem
LCpl	STANLEY George F.	3655202	31/12/1943	Warrington Cemetery
Cpl	LYONS Ernest P.	3450235	03/03/1944	Rochdale Cemetery
Pte	LLEWELLYN Victor D.	4077378	16/03/1944	Greig Meth Cemetery
Pte	WILLS John H.	14654390	10/05/1944	Oldbury Cemetery

"The Battalion during this month completed its preparations for war, and is now ready and eager to seek out and destroy the King's enemies."

13th Para Bn War Diary, May 1944

8.   READY FOR THE REAL THING

Major General Richard "Windy" Gale (Commander, 6th Airborne Division)

"The second visit [on 19th May] was a great one indeed and one which touched us all deeply; it was the visit of their Majesties the King and Queen, accompanied by Princess Elizabeth (below, IWM Duxford). Their Majesties spent the whole day with us, talking to many of the men and their officers. I think the King and Queen and the Princess enjoyed their day. To us all it was a great occasion, one that I am sure none of us will forget."

Lieutenant Harry Pollak (Intelligence Officer)

"During the spring of 1944 the South of England was like a vast military camp as more than 300,000 men and their equipment were assembled for the assault. Morale was excellent. We all knew the tide had turned and victory seemed a foregone conclusion. Italy was at the point of collapse, the North African campaign had been won, the Americans were driving the Japanese back to where they had come from and our own 14th Army in Burma scored heavily against the Japanese, though at very great cost.

"The time was near. In late May my battalion was sent to a tented camp round the perimeter track of an airfield in Berkshire for final training and briefing."

Lieutenant Ellis "Dixie" Dean (MMG Platoon)

"I had completed half of the 6 week machine gun course, when I was recalled and on reporting back learnt that there were only 24 hours before we departed for the transit camp, but the machine gunners would not be going with the rest of the Battalion, instead we were going with the 12th Battalion to Keevil. So on the 25th May, I marched the gunners to the opposite end of the barrack square and reported to Major Mayfield of the 12th."

Captain Padre Whitfield "Boy" Foy

"Not to be so fortunate. For after a proportion of the men had had their leave, the decree went forth and all Leave was stopped. I considered the matter at that time (and in retrospect I still do consider it so) an outstanding example of bad men-management at that time, as I have said., the country, indeed the whole world, knew that the invasion of the Continent was imminent; I venture to say that at that time it was anticipated that the invasion would be a much bloodier affair than it, finally turned out to be. Every man therefore, who knew that he was a possible starter, viewed the venture with a certain degree of apprehension, and then leave was announced and spirits rose; at least there would be ten days at home before anything happened; strange how comforting that was.

"Meanwhile the question was still existed in our minds; would we be in at the beginning of the assault on Europe?

"May 25th and we were in the heart of the English countryside, surrounded by masses of barbed wire and armed guards. All the Battalion, with the exception of Dixie's MMG Platoon, were in the Brize Norton, Oxfordshire, Transit Camp, only a stone's throw from the airfield. The area had idyllic surroundings, so brilliantly revealed in the film 'Memphis Belle', and it seemed a planets distance from war. We spent long days in the June sun sealed inside the camp. Only twice was the Battalion allowed out, heavily escorted. Once we went out in parties for swimming and once we attended a film show at Witney. All communication with civilians was strictly forbidden.

"In the camp was one Nissen hut which Hitler would have given a great deal to inspect. It was small and innocuous looking and as distasteful as every other Nissen hut in the country. This particular one however was labelled "Briefing Room". When we arrived it was the cynosure of all eyes, the magnet which attracted all attention, for inside that room all the secrets were stored.

"There are moments in life when emotional tension reaches a very high level, times when anyone wit a sense of dramatic sense in him feels to be above others. Such a moment occurred to me when a few days after our arrival at Brize Norton, the officers of the Battalion went in past the armed guard to be briefed. We passed through the Model Room; the large model on the floor conveyed no idea as to where we were going, into the Map Room. There, facing us on the wall was what we had waited so long to see the area in France where the 6th Airborne Division was to make its contribution in the high enterprise to which the Allies were committed in Western Europe. We saw the mouth of the river Orne, the towns of Caen and Troarn and the villages of Ranville, Hérouvillette, Escoville, Breville and Sainte Honnorine, names of which we had never heard, but which were to live with us for ever just as Mons, Ypres and the Somme lived in the minds of an earlier generation."

Lieutenant Jack Watson ('A' Company)

"There was a big nissen hut in the camp with "Briefing Room" on the door. We were all dying to know what was going on in there. My men constantly came to me, asking what was happening. Eventually we were told by our Company Commander [Major Cramphorn] that we officers were going to be briefed. By this time it was early June and it all became clear to us what was going to happen. We then spent all our time studying the aerial photos, maps and models to the extent that we knew where every tree was, and in particular the church tower in Ranville itself."

Lieutenant Ellis "Dixie" Dean (MMG Platoon)

"The camp at Keevil in the Wiltshire countryside was at its sparkling best and if the location was meant to be relaxing, it could hardly have been bettered. The transit camp was a tented one in open grassland some 3 or 4 miles from the airfield - peaceful and relaxing with long days of warm sunshine as we made the final preparations for the operation.

"The one nissen hut of the camp housed the briefing room and the door was kept locked, but within days I was to report there. We waited outside, the 12th Battalion Officers, I was the only outsider. The talk was all about where the invasion would take place; with most convinced it would be the Pas de Calais area. Never once did I hear Normandy mentioned. At last we were allowed in and sat around the sand model in the centre of the room. There were maps on the walls and I could work out which part of France we were heading for."

Lieutenant Harry Pollak (Intelligence Officer)

"My battalion's task was three-fold. First of all we had to secure the fields north of Ranville near Caen, blow up all obstacles erected by the Germans to prevent an airborne landing such as we were preparing. Our glider-borne troops were to land there by first light on D-Day. Hundreds of telegraph poles erected by the Germans in the fields were a most formidable obstacle but our 'A' Company had trained for weeks to dispose of them in a matter of an hour or so.

"Our second task was to secure the heavily defended crossroads in Ranville, which was a vital link in our line of communications. Thirdly we had to secure the Château de Ranville, the HQ of the German 21st Panzer Division. Years later, my wife and I had lunch there during a pilgrimage and reunion.

"All this was supposed to happen during the night of 4/5th June."

Captain Alfred "Nobby" Clark (2i/c 'C' Company)

"This concentration camp did not concern, to my mind, the numbers of troops in one spot so much as the amount of briefing, checking and counter checking down to the last detail, almost down to each man's individual role in the forthcoming invasion. We learned that the objective of the 6th Airborne Division was Normandy – in a part so very much resembling the country round Oxon, Gloucester, and Wiltshire where so much of our training over the past months had been carried out."

Lieutenant Jack Sharples (8 Platoon 'C' Company)

"I was amazed at the amount of detail that we were given at the briefing, such things as the tower was detached from the rest of the church and that we must expect to find cows on the DZ. When I came to brief the Platoon and asked for questions, their only concerns were how to find the RV (turn to follow the line of fight and look for the church tower), and secondly the strength of the enemy in Ranville, but were reassured when I said "There aren't enough Germans in the village to give 'C' Company any trouble".

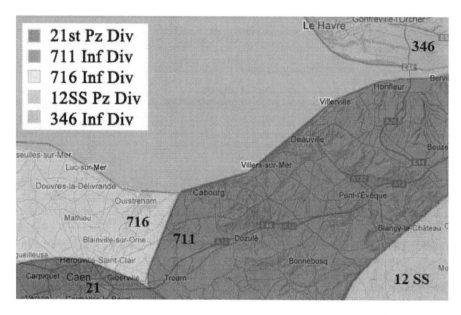

Approx areas of enemy troops (Map created using Google Map Data © 2012)

The intelligence reports stated that the following units were likely to be encountered in the area that the 6th Airborne Division would be operating in:

1. 21st Panzer Division – Around Caen on anti-invasion exercises.
2. 711 Infantry Division – 13,000 troops with coastal batteries, well situated to counter-attack and expected to take up positions on high ground in the east near R. Dives.
3. 716 Infantry Division – 8 Battalions, 2 of which are Russian and each 1,000 strong. Believed to be low category and limited in fighting value. Expected to be completely disrupted by initial landings.
4. 12th SS Panzer Division – Around 21,000 armoured troops and expected to be around Caen within 12 days of D-Day.
5. 346 Infantry Division – Around the Le Havre area and not really considered an immediate threat to the 6th Airborne Division.

Lieutenant Ellis "Dixie" Dean (MMG Platoon)

"I listened intently, particularly to the information that 21st Panzer Division was located SE of Caen. They posed the main threat. To counter this, 6 pounder anti-tank guns would land by glider and the MMG's task was their defence. The anti-tank guns were to be sited outside the rifle companies defensive localities, and if they were outside the defences, then so were we. It was a slightly daunting thought, especially knowing the fearsome reputation the German Panzer Division enjoyed. The Anti-Tank Officers were full of confidence in a secret hollow charged shot called a 'Sabot' about to be used for the first time and was capable of destroying the heaviest Boche armour, even the dreaded 'Tigers'."

L/Cpl George O'Connor (8 Platoon 'C' Company)

"At the concentration camp we were briefed and began to study models and photographs of the area we were going to parachute into on D-Day. When we were fed-up of studying, we checked our weapons time and time again, they were our babies and we knew our lives would depend on them. We held contests to see who could pull his knife out and hit a target of Hitler's head, the head was a blown up French letter tied to a tree. We painted a face on it with the, black grease we'd been issued with to use on our own faces."

Lance Corporal Don "Taff" Jones (MMG Platoon)

"We ended up in a tented field, this was the concentration area. We were not allowed out of the camp and not even within 2 yards of the boundary fence. The only exception was when we were taken out by truck to the aerodrome for a bath.

"We were briefed as to what we were expected to do after the drop near 2 bridges. We were going to drop near the village of Ranville, meet up at a quarry and then form a defensive ring to protect the brigades."

The Pathfinders were to be dropped on all the DZ's from 2 Albemarles per DZ at 0020 hours (the same time as the *Coup de Main* party's 3 Horsa gliders at each bridge would land) along with the 'Advance parties' of the Parachute Brigades (5th Brigade in 5 Albemarles of 296 and 297 Squadron). Half an hour later (0050 hours) the main body of 3rd and 5th Parachute Brigades would jump (The 5th Parachute Brigade carried by 131 aircraft, Dakotas and Stirlings).

The Divisional Headquarters including HQ RA, HQ RE, HQ RASC, FOO (Forward Observation Officer) and FOB (Forward Observation Bombardment) parties and 4th Airlanding Anti-Tank Battery, RA, travelling in 65 Horsas and 4 Hamilcar gliders would come in to land at 0320 hours on the cleared landing zones.

At 2100 hours a further and impressive lift of 226 Horsas and 30 Hamilcars would come in to land. This final lift would carry: the Headquarters of the 6th Airlanding Brigade; 2nd Battalion Ox & Bucks LI; 1st Battalion Royal Ulster Rifles; 211th Light Battery, RA and the Armoured Reconnaissance Regiment; 'A' Company, 12th Battalion Devonshire Regiment; 195th Airlanding Field Ambulance; 3rd Airlanding Anti-Tank Battery, RA; 716th Light Company, RASC.

The remainder of the 12th Devonshire Regiment would come in via the seaborne route along with the rest of the Divisional elements.

Private Ken "Ginger" Oldham ('A' Company)

"I, due to the pre-war jobs I'd done, was often called on to repair equipment, the soldier to see to get your kit repaired, generally speaking. I was not fazed by my comrades' requests. But one day, before leaving for Normandy, Captain Spencer Daisley took me aside and explained that he had had a testicle removed as a result of a war wound and he was anxious not to lose the other, so could I make him a protective shield for it? I made one made of fine leather.

"A few days later, Harry Green, my best mate and I was out digging trenches because of the suspicions flying around about Germans dropping spies and terrorist attackers into the south of England. Harry was using a pick and I was shovelling the soil away. Harry caught my hand with the pick and I had to be sent to hospital, this meant that I was going to miss the drop."

Major General Richard "Windy" Gale (Commander, 6th Airborne Division)

"Once in these camps no one was allowed out. Men were put on their honour and our security police checked up on everything that went on. It was the greatest credit to all that not one single case of breach of discipline occurred."

Private Ray "Geordie" Walker (2 Platoon 'A' Company)

"Now the weather was warm and sunny and we had opportunity to relax and partake in games of cricket or rounders and also visit the beer tent. The entire bar maids had been selected for their attractiveness and their task was to extract information from us about the invasion. No troops fell for their charms or divulged any information. In addition the ever present MP's in the tent made sure that there were no breaches of security.

"Despite periods of relaxation work was now one of regular kit and weapon inspections. We realised the D-Day was rapidly approaching with the issue of ammunition, hand grenades, anti-tank mines, plastic bombs, first aid dressings and rations. Now it was our turn to be briefed, with the use of maps, aerial photos and a model of the area. We were now mentally and physically prepared to take part in the Second Front at long last.

"We had a visit from General Gale to wish us "Good Luck""

Lieutenant Jack Watson (3 Platoon 'A' Company)

"I commanded No.3 Platoon for the assault on Normandy. At Broadwell RAF Station, I gave my stick, which consisted of part of my headquarters and one section commanded by Sergeant Farrell. We were all in good heart."

Flight Lieutenant P.M. Bristow ('C' Flight, 575 Squadron, RAF)

"Once we had been given our first briefing and knew the DZ and the glider targets, a tight security clamp was imposed. No-one was allowed off the camp [Broadwell], no letters were collected though we received incoming mail, and no telephone calls were permitted. On the other hand all our flight commanders went over to Netheravon for a special briefing. This was the operational centre for our part of the show.

"During these days we studied photographs, large-scale maps and then we got a sand table of the coastline with the River Orne running up to Caen. We were even shown a film of the run-in from the coastline to the DZ."

General Gale addressing the 13th Para Bn (© IWM H 39075)

Captain David Tibbs (225 Field Ambulance)

"Day by day we received aerial photographs what showed us exactly the Germans were doing. For instance we could see that each day they were putting up more upright poles in the very area we were about to land and these were clearly designed to prevent glider and parachute landings. You could even see new tracks were people had not walked. The preparations gave us enormous confidence. We were given silk folding maps of Europe in case we were dropped astray, we had small compasses and all sorts of devices to try and help us in unexpected events."

Lieutenant Ellis "Dixie" Dean (MMG Platoon)

"We went down to the airfield one morning, dressed as we would be for the drop and were issued with and fitted out chutes which were then marked out with our names in chalk before being laid in rows in store. For the operation (Operation 'Tonga' to the RAF), the MMG Platoon's allocation of aircraft was 2 Stirlings of 299 Squadron, which were allocated Stick 'Chalk' No.s 204 and 205. I would fly with No.1 Section in Chalk 204, and my Platoon Sergeant, Alf Whalley would go with No.2 Section, under Sergeant Sam Osborne in 205. 204 carried the Squadron letter 'H' and had been nick-named 'H for Hellzapoppin', the title of a Hollywood wacky comedy film of the time.

"We knew from the briefing that D-Day was scheduled for 5th June and gradually everything was finalised, and we were ready to go. Until early evening of 3rd, the weather was perfect, and then the calm was broken by a heavy thunderstorm. The weather on the 4th was rather unsettled. The morning was spent filling magazines of Stens and rifles, grenades were primed and packed away. At midday we thought the operation was still on and the afternoon was given over to organised rest, which for some meant another bout of letter writing, for it was impossible to sleep. It wasn't until early evening that the news of the postponement came through; this meant emptying magazines and de-fusing grenades. The tension showed when one of the senior Privates and one of the few regular soldiers in the Platoon, fired his rifle when unloading. Fortunately the muzzle was pointed downwards and no harm was done."

Lance Corporal Don "Taff" Jones (MMG Platoon)

"On the 4th June we were told to prepare for the drop and early evening we got into trucks and onto the aerodrome. On arriving at the entrance we stopped for, I suppose, about an hour or so. The trucks then struck up, turned around and took us back to the camp. We were told that it was off, that night.

"The next evening came the same routine all over again, only this time we drove into the airfield. Sometime around midnight we emplaned into a Stirling Bomber, a 4 engine job, which you jumped through a large hole in the floor. For the jump I carried a kit bag strapped to my left leg containing a 5 lb tripod and my small pack. The kit bag had a quick release and a rope which attached to your harness."

Brigadier J.H.N. Poett (5th Para Brigade Commander)

"We were delayed for a day by the weather. The next day, 5th June, the weather seemed worse. We well knew the implications of a further delay on security and on the [seaborne] troops who were already embarked and were tossing about in their transports. However, the word came through that the operation was "on" that night. The relief was enormous."

Lance Corporal George O'Connor (8 Platoon 'C' Company)

"After a false start, we left the concentration camp, in the early hours of 5th June, bound for an aerodrome; I think it was called, Broadwell, where we were to embark on planes for our destination Normandy. I was loaded, with so much gear, I had a job to stagger along, I was thinking to myself, that I had been greedy and loaded myself with too much ammunition, there again, I said to myself, "if you're going to war son, you can never have too much ammunition, so carry on as best you can." Here are some of the things I carried:

"A sten gun, 2 spare magazines, filled with 9mm bullets, a bandoleer of .303 rifle ammunition, 2 mark 36 hand grenades, 2 phosphorous hand grenades, my webbing equipment, containing, more ammunition, a pack of plastic explosive, wrapped in 4x2 lint to be used for cleaning my weapon, not the explosive, the lint, a camouflage net, I used as a scarf, on my belt. I had an entrenching tool, a full water bottle and a bayonet.

"In the pack on my back, a gas cape, in which I had wrapped, a one man 24 hour ration pack and a ground sheet. Slung across my shoulder was my gas mask, with my toggle rope tied to it. In my pockets, I had a yellow piece of material, which we were supposed to spread out across our chest, in order that our own aircraft could identify us, 2 pieces of paper, folded around a pencil stub in case I had the chance to write to my wife, a jack knife, a silk map of the area of Normandy, a cheese wire, in case we had to throttle the enemy, a folding hacksaw, enclosed in a piece of rubber, I never found out what the piece of rubber was for. Two handkerchiefs, supplied by the kind WVS Ladies, my fighting knife, enclosed in a small scabbard, hidden in a secret pocket in the side of my trousers, a shell dressing pack, containing a sling, a couple of bandages, a small phial of iodine and a tube of morphia, which had a nozzle fitted with a needle, for injecting the morphia, on the other end of the tube, was attached a small piece of lipstick, to dab on the forehead of anyone that was injected. A few British coins, ten 5 Franc notes, a packet of players Navy cut Cigarettes, a lighter, that I had scrounged, two 2oz bars of Cadburys blended milk chocolate and most important of all a photograph of my wife.

"On my breast pocket, were 2 buttons marked with luminous spots, when you removed the buttons and placed them, back to back, they acted as a compass. In my valise that was fastened to my leg were a mess tin, 2 more packs of plastic explosive, more ammunition, which I hoped wouldn't blow up when it hit the ground before I did. The valise also contained detonators, soap, towel, razor, tin of boot polish and dubbing, a pair of gym shoes, a pair of socks and an extra one man ration pack, I had scrounged. The valise weighed around 65 lbs; I was hoping I wouldn't have to carry it too far, when I landed."

Captain Alfred "Nobby" Clark (2i/c, 'C' Company)

"One thing I do remember about this time, I remember thinking that it would surely have pleased my old Granny, whose concern I could never forget for our personal cleanliness, and also that of our linen, "in case you should ever get knocked down in the street and have to be admitted to hospital, and then what would people think?" Before the final denouement we managed to get a bath. This, I felt, would fit in well with General "Boy" Browning's precept, as well as my Granny's, that no man of the Airborne under his command should go into battle unprepared to meet his maker."

Captain Padre Whitfield "Boy" Foy

"The Brigade Commander and Colonel Luard spoke briefly. "The eyes of the world were upon us", we were making history, let it be well and truly made. I read a psalm and together, under the peaceful evening sky we said prayers. Then into the waiting trucks, a wave of the hand to the camp staff, who were there to say "Good Bye" and we were off to the airfield. The Battalion was in 2 sections, one flying from Broadwell, the other from Brize Norton (below). I myself was with the latter section."

Lieutenant Colonel Peter Luard (Commanding Officer, 13th Bn)

"Our training was exacting and extreme, suffice it to say, that when the Battalion went into the Transit Camp, no fitter or more efficient Battalion of Infantry has ever been seen. They knew, throughout that provided they arrived on the ground they were certain of success. It was therefore, with their spirits high, even though their faces were blackened, that they attended final prayers."

Captain Alfred "Nobby" Clark (2i/c, 'C' Company)

"In the gathering dusk of the evening of 5th June 1944, off the perimeter track of Broadwell Airfield could be distinguished parties of what might have been man or heavily laden camels silhouetted against the darkening horizon. At the rendezvous, the ceremony which was taking place there seemed at that moment to be the most natural in the world. The many shapeless caravans converged, and, like camels, sank to their knees. So all of our battalion, led by Padre "Boy" Foy, acknowledged our need and our dependence, our fear and yet our trust, our inadequacy and yet our resolve. There was another prayer, on the Battalion Flag, a black one, bearing under the parachute badge the red rose of Lancashire and the motto 'Win or Die'."

SUPREME HEADQUARTERS
ALLIED EXPEDITIONARY FORCE

Soldiers, Sailors and Airmen of the Allied Expeditionary Force!

You are about to embark upon the Great Crusade, toward which we have striven these many months. The eyes of the world are upon you. The hopes and prayers of liberty-loving people everywhere march with you. In company with our brave Allies and brothers-in-arms on other Fronts, you will bring about the destruction of the German war machine, the elimination of Nazi tyranny over the oppressed peoples of Europe, and security for ourselves in a free world.

Your task will not be an easy one. Your enemy is well trained, well equipped and battle-hardened. He will fight savagely.

But this is the year 1944! Much has happened since the Nazi triumphs of 1940-41. The United Nations have inflicted upon the Germans great defeats, in open battle, man-to-man. Our air offensive has seriously reduced their strength in the air and their capacity to wage war on the ground. Our Home Fronts have given us an overwhelming superiority in weapons and munitions of war, and placed at our disposal great reserves of trained fighting men. The tide has turned! The free men of the world are marching together to Victory!

I have full confidence in your courage, devotion to duty and skill in battle. We will accept nothing less than full Victory!

Good Luck! And let us all beseech the blessing of Almighty God upon this great and noble undertaking.

Dwight D Eisenhower

Guy Byam (War Correspondent, jumping with the 13th Para Bn)

"On an airfield the paratroops kneeled round their Padre in prayer before emplaning. With bent heads on their knees the men with their equipment look like some strange creatures from another world. Darkness came over the airfield and the men get into their aircraft. They are going to jump with heavier loads than any army has done before. Every extra bullet and every extra grenade will count."

Private Len Cox ('C' Company)

"It always struck me as being so touching, everyone in battle kit, blackened faces and yet everyone was deeply touched by the occasion."

Captain Padre Whitfield "Boy" Foy

"It was June 5th 9pm. We had 2 days previously, visited the airfield, allotted our aircraft and fitted our parachutes. It would have been difficult to find anywhere in the country a better disciplined and keener crowd of men. Then into the waiting trucks, a wave of the hand to the camp staff and off to the airfield."

Captain David Tibbs (225 Field Ambulance)

"We carried all our own equipment with us, for instance my own load was about 80lbs of medical equipment. We were marched over to our planes and there was an air of suppressed excitement, no-one showed the least disinclination to go. When I say we were marched to the planes, I mean it wasn't an act of orders, we knew what we were doing and it was done in an orderly fashion.

"A day or so before I had been involved in inoculating a group of people to make sure they had all their proper medical inoculations and a small group refused to have them. When I told this to the officers in charge of these men he passed it on to their Colonel who came down and said "Well look, if you don't have your injections, I'm not going to take you." These men then promptly stepped forward and got their injections. There was a huge confidence and enthusiasm."

Flight Lieutenant P.M. Bristow ('C' Flight, 575 Squadron, RAF)

"On the morning of 5th June we had a pep-talk from the colonel [Luard] in charge of the paratroops. By 1800 hours all our aircraft were marshalled on the perimeter track and taxi tracks so they could file out in the correct order for take off. I forget how many aircraft went from Broadwell that evening but I think it was 2 or 3 squadrons. I do remember that not only was mine the last Squadron to go, but as I was in 'C' Flight, I was amongst the last. It was a long wait and not without anxiety, for one had no sort of idea what reception we might meet. I do remember a strong sense of occasion and however small the part one felt one was taking part in an historic event."

Lieutenant Ellis "Dixie" Dean (MMG Platoon)

"The actual date of the invasion was supposed to be a secret, but the inhabitants of Keevil village realised something and they turned out in force to cheer us on our way.

"At the airfield the Stirlings, 2 squadrons of them, were lined up at the bottom of the runway. Each plane had a welcoming aircrew, who greeted us with "sooner you than us". There was only one officer, the Navigator; he was the source of amusement among my men. He had left something in the crew room and asked the NCO pilot for permission to fall out. The lads thought this was a great joke, but the pilot, regardless of rank, is the man in charge of the plane and all must do as he says. The crew wore a badge that showed they were proud members of the "Caterpillar Club[6]", on one flight

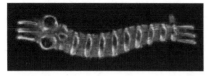

one of the rubber dinghies had broken loose and wrapped around the rudder, so they all had to bail out. The banter past the time until we had to don our chutes, roll berets and, adjust our 'battle bowlers' to emplane.

"Double summer time was introduced in war time, so it was still daylight when we fitted chutes and emplaned. There were 36 Stirlings to take off at 1 minute intervals, so since we would be of the last to become airborne [we] had quite a wait, cooped up in the stuffy fuselage, with the engines ticking away, before we realised that the plane had swung onto the takeoff runway. A sudden roaring of the engines, breaks released, and we thundered down the tarmac. It was 2348 hours, and we were on our way to war, for the first time for most of us."

The Stirling Aircraft lined up at Keevil, 5th June 1944. © IWM CH 13298

Captain Alfred "Nobby" Clark (2i/c, 'C' Company)

"In the dimmed interior of the Dakota and due to a previous application of our faces of brown greasepaint, I could not recognise a single one of the men with me. All were

---

[6] The Caterpillar Club was formed by a young American named Leslie Leroy Irwin who in 1919 demonstrated for the first time that it was possible to fall freely through the air without losing consciousness and open a parachute manually. Irwin joined forces with a silk garment manufacturer to form the Irwin Air Chute Company which began manufacturing safety parachutes. Membership of the Caterpillar Club is still limited to those people whose lives have been saved in an emergency by an Irwin parachute. The club takes its name from the caterpillar, the silken threads from which parachutes of the time were woven, and the way a caterpillar lowers itself safely down to earth by a silken thread it has spun. On being accepted into the club, members are presented with a membership card and a gold pin in the shape of a caterpillar the back of which is engraved with their name and rank (pictured).

70

rendered shapeless by the acquisition of a parachute on the back and a very large kitbag strapped to the right leg. The RAF Dispatcher came aft, carefully checking the equipment of each man, I saw that, praise be to God, he was a 'blue job' and no brash American. A couple of weeks before, he had been supply-dropping to the Chindits. I was comforted by the thought that he was no novice. He indicated to me the large insulated tea container fixed to the floor, conveniently placed for operation by Albert, my batman.

"I remember the location of Private Bamber. He was No.20 in the stick, that is to say right forward of me, the farthest man away from me on the starboard of the plane; diagonally opposite, so to speak. My concern for his whereabouts was two-fold. First, that as he was normally airsick even before the plane was airborne, I had to ensure his fitness to jump at the appropriate moment, and, secondly, since he was the Company HQ 38 set operator on the wireless, I could pass to him as soon as might be after landing a number of 38 set batteries which I had somewhat over generously offered to stow in my own kitbag for him. At the time of packing last minute items, the way he had looked at me for all the world like a little dog put, on trust, by his handler, had roused in me a sense of pity which was really most unsoldierly, at the apparent mountain of kit he was endeavouring to stow away in his kitbag."

Private David "Robbie" Robinson (Anti-Tank Platoon)

"I was a PIAT carrying member of the Anti-Tank platoon with Lieutenant Alf Lagergren, detailed to fly in Chalk 17 with Corporal Simpson as Stick Commander. We were boarding the Albemarle through the exit aperture and were all aboard except the last man. As he was climbing in, the tricycle undercarriage, reared up on its tail and several of the stick slid backwards, out of the hole onto the Tarmac and ending up in a heap under the plane. They scrambled to their feet and tried again but for a second time the plane fell back onto the tail. We were heavily overloaded; we were carrying extra ammo and had full kitbags. After the time we wasted trying to get going, then running around to find a space on perhaps another plane, not being successful and then pulling up wooden posts from around the aerodrome to prop the tail up whilst we loaded, we got the plane moving so that we could take off. But this was all to no avail and the plane did not take off on schedule so we were left behind."

The Armstrong Whitworth Albemarle (The tricycle under-carriage can be seen at the front. The parachutists would exit from a hole in the floor at the rear end).

Major General Richard "Windy" Gale (Commander, 6th Airborne Division)

"We had some grand fellows in the camp with us. I refer to the war correspondents. These men had previously undergone their parachute training and some of them had been attached to units and brigades in the division. I had them in my tent and told them the whole divisional plan."

Leonard Mosley (War Correspondent)

"As I sit amongst my stick of men there is no raucousness, no false gaiety among them. Personally I would not like to be a Jerry destined to meet these boys, for they look pretty grim. For instance there is Jimmy over there, who is a sergeant I used to know from Manchester. He is carrying a Sten gun and ammunition, two .45 revolvers on his hip, a .32 revolver in his crash helmet. He is dropping with a kitbag filled with dynamite and 2 great sausages of plastic explosive around his waist.

"Every man jack in this force is looking forward to hitting European soil a few hours from now. They have been training for it for months. They are fighting fit and fightingly equipped, and they are eager to get to grips with the enemy they have waited so long to meet. I saw a sapper sergeant who was taken off the operation by the Medical Officer this morning because of sickness. He burst into tears."

Sergeant George Butler (3 Platoon 'A' Company)

"On the afternoon of 5th June I was playing 'hooker' in a scratch game of rugby, when the scrum collapsed pinning me underneath and breaking my shoulder. The MI Room was already packed for the drop. The MO Doc Whitley patched me up with some Elastoplasts and put my arm in a sling, telling me I was off the jump.

"This was a blow to my morale but I didn't realise quite how serious a blow it was until the Section I had trained with day and night for the last 9 months, climbed into the trucks and departed for the take off airfield. I was left watching as the convoy grew smaller and smaller in the distance and I walked back through the camp, now empty of troops and organised chaos. It was the loneliest feeling I have ever experienced, before or since.

"I walked into the Mess tent and sat for a long time waiting for take off at the airfield. An RE Sergeant came into the tent and asked about my injury. When I had finished telling him the story, he asked if I would be willing to risk going in by glider; explaining that one member of his team had been stood down on account of illness [probably the one Leonard Mosley had witnessed earlier]. Hence there was room in his glider. I jumped at the chance. I quickly changed my small pack to side fitting, put grenades in my smock pockets and with my Sten and 2 magazines, travelled down to the airfield with the Sergeant and the other members of his squad."

Pte Ray "Geordie" Walker (2 Platoon 'A' Company)

"On arrival at the airfield my Platoon was deposited at our awaiting aircraft, a Dakota. Here we were introduced to the RAF Aircrew who was to fly us to Normandy. I was surprised to see that our Dakota bore black and white stripes painted on the wings and fuselage. This new livery was for easy identification and all Allied aircraft would display similar markings. Hopefully no aircraft would be shot down in error by over keen Ack-Ack Gunners.

"Despite the hive of activity that surrounded us we were able to have a few moments relaxation and enjoy a final cigarette. All too soon the time came to blacken our faces and put our parachutes on before climbing on board our aircraft. We sat on a bench seat which was fixed to the fuselage wall; my seat was on the starboard side and the adjacent a window. When everyone was seated the RAF Dispatcher closed the door and the Pilot started his engines. As soon as the engines reached their operating temperatures the Pilot proceeded to join queues of aircraft leaving their dispersal points and take up their position at the end of the runway. On a given signal from the Ground Controller our Pilot ran up his engines to full power before releasing the brakes, and we roared down the runway and up into the dusky sky. The air armada was on its way to take part in the greatest invasion in history and we were in the van!"

"The 6th Airborne Division planning was done in a specially protected small house, known as Brigmaston Farm House, close to Divisional HQ. Each brigade was allotted a room in the house. Here intelligence summaries, maps and air photographs were kept under conditions of maximum security. An accurate scale model of the whole divisional area was maintained, and also detailed large-scale models of the bridges over the river and the canal, their surroundings and defences. The intelligence material was constantly kept up to date. The number of individuals given passes to admit them to Brigmaston was kept to a minimum. Each individual was briefed at the last possible moment, consistent with his own planning and training commitments."

Brigadier Nigel Poett (5th Para Brigade)

9.   THE FINAL PLAN FOR D-DAY.

INFORMATION

OWN TROOPS

   a) 6 AB Div responsible for preventing enemy penetration westwards over the bridges across the River Orne and Canal de Caen.
   b) 5 Para Brigade to seize intact the bridges and hold bridgeheads to east and west.
   c) 3 Para Brigade is landing at H-4 and infesting high ground between Rivers Orne and Dives.
   d) 1 SS Brigade is landing by sea and fighting its way to the bridges, passing over them at about H+4 hours, and then moving north to attack coast defences east of river mouth.
   e) 6 Airlanding Brigade is landing on LZ at H+12 and will then move south through 13 Bn positions to take up position to secure ST HONORINE, LA CHARDONNERETTE and ESCOVILLE.
   f) 5 Para Brigade plan is as follows:-

   (i)   Coup de main party to land in area of the bridges and seize them at H-5
   (ii)   7 Para Bn lands H-4 hrs 30 min and secures bridgehead on west bank.
   (iii) 12 Para Bn to secure bridgehead on east bank.

INTENTION

13 Para Bn will:-

   a) Clear obstructions on glider landing strips as required and as soon as possible.
   b) Protect the work on the glider strips and the landing of the gliders.
   c) Secure and hold RANVILLE.

13TH PARACHUTE BATTALION - METHOD

Phase I

5 Platoon under command of Lieutenant Jeavons will drop from 3 Albemarles (a/c #3, 4 & 5) on DZ 'N' at P-5 hours (the approximate centre of stick positions where the 3 aircraft dropped on D-Day are marked 'x' on map).

Sections will RV on the DZ and move as follows:-

a) One section to road junction 115749.
b) One section to crossroads 125739.
c) Platoon HQ and one section to area crossroads in RANVILLE 114735

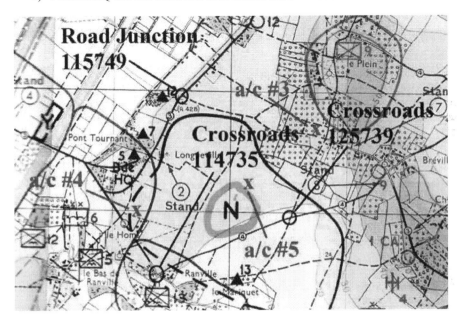

These sections in all cases will prevent entry into the DZ area until relief in the case of:-

a) by 12 Para Bn
b) by 'B' Company
c) by Anti-Tank Platoon

Offensive action will be taken against the occupants of vehicles approaching the DZ, if possible, silently. No vehicles will pass their road blocks. All telephone and telegraph wires will be cut at once.

In RANVILLE great care will be required. It is not known whether or not RANVILLE is held. The position will be approached with great care and offensive action taken against all Germans found, silently if possible. No attempt will be made to clear the village, but only to dominate the area of the crossroads by removal of all sentries and occupation of the vantage points.

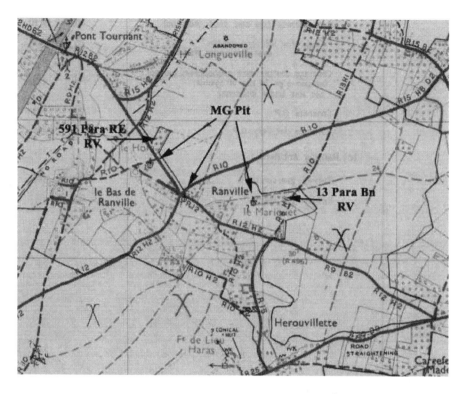

Enemy defensive positions as of Bigot Planning 20th May 1944

Location of enemy defences in the Ranville and Drop Zone 'N' area. Most notable is the machine gun pits located at the RV's and at Ranville crossroads. These were Lieutenant Stan Jeavons' objectives to ensure that the bulk of the Battalion was unhindered when trying to form up. There were also machine guns covering the fields south of Ranville from Ferme de Lieu Haras, but as the Battalion was to drop north of Ranville these were not considered a priority.

Phase II

Bn will drop on DZ 'N' at P-4 hrs 20 min, 1 min 22 sec after crossing the coast. Direction of the run-in is NE-SW. Bn will RV silently and with all possible speed in copse 123735 in the following order from west to east, 'A', 'B', 'HQ', 'C'. Rally will be to hunting horns – Bn call and Company calls at the RV. There will be no homing lights in the RV. Other battalions are using coloured lights.

Company commanders, when they consider that the men from the DZ are in the RV will themselves report to 'O' Group at 'A' Company locality. In the event of an attack during the drop, all men not closely engaged will move direct to the RV.

Companies will retain thirty 75 grenades. All remaining 75 grenades will be collected in Company RV's for use in Phase 4 and left in dumps. One container of 75 grenades is being dropped in the RV area.

Snipers will RV under Lt Bercot with 'HQ' Company.

On orders from Commanding Officer the Battalion will move off.

'A' Company direct to 591 Para Field Squadron RE RV at copse 114738, and commence work with all troops under command and under direction Major Wood, RE. 'B' Company with Anti-Tank Platoon will seize and hold crossroads 114735 and 117733 and will clear all houses on either side of the road. When cleared OC 'B' Company will sound his Company call. 'C' Company and HQ Company on hearing 'B' Company call will move to positions in RANVILLE via crossroads 117733 and track south to Château area to positions. 'C' Company will search all houses south of the north wall of Château Park. Standing patrols will be established immediately and Snipers will move as in directive to Lt. J. Bercot.

If RANVILLE is held in strength 'C' Company will be prepared to attack and clear the village so as to remove the treat to the security of the LZ and working party, and hold the crossroads 114735.

The alarm signal for the working party from the covering party will be 3 red verey lights, duplicated by codeword RED sent by wireless. This signal will only be given on authority of OC 'B' Company from road junction 118737. Until this signal is given enemy activity will not interfere with the continuation of the work. Maximum use will be made of mine warning signs and dummy mines for blocking all roads into the area.

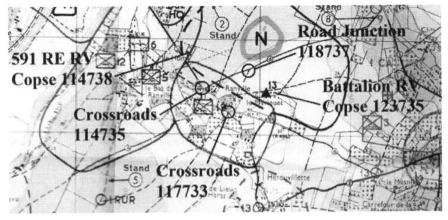

Phase III

By P hour positions will be established. New positions will be dug at once. Battle outposts and patrols will infest the approaches to the bridgehead and by offensive action will force the early deployment of enemy columns.

There <u>will be no withdrawal</u> except on orders from Battalion HQ.

MMG's – One section of MMG will be sited after P hour about track junction 117727, shooting west. One section in 12 Para Bn area at about track junction 109729, shooting SE, will be covering the gap between HEROUVILLETTE and locality 118727.

Officer Commanding the Anti-Tank Platoon [Lieutenant Alf Lagergren] will hand over 3 PIAT's and bombs to 'B' Company at P hour for protection of approaches from E and SE.

About this time it is expected that vehicles of 4th Airlanding Anti-Tank Battery RA, will be moving through the village from the West and every assistance will be given to aid their passage.

At about P+2, 20 men of 22nd Independent Parachute Company may move in through HEROUVILLETTE and 20 men from LE PLEIN area via 'B' Company area to 12th Para Bn area.

Phase IV

As 'A' Company arrives in RANVILLE, after completion of removing anti-glider poles from LZ [formally DZ], all positions will be dug in at once.

'B' Company will lay minefields with type 75 [Hawkins] grenades left in RV from road and wood junction 118733 to NW corner of wood 119734.

'A' Company will lay minefield from west end of buildings 118728, thence west to stream, thence north along line of stream and prolongation of this line to effect a junction with south end of minefield laid by 'B' Company.

Wire available will be erected to cover minefields, and maximum possible use of dummy mine positions and warning signs will be made.

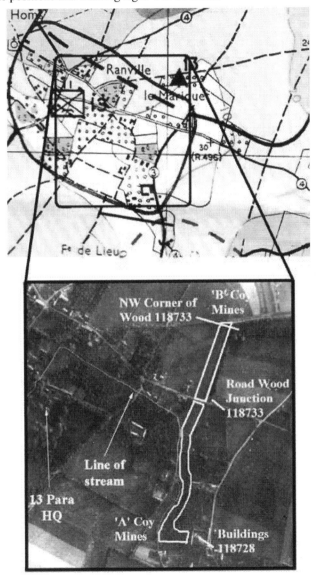

Phase V

'B' Company will be responsible for covering both minefields by fire, day and night.

Points of contact with:-

6 Commando	-	BREVILLE crossroads 134744 by snipers
1 Canadian Para Bn	-	Crossroads 125729 by 'B' Company
12 Para Bn	-	Road/track junct 112737 to road junct 112736.

Crossroads 124724 by 'A' Company

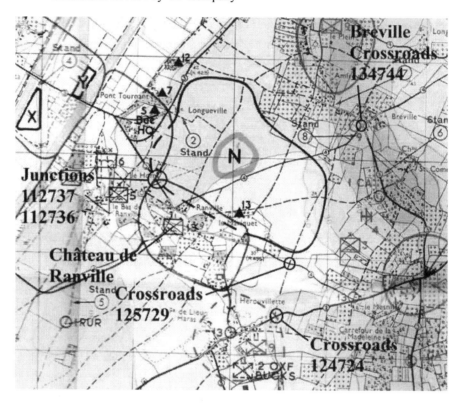

All available transport including captured transport and horse transport will be taken to Battalion HQ (Château de Ranville).

Medical positions

a) DZ CCP   –   Church 111736
b) ADS   –   Building 105735
c) RAP   –   Château 114734

All walking wounded will be directed to the ADS.

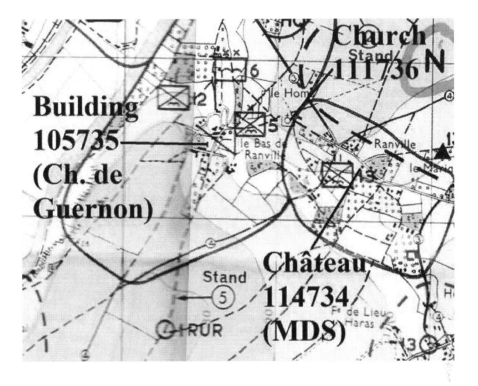

Civilians and Prisoners of War

Civilians will be ordered to remain in their houses and where houses are required for defence, they will be moved to neighbouring houses.

POW's will be brought immediately to the POW compound at the Château buildings at 114734 and the Brigade collecting point for POW's will be in the buildings at 110746.

'B' Coy HQ at road junction 124736
Advance Bn HQ in garden of cottage 114734.
'C' Company will be in reserve for counter attacking purposes.

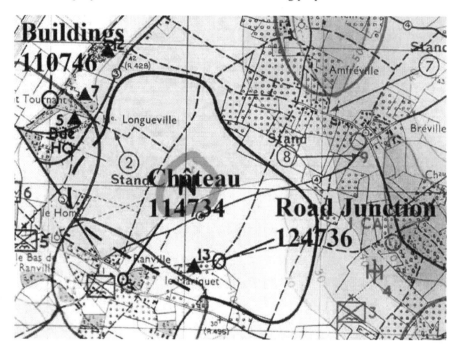

Sniper Platoon

Snipers to cover:

   a) Road junction   133725
   b) Road junction   140728
   c) Château St Come   139740
   d) Road junction   135745
   e) Road junction   128753

Lieutenant Bercot will contact locals so as to obtain information of vantage points for observation, probable enemy movement and any enemy locations.

Snipers will only fire on worthwhile targets, such as officers, despatch riders, drivers of enemy cars, and if certain of a kill: observation posts, recce parties and wireless sets

The "Get Away Men" (who should conceal themselves behind the sniper to take information back) and Lt Bercot and his batman will each have a folding bicycle for swift reporting to Battalion HQ. Each pair will also have a 38 wireless set, but will only use in the most urgent circumstance.

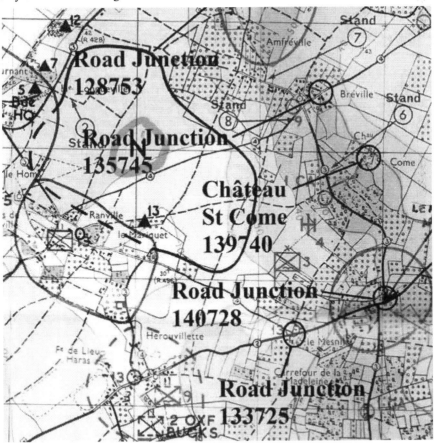

ORDER OF BATTLE - 13 PARA BN

OPERATION "OVERLORD"

BATTALION HQ

Commanding Officer	Lieutenant Colonel P. J. LUARD
Second-in-Command	Major Bill HARRIS MC
Adjutant	Captain Bill GRANTHAM
Quartermaster	Captain "George" DAISLEY
Intelligence Officer	Lieutenant Leslie GOLDING
Assistant Adjutant	Lieutenant Bernard "Shadow" METCALF

ATTACHED OFFICERS

Medical Officer (RAMC)	Captain Neil WHITLEY
Padre (RAChD)	Captain The Rev Whitfield "Boy" FOY
Regimental Serjeant Major	W.O. I. Bob DUXBERRY
Regimental Quartermaster	Serjeant Jimmy HENSTOCK

HEADQUARTERS COMPANY

Company Commander	Major Reggie TARRANT
Admin Captain	Captain. F.A.N. ELLISON
Mortar Officer	Lieutenant Fred SKEATE
Anti-Tank Officer	Lieutenant Alf LAGERGREN
Machine Gun Officer	Lieutenant "Dixie" DEAN
Sniper Platoon	Lieutenant J. BERCOT
Signals Officer	Lieutenant Malcolm TOWN
Company Sergeant Major	C.S.M. MORLAND
Company Quartermaster Sergeant	C.Q.M.S. Ray MEACHIM

"A" COMPANY

Company Commander	Major John CRAMPHORN
Company Second-in-Command	Captain Harry AINSWORTH
No.1 Platoon	Lieutenant Jack WATSON
No.2 Platoon	Lieutenant "Joe" HODGSON
No.3 Platoon	Lieutenant Gordon O'BRIEN-HITCHING
Company Sergeant Major	C.S.M. J. McPHARLAN
Company Quartermaster Sergeant	C.Q.M.S. Harry WATKINS

"B" COMPANY

Company Commander	Major George BRISTOW
Company Second-in-Command	Captain Mike KERR
No.4 Platoon	Lieutenant Bert ARNOLD
No.5 Platoon	Lieutenant Stan JEAVONS
No.6 Platoon	Lieutenant "Terry" BIBBY
Company Sergeant Major	C.S.M. Jack MOSS
Company Quartermaster Sergeant	C.Q.M.S. Eric COOKSON

"C" COMPANY

Company Commander	Major Gerald FORD
Company Second-in-Command	Captain "Nobby" CLARK
No.7 Platoon	Lieutenant Harry POLLAK
No.8 Platoon	Lieutenant Jack SHARPLES
No.9 Platoon	Lieutenant George "Tiger" LEE
Company Sergeant Major	C.S.M. Micky MAGUIRE
Company Quartermaster Sergeant	C.Q.M.S. "Duggy" DUGDALE

"R" Company (IN UK)

Company Commander	Captain "Claude" MILMAN
Transport Officer	Lieutenant "Baggy" ALLEN
Platoon Officers	Lieutenant Ken WALTON
	Lieutenant Cyril BAILEY
	Lieutenant Steve HONNOR
	Lieutenant Dick BURTON
	Lieutenant "Topper" BROWN
	Lieutenant Fred TIRAMANI
	2nd Lieutenant Geoff OTWAY

13 PARA BN – FLIGHT TABLE

A/C	JUMPMASTER	MEN	SUB UNIT	CON	M/C	CYCLE
3	SGT WRIGLEY	9	"B" COMPANY	3		
4	SGT DAWSON	9	"B" COMPANY			
5	SGT BADEL	9	"B" COMPANY			
204	SGT KELLY	20	MMG PLATOON	6		
205	SGT OSBORNE	20	MMG PLATOON	6		1
307	SGT O'BRIEN	17	"A" COMPANY		2	
308	SGT ARMITAGE	17	"A" COMPANY		1	1
309	SGT BRADLEY	17	"A" COMPANY		2	1
310	SGT LLEWELLYN	18	"A" COMPANY		2	
311	SGT ALDER	17	"A" COMPANY		1	1
312	SGT TAYLOR	17	"A" COMPANY		2	1
313	SGT LAWLEY	18	"A" COMPANY		2	1
314	CSM PARRISH	17	BN HQ "A" PARTY		2	
315	SGT TICKELL	17	"B" COMPANY		2	
316	SGT ATKINSON	18	"B" COMPANY		2	1
317	SGT REID	17	"B" COMPANY		2	1
318	SGT CLARK	17	"B" COMPANY		2	1
319	SGT MCGRATH	18	"B" COMPANY		2	1
320	SGT BARRET	17	"C" COMPANY		1	
321	CQMS DUGDALE	18	"C" COMPANY		1	1
322	SGT MUIR	17	"C" COMPANY		1	1
323	SGT BRAY	17	"C" COMPANY		1	1
324	SGT COLLIER	17	"C" COMPANY		1	1
325	SGT STUBBS	17	"C" COMPANY		1	1
326	CAPT TIBBS (RAMC)	20	225 FIELD AMB			
327	RSM DUXBERRY	17	BN HQ "B" PARTY			1
8	SGT BRIMMICOMBE	9	"C" COMPANY	3		
9	SGT SMITH, T.R.	9	"C" COMPANY	3		
10	S.I. HURST	9	HQ COMPANY	3		
11	SGT WEBSTER	9	HQ COMPANY			
12	CQMS COOKSON	9	HQ COMPANY			
13	CPL MONKS	9	HQ COMPANY			
14	SGT HAYTER	9	HQ COMPANY			
15	CPL WADE	9	HQ COMPANY			
16	CPL SANDERS	9	HQ COMPANY			
17	CPL SIMPSON	9	HQ COMPANY			
18	CPL HOLLIS	9	HQ COMPANY			
19	CPL SCOTT	9	HQ COMPANY			
20	SGT MCPHAIL	9	HQ COMPANY			
21	SGT PRICE	9	HQ COMPANY			
22	SGT PRITCHARD	9	MORTARS	4		
23	SGT THOMPSON	9	MORTARS	4		
24	SGT ROBERTS	9	MORTARS	4		
25	CPL PRINCE	9	MORTARS	4		
26	CPL WALKER	9	MORTARS	4		

A/C No.	DROP	AIRFIELD	TAKE OFF
3-5	P minus 5 hrs	Brize Norton	P minus 6 hrs 18 min
204-205	P minus 4 hrs 17 min	Keevil	P minus 6 hrs 01 min
307-327	P minus 4 hrs 24 min	Broadwell	P minus 5 hrs 51 min
8-26	P minus 4 hrs 20 min	Brize Norton	P minus 5 hrs 38 min

0050 hours: 13th Bn (Lancashire) The Parachute Regiment, forming part of
5th Parachute Brigade dropped from DAKOTA and ALBEMARLE a/c on DZ 'N' -
NORTH of RANVILLE, near CAEN, Dept of CALVADOS.

13th Para Bn War Diary 6th June 1944

10.   "TONGA"

Flight Lieutenant P.M. Bristow ('C' Flight, 575 Squadron, RAF)

"The first to get airborne in the last of the daylight were all towing gliders. Never shall I forget the first one of all, for he had just about used up all of the runway and was still on the ground. Around the periphery of the airfield stretched a low dry-stone Cotswold wall and a load of shingle had been tipped against this wall at either end of all the runways. It may have been imagination, and remember the light was failing, it may have been a despairing heave back on the control column or it may have been a bit of both; but it always seemed to all of us who were watching that the Dakota ran its wheels up the shingle bank and was literally catapulted into the air. At zero feet it staggered along too low to make a turn but with a line of electricity grid poles not far in front. Next day the pilot said the trip had been uneventful apart from the take-off. To the best of my memory my take-off proceeded without a single hitch.

"Aircraft carrying paratroops started their take-off about an hour later and not until it was quite dark. There should have been a full moon that night but there was 10/10ths cloud cover so the night was dark. We had normal runway lighting for take-off but no navigation lights were used and we had to observe strict radio silence. Our signal to go was a green light from the control caravan at the end of the runway and we went off at pretty long intervals of 1 minute and 30 seconds. There was certainly no sign of the aircraft ahead of you by the time it was your turn to go. The whole flight was scheduled; So long after take-off and turn on to such and such a course; after another interval turn to a different heading, with times to leave our coast at Littlehampton, to make landfall at Normandy and a time to drop. Streams of aircraft were going off from several other fields, many destined for the same DZ, so they all had to be interlocked. So far as I could judge the staff work must have been good.

"We were supposed to be flying in V's of 3 and I was third in my V so I kept my throttles well opened to catch up the others in front. Formation flying is not a normal part of a transport Pilot's expertise, but we had done a little in the preceding months but not at night, yet here we were on a particularly dark night. I eventually caught up with the fellows in front and found that there were 4 of them. I decided I should be much more relaxed if I dropped back and flew on my own."

Captain Alfred "Nobby" Clark (2i/c, 'C' Company)

"We rolled forward, took a short run, and I felt that lack of bumping which indicated our being airborne, saw obliquely through the open door the ground which should have been below swing upward to my right, and felt the 'clunk' of the wheels as they retracted into their flying position. We were off. We were coming Over Lord.

"It was natural I suppose that as far as the men were concerned silence reigned in the plane for some time. Our RAF despatcher appeared beside me, rather in the manner of a ghost. The look on his face, the only white face in the plane, asked if everything was alright. I asked him how Bamber was. He departed to find out and returned after a couple of minutes to report "OK". To my in incredulous and inane enquiry as to why he had not been sick he could give no answer.

"This passage of words had the effect of starting the general conversation among us, first between immediate neighbours, then soon with buddies on the opposite side of the fuselage. Someone started to sing. The tune was taken up by the whole stick, 'Onward Christian Soldiers'."

Private Bill Rutter (Signaller, 'C' Company)

"The trip was very smooth in the Dakotas although the seats were a bit hard. We drank tea from flasks but there was far too much condensed milk in it for me. The odd thing that sticks in my mind was that although we kept starting different songs, we always kept going back to 'Onward Christian Soldiers' – a hymn that was in the service. For some reason it seemed to have stuck in our minds."

Captain David Tibbs (225 Field Ambulance)

"It was a full moon with a fair bit of cloud which kept obscuring it. The visibility wasn't particularly good and kept coming and going. The aeroplane in which we were in was fairly well lit. We took off as any plane does and obviously ones pulse rates went up a little bit as you realised that this was it. The aircraft was fairly noisy; it was a Dakota, a twin engine plane with no door, just an open area. There wasn't much opportunity for conversation, but most people were trying to rib each other a little bit and some chaps were silent and a bit green, but really a general attitude of cheerfulness was kept up without any problems.

"I was tense and excited, as anyone would be on such an occasion. It was my job as the officer in charge of the 20 men within the plane to keep up their morale and not show any doubts myself, but I felt we were all feeling much the same. I felt that I had the confidence to come through it, although I did think about what my parents would think should I be killed, plus I'd only been married for only about a year so I was anxious on that account as well. I didn't let my mind linger along those lines."

Private Ray Batten (2 Platoon 'A' Company)

"I remember the terrific noise of the aircraft engines when they were struck up, it was still light then in England because we were on Double British Summertime, 2 hours behind. It was perhaps about 12:30 when we crossed over the British coast. I remember there was a war correspondent at No.19 in our stick, I never did find out who he was, but he was going out at No.19. The interior was dimly lit and Lt Hodgson gave us some coffee. All I kept thinking was "Ray Batten the paratrooper going to invade Normandy.""

Guy Byam (War Correspondent, No.19 of Ray Batten's stick)

"In the plane, I'm jumping one but last of the stick. We felt the tremendous vibration of the 4 motors as we start down the runway and all around in the coming darkness are other great planes and row upon row of gliders. The plane is airborne and in the crowded fuselage all you can see in the pail light is the man standing next to you. On we fly, on and out over the channel. The minutes go by and the stick commander told us we are out over a great armada of ships. Then there was something else he had to say, something that gives you a dry feeling in your mouth, "Flak!" The word was passed from man to man and the machine started to rock and jump, but a comforting thought was ahead of us Lancasters were going in to bomb the Flak and coastal batteries."

Lt Jack Watson (3 Platoon 'A' Company)

"Everybody in the aircraft seemed to be extremely quiet as soon as we were airborne. We all wondered what it would be like at this time the next day. We were dropping into the unknown, we had an idea about the defences and who was there, but we wondered what the reaction was going to be like when we got there.. For many of us, it was our first taste of action with the Germans. It was certainly a queer feeling. Suddenly our thoughts were brought back quickly to the aircraft, my batman, Private Harry Gospel was singing his usual Cockney songs, and most of us joined him and forgot about the other side.

"As we were flying over the sea I was impressed by the ships below all signalling to us 'V' for Victory, It was a wonderful sight."

Captain Padre Whitfield "Boy" Foy (a/c 15)

"There were all of us sitting, very crushed, on the floor of our Albemarle. The aperture by which we were to leave the plane was at the back [in the floor] and was covered during the flight by folding doors. Space was so limited that I was compelled to sit on these doors. The atmosphere rapidly became stifling and then the chapter of accidents started. We had left the coast of England and were out over the Channel when, without warning, the lights went out. Groping about in the dark we had to start fastening kit bags to our legs. To do this we had to use the full length of the plane. Once we had completed securing the kit bags we had to start squeezing backwards, in order to get clear of the doors which would have to be opened soon. We laboured and groaned as we pressed backwards, thrusting elbows and rifles into one another as the pressure increased. After much effort, I managed to get clear of the doors. Leaning over I lifted up the 2 parts of the door and fastened them back, letting in a welcome gust of fresh air. Looking down through the aperture I saw the waters of the Channel glistening below, an amazing sight, the white paths cut by hundreds of Allied vessels moving steadily toward the French coast, the vanguard of the beach assault troops."

Private Ray "Geordie" Walker (2 Platoon 'A' Company)

"The flight [a/c 310] to the south coast was uneventful. Up to this point, my comrades and I were in very high spirits; singing, joking and laughing. However as soon as we crossed the coast between Worthing and Bognor Regis the conversation became muted, then total silence. Now each man was alone with his private thoughts of home and their loved ones. Gazing out of the window and silhouetted against the moon, I could see hundreds of aircraft and all heading south, whilst far below a vast fleet was steaming towards France. It looked as if it were possible to use these ships as stepping stones to Normandy."

Lance Corporal George O'Connor (8 Platoon 'C' Company)

"Somebody began to sing the para version of 'Red River Valley', we all joined in, and then carried on singing songs with words I cannot repeat here. Eventually the singing ceased and except for the drone of the engines, all went quiet, I pretended to be asleep, I began thinking, "What was I doing here?" I was about to parachute in to a foreign country and kill or be killed, "What for?" I hadn't done any harm to anyone and the Germans didn't know me from a bar of soap. It seemed stupid to me, we were going to fight and kill each other, Why didn't the Politicians, do the fighting and leave us alone. I only joined the Paratroops for the extra 2 bob a day."

Brigadier J.H.N. Poett (5th Para Brigade Commander)

"Now we were speeding over the coast defences, at about 400 ft and not a shot was fired at us. Surprise was complete. The red light came on – "Prepare to jump" Then the green, "jump" and I was out in the night air and, almost immediately, in fact some 20 seconds, a big bump. I had arrived safely on the soil of France.

"It was all much too quick. I had done none of the things I ought to have done such as identifying Ranville church, or pulling on my lift webs to get a good landing, but I was down and I had not landed on top of one of Rommel's asparagus, set to catch us.

"Then almost at once, to my right, the silence and the darkness was transformed: All the sights and sounds of battle, explosions, firing, signal lights and so on. Now I knew exactly where I was and where I must go, as fast as possible."

War Diary 6th June

0050   13th Bn (Lancashire) The Parachute Regiment, forming part of 5th Parachute Brigade dropped from DAKOTA and ALBEMARLE a/c on DZ 'N' - NORTH of RANVILLE, near CAEN, Dept of CALVADOS.

Cpl Alex Runacres (5 Platoon 'B' Company)

"When I jumped out of the aircraft it was a wonderful feeling! I thought I was invincible and once on the ground I'd have fought the Devil himself."

Cpl Runacres (left) jumped from Albemarle No.5 with Sgt Alan Badel's stick as one of the Advance Party. Under the command of Lt Stan Jeavons, they were to secure and protect the DZ RV's.

5 minutes earlier at 0015 hours the 6 gliders of the *coupe de main* party dived down towards the 2 bridges over the Orne River and Canal de Caen. The *coupe de main* assault of the bridges was a complete success. 3 gliders carrying Major John Howard commander of 'D' Company, the Oxfordshire & Buckinghamshire Light infantry and a team of Engineers, landed 50 yards from 'Pegasus' Bridge and against negligible and startled resistance, with minimal casualties, they took and held their objectives. 2 of the 3 gliders allotted 'Horsa' Bridge, landed close to their objective and took it without firing a shot. The other glider landed at a bridge over the River Dives by mistake. They captured the bridge, realised their mistake and had to fight their way back to the Orne bridgehead.

They now had to wait for the 5th Parachute Brigade to land and reinforce their gains. The 7th Parachute Battalion was to fortify the Western bridgehead of Benouville and Le Port, whilst the 12th and 13th Battalions would protect the Southern and Eastern bridgehead in the Ranville area.

The Independent Pathfinders had been dropped slightly astray on the Eastern edge of the DZ and with little time available, had no option but to set up the beacons. This would result in a lot of the main body being dropped slightly further away from their intended areas, leading to longer form up times.

Lieutenant Jeavons (left) and his advanced party consisting of 3 stick's of 9 paratroopers (aircraft No.3, 4 & 5), dropped on the DZ in the correct place, but were scattered and took longer to form up. At one time only Lt. Jeavons and his batman [Private Eric Prew] were at the 13th Parachute Battalion RV (a small copse at the 'Le Mariquet' crossroads) where Jeavons killed a lone sentry with his fighting knife. He remembered his first words to his batman: "Look around. There's no other bugger here but us." Lt Jeavons also recalls how, "It was terribly exciting to realise, deep down, that we were on our bloody own. We were so isolated I seriously thought the invasion had been cancelled." The RV was passed as clear and they waited for the main body to come in.

Many years later Lt Stan Jeavons was given a letter written by his Commanding Officer Peter Luard, which confirmed that "This most brilliant officer was the first officer to land by parachute in France."

Flight Lieutenant P.M. Bristow ('C' Flight, 575 Squadron, RAF)

"We had taken off at 23:30 and were due to drop at 01:10. Our stick went down within 30 seconds of the exact scheduled time. We were carrying 20 paratroopers and an Alsatian dog. On a temporary rack fitted below the belly off the aircraft we carried a number of small anti-personnel bombs. We had been briefed to drop these as we crossed the Normandy beaches so that if there were any defenders they would be encouraged to keep their heads down. There were also a couple of folding motorcycles in cylindrical canisters. Shortly before we made landfall something exploded on the land right ahead. A vast sheet of yellow flame lit up the sky for a second or two and in that I saw a line of aeroplanes all going the same way, all at the same height, and I was part of this game of follow-my-leader. I made myself think I was all alone on a night course on Salisbury Plain, but kept very keyed up to take smart evasive action if I got close enough to anyone else to see them. I felt the slip-stream from other aeroplanes in front from time to time.

"Bill Dyson and the 'Gee' box brought us in for a perfect land-fall and Robbie Burns and I found we could see enough to make our way visually to the DZ. Robbie was a RAF navigator and was just ex-Ulster university, he was a bright boy. There were not always enough pilots for every crew to have a second pilot, so I was given Robbie as a map reader and that was a lucky day."

Captain Alfred "Nobby" Clark (2i/c, 'C' Company)

"It was the appearance of the despatcher again that caused the singing to die away. He said that there was flak coming up ahead. We were getting near the French coast. I couldn't see ahead from where I was sitting but I did look down through the door and could see in the brilliant moonlight between the patchy clouds the little points of darkness made visible by their tiny white wakes, tire invasion crafts below in the Channel. Then came the long white line of surf, and suddenly as we banked slightly to starboard the flak was visible, the despatcher shouted "Cabourg". Shortly afterwards we were into the flak. It came up at us rather like fireworks. Our aircraft instead of rising and increasing speed seemed to slow clown. It dropped lower, altering course slightly a couple of times. I did think that on this occasion the pilot might just have complied with his orders to drop the bomb not worrying particularly when or where. However he was presumably at last satisfied with his effort, for we started to rise and the engines took on a, for me, much healthier note. The despatcher appeared with what I could feel was a puckish smile on his face as he shouted "Bombs away", with all the aplomb of a bomb aimer who had just released a stick of 1,000 pounders into Hitler's front garden.

"Something hit us. The sound was rather like that of a dustbin being emptied, but there was no apparent damage at the moment. It wasn't until a minute or so later when my next-door neighbour jokingly accused Albert of having made a pool on the floor that we discovered that the tea container had sustained a direct hit from the flak. This was held to be a heinous crime on the part of Jerry, for which we resolved he should pay dearly in due course.

"The despatcher came back from the cockpit saying something to each man as he came. I could not hear until he was 4 men away, although I guessed, "5 minutes to go!" Men began fidgeting with chinstraps and glanced at the hooks on the static lines."

Captain David Tibbs (225 Field Ambulance)

"In the first half hour of 6th June 1944, that is D-Day, the invasion of Normandy, in a Dakota flying in darkness across the channel. It was only one of several hundred planes and gliders carrying the 6th Airborne Division. This particular plane carries 20 medical parachutists. I was to jump first as a young medical officer (MO) who was in charge of the group, and our initial task was to clear the dropping zone of any parachutists injured in the night jump into Normandy. The broad doorway in the fuselage was open and the interior dimly lit. I tried not to give repeated glances to check yet again that myself and the men near me were all properly hooked up, but gave the occasional grin or thumbs up signal to those who caught my eye. There was a sudden stirring and a few joking remarks as a red light suddenly came on and the RAF dispatcher shouted, "Red on!" Everyone stood up and checked the static line of the man next to him - the signal to jump would come within 3 minutes. I looked down and could just see a white line of breaking surf in the half moonlight and knew we were crossing the French coast and the jump would be in about 2 minutes, and swallowed hard."

Lieutenant "Dixie" Dean (MMG Platoon)

"It was unbearably hot inside the plane. My eyes were soon stinging as beads of sweat ran down my face, and I could feel my soaking wet shirt clinging to my back. I wasn't a happy man at all. Then to make matters worse, the 2 large flasks of tea provided by the RAF were too sweet. Sergeant Kelly reported that the rear gunner was complaining that he could see nothing because of the fuselage lights and would not be able to warn the Pilot if any Luftwaffe night fighters put in an appearance. He was told quietly, but firmly "to put a sock in it."

"Everything went as normal until we got the "20 minutes to go" signal. This was received by Sergeant Kelly, who as Stick Commander, and jumping No.10, was plugged into the plane's intercom. As the signal came from the cockpit, it was conveyed personally by the wireless operator who was to act as dispatcher. Once he had worked his way up to the rear, stepping over our legs stretched out on the floor, Sgt Kelly ordered "Stand Up! Hook Up! Equipment Check!" Since we were already hooked up and had fitted equipment, he just waited until we were all on our feet, and then said "Check Equipment!" We checked individually that you were indeed hooked up, and all equipment was fitted correctly. A minute or so to do this, and then came "Sound off for Equipment Check!" From No.20 in the stick came "Number 20... OK!" and as he did so, in case he hadn't been heard, he would grasp the left shoulder of No.19 firmly in his hand. This was a tremendously reassuring action, letting the man know he wasn't on his own, you were right behind him, and come what may you would be facing it together. No.19 would then repeat this, "Number 19... OK!" and so it went on, "Number 18... OK!", "Number 17... OK!" until No.2, in this case L/Cpl Alf Turner grasped my shoulder and called "Number 2... OK!" I would then have reported "Number 1... OK; Stick... OK!" and George Kelly would then have reported to the pilot, "Stick Ready to Jump!"

"Perhaps all of this would have taken 5 minutes or so, and my next task as No.1 was to help the dispatcher open and fasten back, the doors covering the bathtub shaped aperture in the floor just in front of me, through which we were to make our exits. But looking back down the plane, I could see that the dispatcher had not yet secured the strop guard. This is a gate like device, peculiar to the Stirling, which was attached to the underside of the fuselage, and had to be lowered and pinned into position in order to prevent the empty parachute bags getting blown up into the rudder. Alf Turner unhooked me and I went back to where the dispatcher was struggling with the strop guard. I don't know what was troubling the poor unfortunate man, but his hands was trembling so much that he could hardly grasp the retaining pin, yet alone insert the same through the required slot. I did the job for him and went back to my jump position. Alf hooked me up, and I then slid back the front bolt of the aperture doors. But once more I had to be unhooked and go back and release the rear bolt. Hooked up for the 3rd time, I opened and fastened back the upper doors on my own.

"The dispatcher from his position to the rear of the aperture was the only one who could open the lower door, by pulling it up a long handle. This he managed to do. Sometime while all this was happening I should have received the "5 minutes to go" signal. I had not done so, as a consequence, when the bottom door was opened and I was able to look down, much to my surprise, we were flying over land, not the English Channel as I had expected, Because the Drop Zone was only 4 miles from the coast, I had it worked out in my own mind, that once we crossed the French coast, we had less than 2 minutes from jumping, so what was going on? I was completely confused by it all, and still trying to puzzle it out when, from behind me, came a great bellow "GREEN ON!" Half the stick must have yelled out the warning. My immediate reaction was "Why haven't I had the 5 second 'Action Stations, Red' I had asked for?" I glanced up, Green it was, and with another glance down, we were still flying over land and, although I was not happy about it, I took one pace forward and out into the cool night air I went."

Major Hans Von Luck (21ˢᵗ Panzer Division)

"The evening of 5th June was unpleasant, Normandy was showing its bad side; during the day there had been rain and high winds. The general weather conditions, worked out every day by Naval Meteorologists, and passed on to us by Division, gave the "all clear" for 5th and 6th June. So we did not anticipate any landings for heavy seas and low flying clouds would make large scale operations at sea and in the air impossible for our opponents.

"That evening I felt our lot was very unsatisfactory, like most of my men I was used to mobile actions, such as we had fought in other theatres of war. This waiting for an invasion, which was undoubtedly coming, was enervating. But in spite of the inactivity, morale amongst the troops remained high.

"On that rainy evening my Adjutant and I were awaiting a report from No.2 Battalion that their night exercise had ended. This Battalion was in the area Troarn, Escoville, while No.1 Battalion, equipped with armoured personnel carriers had taken up a positions further inland.

"About midnight I heard the growing roar of aircraft. The machines appeared to be flying low. I looked out the window and was wide awake; flares were hanging in the sky. At the same moment, my adjutant was on the telephone, "Major, paratroops are dropping. Gliders are landing in our section. I'm trying to make contact with No.2 Battalion. I'll come along to you at once."

"I gave orders without hesitation, "All units are to be put on alert immediately and the division informed. No.2 Battalion is to go into action wherever necessary. Prisoners are to be taken if possible and brought to me."

"I then went to the command post with my adjutant. The 5th Company of No.2 Battalion, which had gone out with blank cartridges, was not back yet from the night exercise - a dangerous situation."

Flight Lieutenant P.M. Bristow ('C' Flight, 575 Squadron, RAF)

"Rebecca-Eureka was working by now to help lead us in. This was a short-range homing device actuated from a portable ground station. Now the illuminated direction Tee could also be seen and we were almost there. The paratroops had been standing lined up with the red light on - well back from the door opening - and at this point they got the amber and would go on the green. Doug Strake my Canadian W/Op was acting jump-master and was able to speak to me down the intercom and he told me all was ready and well. I had started the drop at the right height, the right speed and all was as right as we could make it, until I lost contact with Doug. I should wait for him to tell me it was OK to open up, but he was silent, we were steadily losing height and advancing on the Germans, who were clearly belligerent as witness the flames in the sky not long before. I was sure it was one of our lot that had bought it, though I was later told that it was a Stirling. A moment later and Doug came through again to say every-thing had gone and I opened throttles, made a climbing turn to port and disappeared into cloud were we all felt nice and snug.

"When he joined us in the cockpit Doug told us that the dog, who with its handler was the last to go, had followed all the others to the door, and as it came to its turn to follow its handler, backed away from the door and retired to the front of the fuselage. Doug had had to unplug himself from the intercom, catch the dog and literally throw it out. Several weeks later he met one of our stick in Oxford who had been sent home wounded and he said they had eventually found the dog."[7]

Official Report - 296 Squadron

"The remaining 8 aircraft reached the area. Considerable light flak was encountered and several suffered minor damage. These aircraft dropped without mishap with the exception of Flight Lieutenant Scott, whose stick also had adventures in the back of the machine. 3 men dropped on the first run in and then the doors collapsed. On the second run the stick was not ready to jump and a third run was made. At the end of this the wireless operator reported from the fuselage that there was still one man and a dog left. A fourth run was made. On the approach to the DZ the W/Op tried to encourage the dog to jump but finally took refuge near the gun turret. The man and dog jumped on the last run in."[8]

Captain David Tibbs (225 Field Ambulance)

"In the moment just before my section was to jump a 4 engine Stirling bomber that had dropped other parachutists elsewhere, but now dangerously off course, suddenly appeared cutting diagonally across our path. Collision seemed inevitable but both pilots took violent evasive action and all the men in my plane were thrown in disarray to the floor.

"As No.1, hanging onto the doorway, I had seen all this very clearly. Our pilot swiftly corrected the plane and the green light to jump came on immediately but I could do nothing to help the chaos behind me, and so jumped out into the darkness. The consequence of this was the men would have to crawl to the door, so instead of jumping out at one man a second, whilst the aircraft would cover the ground at 60 yards a second; they were spread out over a mile or two. Many of these men we didn't see again, only about 5 turned up on the DZ with me. Most were captured and some we never heard of again. Others made their way back a day or so later much to their credit. To my surprise I landed close to an orchard of apple trees, just as my pilot had predicted. The quick reaction of our pilot (FO Peter Hakkansson) saved out lives and his navigation was perfect but sadly he and his crew of 4 all died 2 months later when enemy fire shot down their plane on one of their frequent subsequent flights into Normandy.

"After I landed I had a steady walk in the darkness towards Ranville and in the distance I could hear the thump and crackle of attack going in on the bridges. I bumped into other men, but considering that 2,000 men had dropped in this area it was considerably quiet. It was about ½ hour later that I reached Ranville at my RV point and I waited anxiously for my men to join me. I was fairly soon joined by the chap who'd jumped immediately after me, a man called Clark and soon after that by my Staff Sergeant who had dropped fairly well towards the end of the stick and had been fairly resourceful in finding his way to where we were."

---

[7] Only 3 dogs were used by 13th Para Bn and there is a strong possibility this dog was 'Bing' as he was found approximately 12 hours later after being caught up in a tree and was slightly wounded in the face by mortar fire.
[8] In a letter to "Dixie" Dean after the war, Ken Bailey states that the report by 296 Squadron refers to his dog and himself. He never saw his dog again after the drop. The third dog was killed.

Private Bill Rutter (Signaller, 'C' Company)

"When the green light came on we staggered to the door with our kitbags strapped to our right legs and heaved ourselves out. On my chute opening, I found I had a bit of a swing on, but what was most noticeable was the coloured tracer being fired up at us. I remember thinking it was like bonfire night. I pulled my quick release but it would not leave my ankle, it was hanging under my foot. I reached for my fighting knife to cut it free, when I landed in an apple tree. This was lucky, as I finished up with one leg up in the tree and the other, with the kitbag, just touching the ground.

"I unloaded my gear and draped the wireless set, spare batteries and miscellaneous tackle around myself and started towards the RV. I saw a corporal silhouetted against the sky, in a hedge. When he saw me, he said in his best German "Hande Hock" to which I replied "What's the matter with you?" and nearly got shot."

Lieutenant Ellis "Dixie" Dean (MMG Platoon)

"My chute developed normally and as my body swung into the vertical I looked around. The first thing to catch my eye away to the right were 2 silver ribbons, threading through the dark earth, the River Orne and the Canal de Caen, that was good, I was over the correct dropping zone. To my front, but some distance away, numbers of red and orange balls were shooting up into the sky. They left the ground at speed, but as they rose, slowed down and just 'fizzed' out. This display I reckoned to be the defences of Caen. I stared at them too long, because when I looked down, I was destined to land in one of the orchards on the eastern side of the DZ. I started to pull on the liftwebs, hoping to clear the trees, but realised I wasn't going to make it and prepared for a tree landing.

"I remembered what to do. Head down on the chest, arms crossed in front of it and knees raised to protect my marriage prospects. Down I came, crashing through branches and foliage, without as much of a scratch or bruise. When I stopped, I was completely surrounded in greenery. I felt around for a branch to put my feet on, but found none, so I hit the quick release, the straps flew apart and my Sten (which was broken down into three parts and threaded under them) fell to the ground. I slid out of the harness and lowered myself to the end of the leg straps, and I still hadn't reached the ground. I let go and dropped all of 12" to the soil of Normandy. In doing so, I made a 'stand up' landing, strictly taboo at Ringway!"

Private Ernest Hurst (adapted from his poem)

"Originally I was jumping No.1, but changed to No.2. I looked through the door hole when it was removed and saw the coast was alight. As we left the coast and carried on inland we stood up ready to jump and meet at our copse rendezvous.

"The 'Green' light came on and I followed No.1 out. My helmet came off, then my chute opened and I was on my way. My kitbag wouldn't drop the full length of the rope and just hung below my foot. The next problem was that my chute was starting to twist. Quickly, as trained, I started to twist in reverse. As I was approaching the ground and roughly 20 ft from it, someone landed on my chute. It collapsed as I knew it would and I hit the ground very hard. It was my 13th and worst jump!"

Captain Padre Whitfield "Boy" Foy (a/c 15)

"At nearly 1am. I stood up and gripping the sides of the aircraft, waited for the signal. Suddenly the red light flashed on, we were over the coastline of France. The Albemarle swayed so that we had to cling on grisly in order to keep our feet. A few more seconds passed, the 'Red' light flicked out, the 'Green' flicked on. I took the usual deep breath, stepped forward and my link with England was broken.

"I began to doubt while I was drifting through the air – where were the buildings which should have been the village of Ranville? Why did it appear to be practically unbroken wood down there? And where were all the other aircraft which should have been following us in? It was the railway line gleaming below which brought conviction; there was no railway on the maps and photographs we had been studying for days on end. I might be only 4 miles away from the RV, I might, on the other hand be 14. I expressed a wish that the eggs and bacon which the navigator of our aircraft would get on his return to England might be well and truly burnt. I got ready for the fall and the next moment I was up to the neck in water. It was just after 1am and all was not well!"

Private Ronnie "Rocky" Rhodes (8 Platoon 'C' Company)

"After I jumped the kitbag containing anti-tank mines, Vickers ammo and extra magazines slid off my leg and though fastened to my harness by a 5/8" diameter rope which snapped. I landed in a tree and was knocked out for a while, how long, who knows. When I regained consciousness I was dangling about 12ft off the ground. I made for the rendezvous in the direction of Ranville Church Steeple. All 31 of us made it."

Ronnie and his brother George are pictured together shortly before George transferred to the Parachute Regiment and joined his brother in No.8 Platoon 'C' Company. He was due to have taken part on D-Day, but broke his leg in training and was unable to go. On recovery, George joined 1st Airborne and dropped with them at Arnhem and only escaped capture by swimming the Rhine.

Lance Corporal George O'Connor (8 Platoon 'C' Company)

"There was an almighty thump on the planes fuselage, I looked out of the open doorway and I could see what looked like little red bubbles gently floating up towards the plane, they appeared to be strung out in a line, as they approached the plane, they came travelling towards us at a terrific speed, some of the bubbles shot past us, but some of them exploded near us, I could hear pieces of shrapnel hitting the fuselage and some small pieces of shrapnel entered the plane, one small piece fell by my foot and the lad next to me attempted to pick it up, but rapidly dropped it, as it was red hot.

"The plane rocked and weaved, I thought it was going to crash, the dispatcher crawled along the gangway, shouting, "don't worry lads, we've been through worse than this and you lucky sods will be out of here in a few minutes, so get ready to jump, the red light will be coming on any minute."

"My chute opened with a crack, I looked around. I could see a few of the lads descending and there were tracer bullets, shooting up towards them, I remembered to release my valise, from my leg and it dangled about 20ft below me. I heard the valise hit the ground with a thud, I had been so busy looking around, I had forgotten about landing. I hit my valise as I landed, my legs twisted and I landed flat on my back, with one leg folded under me."

Guy Byam (War Correspondent, Ray Batten and Ray Walker's stick, a/c 310)

"Over the enemy coast and the run in started... 1 min 30 sec... Red light, Green light and out! "Get on! Get out!" Out fast into the cool night and out into the air over France. We knew that the dropping zone is obstructed; we were dropping into fields covered with poles. I lowered my kitbag, suspended on a 40 ft rope, and then the ground came up to hit me and I find myself in the middle of a corn field. I looked around and couldn't be quite sure where I am. Overhead hundreds of parachutes and containers are coming down. The whole sky was a fantastic sight of light and black, one plane got hit and disintegrates wholesale, sprinkling burning pieces all-over the sky."

Private Ray Batten (2 Platoon 'A' Company)

"The man next to me in the Dakota [a/c 310], swore that I had fouled his liftwebs with the sling of his rifle valise when we had our equipment check, he took a lot of reassuring. The pilot then announced that we were crossing the coastline of France.

"After the green light came on and the stick began to jump we were met by a lot of flak and shrapnel rattled outside of the fuselage. The pilot took evasive action throwing us about and the chap in front of me, as he was about to jump, stumbled. I instinctively grabbed him with my left hand and shoved him out of the door. If I hadn't, I couldn't have gone. Anyway, out I went and a second or two later I felt a slight tug on my shoulders, my chute had opened. I could see lots of different coloured tracer coming up into the sky. After lowering my kit bag down 30ft, I pulled forward on my liftwebs to control my oscillation.

"The wind was quite strong and was blowing some of us into the trees on the Ranville side of the DZ. As I approached the top of my tree, I put up my feet, hit it amidst a lot of tearing and ripping noises and bumped down it until I was hanging about 15ft from the ground. I could hear a lot of machine gun fire from Schmeisser and the like. I was suddenly aware of someone looking up at me and I couldn't tell because of the darkness and the shadows if he was friend or foe, so I kept still and pretended to be dead. He soon went away and when I was sure that he'd gone I hit the quick release, but holding onto the straps, I lowered myself until I could no more and hung and dropped the rest only to land awkwardly on my back.

"On the floor I wasn't quite sure which way to go and I was winded so I laid there for a few minutes to get myself together. A search of the area failed to reveal where my kit bag was, this was not good, it contained my sections Bren gun and magazines. I couldn't wait any longer so I orientated myself and set off for the RV."

Pte Ray "Geordie" Walker (2 Platoon 'A' Coy)

"Shortly after crossing the French coast near Cabourg the lights turned from 'Red' to 'Green' and at 00:50 hours I was parachuting down into a Normandy field. It was like a fireworks display, red and green tracer illuminating the night sky. Flares, star shells and high explosives added to the spectacle. On my descent I released my kitbag containing my rifle, spade and other essential equipment. Whilst performing this task a shell exploded nearby and shrapnel severed my draw cord and I parted company with all my equipment. Not a happy start to a new day.

"On landing I discarded my parachute and in haste of cutting myself free from my Mae West lifebelt, I gashed my thumb with my fighting knife. Blood began to ooze and I felt humiliated shedding my blood from a self-inflicted wound. Now I had to find my rifle and the rest of my equipment. Fortunately the Moon came to my rescue; about 90m distant, I saw something standing erect and it was not human. In plunging to earth my spade simply pierced the ground and stood upright. I made a quick dash, pulled my equipment clear and ran back to the line of trees where I had originally landed. Before I could free my rifle from its container, someone was coming towards me through the undergrowth on the other side of the trees. There was no time to get my rifle, if I had to kill someone it was to be with my knife. Whoever was coming my way got stuck in the undergrowth and began swearing in Welsh. My relief was intense and soon I was chatting to my comrade Ray Batten. He too had his share of misfortune, his machine gun and spare ammo was missing."

Guy Byam (War Correspondent)

"The job of the unit which I came in with was to occupy the area and prepare the way for gliders, so we were to rendezvous at a copse... but I can't find it! I went to a farmhouse and ask the way to a farmer and his wife standing on their porch. "We've come to drive the Boche away" I said and the farmer shrugged his shoulders and said "I don't believe it, it's another German manoeuvre." After a lot of explanation, persuasion and reassurance from myself he eventually said "that's your direction" pointing down the road.

"It was tricky business of moving across enemy countryside at night, but the only people I met were our own patrols. I found my unit after only being sniped at once and challenged at a number of times. There was somebody under a hedge and things were happening all around and it was difficult to get what exactly was going on. The sky was crossed and re-crossed with tracer and the distinctive splutter of an MG34 is quite near us."

Sergeant "Taffy" Lawley ('A' Company, left)

"The flight to our objective was uneventful; I was again acting as stick commander [a/c 313]. We arrived over the DZ about 1am and it was then the fun began. There was a deal of flak and plenty of small arms fire, when the green light came on, No.1 jumped, followed by the remainder up to No.10, a Bren gunner who carried a very heavy load. He fell across the exit, preventing anyone else from jumping. The only one who could help him to his feet was the RAF despatcher. This took some considerable time, during which the plane had circled the DZ 3 times before I could jump. The first thing I knew, when I was airborne, was that my rifle, small-kit, spade etc, which were all tied together, had broken away from me when I jumped. I landed in a cornfield and lay quite still for a second, listening, everything was very quiet, although in the distance I could hear the noise of battle and guessed it must be the RV. I got rid of my chute and with my fighting knife in one hand and a 36 grenade in the other, I made for the RV. I had gone a considerable distance, when suddenly I saw 3 bent figures going in my direction. I got up close to them and challenged them and heaved a sigh of relief to find they were our chaps. Guided by the Battalion call blown by Colonel Luard on a hunting horn, we were soon at the RV, where I assisted the CO in directing each arrival to his company area."

Captain Alfred "Nobby" Clark (2i/c, 'C' Company)

"I noticed no opening of the parachute. I strove frantically with the unmanageable kitbag, the rope slipping through my fingers. I thanked God for the provision of double thickness silk gloves. Without them I'd have little flesh left on my hands. The rope, held now in my hands still remained there, but there was no weight of any bag. It had gone. I was coming down into what seemed to be a large wood containing many clearings. Suddenly I was down. Planes were droning overhead. Away to the north I could hear gunfire of some sort.

"I was roughly in the centre of a field of some 50 yards square. I thought I heard voices. A few seconds of absolute stillness on my part confirmed the fact, from just inside the orchard on the south side. They were muttering together, but I could not make out one syllable of their conversation. The breeze changed direction and it brought me their scent. I couldn't describe it, except perhaps to say that the nearest description was that of a cross between plasticine and a cheap brand of soap. I remembered the distinct odour from a course I had previously done. I think that they saw nothing although their suspicions were aroused.

"They may possibly have seen the flash of my arm as it described an arc in their general direction to release from my hand the 36 grenade which I dare not hold any longer since the fuse had been struck for at least a second already. In fact I believe it never reached the ground before it exploded. Although I say it myself, it was a good throw, I didn't wait to see the result, but on the explosion I was up on my feet and running like a hare in the direction I judged northwest to be. After about a minute I pulled up, partly through want of breath but also having managed to subdue my feeling of panic, to say to myself aloud, I believe "You... brave paratrooper".

"I set off in the general direction in which I believed the RV to be and, as far as I could see, I was alone in an uninhabited part of the Calvados region of Normandy. A mile further, I came across Major Bill Harris, the Battalion second-in-command. In crossing a post and wire fence which had not been as taut as it might have been, a lower strand had become crossed over the upper, thereby trapping his foot most effectively, and suspending it 4ft above ground where it was impossible for him to reach it unaided so that he could free himself. I was able to put him to rights in a few seconds. Since he was bound for a different rendezvous from mine we departed our separate ways in the gradually increasing darkness as the clouds covered the moon.

"As I plodded on, suddenly from way ahead in the direction I was going, came a sound as welcome as any I had ever heard, a hunting horn. It was fainter and further away than I had expected it to be. "Dit - dah - dit - dit" the Morse letter 'L' for Lancashire and Luard. I judged it to be a mile away and I eventually arrived.

Lieutenant Jack Watson (3 Platoon 'A' Company)

"At about 0100 hours we crossed the Normandy coast and dropped our small load of 50 lb bombs. The RAF's Halifaxes further up the coast, on my left towards Le Havre, were playing havoc with the German defences as we crossed the coast. It was a pleasant sight.

"The minutes before I got the green light, seemed like years. I remember hearing my batman [Harry Gospel] saying "I'm right behind you Sir." just before I left the aircraft. I was 3 Platoon Commander of 'A' Company and I jumped with my leg kitbag, small pack and carried a Sten gun. Our task as a battalion was to clear Ranville and set out an outpost at a place called Hérouvillette. We also had to clear lanes on the DZ for the HQ gliders to land at 0320 hours.

"I left the aircraft and I was delighted to see my parachute was open and wondered how the rest of my stick was fairing. The kitbag attached to my leg had a quick release pin and I couldn't release it. At this time I wasn't bothered about who was on the ground ready to receive me – all I was concerned about was this kitbag and trying to get it off. If I was to break my leg all my training would be for nothing, I'd be evacuated and be bloody annoyed. Luckily I landed without any trouble and landed in an orchard at the north end of the DZ. I thought to myself have I landed in the wrong place because I was on my own, "what has happened to the rest of my stick?" But within moments, although it seemed ages, I heard a voice which was one of my section commanders saying "Are you alright Sir?", "Yes, how about you?" and he replied "Yes, I'm fine." We looked up, saw the line of the aircraft and started moving in that direction. As we ran forward we started picking up men and formed a battle group and made for the church. I was quite pleased to meet one of my Bren gunners of Sergeant Farrell's section who shattered me completely by saying that he had lost his kitbag, complete with Bren gun."

Private Ronald Minnery (Intelligence Platoon)

"The aircraft never seemed to throttle back and as I jumped the slip stream was too strong and I lost my kitbag. That meant I was landing with no rifle, not exactly ideal for the platoon sniper. I was very upset about this and began to think someone had sabotaged my chord.

"After I landed I began to make my way to the RV and I came across Captain "Harry Ack" Ainsworth who had broken his leg. I took his sten gun and had to leave him there. He wasn't very happy about this at all, but I had to get on with the Company tasks. On the way I met up with my No.2, Hardacre, he had completed his jump with no problems and had his sniper rifle."

Private Dennis Boardman (Signaller 'C' Company)

"In the early hours of D-Day I jumped from an Albemarle. These were normally used for towing gliders, a terrible plane made of wood. It held 10 paras and once inside you couldn't hardly stand up in the dammed thing, only crouch and shuffle along the floor when it was time to jump. To make things even more difficult, we had a kitbag strapped to one leg. I also had a radio set and other gear weighing about 60 lbs. The hole in the floor which we jumped out of was at the rear of the aircraft, in the shape of a coffin.

"When I jumped I went through the searchlight which was directly on the plane with machine gun fire directed at it. Once in the air you had to release the kitbag on a rope, it hung about 15ft below you. I couldn't release mine and knew I was in trouble because of the speed I was falling. I hit the deck and knew my right ankle was damaged straight away. I hobbled for the next 3 weeks and never took my boot off because if I took it off my foot would have ballooned up and I wouldn't have been able to walk. I can pinpoint the exact spot where I landed and still have an aerial photo of Ranville and the drop zone issued to me prior to D-Day (below)."

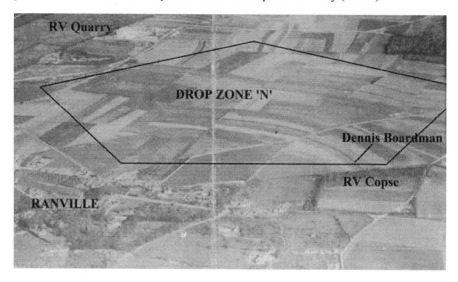

Private William Ellis (Mortar Platoon)

"As I jumped the scene was something like Blackpool illuminations. There were flashing lights all over the place. I saw a plane on fire go down and men with burning chutes falling. The place was an inferno.

"We all had kitbags to carry the extra equipment some carried a base plate; others the legs, others a barrel and the rest carried the bombs. When you got down, you hoped your mates had all the other parts as the mortars had to be built up. But at the time this fellow arrived at the RV, but had lost his kitbag in the jump. The rest of our equipment came down by container. I think there was a casualty or two caused by these containers dropping all over the place."

Lieutenant Ellis "Dixie" Dean (MMG Platoon)

"I'd landed in a tree rising out of a 'bocage' type hedge on the eastern edge of the DZ, now to find the Sten. I searched all around where I had landed, but found nothing and thought what a right 'Charlie' I'm going to look, turning up at the RV without a personal weapon. Fortunately I packed my torch in one of the ammunition pouches. Flashing it around in the bottom of the hedgerow, I collected my Sten piece by piece. I was still enshrouded in the foliage, but could tell from the noise of the planes which side I wanted to be. As I parted the hedge and emerged I saw, only a few yards to my right a large, white French cow staring in my direction with moon like eyes. A shadowy figure, not many yards into the corn was hoisting a machine gun tripod onto his shoulders "Hello Sir, I've just been telling that cow I've come to liberate her."

"It was Lance Corporal Harold Turner a regular soldier with several years experience of skirmishing in North Africa. We pressed on through the waist high corn and soon caught up with Private Bill Price who had jumped No.3, and was carrying the Vickers itself. We set off for our RV [a quarry adjacent to the road on the West side of the DZ]. As we neared a line of bushes we were challenged by a Pathfinder Officer, he identified himself and asked me which RV we were making for. He showed me the direction in which we should be going. We soon caught up with a body of men, so we tagged along in the rear.

"The column halted and the signal came from the front to kneel down. By now I knew exactly where we were and decided to tell the Major in charge of the party, whom I did not recognise. He was organising small groups to dash across a track, they were heading towards the coast and I informed the Major of this fact. "Who the hell are you?" he demanded. "Lieutenant Dean of the 13th" I replied, to be told in no uncertain terms to go and fight my own war and let me get on with his.

"I collected my gunners and headed up the track to our RV, not far along I heard the rallying call of long whistle blasts. Within minutes we were at the quarry, where Colonel Johnson and his IO, Johnny Firth, stood on a mound directing men. We were down near the river and we were the first of the Platoon to arrive.

"Numbers increased slowly, L/Cpl Arthur Higgins arrived, and he was jumping with a Vickers gun tripod and was unable to release his bag. He landed with the 40 lb weight still attached to his leg. Fortunately neither man nor tripod suffered any

damage. Andy Fairhurst arrived informing me that he had been suspended in telephone wires at the road side; he brought the Platoon wireless set with him and opened up a listening watch. Sgt Kelly clocked in, with only a few of his section and no ammunition. The same applied to Sgt Osborne. We had 2 complete guns and also 3 liners of ammunition."

Pte Bill Rutter (Signaller, 'C' Coy)

"I recall crossing the main road in Ranville early on D-Day to get to the rear of the Château, which was our objective. There was a single parachute hanging in the telephone wires. Somehow it struck some of us as being a bit pathetic, hanging there with no occupant. I often wondered who the owner was."

Private John Henry Powell (left) was another who suffered because of the telephone wires. His chute was caught up as he landed and was machine gunned as he hung helplessly in his harness. He managed to free himself and was found 2 days later, still alive but in a very bad way. He was evacuated on the 9th June and spent the next 8 months paralysed in Newcastle Hospital with his wife of 2 years, Winifred, by his side until he died on 15th Feb 1945 aged 26. He was laid to rest with full military honours in Cheslyn Hay Cemetery.[9]

5th Brigade Operations in Normandy Report

In spite of the guiding signals being too far to the East, the drop was made with good accuracy. It was found however, that in general the sticks covered more ground than had been usual in training. This was mainly due to the difficulty the heavy laden men experienced in managing their kitbags in aircraft which were taking evasive action. These long sticks resulted in a very wide dispersion on the DZ.

Had it been daylight the scene on the ground must have presented a remarkable picture; 2,000 troops, of different units, but now completely mixed, some entangling themselves from their parachutes in a fairish wing others searching for their kitbags, many of which had broken loose in the descent, and for their containers. Everywhere little groups trying to locate themselves and to find their RV's. All the while the DZ was under fire from MG's and sporadic mortar and shell fire.

Private Frank Gleeson (12th Parachute Battalion)

"On the DZ I met only one other paratrooper, who was cursing that he could not find any others from his 13th Battalion, Lancashire."

Brigadier J.H.N. Poett (5th Para Brigade Commander)

"The heavy weapons and equipment of the battalions had been parachuted in containers at the same time as the men. Many containers had fallen in the standing corn. In the darkness, and with very little moonlight to help, not much of this heavy equipment was found until daylight. The absence of mortars, medium machine guns and particularly wireless sets was to prove a serious loss to the battalions when they came to repel the German attacks in the morning."

Private Ray Batten (2 Platoon 'A' Company, a/c 310)

"The first person I bumped into after landing was No.19, the chap who I threw out the plane. He thanked me for throwing him out and told me he couldn't have taken the shame if he'd returned to England having not jumped. We proceeded together towards Ranville. On the way I saw a para carrying a bent Lee Enfield rifle and 2 others carrying incomplete Sten guns [these had to be assembled after landing]. A sergeant came by telling me "They got my mate", I have no idea what happened to him. I remember seeing the corpse of an unfortunate chap who appeared not to have hooked up his chute. We met up with Sgt Llewellyn amongst others at the RV and a little later by Major Cramphorn. There was the strange noise of hunting horns being blown by Company Commanders to rally their men; it all seemed a bit surreal."

---

[9] Photo and information supplied by Eddie Dace and Trevor McFarlane, Cheslyn Hay History Society.

13th (Lancashire) Para Bn Landing Positions

Pin denotes approx centre of stick
Not all aircraft are marked due to various reasons

Created using Google Map Data (c) 2012

'A' Company
'B' Company
'C' Company
HQ Company
225 Fd Amb

Pte Ray "Geordie" Walker (2 Platoon 'A' Coy, a/c 310)

"We hurried to our rendezvous and met up with Corporal Stan Braddock (pictured left). As Stan was a veteran of the North Africa, Sicily and Italian campaigns his presence gave us confidence to fulfil our tasks. At the RV we met our first dead German, a young lad about 16 years of age."

Lieutenant Jack Watson (3 Platoon 'A' Company)

"The company commanders had hunting horns, Peter Luard was very much a farmer and hunting man and he decided hunting horns were the thing to rally the troops. By 0115 hours I joined a steady flow to the RV, a wood north of the village I heard the loud and shrill sound of a hunting horn, the CO sounding 'L' for Lancashire and the Company calls of 'A' for 'A' Company etc. I joined 'A' Company just right of the RV and found we were only 40 strong. I spoke to Major Cramphorn and we decided to wait for a few minutes hoping the rest of the company would join us.

"Because it was a night operation there was confusion, with men arriving from all directions and men from the 7th and 12th Battalions were in our RV. One team of the pathfinders for the 8th Battalion landed on our DZ by mistake and as a result some

men of the 8th also joined us. It was quite funny really, men were being pointed to Company areas, "Is this 'A' Company 8th Battalion?", "No, 13th Battalion!"[10]

"At about 0145 hours we were then about 60 strong and Major Cramphorn decided to move off our first task of clearing poles from the landing area for the first wave of gliders. I had one stick completely missing and Sergeant Farrell (left) was appointed my Platoon sergeant. The strength of the Platoon was only 18.

"We formed up just north of the church at Ranville to clear the poles. We knew the drill; we had been practicing it at Bulford so many times a few weeks ago."

Lieutenant-Colonel Frank Lowman (591 Antrim Parachute Squadron RE)

"Two Engineer reconnaissance parties were to drop at 0030 hours to tape out the 2 strips, with the remainder dropping at 0100 hours to prepare the landing strips.

"In general the drop went fairly well. However, one RE reconnaissance party under Lieutenant Pip Mitchley RE was dropped wide and did not arrive in time to carry out its task. The other party under Corporal Stoner RE therefore reconnoitred and set out both strips though they were very short of tapes for this. Also the two Squadron HQ sticks with the Squadron Commander and his 2i/c failed to appear at all. Captain Fergie Semple RE of 3 Troop therefore took charge and got the 2 Troops working with the Infantry party which had arrived as planned."

Private Ray "Geordie" Walker (2 Platoon 'A' Company)

"We worked swiftly as the first gliders were due to land at 0315 hours. Despite being under constant mortar and machine gun fire we had few casualties. In addition we had to cope with wounded stampeding cattle and horses. Fortunately we had the benefit of pale moonlight and could avoid being knocked over by crazed animals."

Private Ray Batten (2 Platoon 'A' Company)

"Those of us who didn't carry part of a Bren gun or other equipment carried a pick or a shovel, to get rid of the anti-glider poles. We were soon organised into parties and busy pulling down the poles and filling in the holes. There was some small arms fire while we were doing this, but I don't recall any being directly at my party. It occurred to me that the sea invasion had not yet started and that when it did start, if it was not successful, we would have 'had it'. We had barely finished removing the poles, when

---

[10] One stick of pathfinders for DZ'K' set up their Eureka Beacon on the wrong DZ (3 miles north on DZ'N') and as soon as they realised it they switched it off but 3rd Para Brigade reported that 13 sticks wrongly dropped on DZ'N' and 8 correctly on DZ'K'.

the gliders came rushing out of the night. They hissed over our heads, not many feet above either. They sent us scurrying like jack-rabbits. Those glider pilots deserved a medal."

Lieutenant Jack Watson (3 Platoon 'A' Company)

"The task was quite easy, opposition was slight and the poles were lighter than expected, but we encountered large trenches which we didn't expect. The men worked extremely well.

"Time was getting short and we just finished filling in the last trench when at 0315 hours the gliders started to come in, but not from the north as expected. They appeared from all directions. It was a nightmare and extremely frightening, I would rather be shelled any day. I remember thinking I was going to be hit by them and had to dodge from one place to another. Some landed well, others crashed into each other. In the darkness we could see the sparks from the skids, and hear the sounds of splintering wood and the yells from the occupants, it was like a scene from hell. Some of our men were hit, and it seemed like a miracle seeing the occupants get out and even drive away with jeeps and anti-tank guns."

Major John Cramphorn ('A' Company Commander)

"My Colour Sergeant, Harry Watkins doing a magnificent job getting the Company organised in the absence of the missing CSM McPharlan. The task proved easier than I had planned for, all the holes had been dug but many of the posts were simply placed in the holes and not yet upright and firm. In many cases all we did was carry the pole away and fill in the hole. We finished the job with about 15 minutes to spare and were digging our funk holes when the gliders started to arrive. As a result we had a ring side seat for the actual landings. Most of the Horsa's made good landings and I was greatly impressed by the speed and efficiency shown by the passengers in unloading the Jeeps and guns. Among the last to land was General Gale's glider, one of the few to make a really bad touch down just off the cleared path and as a result suffered damage from poles still standing. But I don't think he blamed us for that."

Lt-Col Frank Lowman (591 Para Squad RE)

"The removal of the obstruction poles proved easier than was expected. Few of them exceeded 8" diameter, and little more than half of them were in place in the ground. Towards the northern part of the LZ they were securely wired together with heavy gauge wire. In many cases manual removal by 3 men was found to be quicker than using the prepared explosive charges. The 2 westerly strips were ready in good time for the gliders at 0320 hours but lighting by the Independent Parachute Company proved unsatisfactory due to lack of personnel and special equipment. As a result gliders came in from all directions but with the traditional ability of the Horsa glider to absorb punishment, casualties to men and equipment were remarkably few."

Citation: Lieutenant-Colonel Frank Harrington Lowman (RE)

Award: Distinguished Service Order

For conspicuous gallantry and devotion to duty over a period of weeks. Lieutenant-Colonel Lowman has since the moment he landed in Normandy shown the most excellent example to all Engineers in the division. The tasks allotted to the divisional Engineers, both in the initial stages and later in the occupation of the bridgehead have been hazardous. That the has carried out the tasks as effectively and efficiently as they have, has to no small measure been attributable to the close supervision and care of Lt-Col Lowman. He has exposed himself to danger quite regardless of risks whenever he considered his presence desirable. The spirit of his example has been an inspiration to his engineers up to the time of his being severely wounded in a forward position.

Citation: Captain Roderick Ferguson Semple (No.3 Troop, 591ˢᵗ, RE)

Award: Military Cross

For outstanding military efficiency and devotion to duty. While commanding a Troop of 591 Parachute Squadron RE he performed the task of clearing a series of landing strips for gliders in the face of heavy opposition: when the Officer Commanding and Second in Command failed to appear at the rendezvous he took command and reformed the squadron until the arrival of the Second in Command twelve hours later. His courage, his readiness to take command and his example of personal bravery were an inspiration to all.

General Richard "Windy" Gale (Commander, 6ᵗʰ Airborne Division)

"In the glider we all wore Mae West's, and, taking our places, we all fastened ourselves in and waited for the jerk as the tug took the strain on the tow-rope. Soon it came and we could feel ourselves hurtling down the smooth tarmac. Then we were airborne and once again we heard the familiar whistle of the air rushed by and we glided higher and higher into the dark night.

"I suppose all men have different reactions on these occasions. I went to sleep and slept soundly for the best part of an hour. I was woken up by a considerable bumping. We had run into a small local storm in the Channel. Major Billy Griffiths, the pilot, was having a ticklish time and the glider was all over the place. Between glider and tug there is an intercommunication line, so that the two pilots can talk to one another. In this bumping we received, the intercommunication line broke; the problem of cast off would have to be solved by judgement. Griffiths merely said, "The intercom has bust".

"It was only a few minutes after that that he said, 'We will be crossing the French coast shortly'. We were flying at about 5,000ft and we soon knew the coast was under us, for we were met by a stream of flak. It was weird to see this roaring up in great golden chains past the windows of the glider, some of it apparently between us and the tug aircraft. Looking out, I could see the canal and the river through the clouds, for the moon was by now fairly well overcast and the clear crisp moonlight we had hoped for was not there. Nevertheless here we were.

"In a few moments, Griffiths said, "We are over the landing zone now and I will cast off at any moment". Almost as he had said this, we were. The whistling sound and the roar of the engines suddenly died down: no longer were we bumping about, but gliding along on a gloriously steady course.

"Round we turned, circling lower and lower; soon the pilot turned round to tell us to link up as we were just about to land. We all linked up by putting our arms around the man next to us. We were also, as I have said, strapped in. In case of a crash this procedure would help us to take the shock.

"I shall never forget the sound as we rushed down in our final steep dive, then we suddenly flattened out, and soon with a bump, bump, bump, we landed on an extremely rough stubble field. Over the field we sped and then with a bang we hit a low embankment. The forward undercarriage wheel stove up through the floor, the glider spun round on its nose in a small circle and, as one wing hit one of those infernal stakes, we drew up to a standstill. We opened the door. Outside all was quiet. About us now the other gliders were coming in, crashing and screeching as they applied their brakes. It was a glorious moment.

"In the distance from the direction of the bridges, we could now hear bursts of machine gun fire. Except for the arrival of more and more gliders, all around us seemed to be still. It was eerie. Had Ranville been cleared of the enemy? Were the bridges taken, were they intact and safely in our hands? How was Terence Otway and his gallant Battalion faring at the Merville battery? We could still hear intermittent fire from the direction of the bridges.

"Whilst they were attempting to unload the glider, the passing moments seemed like hours. It was still dark and this unloading was proving to be more difficult than we had anticipated. The crash we had had, though not serious, resulted in the nose being really well dug into the ground and the problem of getting the Jeep out was defeating us. Eventually, we had to give up: and so on foot we set out to Ranville."[11]

Sgt George Butler (3 Platoon 'A' Company)

[Travelling in glider after damaging his shoulder prior to takeoff] "I had never travelled in a glider before and in addition to 3 passengers, the Horsa carried a small bulldozer, plus Jerry cans of fuel. After the noise and the crowdedness of parachuting aircraft the silence of the journey was a rare experience. There was the hissing of the slipstream and it was a bit bumpy, but nothing unusual.

"My first sight of France was the flashing around of searchlights and the lazy approach of Ack Ack fire. There was a 'crack' alongside my head and almost 18" square of plywood disappeared next to my port hole. Through this gap I had my first view of the coast. Up forward the co-pilot was silhouetted in the glow of the searchlights. He turned, pointed downwards, followed by the 'thumbs up' signal. We banked, the nose of the glider dropped sharply, then we settled into a steady downwards glide through the

---

[11] 68 Horsa gliders and 4 Hamilcar gliders took off for LZ'N' (formally DZ'N') but only 48 Horsas and 3 Hamilcars landed on or close. A total of 25 gliders reported being hit by flak with no injuries to passengers or crew.

hole in the side I saw Ranville church before the pilot levelled off and we touched down beautifully to the sound of the wheels rumbling through the crops on the Landing Zone. The glider slowed and stopped with the cockpit no more than 2 ft from a stone wall at the far end of the LZ. I had made it.

"Jumping down from the door, I landed in a hole (left from an anti-glider pole) and fell on my damaged shoulder, but such was my excitement I hardly noticed the pain.

"I found the Cabourg-Ranville road and headed for the hedgerow of 'A' Companies RV. I was challenged by a Scottish voice. After identifying myself, the CSM of the Pathfinders asked me where I was heading. "You won't get much further unless you do something about your bloody aiming mark". I then realised that I had been wearing a large white sling. Between us we got rid of the sling and tucked my arm inside my Denison smock. At the RV Colour Sergeant Harry Watkins pointed me towards the LZ. In the half light I saw Jack Watson my Platoon Commander "What kept you, and where are the rest?" he asked. I was the only one of my stick to actually land on the DZ. All my aircraft of 20 were dropped astray. 2 came back after 4 weeks, the rest all ended up as POW's."

At approximately 0130 hours, whilst the various companies and platoons were forming up at a variety of RV's the enemy began to fire from the direction of Salenelles away to the north and near the coast, over the heads of the parachutists towards Hérouvillette. As 'A' Company set off to remove the anti-glider poles the Advanced Battalion HQ along with 'B' Company ventured into and cleared the north of Ranville facing weak resistance. When this was completed the Anti-Tank Platoon came through and occupied the crossroads.

After the sounding of the success signal (the horn of Lt-Col Luard), the Rear HQ party entered Ranville and took up their position in the garden previously chosen in the planning stages. "This garden turned out to belong to the Cure, who may have been somewhat pro-German, and was none too pleased as a result. Later in the day after much mortaring and shelling, he became very anti-British and eventually retired to a dug out in the garden."

Leutnant Gerhardt Bandomir (21st Panzer Division)

"Night time invasion exercises were common and took place almost every night. That night at around 2am a messenger sped into my HQ on his motorbike. I could tell by the look on his face that the real thing was happening. My orders were to head to Regimental HQ immediately and have my Company (No.3 of the 1st Bn, 125 Panzer Grenadier Regt. 21st Panzer Div) standing by.

"At HQ, Major Hans von Luck informed us that paratroopers had landed in the area of the coast. My orders were to fight our way into Hérouvillette and Ranville, in order to assist troops already engaged in that area. For our purpose, attached to us were 6 125mm Assault guns (Self Propelled Guns – SP's)."

Major Hans Von Luck (21st Pz Div)

"We telephoned the company commander, who was in a cellar. "Brandenburg, hold on. The battalion is already attacking and is bound to reach you in a few moments." "Okay," he replied, "I have the first prisoner here, a British medical officer of the 6th Airborne Division."

"By now, we had a slightly better idea of and grip on the situation. Prisoners who had misjudged their jumps and fallen into our hands in the course of our limited counterattack were brought in to me. Before I had them escorted away to division, in accordance with orders, we learned during our "small talk" that the 6th Airborne Division was supposed to jump during the night in order to take the bridges over the Orne at Ranville intact and form a bridgehead east of the Orne for the landing by sea planned for the morning.

"Gradually we were becoming filled with anger. The clearance for an immediate night attack, so as to take advantage of the initial confusion among our opponents, had still not come.[12]

"This general order [see footnote], to attack at once in full strength, hence with my whole combat group during that very night of 5-6 June, in the event of an airborne landing, was known neither to me nor to my adjutant at the time, the later General Liebeskind of the Bundeswehr. Neither, apparently, did the other units in the division

know of this order. Instead, we all adhered to the strict order not to carry out even the smallest operation until it had been cleared by Army Group B. The divisional staff must have known of the other order, as is clear from General Speidel's letters."

Photo: Leutnant Gerhardt Bandomir (3 Kompanie), Major Hans von Luck and Major Willi Kurz (Commander 2nd Bn).

Private Bill Rutter (Signaller, 'C' Company)

"Arriving at the RV we heard a strange noise coming towards us through the mist. It turned out to be the Major Ford's batman bringing in a carthorse. We had orders to pick up any transport, but this caused a bit of a laugh. Now and again a kitbag or container with a load in it would thump onto the ground. Our officers signalled their whereabouts with hunting horns."

Captain Alfred "Nobby" Clark (2i/c, 'C' Company)

"Albert, who had arrived at the RV 10 minutes before me and greeted me, heard my tale of woe concerning the lost kitbag and, after a minute's absence returned with a sten gun and haversack, remarking, "There's bags of these lying about around here" by which I gathered that 2 or 3 of them were spare since their owners had become casualties either on landing or very shortly after.

"There wasn't much time for conjecture or further debate as suddenly the tell-tale sound of mortar fire from the north-east assailed our ears, to be followed within the expected few seconds by the by the crunch of the bombs - too close to be pleasant. 'C' Company No.9 Platoon was to remain at the RV as reserve, until the village was captured and then move in to protect the left flank of Battalion HQ. The only thing

---

[12] Many years later in 1987 Von Luck was given two letters which stated in the first, "Feuchtinger had a general directive to attack at once in the event of an *airborne landing*." And in the second "The 2lst Panzer Division had orders to go into action at once if the enemy made an airborne landing, and with the whole Division, in fact."

that had not gone more or less to plan was that No.9 Platoon was conspicuous by its absence."

Lance Corporal George O'Connor (8 Platoon 'C' Company)

"We approached the edge of the village, the first thing, I saw was a square Church tower, it looked strange, not being attached to the church. Mortar bombs began to crunch down to the rear of us, it was a good job we had moved closer to Ranville or those bombs would have had our names on them. We ran into 4 German snipers at the edge of the village, I'm not certain if we killed them or if they ran away, but the sniping ceased.

"I looked at my watch, the luminous hands glowed 01:55 hours very shortly after that, we met our Company Commander, Captain A.R. Clark, He informed us that he had been unable to find any trace of 9 Platoon, had we seen them. The sad answer was "No sir.""

Lieutenant Colonel Peter Luard (CO, 13th Bn)

"Charley Company, under Major Gerald Ford, had been ordered to mop up the north end of the village, as soon as Major George Bristow's 'B' Company had cleared the southern end. No.7 and 8 Platoon swept down towards the Château, which was attacked by Lt Harry Pollak, a fluent German speaker, who answering the sentries challenge in German, located the post and shot him dead. Major Ford entered the Château where, with his face blackened for night operations and wearing his parachute helmet and smock, was mistaken by the Comtesse de Rohan Chabot for a German trying to trap her. Nor was she satisfied until morning and after that was kindness itself to all ranks."

Lieutenant Jack Sharples (8 Platoon 'C' Company)

"8 Platoon were given the task of clearing the Château in the village, and tracks through the grounds indicated that it was being used by the Germans. When we left the RV (we were the last to do so), 7 Platoon were up ahead and came under machine  gun fire as they approached the crossroads. The Battalion were under strict orders not to open fire until dawn; it would have been so easy in the dark to shoot friendly forces. Major Ford (left) called me forward and instructed me to find a way round and I went along the street trying the door handles. At last I found one that opened. In the room was a still warm bed, a German uniform jacket draped over the back of a chair and a rifle propped up against the wall. In the yard at the back was another discarded jacket. A grenade, landed amongst us and I dashed into the road and called out at the top of my voice "Harry" [Lt Pollak of 7 Platoon] "it's Jack.""

"We quickly worked our way round to the Château [de Ranville], the Germans having scarpered. I left one Section covering the front of the building, another inside on the ground floor and I went upstairs with Privates Orrell and Prince, where I was met by le Comte de Ranville and his wife, protesting about the intrusion of their property. I tried to tell him that it was the invasion, we were British soldiers and that they were to stay indoors. Back came a torrent of French which I did not understand but they clearly did not believe me. Seeing the key in their bedroom door, I took it out and gave it to them saying in my best 4th Form French "Lock the door, I'll talk to you in the morning."

Château de Ranville

Captain Alfred "Nobby" Clark (2i/c, 'C' Company)

"Progress seemed slow. Apart from the very regular and frequent arrival of a bunch of mortar bombs nothing much appeared to be happening. Then we began to advance slowly, into the southwest edge of the village. As we did so the man about whom I had forgotten in the preoccupation of the preceding hours, appeared. So uncertain was I of the period of time that had elapsed since we left Broadwell airfield that I felt obliged to look at my watch, for the first time. It said 0205 hours. Only 3 hours earlier we had been in England.

"The soldier who approached me was Private Bamber. The usual rueful smile was on his face under the paint. "Message from HQ, Sir. Ranville captured", he reported. I felt constrained to ask him how he had enjoyed the flight. "First time in all me life I've never been sick, sir" he said."

Brig J.H.N. Poett (5th Para Brigade Commander)

"With Pine-Coffin's (7th Bn) men in position on the west bank [in Benouville]. I felt confident that, for the time being, the bridgehead would be secure from the west. I left the canal bridge and made for Ranville to see how the 13th Battalion had fared.

"I soon met up with Peter Luard, the 13th Battalion Commander. He was in excellent splendid heart. He had little difficulty in over-running the village and he was in the course of "mopping up" some of the houses which had been occupied by the Germans. He had established his defences on the outskirts of the village. Ranville had been captured at about 2:30am. It is therefore, claimed to be the first village to be liberated in France.

"Luard's Battalion and the Brigade engineers, 591 Para Field Squadron, were preparing runways through the poles of Rommel's asparagus to receive the gliders of General Gale's Tactical HQ, due to begin landing at 0320 hrs. This glider group would also include an urgently needed 6 pounder battery of anti-tank guns for my Brigade. 13 Para would be responsible for the protection of the landing zone for the glider landing. After going round some of the 13 Para positions, I was entirely satisfied and was able to move on to Johnson's 12 Para."

Then & Now: The house in the SE corner of the Ranville Château grounds that Brigadier Poett used as his HQ. He chose this building because many of the villagers had sought refuge in Ranville Château.

0300   Village of RANVILLE now cleared of enemy. Very few enemy were found, as from infm received from inhabitants, it appears that the main body of the enemy were away, and that the majority of those left behind departed with all speed when they saw parachutists Those PW taken were wounded and seemed very young. Identification from PW, dead and documents was 7/II Pz Gren Regt 125.

Captain Alfred "Nobby" Clark (2i/c, 'C' Company)

"As we drew further into the village the gliders landed. We could see them in the dawn light being towed overhead and then released to circle clumsily and sometimes finally crash through the trees before coming to rest on the landing zone. I remember thinking "Rather them than us.""

"The light seemed to materialise quite suddenly as we emerged from the village's southern end with its cover of tall trees, into the north west outskirts with its church on the crossroads, conveniently close by the Château and the presbytery, in the garden of which Battalion HQ was set up, with our Company HQ a trifle close, I thought. Our company was somewhat naked by reason of the non-arrival of 9 Platoon.

"Across the north end of the little orchard in which we had stopped, and separated by it by a 'Gloucestershire' type stone wall, ran the narrow country road. On the other side of this road there stood a rather long, three-storied house. From the windows of this waved hands. A section of No.8 Platoon, having taken up position astride the road, tried their hands at making friends, but the little group of occupants were very scary."

L/Cpl George O'Connor (8 Platoon 'C' Company)

"There were some people staring out of the windows of a large house. Either, they were afraid the Germans would return or maybe, they thought we were Germans, because we did not get any response, when we waved to them. The next time I looked up they had disappeared from the windows.

"My section was detailed to check Ranville again to make sure, that no Germans were sneaking back into the village, this we did, and then rejoined the rest of our depleted Platoon. Our Sergeant Major had joined them, which cheered us up, he decided we should go to the other end of the village, on our short trip through the village, I noticed a café, we all looked longingly at the door, I tried to open the door, but it wouldn't budge, they didn't appear to want any customers. "Keep away from there" warned our Sergeant Major ["Micky" Maguire].

"Ranville looked like a ghost village, exactly like the ones we used to practise in when we were in England. We lay down by a crossroad and hoped a few Germans would arrive, but all was quiet. A runner arrived; he never knew how close he was to being shot and he informed us, that we were to go to a wood on the outer edge of Ranville and dig some trenches, because an attack was expected from that direction.

"The ground was as hard as concrete, after about an hour of digging, my trench was only about 6" deep. I stopped digging when I heard an explosion near the edge of the wood, some crafty bugger had dug a small hole, filled it with plastic explosive and blown a larger hole, it was a good idea, but I thought maybe I could find a better use for my PE later on. I returned to my little trench and commenced to try and enlarge it. I came to the conclusion, that whoever designed the entrenching tool, had never tried to use one, it might have been OK in the desert but on Normandy earth they were useless. Soon after, a Sergeant arrived and told me to move my section to an orchard to the left of us, dig some more trenches and guard the Company HQ. My section didn't go much on that, but I told them to stop moaning and move.

"Once again we commenced digging, one of the lads began to moan, he was told to shut up and get on with the digging, he still moaned as he dug. His moaning was interrupted, a lone mortar bomb landed very close to him, the moaning ceased and he commenced digging like mad. One of my section ran to where the mortar had landed and claimed the hole, uttering the words "They never drop in the same place twice, this is my trench!"

'C' Company, without 9 Platoon, had now cleared the rest of Ranville in a series of small skirmishes and took up position as a fighting reserve on the west edge of the village. From here they could be trust into battle at any point around the village, to plug any gaps and reinforce any part of the line that was weak or threatened.

Private Ernest Hurst (adapted from his poem)

"I unpacked my kitbag that had given me so much trouble and then heard someone coming through the trees. Lance Corporal Medlicott (the man who landed on my chute) and I waited, with our trigger fingers ready. It was a good job we did wait before we fired, because it was our Platoon Sergeant.

"We arrived at the RV and by this time my ankle was giving me pain, I was sure it was fractured. We then moved on, down a lane with a ditch on one side. We passed some dead Germans along the way and then we made our way through a small orchard of apple trees. Hanging from one of the trees was a dead paratrooper, gently swinging in the breeze. It was not a very nice sight and gave us all quite a fright. Eventually we stopped beside a wall and were told to dig in, we stayed here for a few hours then we were on the move again."

Lieutenant Ellis "Dixie" Dean (MMG Platoon)

"We were still at the quarry and a vehicle coming along the road from the direction of the coast was clearly heard. It slowly topped a small rise 50-60 yards away and

halted. An armoured car was silhouetted on the skyline, with its engine ticking over. Johnny Frith then said "The CO wants a patrol to go out and deal with that armoured car." I moved nearer to the road to see how they [12th Battalion] dealt with it. I kept my eyes on it and noticed that it started to slowly move forward, it then accelerated. I thought it was going to get away and pulled a 36 grenade from my pouch, had the pin out and my arm back to throw it, a restraining hand clamped my shoulder and a voice said "Hold it, a party of our men have just gone across the road, you might hit them." It was Arthur Higgins (left). "Another cool head" I thought. The vehicle turned off the road onto the DZ and was destroyed."

5th Brigade Operations in Normandy Report

The normal enemy garrison of the village had been chiefly billeted round the Château (1133733) [Château de Ranville]. During the night 5/6 June, the bulk of this company were away from their billets, but a number of defensive posts on the North side of the town, overlooking the DZ, were held and miscellaneous parties of the enemy were in various houses in the village. The area was finally mopped up by about 0400 hours at small cost to the 13th Battalion.

The medical arrangements made by Lt-Col Harvey, DSO, commanding 225 Parachute Field Ambulance, had been excellent. Casualties from the DZ were collected and taken to an aid post near Ranville Church by Captain D.F. Tibbs and a Medical Dressing Station was opened soon after 0500 hours in Château de Guernon (106734). The fine work and efficiency of the doctors and stretcher bearers under difficult conditions in the first few days and gave a feeling of confidence to all ranks.

During the night of 5/6 June, 3 Organization Todt officers were asleep in their bedrooms in the Château de Guernon and captured. The house and outbuildings then became the MDS under the command of 225 Parachute Field Ambulance.

Private Ernest Hurst (adapted from his poem)

"At last we arrived in Ranville and what I think was a hotel became our Aid Post. The medics took me and laid me on my back on the floor. The pain in my ankle was now getting worse. Next to me was a German and I knew he was dying from the look of death on his face and that decaying smell."

Above : Sketch by Allied soldier depicting Château De Guernon in June 1944

Below : How it appears on www.likhom.com

Captain David Tibbs (225 Field Ambulance)

"We then did what we could in the hours of darkness, collecting up the wounded. At this point we didn't see any Germans, although I had one or two scares when things appeared out of the darkness. I met one rather distressed journalist, who had two Sten gun bullets in his neck, but fortunately not too badly hurt, this had happened as he had given the wrong password. I directed him towards Le Bas de Ranville where the main dressing station was being set up.

"It was the task of my section at daybreak to clear our DZ of injured men and this now had to be done with only the 5 of us who arrived there. The area was covered in wheat that was nearly 3 ft high amongst which it was very difficult to spot an injured man lying flat. A number had fractured femurs due to landing with kit-bags still attached to their leg. Corporal Russell managed get a gas powered farm lorry going which laboured up a long sloping road to collect a number of injured glider troops. On the way we passed 2 dead Germans from a motorcycle machine gun combination which had tried to rush through. These were the first Germans that I saw.

"At first light there was a distant rumble of bombing at the coast 3 miles away and from some higher ground, soon after we could actually see innumerable dots on the sea - the invasion fleet coming in - very heartening! From then on there was a continuous rumbling from the coast of the attack. Most of the injured we brought back in had broken femurs and still had kit bags attached to their legs. We picked up about 12 men in this manner. They would get our attention by waving anything they could as they couldn't stand up in the corn.

"My main memory was the physical exertion caused by carrying the men back by stretcher, sometimes over a mile; it was very hard work indeed. This is where we missed the other 15 men. There was a lot of debris on the DZ, broken up gliders, lots of helmets and lots of gas masks which had been discarded, but apart from that the area was quite deserted because the troops, both British and German were keeping well out of sight in the various houses and woods. We were wearing our Red Cross armlets, so we were fairly distinguished as medics, although a few shots were fired in our direction and a certain amount of mortaring."

Citation: Captain David Tibbs (225 Field Ambulance, RAMC)

Award: Military Cross

On the 6th June, 1944, at Ranville, Captain Tibbs was in charge of a party of twelve stretcher-bearers, with the task of clearing the Divisional Landing Zone and a Brigade Defence Zone.

At first the Defence Zone was subject to light Machine-Gun fire and later in the day the area was heavily sniped. In spite of this and the lack of cover, this party, under the personal leadership of Captain Tibbs, worked unceasingly until 1400 hours, when they had collected all casualties. During the eight hours the party sustained two killed and four wounded, but regardless of personal risk, Captain Tibbs completed his task.

One of the Conscientious Objectors who jumped with Captain Tibbs stick and was also part of his party, was also awarded for his bravery that hectic day.

Citation: Private Geoffrey Brown (225 Parachute Field Ambulance, RAMC)

Award: Military Medal

For Gallantry and devotion to duty.

On 6th June Private Brown was a member of the party under the command of Captain Tibbs RAMC detailed to collect casualties from Divisional Landing Zone and 5th Parachute Brigade. At first the Drop Zone was subject to Light Machine Gun fire and later in the day was heavily sniped. The area was under intermittent but accurate fire all day. Two men of this party were killed and four wounded. Private Brown was unceasing in his efforts all day in collecting the wounded. By his efforts and calmness he set an example to the rest of the men although he himself was in action for the first time. As the gliders and parachutists had scattered over a wide area the duty entailed a period of 11 hours, during which time Private Brown helped materially to enable all the casualties to be collected.

Private William Ellis (Mortar Platoon)

"We set up the mortars in a farm yard and helped ourselves to eggs and cream, the farmer wasn't bothered, he was more concerned about his farm being in the front line. We were also lucky enough to have a butcher in our platoon; he made good use of the cattle strung up in the barn. We had steak on D-Day, our dry rations were forgotten… but they came in handy later on."

Lieutenant Ellis "Dixie" Dean (MMG Platoon)

"Private John Griffiths, a member of the MMG Platoon (later a medic) told me that whilst on 'Drop Zone N', and making his way to the RV, he much to his surprise, came by the body of a dead fox, and was still bemused by this, when only a few yards further on he caught his foot in a trip wire. Clearly, the fox had also caught the wire, and triggered off the anti-personnel mine attached to it. The wild animal had saved his life.

"Around 0300 hours the order "Prepare to move" was given. There were now 29 gunners, myself, Alf Whalley and Andy Fairhurst of Platoon HQ, leaving 26 to man and defend 2 guns. We set off for Le Bas de Ranville and on the way saw the first wave of gliders bringing in the anti-tank guns we were to defend and the advance elements of Divisional HQ.

"Past Ranville church with its distinctive tower we went. I had carefully memorised the route from aerial photos and had no difficulty in leading Sergeant George Kelly to his position. I left them to dig their position and had 400 yards more to go before the planned location of the other section was reached. Arthur Higgins was along side me and a dark figure emerged from the corn. "Halt. Hands up. Advance and be recognised. Password." I demanded. "Punch" was the reply. 'Punch' with the response 'Judy' had been the one set for the night 4th/5th June and a different one had been issued for the 5th/6th June. A very frightened medical orderly from 225 Parachute Field Ambulance joined our party.

"With an NCO and 12 men to search for containers of ammo, we set off to look in the corn in front of our MMG positions. We were disappointed, no machine gun ammunition.[13]

"Not only were we without ammunition but the location I had been briefed to occupy (and told I was not to move from without Brigade authority) was useless. The corn only yards in front of the single gun was 3 ft high and that was the limit of our field of observation and fire. There was also the matter of an unknown number of Germans, only 100 yards to our rear, and there was the problem of shortage of

---

[13] Containers had a signalling device - a tripod arrangement that rose vertically with a flag and coloured light on top. The 13th Battalion containers had blue lights and chutes, they would also of had a blue circle painted on them and the contents of the container would have been written on the band. The containers dropped from a/c No.8, 9 & 10 held the reserve ammunition and were not to be retrieved until Bn HQ ordered them to be.

ammunition. Captain Bowler, the Officer at Brigade, responsible for coordinating the arcs of fire for all the 3 Machine Gun Platoons, had not visited us as arranged back in England to sort out any problems on the ground."

'A' Company having cleared the DZ of poles now had the task of securing the road east of Ranville by laying a minefield to prevent any German armour from entering Ranville. The approaches from the north and south were wide open spaces and offered the 6th Airborne Division perfect killing grounds.

Sergeant "Taffy" Lawley ('A' Company)

"The Platoon was only at half strength due to casualties. In the process of laying a minefield east of the village the mines had to be brought from the gliders some considerable distance away, so off I went and got a wheelbarrow from a house nearby. It took us the best part of the morning to lay the minefield and all the time we were being sniped at, suffering one or two casualties. Eventually we discovered the sniping was coming from the house where I had borrowed the barrow. A well directed grenade quickly brought forth 4 badly knocked about Germans."

Lieutenant Jack Watson (3 Platoon 'A' Company)

"For the remainder of the day I laid the minefield as ordered. The only difficulty I had was shortage of tape. The stick that was missing had most of it. We managed somehow. We completed the minefield by about 2000 hours and I joined my company area where we started digging and preparing my platoon positions.

"Our Company second-in-command, Captain Ainsworth, was missing and was found by the medics in the afternoon, he'd broken both his legs by coming down on one of the anti-glider poles. When they found him he was cursing, not because of his legs but because of his cigars, he'd lost them. I'd jumped a lieutenant and basically landed as a captain."

Private Bill Rutter (Signaller, 'C' Company)

"In Ranville Château's Company HQ grounds, in the dim light, there was a soldier bending over a rockery having a field dressing put on his seat. It seemed a queer place to stop at the time. I occupied a German trench and had a brew, just as daylight began."

Major John Cramphorn ('A' Company)

"It was now beginning to come light and some of the villagers looked on as we entered the built up area in the centre of Ranville. I recall seeing in the windows of one small shop, croissants and Camembert cheese, unknown in England since the outbreak of war.

"I established my Headquarters in the grounds of the Château de Ranville, which had also been the HQ of the German Company in the village. One of the first messages which came over the wireless was to ask if we had any cooks in the Company (our own ACC cooks came over by sea and did not arrive until D+1). During the confusion in the darkness, the German horse drawn ration cart had arrived and been taken to Battalion HQ, they had the fresh food but no one to cook it."

The grounds of Château de Ranville (www.chateauderanville.fr)

Pte Ray "Geordie" Walker (2 Platoon 'A' Coy)

"Our next task was to rush through the grounds of the Château and down a country lane leading to the village of Hérouvillette. The Château had been the billet of the Germans. They had killed several paratroopers who landed in the trees. To see their bodies swaying in the breeze whilst suspended from their harness was a gruesome sight. Several days were to pass before they could be cut down and buried.

"Whilst in the grounds of the Château my Platoon Sergeant [Sgt Llewellyn, left] was wounded beside me, he was shot through the hand and that was the last time I saw him. Sgt Alan Badel took over my Platoon; he was fluent in French, German and had a good knowledge of Italian. He was born to French parents and in later life he became a star of stage, TV and several films."

Private Peter Maynard (4 Platoon 'B' Company)

"When it got light we saw 2 men planting the wooden anti-glider poles in one of the fields. We brought them in and it turned out they were both ether Russian or Polish POW's assigned to plant the 'Rommel's Asparagus'. After they had a bit of food and water that we gave them, they both wondered off and carried on planting the poles, much to our amusement."

Lieutenant Ellis "Dixie" Dean (MMG Platoon)

"H-Hour for the seaborne assault was fast approaching and my binoculars were focussed on a solitary Halifax bomber loitering about in the direction of the coast. Suddenly all hell let loose, from dead quiet to indescribable bedlam in a matter of seconds, it seemed that no-one could survive such a battering. I could now break radio silence, but try as he may, Andy Fairhurst could not contact Brigade. I now know Anton Bowler never turned up and has no known grave. I set off to find my CO with Alf Williams and the medical orderly, who rejoined his own unit. On the way we passed the body of Private Thomas Johnson, the Battalion despatch rider. It appeared that he had dropped in the corn south of Ranville and half a mile off the DZ. He had been killed by small arms fire.

"As we neared the main road into Ranville from the south, smoke and flames were rising from the road which ran through a hollow as it entered Ranville. There was a burning halftrack across the road and a number of soldiers busy relaying a string of 'Hawkins' anti tank grenades. I stopped to congratulate them and recognised an NCO, Frank McLean. We had served together in the same platoon in 1940.

"Before I reached HQ I met Colonel Johnson, and he gave me permission to take all the members of the Platoon, not manning the guns, to go back to the DZ and search for ammunition. I was told I must be back at the guns no later than 1000 hours."

Captain Alfred "Nobby" Clark (2i/c, 'C' Company)

"The area now appeared quiet. But not for long, soon a terrific barrage started from way up in the north as the guns of the Royal Navy opened up. It seemed to me perhaps as well that I had traversed those 2 ½ miles from the spot where I had landed, since the burst of heavy shells seemed to come from just that very spot. 'H' hour had arrived - 0700 hours. I pictured the scene on the beaches as the landing craft grounded, let down their ramps and vomited forth tiny little men into the uncertain and unfriendly surf, to struggle on the beaches against an enemy as tough and determined as any they were likely to encounter. In spite of certain difficulties I had encountered on arrival I preferred my method of getting to the scene of action.

"The occasional mortar bomb still burst uncomfortably close. Now was not the time to forget Brigadier Nigel Poett's words "Dig or Die" How thankful I was to be for the possession of plastic HE. The noise of our beating into the hard stony ground of a 4 ft length of piping was soon heard, interspersed with warning shouts of "Take cover" just in case, as the charges dropped into the bottom of the hole, were detonated. One would blow a nice spherical trench."

Lance Corporal George O'Connor (8 Platoon 'C' Company)

"About 300 yards to the right of us we could see a large Château, from which a young Girl appeared and ran towards a small shed, my finger had tightened on the trigger, before I realised it was a girl, luckily I didn't pull it, she disappeared into the shed and reappeared with a basket. One of my section, nicknamed Chalky, for obvious reasons, was a young impulsive lad and he ran out of the wood towards her to warn her of the danger she was in. On seeing Chalky running towards her, she dropped her basket and ran like hell to the Château; Chalky picked up the basket and doubled back to us, shouting "Eggs for breakfast lads?" I gave him a rollicking for being so reckless; the only answer I received from him was "have an egg Corporal."

"German tanks approaching."

Lieutenant Gordon O'Brien-Hitching ('A' Company)

11. 2nd PANZER DIVISION COUNTER-ATTACKS

Leutnant Gerhardt Bandomir (21st Panzer Division)

"I left Major Hans von Luck and continued with my task of assaulting Hérouvillette and Ranville. After relieving No.2 Company of the 2nd Bn, we advanced further on foot with No.2 on the right and my own No.3 Company on the left. Behind us in the rear were the Assault guns (SP's)."

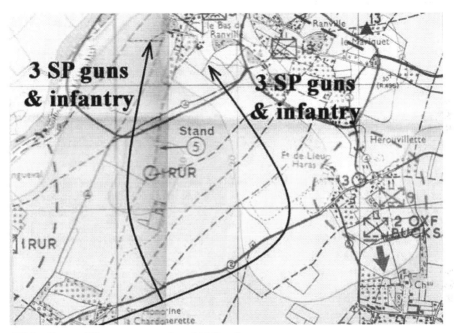

1005 Enemy SP guns reported on 'A' Coy front.

Private Ken Lang (MMG Platoon – 2 Section)

"Shortly after most of the Section went off searching for ammunition, the Brigadier came along the hedge, where we had dug in with a Platoon of the 12th Bn, looking for us. He had 2 anti-tank 6 pounders with him and he took us all up the road and positioned the weapons below the crest of what they now call the 'ring contour' (marked 'B' on diagram "21st Panzer Attacks, Ranville 6th June"). Here we looked back towards the village and to our right was St Honnorine. It was in the cornfields near there, at about 0930 hours we saw the German armour assembling. They were over 1,000 yards away. They stopped and then 2 small groups advanced, one of them in the direction of Hérouvillette, but the second group drove through the corn and the direction of advance meant they would pass immediately across our front. There was just the anti-tank team and the 3 Vickers gun numbers, Bill Price was one of them with Sergeant Kelly the Section Commander. We didn't have very much ammunition, besides our orders were not to open fire before the anti-tank guns.

"We waited and watched as the first group, which had disappeared behind some trees, now came in sight again and they too would pass across our position, but further away. Slowly they drove through the corn and still the anti-tank gunners held their fire; suddenly "whomff!" away went the first round, quickly followed by 2 more. Sergeant Kelly was behind the Vickers, firing short bursts of 10 rounds or so, not the usual 25 rounds we were trained to fire (he only had one belt of 250 rounds). You could see the shells hit their target, a short pause and then they all went up in flames, with the crews scrambling out and dashing away into the corn out of sight. The rest of the German tanks just disappeared into Sainte Honnorine.

"I well remember that our orders were that if they attacked us with armour, under no circumstances were we to open fire before the anti-tank guns did. But, nobody warned us that the gunners were going to wait until the leading tank was only a couple of hundred yards away, before they engaged it."

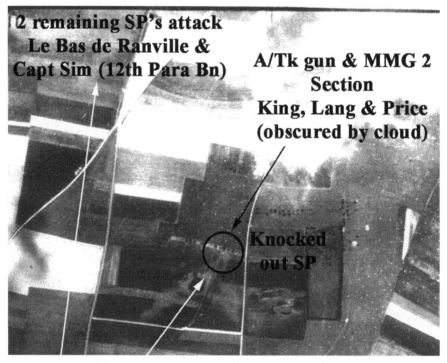

2 remaining SP's attack
Le Bas de Ranville &
Capt Sim (12th Para Bn)

A/Tk gun & MMG 2
Section
King, Lang & Price
(obscured by cloud)

Knocked
out SP

Courtesy RCAHMS

Private Don Jones (MMG Platoon – 1 Section)

"Passing down to these two sorts of fields to a hedgerow, we dug our slit trench there (marked 'A' on diagram "21st Panzer Attacks, Ranville 6th June"). Charlie King and myself had the Vickers machine gun and to our right was a farm house made of red brick. It was now daylight and whilst we were sat there I noticed a patrol of Germans walking along the side of a sort of race course towards the farm house, so we opened fire on them. Whether I hit any of them I don't know. About an hour or two later, at about 10am, Charley and I were sat there and all of a sudden we were shelled. Having never been a war zone up until then, I thought "What the devil is that!" After the explosion I looked up and on the right was a German SP gun and he was firing at us. Charlie turned to me and said "Taff, I've been hit in the shoulder!" and being a bit naïve I said "Come on now Charlie don't bugger me about, we need to get ourselves out of here." because they were continuing to shell our area.

"We went back down towards the houses and one of our sergeants from the intelligence section pointed us in the direction of the first aid post. When we got there they patched Charlie's shoulder and he asked them to have a look at me, "Don't worry about me I've only scratched my leg on some brambles" I said. "Drop your trousers!" was the reply from the medic. There was this old French lady in the first aid post and being only 21 at the time said "I'm not dropping my trousers in front of her!" The medic turned to me and said "Look corporal, I bet she's seen more that you've got!" Anyway, I dropped my trousers and I could see that a piece of shrapnel had taken a gouge out of my right leg. They dressed it up and that was my D-Day over."

1020   'A' Coy attacked by about 40 men and 3 SP guns.
1032   'A' Coy's last LMG wiped out.

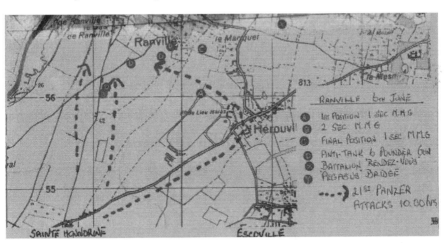

21st Panzer Attacks, Ranville 6th June – Map by Lt "Dixie" Dean (MMG's)

Lieutenant Ellis "Dixie" Dean (MMG Platoon)

"As we returned from fetching the extra ammunition we heard tank engines and they were heading in our direction through the cornfield. As I was scrambling up a bank, I heard the bark of a gun being fired, followed immediately by the "rat-a-ta-tat" of a Vickers, away to our right. By the time I reached the top of the bank several more rounds had been fired. At the top an unbelievable sight met my eyes. Immediately to my front and not 100 yards away 3 self-propelled (SP) guns were stopped and blazing merrily, with another to my right and it was from that direction the Vickers had been firing. My war had begun."

Battery Sgt-Major George Brownlea (4th Air Landing Anti-Tank Battery)

"Sergeant Bert Clements and his 6 pounder gun team on the southern outskirts of Ranville were warned by the Paras [Lt. O'Brien-Hitchin's No.1 Platoon 'A' Company] in the field on their left, of the approaching German armour and infantry. They had a look out posted up a high tree overlooking the corn. "If they keep coming", he thought, "I might be able to get 2 of them, but all 4 is impossible. However if we are undetected and let them advance further, and then Sergeant Portman's gun will also be able to engage them."

After Lieutenant O'Brien-Hitching had announced "German tanks approaching" Sergeant Clements of the Artillery replied "Nobody moves, nobody fires. I'll take the first shot and I'll only do that when either I'm spotted or they are very, very close."

The supporting infantry was wading through the corn and the officer leading signalled to his grenadiers that they should head for the ridge. Sgt Clements allowed the armour to advance.

Citation: Sergeant Bert Clements (4th Airlanding Anti-Tank Battery, RA)

Award: Military Medal

This NCO has rendered consistently meritorious service of a very high order throughout the campaigns in Normandy, Belgium, Holland and Germany. When under fire for the first time, while in process of getting his gun into action on D Day 6th June 1944, he was attacked by a German Mark IV tank at a range of 200 yards. Although subjected to heavy machine gun fire he rallied his detachment and destroyed the tank with the first round. His outstanding coolness and courage shown in this instance inspired great confidence amongst his men and the standard set by his detachment throughout the campaign has been a constant example to others and was instrumental in the maintenance of a steadiness under fire and a high standard of efficiency throughout his Battery. He has never spared himself and on several occasions has carried out more than the normal duties required of him in the furtherance of the cause.

When Sergeant Clements fired, his target was on the top of the high ground 200 yards away and the nearest Panzer Grenadiers were only a mere 100 yards distant. He hit his target, first time, fully in the middle and in the tracks. Almost simultaneously, Sergeant Portman fired his 6 Pounder.

Leutnant Gerhardt Bandomir (21st Panzer Division)

"My Company had to cross the racecourse at La Ferme de Lieu Haras and the armour support followed too close. Our Assault Guns were knocked out, without firing a shot. No.2 Company on the right met heavy resistance (from No.1 Platoon 'A' Company positions) and made little progress, losing many men. Because of this, No.1 Company failed, their Platoon Commander was killed and also another 15 or more men. We had no choice but to prepare defensive positions after the failure of our attacks."

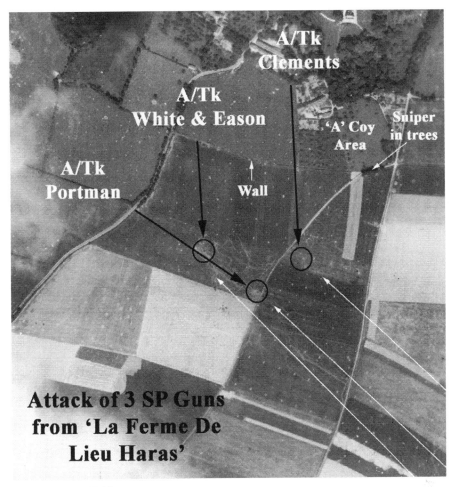

A/Tk
Clements

A/Tk
White & Eason

'A' Coy
Area

Sniper
in trees

A/Tk
Portman

Wall

Attack of 3 SP Guns
from 'La Ferme De
Lieu Haras'

Courtesy RCAHMS

Citation: Staff Sergeant White (Glider Pilot Regiment Chalk 115)

Award: Distinguished Conduct Medal

In the early morning of Tuesday after landing and taking up a defensive position. Staff-Sergeant White was the (sole?) member of a 6-pounder Anti-Tank gun crew. He manned his gun single handed and under heavy mortar and shell fire, he stayed with his gun and fought it entirely himself. He destroyed a Self-Propelled enemy gun with <u>*his first shot*</u> *and continued to engage enemy tanks. Through this man's courage and determination and complete disregard for his own safety he was responsible for delaying the advance of the enemy armour.*[14]

Staff Sergeant White (Glider Pilot Regiment Chalk 115)

"My co-pilot on lookout reported enemy tank movement on our left flank. Our gun was well concealed, but not very well sited. We came under small arms fire and

---

[14] Staff-Sergeant White DCM was killed in action at Arnhem on the 18th September 1944.

127

Sergeant Eason opened up on the Bren gun. By this time the first SP was in range of the gun, but [the] gun layer did not think he could hit the tank.

"In the meantime I had loaded a round and had a look along the sights myself. By this time the tank was almost dead ahead in front at 200 yards and needed stopping. So I decided to have a go myself, Sergeant Eason kept the Nazis heads down with Bren fire and I laid the gun ready to fire. The first round missed so I immediately reloaded and this time I applied 200 yards on the sights. The tank had stopped and I was expecting them to open fire on us any minute, so I quickly sighted the gun and fired. This time it was a hit and the tank went up in flames. During this short time another tank had been hit by the gun on our left flank and also one, which was almost unobserved from our position, was put out of action by a gun on our right flank [most likely the one in Ken Lang's area]. From our position 3 tanks were seen to be blazing and ammo was exploding in each at various intervals. The infantry, who were escorting the tanks, were then engaged by small arms fire for the rest of the day."

S/Sgt R.C. Downing (GPR)

"I landed 50 yards inside the LZ without flap at 6 minutes behind the ETA. I covered the unloading operation with the Bren gun and encountered no opposition, but just paratroops of the LZ force. The crew experienced some difficulty with unloading and it was an hour and a half before we moved off, but were met on the road by an RA major who diverted us to a position in a wheat field 1 mile due south of Ranville and about 500 yards east of the road running south from the village.

"We dug into position and were not bothered by E/A until about 1030 hours when an enemy mechanized (2 tanks and 2 self propelled guns) and infantry. Our 6 pounder scored a hit on one of the tanks with the first round from about 600 yards and the second round blew it up. The infantry were repulsed and mainly by the 13th Para. Bn but I'm certain I nailed one Jerry, and possibly two.

"For the remainder of 'D' Day we were fired on spasmodically by snipers, light and heavy MG fire, mortars and light artillery. Our Jeep suffered a direct hit from mortars and although we saved the Jeep by throwing off the burning kit, a great deal of equipment and ammunition (including my ammunition) was destroyed."

Staff Sergeant W Higgs (Glider Pilot Regiment)

"We moved to the edge of the landing strip and after contacting paratroops made our way to the Battery RV. There was no one there to give instructions so we proceeded to the pre-arranged position of the gun in company of another detachment. The 4 glider pilots acted as scouts on the way up.

"We then dug in and camouflaged our position leaving a look-out with the Bren gun. During this time we never saw any troops (friendly or otherwise) to our front. We were settled in our position (1½ mile SE of Ranville) by 0930 hours.

"About midday we saw 4 SP guns and one Mk IV tank with infantry in support advance over the sky line. We waited until they were within range and before we could fire the guns on our left flank opened up and hit 4 of them. We fired on the tank crews and infantry with our small arms. From then on we were fired on by snipers, mortars and machine guns returning their fire when we could see them, which were not often."

The above photograph shows L/Cpl Phillips (KIA, 19/8/44), Pte Best (KIA, 22/8/44), Pte Watson and Cpl Walter of 'A' Company, take time off during a rest period (5th August) to investigate the remains of one of the German self-propelled gun which they helped knocked-out on D-Day (© IWM B 8791).

Captain David Tibbs (225 Field Ambulance)

"We rejoined the 225 Field Ambulance in Le Bas de Ranville [at Château de Guernon] and I was put in charge of a large barn filled with wounded, many severely and dying, lying on straw. Across a driveway there was another smaller barn (left, as it is today), outside which an anti-tank gun had been positioned (an ideal reverse slope defence) alongside our large Red Cross flag! The frontline was only a few hundred yards away at this point. There was a constant storm of mortar fire coming down and this was causing more casualties. The surgeons were doing their best to cope with the worst wounded. The scene was one of noise, of wounded men, but nevertheless organisation, with people going about ignoring all the mortar fire.

"The barn I was put in charge of contained nearly 100 wounded men. A German attack came in, heralded by shelling, mortaring, and small arms fire close by. The door of the barn suddenly burst open and an excited RASC driver appeared, shouting "The Germans are at the bottom of the lane" (50 yards away), in response to this a badly wounded Glaswegian sergeant levered himself up and pointing a Sten gun at him snarled "Stop yer blathering, ye Fucker, or ye'll be the first to go!", the driver disappeared hurriedly and there was a general movement amongst the wounded as they struggled to get out their guns.

"In a short silence I heard a faint voice at my feet calling out my name and when I bent down heard "David, remove my gun, they will shoot me if they see it." It was Bill Briscoe the Catholic padre, near death with a chest wound. I knew him well, a much loved figure. I knelt down to take his pistol away and kicked it under some straw. I stood irresolute; what should I do if Germans burst in? The wounded should not have been left with their weapons but here they were fully prepared to shoot it out. One grenade tossed in by the Germans would set the straw ablaze and all would die. I had a 9mm automatic which I could use well. Should I join in the shootout, or try to prevent a slaughter by indicating the Red crosses on my arms?

"Mercifully there was a sudden fusillade of shots nearby, some loud explosions, and then sudden silence except for a few shouts outside. The Panzer Grenadiers had retreated because the 2 tanks they were supporting had been knocked out. In the quiet that followed I told my orderlies to collect up and hide all weapons, amid grunts of annoyance. I am sure I was right, the wounded stood a better chance if I depended on the Red Cross to protect them (this would not have been true when fighting the Japanese). Oddly we had been given virtually no instruction upon the Red Cross and Geneva Convention."

The barn at Château de Guernon used by Captain Tibbs

1033 'A' Coy reported attack repulsed. A/Tk guns knocked out 3 SP guns incl 2 destroyed. PW identified as 125 Pz Gren Regt (21 Pz Div).

The excellent conduct and shooting of the gunners was key to the overall success of the morning of D-Day. Had the German armour reached Ranville the bridges may well have been recaptured. The whole invasion could have been compromised.

Private Alf Williams (MMG Platoon)

"After the Vickers gun manned by Taff and Charlie was hit by the SP, Dixie took me along to recover the gun which we noticed was hidden in a bush. As we did so the Germans got interested. Whilst I was busy trying to get the gun sorted out so we could take it back, Dixie started throwing hand grenades and firing his Sten towards the Germans to keep their heads down. To strip the gun took a certain amount of time, but at the end of the day, we got the guns and proceeded back to the British lines. On the way back we came across a German, he just popped up from a field, how come or why he was there I do not know. Once he saw us then turned and ran towards the German lines."

Lieutenant Ellis "Dixie" Dean (MMG Platoon)

"Before we set off to look for ammunition, I had found a position from where 2 Section would be able to carry out its task and led the carriers there. On the way we passed close to one of the 6 pounders responsible for knocking out the armour and I paused to congratulate them. Not surprisingly they were as pleased as punch with themselves. I left the carriers at the new position and went, accompanied by Private Alf Williams, to collect the gun team who had remained behind. Moving up the final stretch of hedge, unexplainably, I took a 36 grenade from my pouch, carried it in the right hand and my left fore finger through the pull ring. I was looking to my left where the German armour had flattened the hedge. Alf was alongside, hissing in my ear, "Jerry's up there". I looked ahead. A party of Germans had come along the track from the farm and were gazing intently at the burning vehicles. Out came the pin and away went the grenade. I grasped my Sten, released the safety catch and in true 'Boys Own' style, charged. Surprise was complete; the Germans ran back towards 'Lieu Harras'. For once the Sten didn't let me down, a full magazine without a stoppage.

"The Vickers had been stuffed under the hedge, I called to Alf to collect it, while I reloaded and got off another full magazine at the fleeing enemy, although they were well out of range by now, but I hit one of them, as he stopped clutching the back of his thigh and two of his companions came back and supported him as they staggered away. Alf hoisted the tripod across his shoulders and picked up the condenser can which left me with only the gun itself to carry. We then legged it as fast as we could back to safety.

"On reaching the track leading to where I had left the ammunition carriers, we slowed to a walk and noticing a rabbit sitting up in the hedge to my left, I halted, lowered the gun to the ground and drawing my .45 pistol took a shot at the animal. Much to my surprise, not 20 yards away in the corn, a German soldier rose up. We looked at each other in silence and then he took to his heels and ran off. Dropping the pistol dangling at the end of the lanyard, I got another full magazine load of Sten fire at the fleeing Jerry.

"The new position for 2 Section gun was near where Private Johnson's body was found. Across the track from his body were three houses. I sent an NCO and a few men to ensure there were no Germans still hiding in the buildings. They were empty but the NCO asked me to have a look inside the nearest one to Johnson's body. A two roomed cottage. The main door opened into the kitchen/living room and to the left another door opened into a bedroom, of a female, judging from the scent. The bedding and mattress was heavily bloodstained."

"A little later I was chatting to Sergeant Gee of the 6 pounders. As we talked the roar of a diving aircraft heading in our direction from the coast, before we could take cover, an ME 109 came into sight, flying at no more than 100 ft. It was completely engulfed in flame and hit the high trees on the road side, somersaulting over, before hitting the ground and exploding not 50 yards away. Wreckage was thrown all around, but we managed to find what was left of the pilot, a charred torso and head, not a pretty sight."

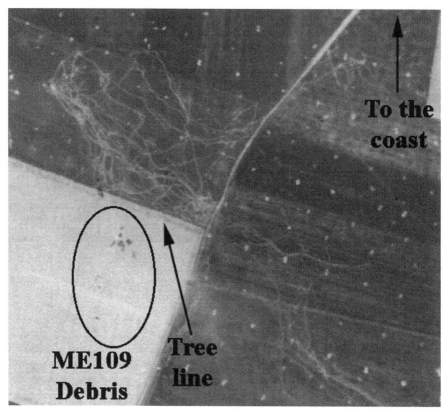

To the coast

ME109 Debris

Tree line

The above aerial photo (courtesy RCAHMS) shows the ME109 crash site 50m south of the tree line. Also the photograph clearly shows the 'paths' made by the SP's and accompanying grenadiers as they were ambushed at 10:30am. At many of the dead ends in the flattened crops would be a dead soldier.

1120   Infm received of counter-attacks against 7 Para Bn and 12 Para Bn. All these attacks are being held.

1200   Arty conc put down on HEROUVILLETTE RACECOURSE to assist 'A' Coy.

1210   'A' Coy reported one more SP gun knocked out.

1212   'C' Coy put in limited counter-attack to assist 'A' Coy. Enemy cas reported as 1 Offr and 42 ORs killed and 6 ORs captured.

1230   7 Para Bn report one Pl of enemy wearing Brit airborne smocks and red berets penetrated part of our line.

'C' Company were still plugging the gaps and because they were well under strength due to mis-drops they had to take up new counterattacking positions frequently.

Lance Corporal George O'Connor (8 Platoon 'C' Company)

"We were told to move to the hedge that was closer to the Château, I went to the hedge on my own to make sure there were no enemy in the vicinity, and I passed 2 dead bodies, I didn't stop to examine them, I didn't intend to be a target for the Jerries. I reached the hedge and opposite there was a cart track, that led to a road, that went to the Château, it was clear of enemy, I placed my hand on my helmet in view of my section and they closed in on me.

"A runner arrived about 2 hours later and told us to make our way back to the orchard nearer Ranville, we were halfway through the orchard, when we heard someone walking towards us, we froze and waited for them to advance, weapons ready, even though we thought, it must be a couple of paras. To our surprise, it was 2 German soldiers, we fired at them at the same time and down they went. I relieved one of them of his Schmeisser and I noticed that the safety catch was still on. I felt no compassion as I looked at the dead Germans, I consoled myself, with the fact that it was them or me and in this case, it was them."

Private Ray "Geordie" Walker (2 Platoon 'A' Company)

"On leaving the Château for Hérouvillette we ran into a small group of Germans, who were promptly killed. Immediately after this incident we had difficulty in silencing a 'Moaning Minnie' [multi barrelled mortar] which was in a wood. Our rifles made little impression and we hoped our artillery would finish the job off."

Private Ray Batten (2 Platoon 'A' Company)

"Our Platoon, under Lt Hodgson was led off to Hérouvillette crossroads to hold back reinforcements for the Germans on the beaches. The crossroads were to be held at all costs and no prisoners to be taken."

"At one point we had to drop flat and one mans Sten gun went off hitting the man in front of him on the helmet. He had a headache for the rest of the day and was not pleased at all! I remember a German patrol running up the hill, they were trying to get behind us and they were firing up the lane, the ricochets flew off the road surface and pinned us down. Despite the fighting around the crossroads a French civilian served us with coffee whilst the bullets flew."

Lieutenant Ellis "Dixie" Dean (MMG Platoon)

"A motorbike with sidecar attachment entered the village unaware of the British presence. Numerous weapons were fired and the vehicle crashed out of control, scattering boxes of Camembert cheese across the road. The riders wounds were treated by David Tibbs, who claimed the bike and had it repaired and repainted."

Private Ray Batten (2 Platoon 'A' Company)

"A little later a German Sergeant Major came along in the sidecar of a motorcycle. His driver was shot dead and he was wounded by two rifle bullets and one Sten gun bullet. He was in a bad way with a balloon of blood and mucus hanging from his nostrils. His life was spared for his great courage by the platoon commander, despite the no prisoner orders and he was taken to the Battalion HQ. Everyone admired this man and we were often passed information regarding his wellbeing. He made a full recovery much to everyone's delight. During the morning we beat off several attacks at the cost of one man dead, Private Arnold Hargreaves was hit in the abdomen by a mortar bomb."

Major John Cramphorn ('A' Company)

"Something always happened when I arrived at "Joe" Hodgson's (No.2) Platoon position, as I made my round of the Company area. The first time they had just beaten off a German attack and at one of the nearby houses I was asked by a French woman, "Who is this General de Gaulle we hear so much about on the radio?" I had to tell her that I did not know him personally, but doubtless she would hear a lot more of him in the future.

"Another time, I had acquired one of the lightweight motorcycles and as I rode down the avenue of trees towards "Joe's" positions, a German 88 persisted in sniping me as I went along."

1330   1 SS Bde Commando tps passed over BENOUVILLE BRS and through Bde posns towards FRANCOVILLE PLAGE.

Pte Bill Rutter (Signaller, 'C' Coy)

"My section took up positions in the grounds of the café on the Ranville crossroads (Then & Now, below). We tried to dig in, but the roots of the trees were in the way. Later we cooked some dehydrated porridge and meat, it was better than nothing. There was plenty of cider to go with it.

"We were pleased to see the Commandos coming up the road later on in the afternoon. With their small packs on their backs they drew remarks such as "What, travelling light?"

Lieutenant Ellis "Dixie" Dean (MMG Platoon)

"Unknown to us, by early afternoon, the complete 21st Panzer Division was concentrated south of St Honorine and the Divisional Commander's intention was to launch his entire force against Ranville and recapture the bridges. 130 tanks and 3,000 infantry; against 3 weak Parachute Battalions, six 6 Pounder and three 17 Pounder anti-tank guns. Fortunately the German Corps Commander over ruled his subordinate and ordered him to attack west of the Orne into the gap between the "Juno" and "Sword" invasion beaches."

1650   4 Schmeisser machine pistols and amn found in RANVILLE sent to 'A' Coy.
1710   'A' Coy again attacked by approx 50 of 3/I/Pz Gren Regt 125. Attack again repulsed.

Lieutenant Rupprecht Grzimek (Reconnaissance Battalion, 21st Pz Div)

"During that same night of 5 to 6 June we were alerted that paratroops and gliders had landed in the sector of Panzer Grenadier Regiment 125 under Major von Luck. Together with the bombing of Caen this suggested the Start of the invasion. We knew the order to attack only on orders from the highest authority. At dawn a liaison officer whom we had sent to von Luck reported that not only had an airborne division landed east of the Orne, but the enemy had brought up a vast armada off the coast and was preparing a landing from the sea.

"Heavy naval guns now joined in the landing operations. The weak units on the coast were apparently already involved in fierce fighting. Soon after came the order: "The Battalion is attached to von Luck's combat group and will move off at once in the direction of Troarn, about 12 km east of Caen." By making full use of cover we reached the area just west of Troarn in the early afternoon more or less without interference."

Lance Corporal Hammel (Reconnaissance Battalion, 21st Pz Div)

"As we moved forward to the northeast we saw toward midday on 6th June 2 Messerschmitt fighters flying north low over the Orne, the only German aircraft that day.

"East of Caen laid the first British paratroops to be killed. From their parachute silk we cut ourselves scarves as protection against the dust. Our commander's deputy gave us the order to attack. We went into the attack practically from the march. Further west we could hear the sounds of battle. That, we heard, was where our armoured group was supposed to attack. The enemy was apparently concentrating his naval fire against this, for him, dangerous thrust. His air force was also in action there. So we made good progress as far as the outskirts of Escoville, hence only a few km from Ranville and the two bridges over the Orne."

Major Hans Von Luck (21st Panzer Division)

"No. 4 Company of the panzer regiment arrived toward 1700 hours on 6 June, Major Becker's batteries not until the night of 7 June. So I had to start without them. My second Battalion was engaged in heavy defensive fighting against the paratroops that had landed, who were obviously trying to extend their as yet very small bridgehead. I could free only limited elements of the battalion for the attack.

"In the late afternoon, almost at the same time as the armoured group west of the Orne, we set off. Our goal: to push through via Escoville - Hérouvillette to Ranville and the two Orne bridges. The reconnaissance battalion went straight into the attack from its march and, supported by the panzer company, penetrated to Escoville against their surprised opponents.

"Then all hell broke loose. The heaviest naval guns, up to 38cm in calibre, artillery, and fighter-bombers plastered us without pause. Radio contacts were lost, wounded came back, and the men of the reconnaissance battalion were forced to take cover."

All day Ranville was attacked from different directions and moving from position to position 'C' Company was busy all day covering any weaknesses in the defences.

L/Cpl George O'Connor (8 Platoon 'C' Coy)

"It was beginning to get dark, I felt like lying down and nodding off to sleep. A runner arrived and said "I've been looking for you bastards every where", he pointed to an orchard and carried on, "Captain Clark is there and he will give you your orders" we doubled to the orchard, situated about 300 yards from the outskirts of Ranville and slightly closer to the coast. We were only operating in an area of about a quarter of a square mile, so we were beginning to know our little patch. The Captain, was waiting for us, he told us the enemy was approaching form the direction of the coast.

"Our Platoon Officer arrived [Lt Jack Sharples], the first time I had seen him since we landed. He congratulated us, for still being alive, he always had a sense of humour, he told us to dig some trenches at the edge of the orchard, facing the direction our Captain had pointed out, then said "dig deep lads it's the only way you will get protection when the German tanks arrive." With that order he marched off, leaving me and my 5 men to get on with it, we began to dig in a half hearted fashion, when bullets began to fly in our direction. Our Captain was right as usual."

2100   Main glider party 6 Airldg Bde, landed on LZ.
2100 to 2130 LZ shelled from SOUTH.
2330   Dakota a/c dropped supplies by parachute.

General Richard "Windy" Gale (Commander, 6th Airborne Division)

"The closing incident for this great day was the fly-in of the 6th Airlanding Brigade. It was a sight I shall never forget. A sudden dull roar of aircraft could be heard. Then they came, hundreds of aircraft and gliders; the sky was filled with them. We could see the tug aircraft cast off their gliders, and down in great spirals the latter came.

"The German reaction was quick. He mortared our HQ, unfortunately my Artillery Commander [Jack Norris] received a terrible throat wound and my Intelligence Officer was also hit. One of my provost men standing just behind me was killed."

Private Ray "Geordie" Walker (2 Platoon 'A' Company)

"A resounding cheer went up from all the troops in Ranville as the gliders landed in nearby fields. Now had support of more men, artillery, anti-tank guns and Tetrarch tanks of the Armoured Recce Regiment. Our spirits were high and we felt confident of winning this first day of battle. At Ranville we dug in and prepared for a counter attack by the 21st Panzer Division."

Château de Heaume, General Gale's HQ in NE Ranville.

Private Bill Rutter (Signaller, 'C' Company)

"In the evening some more gliders came in, what a wonderful sight they were, in the clear sky. The only noise they made seemed to be a whispering and then they landed in the fields like taxis."

Private Ray Batten (2 Platoon 'A' Company)

"When evening came so did more of the 6th airborne division in gliders. We covered their landing as they came in and landed in perfect order. This was a memorable sight, in the morning sun of that summers evening, it looked for the entire world like an exercise. It was hard to believe that so many of them had come to die. We stayed in these positions all day until dusk when we rejoined the battalion at the chateau in Ranville. Our action had earned the Military Cross for our Platoon Commander Lt Hodgson. In the Château grounds we prepared for the night and dug our slit trenches followed by servings of hot stew that had been captured from the Germans. We then settled in for the night, completely surrounded by the enemy."

Citation: Lt William Hodgson (2 Platoon 'A' Coy)

Award: Military Cross

On 6th June 1944 Lieutenant Hodgson held his platoon position with great gallantry and resource, although subjected to many attacks by greatly superior forces and inflicted at least 45 casualties on the enemy and 1 Armoured Fighting Vehicle knocked out. He so manoeuvred his platoon and personally led a counter attack that the enemy was completely deceived as to his strength and position and eventually withdrew. His own platoon suffered no casualties.

137

Throughout all the time he was a constant example of courageous leadership and his disregard of danger was an inspiring example to his men.

Lieutenant Ellis "Dixie" Dean (MMG Platoon)

"Around 2100 there was a marked increase in aerial activity. There were several squadrons of Spitfires circling overhead and then the growing roar of many larger planes could be heard to our rear. Then passed overhead in two streams, Albemarles, Stirlings, Dakotas and Halifaxes; towing mostly Horsa gliders, but also a number of the giant Hamilcars.

"The gliders cast off their tow ropes, 1,000 yards to the south and made a 180 degree turn, lower their flaps and dive steeply down towards their landing areas. Light Ack-Ack guns in the Lieu de Harras farm pumped their shells into the stream of aircraft. Then adding to the noise, our own mortars, with Sergeant Eric Thompson as mobile fire controller, started to engage the Boche guns.

"In a little over half an hour 142 glider loads of Infantry, Gunners, Sappers, Medics and finally the Tetrarch tanks of the Armoured Recce Regiment arrived to strengthen the Division's hold on this vital section of the air bridgehead.

"Just before 'stand to', a complete gun detachment from the 8th Battalion, dropped by mistake on DZ-N was brought to me. Only one small incident broke the night's silence. A twin engine bomber, flying low in the moonlight, dropped containers of small anti-personnel bombs over the village."

Lieutenant Harry Pollak (Intelligence Officer)

"We landed as planned and our casualties were relatively very light. Dawn had not yet broken, when one by one the pre-arranged code signals come over the command net telling us that all objectives had been secured. Great rejoicing followed not only by ourselves, but by the villagers and the French resistance. Had we drunk all the calvados (distilled cider) offered to us we would never have managed to dig in for the inevitable German counter-attack. Furthermore, ground to air radio communications had to be set up to bring in the gliders of the 3rd Air Landing Brigade at first light. The glider landing happened without a hitch and with that our transport, anti-tank guns, fuel and ammunition and a multitude of supplies were secured, not to mention three battalions of airborne infantry of the landing brigade which were required to secure our perimeter."

Capt D Tibbs (225 Fd Amb, RAMC)

"During the night it was possible to evacuate by ambulance to the coast 16 of the critically injured who might possibly survive. These included Padre Briscoe who nearly died on the way but was saved by an emergency operation on a tank transporter ship."

Left: Captains Tibbs and Foy attending the 50th Anniversary D-Day pilgrimage in Ranville Cemetery.

Major Hans Von Luck (21st Panzer Division)

"Now, on the evening of 6 June, it seemed to have become clear even to Hitler that it must be a matter of a large-scale invasion. But Hitler and his High Command still reckoned on a further landing in the Pas de Calais. The panzer divisions and reserve units stationed there were not to be withdrawn, on express orders from Hitler.

"At the same time it was also clear to the last man that the invasion had succeeded, that it could now be only a matter of days or weeks before the Allies would have landed sufficient forces to be able to mount an attack on Paris, and finally on the German Reich. If it were not for that damned air superiority!

"Even by night "Christmas trees" hung in the sky bathing the whole area in bright light. The air attacks never stopped; the navy laid a barrage of fire on our positions and bombarded the city of Caen."

By midnight 'A' Company were dug in on the South side of Ranville, 'B' Company occupied the North and East and 'C' Company were held in reserve in the West, available to strengthen any position as it was required. Battalion HQ and the HQ Company was located in the centre of the Ranville. The Mortar Platoon under Lt Freddie Skeate was sited in an orchard directly behind the Battalion HQ.

Several villagers were killed in that evening's shelling, but during the day only three of the 13th Battalion had been reported as killed, but many were still reported as missing and their fates were unknown. Throughout the day many did filter back through the ranks, each with various tales to tell, most having spent the day with other units. After midnight Captain R.M.T. Kerr, Second-in-Command of 'B' Company brought in a number of men, leaving the Battalion short of half of No.3 Platoon and half of the HQ of 'A' Company, No.9 Platoon of 'C' Company, 9 machine gunners, a stick of 9 from the Mortar Platoon and the Quartermaster's glider party.

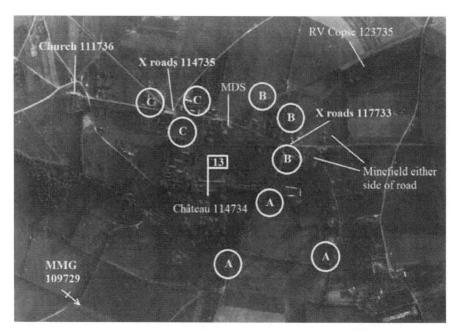

Approximate 13th Para Bn positions, Ranville 2400 hours 6th June 1944

The village of Ranville was the first village to have been liberated during the Second Front. A memorial remembering this fact is erected at the Ranville crossroads:

Veterans and families visit the Ranville Crossroads (114735), 6th June 2011.

From left to right: Sally, Cathy, Claire and Mandy (Major Jack Watson's daughters), Tom Luard (Col. Peter Luard's son), Dennis Boardman, Roy Ritchley, Peter Gospel (Harold Gospel's son), Barbara Longden (Colin Longden's widow), Bill Doherty, Jim Beasant, Bill Sanders, Fred Smith and Fay Robins (Tom Thresher's daughter).

(Picture and text courtesy Fay and Bern Robins Normandy 2011 Newsletter).

This 6th June was a special day for Tom Luard; it would have been his father's, Col. Peter Luard, 100th birthday. His Name Lives On.

ROLL OF HONOUR – D-DAY

Pte	ALDRED John	24	06/06/1944	3656824	QM	St Vaast Chyd 10
Capt	DAISLEY Spencer	40	06/06/1944	133790	QM	St Vaast Chyd 10
L/Sgt	DAY James	28	06/06/1944	5569086	MMG	N.K.G. Bayeux
Pte	FARMER Roy	20	06/06/1944	14627663	MMG	N.K.G. Bayeux
Cpl	HALLAS Joseph	21	06/06/1944	14202729	MMG	N.K.G. Bayeux
Pte	HARGREAVES Arnold	20	06/06/1944	14422876	A	Ranville 3A-J-8
Pte	JOHNSON Thomas H.	29	06/06/1944	4696371	Signal	Ranville 2A-L-10
Pte	MACKENZIE Donald J.	19	06/06/1944	14402094	MMG	N.K.G. Bayeux
Pte	MIDDLETON George R.	25	06/06/1944	249862	MMG	N.K.G. Bayeux
Cpl	PIDDLESTON Raymond R.	21	06/06/1944	3866121	MMG	N.K.G. Bayeux
Pte	POTTER Ernest E.	21	06/06/1944	3663288	Mortar	Ranville 2A-L-6
Pte	SHEPHERD Colin R.	26	06/06/1944	3961383	MMG	N.K.G. Bayeux
Pte	SUCKLEY Harry L.	23	06/06/1944	3663700	MMG	N.K.G. Bayeux
Pte	WAIN Reginald S.	19	06/06/1944	14654376	MMG	N.K.G. Bayeux
Pte	POWELL John H	26	15/02/1945	4917891	?	Cheslyn Hay *

*   Died of wounds.

"I remember what I thought was a French civilian, complete with dungarees and black beret, riding towards me on a bicycle and my surprise when he said to me in broad Lancashire accent: "Can you tell me where the 13th Battalion are chum?""

Private Colin Edward Powell (12th Para Bn)

12. THE MISSING

Not everyone made the Drop Zone or at least, the right Drop Zone. The night of 5/6th June had many extraordinary events, men landed in totally the wrong areas, others got mixed up with different units and some simply went missing.

Numerous aircraft came under fire and were forced to take evasive action, causing navigational errors and slow stick jumping as paratroopers were thrown around in the fuselage. 'Eureka' beacons were set up astray and some were damaged or lost during the pathfinders drop. Many planes developed mechanical problems caused by flak or fell foul of unlucky breakdowns. The Weather in the form of wind and cloud cover added further to navigational mis-drops, and poor visibility for parachutists to orientate themselves towards rendezvous and objectives. Kitbag issues took the minds of the men away from the task of landmark spotting.

Despite the multitude of errors and misfortune, men used initiative and determination to find their way back to their units. Some took hours others took days, weeks or even months to find, fight or stumble back into their own lines. Many fought along side the French Resistance or hid with brave French families. The unlucky ones ended up as POW's, some even escaping and returning to their units to fight again, but the really unlucky paid with their lives.

General Richard "Windy" Gale (Commander, 6th Airborne Division)

"By the following day a good proportion of those missing men had come in. This was the case in all the parachute battalions. The reports of the large number of missing men in the first 24 hours led to an erroneous impression that our casualties had been far heavier than in fact they were. It was wonderful how these men all rejoined their units, many of them having come through the German lines."

Aircraft 15

Carrying 9 members of the HQ Company, this Albemarle mistook the River Dives for the River Orne and dropped the stick between 5-6 miles east of the DZ and into the area the Germans had flooded as part of their defences.

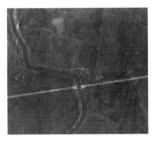

Aircraft 15 landed in the middle of the flooded area of the River Dives. The map over the page shows how easily the Germans managed to flood this area, due to the huge network of dykes and ditches. The only dry land was at Robenhomme, situated on the slightly higher ground NW of the bridge carrying the D224 (which was blown on D-Day to restrict enemy movements towards the main 5th Brigade area and the Orne Bridges, pictured left).

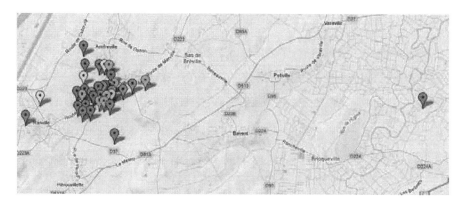

Landing area of aircraft 15 (right) & bulk of the Battalion (Map data © 2012 Google).

Captain Padre Whitfield "Boy" Foy

"I myself had dropped east of the [River] Dives in the swamps. My batman [Private Raymond Whitehead] dropped some 40 yards away, and I contacted him as soon as I was out of my harness. From then (about 0110 hours) until 0630, we didn't see a single soul; we spent the whole of that miserable night trying to find a way out of the wretched swamp – without success. For 5 hours we were never in less than 2ft of water, very often 3 and too often in 5. At one point we were pulling each other through a ditch 4ft deep, with the help of my batman's rifle, when my finger must have caught the trigger; there was a loud crack and the bullet passed between his arm and his body, because he had the rifle pointing towards him at the time.

"At daylight we picked up 2 more of the stick who had also been dropped in the swamps, and together made our way westwards, and arrived on the east bank to find the bridge blown and men of the Canadian Parachute Battalion guarding the area. We chatted in a friendly fashion for a few minutes while we were thinking of some method of getting across the river. While we were chatting we were joined by quite a crowd of men from the Division, almost every unit was represented, and they had all dropped in the swamps.

"After further discussion, it was decided that the Canadians should blow one of the trees standing on their bank, so that it would form a temporary bridge. No sooner said than done and within a few minutes the tree was stretched between the two banks. It was partially submerged and we had to wade, waist deep, in order to get across. There was quite a body of us now and once over, were directed to a spot a mile away, where they said there was a small concentration of personnel dropped astray. We pushed on and when this crowd came in sight, I heard a familiar voice shout "Hello Padre, what are you doing here?" It was Mike Kerr [Captain and 2i/c of 'B' Company], minus all his equipment, but as lively as ever."

Captain Mike Kerr was first to jump from his aircraft and landed in the middle of the River Dives. After a struggle he managed to get out and made for a farm where he picked up 4 paratroopers. A boy, from the farm took them to Varaville at 0330.

Arriving outside Varaville he reported that "Complete chaos seemed to reign in the village. Against a background of Brens, Spandaus and grenades could be heard the shouts of British and Canadians, Germans and Russians. There was obviously a battle in progress."

He decided that they should avoid this area and instead headed for Le Mesnil where he hoped they could make contact with Brigadier Hill's 3rd Brigade. By luck, they met a cockney woman in her 50's from Camberwell and she helped Captain Kerr, by acting as a translator, to a boy who offered to take them to Le Mesnil. The boy was not able to help them for long. The group ran into a German patrol and during the ensuing contact he was killed when a grenade exploded on his head. After dealing with the patrol, Captain Kerr's group found some French farmers and were given bread and milk.

During the next few hours wandering through the swamps Captain Kerr's party steadily increased in number to around 20 as other paratroopers joined their ranks.

Captain Padre Whitfield "Boy" Foy

"From then on he [Captain Kerr] took control of the whole party. We brewed some tea and then had to decide on the next move. The slogan "when in doubt, brew up", was very quickly adopted throughout the Battalion. The Germans were already up to the east bank of the River Dives and we had very few weapons. On the other hand the enemy was also in Robenhomme, directly between us and the Battalion location, if indeed the Battalion had reached its location.

"Finally Capt Kerr made a decision, we would move as soon as possible and would make a roundabout journey (a fairly wide detour to the south of Robenhomme) back to Ranville, hoping that the Battalion was installed in the village. The trouble was that the route chosen involved a walk of at least 3 to 4 hours, through more swamps, as though we hadn't already seen enough water. By this time I was beginning to wonder if France and Holland had git mixed up!

"We set off at about 5pm and plunged into the water; there we were until about 9pm. But as we finally trudged out on to firm ground, we had our reward, for there in the evening sky, away to the north, came streaming in, a gigantic glider armada. We whooped with joy because of the spectacle and because we knew that the gliders coming in meant that the Battalion was almost certainly installed in Ranville. We pressed forward with relieved minds and encountered only one incident. At a track junction in the Bois de Bavent, a drunken Frenchman assured us that one of the tracks was clear of the enemy. As a precaution a small recce party went down and found that it was by no means clear of Germans. So we went the other way.

"The first HQ we struck was that of 3 Para Brigade in the Le Mesnil. There we were assured that we could move down to Ranville with safety and that our Battalion was in possession of the village. At 1am (7th June), Capt Kerr reported to the CO, with his weary crowd of wanderers. Joyous greetings were exchanged; I stripped off my clothes, which by now were stinking to high heaven, got between a couple of blankets and regardless of the possibility of falling mortar bombs, ignored the slit trenches and went to sleep in a house near Battalion HQ. In the morning I awoke to find a steaming mug of tea at my side, provided by Signal Sgt Eric Cookson (right). I sighed out contently. I was home again."

Aircraft 17

Carrying 9 members of the Anti/Tank Platoon, this Albemarle never made it on to the runway. David Robinson has previously told of the events that caused the problems and now he describes what happened next.

Private David "Robbie" Robinson (Anti-Tank Platoon)

"After the pilot failed to take off, there was some confusion about what to do with us, but eventually transport was arranged to take us to some unknown port, most probably Southampton and here we boarded a landing craft.. On this boat there were other Paras, who for one reason or another had been left behind. We landed on the beach at Arromanches late in the afternoon on D-Day + 1. From there we made our own way to join the Battalion in Ranville 3-4 miles inland from the coast.

"When we approached the Canal Bridge [Pegasus] an officer from 7th Battalion pointed us in the direction of the 13th Battalion positions. Some years later I realised that this officer was Richard Todd, the film star who played Major Howard in the film "The Longest Day".

"Arriving in Ranville, almost the first thing we saw were bodies lined up on the pavement awaiting burial. I was surprised to find that there was still a good 30% of the battalion missing.

"The Anti-Tank Platoon arrangement was scrapped shortly after we got to France. Instead, one section was attached to each rifle company that was 3 PIAT's with 3 men to each PIAT and a corporal in charge - 10 men. The officer was still in overall charge but this soon altered as officers were killed or wounded, he was moved to other duties. This then was our recommended set up for the rest of the war. One section of the PIAT's with each company under the command of that company to be used by the company commanders as required. I was with 'C' Company.

"I was positioned on the centre point of the village at a 5-road junction. I was in the garden of a café. The garden was triangular shaped being shaped by two of the roads to the crossroads. This garden had a stone wall around it. A slit trench was dug inside the wall looking over the wall and across the road directly across the full landing area where it was thought that the PIAT could cover the five roads and the landing grounds against tanks. No tanks came thank goodness.

"My slit trench companion was a private named Tarlton who remained with the battalion to the end of its existence but I have not seen or heard of him since I was discharged. This area I visited in 1994 and it has hardly changed, the café, garden with the wall etc. are still there overlooking the landing ground although a few houses have been built on the corner of the landing ground."

Aircraft 20

Aircraft 20 carried 9 troops from the HQ Company. The details of this plane and where the troops dropped are unknown but L/Cpl Casson and Ptes Elston, Higdon, Jones, Whelans, and Wotherspoon from this aircraft are all named in the POW files in the National Archives, therefore they were all captured and most of them spent the rest of the war in Stalag IV-B prison camp.

The 3 remaining members of the stick were not reported as missing, so therefore made it back to the Battalion at some point. They were Stick Commander Sergeant

McPhail (REME Armourer), Private Robert "Bobby" Johns (KIA 23/07/1944) and the other jumper unknown.

Aircraft 204

Taking off from Keevil with the 12th Battalion at 23:48 on the night 5/6th June, was Stirling aircraft No.s 204 & 205. They carried Lieutenant Dean and his MMG Platoon and each carried 20 troops and 6 containers. The first 11 all jumped and were eventually accounted for but the final 9 paratroopers and the plane along with the 6 aircrew were never seen again.

Lieutenant Ellis "Dixie" Dean (MMG Platoon)

"After my chute developed, I had time to look around and pick up my bearings, but Ken [Lang – No.11 and last to actually jump] states that no sooner had his chute opened, he hit the ground. This would suggest that the plane was losing height during the drop. Possibly to confirm this Captain David Tibbs, recalls that as he stood in the doorway of his Dakota waiting for the 'Green' light, their pilot took evasive action to avoid collision with a 4-engine aircraft from which men were already jumping and this aircraft passed below them.

"John Surgey, jumping No.8, recalled that just as Ray Strachan disappeared through the aperture in front of him the light changed to "Red", but he jumped nevertheless. Does this mean that the pilot had realised that he was no longer flying at a safe height for parachutes to develop and decided to abort the drop? But the despatcher took a few seconds to realise this? I have to admit, that he was nervous during the fly-in.

"Back on D-Day, I reported these 9 men as missing. In July '44, when in reserve George Kelly and I were wondering if we could find out what happened to them. George, who was Stick Commander, suggested that he could write to the pilot back at Keevil and ask him where he had dropped the remaining 9 men. Less than a week later came a reply, not from F/Sgt Jack Gilbert, but from the Squadron Adjutant (299 Squadron). Quite simply he said could we help him as it was the only one of the 36 despatched from Keevil that never returned.

"In January 1945, we received notification from the War Office that they had not been reported as POW and finally after the war German Flak records were carefully inspected but no record of the shooting down of this aircraft could be found."

Private Ken Lang (MMG Platoon)

"To my knowledge everything was in order when I bailed out, but the pilot had previously sent the message through that there was a lot of flak about. The approximate position of the aircraft when I baled out was in the centre of the main DZ at a height of about 400ft. There was no indication that anything was wrong with the aircraft.

"I do not know which direction the aircraft was travelling when I jumped and I did not see it crash."

Lieutenant Ellis "Dixie" Dean (MMG Platoon)

"Ken was No.11 and was the last man to actually jump. We have been back together several times and we can both pin-point where we landed. I landed in a tree in a high hedge around an orchard and Ken landed in the 'V' junction of the Ranville-

Pegasus Bridge roads. The aircraft flew across the top [north] end of the DZ and not down the length."

It can only be assumed that the aircraft for whatever reason, crashed at sea and that all aboard were drowned. Did it never regain its height and tried a force landing in the English Channel or receive a fatal hit whilst circling around over the Channel and crash as a result of this?

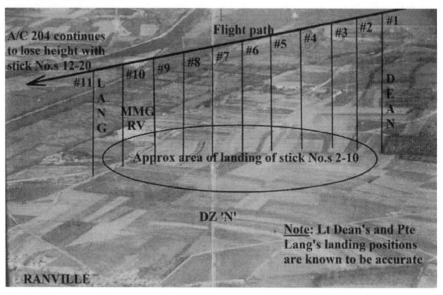

STICK NO	NAME	FATE
No.1	Lt "Dixie" DEAN	Landed on DZ
No.2	Pte Ronnie BOYLAN	Landed on DZ
No.3	L/Cpl Harold TURNER	Landed on DZ
No.4	Pte "Bill" PRICE	Landed on DZ
No.5	Pte "Jock" BARNETT	Landed on DZ
No.6	L/Cpl Arthur HIGGINS	Landed on DZ
No.7	Pte Ray STRACHAN	Landed on DZ
No.8	Pte John STURGEY	Landed on DZ
No.9	Pte "Taffy" PRICE	Landed on DZ
No.10	Sgt George KELLY	Landed on DZ
No.11	Pte Ken LANG	Landed on DZ
No.12	Pte Donald MACKENZIE	Went down with a/c
No.13	Pte Roy FARMER	Went down with a/c
No.14	Cpl Joseph HALLAS	Went down with a/c
No.15	Pte Colin SHEPHERD	Went down with a/c
No.16	Pte Harry SUCKLEY	Went down with a/c
No.17	Pte George MIDDLETON	Went down with a/c
No.18	Pte Reginald WAIN	Went down with a/c
No.19	Cpl Raymond PIDDLESDEN	Went down with a/c
No.20	L/Sgt James DAY	Went down with a/c

Aircraft 312

17 members of 3 Platoon, 'A' Company along with 3 CMP's in aircraft 312 went missing on 6th June when their plane dropped them off target. Only 3 managed to rejoin their unit, one of which was Private Arthur West (left) a bricklayer from Glamorgan.

Private Arthur West (3 Platoon 'A' Company)

"I left England at 2329 hours on the night of 5th June 44 in a Dakota aircraft. The other members of the stick were as follows:

1. CSM McPharlan	10. Pte Brown
2. L/Cpl Pickering	11. Pte Maden
3. Pte Stewart	12. Pte Barker
4. Pte Bevington	13. Sgt Moore (CMP)
5. L/Cpl Cave *	14. L/Cpl Griffiths (CMP)
6. Pte Gardner	15. L/Cpl McGowan (CMP)
7. Pte Bardsley	16. Cpl Bott
8. Pte Pass	17. Pte Oliver
9. Pte West	18. Pte Cave *
	19. Sgt Taylor

*   Note: Pte and L/Cpl Cave were brothers (pictured below).

"Our task was to clear a stretch of land in preparation for our Glider Forces to land near Ranville and to cover their assembly point. However, we were dropped in error at St Samson. I was No.9 of the stick to drop and I landed in a dyke. After struggling for about an hour with my equipment in the water, I reached dry land, retaining my rifle and met Sgt Moore, L/Cpl Griffiths, L/Cpl Cave, Ptes Gardner, Pass and Bardsley. After a talk together we came to the conclusion that we were in the wrong place for we did not know where we were. We all moved together to do a recce in the direction we thought was Ranville (which afterwards we discovered was Troarn), but after moving around for about 2-3 hours we decided it would be better to hide until it was light.

"At dawn L/Cpl Griffiths and Pte Pass moved off in the direction of Troarn to try and contact some French civilians and obtain information. They returned in about 30 minutes with the news that we were in the neighbourhood of Troarn. The same pair again left shortly afterwards to do another recce and to try and contact other members of the party who we believed were in the direction of St Samson. They returned with the news that Sgt-Maj McPharlan, L/Cpl Pickering and Pte Stewart were in an orchard near the church. We then crossed the river by means of a ferry and joined them.

"The Sgt-Major, Ptes Pass and Cave left in the afternoon to do a recce and returned. Guards were posted and we stayed the night in the orchard. At that time we were living on our 24 hour ration packs. During the morning the Sgt-Major left to go to Ranville and obtain help. At approx 1600 hours a Typhoon pilot (Flight Sergeant Tidbury) whose machine had been hit by flak and who had bailed out was brought to us by 2 French civilians and joined the party. News was brought by some more civilians that there was enemy in the area and so we all left with the exception of F/Sgt Tidbury and Pte Gardner. Pte Gardner was detailed to stay behind and tend F/Sgt Tidbury who had sustained burns on the face.

"On the main road – St Samson to Troarn, we suddenly bumped into a German on a bicycle. He was killed but there were another 10 men some distance behind in possession of an LMG. We took up positions on either side of the road but had to withdraw. On our return to the barn near the orchard we found that L/Cpl Pickering and Pte Stewart were missing. Later we were told by the French that they thought they had been taken prisoner. F/Sgt Tidbury and Pte Gardner had left the barn.

"At approximately 2030 hours Sgt Moore, L/Cpl Griffiths, L/Cpl Cave, Ptes Pass, Bardsley and myself decided to leave and work our way towards Brocottes as by this time St Samson was becoming too dangerous for us.

"We re-crossed the river by boat and made our way along the side of the River Dives towards Brocottes which we reached at approximately 0300 hours on the morning of the 8th. We slept until daybreak in an empty barn about 1 mile from the village having dried our clothes as best we could. Sgt Moore and L/Cpl Griffiths left early in the morning in search of food as our own was finished. They returned with the news that they had found a Frenchman who was willing to give us food and let us stay in his barn. We moved to the barn, had some food and stayed there the night.

"During the afternoon we were rejoined by F/Sgt Tidbury and Pte Gardner who told how they heard we were having trouble with an enemy patrol. As a result they decided to leave the area. We learned that a party under Lieutenant Nicholls [8th Para Bn] were in the neighbourhood. We remained here for the night and early the next morning Sgt Moore went off to try and make contact with Lt Nicholls. The Sgt returned shortly afterwards and led our party to the field in which Lt Nicholls was sleeping. Lt Nicholls party consisted of 3 Cpls, 2 L/Cpls and about 10 men. Shortly afterwards 4 [it was actually 6] Privates from 'C' Company 13th Parachute Battalion [from a/c 325 – Lt Lee's 9 Platoon, Privates Sharpe, Hadley, Hodge, Turner, Ryder and Holden] joined us. Lt Nicholls decided to split the party into 3 sections, allotting one LMG to each section.

"We proceeded in the direction of Troarn as we heard that our forces were on the outskirts of the town. We accordingly left about midday, reached and crossed a bridge (221675) without incident and the leading section led by Lt Nicholls were partially across the second bridge (216670) when they saw an enemy patrol consisting of a

German Jeep, 2 motor-cyclists and a motor-cycle combination. The leading section immediately jumped off the bridge to the left hand side of the road, and the second and third sections took cover in the hedgerow short of the bridge. Owing to a slight rise in the ground, neither the approaching patrol nor we were aware of each others presence until they were almost on top of us. It was not until they were opposite our section [2nd] that the whole party opened fire. The 2 motor-cyclists were immediately killed, the occupant of the side car was killed, but the driver managed to get through. The Jeep was knocked out and the occupants took cover in the hedgerow at the side of the road. L/Cpl Cave and the Padre's batman of the 8th Battalion together with myself and Pte Cave advanced along both sides of the road under cover of the hedgerow to draw and locate the fire of the enemy. We lobbed hand grenades where we thought the Germans were hiding, which drew one shot in reply, wounding the Padre's batman in the leg. We eventually wiped the Germans out. The wounded man was tended and left by the side of the road with the French who promised to look after him, but we heard later that he was taken away in a German ambulance. Lt Nicholls advised us to return to the Barn near Brocottes which we reached at about 1400 hours, where we remained until 2300 hours on the night of the 16th."

After the landings of D-Day 17 year old Gaston Le Baron, a local of the area, set off to search for paratroopers in the marshes and found several parachutes which he hid. After wading through the marshes he found a group of paratroops in a cowshed loft. This was Lt Nicholls and his group, which he helped.

Gaston Le Baron (French civilian)

"On June 9th around 8am, they decided to cross Ham Bridge from the right bank to the left, as a column. In front of them, 2 motorbikes and an assault vehicle suddenly appeared, with 6 officers, one of which was a General and 2 escorting soldiers. Instantly, the Paras fell flat in the tall grass. However, one of them was spotted by a passenger in the vehicle, who instinctively opened fire and wounded him seriously in the leg. The riposte was immediate, and the car finished its course in the ditch. The shooting lasted maybe 2 minutes. The Germans were left with 6 dead, 1 wounded and 1 prisoner, who attempted to escape in the marshes but was captured.

"After this feeble victory, we turned round and went back to our starting point and waited, like everyone else, for the Allied Forces advance, hoped for any day then. Our situation was becoming more and more preoccupying. They were completely dependent on the people around them with a lot of risks.

"German reinforcements were arriving night and day from Southern France, from the North and from Germany. Some came for milk, they were constantly among us, they paid with their bread or their packed lunches (or nothing) and I kept everything preciously for our Paras.

"These German units were composed of many men from occupied countries, Poles, Czechs, and Georgians. They made a point of telling us that they were not German, when they were alone. I managed to persuade two to escape.

"All their tackle was handed over to the Paras. Close to these troops, I managed to obtain precious pieces of information, which I passed on to the Para Officer Nicholls, regarding the Allied progress, the size of units, their itineraries and their lack of progress in front of Troarn. We were constantly under the fire of the British artillery, the air-raids, the pounding of German convoys marching to the front, coming across files of refugees."

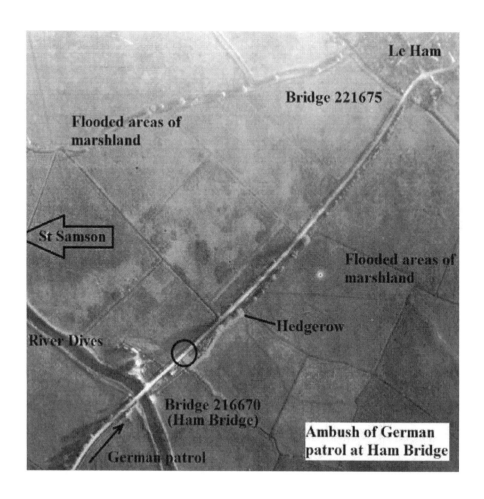

Above: The area of the bridges near Le Ham on the Troarn Road where the German patrol was ambushed. Below: As it looks today (taken from approx area of circle).

Armed with the fresh intelligence the paratroopers made further attempts to reach the Allied lines.

Private Arthur West (3 Platoon 'A' Company)

"A party consisting of L/Cpl Cave, Ptes Pass, Gardner, Bardsley and myself moved off late in the evening across the marshlands towards Troarn, via Le Hain – St Samson with the intention of getting to Bures which we had heard had been taken by the British. We arrived at the bend of the river (173675) at about 0230 hours and slept on the southern bank for the remainder of the night. The next morning we obtained a little food which had to last us for the remainder of the day. At approximately 2330 hours we started out for Bures keeping to the south and then to the west of the river. Just before reaching Bures we encountered several small streams which we had to swim. We sought shelter from 0200 hours until first light in a graveyard and then roused a house in the village and asked the occupants to give us shelter as we were very wet. A man and a woman answered our knock and the man took us to a shed where we dried our clothes and slept for a few hours on the straw.

"At approximately 1100 hours, L/Cpl Cave, Pte Pass and myself went on a recce to gather information and obtain food for the party. As the man and woman who had led us to the shed appeared genuine and helpful we went to them and found there in addition 2 good looking girls age 22 and 20, from the village. We received some milk but no food. They told us that they had heard that the British were just north of Bures in the Bois de Bavent. They returned with us to the shed and we asked them to take the whole party in the direction of our forces. The 2 girls led the way, followed by the farmer who was some 50 yards in front of us. After crossing the railway the girls pointed in the direction of Bois de Bavent. Here they left us and we later made a contact from which point our journey was arranged.

"With the aid of a compass, we made our way into the wood. L/Cpl Cave and Pte Pass were slightly ahead of us, when suddenly crossing a path we saw a party of 10 soldiers. Pte Pass who was on the other side of the path from L/Cpl Cave, thinking they were our own troops whistled, and they turned and saw us. They were Germans. We took evasive action, made a detour round the patrol, and as a result lost L/Cpl

Cave and Pte Pass in the wood. We looked for them, but did not see them again, and decided to go on towards our own lines.[15] On coming out of the wood, we crossed an open field, and I, who was leading the 3, suddenly saw a German soldier outside some farm buildings. He immediately took cover, and I went back in to the wood, and led the party along the edge of the wood. We found a German latrine, which showed signs of recent use, and further examination revealed a newly dug slit trench with a German lying beside it. I warned the others to go back, but Pte Gardner went one way, and Pte Bardsley and myself retraced our steps. I did not see Gardner (left) again."[16]

---

[15] A day later Private Frederick Pass, another brick layer by trade, was captured in Bavent and spent the rest of the war in various POW camps and worked in a paper factory in Sebnitz and a slaughter house in Dresden.

[16] Private William "Alf" Gardner (left) a 20 year old clerk from Carlisle found himself on his own, hiding in barns and was captured in Bavent by a 21st Panzer Div patrol on the 27th June and then was interrogated in a threatening manner in Dozule. From there he was imprisoned until April 1945 in

Private Arthur West (3 Platoon 'A' Company)

"As it appeared too difficult to get through in this direction, Bardsley and myself decided to make our way back through the wood to our original starting point NW of Bures. On our way, we heard German vehicles, and hid for about three quarters of an hour until they were out of earshot. We passed what appeared to be a château, but found German troops in occupation there. Eventually after a difficult march through thick undergrowth, we arrived off Bures at about 1900 hours and I asked a farmer for a drink of water. Having slaked our thirst, we made our way across some fields, until we met another farmer and 2 youths; we asked him for shelter for the night, and he led us to a shed in the fields about 100 yards from the farm, where we slept until noon the following day. We left here for our former wealthy farmer friend who welcomed us and gave us our first decent meal for days and proved helpful in showing us a map of the area.

"At approx 1400 hours we made our way back to the 2 youths, who told us that the British were in Touffreville. We pointed out how extremely difficult it was, making our way about in khaki uniform, and they suggested we should change into civilian. They gave us the clothes, and we handed our rifles and equipment to them and set off for Touffreville.

"On the way we heard such artillery fire, that we concluded we were heading in the right direction. After a mile or so suddenly saw a German some 50 yards away at some crossroads, who looked at us rather suspiciously. Not wishing to be questioned, we moved off the road into the hedge, and returned to the shed of the night before and stayed there until the morning.

"We went out for a look-around, when 2 German riflemen came down the road towards us. We dived into the hedge for cover until they passed. The 2 youths were contacted again and they advised us to try the Bois de Bavent. We were well into the woods, when a single German beckoned us to come to him. However we turned round and strolled back in the direction from which we had come. He fired 3 shots over our heads, so we ran for it and made our way back to our wealthy farmer friend and his two daughters. He again offered us food and after a meal we returned to the 2 youths again. They took us to a house and with the aid of dictionaries we were told that 4 Paratroopers had been taken prisoner in Bures the day before. We realised the 2 youths were not much help to us, and returned to the farmer friend again. He led us to a corner of the orchard and told us to wait there and we would receive food at 2000 hours.

"It was now about tea-time and after the farmer had left we returned to the 2 youths and changed back into our uniforms, as we did not like the situation and preferred a rifle in our hands in case of trouble. We returned to the orchard and the farmer brought us food about 2030 hours, and promised to bring us hot water, shaving kit and food the following morning. We slept the night in one of his barns. We stayed there without incident the whole of the day and night.

"In the evening a French policeman was brought to us, and the farmer explained that the gendarme would lead us to our own lines on the following night. The gendarme examined our pay books and identity discs, and took them from us,

---

Stalag XIIA (Limberg) and Stalag IVB (Muhlberg). He was liberated by Soviet troops but he did not like the Russians, so he headed west and was picked up by the Americans. After the war he joined the ambulance service.

promising to return them later. The following day the farmer provided us with civilian clothes, and food for the journey, and we set out for the journey at approximately 1930 hours. The gendarme was in possession of a bicycle.

"On our way we passed a few German cars successfully. Once we stopped and had a few drinks in a Cafe. After leaving the Cafe, we made our way through Troarn and walked along the main road to Le Poirier via Cagny.

"After some three quarters of a mile, a man on a bicycle caught up with us and started talking to the Gendarme. The 4 of us then walked towards Cagny but about half-way between Troarn and Cagny, the Gendarme turned left on to a side road and told us to follow the other man. He in turn led us through Cagny and we arrived at Le Poirier at approximately 2200 hours. He took us to an agricultural machine shop opposite the church, showed our pay books to the owner, who then returned them to us. He was about 40 years old with a gold tooth and lived in a bungalow besides the workshop. We fed, and when it was dark, the assistant of the machine shop, who was 22, called Jean and rolled his own cigarettes, took us to the vestry of the church and made us comfortable with eiderdowns for the night.

"The only incident during this period was when a German came into the church, he did not see us however.

"During the evening of 5th July, we were brought into the Machine Shop again, where we met a French-Canadian who had come to see us. He spoke English and French very well, and told us he was a Flight Sergeant in the RAF and had been shot down before D Day. He acted as interpreter and was 5ft 6in and 27—28 years old. He was well dressed in a grey double-breasted suit and spoke with slight lisp. He also was in possession of all civilian identity papers.

"With him was a Frenchman who claimed to be a member of the Resistance Movement. He wore black dungarees and carried his coat slung over the shoulder. He spoke little English and I saw him on the back of a motor-cycle behind a French ARP in Caen on Sunday 9th July.

"It was decided that we would be taken to Emieville that night [5th July]. Before leaving, we were given a slip of paper by the French-Canadian F/Sgt to take through with us and hand to the British. It contained the position of an enemy patrol and ammunition dump east of Fruide which required bombing, and it also stated not to bomb the university or the cathedral at Caen, as both buildings were housing refugees. The slip of paper afterwards was sodden and totally illegible while crossing the marshes.

"At about 2100 hours we left with the shop assistant and the Resistance man, who were 100 yards ahead of us in the direction of Emieville. After some 5km the shop assistant cycled off on a side road to see if the way was clear, while we waited with the Frenchman on the bank at the side of the road. After a short while the shop assistant returned with the news that the plan had been altered and we would be going through another way with 21 other evaders. We all carried on and the 2 Frenchmen, who were slightly ahead, were once stopped by some German tanks and asked the way. We were put into the hedges as arranged, in case identification papers were being checked. The Frenchmen shouted for us to come on, the Germans having left, and we arrived at a farm where we contacted three other French youths who were to lead us and the 21 others through the lines. This was near Emieville. Here the shop assistant went home.

"We, Bardsley (left), the Resistance member, and myself, set off with the 3 youths ahead to meet the other 21 evaders. We heard tanks and vehicles in the area, and 2 of the 3 youths went ahead to reconnoitre, but we did not see them again. The remaining 4 of us hid in a hedge, as the Germans were walking about. Our original friend then suggested we should sleep in the hedgerow for the night, and wait until he got further information in the morning.

"At approximately 0500 hours, the 2 Frenchmen went to a farm, to which we were brought a little later. Here we found several more French youths who were all armed and who had tried to get through the night before. Our Resistance friend told us to go with the others that night, and he would do it the following night. We left this farm for another to have some food, where we met another 10 Frenchmen, some of who were armed.

"We slept in a barn until about midday and when we woke up, found that some of the men had already left. After food we moved off in the early afternoon with 2 French youths who were taking us to join some other Paratroops in the marshes east of Emieville. We found them after walking for three quarters of an hour, some 9 men from the 9th Parachute Battalion, one of them was named Sgt Clark. After a talk, we left with the 2 Frenchmen for the farm again, promising to return with food for the Paratroops at 1900 hours. The 2 Frenchmen set off with this about 2000 hours, telling us to remain on the farm until they returned. We stayed there all night, but they did not come back.

"During the morning Germans were moving in all around the farm and after lunch, the farmer's wife came running to us and asked us to leave as the Boche were taking over the farm. We left to re-join the 9 Paratroopers but found them gone. We followed further into the marshes thinking they might be there, passing on the way, 2 naked Boche bathing in the river.

"After struggling through the marshes for 3 hours, we found ourselves back at the farm once again. A German stopped us and asked us something we could not understand which sounded like "Torry---Boom! Boom!" I answered "Oui, Oui" and waved my hand and he went away satisfied.

"We called at a farm for a drink and then decided that the best thing we could do was to make our way back to the machine shop again. We passed through Cagny and at about 2030 hours approximately we met the shop assistant in the main street of Le Poirier. We explained what had happened and the owner hid us in a threshing machine. We stayed there the night.

"Through our peep-hole in the machine I saw many German tanks, Mk IV and infantry, retreating from the direction of Caen. During the afternoon the assistant brought us some food and told us that he and a young woman would set off at 1600 hours and lead us to Caen.

"We agreed and proceeded to Caen, crossing the river into the town by the main bridge which was guarded by sentries. They did not bother us. The town was being bombarded by Allied artillery and there were a number of patrols passing up and down the streets. This was approximately 1830 hours. After walking round the town for about three quarters of an hour the girl went off in the direction of the University, and the assistant took us to what appeared to be a Stadium (Tennis Courts, Football Ground, Cycle Track etc), and told us to wait for an hour and then he would return with something to drink.

"Shells from our own artillery were falling near. The assistant returned with some cider and told us to stay there as the British were expected in the town at 2100 hours. He also said that if our own troops had not arrived within a day or so, he would return bringing some food for us from Le Poirier. He then left, assuring us we were safe.

"However, our position was becoming rather 'hot' for us, due to shelling and numerous German patrols, and we decided to do a reconnaissance. We found 2 German soldiers near some slit trenches, and so we withdrew after behaving as though we had some business and interest in the Stadium.

"We walked up the main road towards the University, and contacted one of the ARP Wardens who took us to the University. There we met a man who shortly afterwards left and returned with the Maire and a Professor of English. The Professor explained that the University was used to hide refugees, and he unfortunately could not allow us to stay there. On asking him where we could go, he took us to the Cathedral. This was packed with refugees. In the morning after listening to a service we wandered around in search of news and met the professor again, who asked us how we were."

CSM Joseph McPharlan did manage to reach Ranville.

Private Colin Edward Powell (12th Para Bn)

"I remember what I thought was a French civilian, complete with dungarees and black beret, riding towards me on a bicycle and my surprise when he said to me in broad Lancashire accent: "Can you tell me where the 13th Battalion are chum?"

Citation: CSM Joseph McPharlan

Award: Distinguished Conduct Medal

He was dropped in - 10 miles from his DZ. Unperturbed he collected others that also dropped astray and organised them into an effective fighting force although cut off from all possible help. He carried out raids on the enemy and captured many prisoners while causing great disorganisation.

With complete disregard to his own safety he disguised himself in civilian clothes and through speaking no French or German forced through the enemy lines and brought invaluable information to the battalion headquarters and organised help for his party.

He returned and directed a raiding party on to enemy AFV's then found that his force had dispersed in his absence.

Dressed still in plain clothes he again returned safely through the enemy lines and reported for duty with his battalion. All this time he was without rest or sleep.[17]

---

[17] He was recommended for a MC, but was upgraded to the DCM

From a/c 312 only CSM McPharlan DCM, Sgt T.I. Taylor (left), Pte A.B. West, Pte. E. Bardsley and Cpl F. Bott returned to the 13th Para Bn. The rest were all captured. Below: Major John Cramphorn (2nd left) with three of his men who evaded capture, left to right Sgt-Maj McPharlan, Pte Bardsley and L/Cpl West (IWM, Duxford).

Aircraft 325

Aboard a/c 325 were 19 Paratroopers and a motorcycle belonging to 9 Platoon, 'C' Company. Captain "Nobby Clark back in Ranville had been deprived of this platoon and was having to move his 'counter attack' Company from position to position to cover all the gaps and possible German infiltration.

Private Len Cox (9 Platoon, 'C' Company)

"We emplaned and were waiting in the aircraft for take off when the engines spluttered and then went silent. We had a mad de-bus and were loaded into another Dakota. The flight as far as the French coast was OK, but then we ran into heavy flak and seemed to fly on and on. It wasn't until the third run in that we actually jumped; something or other went wrong on the first two."

Corporal John Mescki (9 Platoon, 'C' Company)

"Our officer, Tiger Lee, was the first out. No.2 was his batman, Dougie Sharp from Cheadle, No.3 was a fellow called "Nutter" [Pte Charles Hadley from London] who had a water diviner strapped to his leg and this got stuck in the door and the dispatcher kicked him out. I said, "Don't kick me out, don't push me," because I didn't want to spiral. So I just jumped out and when I jumped out it was very quiet, beautiful and quiet, just the noise of the aircraft and my chute popping open.

"When I hit the deck I heard these footsteps. We used to have cartoons stuck up on the wall of the camp showing Germans running at you with bayonets and the caption was, 'Jump to it! Don't just sit there.' So I got up out of my chute and ran off into the hedge and when I turned round I saw it was cows.

"I carried on about another 50 yards and I thought, "Well, I'm lost here," because I realized there was electric and telephone wires going across the field and I knew from the photographs of the DZ that there was no such thing, so I was pretty lost I came to another hedge and intended to jump through it, but I got stuck half-way. Then I heard some footsteps and I thought, "Oh, hell, I've had it," but it turned out to be 2 friends, one who had broken his arm [Pte J. Whittaker] and the other who had burned his fingers on his chute [Pte S. Fell].

"We went straight down this road together and heard a noise like a tank, so I said, "Let's get behind the hedge and throw some grenades." So we pulled the pin from out grenades, ready to throw them over the hedge, and who should come riding past were a man and a woman. Luckily, we kept the pins and rings and pushed them back on, peeked out and they disappeared round the next crossroad.

"We got back on the road, realizing we should go in a northerly direction, when a Typhoon came over. I though it was going to strafe us, so we dived in the hedgerow and found a little path along into a wood. I said, "If we stay off the road, we'll make it." After a while I saw this farmhouse, and I got my binoculars out and looked at it. There, was smoke coming out of the chimney, but it was well protected from the road. I thought we could get round the back without anyone noticing and I went round and saw the door was open. It was now getting on for about 6 o'clock in the morning. I knocked on the door and this French lady came. She didn't look surprised; she just looked at me and said, "M'sieur?" I asked her if there were any Germans in the house and she said no and so I said, "I've got 2 wounded comrades, can you look after us?" She said yes, enter if you wish. I said can you give us any idea where we are and she showed us on a little tiny railway map where we were. I said the British will be here in 3 days, will you hide us? She said yes, and took us out to a barn. We were there for 3 months."

Private Len Cox (9 Platoon, 'C' Company)

"I was dropped at Le Fournet near Bonnebosq after the pilot had made about 5 trips around to drop all members of the plane. I was entirely on my own, so I collected my gear and made for what I thought was the RV. I made off along a road and I met up with Sergeant Tom Smith who had a damaged ankle. We learnt we were at Bonnesboque, close to Lisieux, 30 miles from where we should have been."

Sergeant Thomas Smith (9 Platoon, 'C' Company)

"Sgt Stubbs and I dropped from the same aeroplane on 6th June '44 in the area of Le Fournet. Our objective was the capture of Ranville Château. I sprained my right ankle and hurt my left shoulder on landing and lost my weapons in the descent. I crawled around for 3 hours in an unsuccessful attempt to recover them. There appeared to be no enemy in the area, and I hid in a ditch until 1000 hours. I then contacted Private Cox and together we approached a farmhouse where we received food and were hidden in a small shed for 4 hours. A French farm labourer then took us to his house, where we stayed for 3 days, during which time I rested my ankle. I then endeavoured to get through the lines at Beaufour-Druval, but about a mile outside Beaufour my ankle gave out and I returned with Private Cox to the house we had just left. We stayed there for another 3 days, and on 12th June Private Cox and I were taken by the farm labourer to meet Sgt Stubbs, who was hiding in a hedge about 500 yards away."

Sergeant Arthur Stubbs (9 Platoon, 'C' Company)

"During my descent I was knocked unconscious. When I recovered about 0600 hours 6th June, I found myself in the middle of a field with my harness on. When I had got over the shock I hid in a wood for a few hours and then wandered around the Le Fournet area for 5 days without food, as I did not consider it advisable to contact any civilians at first. I lost my Sten gun in the descent. On 12th June I approached some workers in the fields and obtained food from them, and whilst I was hiding in a ditch Sgt Smith and Private Cox joined me."

Sergeants Smith and Stubbs (9 Platoon, 'C' Company)

"We were both taken with Pte Cox to a small farm and fed and sheltered there for 5 days. We were then removed to another farm at Auvillars where we met Pte Douglas White. Our party was then taken to a farm at Bonnebosq, where we spent the night of 17/18th June. During the night we were joined by Pte Albert Ryder and Pte G Holden, who were in civilian clothes. We were then taken to a deserted farmhouse at Auvillars, where we spent 7 days. Food was brought to us by civilians. On 24th June Ptes White and Ryder donned civilian clothes over their uniforms and armed with one revolver, they went down to a brook for a bathe. We did not see them again. At 2130 hours 5 German were seen approaching the barn and we got out of a window at the back of the barn and ran down the hillside unnoticed. At this point we lost Ptes Cox and Holden.

"We then headed in a westerly direction and on 25th June we contacted the chief of the FFI in the Dozule area and were provided with civilian clothes and hidden in a farm at Druval where we stayed until British troops arrived on 24th August 1944."

Private Len Cox (9 Platoon, 'C' Company)

"We had dropped among units of 2 Panzer Divisions, 21st and Panzer Lehr, and they were out looking for us, so the Resistance kept us on the move. Even then the party got split up when we had to make a hurried getaway as the Germans approached the front of the farm building where we sheltered; we all dashed out of the back, losing the 2 Sergeants in the panic.

"We picked up Pilot Officer Mathews who went along with us and we hid in a barn. In the early hours of the 26th June our hideout was surrounded and we were all captured. We were taken to an HQ about 500 yards away, they had mostly horse drawn vehicles and the troops were largely Romanian. There was a Colonel, who spoke good English. He wanted to know how we were dropped, when, about our unit, he also said we could be shot as spies. During interrogation at the local HQ the place was strafed by Typhoons and I later found other members of the stick had also been rounded up and were in the same building. Next day an attempt was made to escape and some of the guards were shot. Extra guards were brought in and we were all lined up to be shot, but a change of orders and we were herded into covered trucks and driven away.

"On the road we ran into a convoy of Panzers that had been recently bombed and again we were threatened with shooting. Eventually we arrived at a large POW compound of about 500 men, which had been established at the Poutance village stud farm near Falaise. There were about 8 to 10 men in each stall.

"Two POW's, Sgt Coon USAAF and CSM Edwards, No.3 Commando, shot their guard and made their escape. We saw 2 squads leave to go hunt for them and later they came back and we were told that they had been recaptured and shot on the spot. That was 3rd July.

CSM R.W. Edwards (1st SS Brigade, No.3 Commando)

"Sgt Coon and myself were on an outside detail and we decided to make a bolt for it then and there. This we did and from here my story is identical to his."

Sergeant Frank Coon (USAAF)

"While I was at the camp Sgt-Maj Edwards was brought in and as we were senior, we discussed with all others, ways and means of escape. CSM Edwards and myself decided to make a break for it.

"Accordingly I wheeled the guard into selecting he and I to fetch some straw from a nearby farm. We had previously loosened the bars of our window intending to escape that night but this had been discovered, without, however, any suspicion being aroused.

"Arriving at the farm the guard suggested we should stay for lunch, as he was not on duty until 1500 hours. We readily agreed and when the meal was over, I suggested that we should return to the camp. He was rather reluctant but Edwards and I had arranged that we would overpower him while going through the door and disarm him.

"This we accomplished and marched off to a wood nearby. Edwards covered [with the guard's gun] the German in a hedgerow while I went into a farm and asked for food and shelter. These people readily agreed to hide us and give us food, clothing, maps and compasses. We took the German to a thicket, where there was a struggle and we killed him with a bayonet. We then buried him."

From there on they did actually manage to escape and eventually return to Allied lines after more epic adventures, that story cannot be told here but can be found in the IS9 Escape and Evasion files in the National Archives, Kew.

Private Len Cox (9 Platoon, 'C' Company)

"With Pte Bennett I saw a good chance to escape. The guards had to walk posts on the outside and had to go some distance. We also discovered that at the end of the building we were in was a small staircase that led to rooms above. Bennett and I investigated and found a room with a window overlooking the road. The drop was about 30-40 ft. From one other POW who was sent out to bake bread we found out about the surrounding country and where the Germans had gun emplacements.

Bennett and I felt we were going to be moved to another camp, so we decided to give it a try.

"We got a blanket, which we ripped and tied together to make a rope. At 2300 hours the night 7th July, we made our way to the room above the stalls, tied our improvised rope and slid down. We made a dash across the road without the guards seeing us, crawled through three fields and decided to head south to contact the French underground. We had no maps or compass but guided ourselves by the stars. Our plan was to make 20km southwest before daybreak. At the last minute Pte Baker of the Suffolk's decided to come with us, slid down after us and joined us.

"We moved all that early morning of 8th July and had a few narrow escapes avoiding Germans and holed up near Putanges. We looked for a farm and for troops and after watching some French people decided to approach them. They gave us shelter in a barn, fed us and provided civilian clothes. We were there 7 days. Then they moved us to another barn, as SS troops were in the vicinity and we stayed there for 2 days.

"About 17th July the French told us more Germans were coming and advised us to go to Brittany – they provided us with different civilian clothes, food and 150 Francs apiece, as well as a map. After a few hours we decided that 3 of us travelling together was too conspicuous, so Baker, who could speak French and German, decided to go on his own. From Putanges we went to Cramenil and from another Frenchman got aid – lodging, food another change of clothes and some more Francs. We told him where we were heading and he said if we could not make it to come back. The next day we got to Saires-La-Verrerie and made contact with a Cure who put us in a loft for the night.

"We travelled until Sunday 23rd July, making our way to Domfront. After by-passing Domfront we went to La Hte Chappelle where a friendly Italian marked our route for us (Le Teulleul, Garonne, Ernee Vitre, past Rennes and then Brittany). At Desertines we went to a farm. At first the people thought we were Gestapo, for there were many of them about, but we got help. The farm owner was called Duilley. He knew a girl in the village who could speak English and she brought a Frenchman called Maurice Besnard who had been a POW himself and escaped. He said he would contact the chief of the French Resistance. There was a British Officer working with these people and we were told to give our names and numbers.

"On 27th July M'sieur Besnard moved us to the house of another young Frenchman who hid us for 2 days. Meanwhile, some members of the French Resistance had been rounded up as they had been given away by a collaborator. We heard that they had got 14 men and the German SS had found 6 vehicles with arms and ammunition. By coincidence, or design, that same night the collaborator's house was bombed by Marauders.

"We were taken to a forest hide then by motorcycle 15km to Passais and stayed there until 30th July. We were taken to a dugout in the fields, food was brought at dark and we stayed there from 1st to 3rd August when the Germans began to pull out of the area. On 4th August some of the civilians stayed with us in the dugout and we heard gunfire. 6th August the firing got close and we heard machine guns, the next day we were told the Americans were in Passais. We were provided bicycles and made our way there and found no sign of Germans. We ran into a unit of the US 4th Cav Recon. We were told to go back to the farm and report back the next morning.

"Once London had confirmed that I was who I claimed to be, the Americans sent me on my way to rejoin the Battalion. I got as far as Brigade HQ near Pont L'Évêque but they must have had instructions to send me back to England for de-briefing. I reported to MI5 Intelligence in Baker Street, where I was questioned about the two Czech agents, because they had been executed by the Germans. Following that I was sent to a camp for escaped POW's."

Citation: Privates Len Cox & Maurice Bennett

Award: Mentioned in Despatches

After being wrongly dropped on 6th June 1944, Cox evaded capture for 20 days before he and five others were finally apprehended by the Germans near Auvillars. He was taken to a camp at Bonnebosq, where he met Bennett, captured whilst on patrol in Amfreville on 27th June 1944. Transferred to a racing stable near Falaise, they made plans to escape, which they put into effect on 7th July 1944. Climbing up a small staircase, they penetrated the barricade barring the entrance to the rooms over the stables, and descended through a window to the street below by means of a blanket rope. From a prisoner of War who was employed as a baker they had obtained knowledge of the surrounding country and the position of German gun emplacements. For seven days they hid at Putarges before travelling to Desertines. Here they were hidden until they were escorted to American troops at Passais.

I recommend these two men for the award of Mention.

Private Doug Sharp was second out of the plane and was Lieutenant Lee's batman. He also recalled the problems that aircraft 325 encountered as it attempted to drop its load of paratroops.

Private Doug Sharp (9 Platoon, 'C' Company)

"The fact that the jumping lights failed to work properly was probably the reason we landed at Bonnebosq instead of Ranville. We hid our parachutes and harnesses and 'Mae Wests' in a hedge.

"It was not until about 0530-0600 hours that we (Ptes Hadley, Hodge, Turner and myself) could pinpoint ourselves – none of us had a map. I contacted a French woman in Bonnebosq and asked her if she could point out on a map our exact position. She was terribly excited to find that we were British soldiers. She fetched a young girl who could speak a little English and she showed us where we were and pointed out on a map the direction of Ranville. She knew that the Germans were between ourselves, and our final objective – that was all the information she was able to give me.

"I returned to the others who had been hiding in slit trenches and explained the whole situation. After a short consultation we decided to make for Beaufour.

"On the outskirts of Beaufour we stopped a couple of French boys who were terrified when we spoke to them. We asked them if there were any Boche around. They said "No, only in Beaufour itself." Two of our fellows, they said, were in a farmhouse a little way up the road on the left. Here we contacted Ryder and Holden. The farmer put us up for the night in the school, taking us across when it was dark.

"The next morning he took us by a round about route to Dozule. Before entering the town he was informed that about 200 Germans were moving in that day. We stayed the night on the crest of a hill overlooking the town. During the night a member of the 8th Para Bn was brought to us.

"The next morning we decided to move towards Troarn. We ran into a German armoured patrol on the road – we dealt with them very successfully without receiving any casualties ourselves. Our party got split up during the encounter – we immediately made off for the marshes and stayed the night there.

"Next day we were met by a Frenchman who told us that 18 parachutists were hidden in a farm. This was Lt Nicholls and his party. We joined up with them.[18]

"10 minutes after the first party set out we followed. Lt Nicholls remained with his men and F/Sgt Tidbury in the barn. Up to St Samson everything was quiet, but before we reached the bridge we were fired on by sentries who were guarding it. We immediately took cover. The Germans started firing verey lights to locate our position. When the lights died down we moved up the riverbank towards Bures, taking cover in a copse at the edge of the marsh. We saw them mine a bridge; we knew then that Germans held the place.

"On the evening of the 19th we decided to contact a farm in order to get food. We had had nothing to eat or drink for 4 days.

"While we were in search of a farm we ran into a patrol of infantry. We tried to retreat the same way we came. Turner had crossed the river over the marshes; I had not, so I immediately waded the river, which was about neck high. I heard the Germans cross the bridge looking for us. Shooting went on for sometime, ultimately Hadley, Turner and Hodge were taken prisoner. I stayed in the river for about 6 hours, until it got dark. Numerous parties in the meantime carried on the search."[19]

"Eventually I decided it was safe to move; besides I was desperately cold and hungry. I made for a farm and asked for food and drink. A woman who gave me food told me that it was hopeless to try and move from the district. She offered to shelter me in an air-raid shelter in her garden. I actually stayed there for 5 days, coming out only at night for short spells.

"The Germans began to move into the farm on the 26th. For 2 days I was stuck in my dugout as the Germans had completely surrounded the place. On the 29th in the early morning when it was actually light I managed to creep out and make for the Foret Bavent. Here I ran into a patrol of Germans. I tried to hide, they fired at me and slowly surrounded me – I put up my hands and surrendered. I was taken back to the farm I had just escaped from.

"An officer asked me several questions about my activities – Type of aircraft, number of people in the aircraft, where we landed, where our real objective was, also to empty my pockets. No search was made. I said "You've got my name, rank and number in my pay book that is all you need to know." He didn't bother anymore after that.

---

[18] Several members of 'A' Company had dropped astray and were in Lt Nicholls party. See Private West's account previous about the encounter with a German Patrol on the bridges near St Samson. Lt Nicholls group then returned to the barn they had previously hidden in and stayed there until the night of the 16th June. In groups they all attempted to reach the British lines.
[19] Charles "Nutter" Hadley was imprisoned at Mulberg until 20th Oct 1944 then transferred to Faulkener working camp where he stayed until 28th March 1945. He was then moved to Czechoslovakia, where he escaped whilst on the march at Kydne on 28th April. He was liberated by US forces after being helped by Partisans.

"After this short interrogation I was taken by car to a big château south of Troarn, there I was given a similar interrogation except that this time the officer handed out a lot of defeatist talk – the foolishness of trying to invade France and the fact that London was practically flat from Buzz Bombs. After about half an hour I was taken away in an armoured car guarded by 4 men.

"I eventually reached St Pier du Toriquet, the main interrogation camp in the area. For 3 hours or so I was interrogated by a German Officer who spoke very good English. His main worry was to find out the names of the senior officers of the whole division – I saw that he had one or two down correctly but he was still uncertain as to the authenticity of them – he pumped me about my battalion and the whereabouts of other battalions. I gave him little or no help in the matter – answering with non-committal replies.

"Finally I arrived at the brickworks at Bonnebosq which turned out to be a POW transit camp. We stayed here until 3rd July. On the afternoon of the 3rd CSM Edwards, No.3 Commando and T/Sgt Coon made an attempt to escape. They had been detailed to collect straw from a nearby farm under armed escort. On the way they attacked the guard and killed him and made their getaway. We heard later from one of the guards who spoke English that they had been killed.

"We were moved off in the evening to a camp somewhere south of Falaise. The Germans brought in about 150 of the Herman Goering Division and they with fixed bayonets and MG's formed a semi-circle around us. The other guards were evidently terrified of the Commandos and Paratroop boys. There were 30 of us in a small van with the back boarded and nailed up.

"We arrived at the camp in the early hours of the morning. During the time I was in the camp Len Cox [13th Para Bn] and Maurice Bennett of the Commandos escaped. The only punishment we received for this was that we were all kept in the camp for the entire next day.

"Food was poor – our daily menu consisted of – Breakfast (0800) 1 cup of ersatz coffee – Lunch (1230) plate of soup – Tea (1830) 1 cup of usual coffee and 1/5 of a loaf per man and a small portion of butter. Washing facilities were nil. Water was brought by a Frenchman only when we needed it. 12 tubs were filled – this was for washing, shaving and all other ablutions.

"Wounded were uncared for, and there was no medical equipment in the camp. Only 2 orderlies – an American and Englishman tended the wounded – there was no German assistance whatsoever.

"I used to bake bread with a Navy Paratroop boy for the camp at a village about 2 miles away – a guard was always with us. On the first two visits we enquired from the locals the situation and the lie of the land as regards the Germans. On the third visit to the village I was determined to escape. The guard was pretty lenient with us, on the two previous occasions we had behaved ourselves and given him no cause for uneasiness.

"At 1500 hours on 22nd July I made my escape. The guard always sat in the bake house while the bread was baking – it took about 2 hours to bake – on this occasion the heat of the bake house seemed to make him sleepy. I made signs to him that I was going out to the latrine, he nodded approval. I managed to take my jacket as I went. I made for the sound of gunfire which I hoped would bring me to our lines.

"My first stop was in the Habloville area. I made my way across country avoiding all roads and villages. My first contact was a farmer, he was a well built man about 6 ft, dark haired, clean shaven and his left eyelid was permanently closed; with the aid of an issue phrase book I asked him to show me where I was. He fetched a map of the Calvados area and showed me approximately where I was. He gave me the map – Michelin series, and pointed out the direction of Caen. He also gave me some food. I travelled on through fields until I came to a road which the Germans were using. As it was getting pretty late I decided to stay the night in a hedge by the road.

"I set off the next morning at day break [23rd July] reaching St Pierre du Bu about midday, working my way round several concentrations of German transports. Around St Pierre du Bu I almost bumped into a French boy as I was working my way along a hedge. We were both a bit startled at first. He knew I was British and spoke to me in English, saying it was impossible to get through the Falaise area in battle dress.

"He was 16 and his name was Claude Carez. He took me to his family who were living in the area. They had been evacuated from Falaise. I got supplied with food and civilian clothes. I stayed the night near the farm under a hedge.

"The next morning the young fellow and myself set out for Falaise – on the outskirts of the town a French speaking German soldier stopped and spoke to me – as I didn't know a word of French, the French boy answered telling him that we were going to collect some possessions left behind when we were evacuated. We were turned back to St Pierre du Bu. It seemed the safest course was to stay around the place until our troops overran it.

"Supplied with food and blankets I made myself as comfortable as possible under a hedge, digging a trench and roofing it with straw and branches, I stayed in this hide out until 17th August when a Canadian Recce party picked me up. They had been informed by the French people where I was. The Germans happened to be in the same field; before the Canadians and myself left they gave a short burst and slunk off."

Above: Doug Sharp wearing the civilian clothes given to him, speaking with Colonel Gordon of the Canadian Armoured Regiment.

Private Roy Ritchley (9 Platoon, 'C' Company)

"I parachuted into France along with the rest of the stick of 19 from a Dakota aircraft at approx 0030 hours on the 6th June 1944 at a spot between Valsemé and Bonnebosq, which was approx 45 km from the DZ at Ranville. I was 18, alone and very frightened. I didn't meet up with the rest of the stick after I landed.

"After landing I found that the spare Bren gun I was carrying had been damaged, so I took it to pieces and threw most of it in various directions. The barrels I buried with my over-jacket and chute. There was not a sound at all, no bombing, no shooting, and no sound of aircraft - it was eerie.

"A short time passed while I was trying to sort out where I was. I took out the silk map, which was sewn into the lining of my beret, and in the odd moments of moonlight I could read HOLLAND! - That got me worried. I buried the map. I heard a slight noise from the edge of the field where I had landed and peering over the edge of the ditch I was in, saw a figure climbing over a gate by the road and walking up the slope towards me. When the figure got closer I could see that he was carrying a rifle over his shoulder, was wearing a flat cap and a civilian jacket. I had a .45 automatic and ammunition, knife, plus a number of grenades and explosive charges. As it was quiet I decided not to shoot him but perhaps to use the knife. Eventually I decided to play it by ear.

"The figure walked up to the edge of the ditch, looked down and said one word "come". He carried on walking up the field. I decided to follow. I had my knife in one hand, the automatic in the other. The rifle he carried was German. I recognised the difference between the English and German sling attachments. He did not appear to worry about me and just continued walking quickly round the edge of the fields and through hedges until we reached a road which went down into a valley. At the top of the next hill there was a small school on the right. He climbed over some railings by the school and walked round the building to a small shed. By this time it was starting to get light. He tapped on the door and went in, I followed, as I stepped inside, something hard was pressed against my head, a match was struck and a candle was lit. I could see two more men in there and one held a gun at my head. Behind them were two sacks with rifles sticking out of them. I was thoroughly searched and everything in my pockets was taken out and put on the floor. I was absolutely petrified. The man who had collected me spoke a little English and said they were resistant's, gypsies, and his name was Philippe. The other two did not speak to me direct only via Philippe - I never did find out their names, they were too frightened of the Gestapo. We all sat down and just waited. During the 6th June I heard vehicles several times on the road outside the school, aircraft noise and bombing, which was not all that far away. The shorter of the tow men kept me covered with a pistol.

"As night fell a discussion took place and eventually I was given back my possessions, the .45 automatic, knife, ammo and grenades, also a German Walther service rifle and ammo pouches. I loaded the rifle as we got ready to leave. I still did not trust the gypsy with the pistol because he walked behind me all the time. We walked slowly, often stopping. We skirted a village which I later established was called Manerbe and when we came to a road which appeared to be well used we crossed one at a time. I went third with the gypsy with the pistol still behind me. As I crossed, from an incline to my left a German was fast approaching on a push bike and heading straight at me, so I shot him.

"We collected him and his bike and carried him over the gate, and hid the body and the bike under long grass by a shallow stream. We then ran and ran to get away from the area. After some distance we stopped and it was then that I was sick. The three gypsies kicked and punched me; I was totally confused. Philippe explained that we had to move safely and quietly from place to place to avoid the Germans, not to just shoot them - I had a lot to learn. We continued on our journey until it got light; by then we were on the edge of a town called Lisieux which had been bombed on the 6th June.

"During the morning Lisieux was bombed again, and it was obvious from the activity that the Germans were searching the area. We worked our way down a valley towards the town where there was thick smoke and many fires. We skirted the remains of the railway station and eventually got into a builders yard and with a ladder got into the attic of a house nearby. We just pushed the ladder away once inside - I hoped that Lisieux would not be bombed again. The four of us stayed alert and quiet during the time there because the Germans were patrolling the area.

"On the night of 7th June Philippe climbed down the rear of the building and came back in the early hours of the morning with food and a hank of string. We were there for several more days and were fed at night by local partisans. Philippe or one of the others would throw out the string and then pull up parcels of food. Drink in a bottle was usually milk and haricot beans, it was rough but filling. We eventually left our haven and went inland away from the main roads. During the day it was too dangerous to move because of the volume of small German patrols. At night the Germans would try to bring up reserves and equipment which were all heading for the front in the Caen area. We worked mainly at night. I was getting used to the situation I was in and I was now accepted as one of the team. I stayed with the gypsy group, fought with them and followed the general format of behind the lines action - the killing seemed so easy. I discovered that after killing a German, Philippe or one of the others would disarm the body; take the ammo and anything else that could be sold. When several weapons had been collected he would disappear with the weapons and ammo and return with a wad of money, and this was split three ways, but I never got any of it. The arms had been sold to communist resistance groups in the Moult or Mezidon area.

"As time went by we shot German engineers repairing telephone lines that we had cut, sentries or any vulnerable enemy if we thought we could get away with it. As more and mare troops were moving up to the front there were quite a few deserters. If they still had their weapons we would kill them, bury the body, and the arms would be sold. If they had thrown their weapons away we would let them continue, as we knew that German field police would shoot them for us. We were constantly on the move because the Germans were always searching for us. We were in the marshalling yards at Mezidon on July 18th after dodging German patrols. We hid out under a signal box on 17th July after nearly getting caught in the open fields. Unfortunately on the 18th the RAF bombed the marshalling yards. During the confusion we managed to get away. There were fires everywhere.

"The pattern, hit, run and reform the group was continuous. Philippe said it was getting too dangerous because of the volume of German units working their way towards Caen. There were many, many incidents as previously described, some

168

humorous and some tragic, but the three gypsies and I got away with it. That is until the night of 8/9th August when they tried to get me through the German lines near the old Abbey ruins at Troarn.

"We had been out of touch with the local resistance group because we were being chased by German patrols. Philippe had cleared off with several rifles and ammunition. In the early hours of 9th August the two silent gypsies and I closed up behind the German lines when suddenly all hell was let loose with artillery, mortar and small arms fire coming in from our own lines. That was the time that the allies pushed out from the beach-head in Normandy around Troarn. The German front line withdrew so we had to go back as well. When we got sandwiched between the German front line troops and where the German reserves had dug in. We ran across a road to escape the shelling. We were seen and fired upon. I was hit in the thigh and both legs; the two gypsies were killed. I didn't know what happened to Philippe, I never saw him again. A German soldier pulled me off the road into a ditch and got me to a front line field dressing station. I was taken further back on a stretcher eventually finishing up at the German Field Police HQ in Paris. I was drifting in and out of consciousness. My leg wounds had been bound up in crepe paper bandages and though I stuck to my name, rank and number and said I had been separated from a patrol and got lost, and that the two civilians were just showing me the way back to my unit, I was beaten daily. They did not believe the story.

"After several days I was put on a coach and transported to Chalons-sur-Marne. From there I was sent on to Stalag XIID at Trier in Luxembourg. I escaped and was picked up after going about 8 miles, I was then sent further into Germany to Stalag's IVB - IVD. From Stalag IVD I was transferred to Wegstadtl where I worked in a woodwork factory. I also worked at a chemical factory at Chemnitz. It was regularly bombed by the RAF. I was transferred again to a sugar factory in Czechoslovakia where I was accused of sabotaging the factory! Eventually I was sent to a POW camp in Dresden where I worked in the marshalling yards. At the end of the war we heard Winston Churchill's broadcast that the hostilities were over. About half an hour later a force of Russian bombers blasted the marshalling yards. We got out of the area fast.

"I joined up with two other members of our working party, stole an army lorry and, with the aid of a school atlas, tried to get to the Allied lines, However we finished up in Prague and spent 3 weeks with a Russian tank unit. When we were ordered out of

Prague by the Russian authorities we were given a lorry, food, arms, ammo etc., and a sketch map to get to Regensberg. On our arrival there we were shot at by an American unit so we fired back! What a finale to our journey. After debriefing by the Americans we were fed, then flown to Nuremburg by helicopter (Sikorsky's HNS-1 helicopter was test flown at Langley in March 1945, pictured, NASA).

"The following day we were flown to Brussels. Once there we were grounded by bad weather. I met another ex POW Para there so we got together and hitch hiked to Paris where we befriended some French people who ran a chip and crepe shop off Montmafire. They looked after us very well. One evening we were taken to a club near the Sacre Coeur! The police raided the club; we were arrested and handed over to the Military Police. After interrogation we were sent by truck, under guard, to Calais where we were put on a landing barge. This took us to Dover. The date was 9th September 1945. I had hospital treatment for my wounds and was put on special foods as I weighed only just over 8 stones.

"I continued to serve in the Army until September 1947. From the time I parachuted into France on 6th June 1944 I didn't meet any of the few survivors of the stick until after the war. To fill in any more incidents between 6th June and

9th September 1945 would take a lot more space and time. It was a part of my life I shall never forget. As for my comrades in arms, including the resistant's:

> *"Ils ne vieilliront pas comme nous qui sont laissés vieillir:*
> *Âge ne sont pas fatigués eux, ni le mépriser ans.*
> *Au coucher du soleil et dans la matinée*
> *Nous nous souviendrons d'eux."*

Horsa Glider No.35

Captain Spencer Daisley   Private John Aldred

Towed by an Albemarle from Brize Norton, Horsa No.35 carried Captain Spencer Daisley (he was 40 years old and unable to parachute) and his batman Private John Aldred of the 13th Para Bn. Captain Daisley was the Quartermaster Officer and had aboard with him a Jeep as part of the resupply.

They were supposed to land with the first wave of gliders at 0320 hours, but due to navigational errors they were forced to crash land 12 miles NE of LZ 'N'. The glider came down in 'Le Bois de la Ferme du Manoir' a wooded area north of the village St Vaast-en-Auge. The glider could not avoid colliding with the trees and all 5 aboard were killed (the other 3 men were: Glider Pilots S/Sgt Colin Hopgood, Sgt Daniel Phillips and a despatch rider D Davis). This unfortunate event was confirmed by the young daughter of a farmer who owned the woods; she saw all 5 bodies lying in the glider.

The bodies had to remain in the same position until the 10th June because the Germans feared that the passengers of the glider might be hidden in the woods and could ambush anyone entering. They were eventually buried in St Vaast-en-Auge churchyard.

"If I believed that mankind could learn through the exhibition of the results of its folly, I would say that if only people could see the burial ground in a battle area, wars would cease."

Captain Padre Whitfield "Boy" Foy

13. GUTS AND DETERMINATION BEGINS (7th – 8th June 1944)

When General Gale visited each transit camp back in the South of England, his final words of advice to each of the battalions was, "What you win by your stealth and guile, you must hold with your guts and determination."

His first words of advice had become fact and reality, practically all of the set objectives that had been laid out so intricately, had been completed using "stealth and guile". It was now time for the "guts and determination". The two bridges in the 5th Brigade's area and the surrounding defensive 'bridgeheads' would now have to be held with great courage against the inevitable pending German counter-attacks.

General Gale's HQ, Château de Heaume.

Most of the morning of 7th June the 13th Battalion were subjected to shelling, this caused a number of casualties and quickly taught the men that slit trenches were your best bet of survival, but not guaranteed. In between the shelling there was a small interlude of entertainment, an aerial dual that was eventually won by a Spitfire over a Junkers 88 not far from the Battalion's position.

'A' Company were again in the thick of the defensive battle and their positions were attacked several times during the afternoon by armour and were at one time over-run and lost one of the anti-tank guns, shot up by a German SP. The 4th Air-landing Anti-Tank Regiment had Sergeant Guest and 3 gunners killed before a 17 pounder attached from 3rd Battery knocked out the SP. A counter-attack by 'A' Company, with the aid of 'C' Company regained all the ground lost as well as the anti-tank gun. Private Clifford Darby of lost his life during the days skirmishes.

Lieutenant Ellis "Dixie" Dean (MMG Platoon)

"The morning of the 7th June was reasonably quiet with only spasmodic shelling on the south of Ranville. It was always artillery from the direction of Sainte Honorine that troubled us. All the action was away to our left as the Ox & Bucks extended the airborne bridgehead. They cleared the Boche from Hérouvillette, but he was determined to hold on to Escoville and the Ox & Bucks Light Infantry suffered quite heavy casualties in their attempt to capture it.

"During the afternoon Sergeant Kelly's section rejoined us and replaced the 8th Battalion detachment. Before nightfall we received 2 new guns, replacing those lost on the drop, a good demonstration of the meticulous planning for resupply. The new guns came complete with dial sights, which we were never issued with before. Another example of careful planning was the arrival of the Battalion transport and the cooks with their equipment.

"Since we were a detached platoon, we enjoyed the luxury of an Army Catering Corps cook, just for the machine gunners. We located him in the walled yard of a nearby cottage and Ken Lang, who had worked in the ration stores of the 2nd/4th South Lancs, became his assistant cook. No-one had to walk more that 50 yards to collect his food."

Captain David Tibbs (225 Field Ambulance)

"During the morning [7th June], whilst in an upstairs room of the main building, there was sudden rustling noise, immediately followed by the explosion of a mortar bomb in trees outside. I was unhurt but Rickman fell to floor with a large hole punched out of his thigh (mortar fragment). I called to Cpl Russell to hand me a dressing but there was no reply and I then realised that he was lying silent on the floor. He must have died instantly and the only mark on him was a small puncture by a fragment over the heart but sufficient to kill him, a grievous loss."

Left: Cpl Russell's grave in Ranville Churchyard. Note the remembrance cross, placed by David Tibbs, June 2010.

Private Ronald Minnery (Intelligence Platoon)

"The day after D-Day my friend Corporal John Parker, 'C' Company, was killed. He was in his slit trench by a wall at the crossroads and a piece of shrapnel from a mortar attack hit him in the head, it went straight through his helmet."

Lance Corporal George O'Connor (8 Platoon 'C' Company)

"We walked to the cemetery; the noise of the shells exploding was now being added to by the sound of rockets, and you soon learn to tell the difference by the sound. In the cemetery, someone had dumped the bodies of two dead paras, I didn't recognise them, but I could tell they were from our Battalion, because they wore our black lanyards on their uniforms. We commenced to dig two graves with our hated entrenching tools, we managed to dig the graves about 18" deep.

"As we lifted one body in the grave, his helmet fell off, inside the helmet was a gory mixture, grey and red mess of his blood and brains, a bullet had pierced the helmet and ricocheted around inside of his helmet, there wasn't much left of his head so we replaced his helmet and gently placed him in the grave."

Private David Robinson (A/Tk Pl, att 'C' Coy)

"I'd only just arrived in the afternoon [7th June] and found out that one of the Battalion's dogs, 'Bing' had not had a happy landing. He had landed in a tree and was stranded and his owner could not retrieve him because of the shelling. The poor dog eventually rescued later in the morning of D-Day by a number of 13 Para lads. Despite wounds to his neck and eyes he took his place in the line with his handler (pictured left with civilian owner Betty Fetch Bing/Brian, IWM Duxford)."

War dogs were to prove very useful, especially for locating mines and booby traps. They "would sniff excitedly over it for a few seconds and then sit down looking back at the handler with a quaint mixture of smugness and expectancy." The dog would then be given a treat as a reward. The dogs also helped on patrols by sniffing out enemy positions and personnel, hence saving many Allied lives.

Private Ken "Ginger" Oldham ('A' Company)

"I came over a day later [7th June] in an old reclaimed Belgian boat called 'The Leopoldville' with a group of 8 men and a captain, who proclaimed, "Right boys, we're off tomorrow. I'm coming back and so are you!"

"Our battalion had taken the village of Ranville, just next to Pegasus Bridge and were dug in and had held of many German counter-attacks."

The Belgian liner turned troopship, SS Leopoldville (left, Ray Roberts), was torpedoed by U-486 on Christmas Eve 1944, 5 ½ miles off the coast of Cherbourg. It was carrying 2,235 US troops. 763 lost their lives. Captain Limbor went down with his ship and 4 crewmen also died. An unknown number of British personnel (believed to be fewer than 10) were also killed.

Throughout the day's skirmishes, prisoners continued to come in and the 13th Battalion had now taken 15 POW's in the first 2 days. Further to that the War Diary reported that also the 13th had killed 5 Officers and 126 other ranks, 4 tanks had been knocked out and they had captured 3 MG42's, 4 Schmeisser machine pistols, 3 motorcycles, 1 motorcycle with sidecar and four 3-ton lorries.

Lieutenant Ellis "Dixie" Dean (MMG Platoon)

"We had a bit of a panic on the 8th. The order came to "Stand to; German tanks are crossing the bridges." This really was serious, because it meant that our life line was cut and we waited in our slits, Gammon bombs (our only weapon against armour) at hand. For an anxious half an hour we strained our ears, before the order came to stand down and the correction "Sherman, not German, tanks are crossing the bridges". This was far better news and later in the day RQMS Jimmy Henstock delivered another Vickers gun to me and the CO ordered me to site it covering the exposed eastern flank."

Leonard Mosley (War Correspondent)

"What has been particularly refreshing is the officer that commands this force (General Gale - talking to Mosley on the extreme right, IWM). He has been here, there and everywhere controlling his forces, positioning his guns.

"Never by looking at him would you guess that the situation had been grim. His boots are shiny, his jodhpurs immaculate, and come shell or bullet, he has always worn his red Airborne beret rather than his steel helmet. When he runs over the situation his remarks are quite clear, realistic and the way his finger jabs the map as he tells you what he is going to do is confidence inspiring in itself."

From the latest POW's that were brought in, it was realised that the 12th SS Panzer Division Hitlerjugend (Hitler Youth) were now also mobilised and moved into the area. Further prisoners from 857 Regiment of the 346 Infanterie Division (coastal defence unit) was also captured and interrogated.

Private Ray "Geordie" Walker (2 Platoon 'A' Company)

"The next few days would be critical and the Germans made every effort to dislodge us from our positions. Opportunities for meals or sleep were difficult. Fortunately we were provided with Benzedrine tablets;[20] these enabled us to stay awake for long periods. As for food we depended on boiled sweets, chocolate and hard tack biscuits. Water refreshment was from our water bottles until such time as we could make tea from our emergency ration packs.

"During this early period of the fighting our much respected Captain Elliston was killed. As he had been the first Officer that I served under, I felt his loss acutely. Now the days and nights merged under a constant barrage of shell and mortars as the Germans kept up the pressure by a series of counter-attacks."

Captain Padre Whitfield "Boy" Foy

"Domestically things were not too bad with the Battalion. We sat under a more or less continuous bombardment, but we had dug in and construction of trenches was rapidly being brought to a fine art. We had the odd casualties every few hours, they were inevitable.

"Captain F.A.N. Elliston [8th June] was the first of our Officers to be killed in Ranville; he was near his trench when a mortar bomb swished down. He apparently

---

[20] Benzedrine is the trade name of a mixture of amphetamine. Many soldiers are alleged to have become addicted to these tablets.

flung himself down (in a way that one soon learns to do automatically) but a bomb fragment entered his heart and he died immediately. He was among the most respected of our Officers."

Private Ronald Minnery (Intelligence Platoon)

"One time I recall, was the Battalion HQ in Ranville being troubled by a sniper hidden in a copse away in the distance. Hardacre, my No.2 and I were tasked to deal with this. Off we went and selected a good position in which we could observe. We set up the rifles on small tripods and then saw movements up in a tree. We took on the movement and saw quite a commotion amongst the branches.

"We reported to our Sergeant Major the events and as usual he disbelieved us, he was a hard man to convince. He organised and led a patrol and set off to ensure the sniper had been dealt with.

"He came back reporting that he had indeed found a rifle on the ground in the area we mentioned, which had appeared to have been dropped, but there was no sign of any German. "Did you look up in the trees?" I asked, but he replied "I never thought to". Quite often the Germans would tie themselves up in the tree with rope to help support them."

Lt-Col Geoffrey Pine Coffin (CO, 7th Para Bn)

"The gliders were an object of interest to both sides and nothing will prevent a British soldier from looking at things that are a novelty to him. Parties of 2 or 3 would slip out of their position onto the DZ with the object of exploring the nearest glider, but from this one they would pass to the next and so on until they got well out onto the DZ. Several such parties bumped into similar German parties who had, presumably, left their own lines for the exploration of the gliders too. Often the Germans would surrender, but sometimes they would make a fight of it. It was an unnecessary risk for men to take but, fortunately, no harm came of it and the Wehrmacht was deprived of a few of its men as a result. Commandos were at somewhat of a loss when a couple of men, who had not permission to be out at all, returned to their area, proudly escorting a party of prisoners or bringing in documents of Germans, who had decided to fight it out but had lost the fight."

War Diary 8th June

2000   1 OR A/Tk pl killed by shellfire.
2135   Area again shelled. Lieut J.B. Sharples, Lieut H.M. Pollak and CSM Maguire, wounded. MDS hit.

Pte David "Robbie" Robinson (Anti-Tank Platoon, att 'C' Company)

"We lost one of our men on the 8th June; Private Sidney Harbert, he was killed in the evening by shellfire, not much later 'C' Company area, which I was attached to, received a battering and we then lost Lieutenant Sharples wounded."

Lance Corporal George O'Connor (8 Platoon 'C' Company)

"I climbed out of my trench [after the bombardment], to see if anyone else was wounded, Two stretcher bearers, beat me to it, they picked up a wounded man and carried him away, luckily the rest of my mates were uninjured. I could hear moaning in the clearing adjacent to the orchard, I felt unsteady on my legs, but the 3 men I had left and myself went to investigate. Some bombs had dropped in the clearing, the only 2 Platoon officers that we had, our Sergeant Major and a couple of privates lay there wounded. The only Officer we had left was Captain Clark."

Lt Jack Sharples (8 Platoon 'C' Company)

"We were dug in on the right of the road leading to Caen in a little orchard. Back in Larkhill, Private Lloyd Neale of the Platoon had been selected as one of the dog handlers and they were attached to the Platoon for the operation. He was in his slit with a dog and I said to him "That's not your dog" and he replied "No, I lost him on the drop; this is one the Germans left behind." A few days later Neale called out "We're going to be shelled, Sir." I asked him how he knew, "Because the dog's trembling and he was like this last time." Sure enough, over came the shells, all airburst.

"I had warned the Platoon to keep away from the crossroads, immediately to our rear, since they were an obvious target and who was there on 8th June? I still get Christmas cards advising me to keep off the crossroads."

Lieutenant Harry Pollak (Intelligence Officer)

"I am afraid my personal contribution to the invasion of France was not to last very long. On D+3 I was shot in the right arm and within seconds stopped a bit of shrapnel with my left leg. The Airborne Field Ambulance operated on me under the most bizarre conditions, in a cellar by the light of oil lamps. They made a wonderful job and I was evacuated back to England with my leg and arm in plaster."

Lieutenant Ellis "Dixie" Dean (MMG Platoon)

"By the end of the first week, more than half of the Rifle Platoons were led by Sergeants. The born fighting leaders quickly revealed themselves and Lance Corporals and in some cases private soldiers, rose overnight to the rank of Sergeant. 'C' Company, in the middle of the village were particularly badly affected by the mortaring and within days had lost both the remaining Subalterns, also CSM Maguire and CQMS Dugdale."

Captain Padre Whitfield "Boy" Foy

"In war the element of chance or luck is terrifically large. I first knew this on the second day in Ranville. I was walking up the path by the side of the orchard between Battalion HQ and the RAP. I wasn't lingering because a lot of mortar bombs had already fallen. Halfway up the path I heard that well known swish, I dropped flat to the ground and a few yards away, just behind a tree, the bomb exploded. There was no reason why the bomb shouldn't have fallen on me, pure chance."

Private Ronald "Ronnie" Rhodes (8 Platoon 'C' Company)

"One day Wilkinson, myself and the Padre were on burial duties in the church grounds. Wilkinson and myself dug a mass grave approximately 30 ft by 7 ft by 3 ft deep in which we placed 50 bodies over which a burial service was held by the 3 of us whilst under mortar fire. I had my first sleep for 3 days, I was allowed 4 hours (Wilkinson and Rhodes respectively, below).

"I was also given the job of preparing food in a shelled building, there was a set boiler which I scrubbed out with sand and a brick, then filled with water of which, when boiled, I brewed up. I then refilled the boiler, pinched some onions out of a field close by, chopped them up, put in the water and then emptied all the cans into it. Sausages, rice pudding, bacon, everything went in. I brought it to the boil and the blokes could not get enough of this."

"We did not hold Breville. It was my weakest spot and I realized it. What, however, if the enemy did break through that gap?"

Major General Richard Gale

14.   CLOSING THE 'GAP' (9th – 17th June 1944)

The small bridgehead was by now almost fully secured. The 5th Brigade held Ranville and all of its approaches; the Airlanding elements held the southern sector and the Commandos the northern. From the commando positions running south through Le Mesnil was a ridge ending at Troarn. James Hill's 3rd Brigade held most of this ridge, but not the village of Bréville. With a commanding view across DZ-N, this village gave the Germans full observation of Ranville and the Bridges. It was of great importance to General Gale that this 'gap' was closed.

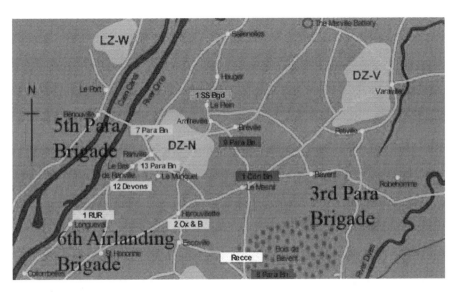

The 6th Airborne bridgehead positions 8th June (www.pegasusarchive.org).

Private Ray Batten (2 Platoon 'A' Company)

"I was sent on patrol towards the [Hérouvillette] crossroads and I heard armoured movements. I reported what I heard and was told that it wasn't friendly because our own armour was not yet in that vicinity. The Navy was called and a heavy barrage was put down in that area.

One time a tank came towards us through a cornfield and some of our chaps were going to go out to take it on. Captain Kerr told them to stay where they were, because there wasn't much we could really do."

Major Hans von Luck (21st Panzer Division)

"At any movement on the battlefield, even of an individual vehicle, the enemy reacted with concentrated fire from the navy or attacks by fighter-bombers. Either our radio communications were being intercepted or the navy had divided up the whole area into grid squares and had only to pass on the square number to launch a sudden concentration of fire.

"I received an order from division [8th June], my combat group was to assemble in the morning, attack Escoville, advance on Ranville and take the bridges. I would have Panzer Reconnaissance Battalion 21, No.4 Company Panzer 22, 3 batteries of Assault-gun Battalion 200, and one company of Anti-Tank Battalion 200 with 88mm guns. Our artillery would support within its ammunition supply."

Von Lucks force was to assemble before dawn to nullify the RAF and Navy threat. The motorcycle escorts from the Reconnaissance Battalion with grenadiers from 2nd Battalion would lead; Major Von Luck decided he would be right behind the Recce Battalion, so that he could make on the spot decisions. Next, following up would be 1st Battalion, the tanks of No.4 Company and the SP guns. The 88mm guns would position themselves on the hill south of Escoville and cover any counterattack attempted by British armour.

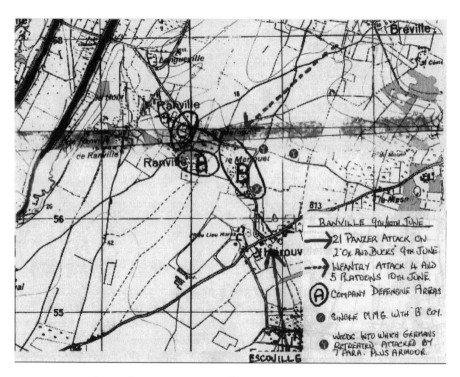

Map of 9th & 10th June attacks on 13th Battalion, drawn by "Dixie" Dean.

In the afternoon of the 9th June approximately one company of Germans were spotted in a wood towards Bréville and Lt-Col Luard gave Captain Kerr of 'B' Company, who were manning the eastern edge of Ranville, the order "Do not open fire on copse without direct orders from me." More movement was seen in a copse to the southwest of Ranville and 'A' Company arranged for the Battalion Mortar Platoon to fire upon the area. After tea, the Germans opened up their own barrage, a prelude of an attack using infantry and armour.

Lieutenant Ellis "Dixie" Dean (MMG Platoon)

"For an hour or more, the Battalion was subjected to the heaviest concentrations of artillery and mortar fire which it had so far experienced. Even while the shells and bombs were still falling on positions in Ranville, from Escoville and Hérouvillette to the south west, machine gun fire signalled the enemy advance. Gradually the sounds of battle from these two places grew louder as the Germans made steady progress towards the Platoons of 'A' and 'B' Companies, holding positions to the rear of the Ox & Bucks. Brigadier Poett drove through the MMG location to take control of the situation and gradually the sounds of battle grew fainter and finally fizzled out all together."

Lance Corporal Hammel (Reconnaissance Battalion, 21st Pz Div)

"With support from the tanks and assault guns [SP] we soon forced our way into Escoville. The remaining civilian population had gathered by the church. We found a few children running around looking for their parents. We took them to the church.

"The British of the 6th Airborne Division put up fierce resistance. When it became light, heavy fire from the navy began to fall on the centre of the village and its southern edge. We could make no progress. Then the news reached us that our beloved commander Major Waldow had been killed, only a day after coming back from his wife. This was a blow to us all. We couldn't even recover his body at first because of the barrage of fire. It was not until after dark that a patrol of volunteers, whom the British in fairness allowed to pass, was able to bring Major Waldow back and bury him further to the rear. Later the British transferred him to their military cemetery in Ranville, where he found his last rest among his former enemies."

Werner Kortenhaus (4 Kompanie, 21st Pz Div)

"That day was for us one of the hardest actions ever. We assembled with about 10 tanks under the trees of the avenue south of Escoville. We drove with closed ports, one tank after the other, to the right past the Château into a large meadow, which was enclosed by hedges. There we intended switching to broad wedge formation for attack, the grenadiers behind and alongside us.

"Then everything happened very quickly: within a few minutes we had lost 4 tanks, knocked out by the naval guns. On my tank [Mk IV, short barrelled] the turret jammed, so that I could only shoot into the hedges with my machine-gun. The fire became more intense, so that on orders from Major von Luck we had to withdraw, as did the grenadiers. The artillery fire continued unabated. Some 30 or 40 grenadiers must have been killed by it.

"On the evening of 9th June we realized that we could no longer drive the British back into the sea."

Private Ray "Geordie" Walker (2 Platoon 'A' Company)

"Throughout these early days we had magnificent naval support from the battleships at the coast. With their massive guns they were able to delay advancing

German reinforcements reaching the front line. When these heavy calibre shells passed over our heads they made a noise like an express train travelling at full speed. I should hate to have been at the receiving end of a naval bombardment.

"Several of the naval spotters trained with me at Ringway, they played a vital part, working with the Battle Fleet in the Channel. These Radio Telegraphists had parachuted into Normandy along with their Royal Artillery Captain and liaised with the Gun Control Officers on the battleships."

Leading Telegraphist E.F.G. Hibberd was one of the men at Ringway with Ray Walker; he was killed early on D-Day and is buried in Ranville. He was part of the group with Brigadier James Hill, who all were dropped astray and had joined up together. As they headed for their objectives, the group was bombed by what was believed to be allied aircraft, leaving only Brigadier Hill (himself badly wounded in the rear) and one other able to continue.

Hibberd's ship, HMS Arethusa (pictured below), was to supporting the 6th Airborne, in doing so she fired 392 rounds of 6" ammunition by 1600 on D-Day alone. HMS Arethusa was part of Bombarding Force 'D' which included the battleships Warspite and Ramillies and the monitor Roberts, 4 other cruisers and 13 destroyers. They provided gunfire support for Force 'S' landing at Sword Beach.

General Richard "Windy" Gale (Commander, 6th Airborne Division)

"By 9pm this attack petered out and the enemy withdrew leaving behind 6 MkIV tanks and 2 armoured cars. Local French civilians reported that many more tanks had been waiting in Escoville and only withdrew when the leading echelon of tanks fell back.

"Thus ended another day. Success elated us. The troops were in grand fettle and their confidence in their ability to hold what they had gained was stimulating to behold."

At around 9pm more of the enemy was seen to be gathering in the woods at the north end of DZ 'N'. A little later as low flying fighters came over and bombed and strafed the 13th Battalion's positions, infantry followed up and attacked 'B' Company from the northern woods. Again, all attempts were fought off.

L/Cpl George O'Connor (8 Platoon 'C' Company)

"I made my way towards the trenches, before I reached them there was a burst of machine gun fire and I dropped to the ground. I crawled to the trench that a Manchester lad was in, as soon as the firing ceased I rolled in the trench only to find the Manchester lad was dead. Yorky shouted, "The bloody fool stood up!" I didn't even know his name."

He was Robert Swindell (pictured) aged 21… He had only just joined L/Cpl O'Connor's Section a few hours before.

L/Corporal George O'Connor (8 Platoon 'C' Company)

[When the shooting died down] "I passed 2 stretcher bearers struggling along with a body, the Medical Officer was there attending a wounded man. The padre arrived he said to the padre, "This ones still alive, he'll be OK when he gets to the field hospital". Pointing to the 2 stretcher bearers, he said, "That's a job for you". The padre followed the stretcher bearers. When the wounded para was taken away, the MO walked around, asking everyone if they were alright, "Yes Sir", replied one para, "we're fit, fit for sod all." The MO laughed and walked away."

The body that the stretcher bearers were struggling with was most probably that of William Clouston, a 28 year old private from Coalsnaughton, Clackmannanshire.

Captain Padre Whitfield "Boy" Foy

"Sergeant Bill Webster was a technician but he was a very fine fighting soldier, and would have made an excellent platoon sergeant. His section had been in a very

vulnerable position, just opposite to the MDS. A Jeep carrying a full load, overturned on the road near his trench. At the time, his position was in full view of snipers and mortar fire was heavy. Webster left his trench immediately and helped in the extraction of the passengers; he went to the MDS, collected a stretcher party and assisted in carrying the casualties to the MDS.

[In another incident] "Our MO Captain Neil Whitley (left) was seriously wounded in the back. Ironically he was hit when helping to carry a wounded German up the steps of the MDS. After a game struggle lasting over 2 months, he died aged 26, in England (Stoke Mandeville Hospital) on 29th August 1944."

The MDS, in Le Mariquet, faces north across the DZ and the steps where Captain Whitley was hit can be seen at the front. In the cellars below, many operations were carried out. During these times in 1944 the building wore a large Red Cross flag across the frontage and the openings of the cellar and the doors were heavily sandbagged.

Then & Now: The MDS Building Château Bruder.

Captain David Tibbs (225 Field Ambulance RAMC)

"The MO of the 13th Parachute Battalion had been badly wounded and I was to replace him. I moved across to join the Battalion about 1½ mile away. Sadly this meant leaving behind the remnants of my original section with the Field Ambulance. The Battalion Regimental Aid Post (RAP) I took over was in the large stone walled stables of the Château in Ranville. One of the conscientious objectors in the new group of RAMC men now with me, showed his inexperience with battle by sitting in a deck chair in the open, reading his bible. When I told him to sit inside behind the strong stone walls he remained where he was and said in broad Scottish accent "If it's the Lords will that I shall die; then I shall die!" I noticed however that after a group of severe causalities came in, some with ghastly wounds, he changed tactics and moved his deck chair inside and never sat outside again. The Château was the home of the elderly Compte and Comptesse of Cabourg, and the upper stories were filled with the local villagers who had fled there for refuge. Soon after my arrival I was asked in for a tea party. The Comptesse was a delightful character and thoroughly enjoyed behaving as if nothing unusual was going on as she sipped English style tea, and I reflected that it was just like some weird film set. The Compte had been a General in the First World War and keep saying "Mon Dieu! Mon Dieu!" as yet another artillery exchange thundered down outside. The Comptesse teased me over the look of distaste she had detected on my face when earlier we had viewed the refugees upstairs, most were filthy and covered in lice. I tried to learn this lesson."

The 6th Airborne Division had solid defensive positions on the eastern flank of the beachhead. The Orne River and Canal protected them from the west. From the south were vast open plains and fields which offered excellent killing grounds. Between Hérouvillette and Le Mariquet large minefields were now in place as was the strip of ground between Hérouvillette and the Bois de Bavent. The Troarn-Le Mesnil road ran through the extremely dense wood called the Bois de Bavent which was impassable to infantry and AFV's. The crossroads in this area at Le Mesnil was covered by a battalion of troops. The ridge to the north of Le Mesnil was also wooded and covered up to Le Plein by the 3rd Brigade. The village of Bréville half way up the ridge however was gained by the Germans. It was in this area that the Germans decided to launch their next attempt to regain the river and canal bridges.

German Order for the Attack 10th June 1944

1. Enemy still holding area east of bridge at Benouville on the Eastern bank of the Orne with elements of 6th Airborne Division. So far it has been impossible to find out whether he will bring up further force in the bridgehead for offensive purposes.
2. 346 ID will make a concentric attack on the enemy bridgehead on 10.6.44 and will destroy the enemy forces east of the Orne.
3. Regt group 657 (with under command II/Gren Regt 857, II/Gren Regt 858, III/Gren Regt 858, A/Tk 346) will push forward with main effort on the left from area Bréville and North of it towards the SW and will occupy the East bank of the Orne near bridge at Benouville.
4. Units will form up as follows:-

II/Gren Regt 857 in area reached on 9.6.44 and battalion will attack along road Sallenelles – Ranville and push on to Ferme de Rearde towards the south.

III/Gren Regt 858 with elements in Bréville and greater part in area Le Plein (1km NE Bréville) will attack Amfreville and push through to the Orne near east of Benouville.

II/Gren Regt 858 in area reached 9.6.44 in order to attack with and protect the left flank of III/Gren Regt 858 and push forward to the crossroads 1500m SW of Bréville.

5. Battalion body between II/Gren Regt 857 and III/Gren Regt 858.
    i.   Longuemare – Le Plein – road fork 1000 in NW of church at Ranville (incl to III/Gren 858).
    ii.   Battalion body between III/Gren Regt 858 and III/Gren 857 church at Petiville – Château de St. Come – church at Ranville.

6. Regt Group 858 will support attack of Regt Group 857 from area Bavent up to the hills near and north of Le Prieure and will give protection with its left flank facing the Bois de Bavent.

War Diary 10th June

0300   Capt Kerr, commanding 2 Pls of 'B' Coy, covering northern approaches, reported enemy MG fire on his posns from woods near BRÉVILLE. Bde HQ confirmed presence of enemy bn in BRÉVILLE and arrangements were made for reception of possible attacks. Intermittent shelling, resembling ranging continued until dawn.

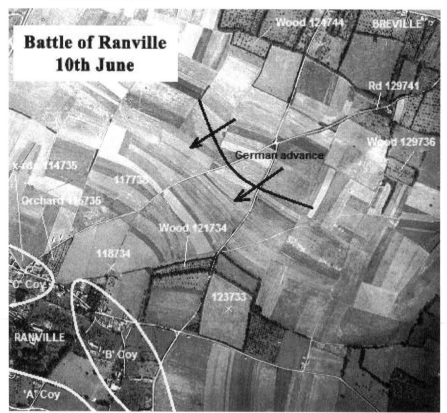

Account - Attack by 858 Grenadier Regt, 10th June, the 'Battle of Ranville'.

At 0300 hours 10th June, Capt Kerr came in to Battalion HQ to report to Lt-Col Luard that there had been some machine gun fire from the same woods [NE] and that he suspected an attack. The Intelligence Officer, Lt L.H.U. Golding, was sent to HQ 5th Brigade with this information and a request for a FOO to be attached to the Battalion. Capt Kerr was told to remain in observation, report all movement and not to open fire and so disclose his positions. The request for a FOO was granted by Brigade who was doubtful about the attack, which was considered to be most unlikely.

0600   Sup arty of 2 Fd Regts registered targets area 130738 - 126744.
0725   Enemy debouched from Woods about 129736 - 2 Coys infantry.
0730   Arty engaged enemy (about 50) 124744.

At 0600 hours, the FOO Lt Hastings[21] (left), South Notts Yeomanry, RA, was reported in position at the Church Tower in Ranville, where 2 battalion signallers, Pte [Alf] John (right) and Pte Thompson were waiting with the Commanding Officers Rover set, to maintain communication.

The FOO was asked to register the openings from the woods NE of Ranville and the 2 crossroads on the DZ, which were considered to be likely Forming Up positions. These registrations were started at once by the fire of one Field Regiment, with one Field Regiment in reserve, which actually was never used during the engagement. The FOO's wireless call was "Easy 6", which became a battalion by-word for efficient artillery support.

At 0645 hours a fighting patrol from 'C' Company under Sgt Holland, was sent out over the DZ to make contact, if possible, with the enemy. This contact was successfully made and it was established that the troops in the woods were in fact Germans. This information was not, however, received until 0800 hours, as the fighting patrol had no wireless.

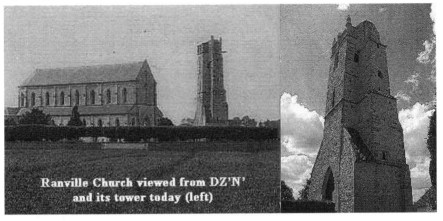

Ranville Church viewed from DZ'N' and its tower today (left)

---

[21] Lieutenant Cuthbert "Pat" Hastings was attached and dropped with the 13th Bn as FOO. He was later promoted to Captain and was eventually Mentioned in Despatches for his part in later campaigns.

Private Ray "Geordie" Walker (2 Platoon 'A' Company)

"Early one morning (10th June) my pal and I were detailed to man an observation post which was located in the roof of a barn. We had a commanding view of the DZ/LZ which was littered with crashed and abandoned gliders. Soon we saw parties of German infantry heading towards our trenches as they dodged from glider to glider using them as cover. We passed this information to our Officer so that he could prepare for an attack. During this melee an incoming shell crashed through the roof of the farmhouse behind us. No-one was killed but an irate farmer gave us a lot of verbal abuse. From all accounts he preferred life under the Germans as life in the village was tranquil. Now under the British his life was shattered under a hail of bombs, shells and bullets."

Leonard Mosley (War Correspondent)

"Watching the dropping zone through his field glasses, I found my old pal Captain Charles Bliss [7th Para Bn on NW of Ranville] "This," said Charles, "is going to be good. Do you remember the gap around Bréville? Well Jerry's found it at last and he's coming through. We have reports of at least 600 Panzer Grenadiers advancing through the woods and we believe they are going to try to drive through to Ranville, break our line and gain the east bank of the river."

0745   *Approx one bn enemy spread about between 117740 - 122925.*
0825   *Enemy now at 118734 - 30 yards from posns. Heavily engaged by LMGs.*

Account - Attack by 858 Grenadier Regt, 10th June, the 'Battle of Ranville'.

At 0725 hours German troops were seen to debouch from the woods, and the crossroads in the village were shelled by the enemy. Stirlings on a supply drop had been fired on from the woods, from which the enemy came, and so it was considered likely that they were indeed Germans and "Easy 6" was asked to engage them, once they came in the open.

The artillery opened accurate fire on the enemy and without doubt caused considerable casualties among them, but the first wave had by now reached the cover of the first gliders on the LZ. Meanwhile the supporting companies had come out of the wood and by 0745 hours the whole battalion had debouched from the woods over a front of about 800 yards and 800 yards in depth with apparently 2 companies up.

Engaged throughout by the artillery, which fired with the most telling results, the enemy attacked the NE corner of Ranville and at one point, come round to attack the North by the orchards by the crossroads. Meanwhile the village was subjected to mortar fire, particularly to the North. The attack on the North was directly broken up by the artillery and never came in, in force, though some men did infiltrate in, some being taken prisoner and one, who had climbed onto a roof being shot by RQMS Hanstock, who took Orderly Room Sgt Ferdinand's rifle to do so, as Ferdinand could not see him on the roof even with his glasses on.

This infiltration was contained by the Anti-Tank platoon, under command of Lt Alf Lagergren.

Private David "Robbie" Robinson (Anti-Tank Platoon, att 'C' Company)

"The Germans put in a counter attack from the wooded area beyond the landing ground. They crossed the open ground, dodging between crashed gliders; I got very, very scared. We had been shelled and mortared up until this time which was bad, but this was my first sight of Germans and it seemed they were very intent in moving us out of the village and back to the sea. And it also seemed that they'd got me, 'Robbo', as their main target. As they got near the full battalion opened up on them and they suffered very heavy casualties. My PIAT was not fired; there were no tanks or transport to shoot at.

"It was a very badly organised attack; I spoke to the IO [Lt Les Golding] after the battle and he told me that the German officers he had interrogated had said that they didn't even know we were there. We must have been that well dug in."

T/Captain Jack Watson (2i/c 'A' Company)

"I happened to be at Battalion HQ at the time when the attack began. They came on with no artillery support and Peter Luard watched them every second of their advance across the DZ. He then gave the wonderful order "don't shoot until you see the whites of their eyes". They got to within 50 yards before he gave the order to fire. They were shot down left right and centre, it was horrific. But they still came forward."

Lance Corporal George O'Connor (8 Platoon 'C' Company)

"I kept peering over the little mound of earth I had surrounded my trench with, someone whispered "Here they come", I couldn't see anything moving towards us, I expected to see a rush of German soldiers, when I did see them, they were crawling through the long grass. Soon as they were about 50 yards from us, someone gave an Indian war cry and we all began shooting. Some of the Germans, stood up and put their hands in the air, but it was too late to stop firing, they were all mown down.

"Another wave ran towards us, they were firing from the hip as they ran. Our Bren gunner swept the field with bullets and the Germans fell down like toy soldiers."

Leonard Mosley (War Correspondent)

"In batches of 10 to 15, spread out over 200 yards, the German infantrymen came on at a run. They plodded through the waving corn until they reached a line of wrecked gliders. Then they fell on their faces and lay there. After a few minutes, they got up and ran forward before dropping down again. It went on like that for 400 yards and still no one fired.

"Now the enemy was gaining in confidence from the stillness. Smelling no danger his loping advances were longer and his periods on the ground of only a few seconds duration. He came on fast; and kept on coming until he was some 100 yards away. And then, at some prearranged signal, every automatic weapon and every rifle in the Paratroops line opened up. It was a roar that set your teeth chattering with shock.

"You suddenly saw Germans, grimacing, wildly clutching their bodies, throwing up their hands and then falling by the dozen into the corn. Then all of them flung themselves down. A rain of bullets surged across those 100 yards of French farm land but the Germans were not beaten yet. The earth was thrown up in showers and the corn went down as if under a flail.

"One of their Officers rose to his feet, called to his men and those still un-wounded, charged once more. This time the Paratroops held their fire even longer and it was from 25 to 30 yards now, when the small arms barrage hit the enemy. With cool, superb and absolute discipline, fingers squeezed the triggers almost simultaneously and down in writing heaps went the Germans again. And now the remnants that remained alive turned and began to flee."

Account - Attack by 858 Grenadier Regt, 10th June, the 'Battle of Ranville'.

Meanwhile the attack on the North East, onto that sector under Capt Kerr (No.4 & 5 Platoons) had been allowed to come on and no small arms fire had yet been opened, it having been ordered that this was to be held "until they could see the whites of their eyes".

Some of the enemy now infiltrated into the Battalion RV, where they were engaged by the Mortars, under Lt F.J. Skeate, with great accuracy and despatch. When they came forward again, fire was opened by all automatic weapons, including six captured

German machine guns and one Vickers of the 8th Battalion which had dropped on the Ranville DZ. At the same time, 'B' Company under command of Major G.W. Bristow, opened fire with light automatics and a Vickers gun from the battalion MMG platoon, onto the supporting companies which were following up.

'B' Company, particularly No.4 & 5 Platoons, suffered the most casualties, No.4 Platoon lost their officer, Lt "Bert" Arnold (left), wounded in the stomach, Pte Frederick Clyne (8 Pl 'C' Coy)[22] and L/Cpl Alfred Brown were killed and Pte Jack Banks was missing, presumed dead and is listed as "No Known Grave".

Private Peter Maynard (4 Platoon 'B' Company)

"On the 9th and 10th June there were big attacks on Ranville where I lost my best mate L/Cpl Alf Brown (left), to what we think was a sniper. No one really knows how he died; he was a runner and was killed taking a message.

"I was sat in my fox hole over looking one of the glider landing zones, when the Jerry's came toward us. I lade out some Bren mags and waited for the order to fire. The OC said, "Don't fire 'till I say. We're going to let them get close." I could see the Jerry's running in and out the gliders in front of me and their officers and NCO's shouting orders. They got 50 yards from us before we opened fire and saw them drop like flees."

L/Corporal Alf Brown was shot on Rue de Chardonnerette (the small road north of the MDS). Where his son (Alf Brown Junior, whom never met his dad) many years later positioned a memorial to him at the end of the road (over: Alf is third from right, courtesy Fay and Bern Robins).

---

[22] George O'Connor records in his own account that on this day his mate "Freddie" was shot by a sniper through the neck. I can only assume this to be Private Frederick Clyne.

190

Captain David Tibbs (RAMC)

"The Germans launched another strong attack on our area the day after I arrived, this time across the DZ, a wide open space. Several hundred of them could be seen crawling through the wheat and they were allowed to approach within a few hundred feet of our positions. When they rose in a final charge they met devastating fire from our battalion. This included the use of MG42 machine guns captured by us when we first took Ranville. The few survivors retreated to a copse where they were mercilessly shelled and I do not think any remained alive at the end. They did not attack in this fashion again."

Account - Attack by 858 Grenadier Regt, 10th June, the 'Battle of Ranville'.

At 0825 hours the attack was completely broken up by the sudden and sustained fire from the NE sector, and 'C' Company, under command of Major G.H.D. Ford, was ordered to counter-attack.

One half, under the company second-in-command, Capt A.R. Clark, to sweep down through the orchards on the North of the village, mopping up as it came and the remainder under Major Ford to counter attack simultaneously on the arrival of Capt Clark's party from the South of the Easterly orchards northwards to take the enemy in the flank.

The counter-attack finally went in at about 1000 hours. The enemy attack had then finally stopped and the counter-attack hit them perfectly and completely disorganised them. Some 20 men surrendered to Capt Clark alone, which caused him slight embarrassment.

0845   *'C' Coy. Pl moved to orchard 115735.*
0920   *Some enemy remnants conc in Wood 121734 and mortar fire falling on x-rds 114735.*
0930   *Wood 121734 being heavily shelled by our arty.*
1010   *18 PW brought in. Identified as II/858 Inf Regt 346 Div.*

Private Ronald "Ronnie" Rhodes (8 Platoon 'C' Company)

"Our platoon was ordered to try and clear enemies from the dropping zone, 20 of us set out, Kirby and myself being the 2 men in the lead. Sgt [William] Collier was killed on the way. We came under fire from the direction of 3 gliders and Kirby covered me while I went to try and clear them. The next thing I knew, I'm in a ditch where I had been dragged by another platoon member.

"I had a useless left arm and bullet through my chest. Kirby had been shot through both eyes. I somehow got back to our first aid post and remember very little about the next 3 or 4 days. Only one person came out of that episode without a scratch, a fellow called Thomas."

1155   'B' Coy report further enemy attacks.
1230   1 Pl enemy moved into EAST end of RV.
1330   Enemy reinforcing RV by infiltration.
1355   Enemy smoke area 117738.
1455   HEROUVILLETTE shelled by enemy.
1530   Several pls of enemy moved astride rd 129741.

'C' Company, especially 8 platoon suffered heavy casualties during the 'Battle for Ranville'. Ptes William Clouston and Robert Swindell were killed on 9th June followed by Sgt William Collier and Ptes Kenneth Alfred Bull and Orrell on 10th June. Pte William Prince lost his life on the 12th June having died of wounds sustained from the battle. Amazingly Pte Kirby survived, despite being shot in both eyes.

Account - Attack by 858 Grenadier Regt, 10th June, the 'Battle of Ranville'.

The execution on the enemy was terrific and none of the enemy who had come forward from the RV ['W' Wood 122735, the 13th Bn's RV on D-Day] was seen to regain its cover. 'C' Company was then withdrawn again into reserve.

It was now appreciated that there were a number of enemy still in the RV and in fact, small numbers, in ones and twos were seen infiltrating into the RV through the crops, which were very high. 'C' Company, the only company available for counter-attack was not strong enough to take this on alone, as the wood was fairly thick. The wood was therefore engaged continually by the artillery and the battalion Mortars in order to contain them in the wood.

The Brigadier (J.H.N. Poett) had arranged, therefore, for one squadron of 13/18 Hussars to support a counter-attack by two companies of 7th Parachute Battalion into and through the wood, followed by 'C' Company, mopping up.

Lieutenant Ellis "Dixie" Dean (MMG Platoon)

"The Quartermaster, Captain George Daisley had in the stores he was bringing with him a spare Vickers gun, but his glider never arrived on the LZ. Instead RQMS Jimmy Hanstock delivered the replacement and the previous day the CO ordered me to site it covering the exposed eastern flank of the Battalion. I found a position in 'B' Companies area along a sunken path. A detachment under Lance Sergeant Tom Donnelly manned the position.

"The shattered remains of the Boche retreated into the two small copses at Le Mariquet, right in front of Sergeant Donnelly's detachment, who engaged opportunity targets before the counterattack by the 7th, supported by armour could finish the job."

Many of the 13th were killed and wounded in the 'Battle for Ranville' and Sergeant John Hughes (right) was one of those wounded that day by small arms fire. He was hit in the foot and during his subsequent evacuation in the back of a truck, was shot again in the same foot after the truck was strafed by an enemy ME 109.

Despite being directly on the road adjacent to the fields which the Germans had used for their attacks the MDS and 195 Airlanding Field Ambulance still carried on with their medical treatment and performed numerous operations in the cellars, all the time under mortar and small arms fire.

Private Lesley Barker (left) wrote a letter home from the MDS. During the German attacks he was wounded once more by machine gun fire to the head possibly after the Germans passed the MDS retreating to the RV copse. His wounds were so severe he was evacuated to England where he never regained consciousness and died on the 28th June 1944 with his sister, who had brought him up since he was orphaned, at his bedside.

After the Commanding Officer was wounded earlier in the campaign, Major Gilliland quickly became Lt-Col Gilliland.

Lt-Col Gilliland (195 Field Amb Dressing Station)

"D+4 was a difficult day. The Germans were clearly visible all morning in the glider field opposite the MDS. On one occasion tracer bullets were seen going down the road outside and the German forces were so near at midday that all secret documents were placed in a fireplace ready to destroy. At 1600 tanks arrived and cleared the Germans."

Major John Watts (195 Field Ambulance Dressing Station)

"We were close enough to the front line to see enemy infantry doubling across the fields. One German soldier, with a foot injury suppurating from a wound received on the Russian front 2 years earlier, spotted the Red Cross and broke off from the battle to come in for treatment."

Lt-Col Geoffrey Pine-Coffin (CO, 7th Parachute Bn)

"When I arrived on the scene, this was in response to a request to open up "on large numbers of the enemy located in the open"; I found that the snipers could fire immediately as they had all preparations in anticipation. I gave the word... The attack was halted and the attackers, being badly shot up, made for the nearest cover, which was a series of small woods which lay immediately between the two Parachute Brigades, but were not occupied by either. Their presence there was highly undesirable as they were, literally, a thorn in the side of both Brigades; a thorn in a very awkward side too, being just beyond the comfortable reach of either Brigade.

"It was not expected that there would be any difficulty in carrying out the job, as the enemy must be considerably disorganised and would be numerically inferior, without food, reserves of ammunition and altogether in pretty poor shape. A bullet travels just as fast though, whatever the odds against the first man who fires it, and in this attack, as in any other, men of the Battalion would be killed and others wounded. It was altogether a thoroughly unpleasant job, generally considered "a bit of cake", with little kudos for success and much blame for failure. It was nevertheless a job and an important one too. It was difficult to determine the nature of the country beyond the woods, it looked like grass, probably was, but might be anything and of any height. Two features were quite definite though, first a road which bordered the long side of the displaced wood, to continue into 3 Brigade area, and second a track which branched off from this road at right angles, to cross the end of the displaced wood at a distance from it of 200 yards. Control would be difficult in the woods, particularly against an enemy in scattered positions and employing sniper tactics, which was more than probable. An extremely simple plan was laid on, which would allow for plenty of modification as the situation developed."

Using tank support from 'B' Squadron of 13/18th Hussars, Lt-Col Pine-Coffin ordered them to fire into the first wood for 2 minutes before laying smoke to protect his 7th Parachute Battalion (less 'C' Company) as they advanced. The smoke was also the signal that the tanks had finished firing. One company of the 7th Bn would then sweep into the wood, clear it and then allow the other company to pass through to carry out the same tactic on the next wood and so on. There were four woods in total and after clearing the final wood, the 7th Bn was to secure the road junction and send patrols to meet the 3rd Para Brigade near the crossroads.

Lt-Col Geoffrey Pine-Coffin (CO, 7th Parachute Bn)

"It was raining hard at the time and conditions for reconnaissance were further complicated by the presence of an unusually large number of Germans in the gliders on the DZ. These were being kept under close observation by the troops in the vicinity, who were having quite a serious shooting match with them and did not appreciate the sudden appearance of various officers, complete with binoculars and a desire to study their battlefield.

"I detailed 'B' Coy to clear woods 'W', 'Y' and 'Z' and 'A' Coy to clear wood 'X' and to secure the road junction.

"The attack started at the appointed hour (4pm) but difficulty was experienced from the start in co-ordinating with the tanks (pictured engaging Germans during battle, © IWM B 5345). They came up in pairs and it was hard to know when they were all up as I understood that a squadron was being used but actually only 6 tanks appeared at any time. It was also very hard to know when they had finished firing because on only one occasion did I see a smoke shell fired and on several occasions there were tanks on fire which produced so much smoke themselves that it was difficult to see what was happening. All 6 tanks were eventually hit and burned out.[23]

"The clearing of 'W' wood went without a hitch and several Germans were killed and 'A' Coy duly passed through and cleared 'X' wood, where several more Germans were killed. Two of the tanks were ablaze at this stage.

"The remaining tanks then fired well into 'Y' wood and 'A' Coy gave covering fire for 'B' Coy's approach to it.

"When 'B' Coy entered the West of 'Y' wood a white flag was raised from the NE corner of it. The wood was thick and it was difficult to sort out the situation as, of course, 'B' Coy in the wood were not aware that the Germans were trying to surrender. About 40 were taken prisoner here and the sorting out of them delayed 'A' Coy, who should have followed 'B' Coy closely into the wood in anticipation of the next stage.

"When I eventually got 'A' Coy on the move again I found that Rear Bn HQ had got ahead of Adv Bn HQ and was, in fact, at the East end of 'Y' wood (which 'B' Coy had completely cleared) and I found my 2 i/c busy marshalling a batch of about 40 more prisoners whom he appeared to have partially stripped. At this stage I modified the plan as the delay over the prisoners had caused a slowing of the momentum which I was anxious to avoid; I therefore ordered 'B' Coy to sweep 'Z' wood immediately and held 'A' Coy for 10 minutes and then sent them off at best speed by the road to secure the road junction. Adv Bn HQ went with 'A' Coy and Rear Bn HQ with 'B' Coy.

"The final stage was something of an anti-climax as there were no enemy either in 'Z' wood or at the road junc. 3rd Para Brigade were in fact at the road junction themselves."

---

[23] No-one who took part on this attack could positively say that the tanks [reported by the 11/13 Hussars as 4 Shermans and 2 Stuarts] were knocked out by anti-tank guns to the north, by 'bazookas' or by anti-tank grenades thrown by troops concealed by the very tall corn in the fields.

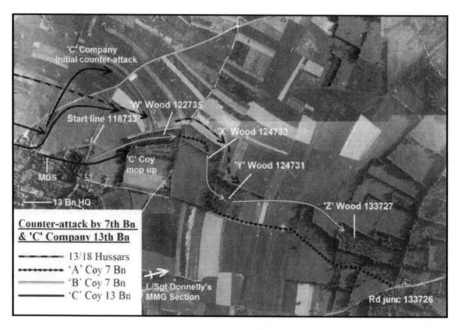

Counter-attack by 7th Bn
& 'C' Company 13th Bn

- 13/18 Hussars
- 'A' Coy 7 Bn
- 'B' Coy 7 Bn
- 'C' Coy 13 Bn

Account - Attack by 858 Grenadier Regt, 10ᵗʰ June, the 'Battle of Ranville'.

Casualties:

| Killed | - | 6 OR's. |
| Wounded | - | 1 Officer & 17 OR's. |

80 German wounded were treated in the MDS, the dead were never counted, but the casualties were very large. When the DZ was finally cleared, 4 light flak guns were found on the crossroads and engaged by the artillery.

Captain David Tibbs (RAMC)

"I walked over the area next day to look for survivors and followed many tracks of crushed wheat left by crawling Germans in their initial approach; at the end of each track was a dead German. The copse was filled with dead Germans, but to my anger I found that several of our men were already there and were stripping the dead of wrist watches or other valuables. I am afraid that it was not unknown to see our own dead with perhaps up to 8 wrist watches on their forearms under their sleeves, a curious irony of war and a reminder not to tempt the gods in this way."

Private Ray "Geordie" Walker ('A' Company)

"By the 12ᵗʰ June we were now receiving a hot meal once a day, thanks to the efforts of CQMS Harry Watkins. Meat and vegetable stew was often on the menu and we appreciated the issue of 'bullybeef', biscuits and jam. About this time we received a tin of 50 Players Navy Cut cigarettes. They were a godsend for calming our nerves and they helped to stave off hunger.

"Now that the days were lengthening and the weather warmer, life was made uncomfortable by swarms of mosquitoes, especially at night in our trenches. The Germans had supplied these insects with a good supply of water to breed in; they had flooded the Dives Valley to improve their defences. At night we developed a method of using smouldering string to drive them away. We received a supply of repellent face cream; the mosquitoes developed a liking for it and ate it like ice cream!"

War Diary 12th June

0600   Fairly quiet night - slight shelling and bombing.
1145 to 1200   Area shelled intermittently.
1430   Our Arty shelling BRÉVILLE.
1530 to 1600   Area mortared - 1 OR killed [Private Frederick Whitehead].
2145   Very heavy arty barrage put down by our arty on BRÉVILLE preparatory to attack by 12 Para Bn and 1 Coy 12 Devons.

General Gale decided it was now the time to close the 'Bréville Gap'. The German 346th Infantry Division had been fighting for days on end and so Gale pressed them whilst they were still tired and unable to organise themselves. He sent the 12th Para Bn to assault and capture Bréville.

The 12th Bn assaulted under a creeping barrage and over open ground, as a result of which caused horrendous casualties, a lot of which was from the creeping barrage falling short. They lost their CO and many other officers. Gale himself went forward into Bréville and was awarded the DSO for his "Conspicuous gallantry" and "his presence among the forward elements, still wearing his beret continued with the utmost coolness and calmness had such an amazing effect on the troops…"

After the very heavy and costly battle had taken place, the area was closed and the perimeter, now finally secured. Later Gale looked down on Ranville from the Bréville position and at once realised the view the Germans had had of his own Divisional area. From there they had watched every movement.

View looking NE across DZ 'N'

Lieutenant Ellis "Dixie" Dean (MMG Platoon)

"The officer casualties suffered by the 12th (Yorkshire) Battalion in their capture of the Bréville feature resulted in promotion and transfer for 3 members of the Battalion. Major Bill Harris MC was new 12th Battalion CO. Captain Mike Kerr a Company Commander and Lieutenant Bernard Metcalf became the Adjutant. Colonel Luard had clearly recognised the potential in the Officers he selected. There were also changes in the 13th Major Ford moved to Battalion HQ as second-in-command with Captain "Nobby" Clark the new OC "Charlie" Company and there were Captaincies for Lieutenants Leslie Golding and Freddie Skeate. Sergeant "Taffy" Lawley was CSM and Charlie Wrigley CQMS of 'C' Company."

Private David "Robbie" Robinson (Anti-Tank Platoon)

"Being with 'C' Company, we dug a position in the garden of the estaminet at Ranville crossroads, looking out over the DZ. I was by the wall when a German plane, an ME 109, flew over very low and very fast over the crossroads before turning towards the coast. The noise frightened us all but no shots were fired at it. I was stood with the PIAT on the wall of the café loaded and a few minutes later, it made the same run, directly towards me. So I fired at him, of course it was a futile shot, the speed of the plane and the PIAT's range made a hit impossible. The bomb flew up over the DZ, landed among the gliders and killed a cow grazing there.

"Being only 5ft 2in, cocking the PIAT was an absolute nightmare. The only way I could do it was by lying on my back, hooking the forward part in my crooked arms, bend my legs and put my feet on the shoulder pads, and then stretch out to the limit. On firing it would re-cock itself 90% of the time, but I carried it cocked ready as it took too long to get ready, quite often I needed help. I couldn't fire it from the hip; it would've broken my limbs and thrown me back yards. The brass primer cap which was part of the tail fin of the bomb would normally come flying back at you when you fired it, so you had to be aware all the time, as I found out later."

Captain David Tibbs (RAMC)

"Another little episode was a small boy who cycled a mile through shot and shell to ask me to see his grandmother who was ill. Somewhat reluctantly I went with him to see grandma. She was clearly near death from cardiac "asthma" and I gave her a small injection of morphine from my limited supply and returned. The next day the little boy reappeared and handed me some Franc notes, making it plain that this was a token of family gratitude for so painlessly dispatching grandma who had died overnight (a long hoped for event). I declined this reward and sent him back to the family."

Lieutenant Ellis "Dixie" Dean (MMG Platoon)

"I had seen no civilians in the village at all, but one evening a middle aged French woman turned up in the Platoon area. My French was very limited, but I was able to understand that she was the owner of a house nearby and she wanted to inspect her property. I detailed someone to accompany her to her house which had taken a direct shell hit, leaving a gaping hole in the gable end. She was soon back, ranting and raving at me and appeared to hold me personally responsible. She demanded to know why we had come to Normandy to fight the war. All the other wars had been fought elsewhere in France. Why hadn't we gone there? She really meant it, but on the whole, considering that Ranville was in the front line, damage to the homes was negligible compared to a lot of the other villages roundabout."

Major Hans Von Luck and his elements of the 21st Panzer Division took the village of St Honorine for the purpose of denying the British a commanding view of the German positions and to provide a view of the British positions. Using a battery of multiple rocket launchers and following in with 2 motorcycle companies, some grenadiers on foot and tanks of No.4 Kompanie, the village was taken.

Major Hans Von Luck (21st Panzer Division)

"I went in close behind the motorcycles and saw the enemy lines for the first time. Hundreds of gliders were lying on the ground. We dug ourselves in at once on the northern edge of the village, to secure the hill for ourselves."

Lieutenant Ellis "Dixie" Dean (MMG Platoon)

"On the morning of the 13th I came across a Brigadier and several other officers of the 51st (Highland) Division. They were spread out along the lip of the small quarry watching St Honorine through binoculars. That evening we were told to expect heavy shelling as a battalion of the 51st Division were mounting an attack on St Honorine at dawn.

"How right they were. The Platoon suffered its first casualties since D-Day. Corporal Egleton and Private Waterworth were both evacuated as a result of their wounds. Later on I went to have a look to see what happened, but all I saw were dead bodies. The attack had failed."

Major Hans Von Luck (21st Panzer Division)

"Then began the heaviest naval bombardment we had known so far. We could see the firing of the battleships, cruisers, and destroyers. The shells, of calibres up to 38cm, came whistling over like heavy trunks, to burst and rip vast craters in our lines. British fighter-bombers swooped down on us unhindered; a veritable inferno broke over our heads.

"Then, taking advantage of the haze and dust of the explosions, the British came back and after hand-to-hand fighting, with heavy losses on both sides, forced us to give up the village again. What more could we set against this superiority in naval guns and fighter-bombers?"

Around this defensive period in Ranville (14th June), Private Albert Cox died of wounds. Albert was in the Motor Transport Platoon and was one of 3 brothers, all of whom were in the 13th Parachute Battalion.

Lance Corporal George O'Connor (8 Platoon 'C' Company)

"Around this time I remember hearing the drone of planes overhead, I looked up through a space in the trees, expecting the worst, I was relieved to see, they were Flying Fortresses. They looked like minute gnats, they were so high in the sky, someone, who seemed to know, more of what was happening in Normandy, than the Generals, said they were "Carpet bombing Caen", and we knew he was right, when we heard the bombs exploding. We could see the tall chimneys at Colombelles, swaying from the effects of the blast.

"Suddenly the air was filled with low flying planes, they looked and sounded like angry wasps, they were marked with black and white stripes, we went to the side of our wood and waved our red berets at them. We watched intently as two Spitfires peeled of and strafed the German occupied wood, with machine gun and cannon fire, another plane followed them, I think it was a Typhoon, it fired rockets into the wood, and we could see smoke and flames rising in the air. As soon as the smoke subsided, we were ordered to advance to the wood. We had a close up of a German troop carrier, as we ran towards the wood. A German was hanging over the side of it and was covered in flies. I passed a couple more dead Germans laying in the long grass, I didn't stop to examine them, I was too intent on entering the wood, the Germans had until now occupied. I doubted if anyone could have lived through the strafe, but we heard a groan from behind a tree, there laid a young German soldier in a pool of blood, he had a large shrapnel wound in his chest, blood was still dripping from it. I removed the leaves away that had fallen on him and knelt down beside him, as he was trying to speak, blood spurted from his mouth and then he was dead. That was one of the moments I was sickened by war, shooting the enemy from a distance had no effect on me, but watching one die as you were holding him sickened me. We dragged him, to where the rest of his dead comrades were and continued our reccie."

In another patrol [15th June] Private Denby-Dreyfuss, a German Jew with the Intelligence Section, found 2 enemy maps on the DZ. These maps contained the plan of attack and order of battle used by the 346 Infantry Division for the 9th and 10th June as shown previously.

Corporal Tom Steer (Motor Transport Platoon)

"I came over with the transport personnel and we reached Ranville on 7th June. The Admin Platoon held their own part of the Battalion's defences north of the crossroads where we were shelled and mortared both by day and night. After Captain Elliston was killed, Sergeant Billy Webster took charge of us. There was a Bren gun post which was manned all the time and each evening before 'stand to' we would be told the time we were to be on guard there during the coming night. On June 15th the Battalion cobbler, Corporal Harry Green, came to me and asked me to change duties with him, since he had a feeling that something nasty would happen, during the time he had been detailed to be on watch. I had no such worries and so we swapped times of duty.

"My time on 'stag' was uneventful and I settled down for the few hours' kip we got during those short summer nights. Later the area was mortared and the Bren slit received a direct hit, killing Corporal Green and Private Melbourne."

Private Ken "Ginger" Oldham ('A' Company)

"The village was mortared frequently and after another bombardment, I discovered that my mate Harry Green had been killed. He'd been in a slit trench by the side of a wall in the village and a mortar bomb hit the wall and killed him."

Captain Padre Whitfield "Boy" Foy

"My own job in those early days was the burial of large numbers of members of the Division. Today, near the church at Ranville, is the 6th Airborne Division Cemetery for the Normandy campaign. When we arrived on 6th June, that site was a green field. By the time we left Ranville on the 17th June, over 160 men had been buried in that green field – and were being added to daily.

"If I believed that mankind could learn through the exhibition of the results of its folly, I would say that if only people could see the burial ground in a battle area, wars would cease. I do not believe that mankind does so learn; its imaginative faculty is so under-developed that it could see such a sight and have almost forgotten it in an incredibly short space of time. There is glory in war; there is amazing courage and patent self-sacrifice; there is a common sharing of hardship and danger which forms unbreakable friendships but the horror of the burial ground remains. Flesh torn flesh and the mangled bones are realities.

"I remember the village priest's reluctance to leave the slit trench that he had dug for himself in his garden. Necessarily in those days there were civilians as well as military casualties; and some of his parishioners were killed. But he himself never left his trench except for the most pressing reasons - and going to his parishioners was apparently not sufficiently pressing. So in addition to burying our own soldiers, we had to bury some of his parishioners. There was the very great kindness of the Comte and Comtesse who occupied the château in the centre of Ranville. They worked unceasingly among their own villagers in a place which had become the front line in one of the major military events in history."

General Richard "Windy" Gale (Commander, 6th Airborne Division)

"The church at Ranville came to mean a lot to us: it was a landmark standing clear above the village, rising above the hubbub of battle; somehow it seemed to stand for us. Though hit by shells it never fell. Coming over the bridges it greeted us. From Le Mesnil as one left the cover of the wood it marked Ranville for us.

"The divisional engineers made a cross, a fine simple cross. This we erected in our own piece of hallowed ground."

The SW wall of Ranville Church still shows its many battle scars today. Adjacent to this wall is the cemetery for the people of Ranville, one can only imagine the devastation that was caused to these tightly packed graves from by the constant mortar and shell fire.

Captain David Tibbs (RAMC)

"The local Parish priest did not distinguish himself but retreated into a slit trench from which he could not be budged to minister to his frightened parishioners. One night a German plane scattered numerous antipersonnel butterfly bombs (these are lethal if touched). To our delight one of these landed right on the edge of the priest's slit trench and I can still recall the look on his face as he peered out past it, lying there ready to explode at a touch. We did not hurry to move it!"

One official report (Account of 13th Battalion 6th June) describes the moment when the anti-British village priest finally came out of his slit trench after several days "He then emerged, kicked his dog, and returned to ground again."

Lieutenant Ellis "Dixie" Dean (MMG Platoon)

"By now life had become so uneventful, that we were all fully convinced that the Division would be soon on its way home to prepare for further airborne operations. Nothing had been said in the briefings about the length of time we would spend in Normandy, but it was generally expected that once the Infantry Divisions arrived in strength, we would be relieved."

ROLL OF HONOUR – 7th – 17th JUNE

Pte	DARBY Clifford V.	23	07/06/1944	14520557	Ranville 2A-J-10
Cpl	PARKER John W.	34	07/06/1944	3651896	Ranville Chyd 24
Capt	ELLISTON Francis A.N.	37	08/06/1944	117615	Ranville 1A-E-2
Pte	HARBERT Sidney	27	08/06/1944	1554318	Ranville 1A-H-18
Pte	CLOUSTON William	28	09/06/1944	408550	Ranville 1A-J-22
Pte	SWINDELL Robert E.	21	09/06/1944	3782725	Ranville 1A-K-22
Pte	BANKS Jack M.	22	10/06/1944	4803038	NKG Bayeux Memorial
LCpl	BROWN Alfred	31	10/06/1944	4449027	Ranville 1A-E-8
Pte	BULL Kenneth F.	18	10/06/1944	14670118	Ranville 1A-H-12
Pte	CLYNE Frederick	22	10/06/1944	3663586	Ranville 1A-B-21
Sgt	COLLIER William C.	22	10/06/1944	911708	Ranville 2A-E-12
Pte	ORRELL Alfred	19	10/06/1944	14417320	Ranville 1A-G-12
Pte	PRINCE William	29	12/06/1944	2047238	Hermanville 1-K-8
Pte	WHITEHEAD Frederick		12/06/1944	3394124	Ranville 1A-K-6
Pte	COX Albert E.	24	14/06/1944	164968	Hermanville 1-N-3
Cpl	GREEN Harry A.	27	16/06/1944	7622507	Ranville 2A-K-11
Pte	MELBOURNE Alexander	23	16/06/1944	3654790	Ranville 2A-C-11
Capt	WHITLEY Edward Neil	26	29/08/1944	252025	Buckland-in-the-Moor *

*   Died of wounds sustained by mortar/shellfire 9/10 June.

"He was quite a big lad when he did his training and it was only when he died that we found out he had lied about his age."

Major Jack Watson ('A' Company)

15. 'THE BRICKWORKS' (17th June – 17th August 1944)

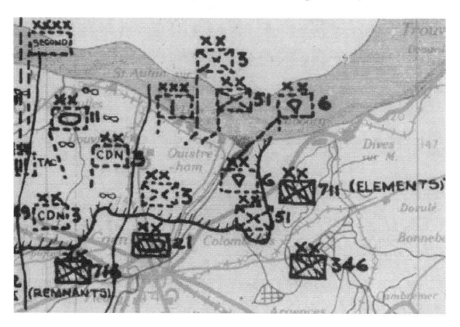

The battle for Normandy was now entering the second phase, one of mainly static defence combined with aggressive spirit comprising of sniping, patrolling and minor raids. The Allied forces had massive air-superiority and so air photography was extensively used to determine enemy mortar, artillery and armoured positions. No other place in the bridgehead in the East typified this period than at the crossroads of Le Mesnil.

The Le Mesnil crossroads in the densely wooded area of Bois de Bavent had been one of constant battle. The Canadians had held this sector and by the 17th June there were definite lines of friend or foe. Both sides had dug themselves in and now the warfare consisted of sniper and artillery fire directed on any movement.

The terrain in this area was made up of very thick undergrowth and dense trees, with many pathways and tracks making movement very difficult and dangerous. On the north side of the crossroads the land consisted mainly of pasture fields separated by thick Normandy hedgerows and ditches, therefore tanks were not really considered a threat; it was, however, ideal sniper territory and visibility was limited to a matter of yards in places and always hedgerow to hedgerow.

The opponents in this area, once again, were the 857 and 858 Grenadier Regiments of the German 346 Infantry Division. This division was now a shadow of its former self after having been battered for nearly 2 weeks continuously, prisoners brought in had told their interrogators that they had suffered 70% casualties and now operated in scratch battle-groups.

General Richard "Windy" Gale (Commander, 6th Airborne Division)

"So it came about that I was able to relieve James Hill and his tired [3rd] Brigade. Poett's brigade took over the southern part of the line, up to and exclusive of Le Mesnil. From there to Bréville were 2 battalions of the Airlanding Brigade."

Lance Corporal George O'Connor (8 Platoon 'C' Company)

"We were told to gather up our gear, as we were moving away from Ranville, we were going to advance towards the River Dives."

Lieutenant Ellis "Dixie" Dean (MMG Platoon)

"The night before we moved up to Le Mesnil, Sergeant Kelly went as our representative on the advance party to take over the existing machine gun positions and to learn a little about the conditions there.

"The means of transporting our equipment were tubular steel and canvas collapsible trolleys, which required one man to hold the handles while the remainder hitched their toggle ropes to hooks at the front and pulled along, sleigh fashion. Not surprisingly the call of encouragement was "Mush!"

"16th June was a glorious day and it was already hot before we set out to march the couple of miles to our new locations. I already knew from the maps that had been issued the previous day, that the long fields of observation enjoyed at Ranville were a thing of the past.

"We occupied the Canadians trenches sited in thick hedgerows with overhead cover. 'B' Company was forward right, 'A' on the left with 'C' in reserve to the left rear. The Anti-Tank Platoon held the crossroads and the Mortars had pits in the yard rear of the kilns. These kilns provided a bombproof shelter for the doctor and his medical orderlies. Battalion HQ occupied one of the brickworks outbuildings."

Private Ray "Geordie" Walker ('A' Company)

"On arrival at our new location a Canadian said to my pal and I "Welcome to Coffin Corner." It was an apt description, for the field in front of our position was littered with dead Germans and cows. Their bodies were bloated, grotesque and covered in flies. They remained unburied as it was too dangerous to remove them as the German frontline was within 100 yards of our trenches. The Canadian warned us that anything that moved was liable to be shot by German snipers concealed in trees."

Captain Padre Whitfield "Boy" Foy

"We were to see a lot of this little village during the 2 months that followed, for we had four spells in the line at this particular place. It was hard and nerve wracking work for our men, not only because of the constant mortaring of our positions, but also because of the interminable patrolling that had to be done. On the crossroads we held at Le Mesnil there was a large notice, which read "Warning Enemy 100 yards ahead". That was literally true. The Germans were on one side of the field and we were on the other. We had a communication trench running right along the front at one point. It was here that we learnt to respect German snipers; several men were to lose their lives because of their shooting ability."

Captain David Tibbs (RAMC)

"When the battalion moved to Le Mesnil, I first met Corporal (later Sergeant) Scott, one of my RAMC men that I had not yet caught up with, a wonderful man who became a legend in the battalion. I was visiting one of the forward companies and was immediately aware that every one was riveted by something happening ahead in 'no mans land'. Then sweating profusely, grinning broadly, in came Scott carrying over his shoulder one of our men. He spotted me and laid the man, who had been out on patrol, at my feet but, alas, he was already dead from a bullet wound that had sliced open his rib cage. My RAMC men would often go out to collect wounded men (including Germans) under the protection of a Red Cross flag or armlets. It was a dangerous game as I found out to my cost later on, but it did mean that the soldiers had an enormous respect for the RAMC who saved many lives in this way."

Private Ray Batten ('A' Company)

"During our stay at Le Mesnil we were shelled and mortared everyday. The Germans knew when it was our meal times and tried to catch us out of our fox holes. They used multi-barrelled rockets, airbursts, you name it. The multi-barrelled were the worst, bump, bump, bump, they would cover an area and there was nothing you could do. All the trees were black, no leaves or anything, it was a horrible eerie place. A horrendous stench filled the place, it was everywhere, bodies, ours and German, were left in no mans land for sometime, they couldn't be brought back in very easily. Add to this a number of dead, bloating cattle, the smell stays with you forever."

Lt Ellis "Dixie" Dean (MMG's)

"In the forward companies the only movement allowed was to collect food and to visit to the latrine. Otherwise you stood in your trench looking across to the other side of the field or orchard, where the Boche was doing the same. We quickly learned to respect their mortars; the slightest movement meant an immediate 'stonk' on that area. Artillery you could hear coming and get down, but all you heard of the mortars was the 'plonk, plonk' away in the distance and seconds later, the final swish and then it was too late to take cover. Most feared was the 'Moaning Minnie's', a multi-barrelled (six) rocket firing mortar (Above: Bundesarchiv, 101I-582-2121-22). You could hear them coming from the moment they were fired and then you prayed as hard as you could. They were an area weapon and heaven help you if they landed near you."

Private Ray "Geordie" Walker ('A' Company)

"As Coffin Corner was to be our new home for some time we made our trenches deeper and protected them with a roof of timber and earth. The Germans frequently used airburst shells and shrapnel was scattered like confetti and at times with fatal results. Across the Troarn Road and to our rear was the local brickworks and that was where our cook house was located. The brickworks manufactured roof tiles and occasionally I had a meal sitting on rows of tiles. On one occasion, whilst having breakfast, a German mortar bomb crashed through the roof and my porridge and I were covered in dust and broken tiles."

Captain Padre Whitfield "Boy" Foy

"The big man of the village was M'sieur Dupont. He was the owner of the large brickworks where the RAP was established and although he was kind in many ways, he never quite gained the confidence of the men. One reason was that he spent a good deal of his time walking round his brickworks not approving of the damage which we, as well as the Germans, were compelled to inflict on his property. This was especially true when the Brigade Sappers blew up the large chimney – it was far too good a landmark and the battalion was all around it. When he saw it totter and fall, he was clearly in a state of mental anguish."

Monsieur Dupont, the potter, had been previously ordered by the Germans to make circular pottery containers for teller mines. These containers were to protect the mines from the sea when mounted on beach obstacles to hamper landing craft. Instead he produced the containers with a clay body that looked like it was strong and suitable, but would dissolve in the sea water.

Then & Now: The unchanged buildings of the "Brickworks"

207

General Richard "Windy" Gale (Commander, 6th Airborne Division)

"We were now in a period of static defence. Consequently my great interest was to build up the enemy order of battle on my front. Where were the boundaries between formations? How wide a front was each formation opposite me holding? What were their intentions?

"Information from prisoners and deserters of which there were a few, generally Poles, showed us what the German morale was like. From them we learned something about their methods and it always seemed to me nothing short of amazing the grip and control a few German NCO's would have over whole companies of frightened, bewildered and war-sick Polish conscripts. We patrolled every night and raided the Germans opposite us."

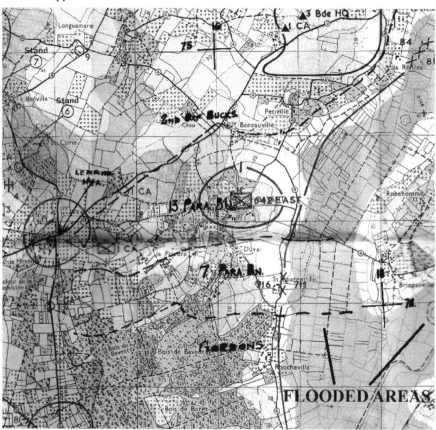

War Diary trace showing patrol boundaries (1/25,000 Sheet 40/16 NW & NE)

Lance Corporal George O'Connor (8 Platoon 'C' Company)

"The Germans came down towards us whilst we were on a patrol, one off them was waving a piece of white material and shouting "Kamerad." When they were about 20ft from us, one of the lads shouted "Halt!" they stopped and the few that had weapons, threw them down And held their hands on their heads. I never thought I would feel sorry for any of the enemy, but I did feel some sort of pity for this lot.

These weren't the proud arrogant German soldiers we had been told about. They were the most bedraggled lot of men I had ever seen, One of them had lost his helmet, he had a gash across his face, that had taken away, half his nose, another had his leg blasted open and blood was running down into his jackboot, as the tall German that was supporting him let go, he fell to the ground, sobbing "Kamerad, Kamerad".

"One of the lads shouted "Look at this". He had discovered an old 6 pounder gun, it looked as if it had come out of the ark, ore of the old cast iron wheels had been shattered by a shell or a rocket, we laughed about it, but never the less, and the old gun could have done us a lot of damage in spite of being so ancient.

"On another patrol we crept across a small field, expecting the Germans to fire at us, any minute, we carefully entered the wood, all seemed Ghostly quiet except for the rustle of leaves, the silence was broken by an explosion at the far end of the wood. I immediately dropped down on one knee, I cursed as I knelt in a puddle. I was about to stand up, when I noticed a dark metal object by the side of me. I called a Sergeant, as he came towards me I whispered to him, to cover his torch, before he shone it on the object, but let a little shaft of light shine on it so that we could see what it was. We both recognised it immediately as a butterfly anti-personal bomb, it's called a butterfly bomb for obvious reasons, it has small wings attached to it, touch one and it explodes, killing or maiming anyone in the vicinity, we had only seen photographs of them, but they were easily recognisable, the word was whispered around and we were ordered to return."

War Diary 19th June

0218   Lieut W.F. Hodgson returned from attempt to reach BAVENT with fighting patrol. Engaged enemy at 147733.

Private David "Robbie" Robinson (Anti-Tank Platoon, att. 'C' Company)

"We also sent out patrols. An incident on one of these patrols that I recall an officer, I think it was Lieutenant Hodgson. About 5 men including me went forward to patrol at night to gain information on German displacements and look for SP's.

"We set out in the dark and after passing through a wooded area in front of our lines we came upon an open meadow. I was sent along a hedgerow on a 15" high bank and took up a position where I could keep watch. I had a Bren for this patrol, and my task was to cover the rest of the patrol should they be fired on so that they might be able to return. They went forward and I lay for a long, long, long time. It seemed like weeks not hours. The patrol had gone forward under the hedgerow, about 50 yards to my right. Each sound made by the wind or wild animals scared me more and more. It was almost dawn when I heard from behind me someone whispering, "Robbie, Robbie". It was a private named Benridge who later went to 'B' Company. He had come to get me back as the patrol had gone back on the wrong side of the hedgerow leaving me stranded on my own in no mans land."

1030   Enemy SP gun reported at 146734.
1200   7 Pl ('C' Coy) attack SP gun at 146734 after mortar preparation. Pinned down before reaching objective and withdrew. Major R. Collins and 14 ORs wounded. 3 ORs missing.[24]

---

[24] Major Collins had only been OC 'C' Company for 6 days and had to be evacuated. Captain "Nobby" Clark took command in his absence.

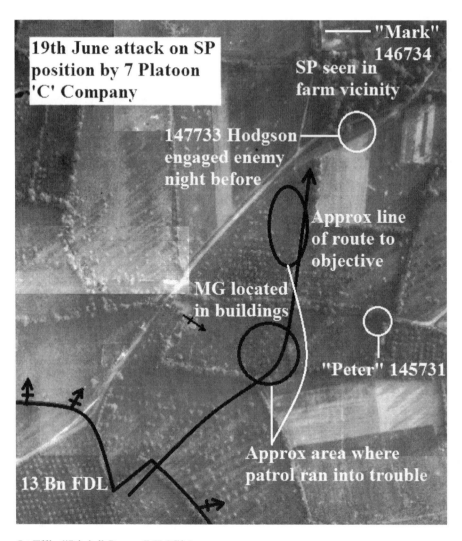

19th June attack on SP position by 7 Platoon 'C' Company

——"Mark" 146734

SP seen in farm vicinity

147733 Hodgson engaged enemy night before

Approx line of route to objective

MG located in buildings

"Peter" 145731

13 Bn FDL

Approx area where patrol ran into trouble

Lt Ellis "Dixie" Dean (MMG's)

"Typical of the patrol activities are the reports for 19th when following the return in the early hours of a patrol led by Lieutenant "Joe" Hodgson of 'A' Company, bringing information on the location of a troublesome SP, 7 Platoon were detailed to attack and destroy the vehicle. After mortar preparation they advanced, only to run into heavy machine gun fire, were pinned down and forced to withdraw. During this engagement Private Stanyon was killed, one Officer [Major Collins] and 14 OR's were wounded and 2 OR's (Sergeant Muir, and Private Denby-Dreyfuss) missing. Stanyon's body could not be recovered because it was too dangerous.

"Contact and Standing Patrols were also mounted day and night by all Companies along likely approaches into the Battalion area, but little was seen of the enemy. The purpose of the Contact Patrols was, as the name implies, to maintain surveillance of known enemy locations and so give early information of any moves by the Germans."

Private R Spooner (Intelligence Section)

"I was very much attached to Peter [Denby-Dreyfuss] no-one could know quite as well as myself the fine work that Peter did during the early stages of the invasion and the information he gained on numerous occasions was of the greatest military value, being instrumental in ensuring our brilliant success and saving the lives of many of his comrades.

"A patrol went out and made contact with the enemy. During the ensuring action they were forced to withdraw and it was then that we found Peter was missing. Several members of the Intelligence Section went forward to see what could be done and two bodies were located, but we were unable to reach them. He was killed by machine gun fire and death was instantaneous."

Lieutenant Leslie Golding (OC, Intelligence Section)

"Wherever the battle was, there he [Denby-Dreyfuss] would be found, giving spirit and encouragement to all around him. He was my interrogator and he had amazing success in all his interrogations, gaining information worth more than all my other sources put together and the means of saving many lives. When he was killed he was in the forefront of the attack instead of at the rear. For a time we did not know his fate, as he was in an unprotected position."

Lieutenant Jack Watson ('A' Company)

"Peter Denby-Dreyfuss was offered a field commission in Normandy, but again refused. He was injured quite badly in the hand on 13th June and was ordered off the frontline, but he refused! As an Intelligence member his place was behind the fighting troops but Peter insisted on trying to get near the enemy lines to gain as much information as he could."

Lt Golding (OC, Intelligence Section)

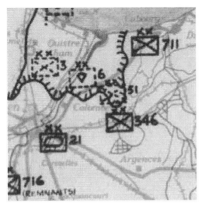

"An ordinary man would have allowed himself to be evacuated with the wound in his hand he had sustained previously, but characteristically he protested so much that the medical people allowed him to remain."

War Diary 20th June

(Situation map, left)

1120   *Quiet morning and afternoon - rifle grenades containing propaganda leaflets fired on our posns.*

211

Lieutenant Ellis "Dixie" Dean (MMG Platoon)

"One morning I heard the swish of bombs and ducked in my slit trench, but the bombs must have been duds I thought. There must have been a slight breeze, for scraps of paper started blowing about. We had experienced a propaganda raid and the leaflets were eagerly collected and were a cause of great amusement.

"They contained the information that London was ablaze, the result of attacks by the secret weapons the Germans had developed. Nobody worried about the leaflets since we were nearly all northerners and we regarded them as a joke. They were put to good use, since the daily issue was only three small sheets per man."

Lt-Col Peter Luard CO, 13 Bn)

"Of the 3 dogs dropped, one was missing and one wounded, but "Bing" (left, IWM, Duxford), though slightly wounded by mortar fire survived. This Alsatian with his handler, Lance Corporal Ken Bailey, held the right hand post, adjacent to the Bois de Bavent. They were on duty all night in their own personal slit trench."

Major John Cramphorn ('A' Company)

"Life at the brickworks was dull and monotonous, so to liven things up and have a bit of fun, we constructed a giant catapult out of timber and twisted ropes. This contraption we used to hurl bricks and stones at the German positions only the other side of the field.

"There was another occasion during the usual nightly mortaring, a haystack at the deserted farm between ourselves and the enemy, was hit and set on fire. The flames were lighting up all our weapon slits and I decided that we must put out the fire. While we were doing so, I turned to give instructions to the soldier working alongside me who turned out to be a German. My opposite number on the other side of the field had obviously the same thoughts about the blaze as I did.

"While some of us were busy fire fighting the Germans tried to infiltrate a patrol, but we could see them coming and put the whole lot in the bag, one at a time as they crawled through a gap in the hedge."

Private Ray "Geordie" Walker ('A' Company)

"It was during our stay at Coffin Corner that our senses of sight, sound and smell became acute. We could smell a German from several yards as they had a distinct body odour caused by the use of ersatz soap and the stale smell of German and Turkish cigarette smoke on their uniforms.

"Life had its moments of drama. One night Lance Corporal Ron Hawthorn and I were detailed to go and collect our rum ration. On our return we came under fire from a German machine gun firing on fixed lines. After having dived into a nearby ditch three times for protection Ron said "If we are to die let's have our rum ration now." Duly fortified with the rum we made it safely back to our trenches at Coffin Corner."

Lt Stan "Jev" Jeavons ('B' Company)

"From the enemy lines 200 yards away, a German officer rose, waving a rifle, bayonet glistening in the Normandy sun. As we watched, the solitary German advanced. Someone pushed a Lee-Enfield rifle into my hands. I, too, climbed out of my trench and awaited the foe. But if the Nazi had some bizarre, noble duel in mind, I certainly had not. After weeks in the killing fields of Normandy I had no illusions of needless gallantry. This bloke seemed to be thinking of a bayonet fight, it was the last thing I had in mind. When he got within a few yards, I shot him dead. I never felt any guilt and never suffered any nightmares."

Lieutenant Ellis "Dixie" Dean (MMG Platoon)

"Late one morning [22nd June] there was a heavy mortaring and someone called from over the road that Sergeant Osborne was wounded. I dashed across and found him out of his trench, lying on his face unconscious. I sent someone to the RAP for a stretcher and knelt down for a closer look. The only sign of wounds visible was a severe bleeding from one leg above the knee and before I could take any action, the medics arrived and I helped to place him on the stretcher before he was taken away. There were other wounds not noticed by me and I was informed the next day that these had proved fatal.

"I had to find a replacement Section Commander and after discussion with Freddie Skeate (Mortars), Lance Corporal Arthur Higgins was promoted to Sergeant and given command of No.2 Section. It was a decision I never regretted and such rapid promotions were occurring throughout the Battalion as the natural fighting leaders revealed themselves."

War Diary 22nd June

2030   *Another party - This time one of our contact patrols located enemy at 146730. They threw a grenade, killing two, and withdrew. The enemy then mortared our standing patrol at the Farm 143731 from 146730 and from Wood 147727. Our mortars promptly put a concentration on both of these, and thereafter every time they fired we replied fourfold (which is now our policy). When all enemy posns were quietened, a further conc was put down on the patrol from 146735 - these bombs actually fell near their own posns at 146730 - before our mortars could reply, 12 Devons put down a concentration on WOOD 146735 which effectively silenced the battery there. Action ended at midnight.*

2200   *During the battle, movement of tkd vehs was heard eastwards from WOOD 146735 - presumably these are SP guns pulling out for the night. In case of tks, 'A' Coy laid mines on rd EAST of standing patrol.*

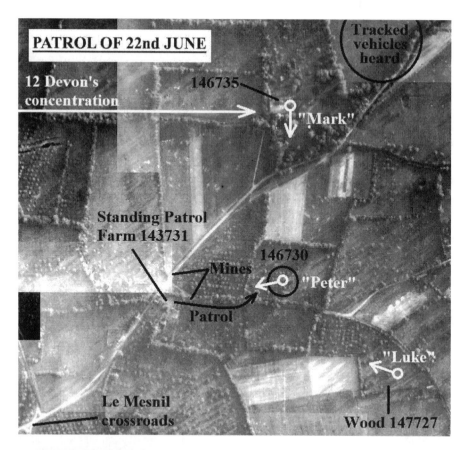

PATROL OF 22nd JUNE

12 Devon's
concentration

146735

**Tracked
vehicles
heard**

"Mark"

Standing Patrol
Farm 143731

Mines

146730

"Peter"

Patrol

"Luke"

Le Mesnil
crossroads

Wood 147727

Private John Frances (left) was eventually evacuated back to England after being mortared. He had suffered shrapnel wounds to the head on the 23rd June. It was not just the mortars that soldiers had to be beware of, as one man of 'A' Company was wounded by a sniper - whilst burying German dead.

One 'B' Company patrol at the farm 143735 was approached by 2 Germans and patrol leader Alan Badel of the Intelligence Section, shot one dead, the patrol them quickly pulled out and then 30 minutes later they returned and recovered the body, from which they found to be from the 858 Gren Regt, 346 Inf Div.

Lieutenant Ellis "Dixie" Dean (MMG Platoon)

"Our first occupation of the Le Mesnil position was coming to its mainly uneventful close and on the 25th June we learnt that the following day we would be relieved by the 12th Battalion and we were going for a 5 day rest on the banks of the River Orne."

Lance Corporal George O'Connor (8 Platoon 'C' Company)

"We reached the bridges and we passed a couple of gliders that had been badly battered about, Military Police, were directing traffic across the bridges. One bridge that had already been named, 'Pegasus Bridge' was being crossed by tanks and troops, the troops were shouting at us, "you lucky bastards you're going home, we'll finish the rest of the Jerries off for you". How wrong they were. We stopped at a small piece of green beside the bridges and were told we would be rested here. We removed our equipment, undressed, jumped in the water and indulged in the luxury of a swim."

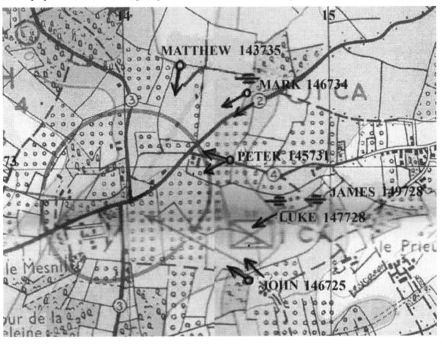

War Diary Night 24th/25th June

2350   Bn area heavily shelled and mortared, 7 Para Bn being shelled also. Sounds of enemy MG fire. 'B' Coy reported attack on their front.

0110   7 Para Bn firing – presumably being attacked.

0025   Area still being shelled and mortared. Our mortars engaged all known enemy locations.

0028   "PETER" on fire!! Lt Jeavons concussed and one OR killed by direct hit on slit trench.[25]

Private Ray "Geordie" Walker ('A' Company)

"On the 25th June the Germans decided they would give 13th Para a night to remember. Just before midnight they opened up with a terrific barrage of shelling and mortaring. This would prove the heaviest bombardment we would endure during all our fighting.

---

[25] The above map (1/25,000 40/16 NW & NE) of the Le Mesnil crossroads, has the appendix trace from the War Diary overlaid. It shows all the known German mortar and artillery positions. They were given the codenames "MATTHEW", "MARK", "PETER", "JAMES", "LUKE" and "JOHN".

"During this action my pal Cecil Smith and I occupied a trench on top of a dyke adjacent 'Charlie's Farm'. Our situation was precarious and we were pleased when our Platoon Commander [Lt "Joe" Hodgson] joined us and gave us moral support, as a couple of teenagers we were glad of his presence. By now our position had become untenable and Lieutenant Hodgson ordered me to run back to Company HQ and inform Major Cramphorn that he was withdrawing from our trench as it would soon cease to exist.

"Running as fast as possible across a field I delivered my message and on making my way back to Lieutenant Hodgson I stumbled across a body lying at the foot of a tree. By the light of the gun flashes I was looking at my pal Cyril; he had been killed by a shrapnel wound to the head. His death saddened me because we had been pals for seven months. Many years were to pass before I learned that his real Christian name was Cecil. It was common practice to identify friends by nickname only."

Private Ray Batten ('A' Company)

"Whilst we were in our trenches we saw a couple of the 'Buzz Bombs' pass overhead on route to London. We were mortared daily and during one heavy barrage at Le Mesnil, my trench received a direct hit. The mortar round blew me about 6 ft in the air, and when I crashed back down, I turned to the Bren gunner, [Cecil] Smith, who was sharing the trench with me and asked if he was ok. He wasn't, he'd had half his face blown off."

Captain Padre Whitfield "Boy" Foy

"From about 11pm the torrent of mortar fire went on; the whole area was literally plastered. In spite of the terrific danger of movement in the open, casualties had to be brought in when trenches received direct hits. The medics had a gruelling task and responded magnificently.

"Stretchers were actually blown out of their hands by bomb blast and yet they themselves were unscathed at the end of the night. The men in the front line sat

waiting to see if this was the prelude to an attack, as well it might have been. Our own mortars went into action and worked themselves to a standstill. The RAP in the brickworks received several direct hits, because of the thickness of the roof the bombs did not penetrate, but sent down the most appalling showers of dust, which on occasions drove us out into the open bombs or no bombs. And all the time casualties had to be collected, treated and evacuated. It was a pitch black night, visibility nil, and the road down to the MDS in Ranville seemed endless.

"Lance Corporal [Stanley] Ware (of 'B' Company, left) was hit in the neck by shrapnel and was brought in to the RAP unable to speak. An urgent tracheotomy was needed to save his life. Doctor Tibbs patched him up quickly and I set off for the MDS with him in a Jeep. Never shall I forget the journey down the hill to Ranville. We crept through the inky darkness slowly because every jolt was dangerous to the wounded man. I felt personally responsible for every bump in the road and every lurch of the Jeep gave me a sick feeling as I thought of the possible effect on the man behind me. The menace of approaching vehicles was terrible.

Neither we nor they carried any form of light, on no less than 3 occasions we stopped with the bonnet no more than a foot or two from the oncoming car. When we finally arrived at our destination, the man was still alive, but two days later at the General Field Hospital, I was grieved to learn that he had died. He had been so terribly brave.

"On the next journey to the MDS on that frightful night, I took a man [Lance Corporal Victor Lightfoot, right] whose legs and thighs had been smashed to smithereens. For 2 miles I heard his agonised screams behind and all I could do was drive at walking pace. He died 5 minutes after reaching the MDS."

Private Ray "Geordie" Walker ('A' Company)

"By dawn the noise of battle abated and with it the realisation that I was still alive. We now waited the final onslaught of tanks and infantry. For some explicable reason they never launched an attack. Now we could relax a little, take stock of our situation and count our dead and wounded. Viewing the field I had run across during the night, I was amazed to see it had a wire barrier and a metal notice bearing the skull and crossbones and the German word "Minen". Luck had obviously been with me that night and for which I was grateful."

Lieutenant Stan "Jev" Jeavons ('B' Company)

"I was nearly killed by a German shell. Suddenly, slap! One landed straight in the trench. They managed to dig out my head but the shelling was so bad they had to leave me. I slipped in to a coma after losing blood from leg wounds and awoke days later in a military hospital in Britain before I was invalided out of the service."

Stan's batman, Private Eric Prew was not so lucky. He was sat having a cigarette in the bottom of the slit trench with Stan when the same shell buried him alive, suffocating him.

Captain Padre Whitfield "Boy" Foy

"There were other casualties that night. Major Bristow ['B' Company] was severely blasted by a mortar bomb that landed close. He complained about his leg but there were tears in his clothing and there appeared to be no wounds. Later we learned that he was close to losing his leg. Many small particles of dust had penetrated his leg. Gangrene set in and he had a very narrow escape.

"Daylight was creeping in by the time the tumult died down. We brewed some tea, lay down in utter weariness of body and soul and called it a day. In a room behind the RAP were the men who had seen their last fighting the men who had not recovered. As I lay down, I wondered if we would be able to afford blankets for their burials next day. Then we slept."

War Diary 25th June

1300   Handover to 1 Cdn Para Bn completed and Bn moved to rest area near RANVILLE on banks of R.ORNE.

Private Ray "Geordie" Walker ('A' Company)

"Shortly after this action we were withdrawn from the frontline for a well earned rest in a field beside the River Orne. Whilst marching past the brickworks at le Mesnil we were met by General Gale, who thanked us for a job well done.

"On arrival at our rest camp we could now inspect our feet for the first time in three weeks. On removing my boots and socks I could see that my feet were in a sorry state. Typical of 'trench feet', I could peel layers of dead skin from the soles of my feet. It was in this camp that we enjoyed our first full nights sleep since D-Day. During this period I had my first opportunity to write home using a 'Field Service Postcard'.

"We were provided with lorries to take us to a mobile shower unit which the Royal Engineers had erected in a field near Hermanville. Here we could have a hot shower and collect a clean change of underclothes."

Private David "Robbie" Robinson (Anti-Tank Platoon)

"We lost a few men around this time. Corporal Simpson, who had been our stick commander on D-Day, was wounded in the heavy shelling and mortaring of late June and I remember that Falkingham, Lt Lagergren's batman, was wounded in an accident involving one of our own grenades whilst we were in the rest area. He did recover, but he never took part in any of the next campaigns that we were involved in."

Lieutenant Ellis "Dixie" Dean (MMG Platoon)

"The MMG Platoon was attached to 'A' Company for the rest duration and we lived on the river bank. I found a suitable piece of ground where we could zero 3 new Vickers guns. The site of this range was half a mile towards the coast and I mentioned to Major Cramphorn what I had in mind. "Good" he said "I've got some Bren guns that haven't been zeroed. I'll send a party along with you." Early afternoon we set off cross the fields for the large sandy bank and zeroed the guns and set off on the return journey. No-one told me that the coastal strip east of the mouth of the Orne had not been cleared and we came under fire from a solitary machine gun."

Corporal Ronald Minnery ('A' Company)

"Sometime later, near the end of June, we were in a rest area on the North bank of the River Orne and Canal. We had at this time acquired quite a number of German equipment in particular MG's, and it was decided that we ought to train with them in order to find out their usefulness. In the marshy land towards the coast there were some firing ranges and it was walking back from these, along the top of dykes and without a care in the world that an MG opened up on us. I was hit in the thigh and the bullet came out through my backside. Private Armitage was also hit, more badly so than me. He complained of a burning in his stomach and died about a week later (7th July). He was a very staunch Roman Catholic and would always help others whenever they needed any assistance. I was eventually evacuated and ended up in Aintree Hospital, Liverpool and was visited by my Mother and Father the day I arrived there."

Captain Padre Whitfield "Boy" Foy

"Nearby was Divisional HQ dug in to the side of a quarry and heavily sandbagged; it was a position which was safe as the Rock of Gibraltar. Again and again I have been amused by the attitude shown to HQ staff at the different levels in the army. The members of a platoon in an infantry battalion make some scathing comments about their Company HQ staff, and this although Company HQ may only be 10 or 20 yards away from forward platoon positions. In the same way all members of a Company have a considerable, if unusually unspoken contempt for those who make up Battalion HQ, because "they are not fighting men". On a higher level, the members of a Battalion roundly criticise Brigade HQ, who are "never in a fight" and whose chief occupation is "sending of wrong orders". Divisional HQ comes in for even more criticism because they are still further back. As for Corps HQ, they haven't even "heard a shot fired in anger", while Army HQ are only "civilians masquerading in service dress.""

"I paid a visit to Divisional HQ to find out whether any welfare amenities were available, and was asked why I had gone through the 'usual channels'. I had already asked Brigade, whose reply was "we are waiting for Division. The Divisional HQ told me "are waiting for Corps HQ". I went directly to Corps HQ and obtained the first of our welfare supplies."

Lieutenant Ellis "Dixie" Dean (MMG Platoon)

"I took a truck load of 'A' Company down to 'Sword' beach; this meant our first glimpse of the vital bridges over the Orne River and Canal and to see the gliders so close to the objectives. Down on the sands we talked to members of the King's Regiment and compared experiences. They regarded us as supermen, but having seen the devastation on the shore line, littered with abandoned landing craft and knocked out tanks, and also seen the undamaged pill boxes and gun emplacements, I know who had experienced the easier way of invading. My young sons comment when he first asked what I had done in the war sums it up nicely. "You cheated; you landed in the dark when all the Germans were in bed asleep!""

"Another evening I accompanied a party to Luc-Sur-Mer, to see in the local cinema, Charlie Chester and his 'Stars in Battledress' show, with the 13th contingent giving their loudest cheers to "Boy" Foy the Royal Command performer on his unicycle."

Private Ray "Geordie" Walker ('A' Company)

"The weather at this time was hot and during the lull in fighting two of my pals and I decided to take an unofficial swim in the canal and in our birthday suits. Whilst in the water two nuns came along the canal towpath with some children. To avoid embarrassment we swam into the reed bed. The leading nun told us not to be embarrassed despite having seen us in the nude. Life had its lighter moments despite the war."

The month of June had passed leaving the 13th (Lancashire) Parachute Battalion well under its operational strength. They had completed the allotted D-Day tasks, fought off numerous counter-attacks, relieved the Canadians in the Bois de Bavent and been subjected to a constant barrage of mortar and shell fire for nearly a month.

Casualties to date numbered 203 and consisted of 40 dead, 125 wounded and 38 missing. On top of these losses, Major Harris MC, Captain Kerr, Lieutenant Metcalf and Lieutenant Bercot were all transferred to the 12th (Yorkshire) Parachute Battalion. Captain Elliston had been killed and Major Collins, Lieutenant Arnold, Lieutenant Sharples, Lieutenant Pollak and Lieutenant Jeavons had all been wounded along with Captain Ainsworth breaking his leg during the drop early on D-Day.

War Diary 25th June to 5th July

Bn resting in Div rest area since 25 June 44. Time devoted to PT, recreation, cleaning and repair of arms, etc. Vacancies for film and other shows were allotted and trips to the beaches were organised. 100 infantry reinforcements arrived 3.7.44.

Private Alfred Draper (South Staffordshire Regiment)

"The division that the South Staffs had belonged to had so many casualties that it was disbanded and on Sunday 2nd July we were paraded in the usual way and about 100 of us were given postings. Nobody told us where but we were loaded onto lorries and driven off. Some said we were going to join the Airborne Division and were laughed at. Then we saw wrecked gliders in fields and all the troops had red berets on. We turned off the road into a field, the HQ of the 13th Parachute Battalion!

"We were distributed round the Battalion two per section. This made up the sections to five, they should have been ten. The section (I went in) was part of 8 Platoon 'C' Company. Our Commander was Major "Nobby" Clark, a first rate bloke who looked after his men. Bob Giles was the lad I joined the section with and because we were outsiders we became very close mates."

Lance Corporal George O'Connor (8 Platoon 'C' Company)

"Some infantry men arrived; they were replacements for the men we had lost. I was allocated 2 men, I found Chalky and Yorky and I now had a section of 5 including me. An Officer arrived, he wasn't a paratrooper, and I don't know if he came with the Infantry men. He looked very smart and clean, as if he had come straight from the Training College."

Private Ronald "Rolly" Pilling (MT Platoon)

"I had landed on Gold Beach in the early hours of the seaborne attack on the morning of D-Day. I was a member of the 8th (Irish) Battalion, The King's (Liverpool) Regiment and our task was the security of that particular invasion beach. Once it was certain the landings were a success the battalion was broken up and I was posted to the 13th as an infantry reinforcement, but I got no further than Brigade HQ where I became driver to Major Lough, the DAQ. I remained there in that job for the rest of the war in Europe and did not reach the 13th until we were in the Far East."

Private Ray "Geordie" Walker ('A' Company)

"Frequently our rest camp was over flown by a lone Messerschmitt 109 on route to strafe targets in the beachhead during the late summer evenings. The unknown pilot was 'lucky' for he avoided being shot down. However, on our return to the frontline and while marching up the long hill from Ranville to le Mesnil, Herr Schnicklegruber, our nickname for this pilot, was shot down. He baled out but his parachute failed to open. Our elation at his defeat turned to sadness as we witnessed his fall to death."

The 9th Para Bn had been in occupation of the Le Mesnil positions for over a week and the first thing they had to do was to repair and improve the battered trenches and dugouts because they took over from the 13th Bn after the heavy bombardment of 25th June. The 9th Bn had been suffering further heavy casualties since D-Day and the taking of the Merville Battery, and now only had 11 Officers [2 of which were the Padre and Medical Officer] and 177 other ranks left. They had to reorganise into 2 Rifle Companies instead of the usual 3. On 5th July the 13th Bn returned to the positions to take back over the from the now very weary 9th Bn. To add to 9 Para's misery, the heavy rains had filled their dugouts in the rest area at Ecarde and they needed to be bailed out before they could at last rest.

The front line in Le Mesnil had now been pushed forward by approximately one field (below) whilst the 13th had been away in the rest area.

During this short 24 hour stay in Le Mesnil, Private Robert Richards (right) of 'C' Company was killed at 2030 hours in one of the frequent mortar attacks.

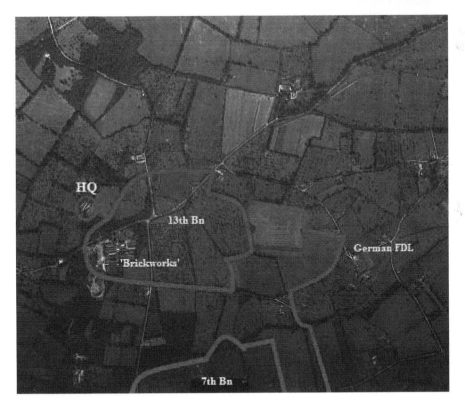

Private Alfred Draper (South Staffs Regt att. 8 Platoon 'C' Company)

"We moved to the front line, Bob and I went in with fear and trepidation. All around us were dead animals and the smell was terrible. There were the occasional shells passing overhead, which the old hands said were from the battleships out at sea shelling the German positions. It seems we were worrying for nothing."

Lieutenant Ellis "Dixie" Dean (MMG Platoon)

"Our second stay [in Le Mesnil] only lasted 24 hours before we marched back again and moved into the grounds of the Château de Benouville. During our rest period the 7th Battalion had failed in an attack to wipe out the garrison of a farm, believed to be the Boche HQ. The 13th were to carry out the task in a night attack and had come out of the line to rehearse.

"First we had to dig shelters and then in the early evening Bomber Command of the RAF put on another magnificent demonstration of air power in yet another attempt by 2nd Army to capture the town of Caen, which was only four miles inland from us. No warning of the attack had been given to us and in the evening sunlight we watched as a single Lancaster flew across our front and then released a shimmering cascade of silver lights, marking the target. Not far behind came a steady stream of other four engine air craft and we could clearly see the bombs leave the bomb bays and start their fall. More coloured markers, red and green added colour to the spectacle and the Ack Ack guns roared into action, with the shells bursting among the Halifaxes and Lancasters. But they flew on regardless of the danger. As the bombs exploded a great cloud of smoke started to rise, getting progressively higher as time went on. We stopped counting the number of planes involved and the later arrivals had the easier run in, as the flak guns either ran out of ammunition or were destroyed by the bombing.

"All together we carried out three rehearsals for the attack and then it was cancelled. The CO had queried the tactical value of the plan, which would result in the Battalion being marooned several hundred yards away, in German held territory and his view prevailed. So it was back to Le Mesnil. Instead of the Battalion attack a Company of the 7th, repeating a previous exploit of theirs, were to carry out a day time raid on the same objective. This would be launched from 'B' Company's area and the Machine Gunners (some one had informed the CO of the Platoons recently acquired ability to provide indirect fire) were to isolate the right flank of the enemy in the farm."

War Diary - 10th July

1100   Take-over from 12 Para Bn completed - posns as before. A certain amount of shelling and mortaring of our posns was caused by a raid carried out by 7 Para Bn on our right. It was noted that the enemy guns and mortars were in action 10 minutes after our arty conc started and 6-barrelled mortars 50 minutes after.[26] During the night contact patrols made contact with enemy posns, reporting no change in previous locations.

Corporal George Simpson (Anti-Tank Platoon)

"I was part of a group detailed to create a diversion on the left, while the real attack went in on the other flank [by 7 Para]. We moved up to the ruined farm ahead of the cross roads and waited for zero hour. 1700 hours, dead on time, the first 3" mortar smoke bomb landed on the enemy just up the road and we opened fire too. Jerry hit back with everything he had a machine gun on a fixed line was firing along the top of the hedge on my right and their mortars came into action. I dived for cover and then

---

[26] Private Donald Lord was killed instantly by a mortar bomb at 1500 hours. Sergeant George Dixon of 'A' Company also passed away on this day in Hermanville Field Hospital, after being wounded by the accidental discharge of a Bren gun.

"thump, thump, thump" I'd been hit in the head, arm, chest and stomach, I assumed by shrapnel.

"Back at the RAP, before I was evacuated, I was visited by both Lieutenant Lagergren and Colonel Luard. This was a big comfort to me. Back in Bayeux in the Field Hospital, they removed two large calibre machine gun bullets, which must have been ricocheted off the walls of the farm. After a week, I was sent back to England and was in hospital until Christmas. I was down graded to B1, and sent to the Reserve Battalion at Beverley. I thought, 4 years training for 4 weeks fighting."

Lieutenant Ellis "Dixie" Dean (MMG Platoon)

"For 15 minutes (the expected duration of the raid) the gunners fired away and then took cover, because as anticipated, the Germans responded with a devastating barrage by guns and mortars. It was every bit as fearsome as the night pounding a fortnight earlier. Fortunately it did not last quite as long and the casualties were not as serious for the 13th. One of the shelters, housing a complete (Vickers) gun team, received three direct hits from mortar bombs on the roof. The occupants, Privates Barnett, Strachan and Stevenson were all in a state of shock and refused to leave the shelter. The detachment commander was rather hysterical also. Of the three Privates only Tommy Stevenson returned. The NCO had lost the confidence of the other members of the Platoon; he had been affected by the frequent shelling we were subjected to. I asked for him to be transferred to a rifle platoon where sadly he was killed a little later.

"But the raid was not a success. The German HQ (a farmhouse nicknamed "Bob's Farm") was protected by a minefield in which the raiding party was trapped and suffered innumerable casualties and were forced to abandon the assault. Imagine how much higher would have been the casualty rate and more difficult the withdrawal, had the Battalion's night attack gone ahead as originally planned in the dark."

Citation: Private Bertram Henry Roe [27]

Award: Military Medal

On 10th July 1944 the forward company position to which Private Roe was attached, was in forward positions very close to the enemy lines. The area was subjected to heavy artillery and mortar fire from 1640 hours until 1930 hours. During this time Private Roe attended to, dressed, and carried to the rear five wounded men. He went about his duties with the utmost calm and disregard for his own danger throughout the worst of the shelling. When carrying a badly wounded man to the rear, on a stretcher, with another RAMC orderly, the road was heavily mortared. The stretcher was put on the ground and one man sheltered in the ditch while Private Roe protected the wounded man, lying on the stretcher, with his own body, though bombs were landing within a few feet of him. Throughout this action Private Roe has shown complete disregard for his own safety and the highest sense of his own duty.

---

[27] Private Roe was one of the conscientious objectors.

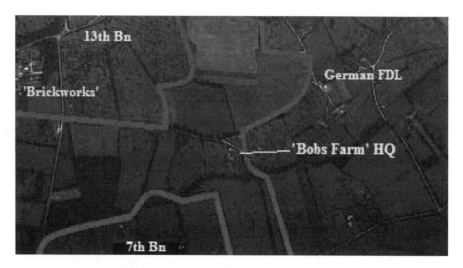

Captain Padre Whitfield "Boy" Foy

"The battalion on our right [7th Para Bn] sent out an urgent SOS for Bren and Sten ammunition. Sergeant Webster personally organised the collection and delivery, under heavy mortar fire, to their forward positions. But finally the Germans got him in the leg. He was brought to the RAP and began to protest vigorously about being evacuated to the MDS. Nevertheless he was sent back. Within two days he was back with the Battalion, he had managed to persuade the MO to let him out, or he ran out, it never really was established.

"Unfortunately when he got back, his arrival coincided with the visit of the surgeon, who took one look at him and sent him straight back, much to Webster's disgust. That was the end of the Normandy campaign for him."

Lieutenant Ellis "Dixie" Dean (MMG Platoon)

"Years after the war ended, I learned what an enormous debt of gratitude all survivors of the Normandy campaign, owed the Colonel for his courageous opposition to the proposed night attack on the German HQ.

"During the final assault by the Company raid of the 7th Battalion, the attacking force was isolated in an anti-personnel mine field covered by machine guns and the casualties were only evacuated with great difficulty. How much more serious would have been the 13th's casualties, had we attacked in the dark

"No medals are awarded for this type of courage shown by Colonel Luard, but he put the welfare of us all, before the chance of military glory, and we must respect him even more for this."

War Diary 11th July

No activity during day apart from occasional mortar and MG fire. At dusk the enemy put up illuminating flares at odd intervals. During the night Bn RAMC personnel assisted by 'C' Coy recovered bodies of Pte Denby-Dreyfuss and Pte Stanyon, which had been lying in disputed ground. Two patrols were sent out to determine extent of enemy wiring, and returned with the required information, having

224

penetrated as far as the houses at 149727, where they heard movement, and hedge junc 146728, where voices were heard.

Captain Padre Whitfield "Boy" Foy

"During the first stay in Le Mesnil, we had a patrol that was split up because of opposition and came back without 3 of its members. It was a month later before we recovered two of the bodies and it was not until the great advance begun, in the third week in August that the third man was picked up.

"One of the first two to be recovered was Private Denby-Dreyfuss, a German refugee Jew himself, who had proved himself a singularly brave man and who loathed Nazis much more heartily than the average Britisher.

"Although living conditions were bad, the officers at HQ ran what we were pleased to call a 'mess'. Battalion HQ was situated in a reinforced barn in a corner of which was a tiny apartment about 10 feet square. There we ate our meals together, the CO, 2nd I/C, Adjutant IO, Signals Officer, the MO and myself. The conversation we had been among the most absorbing I have ever had. The MO (Dr Tibbs) and I actually slept in the brickworks at the RAP and on the way to the BHQ was a lane which became known as 'Bomb Alley'."

Private Alfred Draper (South Staffs Regt att. 8 Platoon 'C' Company)

"Shells and mortars came down quite regularly, but the worst was the 'Moaning Minnies'. These multi-barrelled mortars made a moaning sound. Everyone within ½ mile radius of where they would land felt they were coming straight to him. Eventually I got used to them, but it took time.

"With all the danger and the noise there were a few cases of shell shock – mostly amongst us newcomers. It could happen after a very heavy bombardment or it could come on slowly over several days. One man in the platoon was starting to go and he was put in a dugout with me. He was given a cup of rum and to keep his mind off things until the ambulance arrived. I was nearly as bad as he was by the time it arrived.

"Snipers were another hazard. Any carelessness of exposing yourself brought a bullet your way. It was worth walking the long way round, rather than take a short cut across an opening in a hedge."

Snipers were a constant source of trouble for the 13th Battalion in the Bois de Bavent and to help counteract the problem, Major Steven Sykes from the 'Camouflage Pool' of the Royal Engineers was attached to the 6th Airborne Division on the 6th July and had just finished his first task.

Major Steven Sykes (Camouflage Officer, Royal Engineers)

"My job was to try to organise that [supply] dumps in a large area of the countryside were disposed for quick dispersal as widely and as soon as possible, and I had to make sure that the stores were placed in such a way that they were not obvious – that according to one's knowledge of air reconnaissance they would look part of the countryside.

"On the 10th July I saw the G1, who suggested the concentration on sniper concealment and decoys. This was very satisfactory from my point of view – a positive activity which the fighting troops had requested. It was very easy to proceed too far down the sheltered lanes and into enemy territory. This had now become a sniper war – static, with no attempt to advance. I had to do practical instruction. In fact it was a case of instructing troops in situ. You never knew how close you were to the Germans, and a hedgerow would, over its length, be shared by Germans at one end and the Airborne at the other.

"On 11th July the Airborne G1 wanted, or thought he wanted, a very realistic figure for the sniper decoys he was suggesting. He told me of an artist (a potter actually) whose factory was more or less in the front line near Le Mesnil. I had been astonished at the number of ceramic cats stalking ceramic birds on the roofs of the villas [on the coast]."

Monsieur Dupont, the owner of the pottery as mentioned by Padre Foy, was not able to help with the creation of a sculptured sniper, apart from that, no reasonable sniper would allow himself to be easily seen, so Major Sykes visited the various battalions to find out what exactly the solution should be. He continues:

"In all cases the answers were the same. Could I concoct a good disguise for our snipers which the men could construct themselves; also, could I devise a way of drawing enemy sniper fire on to a dummy, so that the angle of penetration could be noted as we were losing a lot of men among the hedges? When a man has been shot it is hard to know where the shot has come from, whereas clues could be gained from an in or out mark on, say, a cardboard tube. I produced for them dummy figures which were made from available ammunition cartons, with an airborne helmet on top. It looked like a man using an airborne smock. These dummies had to be rather carefully constructed and placed so that they could be raised to draw fire and pulled down again for examination.

"12th July. Diary notes, 'Make sniper hoods at Field Park in morning. To 5th Brigade and 13th Battalion afternoon. Try out sniper suit in most exposed positions. No response from Germans.' Hard work was put into preparing and delivering sniper hoods and printing 70 yards of hessian for 13th Battalion screens.

"To procedure in trying to sell the sniper hoods was to arrange to call the HQ, usually in some deserted house and ask the Colonel and HQ staff to hide their eyes for a few minutes. Sergeant Heath would then put a hood on and quickly take cover among some suitable bushes, generally only a few yards away. They would then emerge from the house and look for the 'sniper'.

"The disguise was remarkably effective. If the mixture of colours, greens and browns in the garnishing of the sandbag smock was near that of the undergrowth it was somewhat impossible, even at very close range, to see where the figure was."

Lieutenant Ellis "Dixie" Dean (MMG Platoon)

"During the morning of 12th July a strange little incident involving Lieutenant Gordon O'Brien-Hitching [OC of No.1 Platoon, left] occurred. He was the only subaltern in the Battalion who held a regular commission and had transferred from a cavalry unit. Lacking knowledge of infantry tactics his answer to every situation was to charge, hence his nickname of "Crasher". According to Dr Tibbs, he also claimed to be bulletproof, but the events of that morning proved him wrong."

Private Ray Batten ('A' Company)

"On one patrol we came across a hedge and saw movement amongst it. We went back and reported what we saw and where it was. Lt O'Brien-Hitching did not believe us and went out to see for himself. He was a bit rash and it cost him, the standing patrol shot him."

Captain Padre Whitfield "Boy" Foy

"Two medical orderlies moved forward along the hedgerow to pick him up, but there was considerable fire at close range and it was impossible to get near him. One of them crawled back to the platoon area in order to get covering fire. The watchers from the platoon saw Private Graham Corbett leave the hedgerow and walk across the open to the wounded officer. Corbett picked Lieutenant O'Brien-Hitching, put him on his shoulders and walked steadily with him into the German lines."

Private Graham Corbett (RAMC)

"I went out to retrieve Lieutenant O'Brien-Hitching after I noticed that he was still alive and badly wounded, as I was picking him up, I noticed a German soldier hiding in the hedgerow nearby and he was pointing his rifle, bayonet fixed, at us. He motioned me with his weapon towards the German positions. I knew the officer was in a bad way and thought it was his best chance to obey the German and hope to get him medical treatment there. Shortly after arriving at the German HQ, he died and they ransacked our pockets looking for cigarettes and anything else useful. They didn't even interrogate me. I spent the rest of the war as a POW."

Lieutenant O'Brien-Hitching never received a Christian burial and the location of his grave was never notified. The incident happened at hedge junction 146725 and one can only assume that his final resting place is in the vicinity of the nearby German HQ ('Bob's Farm') indicated below.

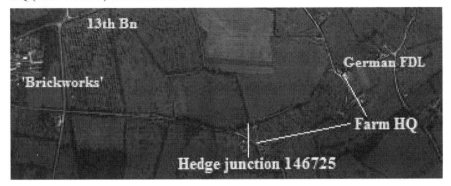

Private Gilbert Smith was also killed on 12th July early, in the evening, during yet another mortar attack, to which the usual four-fold retaliation was issued. The daily multiple barrages from the German mortars was the main cause of casualties which mounted up rapidly. Lance Sergeant Thomas Donnelly, who had transferred to 'B' Company from the MMG Platoon not many days previously, was killed 15th July, again at the hands of mortar fire.

Around this time a deserter from II/858 Grenadier Regiment wandered into the 13th Battalion's positions and during his interrogation reported that Lieutenant O'Brien-Hitching had died soon after being captured. Many deserters entered the 6th Airborne positions, they tended to be Polish, Russian or Eastern Europeans that had been forced into fighting. They were always a good source of information and would willingly point out enemy positions and at what times they ate their meals.

It was during the nights of July that 'C' Company patrolled deeper and deeper in unsuccessful searches for the body of Sergeant Muir, who was lost on the patrol on 19th June. Patrolling was the only real exercise the men had; they were confined to trenches for long hours and short little raids and sabotage patrols operated most nights; they set booby traps with high explosive, snatched a prisoner or observed enemy positions and movements. The policy of these patrols was 'to establish moral ascendancy over the enemy by indicating to him the strength of our patrol activities.'

A few nights later Lieutenant "Steamer" Boyle and two men conducted a patrol and laid delayed action incendiary charges and on their way back they bumped into, and promptly captured, an enemy patrol of one NCO and two men. As a result of the interrogation of these prisoners of the II/858 Grenadier Regiment, a combined mortar and MG shoot was arranged on the Company HQ and Battalion HQ that they disclosed the positions of.

On the brighter side, an enemy aircraft dropped some bombs on his own troops and destroyed a known mortar position. The same day (16th July), Captain David Tibbs and Lieutenant "Joe" Hodgson were decorated with their Military Crosses by General Montgomery himself in the quarry near the River Orne.

Private Alfred Draper (South Staffs Regt att. 8 Platoon 'C' Company)

"We soon found that the worst enemy was lack of sleep. There were so few of us that we had to work a regime of 2 hours on 2 hours off guard. This was alright in the day but at night it was terrible. We also had to sleep in dugouts in the ditches at the edge of the field, which filled with water every time it rained. To finish off we had mosquitoes and flies. Never have I seen so many of either.

"We soon found the paras were good lads. They could be relied on in times of trouble and when asked if we would go back to England with them and do our parachute training, we readily agreed."

Private Ray Batten ('A' Company)

"On another night patrol we went into the German lines and whilst hiding in a bomb crater with Major Cramphorn I could feel that we were being watched. I told him we were under observation. As soon as I said it there was a machine gun burst and we got down in the crater, we were in there quite some time. Eventually we managed to crawl out and get back to our lines."

Lieutenant Ellis "Dixie" Dean (MMG Platoon)

"At the extreme left hand end of the Battalion area stood two houses, one on either side of the road, where 100 yards further ahead lay the German positions. The right hand of the two houses was really just four walls, from the shelling, but we mounted a standing patrol there each night. Across the road, the other smaller property was still in reasonable condition. It was a single floor cottage with a ladder leading up to the loft. One day someone climbed into the loft and looking through a hole in the roof, noticed in an area known to be occupied by the Boche that up the side of a tall tree, ran a ladder, which obviously led to a well camouflaged observation platform.

"The loft was reinforced with sandbags and a sniper installed during the hours of daylight. Any Boche observer up the tree would have a bird's eye view of the Battalions positions; no wonder his mortaring was so accurate. Then the CO had, in my opinion, the crazy idea of mounting a Vickers alongside the sniper. I made a reccie, but saw nothing and the snipers who were there, told me they had seen no-one during the hours of daylight. I reported to the Colonel that it was possible to mount a Vickers, but in my opinion, it was not a suitable task for a medium machine gun. I thought that was the end of the matter, because he did not pursue it any further.

"Our current period in the front line came to an end and while we were in reserve, the Boche brought up an SP and demolished the house.

"Bathing trips were organised and also visits to the cinema in Luc-Sur-Mer. The film being shown was a crazy Hollywood comedy, after which our D-Day aircraft was named, 'Hellzapoppin' and perhaps that sparked it off, but we began talking about the nine missing members of the Platoon. Sergeant Kelly asked if he wrote to the pilot (Sgt Jack Gilbert) would I allow the letter to go. Instead we drafted a letter which did not breach security.

"Less than a week letter, when we were back on the ridge, Sergeant Kelly handed over the familiar buff envelope, marked "On His Majesty's Service". It was from the Adjutant of 299 Squadron, and the gist of the letter was rather than the RAF being able to help us, could we help them, since the aircraft was the only one from Keevil which had failed to return from the mission. I told Sergeant Kelly that I would answer it, and duly informed the RAF of all we knew."

Captain Padre Whitfield "Boy" Foy

"A considerable thrust was attempted by Montgomery [Operation Goodwood] in the Troarn area. Large numbers of tanks were brought over the Orne and established in Ranville and Herouvillette. For several days the roads were almost impassable because of the constant stream of vehicles."

General Gale (Commander, 6th AB Div)

"The plan for this battle included a preliminary softening by the heavy aircraft of Bomber Command. Colombelles and the factory chimneys there (left, 1st July 1944, Bundesarchiv), which the Germans had used for observation posts and Troarn, were the principle targets.

"The concentration of no less than 3 armoured divisions within striking distance, unknown to the enemy was a military achievement of no mean order. The engineers worked all night building additional bridges and throughout the hours of darkness the mass of tanks and guns rumbled over. They concealed themselves under the wings and broken fuselages of our gliders north of Ranville, under trees and in the orchards."

Above: Two sketches drawn by Captain Steven Sykes. A road block on the Troarn Road in the Bois de Bavent (left) and the huge '1000 bomber' raid, during Operation 'Goodwood'.

Lt Ellis "Dixie" Dean (MMG Platoon)

"We stood to at dawn (18th July), displaying yellow fluorescent panels to mark our positions and the sun rose at the start of a perfect summer's day. All we could hear was the drone of engines and the thunder of exploding bombs, but later from a ringside seat (the Platoon's latrine!); I was able to watch the Sherman tanks of the 11th armoured Division moving forward into the attack. The following night we experienced a violent thunder storm and by morning we were all standing in a foot of water."

War Diary 18th July

(Situation map as of 2400hrs)

1650 A patrol sent out to test enemy reaction was heavily fired on.

Lance Corporal George O'Connor (8 Platoon 'C' Company)

"We (the patrol) began to crawl though the cattle feed, towards the German held wood, about half way through the field, the Germans opened fire on us, they must have spotted the cattle feed waving about as we crawled towards them, I ducked so low, I nearly buried myself in the ground. The Germans swept the field, about every third or fourth bullet was a tracer, they lit up the field. One Infantry man made a dash to run back to our wood, he was mown down.[28] We were trapped, it was too far to run back and we didn't have a hope in Hell of reaching the Germans before they gunned us down. We all seemed to have the same thought, keep down and stay where we were and hope. A cluster of shells and mortars fell on the German wood and machine gun fire began from both ends of our wood, I jumped up and made a run for our wood, I could feel one of my legs shaking, but I ran like hell towards our wood."

From the positions at Le Mesnil on the ridge the Battalion had a good view of Operation 'Goodwood'. Heavy rain came and all too soon turned the terrain into an impassable bog with the Allies taking heavy casualties. An even more miserable existence continued at Le Mesnil's crossroads, made worse by the rain.

Two more Polish deserters came through the 13th Battalion's position as the Propaganda Unit broadcasted messages to the enemy in both German and Polish.

Polish and German Addresses - 18 July 44

POLISH

"Men of Poland. Today you have seen yet another demonstration of the power of the Allied armies and air fleets. You saw the bombers go over this morning and some of you may have heard the tanks and guns rolling southwards. Over 1,000 prisoners are now in our cages, and there are more to come.

"Heavy fighting may be ahead, but we are ready for it and backed by the knowledge that we are fighting for a free world, we shall know how to use our air land and sea power to crush the Nazi menace.

"We repeat your simple duty:-

1. Escape now if you can and come over to our lines.

2. Listen to our broadcasts and watch for opportunities to escape.

3. Shoot high, if you are forced to fire on British soldiers.

"Poles, waste no more time. Join the Allies and watch the destruction of everything ignoble, tyrannous and base - everything Nazi. We have never wavered during the dark days of 1940 - 41 in our determination to win this fight for Liberty and now in the day of our power and might, we are marching forward as determined as ever on the road to final victory. Come over before it is too late."

GERMAN

"We promised you later week another view of our bombers. Today you have seen them and today thousands of your comrades have felt the weight of their bombs. Over 1,000 of them have chosen the wise course and are prisoners in our hands. They have exchanged the horror of the bomb craters and the constant strain of a battle fought by you in a vain cause, for the peace and quiet of a correctly ordered PW camp.

"Like most of you, they know that the war is lost for Germany, and there is a better chance of seeing the wife and kids again via the PW camps of England, than by hanging on in a vain struggle against the invincible armies of the Allied Nations.

---

[28] The Infantry man was Private Reginald Gillate a replacement from the West Yorkshire Regiment. Corporal George Lysaght was also killed in this action.

"Choose for yourselves. Stay where you are and be blown to pieces by bombs, shells and bullets somewhere between Le Bas de Bréville and the Rhine, or come over now to our line. If you stay, you can look forward to undiluted hell. If you come over, you will get correct treatment and the certainty of survival. Make up your minds. Come over now."

General Richard "Windy" Gale (Commander, 6th Airborne Division)

"As a result of this battle [Operation Goodwood] our Ranville was no longer in the front line, but what a poor sight Ranville was. The passage of three armoured divisions and the enemy shelling which it received reduced this little Normandy village to a mass of rubble and dust. Rubble and dust in which civilians still lived."

War Diary 21st July

Another very quiet day. The enemy again responded to attempts to draw his fire, when a PIAT was used against one of his sniper posns. Mortar fire was infrequent.

Private David "Robbie" Robinson (Anti-Tank Platoon, att. 'C' Company)

"On the 21st July I was ordered to fire my PIAT at a known sniper position. My comrades who were close by me weren't amused and gave me one or two comments amongst the many insults, because we suffered several mortar stonks in retaliation. Fortunately no-one was injured. 2 days later 'C' Company received a pounding from the German mortars, we retaliated with our own mortars and the PIAT again."

War Diary 23rd July

The enemy was very sensitive all day and fired on the least provocation 'C' Coy were unfortunate in sustaining a number of cas from enemy mortar fire, as a result of very accurate fire from 50mm and 81mm mortars on their forward positions. Two cas were also caused by a troublesome enemy sniper. See attached SITREP.

SITREP: 0800 - 2000 hrs

The only engagement of our one-company front has been a fire fight commencing at 1000 hrs. At this time one of our snipers, working forward, presumably exploded a booby trap at 144725. He was not seen after the explosion. At 1140 hrs an OR of the Anti-Tank Platoon was shot dead by a sniper from the area 146725. In retaliation we attacked his position with mortars and PIAT's at 1400 hrs.

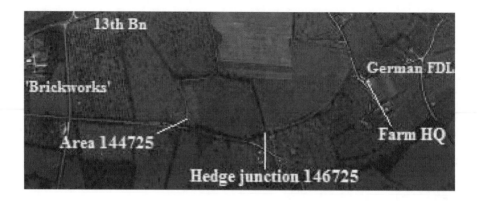

This OR was Private Robert "Bobby" Johns. He became the youngest British Army casualty during WW2 at the tender age of just 16... Jack Watson, Pte Johns and 'A' Company Commander (which Johns was attached) said, "He was quite a big lad when he did his training and it was only when he died that we found out he had lied about his age." Unbelievably, Johns had lied about his age and joined the Parachute Regiment at just 15! He must have been incredibly mature and strong for his age to have fooled his superiors and passed through the hardships of Hardwick and Ringway. He passed jump course 98 in Jan 1943 with the report "Youngest pupil in section, but best performer."

The youngest Allied Army casualty of World War Two, Private Robert Johns aged a mere 16 years old. (Ref: 582, D-Day Museum, Portsmouth)

Private David "Robbie" Robinson (Anti-Tank Platoon, att. 'C' Company)

"I remember being paired with "Bobby" Johns to build a 2-man tent on the last day of an exercise back in England before we had set off for France. We had been in an old mill in Newton Abbot and as it was the last night we were told we could go out until midnight. We were paired off so and me and Bobby headed into the nearest village on the 'Passion Wagon'. We found a pub and the locals bought us pints of scrumpy and the results were quite amusing.

"As we stepped outside the pub door, Bobby collapsed and I bent over to help him up and collapsed on top of him. The 'Passion Wagon' came and we were thrown on and taken to the camp area somewhere in the Buckfastleigh area. Once in the tented area we proceeded to fall over just about every tent, with sleeping men in most of them, until we found our own tent, where we passed out until dawn. I didn't know anything about "Bobby" Johns age or details until after the war."

Private Alfred Draper (South Staffs Regt att. 8 Platoon 'C' Company)

"The weather was atrocious. In the evening it was decided we would be given a rum ration to keep the cold out. Two men in our section didn't drink so the other two of us had a double generous ration. I went to bed and should have been on guard at 4 am, 2 hours before stand to. I never heard the previous guard try to wake me, although he said I had answered him. Come 6 am there was nobody to wake the rest of the section. I should have been court martialled, but the Platoon Officer was new and wasn't sure of himself. Another man committed a far less serious offence a few weeks later and was charged."

Captain Padre Whitfield "Boy" Foy

"The rain made life in the trenches very uncomfortable. Men ate, read, rested and stood to duty knee deep in water. Ina few days the area was saturated and tanks and heavy vehicles were bogged down along every road. Many of these roads were merely tracks cut across fields and these became useless. No further attempt was made to make the important breakout along that axis."

War Diary 24th to 30th July

Bn in rest area. The opportunity was taken to have a general clean-up, which was most necessary after the rains of the previous few days. Whilst in the rest area there was no trouble from enemy bombing or shell-fire. Recreational parties were organised for cinema and stage shows and for swimming on the beaches. As on previous occasions, a Church Service was held.

War Diary 30th July

0930 *Bn took-over from 7 Para Bn in sector SOUTH of line previously held. 'A' Coy is left fwd coy, 'B' Coy in reserve, and 'C' Coy right forward coy.*

1015 *Take-over complete. For the rest of the day there was literally "nothing to report". Only odd rifle shots were fired and only fleeting glimpses of the enemy observed.*

War Diary 31st July

Orders received to handover to No.3 Commando on 1 Aug 44, on 5 Para Bde going into Div reserve. During the day the area was occasionally mortared, but no bombs fell near our posns. The enemy fired bursts of MG occasionally, but with no effect.

Captain Padre Whitfield "Boy" Foy

"We had one more short spell in the line at Le Mesnil, south of our original positions. Major Tarrant (now 'B' Company Commander after Major Bristow was evacuated following a direct hit on his slit trench during the month) had a narrow escape from a 2" mortar. There was a little barn which he used as his HQ and eating and washing. One day, sitting with his feet in a tin of water, a mortar bomb came through the roof and fell at his feet – and failed to explode."

Private Alfred Draper (South Staffs Regt att. 8 Platoon 'C' Company)

"As time went on a holiday camp was started on the coast. Some of the old hands were able to go down for 3 days but we newcomers only had a day. When I went down they were unloading ships out at sea with 'DUWK's'. I managed to get a lift on one and spent the day sailing."

Private Ray "Geordie" Walker ('A' Company)

"After 2 weeks at the front we were given another rest period. This time we had the luxury of a bed in a sea-front hotel at Luc-Sur-Mer. It was 3rd August and we began to wonder as to when we may break the stalemate at the front."

Private David "Robbie" Robinson (Anti-Tank Platoon, att. 'C' Company)

"Whilst in the rear-line away from Le Mesnil in early August, I obtained a 30 cwt Fordson truck, which we put to some good use. We used it to transport the heavy loads like PIAT and mortar bombs, but we used it for other things as well. I took one of the Jewish men from Battalion HQ [Lt Harry Pollak] to collect welfare items such as cigarettes, letters etc."

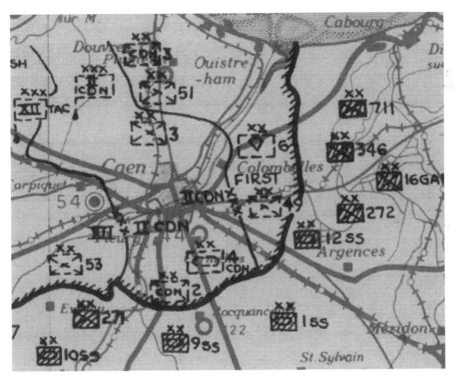

Situation map, 1st August

Lieutenant Ellis "Dixie" Dean (MMG Platoon)

"On the last day of being in reserve [7th Aug] I received orders to view new positions in the Sallenelles area. Doctor Tibbs gave me a lift on his big BMW motorbike that he had acquired on D-Day. We arrived in style at the HQ of the Marine Commando we were relieving.

"They served us with generous tots of gin before venturing out to the tactical positions. The Germans were well away and from an observation post at 'Le Grand

Ferme du Buisson' the Boche frontline could be seen. All around were massive craters, caused by the badly aimed bombs meant for the Merville Battery, which was not far that away. Life here was quiet and we were not subjected to any mortaring or shelling. We even had a visit from George Formby, who put on a show at Battalion HQ, just for us."

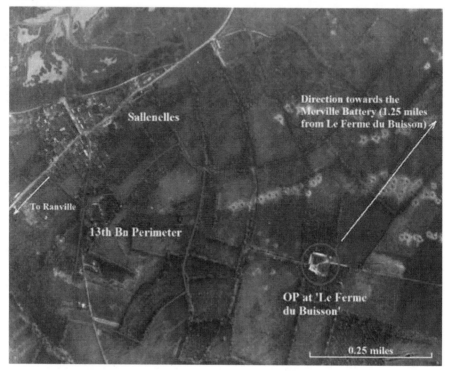

The positions at Sallenelles and Le Grand Ferme du Buisson

Lieutenant Ellis "Dixie" Dean (MMG Platoon)

"By mid-August we were back in reserve at Ranville. A Brigadiers inspection was due to be held on 16th August, so for 2 days we cleaned and polished. The entire Battalion was drawn up in open order wearing best Battle Dress and paraded on a field adjacent to the crossroads, for inspection by the Brigadier.

"The Battalion was a shadow of its former self. We had received a number of non-parachuting men, including 3 officers. These non-jumping Officers had trouble being accepted by the men, who did not take kindly to non-parachutists, but "Steamer" Boyle of the Lancashire Fusiliers proved to be an excellent Platoon Commander and wanted to remain with the Battalion when we returned to England and qualify as a parachutist.

"Next morning, 17th August, we were told that the Boche had withdrawn from the positions on the ridge, retreating beyond the River Dives and the 6th Airborne Division had been ordered to chase the enemy, inflicting maximum possible damage to the retreating force. The days of static defence were over and we were all excited at the prospect of offensive action."

236

ROLL OF HONOUR – THE 'BRICKWORKS'

Pte	DENBY-DREYFUSS Peter C.	22	19/06/1944	13117459	Ranville 4A-K-19
Sgt	MUIR James	29	19/06/1944	987069	Ranville 2A-G-3
Pte	STANYON Roy H.	21	19/06/1944	4928216	Ranville 4A-G-19
Sgt	OSBORNE Samuel	30	23/06/1944	1091335	Ranville 2A-D-1
LCpl	LIGHTFOOT Victor A.	27	25/06/1944	4612433	Ranville 2A-B-1
Pte	PREW Eric R.G.	22	25/06/1944	5619755	Ranville 2A-E-1
Pte	SMITH Cecil	18	25/06/1944	7952781	Ranville 2A-C-2
LCpl	WARE Stanley L.	29	25/06/1944	4922337	La Delivrande 5-A-3
Pte	BARKER Leslie	20	28/06/1944	14631905	Biscot, Luton Churchyard
Pte	RICHARDS Robert D.	23	05/07/1944	14210359	Ranville 3A-B-7
Pte	ARMITAGE John N.	27	07/07/1944	3658191	Ranville 3-E-2
Sgt	DIXON George H.	28	10/07/1944	3714884	Hermanville 2-C-15
Pte	LORD Donald A.	19	10/07/1944	14438786	Ranville 4A-M-21
Pte	BRITLAND Harold F.	20	12/07/1944	14660191	Ryes 5-G-3
Lieut	O'BRIEN-HITCHIN Gordon H.	24	12/07/1944	109882	NKG Bayeux
Pte	SMITH Gilbert	19	12/07/1944	14658563	Ranville 4A-L-19
LSgt	DONNELLY Thomas J.	23	15/07/1944	3663790	Ranville 4A-B-15
Pte	GILLATT Reginald	20	18/07/1944	4546128	Ranville 4A-G-13
Cpl	LYSAGHT George	23	18/07/1944	913145	Ranville 4A-J-9
Pte	JOHNS Robert E.	16	23/07/1944	14434704	Ranville 4A-E-1
Pte	MEARES Thomas	25	07/08/1944	3655805	Ranville 6A-B-22
Pte	CRATES Jack E.	23	08/08/1944	5185579	Ranville 1A-L-16

"Nearly every year I go back to Putot, stand at the top of the hill and look over at where we came from. How the hell we ever got up there I'll never know. The simple reason being, we were in plain view for miles and miles, before we ever got there. It was a disaster for us. To put it bluntly, it was suicide trying to take it, but we had got our orders so that was it."

Lance Corporal Fred Smith ('A' Company)

16.   'HILL 13'

The battle in Normandy had been divided into 3 phases; the initial assault and creating of a bridgehead, from which the second phase was to develop. Wearing down the enemy, division by division, build up the necessary supplies, equipment and men, and enter the third phase, the 'Breakout.'

Nearly 1,000,000 Allied troops were now in and around Normandy. The Americans had captured the port of Cherbourg and now St Lo. Using Caen as the pivot for the breakout, the Allies encircled the German Seventh Army before it had chance to withdraw. The Germans found themselves trapped in the Falaise Plains as the Americans quickly passed south of their positions leaving only one escape route between Falaise and Argentan. Hitler insisted as usual, that no retreat was to take place and that they should hold and counterattack. It was a hopeless situation for the Germans and they lost several thousand men every day.

The German Army after the American breakout on 7th August was expected to withdraw from the Normandy region and it was the Allies intent to push them back not allowing the enemy any time to regroup and organise strong defensive positions.

The objective for the Allied Armies was the River Seine and in order to reach it a series of river and canal crossings had to be made. The two main rivers were the Dives, the Touques and the Risle and in the 6th Airborne Division area (the left flank, towards the Channel) they were wide, deep and tidal. The first river, the Dives, was situated in a wide valley full of marshland, marshland that had been flooded by the Germans for anti-invasion purposes. From the Dives to the River Touques the land was dominated by hills which overlooked any movement across the next valley and would cause any advancing army trouble from artillery. The Touques was situated in a narrow valley in flat meadows leading to the River Risle which had a hill on the east bank which again gave the enemy an excellent defensive position.

General Richard "Windy" Gale (Commander, 6th Airborne Division)

"On 7th August I [had] received orders to prepare plans with the object of taking every advantage of an enemy withdrawal on my front. Owing to the shortage of engineers and equipment, it was obvious that only one maintenance route could be developed. That on the south via Troarn- Dozulé -Pont L'Évêque-Beuzeville-Pont Audemer would be the easiest to bridge and keep our axis with that of the 49th Division on my right. The ground on the east side of the [River] Dives valley rose steeply between 350-400 feet above the level of the river.

"The 3rd Brigade was to move onto Bures, cross the river and then pursue the enemy up to the canal west of Dozulé. The 5th Brigade would then follow up behind. My hope was that the forward move could be pushed with such vigour that no time was given to the enemy to organise positions east of the Dives."

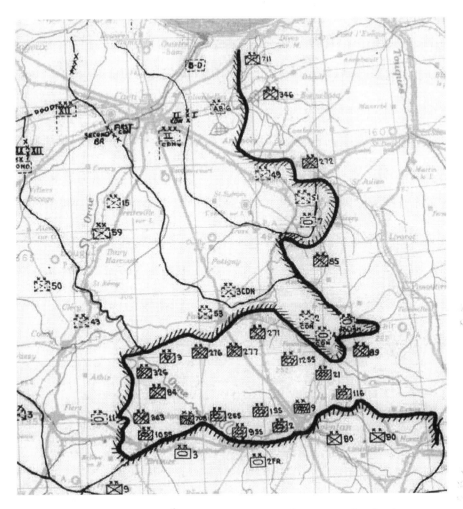

Situation at 1200 hours 18th August 1944, the Falaise Gap can be clearly seen.

War Diary 17th August

1500   Bn moved off to an assembly area in the BOIS DE BAVENT in transport, following information that the expected withdrawal had commenced, and that fwd tpt were pushing over R. DIVES.

Lieutenant Ellis "Dixie" Dean (MMG Platoon)

"17th August saw the Battalion once again assembled on the field at the village [Ranville] crossroads. Back into store had gone the spare battledress and in its place we wore the well worn jumping trousers and Denison smocks, in which we had worn for the greater part of the last 3 months.

"It was a perfect summer's day and we lounged on the grass waiting orders. Major Ford was now second-in-command; Jack Watson was now second-in-command of 'Able' Company with "Joe" Hodgson and "Dick" Burton as Platoon Officers. Major Tarrant had moved to 'Baker' Company when Major Bristow had been evacuated, 'B'

Company were so low in numbers that 10 trained members of the Mortar Platoon were transferred to serve as riflemen. This left "Nobby" Clark in 'Charlie' Company with, 3 non-jumping Platoon Officers, "Steamer" Boyle and 2 Canloan Officers.[29]

"Troop carrying transport was provided and I would move in the second of 2 Jeeps, carrying the CO's Reccie Group, leading the column. The move off resembled the tension of a coiled spring being released. Up the hill to Le Mesnil and there turned right along the road leading towards Troarn. Along this long straight road we raced along in a great cloud of dust. We became aware of a Jeep coming up behind, going even faster than us. As it drew along side, a clearly irate Brigadier Poett was frantically waving us to stop. After we halted Brigadier Poett as gentleman as ever was quick to praise us for the eagerness, but pointed out "the high ground beyond the Dives was still in German hands and the vast cloud of dust we were raising must be clearly visible to them and was a good target for his guns".

War Diary 18th August

0400   Bn moved off through TROARN, and across the R DIVES to area 207703 in rear of 3 Para Bde, where food arrived and the bn. rested throughout the day. Just before midnight the bn moved off from the concentration area to cross the river at 237719 and to attack the village of PUTOT-EN-AUGE.

Route of 5th Para Brigade (Created using Google Map Data © 2012)

Brigadier Nigel Poett (5th Para Brigade Commander)

"Brigadier Hill's 3rd Para Brigade was in the lead, on the right of the Division, and the 6th Airlanding Brigade was to make for Cabourg on the left. My 5th Para Brigade was in reserve, ready to exploit when the time came. The advance eastward by the Division would involve a number of major river crossings. First the River Dives and valley, which the Germans had inundated extensively, making the country exceedingly difficult to cross. These inundations extended from Troarn in the west to Dozulé in the east, and as far north as Cabourg. East of the Dives Valley came the River Touques, which reaches the sea at Deauville, having passed through the considerable town of Pont L'Évêque. Then the River Risle, passing through Pont Audemer on its way to join the mouth of the Seine."

---

[29] One of the Canloan Officers was Lt John Sharman, the other I could not trace. "Dixie" Dean: "The 2 Canloan officers struggled to gain the trust of the paratroopers who don't take too kindly to being ordered by non-jumpers but "Steamer" Boyle was different, he took not time in gaining his men's and the CO's respect."

Captain Padre Whitfield "Boy" Foy

"We arrived at the RV near the Troarn crossroads where we bivouacked for the night. Already we had some considerable experience of mosquitoes; I recall the shocking sight presented by our MT Corporal, Tom Steer's eye. That night we had the misfortune to bivouac in a very wet area, simply seething in mosquitoes. We were gnawed at unceasingly by the wretched creatures and were not a bit sorry that reveille was fixed for 3:30 am. Before daylight, we began the first in the series of long marches; the Germans, after the armoured sweep in the south and the consequent development of the episode of the Falaise Gap, were on the retreat everywhere. We marched through bomb smitten Troarn, now clear of the enemy."

Private Ray "Geordie" Walker ('A' Company)

"On entering the town there was a strong smell of cider coming from an abandoned distillery. Unfortunately we had no opportunity to sample its products. We marched through the town and down a steep hill to the river."

Lieutenant Ellis "Dixie" Dean (MMG Platoon)

"A newly marked track led to a Bailey bridge and most of the leading company ('A') were over to the far side, when the rest of us halted, allowing a bulldozer to move ahead. It was not yet full daylight, but we watched as the outline of the bridge and the vehicle slowly subsided into the water. The Battalion were forced to scramble across at the site of the stone bridge, destroyed by the 3rd Brigade Sappers on 6th June and never repaired.

"We didn't have much further to march and hadn't reached Goustranville when we were ordered off the road and spread themselves round the sides of a lush meadow. As the sun rose the temperature soared. The sky above was cloudless and the larks sang as they must have been doing for centuries, all was perfect peace and the war seemed very far away. And so it was until early evening, when the CO returned from Brigade with orders for a night attack to capture the dominating high hill beyond the hamlet of Putot.

"A daylight assault over the open and under the direct observation of the heights on either side of the road was out of the question."

General Richard "Windy" Gale (Commander, 6th Airborne Division)

"The 3rd Brigade under [James] Hill, got on well and pushed their way forward to Goustranville, about 1,000 yards short of the canal and well under the eyes of the Dozulé heights. Accurate machine gun and shelling pinned them down.

"The strength of the Dozulé position was as obvious as it was frightening. On the other hand it seemed to us that the German intention was merely to gain time and that all we were faced with was a determined but probably weak rearguard. The amount of fire from the enemy and the amount of British movement on what I now called our island bore out this theory.

"The German positions were well concealed and later when I was able to inspect them, I was impressed by the German field works. Their foxholes were neatly dug and were beautifully camouflaged. Where turf had been removed it had been replaced with infinite care. By the 18th we had class 40 Bailey bridges well under way. In a few hours we should be able to get our [artillery] guns up to support an attack on Dozulé."

Brigadier Nigel Poett (5th Para Brigade Commander)

"The night attack was to be a leap-frog, the 5th Para Brigade passing through the 3rd Brigade, when that Brigade had secured the line of the railway east of the canal. This railway line would then become the start line for the 5th Para Brigade attack. It was realized by General Gale and all of us that this was an ambitious and difficult task for my Brigade, but the General judged that it would be impossible for him to remain where he was, with enemy observation over his Division, then spread out in the open country, which was commanded from the heights of Putot.

"In the sector in which Hill's 3rd Brigade attack was to take place there were four bridges over the Dives canal. In the north there was a bridge carrying the railway; some 500 yards to the south there was a smaller bridge; next there came the bridge carrying the Route Nationale 175 over the canal, and finally a much smaller bridge in the vicinity of a farm at Londes.

"Hill's first task was to discover which, if any, of these bridges was intact. He was then to advance as far east as the railway and secure this as a start line for my attack on Putot.

"Hill had decided that it would not be possible to start his advance before 10pm. It was hoped that he would secure the railway, which was to be my start line, by 2am. This would give me, at the best, only three hours of darkness during which to secure my objective - the Heights of Putot. The time was very short; I would not be able to make any firm plan or issue orders until it was known at which bridge Hill's crossing would be made and whether he had been successful in securing the start line for my attack. It was going to be a difficult night.

"I brought my Brigade forward at once to various concealed positions close to the village of Goustranville and from the church tower (left) showed my Battalion Commanders as much as possible of the ground and gave them my general thinking on a plan for the night attack."

At 2145 hours the 1st Canadian Para Bn was to seize the canal and ascertain which of the four bridges were passable to infantry. There were 4 bridges which were labelled A, B, C and D running from North to South. 9 Para Bn working on the information which would be sent back by 1st Canadian Para Bn were then to cross the canal and seize line of the railway.

By 2200 hours the Canadians reported that they had in their custody, bridge 'A' which was sufficient for infantry to cross. Brigadier Hill waited for further information regarding bridges B, C and D before committing 9 Para Bn. By 2245 hours, as no further information had come in, 9 Para Bn was ordered to cross the canal via bridge 'A' and seize the line of the railway. By 2350 hours all four bridges were captured and 'D' bridge was fit for light traffic. 9 Para Bn then crossed the canal via bridge 'A' and by 0245 hours reported that they had captured the railway line including the station.

Led by Captain Golding the 13th Battalion headed for the railway bridge crossing site, but by the time they reached the RV, the tide had risen considerably and was still rising. With the water flowing rapidly, it was deemed to be impassable.

Captain Padre Whitfield "Boy" Foy

"It was as black as ink and one could sense, rather than see, the man in front as we trudged along in single column. We didn't actually start marching until midnight; and after two hours walking, we drew a blank. We came to the expected bridge [Bridge 'A'], but it was blown by the retreating Germans. We retraced our steps (with not a little bad language being used!) and formed up again. Another 'O' group was hastily summoned and this time we made for a different part of the canal."

Brigadier Nigel Poett (5th Para Brigade Commander)

"In the meantime, the Canadian Parachute Battalion patrols had located a second small farm bridge close to the known one. These 2 narrow bridges thus became the only crossing places for the whole of my Brigade. There was now no alternative but to order the return of Luard's Battalion, through the same difficult route he had taken earlier, with a view to him making use of the farm bridges."

General Richard "Windy" Gale (Commander, 6th Airborne Division)

"The 7th and 12th were redirected to this route. Poett's orders were for the 7th to secure the spur immediately east of Putot-en-Auge whilst the 12th were to secure and mop up the village. The 13th were to come into reserve. Their probable task was to pass through the 12th and secure the brigade's final objective, the high ground overlooking Dozulé."

The high ground was defended by a rearguard party of the 711 Infantry Division in well constructed positions offering a commanding view of the valley and main roadway.

Lieutenant-Colonel Peter Luard (CO, 13th Bn)

"Then started a most hazardous march. We had to make the journey at great speed and the only chance we had of doing it in the time was to move directly across the enemy front on a compass bearing. My second in command, Major Ford and myself, both experienced yachtsmen, led the Battalion and on my orders the utmost silence was maintained. I knew we would get shelled along the road as soon as the 7th Battalion made their attack, so I ordered the Battalion to run as fast as they could down the ditch. This we did for 200 yards, until we could move away from the road towards our new RV. By the grace of God, we got away with it and as the first shells landed, the last man was off the road and safe.

"We settled down to rest with our backs against a big bank which ran along the line of the canal. Gradually dawn broke and with it came a mist which slowly cleared and there was the German held high ground, immediately overlooking us. It was unpleasant but unavoidable and there was nothing we could do about it but stay there and hope for the best. The Germans, never fools, saw where we were and shelled us, but their bursts bit the bank, doing no harm and the shrapnel fell mainly away from us and as a result we suffered no casualties. The shelling gradually slackened off but never completely stopped. Brigadier Poett came along and told me we were to cross to the other side of the canal, pass through the 12th Battalion who were in the village and attack the top of the hill."

The 12th Bn was to start as soon as the 7th was in position. 7 Para had to press on; under the frequent enemy flares and machine gun fire they crossed the railway line at the station at 0500 hours.

Then & Now: Putot Railway Station (the railway ceases to exist today)

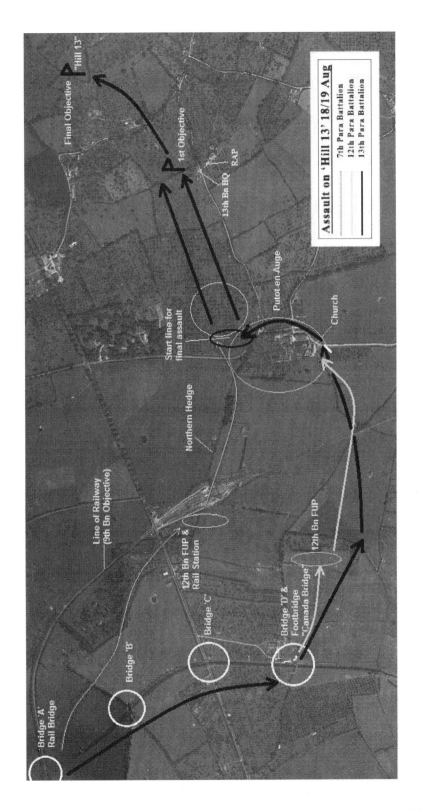

Assault on 'Hill 13' 18/19 Aug

- 7th Para Battalion
- 12th Para Battalion
- 13th Para Battalion

"Hill 13"

Final Objective

1st Objective

13th Bn HQ

RAP

Start line for final assault

Putot-en-Auge

Church

Northern Hedge

Line of Railway
(9th Bn Objective)

12th Bn FUP &
Rail Station

Bridge 'C'

Bridge 'B'

Bridge 'D' &
Footbridge
"Canada Bridge"

12th Bn FUP

Bridge 'A'
Rail Bridge

Lieutenant-Colonel Geoffrey Pine-Coffin (7th Parachute Bn)

"The track which had been decided upon (from the map) to use for direction in the advance did not exist on the ground. The advance was continued however in a SE direction after passing the station. This led through the rectangular field which stretched from the area of the station to within 400 yards of Putot-en-Auge. The northern hedges of this rectangular field, was in fact, the missing track.

"The leading company came under MG fire as it approached the NE corner of the field, and could not get on: this was about 0600 hours. The remainder of the Battalion was massed in the rectangular field at 0615 hours. There was a morning mist at the time and as my wireless link with Brigade HQ was not functioning I had no alternative to fighting my own battle as I found it and to hope for the best.

"The leading company whose head had reached the NE corner of this field was held up by fire from at least 3 MG's, presumably located in the area of the village. There was also fire from another large calibre weapon which later turned out to be 2cm AA/A Tk Guns which were located in the rectangular field itself.

"While 'B' Coy were attempting to work their own way forward, I sent a platoon of 'A' Company to watch the Southern and Eastern hedges of the rectangular field and also ordered them to search two barns which could be seen in the SE corner. This platoon captured a party of Germans who were approaching the SE corner of the field from the village and also captured a 2cm AA/A Tk gun, which they found in this same corner. They then remained in that area and covered my right flank.

"Meanwhile 'B' Company found that the original MG's were beyond their own resources but they had captured a prisoner in their attempts. This prisoner talked freely and gave locations of 3 AA/A Tk guns (one of which had already been captured) and certain German troops in the area. This prisoner was quite certain he would be shot by us and was petrified with terror as a result. When he was sent back with some other prisoners he tried to run away, and was, in fact, shot and killed, not however in the circumstances that he had been led to believe.

"I then gave my orders for dealing with the original MG's but my attention was soon drawn to a party of men approaching the rectangular field from the North, in extended line. It was presumed that this was the 13th Battalion but it was not possible to be certain because of the morning mist. As the party approached closer it could be seen that it included a certain number of Germans and it was thought that the 13th Battalion were bringing in some prisoners with them. Later still it could be seen that they were all Germans and were apparently advancing on the Battalion position with evil intent.

"A curious and not un-amusing situation then arose. The Germans were about 25 yards from the northern hedge when someone in the hedge shouted to them to put their hands up. This dumbfounded the Germans who stopped in their tracks and talked amongst themselves. It seemed possible that the whole lot would surrender, so I held fire to watch developments. However one of them eventually lay down and opened fire with an MG. It then became a shooting match with the Germans outnumbered and without cover - many of them were killed in the first few seconds. It was possible for them to slip back the way they had come in the mist which was very thick so I sent a platoon out on a left handed sweep to bring them in and moved a section to my right flank as a precaution. Prisoners came in very fast and in the end 50 went sent back and the sweeping platoon reported that about 15-20 enemy casualties remained in the field where they fell and about six had slipped back through the mist."

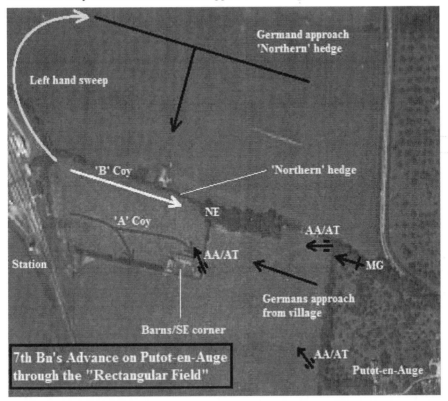

Germand approach 'Northern' hedge

Left hand sweep

'B' Coy

'Northern' hedge

'A' Coy

NE

AA/AT

AA/AT

Station

AA/AT

MG

Germans approach from village

Barns/SE corner

7th Bn's Advance on Putot-en-Auge through the "Rectangular Field"

AA/AT

Putot-en-Auge

7 Para now moved into position at the northern end of Putot. It was now time for the 12th Battalion to take up the battle in the south of Putot and capture the village.

Brig N Poett (5th Para Brigade)

"The church and cemetery of Putot stand on a very prominent mound which dominates the countryside in 3 directions. The ground at the bottom of the mound is, however, 'dead' ground for enemy in the village attempting to fire on the troops waiting to attack."

12th Parachute Battalion Report "Battle of Putot en Auge"

'B' Coy were ordered to attack forthwith and the remainder of the Bn was moved up to the hedgerow under the hill on which the village stood, which leads up to the church. 'A' Coy lined this hedge and covered the west of the village. While this move was on the leading platoon of 'B' Coy had reached the church and the first shots and shouts of alarm rang out. The enemy's defensive fire fell on the FUP. It was almost impossible to bring fire to bear on the Battalion as it was under a hill. Occasional mortar fire fell and that was all.

247

'B' Coy's leading platoon cleared the church and found themselves pinned to the ground by fire from an MG 34 in the graveyard at 25 yards range. This killed one man and wounded CSM Warcup in the neck. The next platoon [Lt Bercot – ex 13th Bn] was then put in and they attacked the group of houses on the crossroad with such ferocity that prisoners were soon streaming down to Bn HQ.

The third platoon (Lt Delany) was then put in round the right as the other platoons were pinned by MG fire. They were led by the Company Commander Major Croker and their movement enabled the other two platoons to move on. Major Croker personally accounted for 3 Germans with his rifle and one he killed with a knife when Sgt Walker was seriously wounded tackling a fleeing Hun. The attack began at about 0610 hrs and by 0700 hrs the village was in our hands.

While the attack was on 'A' Coy had brought accurate Bren fire to bear on fleeing Germans in the open fields to the west. Any escaping this fire were caught by 7 Para Bn on the left. 'A' Coy then passed through 'B' Coy and seized the crossroads north of the village, where they contacted 7 Para Bn. The attack was characterised by the speed of house clearing and the ferocity and courage shown by all ranks. After an arduous night march with no sleep the attack was so swift and well led.

The Bn took about 75 prisoners, 15 of which were wounded and though only 5 dead were found many more were killed in the open field. The booty consisted of 5 MG 34's, 2 80mm mortars, 4 50mm mortars, one Bazooka, and 2 75mm anti-tank guns and one 20mm gun. Bn losses were 2 killed and 6 wounded.

For the remainder of the day the Bn held the village under heavy mortar and shell fire which cost it about 25 more casualties.

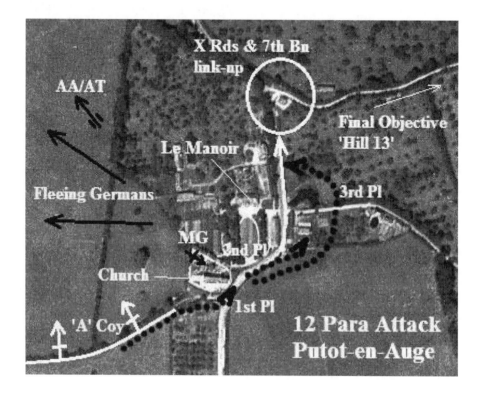

Sergeant Reg Lloyd (12th Parachute Battalion)

"Sergeant Jim Warcup earned the DCM for an act of bravery which he performed when the leading platoon was pinned down by a lone machine gunner in the graveyard at 25 yards range. Without hesitating acting CSM, Jim went forward and led an attack by the leading section on the gun. When only about 5 yards away from the machine gun he was dangerously wounded in the neck by a bullet. Despite the wound he went on until it was destroyed."

Approx Position of MG in graveyard

12th Bn stuck here

Major G Ritchie MC (12th Parachute Battalion)

"About 20 POW's had been rounded up. They seemed quite cheerful and said they were Austrians from a Viennese regiment. The Château area had been held by a about a company under the command of a Feldwebel."

Brigadier Nigel Poett (5th Para Brigade Commander)

"I moved my advanced HQ into the Manoir, a charming 17th century building. Unfortunately, this building soon became a target for German shelling! Soon after we had seized Putot I learnt with great sadness that my Jeep driver, Corporal Leatherbarrow, who had been with me throughout the Normandy Campaign and whom I had left in my Jeep on the outskirts of the village, had been killed by a stray shell. It was a sad blow as Corporal Leatherbarrow had become a close friend."

Le Manoir Then and Now

Captain Padre Whitfield "Boy" Foy

"At first light the 12th Battalion crossed the canal and assaulted the village. While the attack was on, we lay on the west bank, being mortared. The only consolation lay in the fact that the German prisoners taken by the 12th Battalion in the assault on the village, were being passed back through our area and were being subjected to extreme danger by their own guns."

'B' and 'C' Troop of the 3rd Airlanding Anti-Tank Battery were called forward towards the railway station to give artillery support.

Major Joe Woodrow (3rd Airlanding Anti-Tank Battery)

"We were supporting some paratroops who were attacking in an infantry role, a village on a hill that commanded a crossing over a river. Their job was to get into the village as soon as it was captured and consolidate and give support against a possible counter attack as the Germans were known to have tanks in the area. Bert never hesitated for one moment, and started up his jeep just as coolly and just as calmly as if he were going for a Sunday afternoon drive. I myself went with them and as I was travelling in the next Jeep saw everything that happened.

"The Germans had been shelling and mortaring us very heavily all the time and he opened up again just as we were nearly there. One shell fell almost on top of Bert's Jeep, setting it ablaze and wounding the complete detachment. I got the remainder of the men and Jeeps under cover and while I was doing this Bert was carried in. We did everything we could for him and the others put them in a Jeep and rushed them back to the nearest hospital [La Deliverande]."[30]

General Richard "Windy" Gale (Commander, 6th Airborne Division)

"Poett ordered forward the 13th to the eastern outskirts of the village. As it was now daylight (09:45am) and the ground over which the 13th Battalion must move, a prearranged artillery programme to deal with the high ground was put into effect."

Lieutenant-Colonel Peter Luard (CO, 13th Bn)

"Obviously speed was the only way to cross the open space and I called the Company Commanders and issued my orders. 'B' Company to lead, followed by Battalion HQ, then 'A' and finally 'C'. I said in my opinion the Germans would not expect us to do anything so mad and by the time we had started and they had given the necessary orders to engage, we had a fool's chance, but a good one of getting away with it. In any case, we had no alternative since there was no cover. So off we went, the distance was about ¾ mile, with the middle 200 yards the most hazardous.

"We were all very fit young men and there is no doubt that everyone realised that the speed they made was likely to save their lives. And they moved. The whole Battalion was across all except the last section, before the Germans saw the danger and opened fire. Even then, there were only a couple of casualties, neither serious."

SAINT-JOUIN — La Nef de l'Eglise

---

[30] Gunner Albert Dyche died the next day from his wounds in hospital.

Captain Padre Whitfield "Boy" Foy

"On this stretch we had 3 casualties, who we took to the 12th Battalion RAP set up in the little church in Putot. It was a grisly scene in the church, for the place was so crowded with British and German wounded – and dying. The sanctuary was drenched in blood and the MO, Tommy Wilson, was working overtime.

"Meanwhile our Battalion moved on in front of the 7th and 12th and took up temporary positions; hasty decisions were made about the next advance. They were momentous decisions, for the price to be paid within the next few hours was high."

Brigadier Nigel Poett (5th Para Brigade Commander)

"As soon as the 12th had completed the mopping up of Putot, I ordered the 13th forward to secure first the spur running north from Putot, which had been the Brigade's original objective, and then to exploit eastwards and seize the high ground which overlooked Dozulé."

Lieutenant-Colonel Luard had no time to make any reconnaissance and had to quickly make up a plan with the assistance of the Artillery FOO, Captain Saddleton of the 150th Field Regiment.

Lance Corporal George O'Connor (8 Platoon 'C' Company)

"The villagers showered us with flowers, bottles of brandy and calvados, more of them arrived, one old man tried to kiss us, we left the village carrying the odd bottle or two and feeling more light-hearted then when we arrived, we had the Jerries on the run at last. The villagers were still following us as we left the village; they were still trying to hand us lumps of cheese, ham and black bread. I felt a lot drier and warmer a couple of sips of brandy and a lump of cheese had done wonders for my morale, it was the first time I had seen French people excited and pleased to see us. I soon lost my sense of well being, when, bullets came at us, from some high ground, the Germans had retreated to."

Private David "Robbie" Robinson (Anti-Tank Platoon)

"On 18th August the Battalion was mostly moving across country and I had to find my own way by side roads because I was using the 30 cwt truck that I had acquired to transport items like the PIAT's and mortar rounds etc. I had to keep in contact with the Battalion, which was hard to do as I had no wireless. I reached Putot and found that the 7th Battalion was in possession of the western side and the 12th the eastern. From my enquiries I found out that the 12th had taken the village and the 13th had gone through them towards a high point locally known as Les Buttes.

"I moved out from the 12th Battalions positions and turned right up a small road. After about ¾ of a mile I came to another small road on my left. This small road, with banks on either side was at the foot of the high ground of Les Buttes. The Battalion had just reached this point and were deploying to attack. Three PIAT's and ammunition were quietly unloaded, myself handling one of the PIAT's."

Captain Padre Whitfield "Boy" Foy

"In the line of the advance was some high ground, a very dominant feature. The main road was to our left. The object was to gain possession of the high ground straight ahead. The Battalion advanced without opposition, to positions at the foot of the high ground, it was a steep slope studded with bushes and trees. 'A' and 'B'

Companies were forward on the right and left respectively and 'C' Company was in reserve. The distance between all parts of the Battalion was very short. Battalion HQ was in a little house only 200 yards from the start line of the attack. 'B' Company led by Major Tarrant began the attack up the slope.

"In open formation they walked steadily up the hill, weapons at the ready. I stood at the little house 200 yards away and watched intently. For some seconds there was no reaction from the hillside. Then without warning, concealed machine guns cracked into action. A hail of bullets stormed the advancing men. Major Tarrant was wounded in the stomach.[31] After that it was a bitter slaughter. Man after man went down; the remainder never hesitated, but pushed steadily forward in spite of the vicious torrent of fire."

Citation: Major Reginald Mowlam Tarrant

Award: Military Cross

On Saturday 19th August, 'B' Company commanded by Major Tarrant was the advanced Company ordered to lead the battalion under fire across exposed country into Putot en Auge and so to an objective on a hill beyond. Leading his Company with great personal dash he got them across the open country and attacked the first ridges of the hill. This he captured and advanced at once to attack the final ridge. He personally led the charge for the top of this hill showing extraordinary leadership and dash and was seriously wounded in the stomach when on the crest of the hill. Although in great pain he continued to give directions for the attack until he was evacuated. His leadership and dash were an inspiration and encouragement to his men and in the finest traditions of the Parachute Regiment.

The Germans were in well concealed positions just over the top of the slope on the reverse side and had waited until the last seconds to launch a devastating counter-attack. They utilised hidden machine gun nests and threw stick grenades over the summit and down the hill. Being on the reverse side the Germans were out of sight and virtually impossible to attack. With bayonets still fixed after taking the small intermediate ridge, most of the leading platoons were cut down, either killed or wounded.

---

[31] Major "Reggie" Tarrant finally lost the bitter struggle with the three machine gun bullets in his abdomen and died on 28th August 1944. He is buried in La Delivrande cemetery.

Stick grenades thrown over the summit at paratroops 30ft below

The German Positions

The summit of "Les Buttes"

Captain David Tibbs MC (RAMC)

"The Battalion ran into a skilfully set up rear guard action by the retreating Germans and we found ourselves in a hillside valley with fire coming from 3 directions. The leading company suffered heavily casualties including the Company commander, Major Reggie Tarrant, who sustained 3 MG42 bullets to the abdomen. I went to join the company stretcher bearers to help bring out the injured men. Fortunately they lay close to a sunken lane with a steep rise above it so that we were out of sight to the MG42 machine gun but nevertheless it intermittently raked up the turf a few yards ahead of us. By crouching low we were able to evacuate the injured men without having to chance using the Red Cross flag with unfamiliar infantry opposing us. The route back to my RAP was by a sunken road relatively secure from enemy fire.

As I returned, I went to a spot where 3 men had been individually shot down. One was dead, another probably so, but the third was shouting in distress and I went out with a Red Cross flag to pull him in (he had severe injuries by bullet to his genitalia and groin). As I did so I saw the second man was still blowing bubbles of blood, so with great reluctance I returned to fetch him, only to find he had now died. Without thinking I stripped off his bandoleer of ammunition and flung it to the sunken road. As I did so there was a tremendous crack as if a gun had been fired close to my head. I felt a violent shock, like electricity, in my right arm and found myself lying on the grass. After a brief moment of confusion I realised that I had become the fourth victim of the sniper and tried to shift away before another shot followed, but found that I had no strength. Wisely no-one came out to help me but one of my own RAMC men called out "Try hard Sir, Try hard!" This made me redouble my efforts and I managed to push myself on my side along to the gap in the hedge through which I had come where hands reached out to help me. I managed to limp to my own RAP but lost a large amount of blood and felt dreadful (the bullet had gone through the neck of my right scapula, obliquely from front to back, and had severed the sub scapular artery). Pain came later but was not severe.

"Ironically this last shot had allowed our men to realise that the sniper was firing from the upper window of a farmhouse about 400 yards away. Major John Cramphorn took 2 men with a PIAT gun over to it and fired a bomb through the open window, killing the sniper. John came to the RAP to tell me of his success and could not understand why I said "You should not have done that - it was my fault."[32]

Above: 1. David Tibbs outside his RAP barn in the 80's (courtesy David Tibbs) 2. The same barn in 2012. 3. Blended 'Ghost' picture.

---

[32] In removing the bandolier of ammunition Captain Tibbs had broken the Geneva Convention for medical attention under the Red Cross.

Photo taken by David Tibbs MC at the "re-entrant", 3rd left is Sgt Bill Webster, 6th is Captain Bert Hodgson MC and 7th is Private Bert Roe MM a conscientious objector.

Cpl Austin Lyons & Pte Charles Glover (of 4 Platoon, KIA)

Private Jim Beasant ('B' Company)

"I was in 'B' Company, 6 Platoon and was captured. I was helping my mate Tommy Molloy with a Bren gun. I put the last magazine in and Tommy gave it the last 3 bursts when a German got us with a hand grenade over the hedge to our left. I heard a bang and that was it, it killed him outright. I got caught in the thigh. I was taken prisoner and they took me over the Seine in a rowing boat to the hospital but it was full, treating Germans, so they took me to a school which had been converted to a hospital."

Another Bren gun team fell foul of the German grenades. Privates Harold Sands and Cecil Rusdale of 6 Platoon attempted to set up their Bren and died side by side. Harold Sands had joined up as a boy soldier, serving with the 1st Airborne Division before being sent home from North Africa after his age was found out.

Private Harold Sands & Private Cecil Rusdale (both killed by same grenade blast aged 19)

Sergeant Colin Longden (6 Platoon 'B' Company)

"I was with Lt Bibby when we tried to take the hill. All of a sudden the Germans appeared and most of the men around me were killed. I remember telling one man who tried to get up after we hit the deck, to "Get back down!" It was at this time that I lost track of Lt Bibby and didn't see him again."

Private David "Robbie" Robinson (Anti-Tank Platoon)

"The attack had already begun by 'B' and 'A' Companies. 'C' Company was in reserve with us [the Anti-Tank Platoon] in the shelter of the road with its banks. I was surprised that the PIAT's were not asked to support, as the objective was well within range and the PIAT's could be used like mortars if the need arose.

"Wounded began to arrive and after a while we reloaded the truck with the PIAT's and I went back to Putot village."

Private Ray "Geordie" Walker ('A' Company)

"Now it was the turn of my 'A' Company. Our attack was also repulsed and ground to a halt halfway up the hill."

Corporal Dennis Boardman (Signaller, att 'A' Company)

"I only had a Sten which was no good. However, the chap next to me was the company sniper, a great guy who had done a great job since the landing on D-Day. He had been a constable in Leeds City Police. He just threw down his rifle and told me he was making a run for it. He had had enough and he was gone. I tried to stop him but it was no good. I grabbed his rifle and ammunition and starting firing.

"A month later I had to attend his court martial. I was sitting in the hall waiting to go in the court room when this officer appeared. He was my Battery Commander when I was in the Artillery, before I joined the paras. He was a very nice gentleman, we had quite a chat and it turned out he was the prosecuting officer. I told him the guy had been a good soldier until this incident and he promised to put in a good word in for him. He got 12 months instead of 2 years. After the war he became a top London lawyer at the Old Bailey."

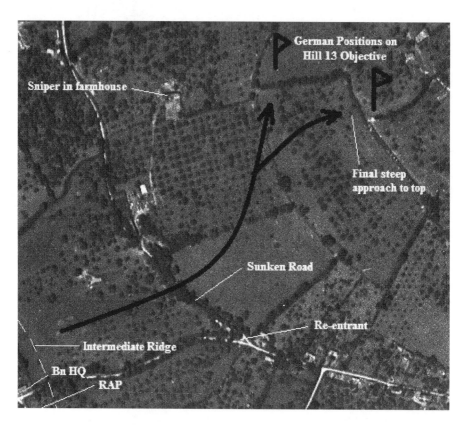

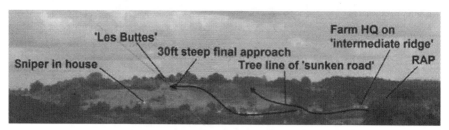

View of 'Hill 13' from Goustranville

Captain Padre Whitfield "Boy" Foy

"Some did reach the top, some actually fought in the enemy positions. Lieutenant Terry Bibby did that with one section and failed to return.

"Orders were given on the spot that the men were to take whatever cover was available. We were to reform for another go. I have very vivid impressions of what happened after the German machine guns opened up. I remember the RSM [Duxbury] doubling round, grabbing hold of any man with a rifle for the purpose of defending Battalion HQ in the event of the leading Companies being over run. I had the strange feeling then, what would happen if the enemy did break through not for the first time I thought that it would be nice at least to have a gun and be able to hit back.

"I can see the stretcher bearers sitting down for a brief moment, absolutely exhausted after carrying repeated loads a distance of several hundred yards in the hot Normandy sun and when men like Ernie Barns and John McCutcheon (pictured left and right) sat down it was because the only alternative was to fall down. They were the most willing and tireless of workers. Came the moment when I heard someone shout "The MO's been hit" and I knew, with a sickening feeling, this was the worst thing that could have happened. Going forward to a wounded man, Captain Tibbs had been sniped. Lying on the floor of the RAP, he went on giving instructions about the treatment of the casualties as they were brought in. But the wound was a nasty one and he gradually became weaker. By this time we were stripped to the waist, having used the top half of our clothing for pillows and covering. The water had run out completely, all water bottles had been emptied and the burning thirst of the wounded had to be slaked with crude cider from the large vat in the farmhouse. Just then as I began to realise the seriousness of the position, came further personally bad news.

"My batman Private Ray Whitehead (who had been used by the RSM to offer defence for the Battalion HQ) had been shot and the wound was deep into his back. When I got to where he lay, I found him temporarily paralysed. We got him back to the RAP, but he was obviously in a very bad way. Although he was still alive when he left us some hours later, he died a few days later [23rd August] in a general hospital."

Lieutenant-Colonel Peter Luard (CO, 13th Bn)

"Most of the leading Platoons were either killed or wounded and 'A' Company fell back to join Battalion HQ on the intermediate ridge. The Germans counter attacked very well. I lay with the men of 'A' Company on the reverse slope of the 'Intermediate Ridge' hearing bullets singing through the grass all around us. There was no fear; we just felt that if the enemy came into view, he was welcome to everything we had in the form of fire power.

"At that moment, I beard a voice behind me in a Bren carrier saying "We must have immediate fire we are being counter attacked". It was Colonel Mitchell [with Captain Saddleton] of the Gunners (150th Field Regiment RA) calling to his Regiment. He had crossed the open ground after us and there he was, cool and calm, calling for support. The Gunners response was marvellous, the fire from them was so accurate, that it stopped the Germans about 100 yards from us. Realising that the initiative might once again be with us, I sent 'C' Company on a right flanking attack, but the re-entrant up which they had to go was well covered by the enemy and they made no progress."

Citation: Captain Steven Saddleton (150th Field Regiment, RA)

Award: Military Cross

At PUTOT-EN-AUGE on the afternoon of 19 Aug 44 this officer was FOO with the 13 Bn 5 Para Bde. During this time the Bn, which was the fwd unit of the bde, was continually shelled and mortared and an enemy counter-attack developed.

Captain Saddleton calmly remained at his post and brought down the fire of the 150 (SNH) Fd Regt RA on the advancing Germans causing severe casualties to the enemy.

By his cool action the counter-attack was broken up before reaching our lines and the Bn was undoubtedly saved from a dangerous situation.

Note: On the citation sheet he was recommended for an immediate DSO by Lt-Col Mitchell, but it was downgraded to an MC.

'Hill 13' viewed from farmhouse HQ on the 'Intermediate Ridge'

Private Alfred Draper (South Staffs Regt att. 8 Platoon 'C' Company)

"I was in the reserve company and we dug in at the bottom of the hill [on the sunken road]. The battle didn't go well for us and 2 of our platoons were called to help out. Our section was right at the back as we only had 3 men that day (Bob had gone down with pneumonia a few days before). The other 2 sections and our Bren gun team had been called forward and I was left on my own. I must say I was very lonely and was pleased when the two men with the Bren gun came back in the evening."

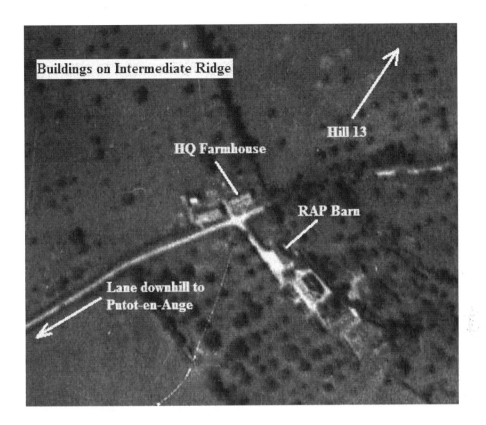

Buildings on Intermediate Ridge

HQ Farmhouse

Hill 13

RAP Barn

Lane downhill to
Putot-en-Auge

Lieutenant-Colonel Peter Luard (CO, 13th Bn)

"I reported the situation to Brigade [1530 hours] and was told to hold where we were. This was no difficulty, since on the intermediate ridge, we were in a commanding position and in any case the enemy counter attack had been repulsed. 'B' Company had lost many men and casualties had occurred in the other Companies.

House used by Lt-Col Luard as HQ

The Battalion had been on the move and in action for 48 hours almost without let up and we were all very tired.

"We dug in where we were. I called an 'O' Group in a nearby farmhouse (left) and in the middle of it; I fell asleep as I was actually talking. They left me sleeping and gave instructions I was not to be disturbed. Two hours later, I woke up and the meeting was resumed, with my apologies."

Lieutenant Ellis "Dixie" Dean (MMG Platoon)

"Early in the afternoon, orders came through for the MMG's to re-join the Battalion. We had heard the sounds of battle and knew that a large engagement had taken place. The farm where we had to report was on a track running up the hill, so we assumed that all had gone well and the 13th were now in possession of the hill.

"Fred Skeate (Mortars) and I set off in the Jeep for Battalion. Once out of the field we turned right and followed the road leading down to the valley floor. Soon we were in the cover of the trees, leaving the metalled road and following a well used track and came to the canal, which much to our surprise we crossed via an undamaged bridge. For the next couple of hundred yards we were sheltered by the trees, but on reaching the edge of the wood saw there was now an open field, before arriving at the railway level crossing. Shells were landing even as we cleared the trees, the driver put his foot down and we raced across those 300 yards, crossed the railway and turned left towards the church standing on a little knoll. Immediately passing "le Mairie", we turned right up the track and soon entered the Battalion position, where the rifle companies were preparing defensive positions. We turned left into the farmyard, halted, jumped out and enquired where we would find the Colonel.

"Nothing had prepared us for the news we were about to hear."

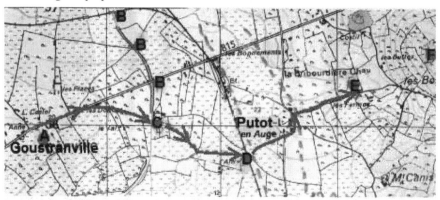

Route to 13th Para Bn HQ taken by Lt "Dixie" Dean
(Drawn by Lt Dean, 2010)

A – MMG Position	C – "Canada Bridge"	E – 13th Para Bn HQ
B – Impassable Bridges	D – Level Crossing	F – Final Objective

Captain Padre Whitfield "Boy" Foy

"For the first time and the last, I used the wireless. The scene at the RAP was indescribably bad. The barns we were using were completely filled with the wounded, dying and the dead. Lying outside were the men we simply could not get under cover. There was absolutely no means of evacuation because there was trouble getting wheeled vehicles over the canal, 2 miles back. My wireless procedure would have sent a Catterick instructor to bed for a month. "Hello Padre here, I want to speak to the CO…... Hello Sir, Padre here, please can you shake Brigade up about transport for the evacuation of the casualties? We have dozens of them here and many of them will die on our hands, unless we can get them back to the Dressing Station… That's all.""

"About 4 in the afternoon the first Jeep arrived, followed closely by two others and we began to get the wounded away. In one of the barns we laid those who had fought for the last time.

"The battle subsided, the enemy counter attack firmly held by the forward Companies. Came evening and all was still, we were not to attack again that night. And that strange after battle tranquillity pervaded the area, a tranquillity which one finds in no other place. The atmosphere is still charged with emotion for men who had thrilled to the excitement of the attack, but instinctively felt fear at the deadly fire they had met and grown hot with fury at the sight of their friends groaning with appalling wounds. And now they brooded deeply on the events of the day, their minds scared beyond imagination. On that lovely summers evening they thought chiefly of those men in the barn and how, but for some stroke of fortune it could have been them."

Private Ray "Geordie" Walker ('A' Company)

"This hill became known as "Hill 13" and was a killing ground for all our companies. During that first night on the hill a wounded German screamed throughout the hours of darkness. I can still hear his cries even after an absence of over 60 years. During this action I came across a barn which contained the bodies of several friends and included "Spit" McCrudden, a Londoner, who had trained with me at Hardwick and "Paddy" Duggan from Northern Ireland (left). "Spit" had taken part in the operation to capture Diego Suarez Bay, Madagascar in May 1942. Yesterday we laughed and joked together, now their voices were silenced forever."

Captain Padre Whitfield "Boy" Foy

"That evening elements of a Commando Brigade came into our position and at midnight attacked the hill, which had now been softened up by an artillery stonk. They succeeded easily."

Lieutenant-Colonel Peter Luard (CO, 13th Para Bn)

"48 Commando passed through in a silent night attack and occupied the top of the hill successfully. The only activity was when they arrived in the evening to recce the positions. The movement was seen and mortar fire came down in our area, wounding 5 Commando key men including the 2i/c. He said "You can not take chances with the Hun."

"Captain Grantham, the Adjutant, took over 'B' Company, and 40 reinforcements, which arrived most opportunely, were drafted in to make up the depleted companies."

Lieutenant Ellis "Dixie" Dean (MMG Platoon)

"With the evening came the first batch of reinforcements from our Reserve Company in England. Ken Walton (left) arrived to take over the Mortars, allowing Fred Skeate to move to 'B' Company as second-in-command.

"The Boche withdrew and over the crest of the hill, in the direction of Dozulé, a bright glow illuminated the dark sky. These are my final memories of one of the blackest days in the Battalions history."

Lance Corporal Don "Taff" Jones (MMG Platoon)

"When my wound had healed, I think it was about August time, I got sent down to Lewis, where I spent the night in the barracks there. Soon after I was aboard an LST again and disembarked at the mulberry harbour at Arromanches. There was a mixture of regiments. I walked along the pontoons ashore and a load of the Cheshire Regiment came ashore as well. I'd been in the Cheshire's, that's where I'd learned about the machine gun. I recognised some of the lads and we had a few words. Soon after I rejoined the battalion and stayed with them until we were brought out of the line."

General Richard "Windy" Gale (Commander, 6th Airborne Division)

"This concluded the Putot-en-Auge Battle. It had proved a highly successful operation for the 5th Parachute Brigade. A night attack had been launched from a start line which had to be secured by a preliminary operation by another Brigade. The route to the start line had been uncertain until the last minute. Information regarding the crossing places of the Canal proved inaccurate and considerable adjustments in the plan had been necessary, these as late as 1:30am. The route to the start had not been completely mopped up, and some opposition had been encountered on it by the leading Battalion, yet the final objective set to the Brigade was secured, though the further exploitation hoped for proved beyond their capacity.

"The fighting spirit of the troops was splendid. They had no sleep during the night 18-19th August and had been up since 2am the previous day, yet throughout the day their dash and energy never diminished, and in the evening the troops were in tremendous heart and well satisfied with their performance.

"120 unwounded prisoners passed through the Brigade Intelligence Officers hands; approximately 40 more were evacuated with our wounded; the dead were estimated at 40, not including those killed on the hill. Equipment captured was 2 75mm guns, 4 20mm AA guns, 2 81mm mortars, 4 50mm mortars and a very large number of MG 34's."

Cpl Dennis Boardman (Signaller, att 'A' Company)

"The last few years I have visited the site, my best French friend lives on the site and I also know the lady who owns the farm at the top of 'Hill 13'. She was about 10 years old and remembers the events. About 20 yards from the farmhouse you look below you and there is an almost vertical hill about 40 feet high, and below open ground of about 30 yards. All the Germans had to do was to throw stick grenades and fire their Schmeissers. Had the platoons taken the route of the lanes they could have come up behind the farmhouse and the battle would have been won with half the dead."

The cost to 13 Para had been very high, 28 lost their lives, approximately 30 were wounded and 6 were missing, one of which was later mysteriously unaccounted for and became the 29th man to be classed as KIA. This was Lieutenant Bibby, OC 6 Platoon 'B' Company.

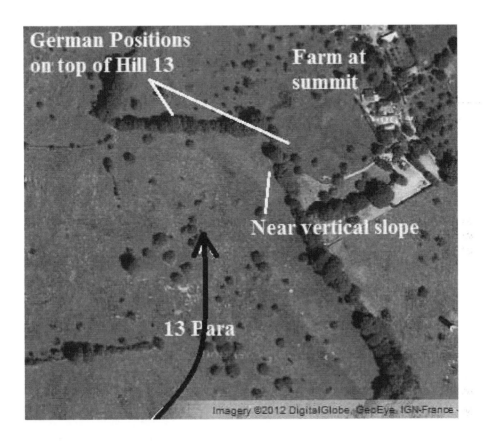

Lieutenant Bibby, OC No.6 Platoon, who had fought gallantly and at times hand to hand in the German positions on Hill 13, was listed as missing in action at the close of August 19th.

Sergeant Wilfred Tickell (left) of 4 Platoon 'B' Company stopped by Lieutenant Bibby who had bad wounds to the head and face and addressed his wounds; he himself was wounded and was later picked up by the Germans along with Lt Bibby. They were eventually transported to the hospital at Château de Gassard, where Sgt Tickell was liberated 22nd August, after the Germans abandoned the Hospital leaving 4 German medics and one member of the British RAMC to care for 6 German and 6 British wounded.

Letter to Wilfred Tickell from Lieutenant Bibby's Mother

June 10th '45
Dear Sir,

I have had word from the War office that my son, Lt Bibby an officer with you, who was wounded and taken prisoner along with you on Aug 19th, must now be presumed to have died of wounds. They inform me that you dressed his wounds and then had to leave him lying. I feel I would like to thank you for what you did for him and should feel very grateful if you would write to me and give me any information about him. Was he badly wounded and did he give you any message. The War Office have kindly permitted to send on this letter to you. Could you put me in touch with anyone who could give me any information? I feel so dreadful not to be able to find any news about him.

Will you please write to me as soon as you are able. If you are anywhere near me would it be possible for me to see you. I've been hoping all this time that he was a POW and it has come as a very great shock to me to hear he is dead.

Yours sincerely

Florence Bibby

Lieutenant Ellis "Dixie" Dean (MMG Platoon)

"I recall that at the first of our reunions, early in the 1970's, asking Colonel Luard, had any more information on the missing officer, ever come to light, but the answer was "no". When Tom Steer was planning the itinerary for our pilgrimage to mark the 45th Anniversary of D-Day, we decided to visit not just the main Military Cemeteries, but also the village churchyards and other places where men of the Battalion are buried, and as a consequence learned that in Pont L'Évêque Town Cemetery were 4

military graves. Two were those of RAF aircrew, one Pte Hinchcliffe of the 13th, and the fourth grave was that of an unidentified soldier. Knowing that "Terry" had been seen alive in the German hospital there, I wrote to the War Graves Commission with this information. Their answer was that there was nothing to link the missing officer with that particular grave. But my interest grew, when we visited the grave, and noted the wording on the headstone "An Unknown Soldier of The Parachute Regiment".

"Some years earlier, I had met Terry's brother Peter, at one of the Newton le Willows Memorial Services, and so before our visit in 1999, I contacted him, and as a result, he and his wife, joined our party, and visited both the grave and the hillside at Putot. On our return, a further enquiry was made, via the MOD, to have the grave investigated and a DNA sample obtained, in

266

the hope of establishing the identity of the "Unknown Soldier". The response was disappointing: "The War Graves Commission do not allow the opening of war graves to DNA test the interned remains".

"However, the letter continued… "I should explain that in this case, the dental records of the unknown British soldier interned within the grave were in the CWGC's archives. In addition, 2 copies of Lt Bibby's (left) dental chart, which were on his personal file (P-file), were recalled from the Army archives at Hayes. It was possible, therefore, to compare the charts in order to determine whether the remains in the grave were those of Lt Bibby. The two charts were studied by an Army dentist, who concluded that the remains in the grave were definitely not those of Lt Bibby."

"The letter then continues with information not previously revealed even to his next of kin. In addition Lt Bibby's 'P' File was found to contain contemporary eye-witness accounts from people who had served with him. These stated that he had been severely wounded in the attack, taken prisoner by the Germans, and transferred to hospital in Rouen. These accounts state that he was then sent by rail to Lille, via Amiens and Albert, and that he was not seen after Amiens.

"And there the story ends…"

Also listed as missing, L/Sgt FC Longden and Ptes AM Burns, AG Heaney, J Ryder and W Watson were all captured by the Germans during the battle for Hill 13.

Sgt Colin Longden (6 Platoon, 'B' Company)

"I was severely wounded and I was eventually carried by a German soldier to the farmhouse at the top, where I was treated by a German Medical Officer who had been trained in Edinburgh and spoke very good English. After treating me I was placed on an old cattle truck and sent to Germany. I'll never forget the MO, he waved as we begun our journey. I was to spend the best part of a year in a POW camp hospital where many died of a diphtheria epidemic.

"The camp [Stalag IV-B] was eventually liberated by the Russians and me and a mate escaped and met up with the Americans. By this time I had lost 3 stone."

Colin (below) passed away in June 2010 and a year later his wife, Barbara, took his ashes to be with his 'mates' buried in Putot-en-Auge churchyard. (Photo's courtesy Fay and Bern Robins)

Lieutenant Ellis "Dixie" Dean (MMG Platoon)

"Next day was generally quiet, on one occasion the Vickers opened up on a party of Boche who emerged from the woods on the far side of a wide re-entrant that we were covering. Our new Doctor [Urquhart] was wounded by a sniper as he ensured there were no untreated wounded of either side still on the actual field of battle. Dr Sheills arrived from the Field Ambulance, 3 doctors in 24 hours.

"The German dead lay everywhere, too numerous to count. For the first time the true horror of the bloody business of war was brought home to me on that hillside above Putot. On the way down, I relieved a German officer of his almost new Luger; he had no use for it."

Captain David Tibbs MC (RAMC)

"I was taken, at first by Jeep, and then by ambulance, back to Bayeux, to the blessed haven of a well organised, tented Hospital with QA nurses. It was wonderful and my fullest admiration goes to the RAMC and QA Hospital organisation. My wound was seen to by an operation and next day the surgeon told me that I would never move my shoulder joint again. I found myself amongst the earliest to receive penicillin, at that time a brick red fluid dispensed by multiple injections from an enormous syringe to everyone, and causing an intolerable ache for some hours afterwards.

"A few days later I was taken back to England in a huge tank-landing craft filled with British and Germans wounded all mixed up; squabbles were inevitable, I was initially placed on a lower bunk with a German above, who delighted in swinging his booted foot over the edge near my face, a situation soon remedied by reminding a medical orderly that I was a RAMC medical officer and wished to be in the upper bunk. At night, before we sailed, a German plane dropped bombs round us making one feel very helpless lying with hundreds of others in this cavernous hold of the ship thinking of the carnage a hit would cause.

"We landed at Portsmouth where our kindly WI ladies, dispensing goodies, were shocked by some young SS German soldiers who spat at them. From there we went by train to Basingstoke for a few nights and here I heard my first buzz bomb which came overhead and then cut off. I felt real fear for an eternity until a heavy explosion nearby let me know it had fallen on someone else, this brought home the unpleasant time the civilians where having, not just the soldiers in Normandy. From here I was transported by ambulance-train to Newcastle on Tyne where I spent three weeks before convalescence leave on the Isle of Wight where I met my newly arrived daughter Teresa for the first time."

Private David "Robbie" Robinson (Anti-Tank Platoon)

"Travelling in my unauthorised 30 cwt truck, I had waited for the Battalion in a sunken road at the bottom of 'Hill 13' as they had attacked. The Germans eventually retreated and took with them many of our wounded, including Colin Longden and Jimmy Beasant, 2 men from 'B' Company who had passed the same para course with me and had become personal friends.

"Following the battle, I went with Padre Foy to pick up the dead and took them to the churchyard in Putot. I helped dig their graves and that is where they lay to this day. I noticed whilst we were loading the dead into the truck, the point at which I had stopped and unloaded during the battle, was plainly in view of the Germans and I could've been disposed of quite easily before the attack took place. I can only think that they did not fire at me so that they did not give their positions away."

Lance Corporal Don "Taff" Jones (MMG Platoon)

"Just after I returned to the Battalion I was called on one morning to go on grave digging duties. It was at some little church and we dug graves in a patch of grass about the size of a decent lawn. I remember that the ground smelled sour. We came across bits of bones, so obviously there had been burials there some time in the past. We only dug very shallow graves, perhaps only 18 inches deep and buried some of our comrades there. It did upset me, but that was war I suppose. You have to do it."

Captain Padre Whitfield "Boy" Foy

"The dead were buried in the little churchyard of Putot. 2 days after the battle, normality was seen to be reappearing when the inhabitants of the farm, which had served as our RAP, came on the scene again; they had moved out when the Germans had retreated through Putot because they feared that there might be a battle. The farmer, delighted because the Boche had gone, went into his garden and dug up several bottles of sparkling white wine and we drank to "la liberation". In and around the barn were blood sodden remains of clothing - the reminder of what that liberation was costing every day."

Left: Private George Attridge KIA, one of the non-jumping reinforcements of the South Staffordshire Regiment

ROLL OF HONOUR – PUTOT-EN-AUGE (19 AUG 1944)

LCpl	ASHFORD Herbert	34	5044455	(Nth. Staffs)	Putot-en-Auge Chyd C-9
Pte	ATTRIDGE George A.	29	4038610	(Sth. Staffs)	Putot-en-Auge Chyd C-7
Cpl	BARTON Frank D.	21	14289691	-	Putot-en-Auge Chyd C-10
Lieut	BIBBY Edward M.	24	242993	-	NKG Bayeux Memorial
Cpl	BOTT Frederick	29	6472489	-	Putot-en-Auge Chyd A-3
Cpl	BRASSINGTON Reginald	29	4920167	(Sth. Staffs)	Putot-en-Auge Chyd C-12
Pte	CRUTCHLEY Thomas H.	27	4919420	(Sth. Staffs)	Putot-en-Auge Chyd B-6
Pte	DUGGAN Francis	22	6985293	-	Putot-en-Auge Chyd C-3
Pte	FUNNELL Ernest W.	24	978870	(Sth. Staffs)	Putot-en-Auge Chyd B-5

Pte	GLOVER Charles E.	21	3606921	-	Putot-en-Auge Chyd B-1
Pte	HELLER Alfred V.	25	6723301	-	Putot-en-Auge Chyd C-14
Pte	HEWITT Walter G.	20	14323799	(Hants Regt)	Ranville 2A-J-9 *
Cpl	HUNTER William A.	20	14314694	-	Putot-en-Auge Chyd C-4
Pte	JENKINSON Stanley	19	14668927	(Q.R.R.)	Putot-en-Auge Chyd A-2
LCpl	KNOWLES Charles W.J.	23	5618171	-	Putot-en-Auge Chyd B-4
Cpl	LYONS Austin	23	3393924	-	Putot-en-Auge Chyd C-15
Pte	McCRUDDEN William P.	23	3387610	-	Ranville 5A-P-2 *
Pte	McNALLY William	21	3663313	-	Putot-en-Auge Chyd C-13
Pte	MOLLOY Thomas W.	21	7021780	-	Putot-en-Auge Chyd B-13
Pte	MORRIS Robert A.	27	2933690	(Sth. Staffs)	Putot-en-Auge Chyd C-6
LCpl	PHILLIPS Joseph	21	4547111	-	Putot-en-Auge Chyd C-8
Pte	PROWSE Alexander	31	3769046	-	Putot-en-Auge Chyd C-16
Pte	PYATT Alfred W.E.	23	14414299	-	Putot-en-Auge Chyd B-7
Pte	RENYARD Roy G.	22	14622344	-	Putot-en-Auge Chyd C-11
Pte	RODWELL Bernard V.	21	6103112	-	Putot-en-Auge Chyd C-2
Pte	RUSDALE Cecil C.	19	14370768	-	Putot-en-Auge Chyd A-1
Pte	SANDS Harold	19	5735323	-	Putot-en-Auge Chyd B-2
Pte	SEDDON Henry	22	3394129	-	Ranville 2A-H-9 *
Pte	TONGUE Harry	21	3606770	-	Putot-en-Auge Chyd C-17
Pte	WHITEHEAD Raymond	26	3657106		Bayeux War Cemetery II-H-24 **
Maj	TARRANT Reginald M	31	58149		La Delivrande 6-B-10 ***

*   Died later in the day, evacuated by the RAMC Jeeps Padre Foy called in.
**   Died of wounds 23rd August 1944 (Captain Padre Foy's batman).
***   Died of wounds 28th August 1944.

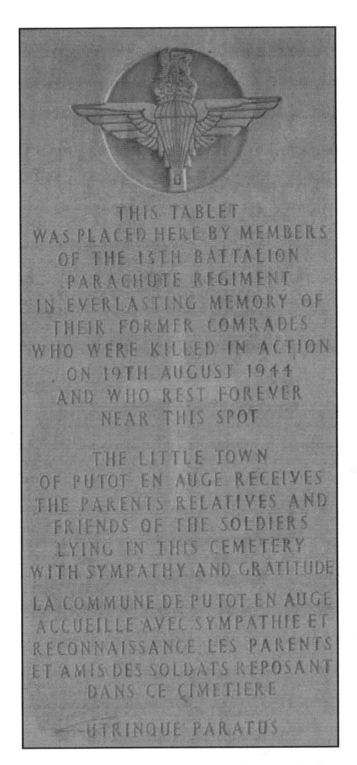

THIS TABLET
WAS PLACED HERE BY MEMBERS
OF THE 13TH BATTALION
PARACHUTE REGIMENT
IN EVERLASTING MEMORY OF
THEIR FORMER COMRADES
WHO WERE KILLED IN ACTION
ON 19TH AUGUST 1944
AND WHO REST FOREVER
NEAR THIS SPOT

THE LITTLE TOWN
OF PUTOT EN AUGE RECEIVES
THE PARENTS RELATIVES AND
FRIENDS OF THE SOLDIERS
LYING IN THIS CEMETERY
WITH SYMPATHY AND GRATITUDE

LA COMMUNE DE PUTOT EN AUGE
ACCUEILLE AVEC SYMPATHIE ET
RECONNAISSANCE LES PARENTS
ET AMIS DES SOLDATS REPOSANT
DANS CE CIMETIERE

UTRINQUE PARATUS

The memorial plaque mounted on Putot-en-Auge Church

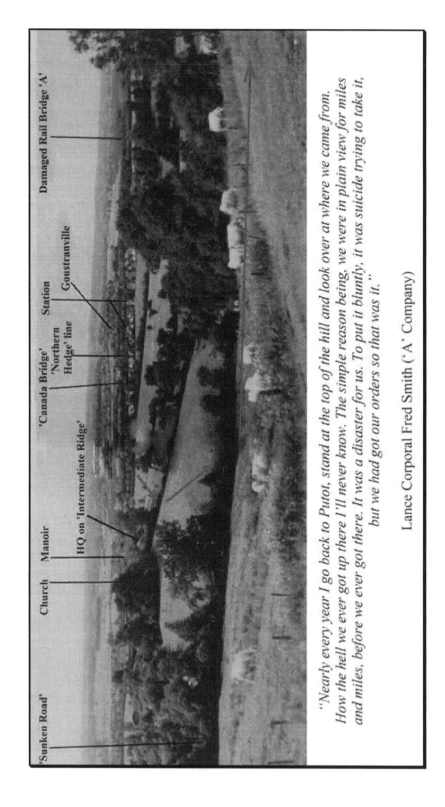

'Sunken Road'   Church   Manoir   'Canada Bridge'   Station   Damaged Rail Bridge 'A'

HQ on 'Intermediate Ridge'

'Northern Hedge' line

Goustranville

"Nearly, every year I go back to Putot, stand at the top of the hill and look over at where we came from. How the hell we ever got up there I'll never know. The simple reason being, we were in plain view for miles and miles, before we ever got there. It was a disaster for us. To put it bluntly, it was suicide trying to take it, but we had got our orders so that was it."

Lance Corporal Fred Smith ('A' Company)

272

Above: The Family of Major Jack Watson MC attending the re-naming of the square at the foot of 'Hill 13' this place was also the 'start line' for the assault.

(Courtesy Fay and Bern Robins, 2011).

Below: The ashes of David Robinson (left) and Harry Watkins (right) are spread by 13 Para veterans Bill Docherty and Fred Smith in 2012.

(Courtesy Fay and Bern Robins, 2012).

"Back at home, just before leaving for France, I had seen my own brother put to rest after dying of rheumatic fever. The comparison was stark. My brother had been washed and dressed and presented with dignity. These boys were still dirty and bloodied from battle, without any coffin, just dropped in the hole."

Private Ken "Ginger" Oldham ('A' Company)

17.   PONT L'ÉVÊQUE

During a very brief rest period, following the costliest day of the Normandy campaign, the 13th Parachute Battalion received 40 reinforcements from the Reserve Company back in the UK. Most of these men were recovered convalescents along with some fresh men who had been left behind prior to D-Day. On top of these additional men a smaller batch joined the Battalion.

Private David "Robbie" Robinson (Anti-Tank Platoon)
"The following day [21st August] I took the Padre to meet 3 of our missing men. They had been hiding after landing miles away from the DZ. Now that the Allied lines had spread across Normandy their hiding place had been over-run. Their names were Len Cox, Joe Whittaker and John Mescki. Len Cox kept a stone he had found in the barn where he had hidden and after the war placed it in his garden. Whilst he was hiding he had carved his name and number on the stone."

Brigadier Nigel Poett (5th Para Brigade Commander)
"The task of the Brigade for 22nd August was to secure the town of Pont L'Évêque and establish a bridgehead over the River Touques. My orders were that the 13th Battalion was to advance on the axis of the Route Nationale 175 and infiltrate into the town. The 12th was to force a crossing south of the town and secure the St Julien feature which controlled the approach from the south."

General Gale (Commander, 6th AB Div)
"The leading elements of Poett's Brigade were pushed forward in what mechanical transport we could collect. This we managed to collect from the Royal Netherlands Brigade and our supply echelons."

Lt Ellis "Dixie" Dean (MMG Platoon)
"Late afternoon on 21st August, we were put on standby for a move forward and transport arrived for the purpose. After the evening meal we moved to the road, where the 3 tonners waited for us, dispersed among an orchard. The decision was made to carry out a rapid debussing in the event of air attack. As we jumped down there was an explosion among the 'B' Company trucks. An insecure grenade in Lance Corporal William Freude's (left, KIA 21/08/1944) pouch had exploded, killing him outright and wounding

several others including Lieutenant Steve Honnor. It was a terrible tragedy, especially as 'B' Company had carried out the final assault and most casualties came from their ranks."

All the units of the 6th Airborne Division were now steaming forward, mostly on foot with the divisional elements following up behind. The move forward was too rapid for the medical units and their MDS at Goustranville was now rapidly falling too far behind the front line, so gathering the dead and wounded as they followed up, they established a new MDS at the abandoned German field hospital in the grounds of Château de Gassard 3 miles SW of Pont L'Évêque (below).

The retreating enemy was denied time to establish their lines in order to minimise the casualties that would inevitably be caused by well sited and dug in defenders.

Lieutenant Ellis "Dixie" Dean (MMG Platoon)

"Our route took us through the small town of Dozulé, where the source of the large fire which had illuminated the sky on the night of the 19th. There was not a building left standing. The place was a mass of rubble and charred timbers, not a single property had been spared and to what purpose? It was really sickening to see the wanton destruction to civilian property.

"The daylight was fading when we reached our RV (La Haie Tondu). Major "Florrie" Ford positioned us and he could be rather short tempered at times and we sorely tested his patience that night.

"Enamel mugs were the cause. We landed in Normandy and carried a pair of mess tins for our food. This arrangement was fine while we lived off 24 hour rations, but the arrival of the cooks brought a problem. The main meal of the day consisted of a meat course, a pudding and also half a pint of tea, and three into two won't go. After a while we were issued a half pint enamel mug. With pouches full of ammo and grenades, where was the mug to be carried? Most of us adopted the same solution; slip it under the fastening tab of the right hand ammunition pouch, where it was always handy for a 'buckshee' brew.

"At the crossroads, Major Ford squeezed through a gap in the hedge and jumped down into a meadow and signalled for us to follow. First the Mortars and MMG's had to unload the trolleys and the delay started his displeasure, but when we jumped down into the meadow he grew very angry indeed. Each man's landing was followed by a "ting, ting, ting" as his mug bounced and struck the metal button fastener on the pouch.

"An 'O' group was assembled in a detached house near the crossroads. We walked into a room where the CO sat studying a map on a table with Leslie Golding. The curtains were drawn and we sat around the table, took out our maps and waited, each with his own individual torch. "There's been a cock up" the CO began, "we've marched through the 3rd Brigade and there are no friendly forces in front of us." An anxious voice then asked "Has this house been cleared?" We switched off our torches and sat in silence as Ken Walton was ordered to check. He went from room to room, we could hear as he opened and closed the downstairs doors, followed by the creaky stairs. I saw the funny side and could barely restrain my laughter.

"The house was reported empty and by first light we were ready to advance. Once again we squeezed through the hedge and deployed in the open field. 400 yards covered later a wire fence was reached, and on it hung triangular signs carrying the dreaded 'skull and crossbones'. The entire Battalion was in a minefield. Perhaps it was a dummy one or an anti-tank one, but we got to the road without a single casualty. From there we stayed on the roads, arriving just short of our objective unhindered."

Private David "Robbie" Robinson (Anti-Tank Platoon)

"I lost the 30 cwt truck getting here. There is a flat high road on the approach to Pont L'Évêque, flat for about three quarters of a mile on top of a hill before a steep drop down into the town. Whilst driving along this part of the road I was observed by the Germans on the hill from the other side of town. The Germans fired at me and the shell landed about 2ft in front of the truck. This blew me off course, through a hedge into a field on the left side of the road. I had 4 burst tyres, windscreen and windows gone, the engine smashed up, the water out of the radiator all over the place, petrol pouring out of the tanks, complete devastation, but I sat there like a window dummy with just glass on me but no harm done! My load of PIAT's and bombs etc were thrown about but none of them were primed, they didn't blow up. Thanks again someone up the top!"

Brigadier Poett (5th Para Bde Commander)

"I concluded that an assault across the open ground south of the town [Pont L'Évêque], which was commanded by the high ground east of the river, would be too hazardous in daylight. Accordingly I issued orders for a night attack. And recce patrols were sent out to prepare for this attack."

Private Ray "Geordie" Walker ('A' Company)

"It was now midday 22nd August and I wondered what fate had in store for us. Lieutenant Hodgson ordered me to act as bodyguard to a Royal Artillery officer [Captain Saddleton, MC]. We entered a field and moved up 100 yards before lying down in the grass to observe a sleepy township in the valley below. It was a lovely summer's day, skylarks were singing and all was peaceful without a gun being fired. On completion of his calculations he ordered me to rejoin my platoon."

276

Private Ken "Ginger" Oldham ('A' Company)

"Moving in a line, under the trees to stay out of sight as much as possible, My Company didn't fool an old French man who came across us. He excitedly waved a large bottle of transparent liquid in front of us; because I was thirsty I drank in great gulps. I collapsed on the floor and thought I was poisoned. It wasn't water, it was Calvados and stronger than any whisky I'd tasted before!"

General Richard "Windy" Gale (Commander, 6th Airborne Division)

"I rushed ahead in my Jeep and found Peter Luard with his battalion already at the river line. Poett's plan was for Luard to infiltrate and to attempt to secure a bridgehead on the east bank. The 12th Battalion were to carry out an assault that night south of the town and secure the rather dominating spur at St Julien.

"I returned from the western half of Pont L'Évêque itself and judging from the reports from the local French people, I concluded that if we rushed the position now we stood every chance of success. I could not find Poett so I sent my orders to him via Lt-Col Harvey."

The people of Pont L'Évêque sense the battle and decide leave.

Brigadier Nigel Poett (5th Para Brigade Commander)

"Colonel Harvey (RAMC) had a personal message for me from General Gale. He had been told by local people that the Germans were about to pull out of their town. Sensing the opportunity of cutting off their retreat, he sent orders, that the crossing was to be forced immediately in daylight and at all cost, I returned at once and issued orders accordingly."

General Richard "Windy" Gale (Commander, 6th Airborne Division)

"It was a decision which may be open to criticism. A commander must be prepared to take risks if he is to grasp opportunities as they appear. As a result of this decision Poett ordered Stockwell [12th Bn] to carry out his crossing at once in daylight."

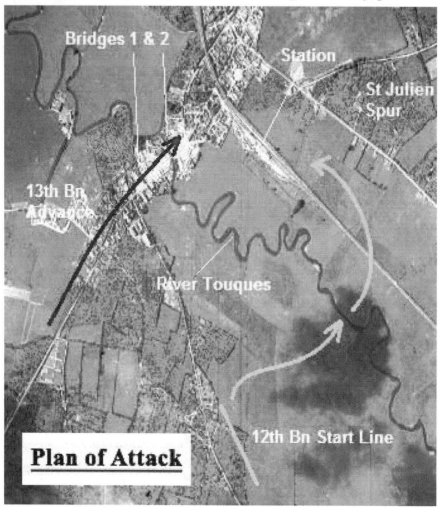

Lieutenant Ellis "Dixie" Dean (MMG Platoon)

"While 'A' Company made sure there were no Boche about, a Jeep came up from the road. Brigadier Poett was driving, accompanied by signallers manning the rover set. He congratulated us on the speed of our advance and went on to say that the Boche appeared to be pulling out of the town and we were to press on in order to seize a crossing over the river.

"Colonel Luard's eyes met mine, "Dixie, go down into the town and find out exactly where the Boche positions are." I called for Andy Fairhurst to join me and entered the town. I moved on the right hand side and 30 yards behind Andy followed on the left hand side. I briefed my escort to keep me in sight and should I be fired upon, he was to ignore me and report to the CO.

"The houses rose directly from the pavement and no gardens at the front, nor were there any gaps or alleyways. If I was fired on, all I could hope to do was to squeeze into a doorway. I went over a little hummock in the road and could now see right into town. Ahead of me, 100 yards away, an excited group of Frenchmen were having an animated discussion. As we approached them all shouting and waving stopped and the party spread across the road to have a good look at the approaching British Army. By now I could see they all wore tricolour armbands, denoting them as members of the Resistance and were all armed with Stens. Doubtless they had listened on their secret radios to the BBC accounts of the advance of the Allies and of their impressive and overwhelming force of tanks and armour, but they were clearly not impressed with the British Army, or at least with its representatives, two scruffy, dusty foot sloggers, one armed with a Sten and the other with a rifle.

"At least my school boy French was understood, since on asking if they knew where the Germans were, the two of us were surrounded by jabbering, gesticulating resistant's. It was completely incomprehensible to me, so I selected the least excitable of them and asked him to show me the enemy positions. He took me first along the side road and there lying on our bellies and peering round the sides of a bridge (pictured below and No.2 on "Dixie's Recce"), he pointed out MMG's on the railway embankment, covering the valley. Then we returned to the main road and now moved into the shopping area, but all the windows were shattered. The reason for this soon became apparent, when we reached the site of the first of the 2 bridges over the river. This had been blown up, but stepping from stone to stone we continued further. Ahead my guide informed me, the other bridge was also destroyed and on the far side was a "cannon". To emphasise the point, the German manning the weapon fired a burst across our front. The heavy "thump, thump, thump" echoed from the high walls and the tracer raced between the buildings. I was also told that machine guns were sited in the houses on the far side of another small square. My guide took me to the open space along the church and pointed out a wooden footbridge, which was intact, but was a trap, machine guns had it covered.

Lieutenant Ellis "Dixie" Dean (MMG Platoon)

"I thought I was in possession of the relevant information regarding the enemy, so I thanked my guide and set off back to the Battalion, meeting them on the outskirts of the town. I informed the CO of all I had learnt, the orders for the advance had already been given out and the MMG Platoon was to support 'A' Company's move up the main street."

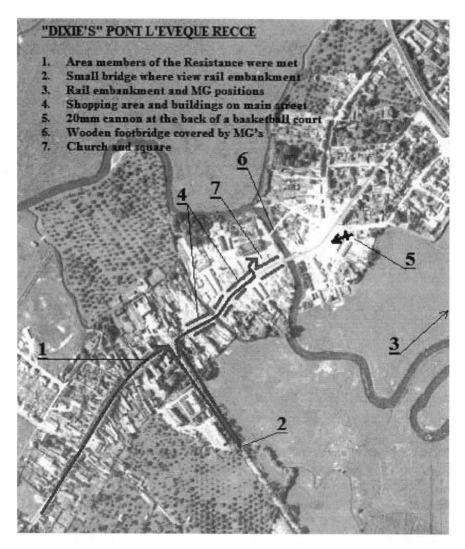

"DIXIE'S" PONT L'EVEQUE RECCE

1. Area members of the Resistance were met
2. Small bridge where view rail embankment
3. Rail embankment and MG positions
4. Shopping area and buildings on main street
5. 20mm cannon at the back of a basketball court
6. Wooden footbridge covered by MG's
7. Church and square

Lt Lack and his party of Para Engineers had also been sent into the town to recce the damage to the bridges, and was most likely be the cause of the gunfire and the 20mm cannon advertising its presence that Lt Dean had heard, and probably why 13 Para had already been given the order to proceed into town and 'ignore' Lt Dean's advice.

Citation: Lt Lewis Lack (3rd Parachute Squadron, RE)

Citation: Lt Lewis Lack (3rd Parachute Squadron, RE)

Award: Military Cross

On 22nd August Lt Lack was in command of a RE recce party in support of 5 Para Bde. 5 Para Bde was following up the German withdrawal with the object of securing crossings over the River Touques in the area of PONT L'EVEQUE. Lt Lack and his party advanced with 13 Para Bn along the road leading into PONT L'EVEQUE. Lt Lack's special task was to report on the state of the bridges and if the bridges were demolished to give an estimate of the size of the gaps and the nature of the bridging equipment which would be required. The leading elements of 13 Para penetrated into the western outskirts and where they encountered small arms fire and mortar fire. Small parties of Germans including snipers appeared to be established on the near side of the River Touques covering the approaches to the bridges. Though under fire Lt Lack crept forward alone and reached the first obstacle where he found the bridge blown, but passable to infantry. He crossed to reach the second obstacle which was 100 yards away. Whilst carrying out the recce he was wounded in the shoulder by MG fire and forced to withdraw after he verified that the second bridge had been blown. Lt Lack made his way back under fire, re-crossed the first obstacle, still under fire and regained his motor-cycle in the outskirts of the town. He reported to HQ 13 Para.

His action was an outstanding example of determination, devotion to duty and utter disregard to his own personal safety. His report was the first information on the River Touques obtained from ground recce and contributed in no small measure to the ultimate success of the bridging operations by the Division over the river.

At 3pm one Company of Lt-Col Stockwell's 12th Bn under the cover of a 20 minute artillery smoke barrage crossed the open ground south of the town. All appeared well as men began crossing the river. The second Company was then sent in to follow.

Major G Ritchie MC (12th Parachute Battalion)

"We were to advance in line across open fields under cover of smoke. 'A' Company advanced and only Captain Baker and 9 other men got across the river where they were pinned down by MG fire. The smoke seemed to run out fast and left a haze. 'B' Company led by Lieutenant John Bercot [who landed in Normandy as Sniper Lieutenant] never even reach the river before being pinned down by mortars and MG's. As Lieutenant Bercot approached the river he was killed."

As the second Company became bogged down as they came under machine gun fire and shelling from the high ground to the east, Brigadier Poett had no choice but to order the attack to cease and consolidate their positions.

'A' Company of 12 Para held on until dusk and only when all their ammunition was expended, did they withdraw. Capt Baker for his actions that day earned the Military Cross. The attempted assault cost the 12th Battalion 1 Officer and 15 other ranks dead and 50 wounded.

During the afternoon as these events were occurring and as it became apparent that another method was needed, the 13th Bn were sent into the town itself.

Major John Cramphorn ('A' Company)

"We were ordered to advance on Pont L'Évêque with all speed and capture and hold the high ground west of the town. This we did with no trouble at all and I set up my Company HQ in a farm, where the lady of the house offered to cook us an omelette. I thanked her and said "Yes please", but before she could serve us, orders came to get down into the town and grab a crossing over the river."

Lieutenant Ellis "Dixie" Dean (MMG Platoon)

"My information that the road was clear even beyond the first bridge was ignored and when we reached the minor road on the right we turned along it and moved down an alley on the left between 2 houses and crossed their back gardens. The women came out to greet their liberators and plied us with cider and small cakes.

"We had to turn back onto the high street short of the first river crossing. If the results of my reccie had been noted, there would have been no need to travel a couple of hundred yards to advance fifty, but we would have missed the light refreshments."

Major John Cramphorn ('A' Company)

"There was no problem crossing the first stream, the bridge had been destroyed but we were able to scramble across. 100 yards further on, all that remained of the main bridge was a single girder, with a multi barrelled 20mm flak gun covering the river bank. The leading Platoon established themselves upstairs in a house overlooking the river. When they first moved in, in the square on the far bank a German officer was conducting on 'O' Group. They quickly dispersed as we opened fire, leaving several casualties behind."

War Diary 22nd Aug

1330   'A' Coy entered PONT L'EVEQUE without opposition until they took up positions fwd of rd junc 518038 just WEST of the br at 520037.

1415   The whole Bn is now in PONT L'EVEQUE – 'A' Coy is heavily engaged from across the river - in addition two MG's and mortars a SP 20mm AA gun has been fired at ground targets.

Lieutenant Ellis "Dixie" Dean (MMG Platoon)

"Dashing up the street towards the main crossing, with the 20mm advertising its presence, we were passing the square leading to the church. Major Cramphorn pointed to a tall house on the left and instructed me to put a machine gun in an upstairs room and cover the way forward. I entered the building via the now missing shop window and led the way up to the third floor. One window overlooked the street and from this high perch I could see beyond the demolitions of the far bridge and was able to pinpoint the location of the 20mm gun. In the far corner of a sizeable open space, behind a typical French urinal of metal construction.

"Since I couldn't engage this target, I looked at the first floor windows of the rather imposing houses across the square to the rear of the gun. In one a machine gun could be seen and we quickly engaged it, and then treated all the other windows to several bursts to prevent enemy observation. All the time the 20mm cannon was blasting away, the tracer flashing across the front and the noise reverberating from the high walls.

"I could see up the road for over 100 yards before it bore away to the left and was surprised to see an SP come round the bend before the driver had second thoughts and backed slowly out of sight.

"Someone came up the stairs behind us, I turned to find Bill Price from the other section. "Sergeant Whalley says can you come quickly Sir? Sergeant Kelly's been wounded." I hurried down the stairs and was led along a cloistered walk towards the church, at the end of which lay 2 bodies. George Kelly and Lance Corporal Harold Turner were dead.

"What a waste of life. They had gone along to watch a detachment of the Mortar Platoon as they carried out assault firing.[33] Clearly this area was under observation and a Boche mortar opened up, accurately around their target. None of the mortars was even scratched, but I lost 2 highly valued NCO's. George Kelly was the most important part in the Platoons development and it was Harold Turner who 'liberated' the cow on D-Day. Tommy Lathom was promoted on the spot."

CSM "Taffy" Lawley ('C' Company)

"A very grim experience for me at this time was the finding of the body of our machine gun sergeant, Sgt Kelly, a great friend of mine; he and another had taken position near the church, which was hit by a Jerry '88'. When we found them, their clothes was smouldering and the heat from the burning buildings had made their bodies swell, making them hardly recognisable."

Lance Corporal Don Jones (MMG Platoon)

"What I remember the most was German and British artillery obliterating Pont L'Évêque, they just blew the place up. During the battle we got caught in mortar fire and that was the last action I saw in Normandy."

Lt-Col Mitchell and Captain Saddleton MC of 150th Field Regiment of the Royal Artillery were still in the forward positions with the 13th Battalion (they had been with them in the thick of the battle to take Hill 13). Captain Saddleton MC got himself involved in the heavy fighting, the war diary of 150 FR states "With a Tommy gun he replied to a snipers fire but was wounded in both hands and evacuated. His OPA, Bdr. Tustin, is missing and believed wounded. His signaller was wounded by a shell splinter in the forehead."

Private Jim Beasant ('B' Company)

"After I had been taken prisoner at Putot-en-Auge, I had been taken to hospital. The French doctor put his life on the line for me. The Germans kept coming back to take me away but he said I had typhoid and so I shouldn't be moved. Eventually the hospital was overrun by the advance of the Allied forces and I was at last liberated."

Lieutenant Shiells the fourth Medical Officer 13 Para had during the Normandy campaign so far, used Pont L'Évêque Hospital on Avenue de la Libération as his RAP. In next to no time the place became busy as increasing numbers of casualties began to flood in (Pont L'Évêque Hospital, below).

---

[33] Firing without the use of a bipod.

Private Ray "Geordie" Walker ('A' Company)

"All hell broke loose. Within minutes we had lost Privates Gregory (left) and Best side by side to a burst of machine gun fire. They were best mates and No.1 & 2 of a Bren gun team sent along the back of the shops via the church, hoping to find a position where they could engage the 20mm cannon. Snipers in the church tower had to be killed quickly to avoid further casualties. The main street had become a death trap and our only movement forwards was by the backs of the houses. Occasionally we were forced to climb over backyard walls. Whilst climbing over one wall the lad next to me got shot in the buttocks. In battle you need a sense of humour to survive, even he saw the funny side of life.

"On our right and near the railway was a 20mm Flak gun that had to be silenced. Lieutenant Hodgson and a Bren team swam across the river to see if they could silence it. Unfortunately they were driven back. Privates "Barney" Wallace and "Geordie" Brown appeared at an upstairs window with a PIAT, but to no avail."

Lance Corporal Fred Smith ('A' Company)

"In Pont L'Évêque, with Lieutenant "Joe" Hodgson; Freddie Beach and I swam the second branch of the river. We boosted Joe up on the bank so he could see over a wall "Get down. Get me down!" was his cry, "Thank god you didn't push me further up. There's an SP just over the wall." We'd nearly pushed him up in plain view of the SP and its supporting infantry. After that we came back over the river, I was carrying the Bren gun. We sheltered in a shop by the bridge as the town by this time was burning. Of course we were soaked to the skin and Joe said "Get stripped off and get some dry clothes on. Help yourself to a pair of dry trousers from one of the nearby shops. And get your own dried out." He did the same and then he went off to check on the rest of the platoon.

"Me and Freddie set the Bren up and along came Major Ford who saw us wearing civvy trousers and said he was putting me and Freddie on a charge for looting civilian property. He then sent someone from 'C' Company (who had come to take over 'A' Company positions) to put us under arrest. I had to leave the Bren and we were taken back to a hill on the opposite side of the road to the cemetery where Battalion HQ had been set up. We were marched straight up in front of the CO, Colonel Luard. Major Ford started going on about the looting and there was no way we could deny it as we were stood in front of them with the civilian clothes on, our own stuff was still drying. From nowhere Joe Hodgson (right) turned up, pushed Freddie and me apart and stood in between us, "If they're on a charge, then so am I. I ordered them to get changed." He said. We were then marched to one side whilst Joe, Major Ford and the CO went into a little huddle. The outcome of which was we were then told that the charge had been dropped and to go back and get changed."

The Germans from 'Place du Marche' bombarded the area of the church (pictured after the battle, below) setting the roof on fire, the bell tower collapsed and the 18th century organ was set on fire. The flames from the church illuminated the town centre and the heat generated became so intense that the bells actually melted.

Lieutenant Ellis "Dixie" Dean (MMG Platoon)

"As I made my way back up to the attic a pile of clothes on the second floor landing were alight and the flames had reached the timbers of the ceiling. We made a hasty evacuation and once in the street, flames could be seen coming from upper windows of other houses."

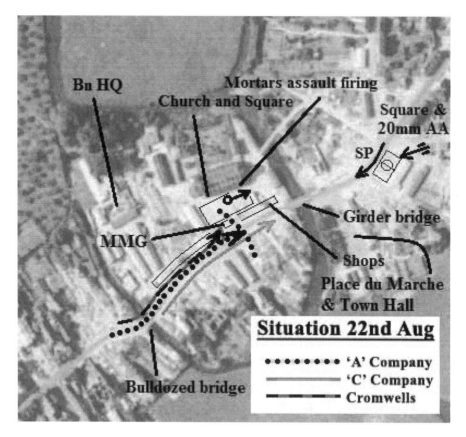

Bn HQ

Mortars assault firing
Church and Square

Square &
20mm AA

SP

Girder bridge

MMG

Shops

Place du Marche
& Town Hall

Situation 22nd Aug

Bulldozed bridge

●●●●●●●● 'A' Company
————— 'C' Company
━ ━ ━ ━ ━ Cromwells

Private Ray "Geordie" Walker ('A' Company)

"Unbeknown to us the Germans had during their retreat, placed incendiary devices in the houses near to our position. With the advantage of an east wind, these charges had been detonated and set fire to the houses we occupied."

Lieutenant Ellis "Dixie" Dean (MMG Platoon)

"Very quickly the main street was an inferno. The occupants of the houses around the square near the cinema were endeavouring to save their furniture by piling it up in the open space. We could neither fight the Boche nor the fire, so we became salvage men.

"Armour support to deal with the "urinal" had been requested and now arrived in the form of 3 Cromwell tanks of the Divisional Armoured Recce Regiment. Accompanying them was a bulldozer which pushed the rubble of the first bridge into the stream, enabling the tanks to cross. They now entered the blazing inferno of the main street and clearly their commander didn't like the look of what lay ahead and they only nosed forward as far as the church square, still some 40 yards short of being able to see their target. The buildings affected by the fire were, by now, becoming unsafe and starting to collapse. Burning timbers cascaded onto the leading vehicle and set on fire the crew's sleeping bags, strapped around the turret. That decided matters; the armour withdrew without firing a shot."

Brigadier Nigel Poett (5th Para Brigade Commander)

"The town was now burning fiercely and, after a reconnaissance with Colonel Luard, I decided that it would not be practicable to make a further attempt to force the crossing of the main river until the fires in the town had died down. At this stage it was thought that the only means of crossing the main river was by the girder and that was under constant fire. I accordingly ordered Colonel Luard to consolidate in the positions reached.

"I then asked for a meeting with the Divisional Commander to discuss the situation. The General sent his GSO1 forward to Brigade HQ where he met me. It was agreed that no further attack should be pressed by Colonel Luard that night and that his Battalion should be ready to seize a crossing place in the morning if this appeared possible. It was also agreed that the proposed attack on the St Julien feature during the night should be cancelled. It was further agreed that, after dark, the 12th Battalion should withdraw from its unpleasant position south of the town. It would then come into reserve and the 7th Battalion assume responsibility for the west and south approaches to the town."

Lieutenant Ellis "Dixie" Dean (MMG Platoon)

"We had been in the town for several hours now and in a short time it would be dark. We moved back into the western end of the town, we came to a field on the outskirts and the supper meal was served. I suddenly realised how hungry I was, the last meal had been breakfast although by now we always carried some 'hard tack' biscuits and part of the previous days chocolate to eat with them."

Lance Corporal Fred Smith ('A' Company)

"I think because of Freddie [Beach, right] and mine's little incident with the civilian clothes, we were sent with Captain Skeate to show him where we crossed the river the previous day. We had to find out if Jerry had pulled out during the night as it had been a quiet one."

Brigadier Nigel Poett (5th Para Brigade Commander)

"In the morning Colonel Luard and I carried out a recce. A patrol under Captain Skeate had succeeded in crossing the river without opposition, the fires had died down

and it appeared that the chance of securing a bridgehead on the far bank was now favourable. I therefore ordered Colonel Luard to secure this bridgehead with the utmost speed."

13th Para Battalion War Diary Appendix

The night was uneventful and at dawn the following day one platoon of 'B' Company was sent forward to find a way through the burning houses and force a crossing of the river, establishing a bridgehead. This platoon under Captain Skeate went forward and reported having crossed and established a bridgehead on the right. The rest of the battalion was therefore ordered over as quickly as possible. This was carried out satisfactorily but almost at once the enemy seemed to have been reinforced, and 'B' Company under Major Grantham reported that they were held up. This seemed to be the vital flank, 'A' Company were sent forward to help and 'C' Company were held in reserve, with one platoon holding on the left where opposition was stronger.

Battalion Headquarters moved to the Safe Deposit of the Bank [Societe Generale, pictured today], wonderfully the only un-burnt building in that part of Pont L'Évêque.

Cpl Dennis Boardman (Signaller, att 'A' Coy)

"We rested for the night, got fed and I slept in the local cinema. I visit the cinema every year when I go over. In the morning 'A' company got the job of attacking, going across the girder. I had the radio and things went well. The streets were very narrow; you wouldn't get a car up them. We found the houses, mostly 18th century and wooden, they had been booby trapped and easily set on fire the previous day and were now looking in a sorry state."

War Diary 23rd Aug

0600   One pl of 'B' Coy succeeded in crossing the br, and made its way forward to the houses at 522037. This pl was quickly followed up by the remainder of 'B' Coy and by 'A' & 'C' Coys until a bridgehead over the river had been formed. Further progress was held up by stiff opposition.

Private Alfred Draper (South Staffs Regt att. 8 Platoon 'C' Company)

"That night we slept where we could and were just going to have breakfast in the morning when the order came to move. No breakfast! Someone had found a crossing and we had to get across quickly. We were immediately pinned down by enemy fire and spent the rest of the day on piles of hot rubble - the remains of burnt out houses."

Area destroyed by fire (Night 22nd Aug)

Lt Ellis "Dixie" Dean (MMG's)

"It'd rained heavily during the night and next morning we found that the rifle companies had disappeared into town. We caught up with the Rear HQ and met CSM Parrish, he'd come back to collect urgently required 2" mortar bombs.

"Together we moved through the smouldering town and towards the second bridge, this was a single girder, 18" wide and 20 yds long. That was the good news. The bad news was that the girder was under enemy fire. However he went first and showed us the way.

"You started running yards short of the girder. "Don't look down, there's a drop of 10 feet into the water." Off he went and he reached the far bank without attracting enemy fire. Now it was my turn, I was on the girder before I realised how narrow it was. I could see the big 'kink' we were warned of. A big leap and I was over it and safely on the far bank. The two of us waited in a ruined building for Ken and then scrambled through rubble of the burnt out shells of buildings to where the Battalion HQ was established in the underground vaults of a bank. The CO was in conversation with Brigadier Derek Mills-Roberts of the Commandos. My task was to cover the valley south of the town and watch for any attempt to bring reinforcements into Pont L'Évêque. The Mortar Platoon had an identical role.

"I took the Platoon to where the Frenchman had shown me the German positions the previous day whilst on my reccie. Here in a little hollow, with the road and stream immediately in front. Any Boche reinforcements would come down the road on the left that climbed upwards along the St Julien spur. The railway embankment on the far side of the valley had enemy plainly visible and moving about. We engaged them and in return we were shelled, but with no casualties.

"All day sounds of battle came from the town. Major Ford emerged from the buildings to our left and gave me fresh orders. The Battalion were to break off the engagement. My task was to find sufficient transport to move the stretcher cases."

Lance Corporal George O'Connor ('C' Company)

"A smoke screen was laid and across we went as we reached the other side of the river, the smoke screen disappeared, we were out in the open and trapped, bullets began to fly around us, the Germans had caught us in a trap and we had fallen for it. At the end of the road was a tank that began firing its machine guns. The tank came rumbling towards us we all dived in to nearest houses for cover, the tank began to fire its heavy gun at the houses, even though there must have been German soldiers in some of them, we ran out of the rear of the house, as I did another smoke screen was being laid so I dashed back into another house, I thought I might be able to throw a phosphorus grenade at the tank, so I dashed up the stairs, I could hardly see my way, the air was thick with smoke and dust, I reached the top of the stairs, through an open doorway was a German soldier leaning out of the window, firing a machine gun, I gave him a burst with my Sten, he fell out of the window taking his gun with him, I looked out of the window, but the tank was out of throwing range."

War Diary 23rd Aug

1240 *After several hours of stiff fighting the enemy has been observed to bring up reinforcements in tpt. Our armour has been ordered up to give covering fire.*
1330 *Orders received to give up bridgehead and withdraw through a covering force of one Coy 7 Para Bn.*

Brigadier Nigel Poett (5th Para Brigade Commander)

"At noon it was reported by Major Ford, the second-in-command, that both Companies were held up and that the Germans were attempting to infiltrate between their positions. It was clear to me that the foothold gained by the 13th Battalion on the east bank of the river was too small and the communications too insecure to make it practicable as a route for a fresh attack. Its retention could only lead to severe casualties. I therefore decided to withdraw the 13th Battalion and that the 7th Battalion should assume responsibility for the western end of the town, and form a firm base through which the 13th Battalion could withdraw."

Private Ray "Geordie" Walker ('A' Company)

"We received an urgent order to withdraw to the river and bring all our wounded with us as they could not be left to be cremated. This was a difficult task and doors were torn from their hinges to be used as stretchers. Two lads yelled "Nobby, Geordie, take this stretcher whilst we go back to look for more wounded.

"Our 'patient' was Sergeant Hughes, he had a gaping wound to the stomach which exposed his intestines and life was flowing from him. To get him to safety we had to take a chance of walking down the main street and hope we wouldn't get gunned down. Nobby was our wireless operator and his movements were slow because of the weight on his back. The street was littered with fallen masonry, broken telephone lines and piles of bricks.

"Whilst passing a burning house I saw a woman in a doorway, she was silhouetted against flames and unable to move. She was petrified by the carnage and in my best schoolboy French; I yelled at her 3 times but to no avail. Her death would be of the utmost horror."

Rue Thouret (above) and Rue Hamelin (below) the streets where the bulk of the German reinforcements and armoured vehicles came down.

The following photographs are a view from the approximate positions where the rifle companies secured the bridgehead:

1. Looking down Rue Hamelin and the building on the left is the one on the corner of Rue Thouret and Rue Hamelin. The man in the road is approximately in the same spot as the soldier in picture 2.
2. Rue Thouret on the left and Rue Hamelin on the right. The German reinforcements came down these streets supported by SP's an armoured cars.
3. Same spot in 2012.
4. Ghost picture.

Lance Corporal George O'Connor ('C' Company)

"Bullets were being fired at us from a window; it was a lone brave German, fighting to the last. A couple of paras ran into the house, just as I was going to fire at him, so I dodged for cover instead, the paras ran from the house, shouting "We got the bastard". Joe Bartram was sheltering in a doorway carrying a Bren gun, I ran to his side, we were about to leave the doorway, when a German tank arrived. I fired my Sten at the tank, one burst and I had run out of ammunition, I dropped down in the shelter of what I thought was a wall to replace my magazine, Joe Bartram stepped over me, firing his Bren gun from the hip, a few shots from the Bren and it seized up, he calmly stepped back into the doorway, checked the gun and returned to fire again. The tank sped off unaware we were there. I looked at my little wall; it was made of cardboard and ply wood, it was full of bullet holes, why I hadn't been hit, I shall never know.

"Those of us that had seen Joe in action suggested that Joe was entitled to a medal, the answer we received was that the medals could only be awarded to the paratroops and not the Infantry reinforcements."

Amidst the ruined and burning town many of the 13th Battalion men earned themselves distinctions fighting many private battles, normally out numbered, to hold on to the very small bridgehead.

Citation: Sergeant John Goodall

Award: Military Medal

On the 23rd August 1944, 'B' Company was in the forefront of an attack against a strong German rearguard holding the crossing over the river Touques in the burning village of Pont L'Évêque. Sgt Goodall was second in command of a section detailed to attack a house on the other side of a street in Pont L'Évêque which the enemy was holding in strength.

During the attack the section came under accurate fire from the right flank and Sgt Goodall and two others were wounded. Still under heavy fire Sgt Goodall bandaged his comrades and took them to safety, one at a time. He then went forward alone and disregarding his own wounds, charged across open ground and silenced the enemy machine gun with his Sten. Not until the end of the action were his own wounds dressed. Sgt Goodall's actions and leadership throughout were in the highest traditions of the Parachute Regiment.

Citation: Private Bernard Batho

Award: Military Medal

On Wednesday 23rd August, while engaged in an attack in Pont L'Évêque, two men of Private Batho's section were wounded and were seen lying in the open in bullet swept ground. Private Batho at once went forward alone with his Bren gun firing from the hip, so as to keep down the enemy's fire. He succeeded in carrying both men to safety, one at a time and in spite of extremely heavy enemy fire directed at him. He rejoined his section with his Bren still in action and was an inspiration to his comrades at a most difficult and dangerous time.

Note: Both Sergeant Goodall and Private Batho were originally recommended for the DCM but again it was later downgraded to the MM.

Around this time Ernest Hurst recorded that his mate L/Cpl Thomas Medlicott was killed after a tank fired from down the street and demolished the house he was occupying.

13th Para Battalion War Diary Appendix

'A' and 'B' Companies concentrated in two big houses and assisted by a couple of PIAT's succeeded in making some progress, but the enemy were too numerous for them to be able to make good their gains and they therefore reported at about mid-day that though they seemed not to be able to make further progress, they could hold on to what they held.

Shortly after this they reported more enemy arriving in Volkswagens round the flank and Brigade was asked for No.48 Commando, which actually arrived five minutes later, as a reserve for the Battalion.

At about 1230 hrs, the enemy counter-attacked strongly and though held, casualties were suffered and the troops were becoming tired.

The troop of Cromwells was therefore requested to move up to the area of the second bridge to prevent enemy armour coming forward through the town and dividing up our forces. This was agreed but, the conflagration from the town was such that it was not possible to bring them forward.

At 1325 hrs, Rear Battalion Headquarters received a direct from a shell and the Brigade set was put out of action.

At about 1330 hrs, the Brigade IO arrived at Advanced Battalion Headquarters with a message from the Brigadier that nothing was being gained by holding on and the Battalion was to withdraw in its own time under orders of the Commanding Officer.

The Battalion was therefore ordered to withdraw in the order 'B', 'A', 'C' Companies and all casualties and spare men were sent back at once. 'B' Company was to be clear by 1415 hrs and 'A' and 'C' to follow when clear. All Companies to be across river by 1445 hrs. The artillery was asked to fire on the Station area and line of the railway at 1415 hrs and on the line of the river at 1445 hrs.

The withdrawal went according to plan, except that the enemy, who had been able to work round the left flank, managed to get a machine gun firing down the river and an armoured car firing down the main street, thus preventing crossing the river by the girder that remained of the bridge and making any crossing most difficult.

Corporal Dennis Boardman (Signaller, att 'A' Company)

"We couldn't go forward into the open ground; the Germans had two MG42's shooting at us. We headed back through the flames back to the river; we couldn't cross via the girder as another MG42 was firing down the river. One of the lads on the other side the river found a long rope in a builders yard, tied it round his waist and swam across, he must have been great swimmer because the water was raging. That's how we crossed, via the rope. The bloke next to me was hit and he was washed down stream. I think it was Private Hinchcliffe."[34]

Lance Corporal George O'Connor (8 Platoon 'C' Company)

"A few paras were running towards the river, we followed, someone had fitted a wire across the river, we grabbed hold of it and ferried ourselves across the river, bullets were being fired at us from all directions, luckily, the blown up bridge gave us some protection, bullets were ricocheting off the girders that were protruding from the water. We scrambled up the river bank and ran through the smoke, until we reached the safety of our tanks, then fell down beside them gasping for breath; I think we were lucky, we didn't lose as many men as we could have, thanks to the smoke screen."

Private Alfred Draper (South Staffs Regt att. 8 Platoon 'C' Company)

"A shell had seriously wounded our Corporal and we had to carry him out at the double. I was one of the 2 front men carrying and was nicked on the knee by a bullet from our own machine gun that was covering us. I tripped and fell, dropping the poor man and the others did the same, thinking we were under fire. We soon recovered and picked him up again and carried on.

"When we got to a safer place we transferred him on to a door and gave him a shot of morphine. The poor fellow was in a lot of pain and it hadn't helped dropping him. We carried him over the river and handed him over to the medics who took him to hospital. We heard later that he had died from his wounds there."

The Corporal was Cyril Eckert. His brother, Stan of the 9th Para Bn, was killed on D-Day.

Back in August 1943 Cyril's brother, Stan Eckert passed his parachute course at the age of 18 and subsequently joined the 9th Parachute Battalion. In October 1943 his older brother, Cyril (21), also volunteered and obtained his wings joining the 13th Battalion. Both jumped on D-Day and helped secure their objectives, Stan at Merville and Cyril in Ranville.

Stan was killed a few hours later, shortly after writing a letter home. It was found on him the next day by a member of the Commandos who had taken over the Merville position. The Commando then forwarded the letter to the Eckert family.

---

[34] It was indeed Private George Hinchcliffe; his body was found later and buried in Pont L'Évêque Cemetery. He lies next to an 'Unknown Soldier of the Parachute Regiment' (the one Dixie Dean thought might have been Lt Bibby, MIA – Putot-en-Auge). After looking through the rolls of honour for the 6th Airborne Div, I could find no soldier listed as 'No Known Grave' killed around the time of this battle; I can only assume that the Unknown Soldier died in the Hospital (which was held by the Germans) or was an escape/evader or even executed.

Letter written by Stan Eckert (9th Para Bn)

Dear Mum,

I am writing this letter at the bottom of a ditch very near the front line and hope to get it posted, pretty soon... as my pal and I have a very good idea that tomorrow we will be prisoners of war.

I am writing this short note here so as if it is ever found by anyone they can forward it for me.

Do you know Mum dear, I have never realised how much you meant to me, until now? If I can get home again, you will see a very different Stan, just wait and see. The same goes for Dad too, and the rest of the Eckerts.

There is one thing that worries me, and that is what happened to Cyril. I hope and pray that he is safe and well.

Well, Mum, just sit and wait for the end of the war when I will be 'home' once again, for good. Don't worry at all, will you.

With love to everyone at home, especially you.

Your ever loving son,

Stan xxxxx

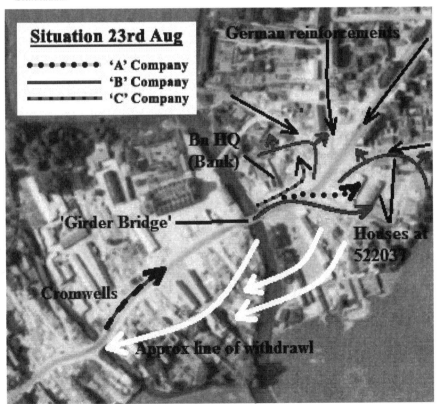

Private David "Robbie" Robinson (Anti-Tank Platoon, att 'C' Company)

"One of the men from the forward groups was delaying us getting across the river. He had been badly wounded in the groin area and his private parts had been affected. His name was L/Cpl Morgan, a man who had been moved from pillar to post within the Battalion. He had been moved from one Company to another and had even acted as batman to Colonel Luard himself. I saw him in about 1980 and he told me that he had fully recovered and had even had children."

Left: View south of withdrawal route. Right: View north of MG and 'Girder' Bridge

Private Ray "Geordie" Walker ('A' Company)

"On arrival at the river [with the wounded Sergeant Hughes] we met Major Nobby Clark who was standing up to his chest in water blazing away with his revolver against a troublesome German machine gunner. Now it was our turn to enter the water and it was with difficult to keep the stretcher above the water, we were almost neck deep. Many hands from the river bank took the stretcher from us. We literally collapsed with our backs to the wall of the opera house [cinema]. Despite being soaked, we needed a few minutes rest and a smoke. I had a tin of 50 Players cigarettes in my pack and they were dry."

CSM "Taffy" Lawley ('C' Company)

"Medic Bert Roe MM swam the river which was under very heavy fire, in order to fix a wire hauser across it, so that we could evacuate the many wounded across.

"When we had withdrawn to the high ground and dug in "Nobby" asked me for a drink of water so I passed him my water bottle. It was only after a long drink that he discovered that it was red hot water. 10 minutes later he was asleep on the grass with a few gas capes thrown over him. Shortly afterwards the CO came along and enquired where my commander was. I very tremulously pointed to the gas capes and told him what had happened. Expecting to be told off, he said "Good work, see he is not disturbed." Later much to "Nobbys" disgust he was evacuated. After, he always cursed my water bottle and never again asked me for a drink."

Lieutenant Colonel Peter Luard (CO, 13th Bn)

"This most difficult operation was carried out under fire with absolute steadiness, no wounded being left on the far bank. The Battalion's casualties in 2 days fighting were 10 killed and 33 wounded.

"In the final phase of the withdrawal a man was wounded and his evacuation on a door across the river was a most difficult operation. Major "Nobby" Clark, gave covering fire with his 9mm pistol, standing up to his shoulders in water, laughing as he returned the fire of a German machine gun and as the bullets splashed all around him. He was not hit and the wounded man was got safely across. That night, while he was asleep, a man stumbled over him, stamping on his ankle, spraining it so badly, he was unable to walk and he had to be evacuated to hospital. Such are the fortunes of war.

"It was Private Bert Roe MM, one of the Medical Orderlies, who was once more to demonstrate the skill, bravery and devotion to duty of these remarkable men, when he improvised a raft using a door on which the stretcher cases were floated to safety."

Major John Cramphorn ('A' Company)

"Major "Nobby" and I were the last 2 members of the 13th to wade the river to safety. We were not able to cross the girder until the early hours of the morning and spent the best part of the day fighting our way slowly forward, but casualties were mounting. Orders came that the Battalion were to break off contact with the enemy and withdraw. A really tricky operation but we pulled it off."

Citation: Major John Cramphorn

Award: Croix de Guerre with Vermilion Star

Throughout the operations in which the 13th Bn The Parachute Regiment have been engaged, Major Cramphorn has led the Company that he trained with outstanding ability and gallantry.

While the Battalion was in Ranville and later in the Le Mesnil areas, 'A' Company, under Major Cramphorn's command was never otherwise than inspired by his personal example of gallantry, under fire, high standard of leadership and personal initiative.

Later when the Division advanced to follow up the retreating Germans, Major Cramphorn once more led his Company with conspicuous ability. Especially was this so at Pont L'Évêque, where by his extraordinary coolness and example under extremely heavy fire, at many times directed at him personally, he refused to run and take cover, but treated the enemy with a contempt that was an inspiration to his men in a most difficult battle when they were at all times hard pressed and outnumbered. His conduct and example have at all times been beyond praise and in the highest traditions of the Service.

Note: Major Cramphorn was originally recommended for the MC, but was changed to the Croix de Guerre with Vermilion Star.

Citation: Major Alfred Reeves Clark

Award: Military Cross

By Wednesday August 23rd, "C" Company, commanded by Major Clark was the Reserve Company of the Battalion which was engaged in attacking strongly positioned and reinforced enemy troops in Pont L'Évêque. His Company area was subjected to continual heavy enemy fire and was, furthermore, seriously on fire in many places. Throughout the action Major Clark moved about among his men, imperturbable and encouraging them by his splendid leadership.

Eventually the battalion was ordered to withdraw and Major Clark's company was the rearguard. During this withdrawal, Major Clark showed the most splendid possible leadership and coolness under intense enemy fire. Finally he was the last to cross the river, covering the crossing standing in the middle of the river while the last man crossed, laughing and using his automatic.

Throughout Major Clark's conduct has been beyond praise and in the finest traditions of the Parachute Regiment.

Note: Major Clark was originally recommended for a DSO but the award was later downgraded to an immediate MC.

13th Para Battalion War Diary Appendix

By 1440 hrs all troops were across except one wounded man, whose passage delayed the crossing of the final few until about 1450 hrs. All was, however, well, as the Brigadier had most wisely told the artillery to fire on order only. As it was then, all wounded were withdrawn successfully and the Battalion was reorganised above the village and the next day passed through and advanced after the retreating enemy.

It was discovered that evening that the enemy had consisted of 800 men fresh from the South, and the next day 127 German graves were found in Pont L'Évêque.

Citation: Lieutenant-Colonel Peter John Luard

Award: Distinguished Service Order

On Aug 23 Lt-Col Luard Commander 13 Para Bn was ordered to force a crossing over the River Touques and secure a bridgehead on the far bank up to the outskirts of Pont L'Évêque. On the previous day his battalion had succeeded in penetrating into the western part of the town but had been unable to cross the river owing to stiffening opposition and the fact that the town had been set on fire and the approaches to the only crossing – a steel girder 80 ft long by 18 ins wide – had become *impassable. Although the fire had died down during the night the town was still burning fiercely and the iron girder crossing was under fire from snipers and mortars; nevertheless Lt-Col Luard succeeded in getting his three rifle companies and a small Bn HQ across the girder and established a small bridgehead which was in reality only a footing on the far bank. The enemy resistance in the town, however was very strong and his battalion was unable to make progress and were themselves being strongly counter-attacked and enemy infiltration was taking place towards the girder bridge. As a further advance was clearly impracticable Lt-Col Luard was ordered to withdraw his battalion to the West bank.*

The return journey over the water obstacle and through the burning streets involved a most hazardous operation in the face of steadily increasing enemy pressure. Lt-Col Luard organised his withdrawal with the greatest skill and by his personal leadership, courage and example completed it successfully. There were some 30 wounded men who had to be got across the river by means of a rope, the crossing by the girder being to vulnerable. He organised this evacuation of the wounded with the utmost coolness and not a single man was left behind.

This fine performance followed close on three months of outstanding work: Lt-Col Luard had dropped with his battalion on the night June 5/6 and had speedily secured the objectives allotted to him. His leadership and example had played a big part in keeping up the morale of his battalion during the difficult period of defensive fighting at Le Mesnil. During the advance to the River Seine and particularly at Putot en Auge on 19 Aug his energy, determination and courage was a source of constant inspiration to all ranks.

Citation: Major Gerald Henry Dearlove Ford

Award: Military Cross

Major Ford was promoted second-in-command of the 13th Parachute Battalion while in France.

He carried out his duties with most marked ability and gallantry. He was always completely calm and collected no matter what the fire or the situation in which the Battalion was engaged. At Putot-en-Auge on 19th August, where he was slightly wounded his conduct in organising the rear of the battalion, which under artillery fire during this advance was beyond praise, again two days later at Pont L'Évêque he moved without hesitation to organise the withdrawal of the battalion, and afterwards returned into the blazing town under fire to recover the body of his batman who had been hit during the action.[35]

Throughout the campaign Major Ford's conduct has been a splendid example to all ranks of the battalion. His leadership and ability are most marked and deserving of recognition.

---

[35] Private Fred Binns/Jack Missing

Citation: Corporal Robert Scott

Award: Military Medal

Throughout the operations in which the 13ᵗʰ Battalion The Parachute Regiment have been engaged, the exploits of Corporal Scott, RAMC, attached to this battalion, have been a constant source of inspiration and encouragement to the men of the battalion. He has never been known to fail to render first aid to any man who has been wounded, no matter what the fire, and he has never been known to consider his own safety for one moment. At Pont L'Évêque he was giving first aid to a wounded Corporal, when a German machine gun wounded him in the fingers while he was dressing the Corporal's wounds. He took not the slightest notice but continued to dress his wounds, after which he carried him to safety. Wherever wounded were, no matter what the fire, there was always Corporal Scott to be found. Several times wounded were encouraged just by being told by their comrades, "It's all right Corporal Scott is here". No example has at any time been finer and there could not possibly have been a greater courage displayed than that constantly shown by Corporal Scott.[36]

Throughout the battle and at Lt-Col Luard's side was the commanding officer of the 150ᵗʰ Field Regiment, RA, Lt-Col Mitchell. He had been helping direct the artillery fire from his guns along with the wounded Captain Saddleton MC. This well directed fire no doubt helped save the lives of many 13 Para soldiers by keeping the SP's and armoured cars at bay.

Citation: Lt-Col James Mitchell (150ᵗʰ Field Regiment, RA)

Award: Distinguished Service Order

This officer has shown most exceptional ability, devotion to duty and resourcefulness in the handling of 150 (SNH) Fd Regt RA in support of 6 Airborne Division during the period Aug 17-25.

At PUTOT-EN-AUGE during Aug 18 and 19, the one Regt directly supported separate attacks by three bdes. As a result this officer was constantly with the fwd infantry under heavy fire, supervising the work of his FOO's, co-ordinating the fire of more than one Regt, and at critical moments directing fire himself – with marked success.

At PONT L'EVEQUE on Aug 22 and 23, he remained in fwd OP's directing fire and controlling FOO's in the attack by 5 Para Bde and later in the extrication of a Bn from the town.

His disregard for personal safety and exhaustion was an example to all ranks of his regiment, with the direct result that arty fire was immediately available at critical moments of the Div's advance.

---

[36] On the recommendation sheet he was originally recommended for the DCM but later had been downgraded to the MM. There was often confusion regarding Corporal (later Sergeant) Scott's decorations, some stating that he held both DCM and MM. I could find no other citation for Robert Scott; perhaps this downgrading is where the confusion stems from.

Private Ray "Geordie" Walker ('A' Company)

"50 years after the battle of Pont L'Évêque I revisited the town and was more than annoyed to see a plaque in the town centre car park, which claimed that the town had been liberated by the Princess Irene Brigade under the command of Lt-Col De Ruyter Van Steveninok. Perhaps the fighting by the 13th Parachute Battalion was a mirage?"

The 23rd August was also an extremely heartbreaking day for the people of Lancashire, on top of the 10 dead and 33 wounded from the battle at Pont L'Évêque, an American 8th Army Air Force B-24 Liberator bomber crashed in heavy rain, into the Holy Trinity School in Lytham Road, Freckelton at 10.30am. 38 children were killed along with 20 teachers and civilians, and also the 3 man crew of the aircraft.

This was the worst aircraft crash in Britain during the war. The bomber, from the American Base at nearby Warton, was on a test flight when the pilot was instructed to land immediately because of an electrical storm.

Above: Rue St Michael (looking west from the 'Girder' bridge, similar position to one showing paras crossing bridge further on, note markings on the right chimney breast) after some of the rubble had been cleared.

Lieutenant Ellis "Dixie" Dean (MMG Platoon)

"I had taken the Platoon motorcycle to find transport to help move the wounded. I drove into an area where the Commandos were resting, and there were several Jeeps and trailers parked under the trees. Before I had finished making my request for help to their officer, one of the drivers got to his feet, started up his vehicle and pulled up along side me. We drove back into town together, through the ranks of the withdrawing rifle companies and up to the main bridge. The last of the wounded was being strapped to the bonnet of a Field Ambulance Jeep. It was [Signals Officer] Lieutenant Malcolm Town (left), he looked ghastly and was heavily sedated, but he was back in action within a few days. Two other officers were wounded in the heavy fighting, Lieutenant Cyril Bailey was wounded by mortar fire and never rejoined us, nor did "Steamer" Boyle, the non-para reinforcement from the Lancashire Fusiliers."

Below: (Then, Now & Ghost) Ambulance crews operate outside of Pont L'Évêque.[37]

Brigadier Nigel Poett (5th Para Brigade Commander)

"The night of the 23/24 August was quiet. Patrols at first light, 6am, discovered that the Germans had slipped out of the town during the night. I ordered an immediate follow-up by the 7th Battalion on the axis of the Pont Audemer road. At 10am the General arrived at Brigade HQ. He gave orders for an immediate advance on Pont Audemer. The 7th Battalion had already got well beyond the first of the Division's bounds and their progress fitted in well with the Divisional plan."

---

[37] Then & Now photographs courtesy Carl Rymen.

Then, Now & Ghost: Members of the Mortar Platoon prepare to move out. The photo was taken from the window (circled) in the building opposite the Old Covenant on Rue St Michael.

The above photograph was also taken from same window as the Mortar Platoon one showing the paratroopers leaving the destruction of Pont L'Évêque behind. (Note the Church in the background). This street was the one lined with shops where Lt Dean had conducted his recce only 2 days before.

Below: The same street before the battle. The building where the Mortar Platoon was pictured was the last to be left standing after the fires, as was the house where the previous two photos were taken from (below, right).

Rue St Michael
(same road Paras leaving photo
photo's taken from window)

Mortar Platoon
photographed here

◄ Old Convent

Below: Hotel de Brilly 'Then & Now' - the last building severely damaged on the opposite side of the street.

Lieutenant Ellis "Dixie" Dean (MMG Platoon)

"During the night the Boche pulled out of the town and the 7th chased him up the road to Pont Audemer. The 13th moved forward as right flank protection to the 7th.

"Plodding slowly down into Pont L'Évêque, now strangely quiet compared to the previous days. Movement through the town was slowed by the lead companies crossing the girder. The buildings bordering the main street were completely gutted by the fire and were empty shells compared to the fine shops 48 hours ago. The centre of the town was just a wilderness of rubble, and for what purpose had this obscene horror been perpetrated upon the civilian population for?

"As we crossed the girder bridge our actions were recorded by an official war photographer. This was the only time that I ever saw one such member of the press."

Lt Dean's MMG was in this top window

The people of Pont L'Évêque suffered terribly. 11 civilians were dead, a further 15 injured and of the 811 properties in the town, 273 were completely demolished and 278 severely damaged. The town was reduced by 68%. As Dr Suleau who had stayed in the town for the duration of the battle, concluded, "I had never seen the Normans crying. A Norman never cries. But Thursday, August 24, 1944, in the ruins of a hot and sorry Pont L'Évêque, the Normans were crying."

Above: The ruins of the Church, again taken from Rue St Michael

Below: Yet more destruction. The Grand Café de Paris.

Below: The 1914-1918 Monument and Town Hall in the Place du Marche, before and after the battle (last view taken from the church).

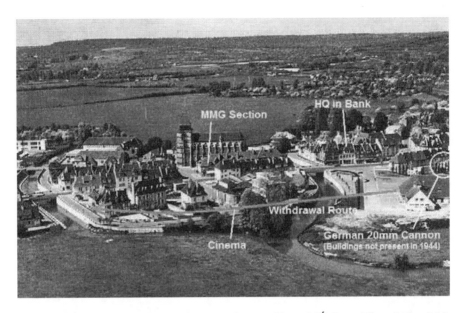

MMG Section

HQ in Bank

Withdrawal Route

German 20mm Cannon
(Buildings not present in 1944)

Cinema

The above photo shows the rebuilt central area of Pont L'Évêque. The whole of this area was obliterated by artillery and fires; very few of the buildings that stood in 1944 still stand today. The photo helps visualise how close the battle actually was. The fields north and south of the town were swept by MG fire and the troops, bottled up in the buildings, were subjected to intense artillery and small arms fire. In 2 days this area was turned to smouldering rubble...

Private Ken "Ginger" Oldham ('A' Company)

"The saddest duty and the one that most affected me most, was burial duty. After Ranville was liberated, there were hundreds of dead soldiers to be buried. The bodies were piled up above ground, each one wrapped in his gas cape and with his face covered so that the grave diggers did not have to see them. But as they were laid into their grave, the grave digger had to open the cape and remove the identity disc for the records. It was when I saw the name of my sergeant, Sergeant Hughes, on the disc I had just pulled off that it got to me. Back at home, just before leaving for France, I had seen my own brother put to rest after dying of rheumatic fever. The comparison was stark. My brother had been washed and dressed and presented with dignity. These boys were still dirty and bloodied from battle, without any coffin, just dropped in the hole. Occasionally, the grave the soldiers dug for their comrades was slightly short for the soldier it was to contain. The grave-diggers had to push the body down with their spade or bend the legs to fit. After 4 days, I sought out the Padré and asked to be taken off this duty."

ROLL OF HONOUR – PONT L'EVEQUE

LCpl	FREUDE William M.	20	21/08/1944	14337733	Ranville 6A-B-15
Pte	BEST James P.	24	22/08/1944	321403	Ranville 6A-B-6
Pte	GREGORY Alan F.	19	22/08/1944	14552474	Ranville 6A-B-10
Sgt	KELLY George E.	23	22/08/1944	3529525	Ranville 6A-B-11
Pte	TURNER Herbert F.	30	22/08/1944	5825861	Ranville 6A-B-9
Pte	BINNS Fred	22	23/08/1944	11263620	Ranville 6A-B-8
Cpl	ECKERT Cyril A.J.	22	23/08/1944	6103133	Ranville 6A-B-13
Pte	HINCHCLIFFE George	21	23/08/1944	14202907	Pont L'Évêque Cem 1
Sgt	HUGHES Eric	35	23/08/1944	3649847	Ranville 6A-B-2
LCpl	LOWTHER John	23	23/08/1944	14209510	Ranville 5A-P-3
Sgt	McKIRDY David	37	23/08/1944	4388377	Ranville 6A-B-4
LCpl	MEDLICOTT Thomas W.	25	23/08/1944	3656200	Ranville 5A-P-4
Pte	MISSING Jack E.S.	32	23/08/1944	1727073	Ranville 6A-B-7

"The retreating enemy fired a last salvo, killing a member of the Mortar Platoon."

Lieutenant "Dixie" Dean

18.   JOB DONE

General Richard "Windy" Gale (Commander, 6th Airborne Division)

"We were now surging forward on a 10 mile front. Flavell [6th Airlanding Brigade] and the Belgians [Princess Irene] on the left directed on Honfleur-Foulbec and the remainder of the Division on the road to Pont Audemer."

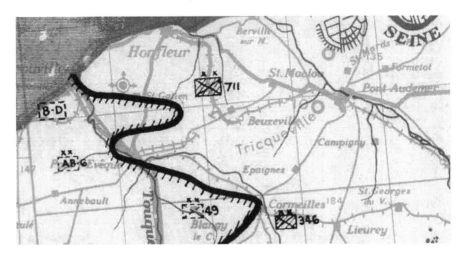

Lieutenant Ellis "Dixie" Dean (MMG Platoon)

"Over the radio came a signal, "Calling all Sunrays" [code name for commanders at all levels] "Assemble in the house immediately above the second 'n' in Colonne [on the map issued]." We took a direct route across open fields and were about to cross a barbed wire fence when a sniper opened up from the far side of the valley. No-one was hit and we ran for cover in a small copse on our right. Someone said "Where's Ken?" In attempting to roll under the barbed wire he [Lt Ken Walton, Mortars] managed to get his small pack caught up. At that moment a tank supporting, located the snipers position and a long burst of tracer was directed into the straw roof of a small building directly across the valley. I put my foot on the bottom strand and pulled Ken out as hard as I could. There was a loud tearing of cloth and he was free, non-too pleased with a badly torn smock, my laughing did nothing to improve his temper.

"The RV was a delightful country villa, surrounded by trees, but of the occupants of the house, there was no sign. We gathered in a room at the front, with enough chairs for everyone. On a side table were several bottles of wine and several glasses. Bill Grantham suggested we quench our thirst, but the CO decided we must wait for the owners and started to give his briefing. After a few minutes he stopped "Perhaps it would be a good idea to have a drink!" Soon we were all sitting with a glass of wine, a really amazing scene, and 10 begrimed, heavily armed officers in dirty, scruffy battle dress, sitting down sipping their wine.

"The front door had been left open and foot steps were heard on the path. An elegant middle-aged lady appeared in the doorway and we all stood up. Before anyone could speak she greeted us in good English "I'm so glad you helped yourselves. The wine was meant for you, our liberators and if someone would be kind enough to pour a glass for me. I will join you in a toast to victory." We felt like guilty schoolboys caught scrumping apples, but she insisted we be her guests. It became Battalion HQ and the rest of the Battalion were deployed around it in defensively for the night."

General Richard "Windy" Gale (Commander, 6th Airborne Division)

"I received orders from General Crocker outlining the operations for the following day. Up to now we had really been fighting this battle on our own. A forgotten army away out on the left flank of the pursuit to the Seine we had been called by certain press correspondents. This to some extent we felt we were. Of course in fact we were very much in the 1st Corps and 1st Canadian Army Commanders' minds. The point was, I think, that in the first instance it was not assumed that we would make much headway, because we were so abominably short of transport; and secondly we were not on the Army Commanders' main line of thrust to the Seine. Just as I pushed all my main effort down the Dozulé-Pont L'Évêque road, taking the gains of the Belgian and 6th Airlanding Brigade as welcome and important contributing factors in my advance, so I think to the Army Commander the advance of the 6th Airborne Division, whilst not the main effort on which he was concentrating, contributed considerably to the general success of the Army operations. With great pride we received the following signal from Lieutenant-General Crerar through our Corps Commander:

"Desire you inform Gale of my appreciation immense contribution 6th Airborne Division and all Allied contingents under his command have made during recent fighting advance. The determination and speed with which his troops have pressed on in spite of all enemy efforts to the contrary have been impressive and of the greatest assistance to the Army as a whole."

"To return to the 1st Corps directive to which I referred above. This gave my southern boundary for the next day's advance and excluded to me Pont Audemer. This latter town was to be on the axis of advance of Major-General Barker and his 49th Division. I received this signal in late evening. At this time I was within 10 km of Pont Audemer and although I could not rely entirely on my information I felt certain that I was nearer than the 49th Division. By piling my soldiers on my tanks and by using every lorry I could lay hands on I was certain I could reach Pont Audemer first. It seemed to me that by forcing the pace I might well be able to reach the village and seize the bridge before those Germans in front of General Barker's division would reach the town. The river at Pont Audemer is of course a major obstacle. If we could seize it before the Germans had made their crossing we might take a considerable number of prisoners. That night, therefore, I decided to disobey my orders and make a dash for the bridge."

Lt Ellis "Dixie" Dean (MMG's)

"In the half light of the morning of the 25th August, following a hasty breakfast we set off on an early 'road walk/run' towards our objective. Several miles down the road, a halt was called as the road was blocked by the demolition of a bridge which carried the railway over the road before it disappeared into a tunnel. Here we passed through the 12th Battalion and as we clambered over the demolitions, two immaculately dressed RAF officers rolled up in a Jeep. The tunnel had been home to a

German long range rail gun, and rocket firing Typhoons had been given the task of sealing the gun in the tunnel prior to D-Day.

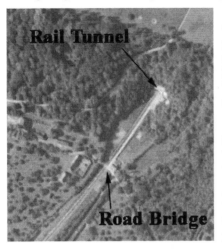

"There was a straight run to Beuzeville, which had already been taken and the population was out in force. They were dealing rough justice to local females who had associated with their hated conquerors. The unfortunate victims were shorn of their locks.

"Clear of the houses and along the open road, we turned right and entered the valley of the River Risle. By mid-morning we were on the outskirts of the town [actually the village of St Germain]. In 3 hours we had covered 12km."

(Left: The rail tunnel west of Beuzeville pictured in 1947, courtesy NIGIF).

Brigadier Nigel Poett (5th Para Brigade Commander)

"7 Para [and indeed the 12th and 13th Battalions], in spite of a most exhausting few days, showed their toughness and marching qualities by the speed at which they reached Pont Audemer. They reached the west bank at almost the same time as the motorized units of the Dutch Brigade and the Armoured Recce Regiment."

This march was no mean feat when you consider that the 13th Bn had been embroiled in 2 months of static warfare in defensive positions and then for the most of August they had fought hard costly battles against the determined German rearguard, of which were generally fought after long marches. They had eaten an early breakfast in the dark with their fingers and then had to push on through clouds of dust caused by tanks and transport that passed them.

Lt Ellis "Dixie" Dean (MMG Platoon)

"We [Mortar and MMG Platoons] were ordered to disperse off the road, as we were under observation from the high ground on the eastern bank of the river. We spread out around an orchard and rested under the trees.

"The ground rose gradually from the river and a stream ran along one side of the orchard (left: in 2012). Over the centuries, a deep gully had been cut in the hillside. I ordered "Everyone wash and shave" and we were all soon along the stream bed carrying out our daily ablutions. The Boche, in what turned out to be his final gesture of defiance, started to shell the area. We all hugged the ground at the bottom of the gully, especially when a salvo landed in the orchard just behind us. I felt a sharp jab in my elbow and pulled out a small piece of shrapnel. I was the only one who had received even the smallest of cuts.

"We climbed back into the orchard, when there was a cry of "Look at that dozy bugger" and the caller pointed towards a tree where a member of the Mortars was fast asleep, propped against a tree trunk. "Wakey! Wakey!" was the universal cry, but he slumbered on.

"Someone went nearer and then called out "He's dead!" Indeed he was. There was not a mark on his body and would not have known what hit him. I could not help but wonder what the casualties might have been had I not ordered that wash and shave, at least 4 shells landed in the orchard. The medics arrived and confirmed he was dead, his body was placed on a stretcher and 4 of his platoon carried him up the road to a nearby church [St Germain] and placed him in the porch."

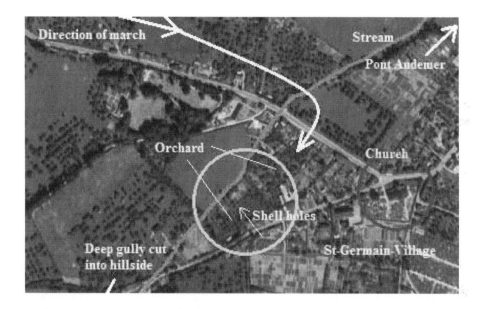

ROLL OF HONOUR – 26 AUGUST 1944

Pte	WOOLHOUSE Walter T.	22	14658854	Mortars	St Desir 3-D-4

Private Walter "Wooly" Woolhouse had been the last 13th Para Bn casualty in the Normandy campaign. The place of his death is now a small park with a pond (the shell holes) and is just down the road from the church. Hours after his death the 13th was pulled out of the frontline and into rest, ready to be sent back to the UK.

General Richard "Windy" Gale (Commander, 6th Airborne Division)

"Pont Audemer was reached without opposition; but we were too late. The last Germans had crossed about 20 minutes prior to our arrival [and blown the bridge]."

Brigadier Nigel Poett (5th Para Brigade Commander)

"The final dash to Pont Audemer marked the end of our Normandy campaign. A message had come to General Gale saying that the 6th Airborne Division would be withdrawn from the line and sent back to England as soon as shipping could be provided."

General Richard "Windy" Gale (Commander, 6th Airborne Division)

"Our task for the time being was finished and we were to be sent back to England there to be prepared for what we knew not. This was no false alarm; with the Germans streaming over the Seine in full retreat our fear was lest the war should end before we could be prepared for another airborne operation. Such was our optimism and I think the general feeling of optimism everywhere.

"It is hard to describe what this day late in August meant to us. The relief was great indeed. Rest was what the men needed and sleep their first thought. The German retreat over the Seine marked the end of a chapter for us all."

Captain Padre Whitfield "Boy" Foy

"We were quartered in a village called Genneville and the villagers extended their hospitality. During the following days I arranged for the making and erecting of crosses for the graves of our men killed at Putot and Pont L'Évêque. In Pont L'Évêque Major Ford and I spent several hours at the home of a charming family called Jufuin; the reason for our visits was that the Battalion had decided to throw a party for the people of Genneville to express our gratitude. In addition to food and fun, there was to be speeches; in particular the CO was to address the whole village.

"It was decided that Major Ford and I should visit Madame Jufuin to ask her assistance in the composition of a speech, which the CO would learn by heart."

Lance Corporal Fred Smith ('A' Company)

"In the rest area in the village of Genneville I remember a small boy about 6 years old who spoke better English than any Lancastrian. His mother was the school teacher. Freddie and I would go out foraging for rations and we went to a farm just outside to see if we could buy some eggs. Unfortunately they didn't have any, but the farmer dug up some cider that he had hidden away since the beginning of the war. His wife did appear some water hen eggs, which she made into a lovely omelette. I often think about returning to see if the place is still there."

Lieutenant Ellis "Dixie" Dean (MMG Platoon)

"The bulk of the unit slept in barns and lofts with the officers in local houses. That night for the first time since we arrived in Normandy, almost 3 months previously, we were able to sleep safe and not be disturbed. For the first time we were out of range of the enemy guns.

"A few mornings later I was called from a game of football, to attend an 'O' group and learned that we were on our way back to England. The weather was good and we visited Honfleur, with its picturesque harbour and its bars."

Private Ray "Geordie" Walker ('A' Company)

"In Honfleur we witnessed the sight of macabre. Women who had taken German soldiers as lovers were marched to the all wooden, St. Catherine's church, sat on chairs to have their heads shaven. On completion they were kicked, spat upon and had to endure much verbal abuse as they ran from their pursuers. We were warned by locals not to interfere."

Private Alfred Draper (South Staffs Regt att. 8 Platoon 'C' Company)

"We stayed for several days in a farmhouse getting ourselves sorted out. During my travels I had acquired a Schmeisser machine pistol. I had broken it down and put it in my pack, some 'friend' had seen it and told the sergeant who joked about it but still took it away. I never did find my 'friend'.

"Bob Giles rejoined us there. He had been walking all over the place trying to find us after leaving hospital. He would never have been able to join us had we left for England and he, like me, had set his heart on joining the Battalion."

Lieutenant Ellis "Dixie" Dean (MMG Platoon)

"For 3 days the Battalion sacrificed their daily ration of cigarettes, sweets and chocolate and on the last night invited all the local inhabitants to the celebration in the village school. It was not possible to fit everyone in, there were as many outside as in. The 'goodie' were laid out on a large table just inside the door and in 5 minutes completely cleared."

Captain Padre Whitfield "Boy" Foy

"The party was a terrific success. The speeches went off to the accompaniment of loud cheers, though there was one slight hiatus. When the Mayor replied to the CO's speech of thanks, he made one statement at which the CO ginned politely and broadly, the famous Luard grin. It wasn't that the CO had understood and found it amusing; he hadn't the faintest idea of what had been meant. It was not until later that he discovered that the Mayor had been referring to the fact that his own brother had been killed in the last war; the Mayor was slightly taken aback that Colonel Luard had found this amusing."

Private Ray "Geordie" Walker ('A' Company)

"Several of the lads could play musical instruments and were able to borrow some and organise a dance. Soon every one was dancing and singing and there was much laughter from the elder spectators. It was a day to remember."

Major John Cramphorn ('A' Company)

"For the party, members of the Battalion dance band had managed to beg, borrow or steal instruments and after the speeches provided music for dancing. This proved very popular until the band started to play "Lili Marlene", whereupon the mayor called "Stop I won't have any German tunes played in my village.""

Lieutenant Ellis "Dixie" Dean (MMG Platoon)

"I didn't get much sleep that night as we were on the move next morning. The entire village turned out to wave us farewell as we met up with our transport. The RV with the trucks was at the nearest main road junction, and here on a wide grass verge we left behind the four Vickers guns.

"Our destination was Arromanches and the route was the reverse of the axis of our advance, so it was lined with memories for us all. Two new Bailey bridges spanned the river at Pont L'Évêque, but nothing could hide the destruction. Next we came to Putot and the terrible hillside of slaughter, but the place slept in peace once more. Back up the hill into Troarn and through the trees of the 'Bois de Bavent' and past the 'Brickworks', followed by the final run down into Ranville.

"Set in the wall at the crossroads, where we turned along the road to Caen was a newly erected plaque dedicated to all members of the 13th (Lancashire) Parachute Battalion killed during the campaign and immortalising our achievement in liberating the first village in Normandy. I'm sure the route had been deliberately selected to take us through the scenes of our battles and leave us with pride."

Captain Padre Whitfield "Boy" Foy

"In Arromanches the now famous floating Mulberry harbour had been installed and we spent a wet and cramped night under canvas in the Transit Camp. On Sunday 3rd September we held our last service in France. When we sang "Now Thank We All Our God" everyone meant it. At 4pm the loudspeaker called us to embark. We staggered with all our kit aboard a landing craft which took us out to the steamer waiting outside the harbour. We made a perilous ascent by scrambling net, found our sleeping places, had an evening meal and retired for the night. By the time we were awake, the ship had begun to move and the coast of France was slipping into the morning mists."

CSM "Taffy" Lawley ('C' Company)

"When we got along side the LCT we had to judge the swell of the water and leap for the scramble net and climb about 20 feet to the deck. Everyone was so heavily loaded and both crafts rolling so badly, made it very difficult. A few rifles went to the bottom, but there was no jibbers – everyone wanted to go home."

War Diary 3rd Sept

1530 Bn moved to embarkation area near ARROMANCHES.

*1700 Bn **(16 Offrs 270 ORs)** embarked via LST on board SS EMPIRE JAVELIN with 7th Bn.*

Lieutenant Ellis "Dixie" Dean (MMG Platoon)

"Next morning we made our way to breakfast and noted that we were sailing up the Solent towards Southampton. As we disembarked in the late morning, ladies of the WVS handed us a packed lunch. The train awaited us across the quay and soon we were on our final leg of the journey home, first to Bulford sidings and finally by road to Newcombe Lines, Larkhill."

War Diary 5th Sept

1645   Bn arrived at LARKHILL CAMP.

Private David "Robbie" Robinson (Anti-Tank 'C' Company)

"Whilst approaching the camp at Larkhill in the trucks, some nearby artillery fired some of their guns during a practice. The sound of the guns sparked off an unusual act, the instincts of some of the men on my truck and I believe some of the others, was to jump off the moving trucks and dive into the ditches and gutters. Those who jumped all ended up feeling embarrassed afterwards."

In a little over 3 months the men of the 13th Battalion had lived through the initial drop, constant mortar and shell fire, ghastly attacks from mosquitoes, a bad mauling on an exposed hillside, house to house battles and had to endure living outside in sun, wind and rain with next to no washing facilities or a change of clothes.

Throughout all this they learned many valuable lessons during the campaign in Normandy. They had learned the importance of clean, well maintained weapons that a lightly armed unit required, even in harsh conditions, as every single rifle, machine-gun and mortar had its part to play. The use of sniping tactics proved extremely useful (due to lack of man and fire power – every bullet had to count) and the use of trees as 'look-out posts' was adopted from their German counterparts. Extra practice in mortar firing was deemed essential, especially in the use of the 2" tubes; good opportunities were lost when putting down smoke screens and mortar tactics were modernised and implemented. Extra training was required in the use of grenades, particularly throwing techniques. Methods of patrolling were altered and lessons learned, sometimes in fatal circumstances. Officers, NCOs and men alike all passed on their experiences and knowledge, such as the use of compasses in difficult terrain such as the Bois de Bavent and the act of using smaller, less visible patrols.

More importantly, they learned how to cope with the horrors of war and the losses of friends and comrades. Hard lessons to learn though, they had lost:

Killed - *3 Officers and 76 men*

Wounded - *11 Officers and 215 men*[38]

Missing - *3 Officers and 51 men*

Total casualties - *17 officers and 342 men*

The Stained glass window installed in Ranville church honours the 6th Airborne Division. Mounted below the window is a marble memorial plaque in recognition of the 13th (Lancashire) Parachute Battalion, who freed the village in the early hours of 6th June 1944.

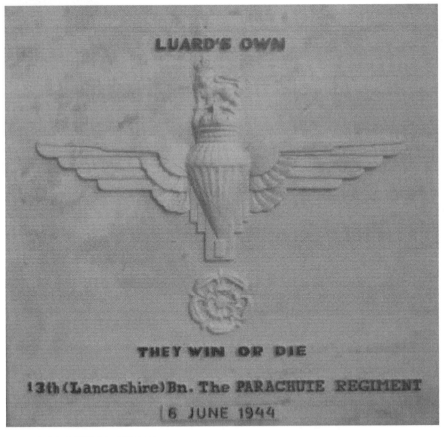

LUARD'S OWN

THEY WIN OR DIE

13th (Lancashire) Bn. The PARACHUTE REGIMENT
6 JUNE 1944

---

[38] 18 Officers and 340 men were actually treated by 6th AB Div medical units and returned straight back to the frontline.

"I was lying in my bed sometime after lights out thinking that in 4 days time I would be spending Christmas at my parents home in Manchester, when the barrack room door was thrown open and a half drunken signaller staggered in."

Private Dennis Boardman

19.   THE CALM BEFORE THE STORM

The veterans of Normandy, September 1944
(Photo restored by pristineimage.co.uk after water damage).

Lieutenant Harry Pollak (Intelligence Officer)

"Whilst I spent one month in hospital in Sheffield [recovering from the wounds he sustained 8th June on Ranville crossroads] and another month on rehabilitation leave, the 6th Airborne Division had spearheaded the British 2nd Army in their relentless advance into France. All this time they saw the deadly flying bombs overhead, making their way without pause towards England. Not only a severe test for the morale of the civilians, but also of the troops whose homes were being destroyed. These flying bombs were soon followed by rockets, an even more deadly and indiscriminate weapon. Targeted mainly on London, they claimed severe civilian casualties and did immense damage to property. Only when the launching pads were overrun by our advancing troops were civilians allowed to relax.

"When I finally returned to duty I had the privilege of welcoming home my own battalion. I was shocked to see their depleted ranks. They had been sent home to be reinforced, retrained and get ready for the next operation."

Private David "Robbie" Robinson (Anti-Tank Platoon)

"Arriving back at Larkhill Camp there were just 6 or 7 of the old PIAT platoon left, but we found some of the lads who had been wounded and brought back earlier for care waiting for us, probably only 3 or 4 though.

"One of the Anti-Tank men waiting for us was a lad called Eric Toogood. During our stay in the brickworks at Le Mesnil we had been severely shelled and Eric had been sent home 'bomb happy' [shell shock]. I remember that he acted very strange and thought he was still sick. In one incident I can remember, we were all due leave after our return from Normandy, but as he had already returned to England earlier in July, and had already had his leave and treatment, he was to stay on camp. He went into a black, blank mood and started to throw his fighting knife at the barrack room door; this kind of knife was not balanced for this, so it wouldn't stick in the door, so he got madder and madder. He was still at it when I left to get on the transport for the station."

Private Ray "Geordie" Walker ('A' Company)

"It was a joyous occasion to see our old barracks and entering 'A' Company block, I met Corporal Kay and Private Bill Mather, as they were not parachutists they remained at Larkhill to maintain the barracks. Every barrack room had many empty beds.

"After a friendly chat with Corporal Kay, I dumped my kit on my bed and went for a meal. The following day we learned that we were granted 14 days leave. Within a few days I had my railway warrant and was on my way to London to catch the train home to Newcastle. In my compartment were 5 soldiers and 2 Swedish sailors who had 2 crates of beer and they kindly shared several bottles."

Lieutenant Ellis "Dixie" Dean (MMG Platoon)

"On Sunday 17th September I was able to turn out for Formby Cricket Club. When I returned home after the game my father jokingly asked "Are you sure it was an extension of leave you received?" I was then told that on the early evening news, the BBC had reported large scale airborne landings in Holland. The fierce fighting at Arnhem was still going on when we returned to camp later that week.

"The Battalion as a whole was only at about half strength, but we did a clean fatigue jump from Dakotas. However, before the end of the month, sufficient reinforcements to bring us back up to strength were posted from the Depot. They were mostly youngsters of 18, who after completing their basic infantry training had then qualified as parachutists and that was the extent of their military experience. But there were also a fair number of regular soldiers who had recently returned to the UK at the end of their overseas tour of duty. Some of these men were veterans of the first "Chindit" operation. In addition to these newcomers were others, slightly wounded in Normandy and now fit again to take their places in the Battalion organisation."

Lance Corporal David "Robbie" Robinson (Anti-Tank Platoon)

"After we had been on leave in England, we came back to Larkhill to find that fresh men were already filling up the camp, very quickly we were back up to battalion strength and training started again, most of which was street fighting. Colonel Luard had thought that we hadn't performed that well in Pont L'Évêque. I remember going to a Great Yarmouth bomb site to practice and also to London on an area of bombed out buildings in Battersea. After the war Battersea fun fair was built on this site but this has gone now.

"It was during this period that I found out that one of my companions was a professional pickpocket who had only joined up to escape the law and had still kept up his profession among the civilian population, but not his battalion. We'd often wondered how he could always find money for fags, beer, going out and to repay his debts etc. his name shall remain anonymous..."

Many of the non-jumping infantry reinforcements who had reinforced the Battalion whilst in Normandy were so impressed by the unit and decided to stay on to become fully fledged paratroopers.

Private Alfred Draper (Ex-South Staffs Regt)

"We were all sent on 10 days leave.[39] When we got back, we non-jumpers were sent to Ringway Aerodrome to do our training. We were lucky in not having to go to the Depot at Hardwick to do the initial training.

"There were 3 pubs around the aerodrome, 'The Sharston', 'The Tatton Arms' and 'The Airport'. Every Friday night a lot of the new lads visited one of these to pick up a girlfriend. Most of the women were married, so how the women explained things when their husbands came home I hate to think.

"After our last jump we paraded and presented with our wings. We were very proud of those wings. We had worked very hard for them. After the ceremony we were sent on a weekends leave. I was very proud going home with my wings and Red Beret.

"Back at camp on Monday morning, training started again. New trainees from the Depot were joining and we had become a unit again. Bob and I were now old hands – we'd seen action, but we were careful though about boasting before the old hands."

The Tatton Arms (above) and The Airport (below).

---

[39] The Bn was given 10 days leave, but was awarded an extra 4 days extension for 'embarkation leave'.

Sergeant Len Cox ('C' Company)

"I was held in a camp for escaped POW's and knew the Division was back training for further operations, so I wrote to Colonel Luard, asking if I could rejoin the Battalion. This was quickly arranged and I reported back to 'C' Company, now commanded by Major Clark, who made me up to Sergeant. I went back to 9 Platoon as a Section Leader."

Private Alfred Draper (Ex-South Staffs Regt now 'C' Company)

"Rob Wilkinson and Reg Lansdell were amongst the newcomers. Reg was posted to 'B' Company but Rob joined our Platoon. We all became good friends and kept in touch after the war.

"Bob, Rob and I decided to become Bren gunners, a job nobody wanted because it was considered dangerous and a heavy gun to carry. We reasoned it out that the section carried the gun in turn on a route march and danger was the luck of the draw anyway. Bob was a Cornishman and the Platoon Sergeant, Chris Hornsey was also a Cornishman and as we were friends we were treated well."

Lieutenant Ellis "Dixie" Dean (MMG Platoon)

"We also received officer reinforcements to bring us up to strength and again it was a mixture of experience and youthful enthusiasm. John Cramphorn was a sick man during the latter days in Normandy and he was forced to take a rest, which allowed Jack Watson to assume command of 'A' Company, with "Joe" Hodgson his second in command. 'B' company remained in the hands of Bill Grantham and Freddie Skeate and "Nobby" Clark held the reigns in 'C' Company and newcomer Desmond "Dizzy" Gethin his second in command. "Claude" Milman occupied the Adjutants chair with Maurice Seal as assistant. Vic Wraight took over the Mortars and Fred Tiramani the Transport Platoon. Malcolm Town continued as Signals and I the MMG's. Harry Pollak was the new Intelligence Officer and Leslie Golding assumed command of 'R' Company. After the first week in Normandy there had been no work for the Anti-Tank Platoon (these weapons were allotted 3 per Rifle Company) and at the same time, the snipers were constructed into the new Scout Platoon, commanded by Arthur Prestt, one of the young reinforcements. Of the others, Lieutenants Frank Sommerfield and Bill Davison joined 'C'. Eric Barlow and Pat Kavanagh went to 'A' and Tim Winser, Alf Lagergren and Steve Honnor were the 'B' Company subalterns. The two remaining newcomers were Peter Downward now Weapon Training Officer and Alan Daborn, a fully trained machine gunner, who was my nominated deputy in 'R' Company."

Lieutenant Peter Downward (Weapons Training Officer)

"In the third week of September, I reported to the 13th Parachute Battalion at Larkhill only to find everyone was on leave after Normandy. My first task was to help Freddie Tiramani and QM Captain Tremlett to sort out the kits of the casualties who had not come back. We separated them into 2 piles, KIA (Killed in Action) and WIA (Wounded in Action). Sorting KIA kits was quite traumatic, particularly in separating personal items for return to next of kin such as wedding rings, watches, photographs, letters and mementoes.

"A couple of days later the Commanding Officer, Peter Luard, returned. The Adjutant, Claude Milman lined up the new officers about to appear before the CO, and through the open door I heard him announce our names, "Barlow, Prestt and Downward". "Downward?" retorted Luard "That's a damned silly name for a parachutist; I hope he knows when to stop!" Eventually I came face to face with the man I had heard so much about. He was a tall impressive military figure with a posture more like a cavalryman, with his ruddy complexion with tufts of hair on his cheeks as an extension to his moustache and a nice smile."

War Diary 2nd Oct

6 Officers and 103 OR's posted to this Unit from AFITC

Lieutenant Ellis "Dixie" Dean (MMG Platoon)

"By the beginning of October the Battalion was fully up to strength and ready to start training again. Training became even more realistic, with rifle companies going to bombed areas of East London for street fighting.

"We received a new HQ Company Commander, Lancashire and England rugby forward, Roy Leyland."

Major Roy "Bus" Leyland pictured here representing the England rugby team in 1935. He played on the wing for Waterloos and East Surrey.

The following day, 17th October, a further 4 Officers and 57 OR's arrived.

Captain Tibbs the Medical Officer had now fully recovered from the sniper's bullet he received in the shoulder at Putot-en-Auge was another man welcomed back.

Captain David Tibbs MC (RAMC)

"I rejoined the 13th Battalion [25th October], to take up again my position as the Medical Officer once again. The whole 6th Airborne Division was being brought up to strength and was being re-equipped ready for its next action."

Lieutenant Peter Downward (Weapons Training Officer)

"In November, after a spot of leave to the Isle of Man and another couple of jumps at Netheravon, I was sent to a weapon training course at Bisley. The weapon I liked the most was the .303 sniper rifle. We took part in a competition, my team won and we even beat the Rifle Brigade who enjoyed the reputation of being the best shots in the Army."

Lieutenant Ellis "Dixie" Dean (MMG Platoon)

"Early in November we were briefed for a Divisional exercise, code name 'Eve' and for the first time in its history; the complete 6th Airborne Division would be in the air together.

"The tactical content of the exercise was to enlarge the bridgehead made by an assault crossing over a wide water obstacle. From our pre-D-Day training, we guessed that the next operation would involve a jump into Germany over the Rhine.

"The promotion of Battalion second-in-command, Major Gerald Ford MC, to Lieutenant-Colonel and his appointment to Divisional HQ, prompted the CO to promote Roy Leyland to second-in-command [20th December]. Les Golding was made Admin Captain and "Baggy" Allen became second-in-command of 'B' Company, leaving Freddie Skeate to take charge of 'R' Company, which meant he would take no part in any future operations. Fred was absolutely disgusted at the way he had been treated.

"I had been moved to take over the Mortars and there was no point in arguing, so I just accepted it. I couldn't do much about it, since all the junior officers were attending a subalterns training week."

Brigadier Nigel Poett (5th Para Brigade Commander)

"We did not have long to wait for another assignment. It was in December, 1944, that von Rundstedt's massive assault burst into the American sector of the [Belgian] Ardennes. The Americans gave way and the Battle of the Bugle began. The 6th Airborne Division was available and we were to be hurriedly despatched to the Ardennes by road and sea to fill the gap."

The situation by 22nd December is pictured below – The Ardennes 'Bulge' had stretched out and was heading towards the River Meuse. The German intention was to make an armoured thrust across this river and head for the port of Antwerp, slicing the Allied lines in half.

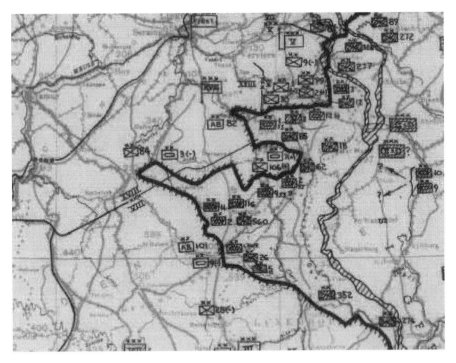

Lieutenant Peter Downward (Weapons Training Officer)

"We were all set for Christmas and a dozen officers including myself were returning back to Larkhill after a tactical exercise. Coming back in a 3-tonner we tried to 'debag' Alf Lagergren who was probably the strongest and biggest of the lot of us. To hold him down on the floor of the vehicle somebody lifted a container holding several gallons of hot tea onto his chest. He ended up being soaked and although not scalded, he had to have cream for the inflamed skin on his chest. But at least he kept his trousers!

"We got back and were immediately summoned to the Officers Mess. I thought we were in for a rocket, but Peter Luard began "In war, things never go according to plan. Christmas is off, and tomorrow, 23rd December, we start moving back to the continent. The Germans have launched a counterattack through the Ardennes and have separated the 21st Army Group in the north from the US Army in the south. We will go by boat and surface, not as an airborne offensive.""

Private Dennis Boardman (Signal Platoon)

"I was lying in my bed sometime after lights out thinking that in 4 days time I would be spending Christmas at my parents home in Manchester, when the barrack room door was thrown open and a half drunken signaller staggered in.

"In a loud, faltering voice he informed the 20 men in the room, who had just settled down for the night, that the German major offensive against the Americans in the Belgian Ardennes region had the Americans on the run, having been badly mauled by strong German armoured forces. We were to proceed to Belgium at once. A lot of abuse was directed at the informant and several boots were thrown in his direction, for nobody believed "Swill" Dugdale who eventually tumbled into bed."

Sergeant John Wallace ('A' Company)

"On the 21st December; I was away from the Battalion on a small arms course and was recalled after a couple of days. I returned to the Battalion wondering what was up, and it was then that I heard the news. The excitement was palpable, and all was hustle and bustle.

"The Sergeant's Mess was ready for Christmas, and it seemed a pity to leave behind the stocks that lay ready in the bar, great inroads were made!"

Lieutenant Ellis "Dixie" Dean (Mortar Platoon)

"Walking across the square towards Company HQ I heard footsteps behind me. "Excuse me Sir, could we have a word with you?" I turned to face 3 members of the MMG's, Bill Price, Fred Lewis and "Taffy" Price. They all jumped on D-Day and were dependable soldiers. They begged me to see the CO and get my old position back and they seemed genuinely concerned, so I agreed.

"The CO was at breakfast and when I was finally ushered into his office, I still hadn't decided what to say. I was encouraged by the CO's relaxed enquiry "You want to see me about the support weapons?" to which I replied, "Yes Sir, I think the fighting efficiency of the Battalion will be adversely affected if we are to go into battle with both heavy support weapon platoons led by officers who are strangers to them." He looked me straight in the eye and when the 'Luard grin' spread across his face he said "In other words you want to go back to your 'Oily Rags'. You're quite right, I'll see the other officers involved, so off you go." I saluted and turned about, hardly able to conceal my delight."

Private Alfred Draper ('C' Company)

"Christmas was coming and it was decided we would have a party in the canteen on Christmas Eve. But orders were received for us to move off on the morning of the 23rd. Plans were hurriedly changed for the party to be held that night. We had a wonderful party, I think! We got back to the billets at about 11pm and were in a mixed state. Some were happy, some went to bed, some wanted to sing and others wanted to fight. I went to bed and laid there smiling watching the antics going on around me. One lad climbed onto a beam across the room and was singing the 'Inkspots' song "Why do you whisper green grass." Another was cutting the strings on the sleeping bags with his fighting knife and he nicked one lads nose who objected."

CSM "Taffy" Lawley ('C' Company)

"My Company was holding a benefit dance for one of our comrades who had been blinded in Normandy when we got the 48 hours notice to get fully mobilised and to be rushed from Dover to Calais under the cover of darkness."

Lieutenant Ellis "Dixie" Dean (MMG Platoon)

"After the advance party had left, we had one deadline that wasn't met, dinner in the Officers Mess at 2000 hours. Before we had dropped in Normandy we had bought some turkeys which the mess staff had reared for us, ready for our Christmas dinner.

"We gathered in the ante-room all with raging thirsts and so it was no surprise that the waiters were busier than usual. Two hours later and the Mess Sergeant announced "Dinner is served" and we followed the Colonel down the corridor to the dining room, and stood behind our chairs as Padre Foy and said grace.

"We were hardly seated when a steaming bowl of cream soup was in front of each of us. The soup was delicious, but we couldn't agree on the flavour. The kitchen door opened and a flustered Sergeant Stubbs went straight over to the Colonel. We thought it was a fresh emergency. The CO listened intently to the message and announced with a roar of laughter, "Gentlemen instead of soup, we have been served the rum sauce!"

War Diary 23rd Dec 1944

0630   Road party left Larkhill.
1015   Unit entrained on Journey overseas [Bulford].
1630   Unit detrained at Dover.

Major Jack Watson ('A' Company)

"We hadn't been able to tell our families that we were going. Padre Foy's wife had come all the way down from Newcastle and as she got in at Salisbury we were on the other platform moving off. A young officer who'd been left behind had to tell her that her husband had gone to the Ardennes!"

ORDER OF BATTLE – 13 PARA BN

"BATTLE OF THE BULGE"

BATTALION HEADQUARTERS

Commanding Officer	Lieutenant Colonel P. J. LUARD
Second-in-Command	Major Roy LEYLAND
Adjutant	Captain "Claude" MILMAN
Quartermaster	Lieutenant Freddie TREMLETT
Intelligence Officer	Lieutenant Harry POLLAK
Assistant Adjutant	Lieutenant Maurice SEAL

ATTACHED OFFICERS

Medical Officer (R.A.M.C.)	Captain David TIBBS MC
Padre (R.A.CH.D.)	Captain The Rev Whitfield "Boy" FOY
Regimental Serjeant Major	W.O. I. Bob DUXBERRY
Regimental Quartermaster	Sergeant Jimmy HENSTOCK

HEADQUARTERS COMPANY

Company Commander	Major Andy McLOUGHLIN
Admin Captain	Captain Leslie GOLDING
Mortar Officer	Lieutenant Vic WRAIGHT
Scout Platoon Officer	2nd Lieutenant Arthur PRESTT
Machine Gun Officer	Lieutenant "Dixie" DEAN
Signals Officer	Lieutenant Malcolm TOWN
Motor Transport Officer	Lieutenant Fred TIRAMANI
Company Sergeant Major	W.O.II. "Duggie" DUGDALE
Colour Sergeant	C.Q.M.S. Charlie FORD

"A" COMPANY

Company Commander	Major Jack WATSON
Company Second-in-Command	Captain "Joe" HODGSON MC
No.1 Platoon	Lieutenant "Topper" BROWN
No.2 Platoon	Lieutenant Eric BARLOW
No.3 Platoon	Lieutenant Pat KAVANAGH
Company Sergeant Major	C.S.M. Bert ALDER
Company Quartermaster Sergeant	C.Q.M.S. Harry WATKINS

"B" COMPANY

Company Commander	Major Bill GRANTHAM
Company Second-in-Command	Captain "Baggy" ALLEN
No.4 Platoon	Lieutenant Alf LAGERGREN
No.5 Platoon	Lieutenant Tim WINSER
No.6 Platoon	Lieutenant Steve HONNOR
Company Sergeant Major	C.S.M. Jack MOSS
Company Quartermaster Sergeant	C.Q.M.S. Eric COOKSON

"C" COMPANY

Company Commander	Major "Nobby" CLARK MC
Company Second-in-Command	Captain "Dizzy" GETHIN
No.7 Platoon	Lieutenant Dick BURTON
No.8 Platoon	Lieutenant Bill DAVISON
No.9 Platoon	Lieutenant Frank SUMMERFIELD
Company Sergeant Major	C.S.M. "Taffy" LAWLEY
Company Quartermaster Sergeant	C.Q.M.S. Charlie WRIGLEY

"R" Company (IN U.K.)

Captain Fred SKEATE
Lieutenant Alan DABORN
Lieutenant Geoff OTWAY
Lieutenant Peter DOWNWARD
2nd Lieutenant "Jock" SIMPSON

War Diary 24th December

0835   Unit disembarked at Calais.

Lt Ellis "Dixie" Dean (MMG Platoon)

"Next morning [24th December] was an even earlier start, it was just daybreak when we disembarked at Calais from the Liverpool – Isle of Man ferry 'Ben-my Chree' (above) and immediately knew the weather warnings had been correct. Everywhere was covered in snow. There we moved to the transit camp and ate our second breakfast that day. We then boarded trucks and waited for the rest of the morning with no-one knowing what was going on. Eventually we were taken round Calais and arrived at what had been a German U-boat barracks and over the main gate arch the Swastika emblem was still in place."

Captain David Tibbs MC (RAMC)

"It was bitterly cold with snowstorms and endless fog. Calais was like something out of hell, freezing cold, foggy, badly war damaged, without electricity or sanitation, and I had to share the large public latrine in an open area with men and women indiscriminately mixed! Buzz bombs on their way to England came over periodically."

War Diary Christmas Day 1944

0900   Bn moved to Dottignies. Route: Cassel – Poperinghe – Ypres – Courtrai.

Lieutenant Ellis "Dixie" Dean (MMG Platoon)

"Next morning, Christmas Day, we fell in on the road and stood around and waited. A convoy of 3-ton trucks came along and halted beside us, but they were clearly not our transport, they had no canopies, leaving the metal superstructure. The RASC subaltern in charge had been given orders to report to Calais, with full tanks of petrol. For the past month his platoon had been carrying coal from Boulogne docks and had assumed he had been sent to Calais to do the same. A phone call to some HQ confirmed that these were our transport. The poor RASC Lieutenant felt the full fury of the Colonels anger."

Private Ray "Geordie" Walker ('A' Company)

"The weather was freezing and we were glad of the protection that our greatcoats gave us. The tear ducts in our eyes were sore due to the intense cold. Driving through the Menin Gate at Ypres (below) was awe inspiring to see the names of 55,000 men killed during the battles in the Flanders fields in 1914-18 and had no known grave. Here we were, another generation moving up to the frontline that our fathers had walked; nothing had changed in 30 years."

Lieutenant Ellis "Dixie" Dean (MMG Platoon)

"Past Ypres and Mons we went. It was evident the civilian population was worried by the Boche offensive and they turned out to cheer us on our way. In some places we were lucky enough to have cakes and apples thrown up to us. Somewhere along the route we stopped to have our Christmas dinner – one cheese and one luncheon meat sandwich."

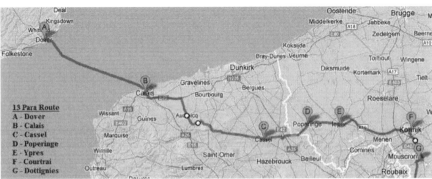

The route taken from Dover to Dottignies (Google Map Data © 2012).

War Diary Christmas Day

Night spent in civilian billets.

Pte Ray "Geordie" Walker ('A' Coy, top)

"In Dottignies our convoy halted in the town square adjacent the bandstand. Nearby was an abandoned 88mm German AA gun, with its barrel pointing harmlessly into the sky, never more to shoot Allied aircraft. The advance party was there to meet us and within minutes Private "Yanto" Evans (Ray & Yanto, left) and I were escorted to No.17 Rue Alphonse Poullet and told the owner, Cyrille Trenteseaux-Landrieux that we were his guests for the night. This was a Christmas to be remembered.

"Cyrille ushered us into the kitchen and we met his wife and daughter Odette. We dumped our kit on the quarry tiled floor and sat huddled around a cast-iron stove. They made us welcome and gave us a cup of hot chicory coffee. I kept up the conversation with my schoolboy French and we talked into the night. Before retiring to bed we gave them sweets, chocolate, cigarettes, soap and toothpaste, luxuries they had not know for 4 years."

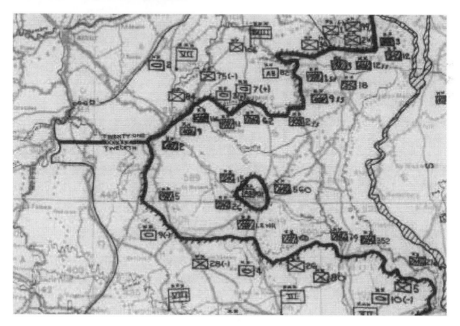

The 'Bulge' on Christmas Day (note: US 101st Airborne surrounded in Bastogne).

335

Private Ken "Ginger" Oldham ('A' Company)

"Me and my mate knocked on the door of our billets and were invited in, the Belgians were most hospitable. However, the poverty in which this family lived astonished me. The flagstones on the floor were strewn with straw as bedding for the soldiers. The youngest children were put in open drawers in a huge sideboard to sleep. There was a huge tiled stove in the corner into which the father kept throwing logs and pushing them down into the fire with his bare hands. He turned to tell us about his stove. "My son is in the resistance here in our village," he said, "and there was a German soldier in the occupying force that made a nuisance of himself. He was chopped up and ended up in this stove!"

Lieutenant Ellis "Dixie" Dean (MMG's)

"Christmas Day 1944 must have been a record one for the bars of Dottignies, it was difficult to find a seat in any, but along with a number of my fellow subalterns, finally managed to do so. I have never considered myself lucky when playing cards, but I was that night, ending up with a wallet full of Belgian francs and nothing to spend them on.

"The coal trucks had disappeared and next morning another RASC Platoon arrived to further us on our way. Our destination was Namur on the banks of the River Meuse. It was dark when we arrived, but it had been a more comfortable journey, as these 3-tonners had canopies." Next morning [27th Dec] we were eating our breakfast in the [Namur] schoolyard when through the gates came Roy Leyland, 2 men of the Scouts and a German prisoner. Earlier an agitated woman was taken to the Intelligence Officer [Harry Pollak] to translate and he found that the woman had been roused by a knock on the door during the night. The German, brandishing a gun had forced his way in. She waited until he was asleep, and then crept out to warn the nearest army unit. The young Luftwaffe pilot was a source of great interest for the young reinforcements.

"After breakfast I attended a briefing, a Brigadier, informally dressed and wearing a black beret entered the room and introduced himself as Commander 29th Armoured Brigade, under whose orders we were now operating. I was not impressed either by the Brigadier or the manner in which he gave his orders. Everything seemed 'airy-fairy' to me, with no-one in control."

Private Dennis Boardman (Signal Platoon)

"The Yanks were pulling out in their thousands. They were going one way, we the other towards the enemy, the whole area was one of disorganised chaos. The snow lay thick and the temperature was well below zero, conditions were extremely unhealthy."

The 6th Airborne Division took over the sector of Givet – Namur on the apex of the German salient, 50 miles away from where the Germans had begun their offensive 11 days previously. The US 101st Airborne, the "Screaming Eagles", were finally relieved on 27th December by General Patton's 3rd Army. They had been surrounded for 7 days holding the vital 'crossroads' there, denying the German armour and supply trucks the use of the main highways.

The Allies had turned the battle on its head. The 'Bulge' was now being squeezed and slowly pressed back. The 2nd Panzer Division had bypassed Bastogne and continued their advance only to become isolated and running out of fuel. Having lost most of their tanks they were in danger of being cut off and had to withdraw towards St Hubert, fighting many fierce rearguard actions as they did. The 9th Panzer Division to the north and the Panzer Lehr Division to the south held open a corridor through which the 2nd Panzer Division could pull out.

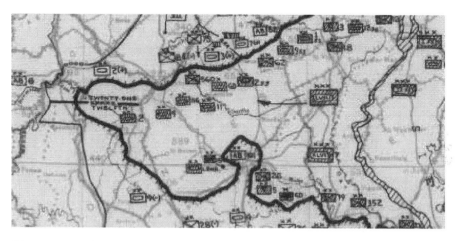

Lieutenant Ellis "Dixie" Dean (MMG Platoon)

"The Panzers were halted 30km to the east by shortage of fuel and there were no friendly forces in between. We were to hold the bridge at Namur. On one side of the river there was a large outcrop of rock and perched on top was a fortress known as 'The Citadel'. Who ever occupied that controlled the crossing (view from the Citadel, below). The MMG's task from the Citadel was to cover the river and the approaches to it, north and south of the bridge. The next day [28th Dec] we were relieved by a unit of the 53rd (Welsh) Division."

Namur
La Meuse et panorama de Jambes.

War Diary 28th Dec

1800   Unit moved to Morville preparatory to a further move up the line. 1 troop 4th
Airlanding Anti-Tank Battery under command.

War Diary 30th Dec

0900   Move in 'Kangaroos' to Houyet to take up defensive positions.[40]

Lieutenant Harry Pollak (Intelligence Officer)

"The CO and I with our batmen went on ahead in our open Jeep. To save loading weight in gliders, Jeeps of the airborne troops had no windscreen or superstructure. It was the coldest journey I have ever had, non-stop to Dinant on the River Meuse in Belgium. There we met with the Divisional Commander [now Major-General Eric Bols] and were given our orders."

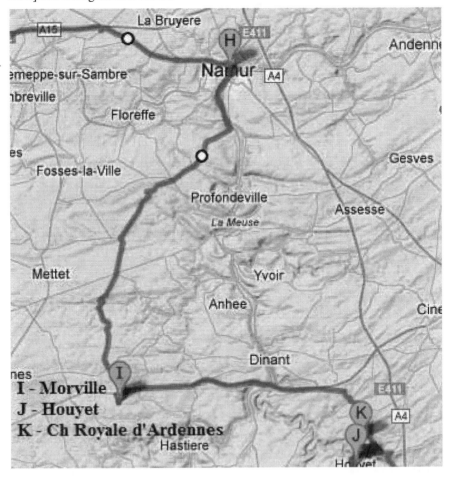

I - Morville
J - Houyet
K - Ch Royale d'Ardennes

Route: Namur to Château Royale d'Ardennes (Google Map Data © 2012).

---

[40] 'Kangaroos' – Tanks minus their gun turrets for troop carrying purposes.

Private Bob Fife ('C' Sq, 49th APC)

"Our main concern was trying to keep warm; it was deep snow and well below freezing. We were lucky that we had airplane engines in the 'Kangaroo's', 9 cylinder Wright Whirlwind radial engines, so we were not troubled with freezing radiators, sometimes the tracks froze solid, but a bump with another 'Kangaroo' cracked the ice. The rear of the vehicle was the outlet for the hot air off the engine, so we used to get the engine going, sit at the back and enjoy the ducted heating. Our bedding was wrapped in waterproof sheeting and stored at the back right over the engine, so at night we had lovely warm bedding!"

Sgt Jimmy Parker ('C' Squadron, 49th Armoured Personnel Carrier Regt)

"A very early reveille was necessary on 30th December to meet the 13th Paratroop Battalion [in Morville] of the 6th Airborne Division to whom we were now attached, and with them aboard we were to cross the River Meuse and take up station at the famous Hotel Château d'Ardennes."

Lieutenant Ellis "Dixie" Dean (MMG Platoon)

"The move took us via Beauraing and the bridge here had been blown by the Americans as a Boche recce column approached. The German offensive had run out of steam and come to a halt. The next task of the Battalion, was to provide protection for a Sapper unit, while they constructed a Bailey bridge in place of the blown one. During a recce of my own I witnessed on the road between Beauraing and Dinant the evidence of an armoured battle in which the Americans had been the losers, as the numerous burnt out Shermans indicated. Along a woodland track 100 yards from Beauraing Bridge shattered remains of Panzers who had attempted to rush it could be seen, the Allied Air Forces had put an end to their plans.

"The HQ of the Battalion occupied the Château Royale d'Ardennes, a country retreat for the Belgian Royal Family, but now a luxury hotel. Some of the HQ even went out shooting wild boar during their stay."

Captain David Tibbs MC (RAMC)

"We stayed at the hotel, Château d'Ardennes, literally between silk sheets! The hotel manager told us with relish that a German Major had been playing the grand piano half an hour before we arrived. Just down the road an American Jeep had been blown up by a teller mine left by the Germans as they retreated and the remnants of the 2 occupants could be clearly seen hanging from the branches above the shattered vehicle."

Major Jack "Whipper" Watson ('A' Company)

"We had our Christmas dinner in the "Château d'Ardennes" and it was a very pleasant way of enjoying Christmas, especially as there was a lot of snow around us - one got the festive feeling."

Château Royal d'Ardenne.   Edit. F. Colle, Dinant.

Private Ray "Geordie" Walker ('A' Company)

"We came to a halt at the Hotel d'Ardennes and rested for 3 days and enjoyed Christmas dinner on the 30th December. The Hotel has dust sheets on the red carpeted corridors and magnificent bathrooms with marble tiles and gold plated taps.

"My platoon was ordered into the valley below to defend the railway bridge at Houyet. After setting up the Bren guns we moved into a hotel. My 3 pals and I found an American 'K' ration box which had a few tins of baked beans and 2 packets of Chesterfield cigarettes inside. We had a hot meal of beans before settling down for the night."

War Diary New Years Day 1945

Warning order received to move to Dinant. No enemy activity on Bn front.

War Diary 2nd Jan

0900   Unit relieved by 12 Devon and moved towards Dinant.

Lieutenant Ellis "Dixie" Dean (MMG Platoon)

"The morning of 2nd January dawned bright and cold as had most of our days. There had been continued frost, but it remained dry. Greatcoats had been handed in as they hindered mobility. There had been no fresh snow falls but the land was covered several inches deep and the roads were packed hard. Beauraing only had one street and after breakfast the Battalion began forming up along it, ready to march to Dinant."

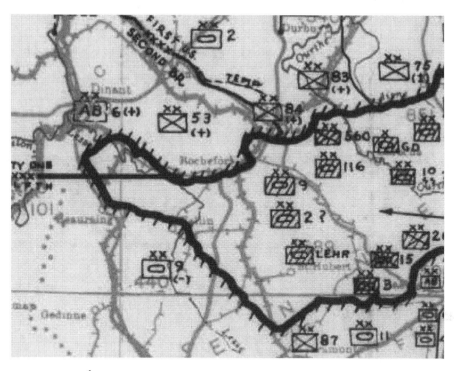

War Diary 2nd Jan

1100   Orders received during move to proceed to Pondrôme preparatory to moving up to front line.

2030   Orders received to attack Bure and then attack Grupont.

Lieutenant Ellis "Dixie" Dean (MMG's)

"Because of the threat of aerial attack we marched well spread out, the Mortars and MMG's at the rear, pulling their trolleys dog sleigh fashion and given the condition of the roads, cries of "mush, mush", were not inappropriate. We virtually had the road to ourselves until an Army staff car, flying the Divisional Commanders flag approached from the direction of Dinant. The car stopped in the column near Battalion HQ and someone got out and marched with us.

"Just before we left England, we learnt that General Gale had been promoted to Deputy Commander 1st Airborne Corps and Major General Eric Bols was now GOC the Division.[41] I thought he had come along to have a look at us.

---

[41] Major-General Eric Louis Bols DSO had previously been in several military positions and had been part of the planning team for Operation 'Overlord'. He had then been given the command of 185th Infantry Brigade in the 3rd Division where he earned his DSO in the Battle of Overloon. The DSO was gazetted 1st March 1945.

He walked with us for a while and then his staff car, which had crawled along in the rear, was called forward, the CO joined the General in the car and drove off towards Dinant. The Battalion turned off the main road and took a minor one to the left. I guessed there had been a change of plan. On entering a small village, we found the colour sergeants had already set up shop and were waiting to serve haversack rations and tea. Roy Leyland called an 'O' group and told us our rest was cancelled and that instead we were to be part of a counterattack."

Private Ken "Ginger" Oldham ('A' Company)

"We were billeted in a convent near Namur and Dinant [it was in fact the convent in Beauraing[42]] south of Brussels. Although the nuns had to take in 30 or 40 men, who must have thoroughly upset their routine, they were magnificent. The army language was a bit rough, but the men assumed the nuns wouldn't understand. There was a lot of swearing and joking going on whilst we cleaned our kit and prepared for fighting. As we were leaving one of the sisters came up to us. "Good morning chaps," she smiled, "I do hope things are not as bad as you obviously expect!"

"During that same cleaning session the night before, one fellow started singing, "Abide With Me". Everyone jeered and shouted at him to shut the 'heck' up but he insisted that, "it's very likely, I'll be dead this time tomorrow. So I'm singing for my own funeral." So he did, and he was - prophetically enough."

Private Ray "Geordie" Walker ('A' Company)

"On leaving the town of Beauraing, we had to march up a hill and whilst doing so one of our support tanks slipped sideways on the icy road and knocked over one of our lads. Fortunately his injury was not too serious."

View looking down the hill towards Beauraing centre

Sergeant John Wallace ('A' Company)

"We were advancing either side of the road in single file before we came to a quite short steep hill where the snow had been battered down by armies travelling over it.

---

[42] In 1932 near this convent and opposite the railway bridge became the site of one of the modern apparitions of the Virgin Mary. These sightings were made by 5 children and happened over 30 times.

We were overtaken by some Sherman's, but they couldn't get up this steep road, they were sliding all over the place like an ice skating rink and believe me it makes you jump when you see a tank sliding back at you."[43]

Lieutenant Ellis "Dixie" Dean (MMG Platoon)

"We marched all day through the rolling country of low hills and wooded valleys. We didn't know our destination and late afternoon we entered the large village of Pondrôme, where the colour sergeants had found billets for everyone and the evening meal was being prepared, and more welcome still, the first mail from home since arriving in Belgium.

"After a few hours sleep, we were roused and called to an 'O' group. Battalion HQ was in a large farm in the village centre and the 'O' group assembled in the kitchen. Harry Pollak was busy handing out maps, with instructions to fold them to include the villages of Tellin, Bure and Grupont. I realised from the maps that a few hours earlier warning of the change in plan, would have saved us a day of marching. Pondrôme was only a few miles east of Beauraing.

"The CO informed us that for some days the Panzer armies had halted due to lack of fuel and were receiving a hammering from Allied Air Forces. Monty was in command and was ready to mount a full scale counterattack.[44] Our task was to seize intact the bridge over the river at Grupont. In order to do this, it would be first necessary to clear the enemy from Bure, which was reported to be defended by an enemy platoon.[45] Simultaneously the 8th Battalion the Rifle Brigade with 2nd Fife and Forfar Yeomanry, with Sherman tanks would seize 2 hill features codename "Gin" and "Orange" which dominated the area. In support of the Battalion there would be a regiment of 25 pounders and an Officer controlling their fire would travel with the CO.

"Next morning we would move by transport to Resteigne and then march to Tellin, there we would leave the main road, take a minor one running south, before turning east to approach Bure along a wooded ridge. Keeping in the woods it was possible to get within 200 yards of the village, hopefully unobserved. The eastern edge of the wood was the start line of the attack 'A' Company would be first to cross and they would clear the Boche from Bure. Immediately 'A' was on their way, 'B' with the scouts [snipers] and MMG's would continue to advance along the un-wooded ridge

---

[43] This road/hill was Rue de Bouillon (pictured) heading east out of Beauraing towards Pondrôme.

[44] The American 3rd Army was forcing the 'Bulge' in the south and the British 53rd Welsh Division and the American 1st Army were pressing in the north. The Germans could now only escape towards the River Ourthe eastwards and the 6th Airborne Division was to attack from the west and head east. It was imperative that the German forces be allowed no time to consolidate and to inflict maximum damage and confusion to the already battered units, and at the same time close the salient.

[45] Patrols on 31st Dec had seen an SP gun at the west end of Bure and took 6 prisoners from the Chapel Notre-Dame which is north and overlooking Bure. Further patrols the following day reached the edge of the wood south of the Tellin-Bure road and found that the SP was no longer in sight but 2 sentries guarded the edge of the village instead. The patrol was later shot and mortared at by MG's and 2 mortars from a reoccupied Chapel Notre-Dame. Another patrol operating further south from Tellin saw enemy troops enter the wood from the south. These patrols estimated that there was a force of about 60 men in Bure made up of the remnants of 3 and 5 Kompanie of the 2nd Panzer Division. This unit had suffered badly at Celles and was reduced to a battle group in strength. They had at least 2 SP's and the remainder of the Division was thought to be occupying Grupont, immediately east of Bure. It was not known, however if there was any running tanks, but estimated that there was "not more than 15 Mk IV and 10-15 MkV's."

until they occupied a position overlooking Grupont Bridge. They would provide fire support for 'C' Company who would pass through Bure and capture the final objective. "Finally the CO asked "Any questions?"

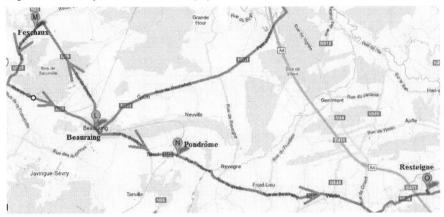

Final route to Resteigne (Google Map Data © 2012).

Lieutenant David Clark (225 Field Ambulance)

"I was told to set up a dressing station in the village of Resteigne. The Germans were in one of the next villages called, Bure and were to be attacked the next day. Companies and Platoons of the 13th Parachute Battalion, many of whom I knew personally, came marching through the village for the assault, full of cheerful confidence. Sherman tanks rumbled through, massive and effective looking; the drivers had fought all the way up from Normandy. The tanks looked like tinker's caravans, with cooking pots, wine flagons, bed rolls and miscellaneous loot dangling from the camouflage netting."

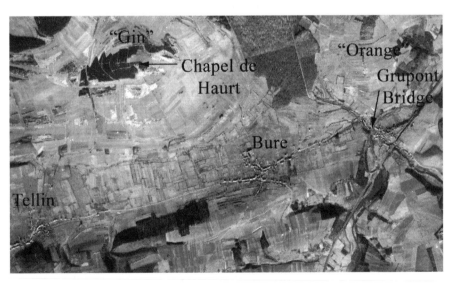

13th Parachute Battalion Objectives

The march from Resteigne to the start line

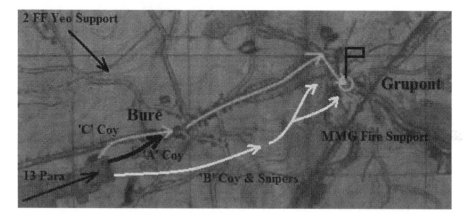

Plan of attack

"When the German Panzers finally withdrew from Bure and the villagers were able to resume their normal lives, the following message, written in German was found chalked on the blackboard of the schoolroom:"

Never again must the world endure such a Christmas
A son separated from his mother
A husband from his wife
A father from his children
Nothing could be more cruel
Life must be for loving and giving.

Lieutenant "Dixie" Dean

20. THE BATTLE OF BURE

Pierre Lardinois (Villager)

"From October, despite difficulties finding building materials, I carried on repairing the damage to my house caused on 8th September [as the Germans retreated through Belgium in the autumn of 1944]. I applied the last coat of paint on the 20th December and we begun to plan a family reunion for Christmas. However many alarms and rumours about the German offensive were sweeping through the village.

"On the 23rd December many of the children left to escape the inevitable reprisals."

L'Abbe Hubert (Cure of Bure)

"Panic broke out when the fighters flew over towards Dinant and all the members of the resistance left. Refugees came through from Clairaux and on 23rd December we heard that the Germans were at Jemelle and by mid-day an American convoy arrived which caused confusion amongst the villagers. At 2:30pm artillery and gunfire broke out and the villagers hid in their cellars and the cellars of L'Alumnat."[46]

---

[46] L'Alumnat (pictured, in 1938, courtesy College d'Alzon) is the large building in north Bure that is College d'Alzon today. It is referred to as the Château, College or L'Alumnat in many of the following accounts.

Father Jean-Marie Decorte (L'Alumnat Superior)

"The railway workers in Jemelle returned with the news that the Germans machine-gunned the loco engines. Around noon, a US convoy passed through our village and immediately told the population to seek refuge in the cellars."

Company 'K' of the 3rd Battalion, 335th US Infantry was the unit that passed through Bure. Their mission was to establish a road block in Grupont. Two platoons waited in Tellin and two went off towards Grupont via Bure. They passed through Bure without incident and were travelling between Bure and Grupont when the leading Jeep was fired on. Speaking to a civilian, 1st Lt Carpenter [Company Commander] learned that there were 9 Germans with a half-track in Grupont. The civilian then offered to lead 2nd Lt Prewitt's 1st Platoon to Grupont in order to ambush the half-track.

1st Platoon headed off towards Grupont and whilst they were away Lt Carpenter (left) set up his command post in a stone house overlooking Grupont. A German tank approached Bure and fired point blank at the CP, all the men escaped, but Lt Leonard Carpenter ended up hiding in the house whilst 3 Germans dismounted the tank and searched the building. To evade capture he hid amongst potatoes in the cellar and was eventually aided back to Tellin by a civilian. He was unable to contact 1st Platoon to inform them of the situation and they continued making their way to reccie Grupont.

Pierre Lardinois (Villager)

"Some Americans who hadn't got away were hidden by brave families, who during the following nights led them to safety. I know for a fact that Leon Thungen, Edmond Jacquemin and Eugene Rondeaux helped men escape and there were plenty of others. An American officer called Carpenter had an observation post in Leon's attic and watched the enemy approach and was then trapped. When it was dark Leon guided him to the outskirts of the village, where he hid his wireless and binoculars until he could return to collect them. Leon was very lucky that night. After he had sent the officer on his way he came face to face with a German patrol as he returned home. Asking why he was breaking the curfew he replied that he was visiting a sick relative in the next village, which satisfied his interrogators. Edmond and Eugene helped a dozen or more Americans evade capture."

2nd Lt George Prewitt (1st Pl, Coy 'K', 335th US Inf)

"We started out for Grupont along a railroad track that bent away from the road into the town. I had 30 men. We came to a wooded bluff. I looked over the edge. Shit! I didn't see 9 Germans and a half-track. I saw a whole company of infantry, 5 German tanks, 2 Shermans, 15 damn half-tracks, 2 of our Jeeps, one of our 2 ½ ton trucks, and 3 German ambulances. Hell, it looked like a whole goddamn army. They were going across the bridge toward the town we'd just left. I looked at the Belgian guy and he was embarrassed. Looking at me like I thought he couldn't count. I sent him back to Bure. It was no place for a civilian.

"I put Clyde Wright's squad on the side of the bluff facing the road going to Grupont from Bure. I told Buckley to take his men along the bluff overlooking the town. I put Rygh and his boys, my first squad, at the foot of the bluff along the river bank to keep the Germans from coming along the face of the bluff and getting Buckley. But, hell, I was outnumbered. I sent a man to find Carpenter and get orders. While he was gone a Kraut posted near the first squad spotted them and started to fire. Rygh made short work, with one shot. Man, the good Lord was with us. When Rygh fired the noise of the German convoy muffled the sound. They didn't know we were there.

"The man I sent to Bure came back in about 15 minutes. Said he didn't find anybody in Bure. About that time a German on the bridge spotted Clyde Wright's men along the side of the bluff. Wright had just started leading the squad after Holland got shot in the gut. The German on the bridge started hollering and waving his arms toward Wright. A German officer started strutting around like Hitler. He was organizing a patrol. The patrol went into the woods after the second squad but ole Wright and his men eluded them. I knew I done good when I put him in for Holland. The Germans sprayed the woods pretty good and withdrew. Nobody got hit.

"I had the BAR team cover us and we went along the river running perpendicular to the road from Bure to Tellin. I thought I could follow the river and then cut back and go parallel to the road until we were opposite Tellin. There we could hook-up with the company. I thought that's where they must have gone. We couldn't get too close to the road because of the German armor. In about 20 minutes I figured we had gone far enough and turned right.

[Prewitt continues] "It was almost dark and getting cold. We had shed our overcoats and had no overshoes. The men had no food and the water in the canteens was frozen. At a point where I thought we were opposite Tellin we turned right toward the road. When we got there the Germans were all along it. We had missed Tellin. But it was pitch dark and we had to do something. I thought I saw shapes that might be haystacks in a field on the other side of the road. We quietly worked our way across. The haystacks were 200-300 yards ahead up a little rise. I put a squad in each stack and

348

used one for a platoon CP. From the higher ground we could see a little better. There was a town off in the distance. But we had no maps and I didn't know what it was.

"I sent a patrol to the town to see if it was Tellin. The Germans in the place must have been asleep. My men eluded them and got to a Belgian house. The town was Bure. The Belgians gave them the route to Tellin. By now it was about 2300 [23rd December]. I sent out 4 men to reconnoiter a route to Tellin. I told them to be back by 0100. We had to move.

"At 0430, 2 of the 4 men returned. They were damn good men; I knew they would. They had, after hours of foraging, found a safe route to Tellin. The other 2 were in a barn in Tellin waiting for us. The company was gone. But no Germans were in the town either. We took off. When we got to the barn at Tellin there were sandwiches and wine waiting for us. As I said, I sent good men."

Pierre Lardinois (Villager)

"An American battalion had taken up positions in the centre of the village and advised us to get off the streets to seek shelter as fighting could break out at any minute. The Americans only had rifles, machine guns and bazookas. We fled to the woods above the village and waited. At around 3pm the shooting started, quite a lot at first, but soon died down and I ventured back down. I entered the yard through the back gate and found lots of equipment that the Americans had left behind when they fled. This confirmed my suspicions that they didn't intend to stay and fight, but were in more of a rush to reach safety.

"By now there were a few Germans already in the street and more were arriving. The first one I saw had a machine gun and belts of ammo across his chest; he fired several bursts in the air in front of the church."[47]

Father Jean-Marie Decorte (L'Alumnat Superior)

"The first German that came to L'Alumnat was a young fellow dressed as an American. "Yes", the Germans said "were here again!" it's wasn't a bad dream, but the sad reality! He came to see if there were any Allied soldiers and asked if there was any room for 80 men, fortunately I managed to turn him away.

"The Germans settled in the village. They were all young men, who seemed to be only 15, one stood guard outside the parish church and he harangued passers by in impeccable French. The Cure was stripped of everything he owned, they even took his spare coal and potatoes."

Felix Despas (Villager)

"December 23, 1944, there were 3 of us in front of the church exchanging our impressions about the rumours of war. It was about the return of the Germans, who had mounted a new offensive. None of us believed the words of some people in the village, who told us that the enemy was in Grupont. We had mixed emotions.

"Suddenly, we heard the characteristic sound of a tracked vehicle from the direction of Grupont. The sound was amplified then multiplied; soon 3 Panther tanks covered with branches appeared and came straight at us. The first one stopped next to us and a tank driver in black uniform and cap appeared in the hatch. He addressed us, "It's us!

---

[47] This unit was most probably part of the Panzer Lehr Division.

Are you happy?" Suffering from the shock of the surprise, we couldn't answer. The 3 tanks then continued their journey towards Tellin."

Celestine Limet (Villager)

"A column of tanks drove towards the outskirts and where the road divides, one half carried on towards Rochefort and the others moved forward into Bure. My brother, Camille, who lives along the road to Grupont watched as the leading tank with a file of infantrymen on either side approached the church.

"I was living with the Vinkboom family in the house next door to 'Dufong' – a farm, which had been burned down during the fighting in September. The leading tank stopped at the foot of the steps. Some Americans trying to escape along the hedges across the road from us and running up the hill to Renkum Cross were shot at by the Germans."

L'Abbe Hubert (Cure of Bure)

"I saw 2 'Tiger' tanks and several smaller ones [most probably 2 Panther IV's and several SP's] and that evening there was 4 of the smaller ones in the village and between 100 and 200 Germans who then laid mines on the approaches to Bure."

Charles Magnette (Villager)

"I was 16 years old and lived on the road to Lesterny, near the cemetery. Built in 1937, ours was the only house on this road. In December, we heard the sound of cannons in the distance. We did not see the Germans enter the village by the road from Grupont, but my brother saw a column of tanks that rose from an old path from Grupont to Wavreille. We heard the noise of battle and saw houses burning. From our house, we saw the impact of shells on a small hill near Grupont. These impacts were close to our house so we then went down the cellar. One shell landed very near the exit of the cellar. The water level rose so dad made a kind of small floor on blocks to keep us dry."

Felix Despas (Villager)

"On Christmas Eve the Germans settled into different locations in the SW half of Bure. One tank climbed the steep pathway in front of my house and parked 50m away under a big ash tree. In this position, he had an excellent overview on the hill called Haurt, on top of which stands the Chapel Notre-Dame de Haurt."

Father Decorte (L'Alumnat Superior)

"On Christmas Eve from 4am, our chapel (left, courtesy College d'Alzon) was packed with people for Mass."

Celestine Limet (Villager)

"It was a bitterly cold night and in the morning, the sentry [standing outside near the steps] saw me light the fire, came in for a warm. He watched me cut someone's hair and asked me to his, which I did. Word got around and I spent the rest of the day as barber to the German Army. At 8pm there was a knock on the door and a German officer and his orderly asked in perfect French "Is it true that you are the village barber?" I replied that although I was not a professional, I do cut hair when asked to do so. He asked me to shave off the several days' worth of stubble from his face and tells me about the battles against the Americans at Rochefort and that he had been in the lead tank. When I finished he asked me how much and I shrugged my shoulders. He left a one mark coin on the table.

"The next morning (25th) more soldiers wanted haircuts and whilst one of them was waiting, he lifted my niece on to his knee. Her father had been deported to Germany; the German soldier said that she reminded him of his own daughter who was spending Christmas without him."

Father Jean-Marie Decorte (L'Alumnat Superior)

"On Christmas day, a lieutenant with a hard face of an old Prussian warrior, broke into the cellars and claimed that he had brought a beggar from the neighbouring village and he did it with such clamour that the people in the cellars were terrorised. Minutes later, the same lieutenant reappeared, accompanied by soldiers and shouting "Man hat geschossen!" "One shot!" He claimed that someone had killed 2 Germans in the nearby meadow and the shots were from our house! This was the excuse for a massacre, the situation was serious. The Germans did not see in the room of a Father, who was absent, an old radio transmitter."

Felix Despas (Villager)

"The Germans came in numbers to search the suitcases and other luggage we had brought. We knew they were looking for a hidden radio transmitter, the soldiers thought that the Allied artillery was being effectively directed by an observer. Personally, I think the tank who had settled in front of my house had been the main target of the guns.

"The grenadiers completed their search and found nothing. Yet we learned later that there was indeed a radio station in the Château. The small towers on the roof of the building (left) were used as watch towers. From that day they refrained from further acts of courage, because of the fear of retaliation on those in the cellars. The artillery fire increased and the building was hit many times. There were many moments of panic, during which everyone began to pray. I remember that strong voice of Bertha Pigeon, leading the prayers."

Pierre Lardinois (Villager)

"Christmas Eve is a family occasion and we eagerly awaited their arrival in our newly decorated home. At 9pm a German walked straight in and proceeded, without speaking, to inspect our home from top to bottom. When he'd finished he left, again without speaking. We thought that was that, but he returned 15 minutes later with 2 senior officers who took over our house.

"My brother, his 5 children and my oldest sister, who came to visit us for Christmas, had to move out. They stayed at Leon Thungen's house in the centre of Bure. My wife and I stayed behind and had to listen to endless clicking of heels and "Heil Hitlers". Away in the distance we heard the sound of artillery and not long later a German cook arrived to cook a pig that two other Germans brought.

"I spoke to the chef and told him how appetising it smelled, and my wife and I was invited for supper. My wife did not want to be associated with the enemy, but eventually agreed. We were served wine in some glasses and I wondered where they came from, they were not mine. I asked where they were from and was told that the wine was from the Cure's cellar and the glasses were his also. A few days previously Justin Petit had told me that he had killed his pig so that the Germans couldn't get it, should they come back!

"The Germans burned our coal supply and my wife and I decided to go to bed and I told the senior officer that he is responsible for our safety. The other officer insisted we drink a toast for Christmas and at midnight we drink to "Peace on Earth and goodwill to all men." For the rest of the evening it was calm.

"I have told the tale to the Cure of how we drank his wine and told Justin how delicious his pig tasted and they roar with laughter every time."

Felix Despas (Villager)

"Since late December, the snow began to fall and I went home every day, enjoying the quiet passing moments. I took the risk of the crossfire or being hit by shrapnel. I had a cow and a pig to look after and I wanted to monitor my property. On December 26th I was surprised to find German soldiers in my home. They seemed to be in high spirits and to my dismay, I realised there was a strong smell of tobacco in the air. These Boche had discovered my big cooking pot, and were smoking and feasting. I had no choice but to accept the situation."

Celestine Limet (Villager)

"Towards the end of December the Germans dug trenches in the hedge at the back of our house running up the hillside above the village. One sunny morning I was walking along the path from the home of Felix Despas to the Chapel Notre-Dame de Haurt, when a German officer called to me, pointing at vapour trails in the sky, he said "Americans.""

"Late on the night of 28th we heard a lot of rumbling outside and watched a column of armoured vehicles, 25-30 of them, tanks and personnel carriers. They drove towards Tellin but came back at 3am. Several men came in and helped themselves to our frying pan, which they put to good use before settling down to sleep on the kitchen floor."

José Rondeaux (Villager)

[His mother had just given birth] "It was a little girl. Next door to us lived a cripple, Mathilde Eloy, who had 2 wheelchairs. One was powered and the other was a push type. I borrowed the latter to be able to take my mum and little sister to the college. It was December 28th and we moved along in the snow amongst the Germans. Upon arrival at college, we were received by Father Rénald "Come to the kitchen," he said, "we will try to find a bed for your mother." It was hardly safe in the room for when the fighting started, the tiles broke and it became very dangerous for her. We were then moved to the basement, below the stairs. But of course there was no crib for the baby. We found a kind of shoe box which, when Mum could not take care of my sister, was placed on a shelf along the wall. She was baptized and of course I was the godfather."

Pierre Lardinois (Villager)

"We sometimes heard planes and the Germans took no chances, barn doors were left open so that vehicles could be put under cover. There was a tank at the side of the church, hidden under a pile of Joseph Despas' firewood. Every time there was an alert, the tank rumbled forward to a position where it could fire down the main street. When the 'all clear' was given it moved back and was hidden under the wood again. Each time it did this, the wood was smashed and the stock got less and less. Joseph eventually had had enough of this; he grabbed one of the tank crew and shook him screaming "For heavens sake man! If you want to fight, go do it out in the open, but don't break up the pavements and destroy my fire wood!"

Marie Decarme (Villager)

"We had a house full of soldiers. Sometimes it was very difficult to distinguish one from another, because sometimes their uniforms were similar. So sometimes we did not even know who was with us.

"In the early days, before going to the college, some other Germans came to our house. Mum stared suddenly in shock and she said "Marie. My God I know this man!" And the soldier replied in perfect Walloon [local dialect, hence he must have been from the region]. "Yes ma'am, I came to your home to sell shoelaces the other day."

Felix Despas (Villager)

"A few days later, around December 29th, when we had lived a few days of relative calm, the tank outside my house was set upon by exploding shells. The crew realised that its cover had been recognised and it moved to the village. The artillery continued to fire. That day the Germans occupied the half of the village in the NE. My house seemed to be the extreme limit of their presence to the SW. The shells rained down more and more and many of us took refuge in the cellars of L'Alumnat. For 10 days we stayed confined, 400-500, occupying the great, solid cellars."

Simone Herman (Villager)

"We were in one of the many small cellars of the college with probably 60 people. We were sitting on benches and we were packed so we couldn't move. One of the few activities that we had was to pray. Mum would not even let us go home to eat. She was afraid the Germans would pick us up. So we lived on soup and the little we could find. Days were reduced to their simplest form and we had no sense of time. Sometimes we didn't even know if it was day or night."

Felix Despas (Villager)

"We began to get hungry in the cellars of the L'Alumnat and this in spite of provisions of food, albeit limited, from the nuns of the Convent. Marcel Petit and I went to my house to bake bread. The risks were great; because it seemed to me that the shells were falling more and more. Before leaving the basement, we were reminded to knead the dough. I believe that the growing danger and panic made us forget that detail. Being back at home, we hurried to turn on the oven. I don't know if the smoke from the oven had attracted the attention of the artillery observers, but we felt that the shells were falling nearer and nearer. This is precisely what made us forget to add the yeast and we baked the bread in haste. They were woefully flat and were as hard as wood when we tried to eat them in the cellars. Marcel Petit had the misfortune of dying a few days later, when a mine exploded.

"On December 28, two girls Leonie and Marguerite Dietrich, living in my neighbourhood, wanted to go and see what the fate of their cows was. I had warned them of the danger and I assured them that I had seen to them myself. Still, they came out of the cellar and nearly became the victims of an explosion, a high calibre shell ripped through a wall just a few meters of them."

The day before 2nd Panzer Division had reached as far as Celles, but in doing so was almost wiped out. They now consisted of one armoured car battalion [what was left of Panzer Grenadier Regiment 2], one armoured company [the remnants of 1st Bn, 3rd Pz Regt, with 12 Panther tanks and some SP guns], one light artillery battalion, two week armoured engineer companies and the remainder of the anti-aircraft battalion. They held defensive positions in Rochefort as ordered, despite the 2nd Panzer Division's Commander, Lauchert's request asking if he could pull the Division back. He was told in no uncertain terms he must hold.

For 2 days the Allied Air Force and heavy artillery proceeded to batter the town of Rochefort, but for no real gains. Then on the 29th December Lauchert moved his troops to the line of Wavreille-Lesterny-Bure and the following day took over the heights between Grupont and Bure from the Panzer Lehr Division.

In his book "Friedens- und Kriegserlebnisse einer Generation, ein Kapitel Weltgeschichte aus der Sicht der-Jäger-Abteilung 38 (SF) in der ehemaligen 2. (Wiener) Panzerdivision" F. J. Strauss a former member of 2nd Panzer Division wrote:

28th December: "The 2nd Pz Div moved back into the line Wavreille - Bure - Mirwart. Repaired assault guns of the 1st Kompanie were committed into the frontline."

31st December: "Enemy attacked 2nd and 9th Pz Div, especially Bure. 1st Company (Zug Nickel) 2nd Pz Div destroyed 2 enemy reconnaissance vehicles."

Pierre Lardinois (Villager)

"The original German unit [Pz Lehr] moved out of Bure and was replaced by another [2nd Pz Div] and the situation became tenser, we felt that we could be caught up in the fighting at any minute.

"Towards midday on the 31st there were explosions and the Germans rushed to their defences. The bombardment was not only on the hills but on the village as well. British armour engaged the Germans, causing damage to one vehicle which had to be withdrawn up the main street. Many houses lost their windows and it was during this fire fight, that 3 members of the Belgian SAS were killed."

Lieutenant Bill Cunningham (61st Recce Regiment)

"I found myself driving doing a recce for the 29th Armoured Brigade. Our mission was to capture a church which the Tanks of the Brigade wanted as an OP. The church was above the village of Bure. I left my [armoured] cars, took my troops and set off through the snow to the church.

"I guessed that the chapel was held by the Germans as we got there I put a PIAT round into the church where I thought a machine gun post might be and I then sent my PIAT team back to their car to radio the tanks, telling them they could have their OP. I then moved my men back away from the building because when a position has once been occupied by the enemy, they will sometimes mortar the position.

"I was then pleased to hear a tank coming from the direction of the calvary[48] and presumed that it was the Forfar's, but it wasn't... it was a German tank, I'm pretty sure it was a MkIV. Their officer, who had left a pistol as one of my chaps had picked it up, jumped down, and we immediately shot him and his gunner then started firing. This all took place at 20 yards. The gunner was firing high and I managed to take my people back the way we had come."

Several villagers witnessed these engagements.

Celestine Limet (Villager)

"British tanks moved along the road to Cambuses towards the Chapel Notre-Dame de Haurt [Chapel Hill[49]] and took up positions on the hillside. I had just left the house to feed the cattle and I heard machine gun fire from Chapel Hill. Several rounds struck the front of the house and others in the field behind. I shouted to my mother to find shelter and ran to Justin Ligot's house near the centre of the village. From a rear window I saw what was happening. A Jeep drove towards the calvary and when it was close to Liegrous Farm a German tank, hidden behind Alphonse Magnos house, opened fire, but missed and the Jeep accelerated to safety, behind the calvary.

---

[48] The Calvary is at the site of Bure's football field halfway up the road that leads up to the Chapel Notre-Dame de Haurt.

[49] 'Chapel Hill' or Haurt Hill is a 2000ft dominating high feature north of Bure. The hill has a small pine wood at the top and one building, Chapel Notre-Dame de Haurt, hence the name.

"Later I found the body of a German soldier buried only a few meters from the Chapel. The ground was frozen so hard they couldn't have been able to dig very deep, and his feet were sticking out above the snow."[50]

Felix Despas (Villager)

"On December 31st, I was able to report that an Allied patrol went by the Panther. Several Jeeps appeared on the hillside of Haurt and I could see the black impact marks in the snow, caused by the explosions of shells. The small vehicle escaped by zigzagging. This indicated that an Allied attack was imminent. Several years after, by a coincidence, I had the pleasure of getting to know who was driving that Jeep. It was Michel Maes, Belgian SAS, who still had moving memories of the re-conquest of Bure."

Lt Paul Renkin of the Belgian SAS, assigned to the 61st Recce Regt, with his section of 4 semi-armoured vehicles, was placed as a mobile flank-guard unit and they carried out many reconnaissance patrols. On 31st December 1944, on the outskirts of Bure, Pte Lorphèvre, with disregard of the personal danger, went on foot to make a reconnaissance in the immediate proximity of the enemy. When he spotted an enemy position, he opened fire in order to indicate to his section the enemy position. Lt Renkin decided to attack it with all 4 Jeeps. Pte Claude de Villermont helped to reduce the anti-tank position to silence, by bringing his vehicle close to the enemy, and by engaging it with violent and precise shooting. With the enemy having been destroyed, Pte Lorphèvre returned to his vehicle. Unexpectedly, another enemy battery opened up on Renkin's party and he calmly gave orders for his group to withdraw. Lt Renkin's Jeep was last to leave the area; and as they did his vehicle was hit by a shell. Lt Renkin was killed along with driver-machine gunner Pte Claude de Villermont and machine gunner Pte Emile Lorphèvre.

Left to right: Lt Renkin, Pte Claude de Villermont & Pte Emile Lorphèvre. All 3 men were awarded the Croix de Guerre 1940 with Palm.

Lieutenant Winzer (61st Reconnaissance Regiment)

"We were entering a village by the name of Bure when I saw my leading armoured car shot up by an enemy anti-tank gun from a wood on our right. It was an open road

---

[50] Probably the German Tank Officer mentioned by Lt Bill Cunningham.

and I was not far behind. We tried to reverse but got only a few yards when a shot came into my car broadside on. The car caught on fire, the operator and I managed to bale out, although we were both wounded. We were being fired at and had to get to cover. It is very difficult for the driver of an armoured car to get out, especially when the car is on fire and there was no way we could get at him. The shot came in just behind the driver's seat and I think Trooper Collingwood must have been killed outright. I managed to crawl back to my own lines and sent a party of men to try and rescue the crews, but the cars by then were surrounded by a strong body of Germans and they couldn't get anywhere near them. I heard later that the Germans moved my car so his body was never found."[51]

F.J. Strauss, 2nd Panzer Div, reported in his book that on New Years Day English troops were first recognised in the area. They believe that this indicated a major attack was due in the next couple days. They formed into small battle groups and repaired SP's were sent to the frontline.

Louis Limet (Villager)

"We lived in the Rue de Grupont, halfway between the church and outside the village towards Grupont. For my parents [he was only 7 years old] it was a painful ordeal. For my sister, my two brothers and me, our memories are very vivid, but full of recklessness due to age. In the earlier fighting, we fled into the cellar. Potatoes harvested in September and apples picked in October were our main food. We couldn't cook. We were afraid. These reasons led us to our neighbours, the Louviaux family and their cellar. Other people in the neighbourhood were there too, including Clovis Poncelet with a leg in plaster, and Eugene, a Frenchman. A wood burning stove with the chimney flue going out through the window warmed the cellar and allowed us to cook some food.

"During the lulls, we went up to the ground floor. Mum allowed us to look out the kitchen window, from a distance by standing on the table. Thus, we saw the Germans

---

[51] The Cure of Bure reported that he buried a British soldier near the church after the Germans had left the body in front of the Presbytery and told him to bury the corpse.

take the Laffineur's pig, kill it and place it on a vehicle, while others carried away toys that Albert had received from 'Saint Nicolas' 3 weeks earlier. We observed the Germans advancing towards the church, brushing against the frontages of the houses opposite.

"Things got intense when 2 Germans came into the house; they hung their guns on the coat rack in the corridor, took off their coats, sat in the kitchen and asked for coffee. Mum served them and one of them made me sit on his lap. What a relief for my parents when they left."

Yolande Despas (Villager)

"At first, we stayed at home. Then a shell fell on the rear gable and that's when we decided to do as the majority of people in the village and we went to the basements of the college. We had the handiness to get there as it was only across the road, where we found ourselves below the tower. A chair allowed us to reach the window. We spent the time mostly in prayer. We sat still. At certain times, often day by day, the bombing resumed. Sister Marie-Ange and Sister Augustine were with us also. It was very cold and, initially, I had my dog with me. It warmed my feet."

Celestine Limet (Villager)

"On the morning of 2nd January, Mother and I went home, so I could continue to look after the cows and sheep. All was quiet, but later in the day, we heard firing, so we made the decision to take shelter in the safe cellars of the Château. It went quiet again as we made our way there."

Lieutenant William Steel Brownlie (2nd Fife & Forfar Yeomanry)

"2nd January, the Germans were holding Bure, 6 miles up the valley, and we were to attack them from a favourable direction, perhaps by way of a ridge running east on our left front. I was to be taken by a small force of 61st Recce Regiment, in Bren carriers, to see if there was a route suitable for tanks. The officer in charge gave me a Bren and said I was his gunner as well as his guide.

"We motored through a Christmas card landscape of snow, pines and glades, except that at one point I was out on foot and a small shell exploded nearby. There were signs of German patrols, also the tracks of wild boar, which didn't matter so much. The important thing was that there was no covered approach for the tanks on the left and right of the ridge, as the country was too thick. We veered off to the right, ended up in a village. The bridge was blown; the locals said that the Germans always occupied the place by night. Suddenly a shell crashed right among us, bowling us over. When the smoke cleared there was one carrier less, its crew of 3 blown to pieces. We scattered, but nothing more came over.

"I had to get word back and used the carrier's wireless. There, control promised to pass the message, he added that we were to stay there all night and try to keep the Germans out of the village. I also learned from the very nice platoon commander that they had no rations.

"A sudden alarm and 4 small vehicles were seen coming up the road from the direction of the enemy lines. They were SAS Belgians, who had been dropped in weeks before and operated beyond the front in Jeeps. Their leader agreed to take me back to Chanly. Off we went, myself sitting in a pile of ammunition, grenades and explosives, the others continually smoking and holding Sten guns."

"We reached the start line and looked down into this silent and peaceful village."

Major Jack Watson

21.   DAY ONE: 3rd JANUARY 1945

Lieutenant Ellis "Dixie" Dean (MMG Platoon)

"3rd January was again cold and sunny. The move to the 'start line' went without a hitch and after debussing at Resteigne we had a 6 km march. In Tellin we passed through the 8th KRR's[52] who were gathered around 'biscuit tin stoves' to keep warm. They looked cold and miserable in their long greatcoats and cap-comforters under their steel helmets. Whenever we passed through another unit of our own Division, there was always plenty of none too polite banter and insults, but we passed through Tellin in silence.

"Just clear of the village, 'A' Company, in the lead, turned off along the minor road running up into the hills, and we ran into deeper snow. It was hard work with the trolleys in the snow covered fields. In the woodland we had to unload the trolleys as the planting of the pine trees was too close for the trolleys to pass."

Over on the 13th Para Battalion's left flank the Sherman tanks of the Fife and Forfar Yeomanry were getting into position to cover the advancing paratroopers.

Lt William Steel Brownlie (2nd Fife & Forfar Yeomanry)

"I do not know if my report that there was no covered approach towards Bure by tanks had any effect, but certainly the decision was to move to high ground, with no element of surprise, overlooking Bure. From there we were to support by fire, the paras. They were to attack up the valley to our right, while we took on targets ahead of them. When they got to the edge of the village, we would come and join them.

---

[52] The 8th Rifle Brigade was detailed as the supporting infantry for 'A' Squadron, 2nd Fife & Forfar Yeomanry's Sherman tanks. Together, their task was the assault and clearance the 'Chapel Hill' (codenamed "Gin") feature that overlooked Bure.

"We moved at first light, the snow had stopped so we could see the whole area over which the battle was to be fought it was a panorama of black and white. It was a dominating position. We were overlooked only by the top of our own feature, where there was a thick wood almost enclosing a church of some sort. We called it Chapel Hill and were assured that it was occupied by friendly troops. It was not."

"As we settled down waiting for the battle to begin, there was a roar and Guy Wilkes' tank was hit by an armoured piercing shot from the Chapel. We scurried round, looking for positions giving us cover from Chapel Hill on our left, and still a good field of fire to our front. Jimmy Samson's 3 Troop was sent to deal with Chapel Hill, while the main attack was postponed by 30 minutes. Our Desmond Chute was with the paras as liaison in a scout car and kept urging us to clear up the nonsense on our flank, so that the attack might start. Easier said than done. The Chapel was guarded on 3 sides by thick woods, and the SP or whatever it was had a field of fire

down the avenue on the fourth side [facing Bure]. Eventually Corporal Dave Findlay motored into the open gap with his gun already traversed and shot out at a range of 200 yards. He knocked out the SP, but received a hit that bounded off his turret, showering him with fragments and wounding him in the face (diagram © aerial photo March 1945, RCAHMS)"

The Chapel de Haurt with SP gun superimposed.

Citation: Lieutenant James W Samson (2nd Fife & Forfar Yeomanry, RAC)

Award: Military Cross

On Jan 3rd 1945, Lt. SAMSON was ordered to seize the top of Chapel Hill from where one of our leading tanks had been knocked out by SP guns concealed in the woods at the top. Lt. SAMSON moved his Troop up as close as possible and halted under cover whilst he dismounted and went forward on foot to locate the exact position of the enemy. He then moved up his Troop and destroyed the SP. He then went on a further recce and located another. This time the enemy withdrew and the SP was found abandoned in the woods. This was extremely difficult country for tanks unsupported by infantry and the capture of this vital feature without further loss was entirely due to the courage, initiative and efficient action of Lt. SAMSON.[53]

Private Dennis Boardman (Signaller, att 'A' Company)

"The going was tough as we headed towards Bure across open country, the snow some 2ft deep in parts and we only saw one person during the gruelling march. Was he a German or a Belgian civilian? He was too far away to identify, but I'll always believe he was the person who warned the Germans in Bure. The plan of attack was for 'A' Company to go in on the left flank (I was attached to this Company) and 'B' Company was to go in on the right. 'C' Company would remain in reserve along with Battalion HQ.

"A squadron of British Sherman tanks would move up the road, once our attack had got under way. This boosted our moral as most of the actions we had fought were without armoured support. In an emergency we would be able to call on the support of a battery of 25 pounder guns of the Royal Artillery."

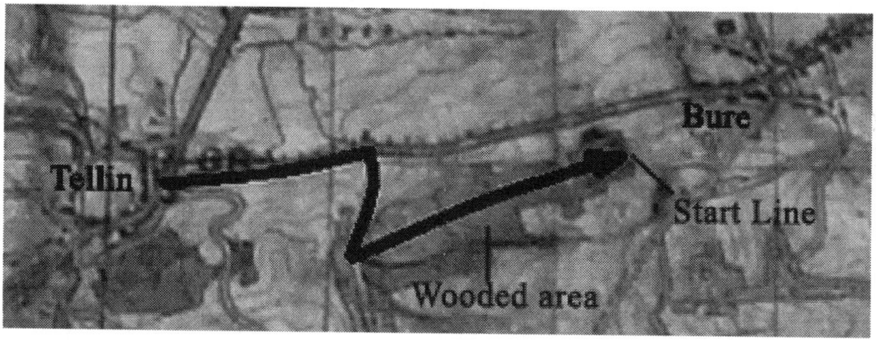

War Diary 3rd Jan

1300 *Bn formed up for attack on BURE 2368 with 'A' Coy clearing village, 'B' Coy covering from high ground 2268 and 'C' Coy in reserve.*

Private Dennis Boardman (Signaller, att 'A' Company)

"Zero hour was approaching as we crouched on the edge of the thick pine woods. As we looked down on the picture postcard village not a civilian or German could be seen. Major Watson our Company Commander gazed at the hands on his watch. He

[53] The actual citation sheet states the date as 4th Jan, but in fact it was the 3rd Jan.

gave the signal and the first platoon moved out into the open field and headed towards the road, about 200 yards away. The other platoons followed and I went next with Major Watson. By now, the radio I was carrying was beginning to hang heavily on my back. About a 100 men, their heaviest weapons, the Bren and the PIAT, were on the move."

Approximate view of Bure from start line

Major Jack "Whipper" Watson ('A' Company Commander)

"We reached the start line and looked down into this silent and peaceful village. The Germans knew we were there, they were waiting for us and as soon as the first Platoon broke cover, we came under heavy fire I looked up and saw the branches of the trees being shattered by machine gun bullets and mortar bomb fragments. Machine guns on fixed lines had us pinned down, even before we crossed the start line. This was the first time I had led a Company in battle. We were held up by the dead and wounded among us but we had to get away.

"Within minutes I'd lost about one-third of my men. I could hear the men on my left-hand platoon shouting for our medics. We were held up for about 15 minutes because of the dead and wounded around us. The village was some 400 yards away and as quickly as I could; I got a grip on the Company and ordered the advance to continue. Whatever happened, we had to get into the village as quickly as possible but we suffered more casualties on the way."

Private Ray "Geordie" Walker ('A' Company)

"We had some shelter from observation by passing through a wood and on descent on the other side of the hill 'A' Company would lead the attack. As soon as we left the shelter of the wood and ran across a farm track and into a field the Germans had spotted our khaki clad figures silhouetted against the snow. They knew where we were and guessed our plans. My section laid in the snow adjacent a hedgerow that overlooked the first group of houses in the village. It was now 1320 hours and our battle had commenced."

362

Private Dennis Boardman (Signaller, att 'A' Company)

"Then it happened, a series of plop like sounds came from the woods on the far side of the village and seconds later mortar bombs rained on our positions closely followed by the scream of shells. This was followed by machine gun fire and by the sound we knew it was an MG42. It seemed as though all hell had been let loose. I flung myself down into the snow, the noise in my ears was deafening. I felt my hands gripping the ground below the snow. As the first rain of bombs and shells subsided, I heard one groan of pain, then a second and then the cries of "Medics! Medics!!" filled the zero temperature atmosphere. I slowly lifted my head and gazed around me, mortar bombs had landed around me and I hadn't even a scratch, by the noise it my headset, my wireless was still in working order.

"The medics, just 3 of them, were attending the wounded some of the injuries were worse than those I had seen in Normandy. The Medics could not cope so I sent a message to Battalion HQ for urgent medical help. A fresh barrage of mortar and shells arrived but these were aimed at 'B' Company, on our right flank, they were getting their share of the German attack. Those medics were the bravest men I ever saw. The lives these men saved will never be known and medals will never recognise the personnel risks those unselfish men took."

Major Jack Watson ('A' Company)

"We had to get under the firing and get into the village as quickly as possible. On the way down I lost more men, including my batman [Harry Gospal, wounded]. One man took a bullet in his body igniting the phosphorous grenades he was carrying. He was screaming at me to shoot him. He died later."

The No. 77 Grenade was a British white phosphorus grenade and was introduced in 1943. It had 8 ounces of white phosphorus, an impact fuse and a tin casing. It was intended for laying down smoke screens but was also very effective as an anti-personnel and incendiary weapon. Once exploded, the contents (the white phosphorus) would disperse and ignite as soon as it came into contact with the air. This made the grenade enormously dangerous — hence its effectiveness in battle.

Pte Dennis Boardman (Signaller, att 'A' Coy)

"Major Watson conferred with his second-in-command [Capt "Joe" Hodgson] and seconds later, someone not far from me yelled out "For God's sake let's get into the village before the next lot comes down on us.

"Suddenly we found ourselves running at full speed, leaping a hedge, towards the road, having left the medics to stay and tend the wounded. We jumped over several mines lying across the road as another batch of mortar bombs landed around us. Breathing heavily, we rushed towards the houses, passing several dead Germans, one of the sections having disposed of the machine gun crew that had been firing in our direction and had caused some casualties."

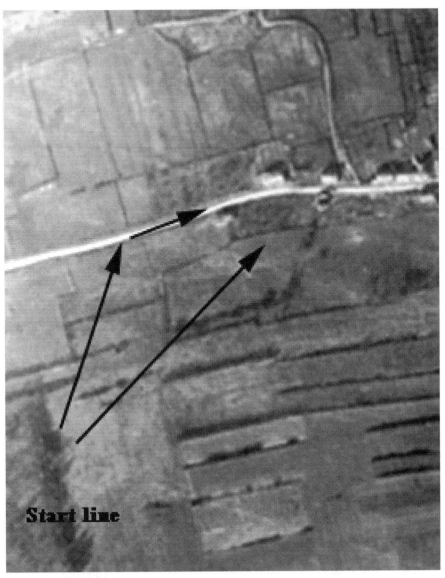

Start line

Courtesy RCAHMS

Sgt John Wallace ('A' Company)

"3rd of January 1945 – A day I shall never forget! The reconnaissance group had been to Bure and we were told that there would be a sniper or two and possibly a machine gun. I set off from the start line, down the steep hill and across some open ground ('A' Company's route, above). Our Platoon Officer was a Lieutenant called Pat Kavanagh [No.3 Platoon], who later became a very senior Police Officer. The signal was given and following Lt. Kavanagh, we set off.

"That very instant we were shelled, mortared and got hammered in all directions. There was a sergeant in the Company called McGrath, and there was quite a deep ditch either side of the road and we were crawling along either side of it. For some reason he climbed out of the ditch and tried to cross the road, he hadn't an earthly chance… He got shot down there and then. While he was lying there in the middle of the road and was moaning and groaning, a mortar bomb came over and landed on his stomach and literally blew him into two. This was quite a sight. We then gained a foothold in the first houses of the village.

"We had lost, I am told, 60% of our strength and this was no surprise to me because there were bodies lying all over the place. The one thing that struck me at the time was that blood goes a long, long way in the snow."

| Sgt Frank Chadwick | Sgt William Greendale | Sgt Arthur McGrath |

The 3 Sergeants of "A" Coy KIA during the first few minutes of the assault on Bure

Pte Fred Wilcock ('A' Coy)

"I was also with 'A' Company in Pat Kavanagh's platoon and as we assembled on the start line the shells started to land nearby and I started laughing, I thought it was funny. I didn't laugh very long… Men were screaming wild, heads were blown off, and men torn in two. I was only a kid, just 19. We then crossed the open fields and fought our way to the first houses."

Private Ray "Geordie" Walker ('A' Company)

"Within minutes of crossing the start line of the attack we came under heavy machine gun fire and salvoes of mortar bombs, intermingled with shelling from concealed artillery. For a few moments we were pinned down and unable to move

| Cpl Jones | Pte Morris |

forward. Whilst trying to resolve our predicament, my section received a direct hit from a mortar bomb which killed and wounded most of my friends (left: Cpl Reginald Jones and Pte John Morris, two of Rays friends killed).

"At the time of the explosion I thought I had been kicked by a mule as a piece of shrapnel tore a hole through my left upper arm. Stan Braddock my Sergeant, who had lain beside me was the only one uninjured. Stan cut my clothing with his knife and applied a field dressing, then said "Good luck and get the hell out of here Geordie lad." I set off amidst a hail of bullets and within seconds I met my Company Commander, Major Jack Watson and he too wished me luck."

Lieutenant William Steel Brownlie (2nd Fife & Forfar Yeomanry)

"The airborne advanced from their start line and we saw small black figures running out of the line of trees across the white expanse of snow, one or two dropping here and there, the rest soon disappearing into the jumble of houses and gardens of the village. There were little puffs of smoke as the Germans tried to keep back the flood, but we kept a stream of fire on them."

'B' Company on the right flank were attempting to advance across the hill eastwards to the south of Bure, came under fire at the same time as 'A' Company on the left flank.

Lieutenant Ellis "Dixie" Dean (MMG Platoon)

"H-Hour was almost upon us as I raced to catch up with Bill Grantham [left, OC 'B' Company], and even before I caught up 'A' were on their way and it was clear they were being opposed. Bill Grantham and his 'O' group were emerging into the open as I reported his lack of machine gun support to him. He continued to walk towards the top of the ridge as I spoke to him. All he said was "Follow on as quickly as you can" and with that he was gone, and the mortar bombs started to rain down on that exposed ground they were advancing over.

"I turned and hurried back to the Platoon. They were leaving the woods to follow behind 'B' Company, when the CO from his position on the 'start line' overlooking the village, called on us to halt. "We've lost radio contact and the situation with 'B' Company on the right flank is not at all clear, so wait until I know more about what is happening over there." He explained. I moved the men and guns back about 100 yards, in the cover of the trees and went back to join the Colonel.

"As I arrived the first walking wounded members of 'B' Company came down from the ridge. Arthur Prestt, Scout Platoon Commander was one of them and he was able to give the CO an accurate account."

Lieutenant Arthur Prestt (Scout Platoon)

"We moved out of the wood onto the snow covered hillside, adopting an open formation as we did so. I was moving slightly to the rear of Major Grantham and his Command Group. After we had advanced about 100 yards, he must have seen something suspicious and moved down the hill to the shelter of a hedge. He appeared to speak to his signaller who already was in contact with one of the other stations. There was a single shot and Major George "Bill" Grantham fell dead at our feet. Then the shelling and the mortaring started. The hedge gave us no protection at all and very quickly the casualties mounted. I was one of the lucky ones, I was only wounded, but there were quite a number killed outright in the first salvoes. Too many for the 3 Company medics to deal with but they went about their task fearlessly and devotedly; laying us down in hollows in the ground. Alf (Lieutenant Lagergren) came forward and took charge, ordering all those capable of movement to run for shelter in the village and he led the rush to the nearest houses.

"From time to time a German tank appeared to our front, but never fired. We lay there for the best part of an hour and then Corporal Charlie Bryan (RAMC) had run out of dressings, so he collected the walking wounded and moved us back to the start line, where I was able to give the CO an account of what had happened."

Private Peter Maynard ('B' Company)

"As we were advancing along the hill the Germans knew exactly where we were and they gave us everything they had, small arms fire, 88's, mortars and moaning minnies."

Private Bill Holding (Scout Platoon)

"I was a sniper with the Scout Platoon and moved out with 'B' Company onto that snow covered hillside. When the bombs and shells started to land among us we got a bit mixed up. [Under Lt Alf Lagergren orders] Sergeant Tommy Hindle of 'B' Company (left) took a 2" mortar off one of the casualties, shoved it in my hand with some bombs and told me to put smoke down across the front. Once it was thick enough, we all ran as fast as we could for the houses on the right of the village."

Corporal Fred Smith (Scout Platoon)[54]

"For the start of the Ardennes Campaign I was in the newly formed Scout Platoon [snipers] and was attached to 'B' Company. Our task was to establish a "fire base" in order to support the attack of 'C' Company against the bridge at Grupont.

"My partner, as ever, was a young lad from Hull called Freddie Beach and from the start line we set off up the hill to our right. Unfortunately when we got close to the top of the hill, from which we could see all around us, we got very badly shelled and mortared. Major Grantham and Lieutenant Tim Winser were both killed. There were a hell of a lot of big bangs going on all around us and 'B' Company Sergeant Major [Percival] Jack Moss[55] was hit; he died of his wounds the next day. Our dog handler had the misfortune to lose the cheeks of his rear portion, sliced off by a large piece of shrapnel. We took heavy

---

[54] Fred Smith, pictured as a Royal Welsh Fusilier joined the Parachute Regiment after returning from the North Africa Campaign.
[55] CSM P.J. Moss was an ex-East Lancashire Regiment regular soldier, from Preston. He told one war correspondent on the eve of D-Day that he wanted to "get another crack at 'em" because he was "kicked out at Dunkirk and joined the paratroops to get back again."

casualties up there and the few of us that were left received orders to get down to the bottom of the hill, towards and into Bure where we should join up with 'A' Company. This we did… as fast as we possibly could! From then on we would come under the command of Major Watson's 'A' Company. This suited me, quite frankly, because Captain Joe Hodgson was one of the officers in 'A' Company, and we got on very well, Joe and me."

Private Anselm Snelham was a bright and cheerful, happy go lucky character, who always had a smile on his face and his sniping partner Private John McAndrew were two members of the Scout Platoon killed on the hillside during the first day of the battle, although McAndrew died the following day of his wounds. Snelham had also been particularly good sportsman - he could box and was a footballer before the war having been with Liverpool FC as a youngster. His photograph (left, apologies for the poor copy) hangs today in the Bure FC changing rooms halfway up the track leading to the Chapel Notre-Dame de Haurt.

Those still capable of standing after the barrage stormed down the hill and through the smoke screen towards the southern side of the village. 17 members of 'B' Company (nearly half of the Battalion's killed in action that first day) were cut down just short of the village, almost side by side, by MG fire from well placed defensive positions near the Chapel de Salette (over).

Father Jean-Marie Decorte (Bure civilian)

"Finally I recognised the English advancing from my window. I wished I could have shouted at them not to advance, but we daren't make a move. The enemy surrounded us on all sides. The tanks and guns were well placed. Also in this key position, the German general used elite troops whose members wore the Cross of Stalingrad. Bure is surrounded by a circle of hills and the Germans used these in a state of defence, mining smaller trails, lining the hollow roads with well posted machine guns and small cannons. The English were mowed down before our eyes only a few hundred meters from our house."

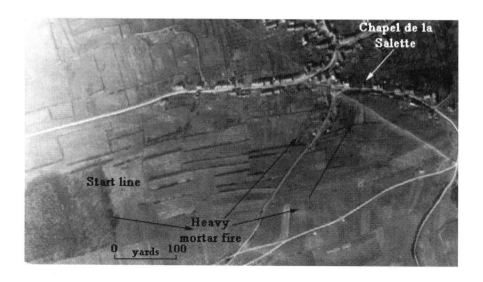

Chapel de la Salette

Start line

Heavy mortar fire

0   yards   100

Chapel de Salette

17 shot down running through smoke as they entered Bure

Remaining men entered houses from rear

MG34

Rue de Mirwart

Note: Bushes and trees not present in 1945

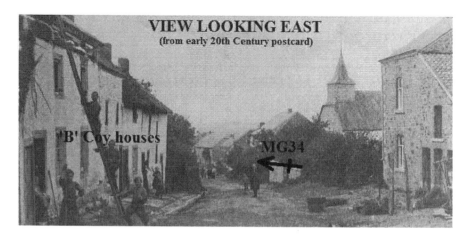

VIEW LOOKING EAST
(from early 20th Century postcard)

'B' Coy houses

MG34

Lieutenant Ellis "Dixie" Dean (MMG Platoon)

"Clearly any further advance on the right flank was out of the question and the situation in the village wasn't clear, so Harry Pollak [Intelligence Officer] was sent to contact Major Jack Watson ['A' Company in the village] for an up-to-date report."

1400 *'B' Coy advanced towards village and were intercepted by Tiger tk and by concentration of MG and mortar fire. Heavy casualties suffered but succeeded however in reaching village, and occupied isolated positions. 'A' Coy were now fighting near X rds in village.*

Major Jack Watson ('A' Company)

"Once I had got into the village it was difficult finding out just what was going on. I pulled in my platoon commanders to establish that they were secure and to start movement forward. It was eerie. We would be in one house, myself on the ground floor, and my signalman telling me that there were Germans upstairs, and at other times they would be downstairs and we upstairs. It was a most unusual battle."

Sergeant John Wallace ('A' Company)

"After that it was very close quarters stuff. The Germans were very close; we were firing across the street and at some stages, some members of my company were in the downstairs of a house while Jerry was upstairs. I remember it was literally across street stuff, we on the right hand side and the Germans on the left. Lieutenant Pat Kavanagh seeing Germans occupying the house opposite said "Look, that house across there, we've got to clear them out." So 3 of us simply followed the drill... dash across the road... open the door... chuck a grenade in... wait for it to go off... then charge in firing the Sten at random in all directions. We then went upstairs and threw a grenade through a hole knocked through the wall, I don't know if it did any good. We never went through after it.

'Hull down' position of 'Tiger' tank at crossroads looking down Rue de Tellin

'A' Coy

"I can also remember one Tiger tank, kind of hunkered down, between 2 buildings, all you could see was the gun muzzle. When he engaged, it was literally at point blank range."

Report by Victor Thompson (Herald War Correspondent)

"They had turned the first houses into fortresses when enemy 'Tiger' tanks rumbled up the main street and began to shoot along it. "The fire was so intense," one paratrooper said, "that it was suicide to try to cross the street. Medical orderlies had several times to throw morphia across it to be administered to the wounded on the other side.""

The aerial photo taken in March 1945 (RCAHMS) shows the houses and buildings of Rue de Tellin in which 'A' Company fought and held. Most of the buildings still stand today and still show signs of battle and repair. The houses completely demolished are those shown in the old photograph shown previous.

In the relative safety of the wood on the hillside from where the attack had begun the MMG Platoon, Mortar Platoon and 'C' Company had to wait for further updates before they could be deployed.

Lieutenant Ellis "Dixie" Dean (MMG Platoon)

"The news [via Lieutenant Pollak] from 'A' Company was more encouraging, but they too had suffered casualties, as they had crossed the open fields. There was a large tank, suspected, 'Tiger', sited at the crossroads of the village in a 'hull down' position, making it impossible to move along the street, and the advance had to be through gardens along the backs of the houses. Some houses had been wrestled from the Boche, but it was slow going, every yard of advance was fiercely contested. Some properties were small farms with out buildings, all of which had to be cleared. There were enemy SP's prowling around on the yet un-captured heights of 'Gin' and 'Orange' adding to their difficulties."

Celestine Limet (Villager)

"On 3rd January we [Mother and I, from the cellars of L'Alumnat] had returned home to tend to the livestock, but shooting started again. Only this time, it was a lot heavier than before. Once more we made a dash for the cellars of L'Alumnat, but the firing became so intense that we were forced to seek shelter with M'sieur Defaux-Goffinet in his cellar – we were not the only ones."

Louis Limet (Villager)

"After 2 stressful days, my parents decided to take refuge in the Château. We spent one night with fires and flashes of tracer bullets. In the morning we returned to the house despite the danger. The house, barn and stables of the Volvert's had finished burning. Numerous houses in the main street partially or totally destroyed testified the fierceness of the fighting. Ours was occupied by the English. Tin cans and straw littered the kitchen floor and the floor of the next room. The front door no longer closed. My uncle's pig had escaped, leaving footprints in the nearby gardens. Dad and my older brother, armed with a rope went to recover the precious animal in front of some mocking Germans in a trench."

Celestine Limet (Villager)

"My brother Camille had sheltered in his own place towards Grupont, where the Germans had dug trenches along the track. During the fighting one of his pigs got out and was loose in the German positions. Ignoring the danger, Camille ran after it. The Germans told him to stay indoors, but in the end with the help of laughing Germans, they managed to get the pig back by using a length of rope tied round one leg."

Back on the hillside to the south as the wounded were still being rounded up by the medics, the British armour now attempted to join the paras who had made it into the village to help push out the Germans.

Private Ray "Geordie" Walker ('A' Company)

"On reaching the crest of the hill and beyond the tree line I dropped into a slight hollow in a field and joined other wounded men. We nestled close together for warmth as it would be several hours before we could be evacuated. From here I lay and watched as tank after tank of the supporting Shermans were knocked out."

Lieutenant William Steel Brownlie (2nd Fife & Forfar Yeomanry)

[After giving supporting fire from Chapel Hill] "Geoff Hales' Troop [No.1 'A' Squadron] was sent down the track in front of us, to go into the village and give close support. He had gone about 300 yards when his own tank was hit. Sgt Robinson took cover in a hollow. Geoff and his crew came struggling back up the slope. Amazingly none were injured, while only one man in Guy's tank had been hurt, hit in the leg by a second shot as he was bailing out. Geoff had rescued nothing from his tank but a large carton of 'Mars Bars' – he had a friend in the factory in Slough.

"The battle in Bure raged furiously, and the Airborne were in danger of being pushed back. Desmond was still with them in his scout car and reported a 'Tiger' at the far end of the street which was proving unassailable. He didn't sound happy and then fell silent, it's difficult to continue fire support, not knowing who was where."

Private Dennis Boardman (Signaller, att 'A' Company)

"We were winning ground when we heard the roar of the Sherman tanks coming up the road. We cursed as we saw one, then two, burst into flames. Only two of the British tanks managed to escape. Seeing our support pull out we thought for a moment our heaviest weapon was the PIAT, against the 'Tiger', no match. The only way was to get very close and aim for the tracks. The fighting grew fierce and hand to hand was the order of the day."

Account by Units of the 29th Armoured Brigade supporting 13 Para

The tanks slithered from side to side on the glassy road. 200 yds short of the village the leading tank went up on a mine and this gave the reminder of the Troop some cause for thought. However, a diversion was found, the village was entered from another quarter and another of the tanks was hit, this time by an armour-piercing shell. The unfortunate airborne troops were also meeting trouble from a strong and determined enemy. Major R.L. Leith, who had to come up with the 'C' Troop, made liaison with the OC Parachute Battalion, and as darkness was falling the attackers could not hope to make further progress that night. So, with the British holding a third of the village and the enemy the rest, a halt was called to the fighting. One Troop of 'C' Squadron stayed with the infantry throughout the night, the rest of the Squadron proceeded by a series of intoxicated slithers back along the snow-filled road to Tellin.

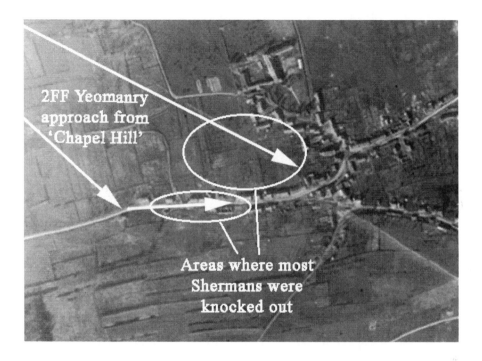

The 8th Rifle Brigade and 'A' Squadron, 2nd Fife & Forfar's went back up Chapel Hill during the day to ensure that this vital feature was held against any counter attack which would result in the village being surrounded by the Germans.

Private Donald Gillate (8th Bn The Rifle Brigade)

"We were ordered on to the pine-wooded and snow covered mountain of the Chapel de Notre-Dame of Bure. It quickly became known as 'Chapel Hill' but was later nicknamed 'Hill 113'. 'Hill 112' had been the scene in Normandy of our first and possibly most bitter action so far and Chapel Hill certainly rivalled it for unpleasantness. Bure was occupied by the enemy who clearly resented us as neighbours prying on them from the hill that overlooked them.

"For our part we were ordered to hold the hill come what may, but in this encounter the Germans held much better cards. Not only were we a narrowly concentrated target but they had the great advantage of elusive SP guns which could move about at will without fear of reprisal from our own artillery. Furthermore the pine trees turned every shell they fired into an 'air-burst', that is to say that when their shells hit the tops of the trees, they threw the blast and shrapnel downwards among us."

Private Dennis Boardman (Signaller, att 'A' Company)

"As darkness began to fall [it was winter and double GMT] the situation appeared to become critical. We requested reinforcements, but they were not available. We were cut of from the rest of the Battalion. I tried several times to contact 'B' Company on the wireless, and as the hours past, I knew it was hopeless. Later, a pal of mine found his way to our HQ, in the cellar of one of the houses. The news was bad; 'B' Company had almost been wiped out.

"During the late afternoon as the fighting eased off, we blew holes in the walls of the line of terraced houses, in order to maintain contact with the forward sections of the Company. To venture outside the houses we were met with a burst of machine gun fire from the road junction ahead. In between, 'Tiger' tanks rumbled up and down the

road firing their 88mm guns at point blank range into the houses. It meant we had to move from house to house or seek temporary use of the cellars. The cellar, in which we established Company HQ, was full of potatoes."

What was left of 'B' Company had reached the southern edge of Bure so they could attempt to fight back against the well sited German machine gun positions and attempt to link up with 'A' Company occupying the western half of the village. The fighting was again at close quarters, from house to house and garden to garden.

Private "Bill" Holding (Scout Platoon)

"We had worked our way towards the crossroads and I was with Lieutenant Lagergren (left) and several others in a barn. The Germans were advancing towards us supported by a tank, which put a round through the barn door, killing 3 men and I got splinters in my thigh. Now the Germans were only yards away, Lieutenant Lagergren threw the door back, stood in the open firing either a Bren or Sten, while the rest of us scrambled out the back through a low opening into a pig sty. We reached safety but we never saw Lieutenant Lagergren again."

Sergeant J Munro ('B' Company)

"I was a section Sergeant when we attacked Bure. My section was intact and fought intact, until half way through the village just to the right of the church [Chapel de Salette] where we met very heavy enemy MG fire. From then on I did not see private Pope or Docherty and cannot say whether they were wounded or not, as we had to push on as fast as possible to overcome the enemy MG posts. This we did, and in the village, just beyond the Chapel de Salette, we again met a very heavy barrage of MG, in this Private Bentley was wounded by MG bullets but Private Woolley was alright. After searching the houses I came out into the field again where I told my section to consolidate. As they were reporting to me a tank came over the hill and fired. With

374

this I was wounded. I never saw these men again and the last thing I did was to send medical attention to where Bentley was wounded."[56]

'A' Coy in houses on Rue de Tellin

'B'

'Tiger' at crossroads (Behind houses)

'B'

Route of 'B' Coy (photo looks west from area of 17 KIA)

Fountain

Rue de Mirwart

Private Dave Beedham (5 Platoon 'B' Company)

"We had to keep dashing from house to house, because there was this German 'Tiger' tank which was roaming up and down the street. It would drive right up to a building we were using, poke its big 88mm gun through the window and then blast away, we had to nip smartly out of the back, all very disturbing. After we reached safety I looked out of a bedroom window and there was Billy Roper, one of the Company Medics, walking calmly up the street, looking into the now half demolished houses to see if there were any wounded. Sometimes he was no more than 20 yards away from the 'Tiger', but the crew respected his Red Cross armband and didn't try to stop him. He was the real hero he was completely unarmed and wouldn't even carry a pistol which he was entitled to do."

Lieut David Clark (225 Field Ambulance)

"We took over a café as our dressing station [in Resteigne]. This was the first time I had set up an aid post in action, so I left it to the veterans in my section. They rapidly smashed the plate glass windows, and then cleared the furniture from the rooms, either by piling it up against the windows or throwing it into the street. Shells were beginning to fall on the village and a building opposite was hit and collapsed. Our first casualty was a middle aged woman screaming continuously in French (until the morphia took effect). Others soon came, at first civilians and soldiers from our village, then casualties

---

[56] All 4 of the privates were captured by the Germans and survived the war. Sergeant Munro was eventually sent back to the UK where he spent the rest of the war in Edenhall Hospital.

from the battle area just up the road.

"We soon learned that things were not going well; the village was held by experienced troops backed by a 'Tiger' tank. This enormous tank outgunned the Shermans, burned and wounded tank men were amongst our early casualties.

"The 13th Battalion men had approached the village across snow covered fields; the experienced Germans had let them get well out into the open and then opened up with mortar fire, which proved devastating on the frozen ground. Many of those who had chatted with us that morning were now dead or severely wounded.

"The casualties poured in, walking, carried by their friends, slung across Jeeps. We had to sort them out, bandage their wounds and pack them into ambulances to go back to the MDS. All were injured badly, bleeding and shocked. Many were severely wounded, shattered and broken limbs, injuries that would probably cripple them for life. It was here that I had my first experience of acute battle breakdown.

"A stretcher was brought in with a parachutist lying on his face. I went to examine him and found him shaking all over; his eyes were tight shut and he was moaning and whimpering. I said to the stretcher bearers, "What's this? Where are his wounds?" They replied, "Oh, he hasn't any. He's got a twitch!" I looked at the casualty card; on it the battalion Medical Officer [Capt Tibbs] had written 'acute battle exhaustion: evacuate.' I tried to speak to him or to comfort him, but got no response, only further shuddering. So I ticked the card and told them to put him on the next ambulance."

Private Ray "Geordie" Walker ('A' Company)

"I was more than pleased to be evacuated from Bure. I along with 3 others we were eventually picked up by "Jock" Weatherspoon and driven in his Jeep to a RAP established in a café in a neighbouring village. Here the Medics attended to our wounds and applied fresh dressings. We were given mugs of tea whilst awaiting the arrival of an ambulance to take us to hospital. Within an hour we were loaded into an ambulance along with the stretcher cases. I was one of the 3 men classified as 'walking wounded' and we sat on the floor whilst being driven to a final destination.

"Our journey was slow and laborious owing to the amount of traffic passing to and from the front line. In addition the road was packed hard with snow and ice. Our driver took a wrong turning and we ended up in the French border town of Givet. With the help of a local man we were put on the road to Namur.

"Somewhere along the Meuse valley we stopped at a small village school as one of my comrades was dying from his wounds. I accompanied the medics into the school hall and within a few moments he was dead. He was laid alongside several other bodies which were to be collected by men of the Pioneer Corps for burial. On climbing back into the ambulance, the driver told me that we should reach the hospital in about 1 ½ hours."

Lieutenant David Clark (225 Field Ambulance)

"I still have the record of that night, written on the pages of the French Hotel register in Harry Abbott's clear architectural gothic hand. There were 118 of them in 36 hours, all sent back except for a corporal, who died slowly in the middle of the café floor. By the end, my hands and clothes were stiff with blood and I was dizzy and exhausted. But we had coped."

F.J. Strauss (2nd Pz Div) states in his book that "An attack by British airborne troops was repulsed by Nickel's platoon [1st Kompanie], the enemy suffering about 250 men KIA, whereby NCO Orleth showed himself particularly useful." And that "On 3 January 1st Kompanie was embroiled in house to house combat in Bure, in which a Sherman was knocked out."

His figures of 250 are nowhere near the actual number of KIA, but in terms of killed <u>and</u> wounded that terrible day, he is not far wrong. The 13th Para Bn alone suffered 41 KIA with around 3 times more wounded, many of which died of their wounds. Add to this the KIA and wounded from the 2nd Fife & Forfar Yeomanry and the casualties could add up to 250, but debatable.

On Rue de Tellin, 'A' Company were making very slow progress towards the crossroads against the German tanks and had to fight off numerous counter-attacks.

Sergeant John Wallace ('A' Company)

"I soon learned why cowboys in the movies smash the windows before a gun battle starts! The glass flies everywhere. By this time it was beginning to get dark, we had set off from the start line at 1:30pm and being the middle of winter, the dark came very quickly."

Private Fred Wilcock ('A' Company)

"We were trapped in a cellar and the Germans roamed above us and a box of apples in the corner was all we had to eat. One poor chap had to lay on the floor all night with a bad stomach wound. We run out of morphine to give him so we pretended to give him morphine by using a knife to prick him in his leg. The soldier believed that he was receiving morphine and settled down. Sadly he died later.

"When it was my time to go on watch, another soldier stopped me and said he would go on watch instead. Minutes later a shell exploded and I scrambled to the watch point. I felt a warm sticky substance on my hand… It was the soldier who had stood my watch. He had been blown to pieces."

As the 'Tiger' tank crawled down the street, systematically blowing up houses, Private "Bobby" Macgregor and his friends were cut off from the rest of their unit. Supporting Panzer grenadiers quickly closed in on them, and with little firepower and out numbered, surrender was their only option. They were marched into the enemy lines and into a make shift, barbed wire POW camp.

The 2nd Panzer Division attempted to hit 'B' Company's area of in another counter-attack, this time from the direction of Grupont. Watching from 'Chapel Hill' the Fife & Forfar's saw the critical attack begin.

Lieutenant William Steel Brownlie (2nd Fife & Forfar Yeomanry)

"On the hill south of the village, down which half the paras ['B' Company] had come in the first rush, there came a counter attack. 3 SP's followed by bunches of infantry were mowing a patch through the Airborne, who were scattering in all directions. We hit the leading SP with our third shot, range about 2 miles, and it halted. The second was soon also stopped and the third, having been hit 3 or 4 times, disappeared. The counter-attack was over and we felt that we had done our job. We were shelled, with no damage."

As 'A' Company won ground the Germans slowly fell back towards the crossroads and many villagers caught up in the war torn area of Rue de Tellin headed to the cellars of L'Alumnat.

Renie Lambert (Villager)

"Back in December, we had taken refuge with an aunt living 4 houses away from our house. We were 3 families totalling 13 people. An old uncle of mine was sick and would sometimes sleep in a bed upstairs. He discovered to his surprise, one day, a large shell lying on the bed which had not exploded. We decided to leave and started toward the college, among the Germans retreating. Houses were burning on Grupont Road ahead of us. Arriving near the church, we heard the bullets whistling around us. Immediately we lay down in the snow. Then when it was less risky, we turned left towards the L'Alumnat.

"Part of the village was already there. There were several cellars and many similar small ones, but everyone was already very tightly packed and so we found a place in the hallway."

1700   'C' Coy ordered to move into BURE in support of the other two Coys. Arty fired by concentrations on high ground overlooking BURE to cover them in.

Major Jack Watson ('A' Company)

"Our numbers were getting extremely depleted as we moved forward from house to house. I eventually got to the village crossroads by the old church. In the meantime I had informed my CO exactly what was going on, and he decided to send in 'C' Company, who were in reserve, to support me. By this time their 60 ton 'Tiger' tanks were all over us."

Lieutenant Ellis "Dixie" Dean (MMG Platoon)

"In an effort to at least clear the village before nightfall, the CO sent in 'C' Company, ordering them to pass through 'A' and complete the task of seizing Bure. To cover their dash across the open, the artillery were called on to lay a barrage on the eastern end of the village and on the 2 hills where the mortars and SP's were lurking. As the shells screamed over, 'C' Company ran from the wood and advanced on the houses. Reports on the radio told of slow progress and it was clear that as night began to close around us, that Bure was not going to be captured that day.

"The only uncommitted troops were the Mortars and the MMG's, as they really have a limited role in street fighting."

1830   'C' Coy had pushed forward as far as X rds 229685.
1930   Enemy counter attack supported by Tiger tk forced 'C' Coy to withdraw 100 yds.
1935   Tight bn perimeter formed, occupying approx ½ of village.
1940   F & F.Y. report 6 enemy SP guns disabled during day.

Sergeant Len Cox ('C' Company)

"Along with the rest of 'C' Company I waited in the woods while the other 2 Companies cleared the village and high ground so that we could pass through and attack the bridge at Grupont. We could see the flashes of the German guns away to our left as they were firing and the shells were landing in the trees. After a time, orders came that we were to make a run for the houses and assist 'A' Company in evicting the Germans.

"We moved to the front edge of the wood and on a signal we raced across the open fields as fast as we could, across the road and started to work our way along the backs of the houses. There was a German tank firing down the main street. The first few houses had been cleared but after that it was grenade and Sten all the way, with no-one daring to use the road because of the tank. Progress was slow and we had many casualties. The final orders were to clear the area around the church and then hold as it was getting dark. We finished up in the house next but one to the church (above), clearing 'Jerry' out with grenades and then found 4 civilians in the cellar. Wireless contact with Company HQ had been lost earlier and we didn't know where any one else was. All that was left of 9 Platoon was Lieutenant "Dick" Burton, Sergeant Bill Railton, myself and 12 others were marooned in that house for 36 hours."

CSM "Taffy" Lawley ('C' Company)

"It was my Company's turn next and we got through to the centre of the village. It was getting dusk now and it was then things began to happen, everything became mixed up, something that can easy happen in street fighting. We had sent 2 platoons forward and had lost touch with them, through their 38 sets breaking down;[57] it was very difficult in the darkness to discern friend from foe; sometimes we would be in one house and the enemy in the one next door."

2000   *All occupied buildings formed into strong points and aggressive patrolling ordered during night.*

2015   *Tiger tk advanced beyond X rds 229685 to support infantry counter attack which was broken up by – 'C' & 'A' Coy. Four counter attacks were broken up during night.*

Private Ray "Geordie" Walker ('A' Company)

"On arrival at the 101st British General Hospital at Heverlee, I was met by a nurse who checked my ID and medical cards, before escorting me to a nearby room. She cut my bloodstained tunic and clothing from my body. It was at that stage that my wound began to really hurt. I was so numb from the cold, that I could not feel pain, but now in the warmth of the hospital, my body and particularly my arm, was regaining other feelings. The nurse treated me gently as she washed me from head to toe in preparation for surgery. She wrapped me in a surgical gown and placed me on a trolley, which was wheeled by two orderlies to a room adjacent the operating theatre. This room was already occupied by several unconscious men ready for theatre. A

---

[57] The 38 Radio Sets was well known for being temperamental, it was awkward to carry and composed of too many parts and often a slight knock could send a set off net.

nurse gave me a premedical injection, but before loosing consciousness, I was aware of a man standing over me; I thought I was in heaven."

Report by Victor Thompson (Herald War Correspondent)

"In all the Germans counterattacked five times that first day and each time there was hand to hand fighting with knives, grenades, Tommy guns and even gun butts. Sometimes the Germans got into ground floors while the British held the upper storeys to which our men had gone to escape from the tanks, which were firing through the windows. Sometimes the British held a parlour while a kitchen contained Panzer Grenadiers. There was fighting over garden walls and in hen houses. There was much killing and no prisoners were taken."

Yvonne Louviaux (Villager)

"I was 14 and lived in the heart of the village. During the battle, we were forced to stay for 3 days in the cellar without ever being able to go back up because the fighting was violent. We heard the commotion above us, sounds of clashing metal weapons. Mum told us to keep close to each other and if we die, we would do together. I told Mum "I don't want to die!" An Englishman came to our cellar. Then another came down and told us it was better and for our sakes to get out. When we got back, days later, I remember seeing our couch filled with blood."

Lieutenant William Steel Brownlie (2nd Fife & Forfar Yeomanry)

"With darkness we harboured near the Chapel [on Chapel Hill], which was in ruins. There was body laid in the brushwood, apparently the commander of the SP [destroyed by Samson's Troop]. We sat and ate in the tank. There was no wind, no more snow, but it grew colder and colder."

Extract from: An Account of Ops 29th Armoured Brigade in the Ardennes

By midnight, the situation at Bure was still somewhat obscure. It appeared now that only about a quarter of the place had been cleared of the enemy; 2 platoons of 13th Parachute Battalion which had penetrated to the eastern end were cut off.

Private Dennis Boardman (Signaller, att 'A' Company)

"During the night the fighting continued in the houses and German voices were clearly heard giving one another instructions, in between a piercing scream would stir the icy cold night. The Germans knew we were still a fighting force. The position by now seemed hopeless and I remember the occupants of the cellar, which now included many wounded, emptying their pockets of documents which might help the enemy if we were captured. Major Watson took over my radio and spoke to Colonel Luard outlining the situation. We were told Bure must be taken at all costs."

Major Jack Watson ('A' Company)

"It became difficult to keep the men awake - after all they were tired, we had no hot food. All through our first night they were shelling and firing at us, and we were firing back. When we told HQ we had German tanks in the area they decided to bring in our own tanks in support, but they were no match for the 'Tigers'."

Now that everything was a lot quieter and under the cover of darkness the remaining personnel in the woods could get down into the village to strengthen the position and for Lt-Col Luard to take a firm grip on the situation.

Lieutenant Ellis "Dixie" Dean (MMG Platoon)

"We waited in the trees until it was dark, before any move was made to get the rest of the Battalion into the village. We moved back into the wood and formed into a long snake and holding onto the man in front, we finally emerged from the wood without mishap. Now at least we could see where we were going, but there was still some distance to the road.

"All was quiet in the village and moving quietly we eventually entered the built up area. The houses on the outskirts, stood well apart, straggling the street. On the left, the RAP occupied the first one, Battalion HQ the next, while the rest, Major Andy McLoughlin with his HQ, Mortars and MMG's, pushed on until we bumped into the rear positions of those already there. The Mortars, who were leading, were allotted 2 houses on the north of the road, and we were given 2 next to the rear, while Company HQ was on the opposite side.

"I had been given the task of covering the main street, so leaving Sgt Whalley to check the houses; I went forward with my 2 Section Commanders to have a look around. All was quiet, the road was littered with debris of mortaring and shelling, but there was no-one about. Forward of Company HQ on the right, a flight of steps ran up to a front door and underneath them was a small chamber open to the west, and I sited one gun here, firing back down the axis of advance. Forward of this position, the pavement on either side was blocked by fallen masonry and I sited a gun on either side behind this cover.

"Alf Whalley had searched the houses, finding them empty. Thinking we would only be there for the night, we stretched out in a broad passage that ran the length of the house. It was a long sleepless night. Information about the actual location of the Boche was lacking, so every movement had to be treated as suspicious. On one occasion, a burst of Sten gun fire broke the night's silence. A Boche patrol had approached the right hand forward post through a derelict house to their front. "Rommel" [Private Rodden] waited until the leading man was only 5 yards away and then fired. The corpse, with an MG42, was there when daylight came."

Headquarters
Company HQ

MMG
Facing west
- stairs altered
since 1945

Major "Nobby" Clark ('C' Company)

"I sheltered in the house of a brave man who gave us everything he had. We did have some pieces of artillery in support, but the Germans had artillery also and one of their tanks, a Tiger, was circulating in our half of the village to identify and direct their artillery. From an upstairs window, I tried to get out a grenade, but the next house was full of Germans. And I could not throw my grenade on the tank."

Sergeant John Wallace ('A' Company)

"Things seemed to quiet down a little. Major Clark ['C' Coy] sent me out, he said "Take two blokes and go and find out what's going on. Don't run into trouble. There's no point finding out if you don't come back to tell us!" I took these two blokes out and along the street I saw what I think was the school burning. To avoid being seen we sneaked along the back of the houses, two of us got past the burning building and then we were fired on. The third man Lance Corporal Corrie decided that we'd got into trouble and he went back. The remaining two of us decided that we couldn't go back past the machine gun that was in the back room of a house and so went a little further until we reached a big thick hawthorn hedge. On the other side of the hedge Jerry was digging in, we sneaked down further still, keeping very quiet indeed. It was a black, black night and eventually we got clear of the hedge. Down at the bottom, clear of the hedge there was a German halftrack and the crew were out having a smoke, the lad I had with me, his name was Byrne said "Shall we throw a grenade in?" and I replied "No, certainly not!". I think he was a little disappointed! We then sneaked back to our own lines and got fired on by our own boys, they weren't expecting us! I eventually got in my slit trench and sat there with my knees up near my ears trying to keep warm as my clothes froze on me."

CSM "Taffy" Lawley ('C' Company)

"My Company Commander established Company HQ at a house in the centre of the village. When night finally came, Major Clark decided we would move forward and if possible find out what had happened to our 2 lost Platoons. After we had gone some distance (down the back of the houses) Major Clark decided we would enter the house we were immediately behind and try to make contact on the wireless, but we soon found that all the doors and windows were bolted. I saw a passage along the side, so we went along it, with the intention of getting in at the front. I tried to open the door, but found it locked, and then I beard voices in a strange language which I knew to be German. I tip-toed back and reported to Major Clark. We both went back up the passage and listened; they were Germans all right and a large number too. They had a tracked vehicle with them and were busily loading it with documents from the building opposite. We went back to the others to formulate a plan of attack when suddenly we heard footsteps coming down the side of the house. We were only 6 in number, so we had to think quickly. We all stood still and waited until the footsteps came very close. Major Clark shone his torch in their direction and we all opened fire. When the torch went out I dashed back across the opening to the next house and gave covering fire while the others got across. We then returned to our original position. All that night we were heavily shelled, and had one direct hit on the house we occupied, killing one of our signallers and wounding some others."

In charge of one of the lost 'C' Company platoons (No.8 Platoon) was Lieutenant (later Captain) Wilfred "Bill" Davison.

Citation: Captain Wilfred Davison (8 Platoon, 'C' Company)

Awards: Chevalier of the Order of Leopold II with Palm & Croix de Guerre 1940 with Palm

Captain W. DAVISON served in the Campaigns in Belgium and Holland as a Platoon Commander in the 13th Battalion (Lancashire) The Parachute Regiment. His work at all times particularly able and fearless. At Bure on 3rd January he led his platoon in the attack with great personal dash and courage. After the capture of the village, during which time he was wounded, [he] defended his sector with outstanding ability and courage. He directed the artillery fire so well and fearlessly that German counter attacks with Tiger and Panther tanks were stopped right in his own position, with shells bursting in the houses that he was occupying. He personally led platoon counter attacks, more that once, with only one other man, and repulsed the enemy. He refused to leave the positions in spite of pain from his wound until ordered to do so.

Private Alfred Draper ('C' Company)

"Our Company went in about tea time [double summertime – just getting dark] and managed to get to the crossroads at the centre of the village. My section was sent to a house on the other side of the crossroad held by some of 'B' Company. We were under fire from a German machine gun across the road and we kept firing back at it. I thought this was silly, it was going to attract the attention of a German tank that was roaming around and sure enough it did. He rolled up outside the house and fired 5 shells into the house. Luckily they were armour piercing and didn't explode. An officer [Lt Steve Honnor – 6 Platoon 'B' Company] shouted "Everybody out!" and 6 of us scrambled out. I was the only one from 'C' Company the others were 'B' Company (the rest of my section stayed for some reason). Nobody seemed to know what to do including the officer so two of us said it would be better to go to the village we started from [Tellin] for the night so we did.

"On the way we met another group and who should be there but Bob Giles and Bob Wilky. They had been cut off in some way and had the same idea that I had. The next day we went back to Bure and joined our Companies.

"The lad who had agreed with me that we should go back to the village was awarded the Military Medal. In reality we should all have been Court Martialled!"

It was Eric Toogood who for his part in the battle on that first day earned the Military Medal. He was the member of the Anti-Tank Platoon who back in July 1944, had been evacuated from Normandy after suffering from 'Battle Exhaustion' caused by the constant mortar and shell attacks at Le Mesnil crossroads.

Citation: Private Eric Toogood (Anti-Tank, attached 'B' Company)

Award: Military Medal

On 3rd January 1945, during the attack on BURE, Pte TOOGOOD's platoon was clearing the south side of one of the streets. Fighting had been intense, casualties heavy, and not half of the village had been cleared. As darkness fell, Pte TOOGOOD's platoon, holding firmly on to houses they had captured, were cut off from their company by enemy infantry and tanks.

The platoon position was attacked fiercely by the enemy, including a Tiger tank. Pte TOOGOOD was manning a PIAT and, searching for the tank, found it to offer only a head on shot. Nevertheless he engaged the tank, killing two of the crew and forcing the tank to withdraw.

The enemy infantry covering the tank counter-attacked the PIAT position in greatly superior numbers with grenades and small arms fire, blast from one grenade rendering Pte TOOGOOD unconscious. His position was subsequently over-run and the PIAT put out of action. Pte TOOGOOD, on regaining consciousness made his way back to his company and while doing so met three of the enemy who attempted to stop him. Although suffering from the effects of the grenade explosion, Pte TOOGOOD shot one with his pistol and brought back the remaining two with him as prisoners.

Throughout, Pte TOOGOOD showed courage, determination and cheerfulness in particularly unpleasant circumstances and constantly encouraged his comrades, contributing largely to the final success of the attack.

The two German prisoners from 2nd Panzer Grenadier Regiment were taken during the afternoon and one, an NCO, during his interrogation, reported that there were 3 rifle companies and a heavy company, each 80-90 men in strength operating in Bure. Tanks and SP's were working in pairs (Mk IV and Mk V) and some were possibly from 9 Pz Regiment. He also said that he had heard that 9 Pz Recce Unit were due to take over the Grupont area that night, although this 'rumour' was ignored as information of this kind was often rife in prisoners.

He stated that the rifle companies were named 1, 2 and 3, and the heavy company retained its former number, 10. Each rifle company was split into 2 platoons of 5-6 sections and had 5 halftracks, 1 MMG and 2 LMG's per section. The 10th (Heavy) Company had 6 SP guns, 4 heavy mortars and "some" anti-tank guns.

During the interrogation he also spoke of arriving from Germany on 29th Dec 1944 in a draft of 25 men, which were split up between the companies. On the 2nd Jan

another 50 men from an unspecified unit arrived. He maintained that elements of the 9 Pz Div were to relieve them during the night of 3rd/4th or 4th/ 5th January and that they would withdraw 20 miles to refit and that they should hand over their tanks to 9 Pz Div when relieved.

Lt Freudel (left) was part of the 10th Heavy Company and joined the army in 1938. In Sept 1944 he had encountered the 1st Airborne Division in Arnhem and now as he was waiting for a court martial [unknown reason], he became involved in another intense street battle with the 6th Airborne Division. He survived the Battle of Bure only to be captured shortly after by an American unit.

Private Thomas Holt | Private Ernest Jones | Private Dennis Kenny | Private Daniel Regan | L/Sgt Douglas Shales

Five of 13 Para Killed In Action 3rd January 1945

"The night 3rd/4th January was a terrible one and we sheltered in the cellar. Outside we heard English voices; bursts of fire and the wounded could be heard calling for help. The Bourtenbourg family were also in their cellars with some English soldiers. Some German soldiers returned and took over the ground floor, so they all kept quiet. When the Germans moved out the English emerged and carried on the fight."

Pierre Lardinois (Villager)

22.   DAY TWO: 4th JANUARY 1945

Guy Jacquemin (Villager)

"During the offensive, we stayed in the cellar. We had protected the ventilator grating with large pieces of wood, and we were down to a few mattresses and blankets. However, there was a fire in the oven...

"Albert and I slept on a pile of potatoes. We were with Pierre Lardinois and his family, and we were a little cramped. During the battle, we heard the rattle of weapons, shelling and explosions. I remember a machine gun installed in front of the house shooting continuously.

"We also heard a tank. He fired, left, came back, and pulled off again. The Allies responded and as expected a shell hit our home. You could hear the cows bellowing, screaming soldiers, and the wounded groan..."

Celestine Limet (Villager)

"Fighting went on throughout the day and night which I was able to watch through the cellar ventilator. At midnight it was as bright as day, with tracer bullets and fires. Several houses across the street were in flames, the 'Liegos' garage, plus the homes of Jules Grandjean and the Marione's. Jules was sheltering with his wife in the pig-sty when he was told by soldiers that his house was on fire. They tried to save some buildings from being destroyed, but were driven back by the flames, and they too found shelter with us. Jules wife received a bullet wound on the way.

"Jean-Baptiste Marione and his wife, both elderly, were in the cellar with us and from my reactions he could sense something was wrong "What's going on out there, Celestin?" he asked me. "I'm watching your house go up in flames" I told him. They wanted to go and salvage what they could, but there was gunfire from both ends of the street and it was not safe to cross the road."

Louis Limet (Villager)

"3rd and 4th January, at the height of the battle, we were in our basement. Shells fell close to our home. Filled with fear, father, a man of strong character, fell on his knees with clasped hands and prayed "Our Lady of Haurt, change the direction of fire." During a temporary ceasefire, we came out of the house safely. A thick layer of snow covered the ground and was blackened with electric poles and with the debris from our homes. A destroyed tank was stopped at the pump across from the Laffineur's. As children, we were sad to see our toys hidden under the roof in one corner of the bakery had been hit by a shell which had also destroyed the floor.

"Our cellar had not been damaged by the shelling so we sheltered there. Alternatively German and English soldiers were shooting and then came violently on to our ground floor. To protect us, Dad shouted "civilians" at the foot of the stone staircase. He was afraid of grenades being thrown down by the fighters. We remember a German machine gun crackled for over 2 hours adjacent the cellar vent. During a lull, we went to an English para lying on his back; we grabbed his belt and dragged him in between Lannoy's and Louviaux's."

Lance Corporal David "Robbie" Robinson (Anti-Tank 'C' Company)

"Major Clark, now CO of 'C' Company, sent me with 2 men. I was then a lance corporal, it having been decided back in England that the No.1 on the PIAT should be a lance corporal, and as I had always carried the PIAT although I was only 5 ft 2 tall, just skin and bones with the weight of 110 lbs, I was chosen.

"I was asked to move through the back gardens of the houses on the main street towards the centre of the village where a 'Tiger' tank was hull down in a dip in the road and under the shadow of the church wall with just his turret showing. The only place we could have any effect on this tank was in the rear so I was to try and get behind him and knock him out so that our advance could progress more easily.

"We moved out on the right hand side of the main street, along the back gardens furthest from the buildings along a hedge and a fence on a small raised bank. Our objective was a building that had been burned out during the day and was believed to be just beyond the tank on the other side of the street. Progress was slow with various obstacles like sheds, rubbish, chicken runs etc. At the chicken run, we carefully lifted the wire to crawl through on both sides of the run and progressed about 200 yards. Then the Germans spotted us and fired at us with an MG starting from our rear and sweeping along our line of three. We dropped down behind the small 18 inch bank. The men with me, who were fresh this being their first contact with the enemy said, "what do we do now corporal?" Knowing that if I moved forward the MG would be lined up to receive us and if I didn't move the mortars would soon be dropping in on us I decided to go back.

"I said to them when I give you the signal, run like hell back to where we came from. I took a long breath and said "Go!" and we went. As I bent to pick up the PIAT the MG opened up, one tracer going across my knees though both trouser legs but not hitting me, but the tracer burnt my skin on both kneecaps, the scars still show. I was so scared that, as I ran, I forgot about the chicken run, but I never did find it so it was either flattened by my 2 companions or I went round it. This has always been a mystery to me!"

Private Dennis Boardman (Signaller, att 'A' Company)

"The night must have been the longest of my life. As dawn approached we were reinforced by some sections of 'C' Company and this boosted our will to carry on the battle. We started the day with fresh energy.

"The quietness which had persisted during the latter part of the night was abruptly broken by the sound of tanks; 2 Shermans were coming up the street to supply us with ammunition. That done, they moved forward. The 'Tiger' was waiting at the junction, its 88mm gun was fired and the first tank caught fire, the other Sherman hastily withdrew. The 'Tiger' tank commander knew the Shermans were no match for him. Slowly he moved his machine into the road, he stopped at each house turned his 88mm gun and fired, this was followed by a heavy burst of machine gun fire. He repeated this operation to every house in the street."

Private William Ellis (Mortar Platoon)

"I remember being trapped in an isolated house with some of the lads, we were upstairs and you always went upstairs if you could. The house was hit by a tank shell and we had to jump down below, we had to make our escape that way, well what was left of us."

Celestine Limet (Villager)

"Through the cellar vent I watched the British soldiers advance along the backs of the houses and get near the church. They couldn't move down the road because of the tank, which is pointing straight down the road. Dead bodies, both British and German could be seen lying in the street. The tank was behind Defaux-Goffinet's house, where there is a slight bend in the road. One British tank had driven straight up the road from Tellin, until it was outside Felix Despas' house, where it was stopped, by a direct hit, which blew off the turret. After the fighting was over, we found a piece of hairy scalp in the branches of a nearby walnut tree. Another tank was hit right outside our front door, but was able to withdraw."

The above (Then, Now & Ghost) photographs taken on the junction of Rue de Tellin and the lane that leads up towards Chapel Hill, shows the Sherman that Mr Limet refers to. The turret can be seen on the right. The house on the right was used as Headquarters Company HQ.

Captain David Tibbs MC (RAMC)

"On another occasion I was further down the street standing next to the Firefly Sherman tank, when its was hit. The noise was terrific, first, one solid 88mm shell hit it, ricocheted off and screamed away, but the next shot came within seconds, dislocated its turret, forcing it to back off and the crew to abandon it hurriedly. However, they brought its heavy machine gun with them and set up an improvised position."

Father Jean-Marie Decorte (L'Alumnat Superior)

"British paratroopers attacked the houses full of Germans; in each house was a violent struggle and scenes of horrific melee. When morning came, the English were in the village, but around the houses corpses lie, with English and Germans in grimacing postures or threatening gestures, killed by a stabbing, a grenade or a bullet. The floors and walls were stained with blood from the hard battle of bayonets, knives, grenades, bullets."

Those 10 ½ hours (0130-0000 hours) since the battle begun were the worst ever in the 13th Battalions history. They had suffered 41 killed and approximately double that in wounded and missing. It is nigh on impossible to determine how each man lost his life or for that matter where he might have fallen. First they were caught in the heavy shelling and mortaring on the exposed hillside, where they had no cover. Then, any of those surviving this deadly barrage, were forced into storming the village under smoke screens but also through intense machine gun fire.

But to mention a few, Private William Murray was to remain MIA and subsequently has no known grave to this day. He is remembered on the Groesbeek Memorial. James and Alice Waddell of Cambuslang had to endure the loss of their 3rd son, Private Alexander Waddell (19). James Jr (19) had been killed in N. Africa with the 1st Para Bn in March 1943 and John (unknown age) was lost over the skies of Germany with the RAF the previous January.

Lieutenant William Steel Brownlie (2nd Fife & Forfar Yeomanry)

"[We moved] out at dawn to our previous positions, just in time to avoid a tremendous stonk by enemy medium guns on our harbour area in Chapel Hill. I sat chewing my fingers to keep them from freezing up. Jimmy Samson walked over to discuss some point or other, and I hardly recognised him. He seemed to have shrunk to half his normal size, face black and blue, encrusted with dirt and icicles on his beard. But then how did I look?

"Dick Leith's Squadron joined in further attempts to push through Bure, coming in on a flank along with a unit of tank destroyers (Archer SP gun, pictured below). Dick had a dispute with them, on the air, saying they were just getting in the way. His flank attack failed, but one troop penetrated up the main street into the village, where it was knocked out by the 'Tiger', if that is what it was. One tank did not brew, but ran against a house with engine running and gear engaged, where it scraped away with its track for 12 hours until the petrol gave out."

Account by Units of the 29th Armoured Brigade supporting 13 Para

From early light on 4th January there was enough excitement to satisfy anyone. All three tanks which had been left in Bure were knocked out by well directed enemy fire, and when 'C' Squadron, now in position to the southeast of the village, pushed another troop forward with the intention of out flanking the village, another tank was lost. There, for hours, the situation remained deadlocked. Each side resorted to heavy shelling. It was certainly remarkable that relatively few casualties were incurred by the Yeomanry, for their position was simply plastered. There were times when it seemed as though the whole Squadron must be out of action. The vehicles looked so shrapnel-scarred and must-bespattered that they had the appearance of being knocked out. Corporal Gorman and Trooper Lines were killed in this action and Lieutenant Jones and several troopers wounded.

Josette Joris (Villager)

"We had a good relationship with the Germans [Josette lived near the gendarmerie]. In fact it was they who'd tell us when the battle promised to be more difficult. We were part of the 37 in the basement at Rosa Gillard's. The Germans defended Bure with a big tank that used the backside wall of the house for protection, so we occupied the basement. When it fired, it shook the house so much that we felt that the house had collapsed on us.

"One day Mum went up into the house, she came face to face with 2 Germans, the youngest burst into tears in the arms of my mother. Over her shoulder, she looked at the other who, with his fingers, made it clear he was only 15 years old! 15 years, just the age of myself! These two from time to time came down to protect themselves in the basement with us. It was there they were, asleep, when the English arrived. Someone said to the British there were two Germans in the cellar. Immediately, they descended the stairs, and crying very hard, they pushed out the two Germans, without giving them time to put on their boots. They took them, barefooted in the snow. I felt very sorry for them, because these two men were extremely friendly."

Lieutenant Ellis "Dixie" Dean (MMG Platoon)

"The main street was deserted. I couldn't see too far up the street, as it veered off to the left, but I knew from the map there was a crossroads up there. In the opposite direction, looking back the way we had come, there were very few houses, perhaps a gap of 40 yards to the nearest, and this was Battalion HQ. Almost opposite 'our' house, but across the road, stood a farm cart, loaded with hay and the shafts were locked, rising diagonally upwards. On the far side behind Company HQ, the ground started to rise just to the rear, but at the back of the buildings on our side of the road, was an open aspect of snow covered fields, slowly rising in height towards the two hill features (code named "Gin" and "Orange"). It was also possible to observe the rear of the houses running up to the crossroads. Further still to the right, could be seen the country leading towards Grupont. I had one gun not yet committed; their task would be to cover this flank.

"I was upstairs working this out, when away in the distance I heard the noise of a truck, slowly grinding its way up the street. "Stop that truck" I called down the stairs, and even before I reached the ground floor, in bounded Fred Tiramani, "Christ Fred. Where do you think your going?" I asked, "I've brought the Battalion their breakfast." He replied. All of us present set to unloading the food containers. "What on earth has happened to the Battalion?" Fred wanted to know, "the talk at Brigade is that the Battalion has been almost wiped out." "It's not as bad as that" I assured him, "but we have taken a battering."

"By now the passage was filled with the Battalions breakfast. I pointed out Battalion HQ to Fred "As you go by, tell them where the food is." For the next half hour a steady stream of carrying parties collected their company's rations."

Lance Corporal David "Robbie" Robinson (Anti-Tank 'C' Company)

"We were bogged down in buildings, with no chance of going forward. It was very, very cold and we had had no sleep or food. When up the street in full view of the Germans, in the centre of the road a certain Sergeant Scott [not Sgt Scott of the medics] arrived with Fred Tiramani in a truck. They were carrying the Battalions breakfast – a stew. This was the most heroic sight I think I ever saw."

Major Jack Watson ('A' Company)

"I will always take off my hat to Colour Sergeant Harry Watkins (left). How the hell he found us I do not know, but he did. We were still scattered in the houses along the main road in the centre of the village. He brought us a stew which was good and hot, and we were able to get men into small groups to have food and then get to their positions in the houses."

War Diary 4th Jan

0800 *The whole bn area was subjected to very intense arty fire causing numerous casualties. During morning 5 enemy counter attacks were broken up although enemy Tiger tks still operated in village, making moping up extremely difficult.*

Sergeant John Wallace ('A' Company)

"The next morning Fred Tiramani drove in with the breakfast, it was stew, I never got mine, but apparently it started hot and got cold before it was eaten, that's how cold it was. It was about 11 o'clock when I got wounded; I had my section out on the left flank [north of Bure in the back gardens] and was sending them back two at a time for the stew. Then my corporal (George McPherson) who was a regular soldier and I got our turn. The shelling became quite hot and we dashed across a bit of open ground to the house which was being used as Company HQ. As I got through the backdoor my corporal was in the doorway when a shell landed on the door step. I ended up on the floor with my corporal lying next to me, he had lost his head. My Sergeant Major

[Bert Alder] came from down the cellar and tripped over Mac's helmet with his head still inside it. My Sergeant Major later came to visit me in hospital and told me that he had moved Mac's body himself and that "a head is surprisingly heavy!"

"I never lost consciousness and remember being carried by the stretcher bearers. They took me to the RAP and I was patched up there before an ambulance came along to take me away. Four others were in the ambulance with me, three of my battalion and a German soldier who was wounded. He was lying in the middle of the floor of the ambulance and was communicating with the others in mixed English and German as well as exchanging cigarettes. Strange really, not long ago we were trying to kill one another!

"A corporal from 'B' Company turned up in the hospital. He told me his story, he had been shot through the lung, his friends had done what they could for him during the severe fighting, and they had dragged him into a house and had had to leave him there because they were in deep trouble. He was with two other wounded in the house and they huddled together through the night for warmth, but they both died. In the morning he woke to see a German looking through the window at him. The Jerry went away and he lay there expecting a grenade at any moment to finish him off, but it never came. I was to spend the next 2 years in hospital."

Lieutenant Ellis "Dixie" Dean (MMG Platoon)

"Not soon after we had finished eating, the snow started. I was upstairs at the front, looking up the street, and from the crossroads came the crack of a large gun being fired and a red hot projectile flashed across in front of me, followed by another, then yet another. The hay cart was the target, but the shells passed straight through and came out the back. Private (Rommel) Rodden was crossing back to his post, when the first shot was fired. He immediately rolled under the cart, crawled to the front and let off a full magazine of 'Sten' up the street. What ever was firing, in the half light and swirling snow, had taken the cart with its load of hay and raised shafts, to be a tank.

"The two forward guns on the street were in great danger. Somehow or other I had to get them back into the shelter of the houses. Getting as far as the gun under the steps was no problem. Snow was no longer falling, improving visibility for both sides. Tommy Howell and "Rommel" was the gun crew under the little chamber, and I crouched down looking over the steps. A monster of an armoured vehicle was clearly visible, not much more than 100 yards ahead, standing at the crossroads. It was far larger than the tanks and SP's we had encountered in Normandy, and was a 'King Tiger'.

"I watched 2 Shermans of the Fife and Forfar, come racing up the road behind, oblivious to the 'Tiger'. They roared past where I stood and I thought I was about to witness a spectacular tank shoot out, but not so. The first Sherman must have seen the enemy tank and in slamming on the brakes, stalled the engine, a sitting duck of a target. The second Sherman was forced to swerve, drove off the road to the right, circled and then drove at speed back again, pushing the halted vehicle through a gap between two houses, the two then turned and raced off to the rear. It was all over in a minute and the 'Tiger' crew must have been as bemused by this as I was. I had missed the opportunity to get the guns off the street.

"The tank team, too, must have been ashamed of their inactivity and sprung into life. The left hand Vickers was the first target, suddenly there was a rush and a roar, something struck the masonry piled in front and exploded. I saw the gun and tripod thrown upwards and backwards and a man ran scrambling to safety. Next it was the turn of the gun up the road in front of me. The same rush, roar and explosion, and then a voice calling for help.

"I was up and running. As I raced up the street, I was conscious of a string of brightly coloured lights coming towards me and passing silently over my head, it never occurred to me that they were bullets and I was their intended target. I reached the gun position, and the lights followed me. Sitting behind the gun was Alf Williams,

and it was he who had called for help. Crouched alongside him were two young reinforcements. The lights missing Alf and I, were slamming into these 2 bodies with a peculiar hissing noise.

"Then all was quiet. Somehow I wrestled Alf onto his feet. He was wounded in the legs and half carrying, half dragging; I started back up the street. A door to the left opened, and a voice called "In here". I turned to see CSM Dugdale (left) and other eager hands helped me carry the wounded corporal inside Company HQ. We laid him down and a Company clerk injected him with morphine – we all carried an ampoule in the field dressing pocket."

Corporal Alf Williams (MMG Platoon)

"By this time I was a corporal and I got wounded, in a place called Bure. I was manning the machine gun with Scott and King. The German 'Tiger' armed with its 88 put some rounds into our two positions, killing [Pte Norman] Scott and [Pte Ron] King, and wounding me in the legs. Dixie came out of a house nearby, got hold of me and carried back to safety. He did all this directly in front of the German tank commander."

Lieutenant Ellis "Dixie" Dean (MMG Platoon)

"Private William Sears, a regular soldier who joined the MMG Platoon on our return from Normandy, was a 'gentle giant' of a man and with his experience, was a good example to the younger lads of 18 or 19. He was affectionately called "Pop". He was killed by cannon fire from the same 'Tiger' tank that killed Scott and King, but the position he was manning was on the opposite side of the street."

Celestine Limet (Villager)

[Watching through a cellar vent] "A British machine gun had been sited on the pavement, between my house and the barn next door at Dufong's farm. From there they can sweep the street as far as the bend. They were spotted and engaged by the 88mm gun, killing two of the crew. After firing 4 or 5 rounds the 'Tiger' pulled back and replaced 5 minutes later, by another. The tank commander gave orders to open fire with a revolver, which made a noise like a chirping cricket. As well as the 88mm, the tank was armed with a rapid firing machine gun, which fired in short bursts."

Lieutenant Ellis "Dixie" Dean (MMG Platoon)

"I turned to go back out of the door, "Where are you going?" Major McLoughlin wanted to know. "Back for the others" I replied. "Oh, no you're not, it's sheer stupidity going back on the street, the Colonel's worried because we've lost so many

Officers already." He was right. The two other lads, I knew were dead. No human body could take as many bullets as theirs had done and survive. I hoped they hadn't suffered, I didn't think they had. Death would have been instantaneous but there was still a nagging doubt in my mind. I had to go back.

"Not through the front door though; there must be another way out. In the corner, on the outside wall, was another doorway, but a large chest was drawn across it. "Where does this door lead?" I asked and started to remove the obstruction. CSM Dugdale came and gave me a hand. To my surprise, the door opened as I turned the handle and I found myself in an alleyway running diagonally towards the street, at the end of which, I could see the deserted gun position. Together we approached the gun site, crawling the last few yards through the snow. The lads were dead, but the gun was intact, so carefully we (the CSM had been an ex-machine gunner) dismantled the gun and tripod, and then dragged the whole lot back to the house.

"David Tibbs had come to attend to the wounded NCO, who was sleeping because of the morphine, and after dressing his wounds he said "He will be alright here, and I will arrange for him to be evacuated as soon as possible."

"Major McLoughlin asked the CSM to leave and I thought I was in for a right rollocking for deliberately disobeying an order, but instead he was almost apologetic, explaining that this was the first time he had been in action, and even years as a Battle School Instructor had not prepared him for the real thing. What should he be doing in the situation we found ourselves in?

"Sergeant Egleton was waiting with more bad news; Alf Whalley had been wounded and evacuated. A report had reached him that I had run up the street, with tracer bullets coming out the back of my head before collapsing behind the right hand gun, and he had gone out to investigate. He was caught in a mortar stonk and wounded in the thigh."

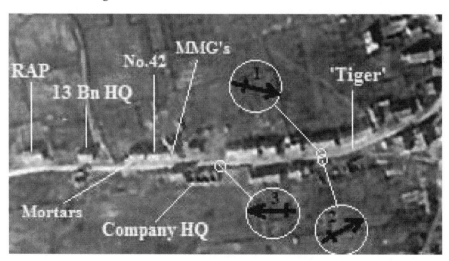

No.1 Section: Covering Rue de Mirwart (Pte Sears KIA)

No.2 Section: Covering Rue de Tellin, East (Pte King KIA & Pte Scott KIA)

No.3 Section: Covering Rue de Tellin, West

Captain David Tibbs MC (RAMC)

"I used No.42 Rue de Tellin as one of my RAP's, and fortunately it had a cellar which gave us good protection. The front door and downstairs windows were perforated many times by shell fragments which would have been lethal to anyone above ground.[58]

"I had to take shelter behind the stone steps of the house, when the 'Tiger' opened up on me with its MG42 as I was crossing the road. The smoke from a burning hay cart[59] that had provided cover, suddenly lifted and I had to hurl myself onto a pile of broken grass when the tank fired."

CSM "Taffy" Lawley ('C' Company)

"Next day [4th Jan] things were a little quieter, but still not safe to shown even one's nose outside. There were many wounded and dead lying around, amongst whom moved our padre administering morphia and first aid at great danger to himself.

"It was during this period that Major Clark's cool courage and determination reached its peak, in that he took the bearing of every shell that came over and had it sent back to Battalion HQ and at one time brought our own guns to bear on targets only 20 yards from our position. Our 2 lost Platoons eventually got back to us, looking very much as if they had been down a coal mine and in very bad condition. They had been unable to get out of some cellars owing to the 'Tiger' tanks, and it was not until these had to move because of the fire Major Clark had brought on them, that they were able to get out."

Extract from: Regimental History of 53rd Medium Royal Artillery

Early on the 4th, breakfast, a 'Tiger' tank and a German counter-attack arrived simultaneously and we defied Larkhill by taking on the 'Tiger', single gun close target, with 210's D Sub (Sgt Davies) and infantry observation by a Company Commander. His final order deserves record: "Can you go south 12 ½? I'm south 25 from the last round and the target is between that round and me." Sgt Davies' layer breathed on his dial sight, the 'Tiger' withdrew and the Company Commander came back to congratulate us with that glow of delight on his face which is the finest compliment that any infantryman can pay to a gunner."

---

[58] This house was also used by Major AR Clark as his 'C' Company HQ.
[59] This was same hay cart that Lt Dean explained that the German tank had earlier mistaken for a Sherman tank.

Extract from: An Account of Ops 29th Armoured Brigade in the Ardennes

The enemy put in several counter attacks during the day in terrible weather it was snowing hard and visibility was reduced to nothing. These attacks made by infantry supported by SP guns, were beaten off by artillery and tank fire though not without loss; 2FF had 3 more tanks knocked out in Bure and on the high ground to the south [Mentioned earlier].

Trooper Les Dudderidge (2nd Fife & Forfar Yeomanry)

"I replaced Les Lines as gunner, he'd been killed. We reversed our tank through a shop front window and parked the tank inside the shop. As we pulled out later in the morning of the 4th Jan, we were hit on the turret above my head in the gunner's seat. Being the gunner I was the last to bail out. Me and the wireless operator got into a house near the tank and found a dozen or so Lancastrian paratroopers there.[60] I did not know any of the name of the paratroopers or even the crew of the tank as I had only just replaced the previous gunner.

"We stayed in the house all day on the ground floor and fire was exchanged between the Germans and the Paras. I saw Germans in the houses opposite through the window and the paras were popping them off. When it got dark we [the wireless operator and I] ran back to the first aid post further down the road, which was littered with broken slates and various other debris, and radioed for a scout car to collect us."

Jean-Marie Decontie (Superior of L'Alumnat)

"On the 4th January, a German SP, hidden behind our garden wall, draws a lot of fire directed onto L'Alumnat. Shells fall all around us and the building suffers 30 direct hits, damaging the roof and shattering the windows, but the walls are solid and the shells make little impact."

Yvonne Louviaux (Villager)

"We had a fashion store (clothes and hats) and everything was destroyed. There was one particular hat, a lovely plum coloured one that I really liked. Mum never wanted me to wear it because it was too expensive. Following the fighting, it'd received a small hole. It was repaired and I still have the hat today. Shells fell in front of the house and literally pulverized the big oak door of the entrance.

"Grandpa was still with us. One day, Louise George's sister, mother, living a little further along the road to Grupont, was ill. He took advantage of a lull and wanted to inquire about the health of his wife's sister. He was arrested by the Germans who occupied the area around the police station. He explained why he was out and the soldiers told her they knew that a lady was sick as one of their doctors had gone to see her. He had not returned and Mr. Rose, who spoke good German said: "I will go after Joseph." He was also arrested by the Germans."

Marie-José Pigeon (Villager)

[Her 2 brothers had been captured by the Germans when war first broke out, so she had to take care of the farm with the help of her cousin Edmond] "My uncle Joseph Lambert, my god-mother Martha and their 3 children lived in a house opposite the church. As it was far more dangerous in the village centre, they came to join me. At

---

[60] Most likely to be Sergeant Len Cox's party of a dozen, one of the two 'lost' Platoons of 'C' Company.

the same time, it allowed me, not to be alone. The Puffet family also came to join us and we ended up with 11 in the cellar. Sometimes there were more people as young soldiers arrived with some Alsatians. "Where are they now?" Edmond advised them so they could leave. There was panic every day in our basement and it was always the same meals. We did not really eat, but even if it was not much, I do not remember being hungry. The English were on the side of Notre-Dame de Haurt while on our side, we had the Germans. Sometimes Edmond went down the village to see his mother. He saw one or two English, but rarely. And then one day the Germans came to say that we had to leave. Apart from the Puffet's and Edmond, we all left for Tellin.

"Around us we could see tracer bullets go everywhere. It was horrible. In Tellin, we stayed one night at a baker's and then with my cousin, continued towards Resteigne. But we did not stay, returning to Bure and finding Edmond who had remained to look after cattle."

Felix Despas (Villager)

"The first days of January came and it was freezing to minus 15 degrees Celsius. The sounds of automatic weapons, explosions of shells and grenades followed each other constantly. On the morning of January 4th, there was a lull, I returned home. I was surprised on entering the kitchen, because there was a strange shape sitting on a chair with an oil lamp before it, which dispensed a little bit of heat. I shouted, "Who's there?" and a man covered with a blanket showed himself. I saw he was wearing a British uniform and it made me realise he had been wounded by the explosion of a landmine in the snowy path, not far from home. His right leg was red with blood and he had 2 pieces of tree branch attached to his leg as splints. The man suffered terribly, and he asked me to drive a Tellin. His unit had attacked the village at night, from this locality. I was puzzled because I had no means of transportation. Knowing there was an infirmary at the Château L'Alumnat, I told him I was going to take him there. He understood very quickly and was in agreement. I returned to the cellars of the monastery and asked for help. Despite the danger that occurs even outside, Auguste Hamaide, one of my neighbours came to help me.

"We assembled some pieces of wood together to make a stretcher, on which we placed our patient. Our patient was a Captain belonging to the British Army.

"The fate was cruel to this man and for many others. Some time later, an ambulance of the Red Cross, who had come for him, hit a mine outside the village. Several medics died with him. Very close to where this happened, a Sherman tank also hit a mine. We realised very quickly that the perimeter of our town was heavily mined by both anti-tank mines and other anti-personnel devices."[61]

Unknown rank – Robert Stubbs (6th Field Regiment)

"It was around this time that I was ordered to drive alone, in the Troop Leader's wireless truck, in precarious road conditions, from our hilltop to another hilltop. I was looking for the 6th Airborne's Division Observation Post. I informed the 6th Airborne's commander of my orders, which were to try to contact our OP's Bren

---

[61] The Captain in question was John Patrick Milner of the 6th Field Regiment (RA) and is buried in Hotton along with L/Cpl George Marshall a medic attached to the 12th Devons who was also killed; the 12th Devons had sent a recce into Bure on the 7th Jan to extract the wounded officer after learning of his presence in the L'Alumnat. L/Cpl Philip Bingham, and Privates Frederick Hendy and Bertram Squibbs were the other members of the 12th Devons that were killed in the Jeep.

carrier. I called but received no response. The shells started coming with intensity and the 6th Airborne blamed my truck and me. I was told to leave sharpish, which I did, sliding all the way back to my Command Post.

"Later, we found that the Captain [Milner] of the OP I had originally been sent to try to contact had been killed previously and their wireless operator, a Harry Theakston from Bradford, taken prisoner."

Lance Corporal David "Robbie" Robinson (Anti-Tank 'C' Company)

"My section was positioned in a barn with double doors. The barn had cows in the left hand side, and us in the right and we often snuggled in with the cows to keep warm, it was that cold. During the day a warning sounded "Tank nearing!" We got into position and waited to fire the PIAT into his rear, where the radiator was. One 'Tiger' tank came down the street and stopped at the barn. I don't think he would have risked coming any further because he was getting into hostile ground. He must have heard some movement because he bought his gun round and pointed it at the cow section of the barn where I was lying at the time. He fired. The shell went through the front window and out the back window and exploded in the dung heap out the back. The cows all reared up and dashed around in the barn, banging and crashing and making as much noise as a cowboy stampede on some of the films. The tank commander must have thought "I'm getting nervous its only cows" so he didn't fire again but retreated back to the hold down position at the church."

Private Alf John (Signaller)

"We were in a house on the main street, where the ground sloped steeply down at the rear [Northern side of Rue de Tellin]. You entered the front at ground level, but towards the rear, this became 'upstairs' and the lower room was the cowshed, complete with cow. During the battle a Jerry tank roamed up and down along the back, systematically firing into the houses. The pattern of firing led to us to move from room to room for safety and eventually we ended up sharing the room with the cow. Unfortunately, every time a shell exploded nearby, the cow either shat or urinated. As a result, we spent as much time dodging the cow's backside as the tank's gunfire."

Major Jack Watson ('A' Company)

"It was the first time I had seen 'Tigers', and now here they were taking pot-shots demolishing the houses. I moved from one side of the road to the other deliberately drawing fire. A tank fired at me and the next thing I knew the wall behind me was collapsing. But a PIAT team came running out, got within 50 yards of the tank, opened fire and smashed the tanks tracks. They were very brave. It went on like this all day - they counterattacked but we managed to hold them. They pushed us back - we pushed forward again."

Sergeant Len Cox ('C' Company)

"As soon as it was light the shelling started, and the massive German 'Tiger' tank took direct aim at the house and put several rounds into the upstairs rooms. Some of the lads were wounded, but could not be evacuated. When the 'Tiger' got within range, Doug Sharpe and I got a couple of PIAT bombs off, hitting it on the side. Later I heard from 'A' Company that it had to be towed away. All day long the area was bombed and shelled and there were more casualties, mostly as a result of blast, but Corporal Ryan was severely wounded and later died. All that day and the night that followed we remained cut off from the rest of the Battalion."

Report by Victor Thompson (Herald War Correspondent)

"Another outstandingly brave man was the corporal who lay dying from serious wounds. He would not let his comrade's fuss about him. "I'm alright," he told them, "only cut my bandolier loose because it's hurting me. I know I've had it, so you go and look after the others." Then he said "Give my love to the wife," and died."[62]

'A' Company earned several bravery awards for their critical actions in the battle. Right from the start they were involved in a non-stop fire fight, in extremely close quarters and against the 2nd Panzer Divisions armour with its highly skilled supporting grenadiers.

Citation: Major Jack Watson ('A' Company)

Award: Military Cross

On January 3rd 1945, Major Watson was commanding 'A' Company of a Parachute Battalion, which was leading the assault into Bure. When the Company was formed up on the start line, very heavy and accurate fire from enemy mortars, artillery and machine-guns came down on it. Some 28 casualties were incurred immediately, but

---

[62] Believed to be Corporal Peter Joseph Woods.

Major Watson, completely disregarding the enemy fire, ran up and down the line reorganising the forming up, and by his personal leadership and example enabled the attack to be launched.

He led the Company several hundred yards down a slope and stormed into the village in spite of fire from enemy machine-guns from the nearest houses. Once in the village he kept the Company moving forward, clearing the houses constantly moving himself from place to place, with complete disregard for enemy fire and continually encouraging his men. Almost at once the enemy counter-attacked with Tiger tanks and infantry, but Major Watson immediately organised his PIAT teams and beat off the tanks. At one time in order to make a Tiger tank move its position and give a better shot to a PIAT, he deliberately drew attention to himself, though only 50 yards from the tank.

Although the enemy counter-attacked time and again, Major Watson coolly organised the defence, and having repelled the attacks, again advanced and eventually completed the clearing of that part of the village allotted to him.

His conduct, energy and gallantry throughout were beyond praise, and without him the attack might well have failed.

Citation: Private Ronald Hawthorn ('A' Company)

Award: Military Medal

On 3rd January 1945, during the attack on BURE, Pte HAWTHORN was manning a Bren gun with 'A' Company. During this attack the company was very heavily counterattacked, by both fire and infantry, tanks and SP guns. During this time Pte Hawthorn manned his gun with most remarkable coolness and efficiency, engaging target after target with absolute disregard of the enemy fire.

During one attack made by his platoon, Pte Hawthorn saw an enemy SP gun moving up to engage his company. He immediately moved his own position so as to fire at point blank range at the gun. In doing so he exposed himself to almost certain death from the enemy gun's fire, but so accurate was his own fire that he inflicted heavy casualties among the gun's crew, forcing it to withdraw and without doubt saving his platoon and making possible the success of their attack.

Citation: Lance Sergeant Frederick Gilbert Burton Eales ('A' Company)

Award: Croix de Guerre 1940+Palm

Sgt Eales was wounded during the campaign in Normandy and returned to the 13th Battalion (Lancashire) the Parachute Regiment just in time to go to Belgium in December 1944. He was then a Corporal and second in command of a section.

During the battle at Bure on 3rd January 45, his section met withering fire during the *advance into the village. All except himself, who was wounded in the arm and leg, and one man, were killed. Undaunted he, with his one man, occupied the section objective, personally driving the Germans out of the area. Gathering isolated men round him, he fought with the section and repelling all local counter attacks kept his sector. He refused to be evacuated in spite of his wounds. On the morning of the last day he was found by his Company Commander, unable to move, still commanding the section sector and by his cheerfulness and courage keeping up the morale of his men. He was eventually evacuated by order of his Company Commander.*

Lieutenant Ellis "Dixie" Dean (MMG Platoon)

"Stan Horton originally joined the Battalion in Normandy. We were never told how long our stay in Normandy would last, but assumed that once the link up with the seaborne assault forces had been made, we would return to UK and prepare for further airborne ops. But of course that did not happen, and as causalities mounted, there was a serious need of re-enforcements. They came, but were non-jumpers from 21st Army Group Re-enforcement Pool. Stan Horton was one such, and already a trained signaller. He was one of the few such men who wished to qualify as a parachutist and continue his service in the 13th. So, in September he came back with us, while the rest of his group were returned to the army pool. Both he and Dennis Boardman would have been signallers with 'A' Company. On operations, "out-stations" (as they were called), consisting of a Corporal and 2 Signallers, were attached to each HQ."

Citation: Private Stanley John Horton (Signaller, 'A' Company)

Award: Croix de Guerre 1940 with Palm

Pte Horton was a signaller during the campaign in Belgium with 13th Battalion (Lancashire) the Parachute Regiment. No matter what he was called upon to perform he did his duty cheerfully and with absolute efficiency. Especially was this so in the battle at Bure on 3rd January 1945. He was attached to Company Headquarters.

On the start line the Company was met by very heavy and accurate fire, from artillery and small arms, suffering forty casualties immediately. The Company Commander ran up and down the line encouraging the men. Private Horton, who could have stayed with Company Headquarters went with him carrying the set and transmitting vital information of the progress of the attack. In order to obtain the best results when in the village, he constantly moved to exposed positions, disregarding his personal safety. At one time, unheeding apparently certain death, he moved within point blank range of a Tiger Tank that was firing down the street, in order to send his message with certainty. One set was shot off his back. Unperturbed he took a spare set and continued. He is of small stature and his physical effort was prodigious, and though almost exhausted he never failed in his communications. The information that he sent back was of the utmost value.

Celestine Limet (Villager)

"Whenever there was a lull in fighting, the British Medics could be seen [he was still watching through the cellar vent] dashing around, collecting and treating wounded.

"Not too far away there was a cry of pain as a German soldier had been hit. Two of his comrades dashed out and dragged his body into the hallway of the Bourtembourg's house, shortly after he died there. The Germans didn't know it, but there were some civilians in the cellar and British in the attic. The British fought their way further into Bure and killed 2 Germans in the cellars of the village hall."

1400   Situation a little more quiet. Enemy still infiltrating, positions were however held without giving any ground. Any enemy movement or infantry or armour subjected to heavy artillery fire.

Private Dennis Boardman (Signaller, att 'A' Company)

"German infantry and tanks [SP's], we believe they were the 2nd Panzers, were closing in, they ran across the back gardens of the terrace houses and were easy to deal with, but for how long?

"Major Watson came across to where I was sitting and took the microphone of my radio and after several minutes contacted the officer in charge of the 25 Pounder Battery, which had promised support where necessary. He was instructed to fire a barrage on to the road junction and on to our own positions. This would, he hoped, clear the enemy which were now almost on top of us. This was at the risk of suffering some casualties ourselves. A runner was sent to the forward positions to warn everyone of the bombardment of our positions and to get to the cellars once they heard the scream of the shells. Once the barrage was over, resume the action. One main concern was the wounded, 8 or 9 men, who should have been evacuated hours ago, some of which were in agonising pain. Many of the fit paratroopers had already given their morphine supply to the wounded.

"Presently the whine the shells came to our ears followed by the explosion of them bursting in the air above us, yet we felt invigorated we were not alone, support was available. We were hitting back with something more than machine guns, rifles and grenades. And the enemy were getting the full blast of the artillery fire.

"For a full 15 minutes shells tore into our and the enemy positions. Two of the wounded received fresh injuries from shell splinters which burst through the floors above. Then there was a stony silence and all the fit men rushed up from the cellars, ready to renew the battle and let fly with everything we had. The enemy infantry were already withdrawing from the gardens, leaving their dead and dragging their wounded with them. Even the 'Tiger' tanks were moving to safety. A paratrooper dashed into the road with a gammon bomb and from almost point blank range, threw it onto the tracks. There was a cheer when the smoke cleared, and the track was blown apart, and the tank turned helplessly in a circle, while the crew were finished off as they abandoned the vehicle.

"In the midst of the confusion, one of the Medics came across to me pleading with me to get on to Battalion HQ for help in getting the wounded out for urgent medical aid."

Captain David Tibbs MC (RAMC)

"The tank commanders were courageous and resourceful with active groups of panzer grenadiers clearly experienced in street fighting. Our men proved equal to this but there were many casualties. At one stage there were 5 badly wounded men in the cellar of a house about 30 yards in front of the tank. We knew of this but saw no way of getting them out. At this stage Sergeant Scott came to me and asked if he could take an ambulance up to the house and remove the wounded men, and the Padre said he would like to go along as well. If I had known precisely what was planned I might have stopped such lunacy but off they went."

Private Dennis Boardman (Signaller, att 'A' Company)

"We couldn't believe our eyes, for 10 minutes later we saw an ambulance coming up the road. We stopped it outside the front door; it was Sgt Scott, of the medics and with him was Padre Foy, a man loved and respected throughout the unit. Scott was one of the bravest men I ever met."

Captain David Tibbs MC RAMC)

"As the ambulance (with large red crosses) approached the tank a hush descended and the ambulance came to a stop outside the house, only 20 yards away from the massive 88mm gun of the tank, and for that matter its MG42 machine gun. The tank moved up alongside the ambulance and to everyone's astonishment (including the German troops) the top hatch of the tank opened and the tank commander emerged, head and shoulders showing, a prime target for our men. He called out in good English "You are a brave man sergeant, but you should have waited until the fighting was over before you collected any wounded. I will allow you to come once, but if you come again, I will shoot you off the street." The ambulance reversed and the wounded were piled into it."

Lieutenant Ellis "Dixie" Dean (MMG Platoon)

"The Battalion Padre was driving, and he was accompanied by the Battalion Royal Medical Corps Sergeant. The Padre made a three point turn and the wounded were loaded onto the ambulance."

Private Dennis Boardman (Signaller, att 'A' Company)

"There was a cold silence mingled with the odd joker who still kept his sense of humour. The German kept a watchful on the proceedings. It didn't take long to fill the ambulance. As the Red Cross van was reversed the last word I heard from Scotty was, inviting us back for a cup of tea at HQ. Anyone would have thought he was out for a morning drive. With a final wave, the ambulance departed, the tank commander nodded his head and disappeared inside the tank. Seconds later the 88mm gun was swung round and a shell blew the front wall out the next house to us. The cease fire was over."

Lance Corporal David "Robbie" Robinson (Anti-Tank 'C' Company)

"During the second day in Bure, we went out whenever the shelling stopped to try and get a shot at the German tanks, but were always spotted and fired on before we could get within range. In the afternoon I had just taken a chap called Lord over to the Company Medics at HQ and was on my way back to the barn we were occupying. I was in the passage way between the two buildings and the tank blocked my exit, I cowered there until it withdrew."

Captain David Tibbs MC (RAMC)

"The ambulance heavily laden lumbered back down the main street, past my RAP (David Tibbs photo) and back to the 225 Field Ambulance 2 miles away. Two men were the heroes of the hour - Sergeant Scott (with Padre Foy in strong support) and of course, the enemy tank commander... What men! It is said that later (but it may be legend) when the tank commander showed himself through the hatch to direct his men once too often, and was shot, some of our men shed tears at this. Such is war and the strange bonding it can create between the men of both sides!"

Company HQ (First Aid Post in cellars)

Passage way

Citation: Capt Rev Whitfield Foy (RAChD)

Award: Military Cross

During the attack on BURE on 3rd January 1945, 'A' Company of the 13th Parachute Bn received very heavy casualties on the start line. When this information reached the Rev FOY he at once went forward to help. In spite of the fact that most of the casualties were lying in a very exposed position on the forward slope of a hill and the enemy artillery fire was both accurate and intense he moved about, completely disregarding the fire and his own danger, and moved the wounded to safety, meanwhile reassuring them and keeping up their morale.

On moving into the village he several times joined parties bringing in casualties under heavy shell fire, was untiring in his attention to the wounded, and completely without sign of fear in his movements and actions.

403

During the action volunteers were called for to obtain identifications of dead and to search for wounded in positions still under enemy observation and heavy fire. Rev FOY at once volunteered and taking a small party boldly went out.

Then, in spite of most vicious fire directed against him, he moved about from place to place in his search, and finishing his work returned to the Battalion bringing with him two wounded men.

His example and extraordinary courage and devotion to duty were of inestimable value to the morale of all ranks throughout a most bitter engagement.

Citation: Corporal Charles Bryan (RAMC, att 13th Para Bn)

Award: Military Medal

During 3rd January 1945, 13th Bn Parachute Regiment advanced to attack BURE.

During the afternoon, when 'B' Company was moving down an open slope to attack BURE it was very heavily mortared and shelled, so that more than half the Company became casualties. Quite regardless of his own safety, Cpl BRYAN walked about on the open hillside during the height of the enemy mortar fire and collected all the wounded on a strip of road which was slightly sheltered by a bank. But for his superb bravery many wounded would have been left on the open hillside with no protection against continued enemy mortar fire and in positions difficult to find and collect in the approaching darkness.

Cpl BRYAN remained in the open with his wounded men until at dusk they could be evacuated on Jeeps. He continued throughout this battle to do his duty as a stretcher bearer unflinchingly, going repeatedly through the streets of BURE to collect and evacuate casualties to the RAP, when those streets were being shelled and swept by enemy small arms fire.

His superb gallantry and devotion to duty, besides undoubtedly saving many lives, materially supported the morale of the infantry while they were facing great odds.

Captain David Tibbs MC (RAMC)

"Two soldiers out on patrol in daylight were shot at and lay inert on the snow 400 yards out from the village of Bure. Two RAMC men, one a Conscientious Objector, went out with a Red Cross flag to see if there was a survivor. When they reached the casualties they found one was dead and the other was unhurt but was feigning death. He muttered "Get me out of here". The 2 medics solemnly loaded him onto a stretcher and carried him back to Bure, a very relieved man. No further shots were fired and it is not known whether the episode was being watched by the enemy marksman. Possibly he wished to remain concealed. Were the medics misusing the Geneva Convention even though they were saving a life and not assisting any military action? Maybe it was cheating but to do this must have been irresistible and the 2 medics had a good sense of humour."

The tanks of the 2nd Fife & Forfar Yeomanry had themselves taken very heavy casualties in supporting the 13th Para Bn and in trying to hold the high ground dominating Bure. The War Diary of the 13th Para Bn on the 4th Jan shows the extent of the armoured losses.

1700 Own losses 16 SHERMANS, enemy tks still operating in village. Fighting throughout day extremely hard and costly. Throughout hours of daylight 'A' &

'C' Coys sent fighting patrols into unoccupied part of village without however managing to hold onto ground gained outside bn perimeter

Citation: Major Richard L Leith (2nd Fife & Forfar Yeomanry, RAC)

Award: Military Cross

At BURE on the evening of Jan 3rd 1945, Major Leith's Squadron was supporting a Para Bde who were attacking and meeting strong opposition from SP guns and MG's. 2 tanks of another Squadron had been knocked out at the western end of the village. Major Leith went into the village with another Troop and in spite of heavy fire did a dismounted recce. The following morning he led the remainder of his Squadron to the high ground to the south. When the Troop in the village were all knocked out, Major Leith immediately led another Troop into the village and placed each tank personally. Throughout, major Leith showed complete disregard for his own safety and his calm leadership restored the situation.

Citation: Gunner Arthur Miles (53rd Medium Regiment RA)

Award: Military Medal

On 3rd Jan 45 Gunner Miles was wireless operator working in a tank OP in support of a Squadron of the Fife & Forfar Yeomanry. This unit had the task of capturing the dominating feature known as Chapel Hill, about 2 miles north of the village of Bure, and an OP was required to accompany it.

On arrival on the objective the Squadron was subjected to heavy and accurate fire from SP guns concealed in the woods on top of the feature and firing from close range. Gunner Miles who was operating in a tank for the first time remained completely unperturbed by the situation, and by the cool manner in which he passed fire orders induced quick response from the guns, which undoubtedly saved a number of tanks from being hit.

The following day the OP was subjected to accurate 15cm artillery fire and the tank was hit. In spite of this the team continued to operate from it, and Gunner Miles conduct throughout was beyond praise. At no time during the day did communications fail and his standards of operating under these extremely difficult conditions was faultless.

The devotion to duty and behaviour of this man was an example to the whole crew, and by his actions he was directly instrumental in enabling the Squadron to extricate itself from an unexpectedly serious situation.[63]

Sergeant Walter Loydall (53rd Medium Regiment Royal Artillery)

Award: Croix de Guerre with Palm

In the Ardennes battle in Dec 1944 and January 1945, Sgt Loydall was in command of a gun which never failed to carry out its allotted task. His battery did a considerable amount of firing, firstly from positions just east of Dinant, when contact was first made with the enemy, and some most successful shoots were carried out, and later in the advance to the Bure area and beyond Sgt Loydall's gun was never out of

---

[63] The actual citation sheet states the date as 2nd Jan, when in fact it was the 3rd Jan.

action during the whole period and in spite of very severe weather conditions the response from it was always excellent.

Lieutenant Ellis "Dixie" Dean (MMG Platoon)

"Around the crossroads, fighting was apparent from the sounds coming from that direction. We had one gun sited to fire back down the street, one gun in each house observing the open country to the rear. The other gun which had been knocked flying by the 'Tiger' could only be used in emergency [split water cooling jacket and only capable of firing until the barrel overheated].

"Early in the afternoon I was called to join the gun team in the back bedroom. A large sash window was open and a group of German soldiers 200 yards away, crawling along a threadbare hedgerow, was pointed out to me. They halted and started to set up 2 machine guns – a preliminary to an attack along the rear of the houses? I thought. The gun was quickly laid on the target and the order to "Fire!" was given.

"The gun fired one or two rounds and stopped with the crank handle back on the roller. The man firing, immediately recognised a No.1 position stoppage, correctly and efficiently pulled the crank handle back, released it, tapped it home, re-laid and carried on firing. His actions could not be faulted, but the gun stopped again. Again it was pull, tap, followed by 3 upward and outward turns of the 'Fusee Spring'. Hardly had the gun re-commenced firing, but the regular rattle of the Vickers was drowned out by the sudden incoming scream of high velocity shells, followed by deafening series of simultaneous violent explosions overhead and we were in a heap on the floor. Dust and plaster showered down, broken timbers laths and slates were all around; the room was a complete shambles. There must have been a Boche SP lurking on the hillside and seen where we fired from, and then proceeded to engage us. Several shells hit the roof over our heads, had the gunner put them through the window we would have been massacred.

"Is everyone alright?" I called out. "My hand's bleeding..." that was Private O'Brien, who had joined the Platoon after the Anti-Tank Platoon was broken up. We staggered to our feet "Get the gun in another room and carry on engaging those guns." I ordered. I turned to treat O'Brien's hand. One of his fingers was almost severed from the hand. Using a field dressing, I tried to bandage it, but the finger would not stay in place. I led him to a chest of drawers and cleared the rubble with my arm, "Look away" I said, and taking my fighting knife, I cut off the finger and then was able to dress it, and sent him to the RAP. I rejoined the gunners in another room but there was no sign of the enemy and no attack was made."

Pierre Lardinois (Villager)

"Daytime on 4th January was hell – shells fell constantly on Bure. A [German] field telephone had been installed in the room above and operators shared our cellar. Orders were received by wireless and then transmitted to the tanks, which would then open fire. We could also hear the British armour as they noisily manoeuvred outside."

Celestine Limet (Villager)

"In the late afternoon, just before it got dark, there was a strange silence. By then there was a total of 16 of us in that one cellar, including some children. Victor Petit came across and asked what was happening. At that moment a German tank rolled up and stopped right outside the door. M'sieur Mullesch, finding these parts too dangerous, had a word with the tank commander and asked him if we could move to the château. He agreed, but told us to hurry as fighting could start up at any moment.

"Off we went and I couldn't believe the amount of destruction there was. We saw a troop of tanks outside 'La Pauche', whilst in the vicinity of the church; the Germans were lined up being served a hot meal. We reached the château and stayed there for the rest of the battle.

"Alice Hody, my fiancée, was sheltering with others on the far side of Bure, near 'La Pauche'. The fighting there was just as fierce and at sometime on the 4th, the Germans were passing with some of their wounded, so she went out and asked the Officer in charge, if they could move to the château. "Not just now" she was told, "it's far too dangerous. I'll let you know when it's safe to move." He was as good as his word, returning later when all was quiet and telling them to go as quickly as they could."

Marie Decarme (Villager)

"We did like everyone else, and went to the college, but almost every day, we went back to take care of our animals. One day my brother, who was 26, went to treat the cows. When he wanted to return to the college, the battle hardened, and he had to lie near a water pump along the road [Rue de Belvaux] and wait. Every time he lifted his head a little, he saw spinning tracer bullets above him. This lasted for at least an hour. Dad, from the college, where you could hear the battle, imagined the worst, especially as it normally only took 15 minutes at most for this task."

Pte "Bobby" Macgregor (left) had been cut off and captured the previous day. He and his fellow captives were marched out of their makeshift camp as daylight came on the 4th. During the night they noticed that only one sentry guarded them, but it was now too late to do anything about it. They were forced to follow a German Officer, and fully aware of the order that Hitler had issued previously, an order to shoot all Paratroopers as spies; owing to the covert way they entered combat. All of the Para's where lined up and threatened that they would be shot. Fortunately they were all marched back to the camp.

They were then joined by more prisoners, making the total around 40 men, all Allied soldiers, but not all paratroopers. Night fell and once again they were guarded by only one German guard. One of the new prisoners had smuggled in an Italian Beretta pistol and shot the guard dead. Around 20 of the 40 prisoners made a dash for freedom, Macgregor one of them.

During the night they split into smaller groups and Macgregor's group asked for assistance at a farmhouse and were given some food. The owner of the farm, unbeknown to the small party contacted the US Authorities and some American troops arrived and took them away. After a short interrogation they were released and returned to the British Sector.

Back in the village the battle still raged. Without total control of all the heights around Bure and Grupont it was now clear to the 5th Para Brigade HQ that more help was needed to take the village in order to push on towards Grupont.

1800   Coy of 2 Bn Oxf Bucks LI joined unit as reinforcements.
1900   Enemy withdrew to EASTERN edges of village and Oxf Bucks cleared buildings in that part of village.
2200   Heavy enemy counter attack with 2 TIGERS in support forced Oxf Bucks to withdraw towards 'A' Coy positions.

Account of 'C' Company 2 Bn Ox & Bucks Light Infantry

The Company left Custinne at 1400hrs 4th Jan 1945 with orders to report to 5th Para Bde HQ's and then to go into Bure to assist Lt Col PJ Luard and 13 Para Battalion. We debussed in Tellin and marched to Bure, where we arrived just after dark. The Company Commander, Major J Granville, met up, having gone on ahead to recce the position with Lt Col Luard.

20 Platoon (Lt FH Wood) moved in first and took over from the left forward Pl of 13 Para Bn, without incident.

21 Platoon (Lt G Hill) then pushed through them and got as far as the 'S' bend in the centre of the village, where they contacted the enemy.

22 Platoon (Lt J Leadsom) moved in on the right and established itself in a school building, opposite 21 Pl.

23 Platoon (Lt JK Stone) moved up into reserve behind 20 Pl.

The enemy had two patrols in the village, one on the other half of the 'S' bend consisting of an SP gun, with fairly strong flanking protection, of MG groups and snipers. The other was a similar force on the road running SE from the centre of the village. The latter kept the main road covered, but we were able to move fairly freely behind the buildings on the left.

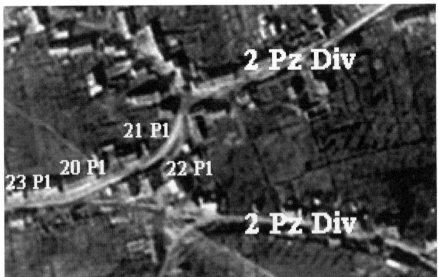

The 12 Para Bn moved into Bure with the intention of going through to attack Grupont, but moved into the buildings behind 'C' Company when they found the village still occupied. PIAT patrols from both ourselves and the 12th, tried to get round the buildings to attack AFVs from the flank, but were unable to do so owing to the enemy's good use of his snipers, LMG gps, etc.

The enemy then eased his way forward round the bend until he located 22 Pl. His flank towards 21 Pl was covered by buildings into which he got some infantry. The SP opened up on 22 Pl's house, from about 50yds range with its MG, and then its 88mm gun.

At this range he scored 4 direct hits on the house, doing a lot of damage to it and the Platoon inside, who had 2 killed and about a dozen wounded. Lt Leadsom himself wounded in the leg moved the remnants of his Platoon into the next building. The SP then came further forward using its MG at random down the street but doing no damage.

Pte Cooke, on 21 Pl's PIAT could not engage the vehicle from the area of the school, so took his PIAT down the road and hit the SP which started to back away, he rushed back calling for another bomb "as the bastard's were getting away" with his fourth bomb, all of which hit, he broke the track, but the enemy were able to tow the vehicle away with another one which took its place.

The rest of the night was very cold and dark, was spent in the positions without a great deal of activity, save for light probing by enemy infantry, several of whom we eliminated. During this time L/Cpl Short MM, was killed by an odd shell from an enemy SP 88mm.

Citation: Private James H Cooke (21 Platoon, 'C' Coy, 2nd Ox & Bucks)

Award: Military Medal

On the night of 4th January 1945 Pte COOKE was the PIAT man of the leading platoon advancing up the street at BURE. The enemy was holding the crossroads in the centre of the village and counter-attacking supported by a Tiger tank. This tank was systematically destroying the houses on the opposite side of the road. The enemy was also covering the street with automatic and rifle fire.

Pte COOKE, without hesitation and showing incredible gallantry and disregard of his personal safety, took his PIAT out into the street, where he was under direct fire, so that he could get a shot at the tank. He fired two bombs and hit the tank but did not disable it. He then returned to his platoon, collected three more bombs, and returned to his position in the open. Having fired three more bombs, the tank was knocked out and ceased firing. Owing to this gallant action the company was able to infiltrate forward and the other platoon was relieved from a very difficult position.

Pte COOKE's action had a definite effect to the future success of the operation, and saved the lives of many of his comrades. As a result of his action, casualties were inflicted on the enemy, since the tank crew was wiped out by small arms fire as they got out of their vehicle. Pte COOKE's action was a fine display of courage and an example of determination and personal bravery which had a stirring effect on his comrades.[64]

Lt Archibald J.W. Leadsom (22 Platoon, 'C' Company, 2nd Ox & Bucks)

"I was in one of the Platoons that were sent into Bure, we went in at night and along the village's main street on the right hand side. We went along until the pavement rose up above the main road and I could see shadowy figures across the road, the village was burning at this time in places and because of the snow on the ground we could see. I saw the figures on the left hand side across the road. I called out to them "Bon nuit", but got no reply, so I didn't know who they were, I just presumed they were civilians, anyway we carried on until we reached what I thought was a village square. There, I saw that there was a half-track and it wasn't actually a village square it was a kink in the road [the 'S' bend in front of the church]. The Americans had half-tracks and in the darkness it was hard to tell if it was friend or foe as they were very similar, the German and the American half-tracks. Because of the path which had risen by about 4 feet above the road, I was looking down on the vehicle. I still couldn't decide what it was so I put my men in a house that was behind us and went for a look around the place a bit more. I went to the side of the house where I put my men, with the intention of going around the back, as I went round the corner I met a German wearing a black uniform and I could see that he had a skull on his cap, I did not fire at him, nor him at me, we were both so shocked, he turned and ran, and I turned and ran the other way, back into the house.

"Later at one stage we heard some shouting and yelling in German outside that seemed quite intense, it was if they were laughing and joking, so I went outside with one of the others with me, but I cannot remember who. I stopped overlooking the area that earlier I had thought was the village square. Suddenly a whole crowd of them came charging down the street to my right, all yelling and whooping, they all seemed rather excited. When they got level with me I lifted my Sten gun, fired a full magazine into them and then rapidly retreated back to 'my' house. They then brought a tank up to what I had thought was a square [the 'S' bend], which then fired its main cannon and its machine guns into the houses. The house that I was in was like a small workman's cottage with a typical solid wood door, which the German tank fired his machine guns through. The door was that solid that it took most of the impact out of the bullets, but I still got 2 bullets in my leg one of which is still there today. I put some field dressings on and then when to see the MO, who told me that I would have to go to hospital and I spent the rest of the night on some straw somewhere in a barn.

"The next morning my Colonel came up to me and asked, "Do you want to go and have a look? They've gone. We've got some prisoners; do you want to see them?" I went to see and one of them spat at me, you can't really reply to that, I didn't spit back, I just ignored him. After that I went to hospital for a while."

---

[64] The citation conflicts with the Ox & Bucks report, which states that an SP gun attacked 22 Platoon, not a 'Tiger' tank, but ties in with other reports and Jim Leadsom's version of events.

Above: View east of Jim Leadsom from "raised path" towards crossroads
Below: View west - route of German soldiers towards Rue de Tellin

Citation: Lt Archibald J.W. Leadsom (22 Platoon, 'C' Coy, 2nd Ox & Bucks)

Awards: Chevalier of the Order of Leopold II with Palm & Croix de Guerre 1940 with Palm

On 4th Jan 45 Lt Leadsom's Platoon was the leading platoon of this Company sent to assist 13 Para Bn at BURE. Lt Leadsom was ordered to capture and occupy two houses. This action was carried out successfully largely due to this Officers dash and bravery.

Shortly after the houses were occupied, the enemy brought up a tank to within 25 yards of the house. Lt Leadsom continued to hold his position, although the two houses were blasted under him. During this time he showed great leadership and dauntless courage. He himself eliminated a number of enemy with his Sten – calmly standing under direct fire at the doorway of the house. He himself wounded in the leg, but refused to have it attended to until his position was secure, and other casualties had been evacuated. After having his wound dressed, he remained with his platoon until the end of the action, when he was evacuated to hospital. It was due to this great exhibition of personal bravery, leadership and courage that a difficult situation was averted and the position held. Throughout the action Lt Leadsom's actions were an example and inspiration to his platoon.

Private Dennis Boardman (Signaller, att 'A' Company)

"Further badly needed help came with a Company of the Ox and Bucks Light Infantry. They took over the role of our lost 'B' Company. Night came and the fighting continued, with hand to hand fighting and most important of all, someone had crept up to the 'Tiger' tank with a PIAT and blown off one of his tracks. It was now useless. During this period we advanced and took the road junction. And most important of all… we had a hot meal, the first for 2 days."

Pierre Lardinois (Villager)

"We were wondering who controlled the village, then during the early evening there was a let up in the fighting and we heard more German soldiers arriving. One of them came down to the cellar, where he received a warm welcome from his comrades who were already down there with us. They congratulated each other on their survival and had something to eat. The new arrival gave an account of his adventures during the day, which he had spent on 'Chapel Hill' [Codename 'Gin.'] in an observation post. We also heard what else had been happening in the battle. He informed the others that they were threatened with encirclement by the Allies, since Wavreille and Rochefort had already been recaptured and the road from Wavreille to Tellin was open to traffic.[65]

'A' Company of the 12th (Yorkshire) Parachute Battalion had by this time (2300 hours) joined the battle on the eastern edge of Bure from the south. Fighting in this area was met by armour and supporting infantry. The armoured attack was fought off with the help of 'C' Company 2nd Ox & Bucks PIAT (mentioned earlier).

Private Eric Barley (12th Parachute Battalion)

"We then moved up to Tellin with orders for the 12th Battalion to attack through the 13th Battalion who had taken half of Bure. I was told in the evening to accompany the CO [K.T. Darling] and the Intelligence Officer [Lt Wentworth] in a Jeep taking the wireless with me. The destination was the 13th Battalion HQ.

"We were stopped by a sentry on the road and he told us to travel on the side of the road as a German MG was firing on fixed lines. Shortly after leaving the sentry, the Spandau, the

---

[65] When the fighting was completely finished Pierre recalled seeing 17 knocked out Allied tanks on this stretch of road near Les Cambuses.

'diarrhoea gun' as we shit ourselves when we heard it, opened fire. It was pretty close as we could see the muzzle flame. Eventually we reached 13th Battalion HQ, dropping the CO off with orders to the Intelligence Officer to contact 'A' Company [12th Bn on the hill south of Bure].

"At the crossroads, the Jeep crawled to a halt. Getting out, we could see that we were tangled up in barbed wire. A couple of Germans came walking down the road. The IO shot them and sent the driver back to raise a patrol to come and get the Jeep.

"A German came out of a house and was challenged and shot. I crouched down at the side of the road and waited for the patrol. My companion walked across the road and a German came quite close to him. I fired my Sten and he rolled over. We had another look at the wire around the Jeep, and as we were doing so, a German tank crossed the road so we dived behind a boulder. A German looked out of the turret at the Jeep and pulled across the road, where there were more Germans in a house. We climbed a hedge and made our way in the direction of 'A' Company. We crossed a couple of fields covered in snow, this was at night. In one field we came across some 13th Battalion dead and the Intelligence Officer decided to retrace our steps. When we reached the hedge at the front of the house, the tank crew were still talking to the other Germans. We decided to get on the road and just walk past them, which we did and eventually reached 13th HQ where we bedded down for the night; a shell killed 2 signallers upstairs. In the morning the Germans were seen driving our Jeep away."

Lieutenant Ellis "Dixie" Dean (MMG Platoon)

"It had already been dark for several hours, when I was summonsed to Battalion HQ. The cellar I was directed into was crowded, apart from the CO and his Gunner Fire Control Officer, Adjutant and Intelligence Officer, there were also wireless sets with their operators. "Dixie, I've got a job for you oily rags." He went on to explain that at first light next morning [5th Jan], the 12th Battalion were going to continue the advance towards Grupont, and the start line was to be the road running southeast from the centre of the village. One of their companies would be digging in to hold this position and we were to support them.

"Vic Smith had only become my batman prior to leaving Larkhill and was one of the newcomers, and this would be the first time we had done a recce together. Initially we moved off down the street, to the first of the houses on the right hand side of the road, and behind it, started to climb the hillside. Some yards from the crest, a straggly hedge ran in the direction of the proposed positions. It was a line of bushes at irregular intervals. As I moved to the next bush, my batman would cover me, and then he would join me etc. I reached the last but one bush, there was now a considerable gap before the last one, and what is more I sensed there was someone behind it. When Vic joined me, I told him of this and said if I was fired on, I would dive to the left and roll down the hill and he was to report what happened to the CO.

"I stepped off finger round the trigger. The nearer I got the more certain I became there was someone behind it. The challenge came, thankfully in English, "Stand still! Hands up!" I obeyed and exchanged passwords. They were two of the Scout platoon seeking any signs of members who had become separated from them, during a Boche counterattack earlier in the day.

"We returned to the house at the west end of Bure and I sent Vic to bring the Platoon to join me there. I had other urgent business to attend to. Despite the cold in the rear garden, I scrapped a hole in the snow, dropped my trousers and emptied my bowels."

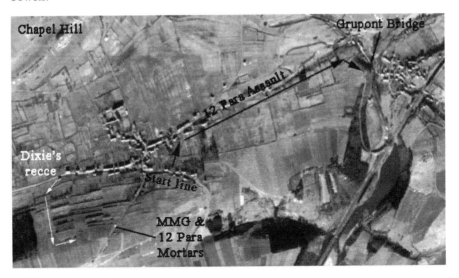

Private Robert Butcher (12th Para Bn, Mortar Platoon)

"We were told that the 13th was having a hard fight and that we would attack next morning to help them. As darkness fell, the Mortars marched up a hill near the village and commenced to dig in preparatory to giving covering fire in the morning. The situation was very fluid and confused; we could hear machine gun fire nearby as well as the sound of tanks moving about, but did not actually come under fire."

Private Bert Marsh (12th Para Bn, Mortar Platoon)

"Our orders was to support the 13th Battalion, our position was on a ridge [south of Bure], it was night time, lots of action going on in the distance we dug pits and slit trenches, no sooner had we finished, order was to withdraw to a cottage. We did not take part in the battle, but we felt for the men of the 13th Battalion. We knew they were going through what we had when taking Breville. It must have been hell for them. Next morning we were all stood outside, Jerry started to shell the position we had left, they just rained down."

Sergeant Harold Cammack (4 Platoon, 12th Para Bn)

"After the street fighting in Namur we were sent to Bure. Bure was a lot more hectic and the opposition was stronger. I had a couple of my section wounded but none killed. The calibre of the Germans was good, they were good soldiers, there's no denying that, especially the tank crews and the Panzer Grenadiers, and they were first class soldiers. No doubt about it.

"To get information about who we were fighting we had to get a prisoner. To do this we would just stalk them, maybe for 2 or 3 hours, undetected and when the opportunity arose, as he [a German] relieved himself three of us simply overpowered him. We knocked him out and then took him to HQ."

Lieutenant Ellis "Dixie" Dean (MMG Platoon)

"What had proved to be the most hazardous day of my life safely ended. Throughout the day, I felt that no serious harm would come to me that day, and it hadn't, though on two occasions, downright bad marksmanship had prevented death or serious injury. There was a special reason for this – January 4th was Mother's birthday and I knew that if anything happened to me on that day, the date would never be a happy one for the family."

Three of the Killed In Action 4th January 1945

"The battle for Bure went on all day Friday, one male crossing the street was hit by machine gun fire and the phosphorous grenade in his pouch ignited. Two Sergeants in a house nearby threw smoke grenades near him and under their cover dragged him to safety. It was a struggle of life and death few prisoners were taken. It was the spirit of Arnhem all over again."

J. Illingworth, Liverpool Daily Post

23.   DAY THREE: 5th JANUARY 1945

War Diary 5th Jan

0100   Position stabilized with one Tiger tk still operating in village.

Pierre Lardinois (Villager)

"It was a long night, with the Germans in the cellar with us until about 3am, when they collected their equipment and left. I didn't know if they had evacuated Bure because the rest of the night was quiet and when it was getting light I ventured upstairs. From the front room ground floor windows, I saw British soldiers moving along the Presbytery wall, and later learned from them that they had been occupying some of the nearby houses since the previous evening.

"Then more British soldiers came into sight and I returned to the cellar to announce the good news. When I went back up the British were in the house opposite and I was bold enough to call "Bonjour" to them. One called back in French and asked me to go over to them, which I did. They wanted to know where the German positions were and what time in during the night they moved out of that area of the village. As I started to tell them, a burst of fire came from nearby. I could see a German soldier in the gable end of Mr Hérin's house only 50m away. He fired at the British soldiers along the Presbytery wall and they returned fire. Everything went quiet again and the British took up positions, looking for the slightest movement."

Jean-Marie Decontie (Superior of L'Alumnat)

"After a fearful night, when every house was the scene of fierce hand-to-hand fighting the British arrived [at L'Alumnat]. We gave thanks to our Lady of Bure, kissing each other and weeping. A British Captain advised caution and ordered us to stay inside. Everyone obeyed, except one brave man, who went to feed his cattle, and found that some of them had suffered wounds.

"A British tank was burning outside and the houses in the nearby cul-de-sac were engulfed in flames. The glare of the fires lit up the building and our crowd of refugees panicked and made for the exit screaming "the place is on fire!" It required all of my strength to stem the mad rush for the doors and to restrain the poor hysterical creatures."

0830   A determined attack succeeded in pushing the bulk of the enemy out of the village, with only odd snipers remaining behind. Tiger tk still in village in spite of repeated attacks by PIAT's.

Extract from: The Story of the 23rd Hussars 1940-1946

On the following morning 'A' Squadron moved out very early indeed, with orders to have another crack at Bure. 'A' Squadron were ordered to reconnoitre the high ground in order to cover infantry into Bure from the right flank. This hill, steep, wooded and covered with snow, lay half shrouded in mist. The infantry, 12th Para Bn was contacted, and the plan discussed.

It was now time to withdraw the Fife and Forfar armour; they had been exposed on the snow covered hillsides and had suffered the losses of many vehicles. Still watching the battle they had an extremely good view of the entire battlefield.

Lieutenant William Steel Brownlie (2nd Fife & Forfar Yeomanry)

"Meanwhile we sat and shivered, with no word from Desmond. His scout car had in fact been destroyed by a shell while out conferring with the paras. 3 miles away on our left front was a huge round hill, code named 'Orange', all white except for a wood on the summit. There was a discussion about who was occupying it, but in the afternoon I saw a platoon of infantry advance up its lower slope in arrowhead formation, the size of ants at that range. A grey snout emerged from the trees above them; there was a flash of flame and a puff among the little figures, who ran back the way they had come. The snout fired again, and one little black figure seemed to leap into the air and fall back into the snow. He lay there until we left the area of Bure. I was able to report that 'Orange' was not held by our troops."

This was the small force under the command of Lieutenant Clements which was sent to observe enemy movements and relay vital information by use of a 68 Radio Set. The positions they took up were also occupied by the Germans.

CSM "Taffy" Lawley ('C' Company)

"After the battle, I learned that a platoon of the 12th Battalion commanded by my old pal Clements, had been sent out to the high ground between Bure and Wavreille to make a reconnaissance and had got badly shot up. Only he and one of his men were able to crawl back to an old Château, although both were badly wounded; they were found by our padre who had gone back to bury the dead."

After being engaged by the enemy they were given the order to withdraw over the radio. Only 8 men succeeded in withdrawing and Lt Clements and 18 men were missing at the end of the day. Of these only Lt Clements and one other man made it back and 9 men were found days later killed.

Citation: Lt P Clements DCM (12th Para Bn)

Award: Military Medal

On 5th January 1945 Lt P Clements commanded a platoon which was given the task of occupying a position on the feature north of Grupont dominating the area in which the 12th and 13th Parachute Bns were operating. The patrol reached its objective by 03:00 hours and took up a position as ordered. During the following nine hours the platoon lay up in a wood on the feature, which was also occupied by the enemy, reporting enemy movements and inflicting casualties including the killing of the officers of a recce group which approached the position. At about 12.00 hours the platoon came under accurate fire from close range. Lt Clements although fully exposed to enemy fire personally passed the necessary fire orders for the artillery to engage the area held by the enemy. The enemy then brought up at least one Tiger Tank which engaged the area held by the platoon. By this time the platoon was coming under accurate fire from the rear as well as the front. Lt Clements then decided that the platoon must withdraw. He organised the withdrawal down the very exposed slope of the feature. At the first bound he was wounded in the stomach. Although he could not move himself he continued to command the platoon and issued necessary orders for the remainder to withdraw. Throughout this period the platoon had no food and was exposed to very severe weather conditions. It was entirely due to the fine leadership, determination and example of this officer that the platoon carried out its task and was able to withdraw when this task was completed.

Private Eric Barley (12th Battalion)

"One of our larger patrols was attacked on a hill by tanks and infantry. They retreated leaving 6 wounded, some dead and 2 medics to look after the wounded. The hill was later recaptured; the wounded had been shot together with the 2 medics."

Nestor Jabot (Villager)

"Before the invasion, there was always some panic. Some came out with the worst scenarios like: "When the Germans come, they will take the young men..." My Mum then advised us to leave. We made a small group composing of Arthur Libioule, Joseph Libioule, Emmanuel Despas, Joseph Bodson, Dad and me. We set off to meet an old priest called Warnotte at Feschaux, who my dad knew.

"We went through Dinant and noticed a Jeep destroyed at the foot of the Bayard Rock (left, the Jeep had carried 3 German soldiers dressed in US uniforms, they hit a line of mines trying to force their way through Dinant).

"Eventually we had had enough and on Sunday, we left for Tellin with Dad and Emmanuel Despas.

"From the steps of the church, we could see Bure, but to see what? We could see absolutely nothing but you could hear muffled sounds. At Tellin we saw German prisoners with their hands on their heads. Then Emmanuel said he was tired of not having heard from his mother. He then went to Bure taking a circuitous route, imagining that he'd escape danger. Subsequently, we had no news of Emmanuel. Dad said that things might still go wrong. We later learned why we have more news of Emmanuel. He was caught by the Germans and led to Grupont. Arriving at the T-junction [now the roundabout near Parc La Clusure], the vehicle in which the Germans took him missed its turn and went straight from the parapet and fell into a hole. Emmanuel was wounded in the shoulder and cared for by a German doctor in the house of the Collignon's, very close to the house of Joseph Bodson who was with us at the beginning of the trip. He stayed there a while and Arthur Rose had a long talk with the Germans for his release [this confirms the story of Charles Magnette].

Charles Magnette (Villager)

"After a few days of battle without seeing a single soldier, 2 young Germans descended the stairs of our basement. They were nervous and probably drunk. They told us to leave, but where would we go?

"We placed a few things on a handcart and went to the village. Houses were burning and they shone miserably on the snow-covered ground. Germans at the entrance to Bure made us realize that we had to leave towards Grupont. On the roads, there was a crowd of Germans in conversation with Arthur Rose, the coal merchant. We tried to find some accommodation, but nobody wanted to welcome us. Finally, the last building was a hotel [Ry de Belle Rose], which was good enough for us. It was the first time we had ever walked into a hotel.

"In the hotel, by entering through the porch, we looked right and left, the place had been turned into a German hospital. We could hear screaming day and night. And outside, there was a huge pile of bandages mixed with body parts following numerous amputations made by the surgeons. My dog did not hesitate to utilise these.

"We stayed several days. We washed in a small stream passing close, the water in the hotel being frozen, we had no other solution. This frozen water had other consequences as the pretty toilets of the hotel did not work."

'Ry de Belle Rose' - the Grupont hotel used as a German Hospital.

Fortunat Zune (14 Year old Villager)

"Our cellar was only covered with planks and was therefore not very safe when the bombings were quite large. So we decided if our cellar was damaged to go to our neighbours. Mum had decided we could make it if we evacuated quickly. We wrapped the food we had baked in towels and placed them on the table. We quickly went to our neighbours, but in the hurry forgot the food. The firing had increased and we could not return to fetch it. We stayed there a few days and ate the neighbour's food. When we did return, our food had gone.

"One day while we were in the basement, we heard people above us in the house. It was the Germans who were bringing their wounded. One of these soldiers, 'Alsatian' they called him, sometimes sat down on the stairs next to us. He explained that they were being given first aid, and then they were to be taken to a hospital in Grupont, the Hotel 'Ry de Belle Rose' (Repos du Linçon, mentioned earlier). One day he asked me for a wooden board, with which he made a makeshift splint for a comrade with a broken arm. Then there was a lull in the fighting and he asked if I would lead his comrade to Grupont. I went outside and I saw that there were 4 killed Germans tied on an American Jeep [possibly the one taken belonging to Eric Barley, 12th Para Bn or seen previously by Lieutenant George Prewitt, US Army], driven by the Germans. Then, this Jeep drove off towards Grupont."

1000   Intensive shelling of village by enemy.

Trace of positions taken from 13 Para War Diary

Lance Corporal David "Robbie" Robinson (Anti-Tank 'C' Company)

"I was near Major Clark when he was wounded. A shell hit the house we were in [No.42 Rue de Tellin, the HQ & RAP with the steps] and the explosion blew him out of the window and into the street."

Major "Nobby" Clark MC ('C' Company)

"An artillery shell passed then through the roof ['C' Company HQ]. Luckily, I was alone with my batman on the ground floor. The others were in the cellar. The explosion was so violent that we were thrown into the middle of the street. Some days later I became blind. My ordnance spitted chips of tooth for several days before he died.[66]

"The civilians are those who suffer most from war. Soldiers are armed and know they may die, it's completely different. Luckily, in Bure the whole civilian population sought refuge in the cellars of the school (L'Alumnat) at the edge of the village. Young people went courageously back to their own houses at night to look for food. They risked their lives because once they ran into Germans, and once into British who were as dangerous as the Germans because of their nervousness. The battle of Bure was hard, but we behaved well."

Lieutenant William Steel Brownlie (2nd Fife & Forfar Yeomanry)

"We were told that the enemy were pulling out, so I sent Jimmy Samson's Troop round to the far side of Bure, to take on any enemy withdrawing. His Sgt Robinson blew up on a mine, but the rest moved round to the rear and spent the day firing at odd packets of Germans.

"Colonel Alec came up in his tank, and said that we would probably be relieved by 23 Hussars. They arrived late in the afternoon, and haggled about where they were to position themselves.

"This was the small part we played in pushing back von Rundstedt's 'Bulge' in the Ardennes. My abiding memory is of the tiny black figures labouring in a white landscape, while we did our best to support them, that and the cold!"

Extract from: An Account of Ops 29th Armoured Brigade in the Ardennes

By 1015 the following morning 'A' troop 2FF Yeo had managed to work its way forward from Chapel Hill into a position where it could shoot at anything moving into or out of Bure on the eastern side: a number of targets were successfully engaged during the day. By late afternoon 23rd Hussars had completed the relief of 2FF Yeo and were in position in Bure and on the ridge to the south. Enemy bazooka men were still lurking both in the village and on the hills.

1030 *Systematic clearing of village house by house ordered by CO with 'C' Coy to occupy NORTH, Oxf Bucks EAST and 'A' Coy SOUTH of village, 'B' Coy in reserve. 4 counter attacks with sp of 4 Tigers dispersed by own arty concentration on FUP.*

---

[66] Private Harold Hughes died in Hospital on the 7th January and is buried in Brussels Town Cemetery.

Lieutenant Ellis "Dixie" Dean (MMG Platoon)

"The next morning was a lot quieter in the western end of Bure. The battle had advanced beyond the crossroads, which was no longer dominated by the 'Tiger'. It was relatively safe to walk down the street. I was up in the back bedroom with Sgt Drew. The burnt out shells of Sherman tanks of the Fife and Forfar, shot up whilst trying to out flank the 'Tiger' littered the landscape just to our rear. Away to our right, towards Grupont, a group of tanks were circling a large isolated building. They were too far away, even with binoculars, to identify, and as we discussed this, someone came up the stairs and entered the room. I turned to see 2 members of the 'Scouts', one of whom I knew well. In 1940 Fred Smith and I, served in the same Company of 70th Battalion Royal Welch Fusiliers. After that we went our own ways, but by late 1943 were both serving together in the 13th."

Corporal Fred Smith (Scout Platoon)

"On the 5th of January Joe [Hodgson] asked Freddie and me to do some street clearing, ready for an advance. So off we went on a street clearing exercise. I cannot remember who the pair was on the right hand side of the street, but Freddie and I were to operate on the left. But before we went out I went to see Dixie Dean who had his Vickers machine guns set up in a farm house on the main road."

Lieutenant Ellis "Dixie" Dean (MMG Platoon)

"His own Platoon Commander [Arthur Prestt[67]] had been wounded and now he was going on a sniping assignment. He knew something was going to happen and he had to confide in someone. Since Arthur was wounded, he had come to me. I tried my best to persuade him that he was imagining things as we all did now and again, but I can't have sounded too convincing, especially after my experiences the previous day. "What will be, will be" was Fred's philosophy. We shook hands and off he went."

Corporal Fred Smith (Scout Platoon)

"We went a few houses forward at a time and then we would wait, watching the troops on the other side, giving them cover as they moved forward. Eventually we got down to the crossroads as we called them, in fact the main road turns to the right and a minor road veered off to the left. We got just past the crossroads, maybe only 20 or 30 yards past the church itself and Freddie and I saw some Panzer Grenadiers in a house on the corner of the junction and then from nowhere a tank appeared about 50m away. We had no kind of anti-tank weapon in our position and watched as the tank poke its barrel into the window of a house on the corner and blast away. The monster then turned and headed our way with its large barrel indicating it was going to do the same to the building we hid in. Freddie and I were paralysed with fear because we had no way out and thought we were about to be killed. We came under fire from an MG34 or an MG42. We were in a doorway of an out building a bit like a garage, whilst we crouched behind the wall the bullets were chipping away at the brickwork which was

---

[67] Lt Arthur Prestt had been severely wounded in the hand during the intense shell fire on the hill south of Bure as they had emerged from the woods on the start line. He did not return to the 13th Battalion until after the war in Europe had finished. After the war he went on to become a prosecutor for the Judge Advocate's Department and dealt with many war crime trials in Malaya and eventually witnessed more than 40 hangings. His even-handed approach won him the respect of many Japanese soldiers. His legal career eventually saw him become the Honorary Recorder of Manchester.

only one brick thick in the reveal. We knew that the wall couldn't possibly cover the 2 of us forever; an unexpected burst of reassuring fire came from about 50m behind us. I instantly recognised the sound of a Bren gun as it sprayed the tank around the drivers hatch. The tank, fearing an anti-tank attack backed up and took cover behind the rubble of the house it had just demolished, it then withdrew up the street towards Grupont.

"After being saved from the tank we decided not to push our luck any further and decided that the best thing to do was to withdraw back towards Rue de Tellin by the back of the houses, so I said to Freddie "I'll cover you, make a dash for it and get back. Then you can cover me." Off he went.

"My turn came and unfortunately, I got no covering fire from Freddie. I ran back towards our lines and ducked into a gap between the church and a house that was there. I then tried to make my way back and in one of the houses we had already cleared I saw the man who shot me at the window. Most of the houses only had 2 rooms upstairs and downstairs, they weren't big houses but most had cellars. Straight behind the houses was fields and as we were clearing the Germans out from the front

 they were ducking out from the back, waiting until we had gone then reoccupying their positions again. I spotted him, but because of my position, thought I'd never be able to get him. There was a cart just outside so I decided to duck down behind it. I felt a tap in my back and thought it was Freddie throwing stones because he did that sort of thing. As I turned around and started to drop, he fired and that was more or less it. It wasn't until much later that I found out Freddie had almost been cut in two by the rapid firing Spandau. (Inset: Freddie Beach KIA 5th Jan 1945).

"I thought that I was finished. All I felt, was a pat on the back, which was caused by the bullet coming out. I never felt a thing when it went in, just as it was coming out. I dropped on the floor and could see blood on the floor, bright red blood in the bright white snow. My only thought at that time was, I'm not getting caught with this rifle in my hand. It still had a sniper sights on, so it was a case of getting the scopes off quick and throwing them. If I had have been caught with the sights, I'd have been shot instantly. No-one likes snipers; we probably would have done the same. I got rid of the telescopic sight, got up and started making my way back again or attempted too. I only made a couple of paces and the houses seemed to be coming in on me, it was like I'd had 14 or 15 pints. I'd take one step forward and three back, then I just went down. Joe Hodgson had seen me go down and sent a couple of his men to fetch me back in. They came out with somebody's bedding, rolled me onto it and carried me back. The snow I was laying in was very cold and thankfully that's what apparently saved me because my blood wouldn't flow as quickly. The next thing I remember was being outside the battalion aid post and Charlie [Bryan] the medic touching my chest with the toe of his boot and saying "There's not much point in sending him back." Joe Hodgson played holy hell with him and made sure he put me on the next Jeep out and that was over the bonnet of the Jeep.

"I woke up in another aid post in some stables with a sky pilot [*Slang:* a chaplain in one of the military services] over the top of me, but I cannot remember where. From there I ended up in a hospital in Brussels which used to be a convent. On my big toe was a tag, it basically said "Your going home!" Soon after that I ended up on some dockside on a stretcher, put on a boat and sent home to England, where I was placed on a hospital train and taken up to an Edinburgh hospital. That was it. I never got back in the war again.

"Apparently the bullet had entered my body close to my arm pit, ricocheted close to my vital organs and rib cage, before coming out of my body through my back and hitting my belt."

House demolished by tank

Panzer Grenadiers

Smith & Beach

In March 2013 Fred Smith (previous photo, in wheelchair) found the doorway and told his story to John Hutton (on left) another ex-13 Para and later RSM in the SAS. They had travelled to Bure together and John immediately recognised the events Fred spoke of (picture courtesy Serge Loslever).

L'Alumpat

'Pig Pens'

"Jock" Hutton's Position

Cpl John "Jock" Hutton ('A' Coy)

"Ha-ha... What? I remember that! It was me manning the Bren; it was in my barn 50m over there, down the road! [pointing towards the farm entrance further down Rue de Belvaux]

"I remember being trapped in the barn for 2 days and nights during the intense street fighting. The barn back then was full of pigs and troughs, and was close to the college, traces of the walls are still there today and you can still see where the troughs were attached to the wall. From that barn we held off almost constant attacks from the Panzer Grenadiers. There were 5 of us in this position and I manned the Bren gun firing at the Germans through a hole in the east wall.

"As I said the battle went on for days and we had to take turns to rest and take watch. One time on my watch I heard a noise in the snow covered ground outside. Looking out I saw a German who must have thought the barn was empty and was obviously looking for somewhere to get out of the harsh conditions outdoors. He was crawling towards one of the trough entrances and I couldn't risk using the Bren on him because I didn't want to draw the attention of the tanks and the MG's. I drew out my Fairbairn–Sykes fighting knife and waited patiently for the German to stick his head through the door, as he did I stuck the knife under his chin and up through his brain. I hit him so hard that the tip of the dagger went through his skull. I then dragged the body in, using the knife's handle. A little later we had to move the body; it was starting to attract a number of hungry pigs..."[68]

Ex 13 Para & SAS RSM veteran "Jock" Hutton inspects the remains of the old 'Pig Pen' his section occupied for 2 days & nights. The rusty marks on the walls indicate where the troughs were attached.

Picture Serge Loslever

Sadly Fred Smith passed away a few weeks after fulfilling his lifelong wish to find the spot where his mate Freddie Beach was killed and where he himself was shot.

---

[68] "Jock" Hutton parachuted in on D-Day and was wounded in the stomach from mortar fire during the patrol on 22nd June (reported on page 211). He was evacuated back to England and rejoined in time for the Ardennes. On the first day of the Bure street fighting he was captured, but escaped almost straight away. He was a career soldier and served with the Rhodesian SAS as the Regimental Sergeant Major.

L'Alumnat
(Collège d'Alzon)

Hutton in pig sty
(no longer there)

Tank

Smith
& Beach

Church

Courtesy RCAHMS

Sergeant Len Cox ('C' Company)

"Another day and we were still isolated. The mortaring and shelling was as bad as ever so we decided that since the rest of the Company hadn't come for us we would have to go looking for them. We had no idea at all where they were, nor if it was safe to move outside. Gammon bombs were used to hole the walls and that was the method we used to get us back to Company HQ. They gave us a hot meal, the first for nearly 3 days and then sent us back the same way to reoccupy our old position.

"Later in the day, I went out with a patrol to a crossroads on the outskirts of the village, where some Belgian civilians reported a party of Germans waiting to surrender. They guided us to the spot and then ran off only seconds before a mortar stonk landed around us. We sheltered against a high bank close to where 'B' Company had been caught in the open on the first day of the battle. The dead bodies were lying there, now covered in snow. Our patrol returned without any casualties but neither did we have any prisoners.

"While we'd been away, fresh orders to clear the other half of Bure had been given with 9 Platoon made responsible for the road running to the right away from the church. We systematically checked every house and ended up in an isolated farmhouse, in quite a commanding position, which we were ordered to hold. The German infantry made several attempts to eject us but we held out."

Guy Jacquemin (Villager)

"During a lull, we went up to the kitchen to see the damage when suddenly 5 or 6 Germans were stood at the door and one said in good French, "Open the door, Madame!" Mum answered that the door wouldn't open and we headed back towards the cellar. Carmen, the wife of Pierre Lardinois was worried and said that Peter was in the street with the English. Just as we intended to run down the stairs... shooting broke out, Carmen started to cry and shouted, "It's Pierre ... he been killed…" Fortunately, he was not."

Guy Jacquemin (Villager)

[Summing up his own experiences of the last few days] "During the lulls, we would go and get news of our grandmother or our brother Edmond. Albert and I went up the alley. We have overview of the Allies in the Henrot Wood. We were not worried. Reaching the top, we see the Germans, and immediately there's a burst of gunfire. We ran to the farm. The battle became so violent that we had to spend the night at the farm. Shells rained down from all sides. We were in the cellar of the farm. There was a man who relied on 'Our Lady of Hauff'. The nearer the shells fell, the more he cried. A shell fell very close and the man shouted in such a way, that Albert and I couldn't stop laughing. The next day, Edmond got us back to the house and consoled mother who had spent a night of distress.

"A second sleepless night was waiting for us. Victor Lardinois had gone home came back to tell us part of the village was burning and that the battle would be terrible. We had no alternative but to go to the Château. We took some clothes and ran there. There was fire on all sides. We had to step over electric poles lying on the ground. At the Château, there were already many people. We found a place in a hallway that overlooked the courtyard. Through the glass in the door, we saw the shells falling in the yard. People prayed, cried and cried. Some even shouted. We said, "If a shell shows up in the hallway... that's it!" We also said we were not so bad in our cellar. So the next day we went back home."

Celestine Limet (Villager)

"Felix Despas and I went to inspect our homes. The doors and windows of my ground floor had been boarded up with timber taken from the barn. Felix being braver than me, entered first. We found blood on one of the bedroom floors – a wounded man must have been treated there, and left his rifle behind. The house itself was badly damaged; most of the roof and one gable end were completely destroyed.

"My cows had gone, who released them I'll never know. I recovered them later; one had a piece of shrapnel in the upper leg. My goat had been tethered to a post and had been left water.

"We carried on to Felix's house, but leaning on a barn door at Henri Ligot's was a wounded British soldier (either an Officer or NCO) who called out for help."

Felix Despas (Villager)

"To make me understand that he was wounded, he took my hand and placed it into the opening of his battle-dress. My hand came out red with blood. He asked me to drive a Tellin. Again, I said I would "take you to a hospital." I placed a thick layer of hay on my wheelbarrow and I placed him on it."

Celestine Limet (Villager)

"Felix tried to tell him that it was too dangerous, but he didn't seem to understand, so Felix made the sign of a cross, hoping to convince him that we were taking him to safety. We managed, with some difficulty, to lift him onto a low cart. He was a big man, and pushing him through the snow wasn't easy and near the church we had to take a breather. From here we could see 2 British soldiers sheltering in the porch of the Jacquemin's house and we called to them to give us a hand. They indicated that they daren't show themselves, pointing out to us a German patrol not too far away.

"Before we reached L'Alumnat, we met Louise Vanderbil, who spoke very good English and she explained to him where we were taking him. He must have survived the war, because after it was over he used to write to Marie Lens."

Private Dennis Boardman (Signaller, att 'A' Company)

"Late in the afternoon we saw what appeared to be 4 civilians coming down the hillside road, they waved to us, and as we went towards them a rain of mortar bombs came our way. We never saw the civilians again."

Report by Victor Thompson (Herald War Correspondent)

"Nearly all the time," said one Londoner, "we were so close to each other that each side could hear the other's orders and all the time too there were a few civilians hiding in the cellars. Germans broke into a shop and took overcoats and berets to cover their uniforms. We dealt with them."

Unknown name (341 Battery 86th Field Regiment, RA)

"January 5th - Slightly less cold, but dark menacing snow clouds hung low overhead. Activity around Bure continued all morning. About 1400 hours the enemy made a desperate attempt to recapture Bure. A company of enemy infantry supported by some tanks and heavy mortar fire attacked down the snow-covered hill slopes. Major Whitmee, who was our OP in Bure spotted the attack in sufficient time to bring down the Regiment's concentrated fire with very great effect. One tank was hit and reversed, causing the others to withdraw. The enemy made repeated attacks all afternoon, using their mortars with harassing effect on our troops and OP Each time, however, Major Whitmee's efforts brought the Regiment's fire down on the attackers and broke up each attack. At night the enemy gave up the unequal struggle and Bure remained firmly in our hands. Major Whitmee was awarded the MC for his gallant actions on this day which undoubtedly saved Bure and our troops."

Major Whitmee of the Herts Yeomanry was attached to the 13th Battalion as a Forward Artillery Observer, conducting the support of the gunners. For the massive help given to his men, many of which owed their lives, Lt-Col Luard placed the following recommendation:

Citation: Major Herbert N Whitmee (86th Field Regiment, Royal Artillery)

Award: Military Cross

During the engagement fought by the 13th Bn the Parachute Regiment at BURE in January 1945, Major Whitmee was attached from 86th (Herts Yeomanry) Field Regiment RA, in support of the Battalion.

From the beginning to the end of the action, the support given by Major Whitmee's guns, which were entirely under his direction, was quite exceptional. Time and again during periods of almost continuous enemy counter attacks, the quick and accurate fire of his guns broke up the attack, often right on top of our positions.

This quick, close and effective artillery support was of incalculable value to the morale and confidence of the troops.

During the whole action the conduct of Major Whitmee was beyond praise. In the most difficult and dangerous circumstances, when enemy shelling was particularly accurate and heavy, he remained extraordinarily cool, calm and collected, and his cheerful personality was an outstanding example and inspiration to all around him.

Pierre Lardinois (Villager)

"The fighting had moved to the top [Grupont] end of the village, with the Germans desperately clinging on in that area. As it got dark and the fires continued to rage, getting nearer and nearer, we decided that we would move to the cellars of L'Alumnat. It was dark before we moved and as we went I noticed that the British were now in control of the centre, having being forced out for a short while the previous night. Most people had already sought shelter in L'Alumnat, their dogs as well. Our party added another 17 to the total, plus 2 more dogs.

"Shortly after our arrival, the Holy Father served a meal of boiled rice with raisins and a drink of tea, but there was not enough to go around. I wasn't sorry that I missed out, because all those who ate were taken ill with diarrhoea. They suffered badly, having to relieve themselves in the snow and the courtyard became a stinking sewer. This went on all night and an old lady who arrived at the same time as us, acted as door keeper. Growing tired of this, she shouted "Shut the door, for heavens sake!" whenever someone failed to do so. Soon the children in our party, made a game of this, chorusing "Shut the door, for heavens sake!" before she had time to open her mouth.

"Whenever there was shelling or machine gun fire, we all prayed aloud, just as we had done back in our own cellar. As soon as the shelling stopped, you could not hear yourself for the noise of people talking."

Felix Despas (Villager)

"On January 5th, I was again going to my home. I saw with dismay that the British had lit a big fire in my barn. It appeared to me with certainty, that at any moment, the fire was going to spread to the parts of the main building that I had left. I approached them and said to put out the fire. One of the soldiers had a vicious reaction and pointed a pistol at my head. I pulled myself together very quickly and went to find an officer. I found one and explained the situation that I had found myself in, and he went to the scene and put out the fire. Later, I realised that all my furniture had been burned. The British were not all unpleasant, because just before this incident, I'd had a long talk in great kindness with some others, who were wondering where the Germans were in the neighbourhood."

Renie Lambert (Villager)

"One day we had soup. Everyone lined up to get some, but the soup will remain engraved in the memory of each person who had it. Everyone had incredible diarrhoea. Some couldn't get to the toilet quickly enough.

"Intimacy was gone. One of my aunts, Jeanne Lambert gave birth to a baby girl in the basement, in front of everyone and Odile Damblon also had a little boy. I still remember my aunt arriving at the college; her legs were blue with cold. She had first hidden at the water tower in the woods before coming from Mirwart Road to us at the college. I think she gave birth on the same day of her arrival. And then there was the drama of when Louis Laffineur. He wanted to go find food for the people; he ended up being shot in the stomach and died."

Pierre Lardinois (Villager)

"I was very worried, caught on the wrong side of the street and separated from my family at an anxious time. I was wishing that I was back in my own cellar. I wasn't feeling very brave, but after a while, I decided that I ought to try and get back home, making a big detour to avoid crossing the street near where the firing was going on. Even then I had to take shelter from shooting in M'sieur Depais home. The house was badly damaged and all the cattle in his barn had been killed, the place was a complete shambles. There was another lull in the fighting and I made a dash for it. Running down the passage leading to the door, I sensed someone was there and a German soldier raised his hands shouting "Kamerad! Kamerad!" I knew he wouldn't be the only one, so I pushed him ahead of me up the passage and called to the British across the street to take him. He was screaming at the top of his voice all the time and must have been hoarse by the time the Tommies came out and roughly bundled him inside.

"Eventually I reached the safety of my own cellar and was welcomed with tears of joy by my wife and the others, Madame Louise Jacquemin and her children. They told me that when they saw me cross the street to talk to the Tommies, they had left the cellar only to come face to face with Germans coming in through the back door. They fled back down the cellar and heard shots from the room above and were convinced that they were at me and I had been killed.

"I made a promise that I would never leave my wife on her own in the cellar again, but less than an hour later we heard cries from behind the house. The cries became more urgent, and I went to investigate. My neighbour Joseph Hérin needed my assistance because Louis Laffineur was lying wounded in the street [had gone out to fetch food and see to his cattle]. The two of us carried him back to his house and had a look at his injuries. A bullet had passed right through him, via his stomach. He stayed conscious and we managed to bandage him, but we didn't know what to do for the best – both the British and Germans wasn't far away, but there was no sign of them. I looked up and down the street and couldn't see a soul. Fortunately alcohol quietened him down and we prayed that help will soon come. Time dragged on and I kept a look out through the corner of the window, until about 1pm, when I caught a glimpse of a British tank advancing slowly up the street, flanked on both sides by a file of soldiers. The Tommies kept close to the front of the houses, searching each one in turn. Eventually they reached us, and one of them looked at our patient and assured us that he was ok.

"The fighting continued all around us and once again, despite my promise, I had got involved yet again. In the end another British soldier, either a doctor or a medical orderly turned up and gave him a thorough examination, followed by an injection and wrote the time, 1415, on his forehead. Two other wounded British soldiers were also treated in the room. Louis was quiet now and arrangements were made to evacuate him to hospital after dark.[69]

"Before the wounded were moved, a British tank in front of M'sieur Bodart's was hit and exploded, setting fire to the house. Before the fire had died out, 7 properties, stretching for 70m along the street had been destroyed. Lots of cows perished in the flames, some lucky ones were let out – God knows who by. They wandered about, bellowing mournfully. Those still trapped, especially M'sieur Herin's, replied in equal mournful fashion.

"My brother's family, lodging with Leon Thungen, had like everyone else taken to the cellars and were not aware that the house was on fire above them. They were forced to run through the flames to safety and as they ran, they saw the British 50m away on one side and the Germans the same distance away on the left."

Account of 'C' Company 2nd Bn Ox & Bucks Light Infantry

The next morning was fairly quiet except for patrols, until we received orders to clear the rest of the village. 'C' Company was to clear the right of the main street [Rue de Grupont], and 'A' Company of 13 Para the left. 3 Shermans were to assist us forward.

The enemy had a well dug in MG post at the far end of the street, some 300yds away, and there were snipers in several houses, one of whom had wounded L/Cpl Jerome and a Gunner officer.

The assault went quite well to start with, and the tanks set the far end of the village on fire and eliminated the main MG post. Unfortunately we lost all 3 tanks shortly afterwards. Two were knocked out by bazookas and one 'brewed' up by another SP gun [it was this action Pierre Lardinois had witnessed and had set several houses on fire].

Roger Vulvert (Villager)

"Our house was perpendicular to the road and from here the view of the intersection of the church was very interesting for the Germans who had made an observation post [it was in fact the German MG strongpoint]. It is likely that the tracer bullets fired by the English to dislodge the Germans, set fire to our house and the neighbours. The cowshed and horses stables also began to blaze. The horses managed to break their halters and flee. We managed to collect them. But all the cattle perished in the fire and the house completely burned down." (over)

---

[69] Louis Laffineur died in Ciney on 10th January. His last message was for his son, Lucien, who had been rounded up by the Germans on 8th August 1944. He too never returned to Bure.

1. MG's positioned in windows on the right firing towards 'crossroads'.

2. MG post viewed from calvary on Rue de Grupont.

3. The house was demolished and rebuilt (shown in 2012).

4. The view of the German machine gunners towards 'crossroads'.

Account of 'C' Company 2nd Bn Ox & Bucks Light Infantry

The enemy was installed in the far end of the village in some strength, but 21 Platoon got to their objective just after dark. 23 Platoon, who were behind them, established themselves on the right flank, with Company HQ on their left and 20 Pl in the building covering the length of the road from the Western end. 22 Pl's remnants were in the rear area in reserve.

Lt Stone took a patrol of 10 men to contact 21 Pl with orders for a temporary withdrawal, to allow a Medium Artillery stonk to be put on the remaining positions just east of Bure. They reached the house alright but the enemy had both entrances covered by MG and snipers, who opened fire as soon as the patrol was clear on its way out. The darkness of the night and wire fences made it difficult for the patrol to manoeuvre freely and they lost Cpl Boyce (killed) and 3 men wounded. The patrol got back with its wounded, and shortly after Lt Hill extricated his Platoon.

Lt Wood with Lt Stoke as guide then took 20 Pl to the forward position unmolested. The 13th were established left of the road, thus after 30 hrs during which we had no rest and not too much food, the village was ours.

Extract from: The Story of the 23rd Hussars 1940-1946

In the meanwhile First Troop was fighting its way through Bure. But the enemy still clung to the eastern edge of the village and some of the remaining ruins. The attack to clear these positions at first went well, and good progress was made towards the river at Grupont. There, however, the tanks moved forward more warily down the narrow village street. The Troop leader, Lt Goss, led with distinction and bravery. But it was all in vain and both his own and the tank following were hit and destroyed. Four of the crews were killed, the wounded having to make their way back under fire. Bure was, in fact, one of the nastiest spots the Squadron had ever been in. The Germans clung to the houses and ruins, hid in cellars and catacombs, fighting and sniping grimly to the end."

As the 23rd Hussars Third Troop reached the top of 'Chapel Hill', to cover the attack, they ran into an enemy ambush hidden amongst the snow, mist and woods.

Citation: Lance Sergeant Arthur Huthwaite (23rd Hussars, RAC)

Award: Military Medal

On 5 Jan 45 L/Sgt Huthwaite was commander of a tank which was advancing in difficult country to some high ground near BURE.

As it passed between 2 small copses there was an explosion and the tank appeared to be hit. Sgt Huthwaite ordered to driver to speed up but immediately there were 2 more explosions and the tank was immobilised. Sgt Huthwaite ordered his crew to evacuate the tank. Regardless of his own safety and in spite of being shaken by the explosion Sgt Huthwaite ran back to the tank following to warn it not to enter the copse. This tank was then hit by a short range anti-tank weapon & the crew evacuated it. Sgt Huthwaite, seeing the Commander was not with the rest of the crew, jumped on the tank to see if he could help him. He found the Commander dead and although he knew the enemy must be close by remained on the tank and ordered the driver back into the tank. Under Sgt Huthwaite's guidance the tank was reversed out of range of further attacks.

Sgt Huthwaite had meanwhile reported the action on the wireless. Later, though under MG fire, he helped to remove the body of the dead Commander and supervised the evacuation of his own tank.

Throughout the action Sgt Huthwaite was an example to both crews when they were all shocked and his leadership and clear reports on the wireless prevented further casualties and was responsible for the safe evacuation of the two tanks.

Four more Germans were captured and interrogated, they were from Battle Group Schöngrunder, a unit comprising of the survivors of 2 Pz Recce Unit which had suffered heavily before Christmas. They had been withdrawn, reorganized and then sent forward 1st Jan to Bure, which they reached on 4th Jan. They reported that 3 and/or 10 Pz Gren Regt was already there. They all withdrew to the east of Bure early morning 5th Jan, dug in and then later withdrawn further.

They said that their unit was 50-60 strong when they entered the battle on 4th Jan and by noon 5th Jan they were down to 30-35. They estimated that the German strength in Bure on the evening 4th Jan was about 120, but further casualties had been caused during the night.

Extract from: *An Account of Ops 29th Armoured Brigade in the Ardennes*

By 2030 Bure was reported clear but during the night infantry and at least one SP gun infiltrated into it and once more the situation became confused; the attack by 12th Parachute Battalion towards Grupont was cancelled.

Private Dennis Boardman (Signaller, att 'A' Company)

"We lost 2 more of our tanks during the day, but by 7pm Bure was almost in our hands. In the village church, which was full of civilians, we found one of our Officers [possibly Lt Lagergren], shot through the head when caught by a German.

"During the third night we were ready for the final push on Bure. We were in the hall of a house, keeping very quiet when a German soldier walked past us on the opposite side of the road. We let him carry on as we didn't wish to give our position away. It was while we were watching him that I heard the voice of Colonel Luard on my radio. Sgt-Major Bert Alder signalled me not to answer as the Germans would hear me and I would give our positions away. Finally, when I did answer, the message was for Major Watson to report to Battalion HQ as soon as possible."

2100   Last enemy outpost eliminated by 'A' Coy and all enemy resistance in village ceased.

Lieutenant Ellis "Dixie" Dean (MMG Platoon)

"Finally when the Germans were pushed out, 'A' Company occupied the south of the village, with 'C' Company in the north and 'C' Company of Ox & Bucks in the east. What little was left of 'B' Company were in reserve."

2200   HQ 5 Para Bde ordered evacuation from BURE to start at 2359 hours. Total casualties 7 Officers, 182 Other Ranks.

Lieutenant Ellis "Dixie" Dean (MMG Platoon)

"Shortly before midnight, I was making a routine tour of the sentries and entered the house occupied by Sgt Higgins. By the glow coming from the back room I knew a fire was burning, and from the aroma, that something was cooking. "Higgy" was standing in front of the stove, on top of which was a cooking pot, chicken and mixed vegetables. As we talked a runner from Company HQ summonsed me to an 'O' Group.

"Vic Wraight was already there, the CSM too. "Listen very carefully as there isn't much time." Major McLoughlin began, "The Battalion is to withdraw at 2400 hours. Prisoners captured this afternoon say they had been ordered to hold on, as a big counterattack was to be mounted at first light. When this news was given to the Brigadier, he decided the Battalion is too exhausted to resist a major attack, and so we are to pull out. Anything that can't be carried for some distance is to be left at the last house on the right, where a party under the RSM will destroy it. Nothing of any value to the enemy is to be left behind. The Machine Guns to lead, followed by the Mortars, any questions?"

"Yes, where are we going?" I asked. "I'll move with you and lead the way" He replied. Realising how dark it was I then asked "How will I know which is you?" Major McLoughlin paused for a second and replied "Listen. I'll hoot like an owl." It was a most convincing impression he gave. "Synchronise watches" a pause "2353 hours in 5, 4, 3, 2, now. You are to be on the street ready to move in 5 minutes, we go at 2400 hours."

Private Dennis Boardman (Signaller, att 'A' Company)

"It was midnight when Major Watson returned and the news he brought shook the whole Company. We were to withdraw from Bure, at once, and as silently as possible, in order that the enemy didn't know we were pulling out. The village, almost in our hands, a third of a battalion lost for nothing. The men were cursing, they were disgusted, and they felt cheated. The grumbling grew worse as the withdrawal from Bure continued. Who was the stupid senior officer responsible for this order? Faith in our superiors was at the lowest and we felt our bitterness was justified."

Lieutenant Ellis "Dixie" Dean (MMG Platoon)

"How the NCO's got the men into the street on time I'll never know, but they did. I walked back, counting as I went. 3 killed, 4 wounded – that made 34, including myself. I then heard "Towitt, towhoo. Towitt, towhoo", coming from behind me and getting nearer each time. By now I had seen the funny side of it, for the hooting was only known to the members of the '' Group and I was imagining the reactions of the members of the Company, when this figure halted in front of them and hooted like an owl!

"The OC gave a wave of his arm and we set off, making as little noise as possible. We were very vulnerable, for the village must be a registered target of every Boche gun within range. Passing the last house the second-in-command checked us through. We couldn't march, we shuffled. The surface of the road was packed ice, from the passing of armour and keeping ones feet was hard enough. I reckoned the heavily laden gunners must be finding it hard. They were really struggling, because not a single thing was left for destruction, even the damaged gun and the ten belts of ammo carried by the casualties had been brought. Some men had 80lbs extra on their backs.

"The next 3 hours was a real nightmare. Men were continually falling and landing flat on their backs, having to be hauled up by their mates, cursing and swearing (quietly). Nor was there any chance of sharing the heavy loads. We passed through Tellin and there were no more built up areas on the move.

435

"Out of the night ahead of us, a jeep appeared. Out stepped Mike Brennan, Brigade Major "Well done. Well done." He encouraged us. "Not much further now. Here let me take your load and put it in the jeep?" He asked the first man. "I'm alright, the man behind's carrying more than me." He went down the line, asking each man in turn, but not a single one would hand over his load. I experienced a surge of pride in these young soldiers in what they had achieved and their behaviour. Surely this was the British soldier at his best. For 3 days and nights, we had been battering away at the Hun, taking a hammering, but giving a harder one in return. Now dirty, dishevelled, exhausted in mind and body, with little sleep or food for 72 hours, having seen their pals and comrades killed and wounded close at hand, they had felt the shame when ordered to withdraw – they knew they had beaten the Boche yet again, and so unconquered, un daunted, we marched on."

Private Dennis Boardman (Signaller, att 'A' Company)

"The 6 mile walk from Bure was a nightmare; it was like walking on an ice rink, men were falling every few yards, cuts, bruises and sore backsides. The walk was sheer hell. In the early hours of the morning we enjoyed hot food and sweet tea in a school not all that far from the battle area. Though everyone was tired and thoroughly worn out, the only topic of conversation was that of being let down by the higher-ups. An explanation must be demanded. Someone must provide a satisfactory explanation!

"The explanation was eventually given. Our attack on Bure, the further-most point of the German Ardennes offensive had been a resounding success. The 2nd Panzer Division had been moved from another sector of the front to our area. This had left the Germans weak in that area enabling British troops to cut off and capture large Germans forces. The men felt a good deal better after hearing the statement; how true it was we will probably never know."

Account of 'C' Company 2nd Bn Ox & Bucks Light Infantry

At 0010 hours we had orders to withdraw from the village starting to thin out 0015 hours, and 'C' Company to be clear by 0030 hours. We marched back to Tellin, where barns were found for a well earned 'kip', after a hot meal which the CSM and CQMS had waiting for us.

During the action our own casualties were:

Killed:	Died of wounds:
Cpl Blower J.	L/Cpl Short H. MM
Cpl Boyce F.	Pte Morris J.
Pte Reeve K.	

Sergeant Len Cox ('C' Company)

"The farm house we now occupied was some distance from the village and once again we lost wireless contact with HQ, so we never received the news that Bure was to be evacuated. It was only when the Company were on the move and clear of the built up area that miraculously, contact was made and we were told to make our way back on out own. We moved cautiously back into the village, which was now deserted and then out on the road back to Tellin. The surface was like a skating rink but finally about 0300 hours we reached the safety of our own lines."

Extract from: An Account of Ops 29th Armoured Brigade in the Ardennes

Information was received that the 53rd Welsh Division on the left were meeting with some success and 6th Airborne Division were ordered to take over one of their brigade sectors. It we therefore decided to withdraw from Bure and extend the frontage in the defensive rather than an offensive role. The withdrawal was carried out during the night, without incident, 23H taking up positions in the Tellin area and one company of 8th Rifle Brigade on Chapel Hill.

"Saturday 6th, the British had pulled back towards Tellin, with the Germans as far as 'Le Gendarmerie' near the burial ground. The village was in 'no man's land'. I returned to the Presbytery which was in ruins. I went as far as the end of 'Tiran Rue' and then as far as 'Henrot' house, I could see the dead lying in the streets and in the houses, also burnt tanks. The shelling and the machine gun fire faded away and patrols from both armies operated around the village."

L'Abbe Hubert (Cure of Bure)

24.   THE AFTERMATH

War Diary 6th Jan

0200   HQ 5 Para Bde [Resteigne] reached and taken as quarters for rest of night.

Pierre Lardinois (Villager)

"The morning of 6th January was a lot quieter and my brother and I decided to go back to see what we can salvage from our belongings. On the way we stopped at Louise Jacquemin's house and came face to face with a British soldier, who assured us that there were no Germans in the area. He pointed to a nearby house in which he had spent the night in the cellar, with the Germans in the room above. We congratulated him on his lucky escape.

Leon Thungen's house [near where the 'Tiger' had operated] was a pile of smoking rubble and the cellar was full of debris. The family before they left had the presence of mind to throw all the valuables into the garden and now these could be recovered. Included in these souvenirs, were some photographs he had taken, recording the course of the war.

"From where we were, we could see Germans 100m away across the fields, where they held the 'Gendarmerie'. 200m in the opposite direction, from the edge of the wood, we heard a cry for help. Eugene Rondeaux went over and came back with a wounded British soldier, who had lain all night in the snow, unable to move. I am sure the Germans watched this incident, but they didn't interfere.

"Henrot's house was a shambles, with lots of evidence of the fighting that had taken place within those 4 walls. There was blood everywhere and corpses lay side by side. In another room, there was another body with the hand mutilated by someone removing a ring, and further along the street, another dead man had suffered the same treatment.[70]

"Arthur Rose was also about and as he passed the Gendarmerie, he was apprehended by the Germans and taken into custody. It was 7 days before they released him."

Charles Magnette (Villager)

[Taking refuge at the hotel Repos du Linçon, Grupont] "Then one day, we heard a lot of vehicles and from that moment, we did not see any Germans. They were gone! When we made our way back, we met outside the railway station, a fine officer, probably English. We stopped and he asked Dad to accompany him and show him the

---

[70] "Dixie" Dean: "Rings were often removed by a soldier's comrade for return to wives and families; and during fierce battles, there is little time for niceties."

way to Mormont. At that time, Omer Martin arrived and volunteered to accompany the officer. They were both found shot later in the woods.

"We arrived at the house and we crossed a British column which had installed 2 tanks on each side of the house. They had a fire on which they were warming their food. We were starving, but they did nothing. On entering the room, I had a funny feeling. Hanging in the middle of one of them, I at first thought there was a naked man. Then, I realized it was one of our pigs. It had been killed and had pieces removed."

Nestor Jabot (Villager)

[After fleeing to Tellin and deciding to return] "When we finally got back to Bure, we were affected since shells had fallen on the corner of our home. We went to sleep under a table at the college. There was then no longer fighting, but there were ruins everywhere, hanging electric poles, constant troop movements, and death everywhere. For example, between the presbytery and the boy's school, there would certainly be a death every 10m [most would probably be caused by Jim Leadsom]. Negative temperatures were ultimately a godsend for keeping the bodies until they could be buried."

Unbeknown to the 13th Battalion, the Germans had decided to pull back at the same time. Lieutenant-General Lauchert had decided after the heavy house-to-house fighting that he would give up Bure to save his remaining men's lives. Learning from prisoners, Lauchert found that his opponents were fresh British Airborne troops who had recently arrived via the sea from England. He realised that he could not possibly have the men and equipment to hold on for much longer. For the following days and weeks his division had to slowly retreat, fighting many more rearguard actions as the salient of the bulge was reduced.

The 13th Parachute Battalion on the other hand were afforded the luxury of being sent into reserve, where they could lick their wounds and recover from the traumas of Bure. The 12th Devonshire Regiment took over the position in the frontline from the 13th Para Bn and sent several patrols into Bure to ascertain the enemy in the vicinity.

Captain David Tibbs MC (RAMC)

"The next day a recce party found that the Germans had left and were told by the much relieved beleaguered villagers that they had left at the same time as ourselves the night before, On hearing that the Germans had gone I felt compelled to go back and ensure that there were no wounded men left lying in the surrounding area.

"I drove a Jeep and had Billy Roper with me. He was one of the Conscientious Objectors, a simple man but a deeply committed Christian. We motored up the hillside about quarter of a mile from the village where an number of casualties had occurred when suddenly Billy asked me to stop, with such intensity in his voice that I did so and asked "What's wrong?" and he replied "The Lord tells me we should turn back." Again there such intensity in his voice that I decided we had probably covered enough ground, and, anyway, I did not wish to scoff at his beliefs. I reversed the Jeep, to Billy's enormous relief, and motored home. That evening when the officers all met for a meal, Fred Tiramani, who had been assigned clearance of mines from the roads around Bure, said "Do you know, I found the most extraordinary thing today? I had followed the tracks of a Jeep in the snow and came to a spot where it had reversed and come back. Just 2 yards beyond here I found 2 stacked Teller mines that would have blown the Jeep to smithereens." Feeling very apprehensive I asked him to show me where that was on the map, and sure enough it was the exact spot where we had turned! When I told Billy he smiled at me without speaking!"

Report by Richard McMillan (War Illustrated War Correspondent)

"I watched them go into action in a wilderness of snow and ice resembling the Russian front at its worst. The Germans hung on at the cost of great bloodshed until they were forced back yard by yard by the superior fighting power and superhuman valor of the British. For a whole day and a whole night the British hurled themselves in waves against the fiercely defended fortress into which Bure had been converted.

"The fighting was grim, but it was hardly grimmer than the weather. The whole battlefield was like a cake of ice, with snow several inches deep and a frost which turned the normally gentle landscape of the Ardennes into a scene of iron. Against this background, fierce for human beings but fairy-like as the snow-clad trees and frosted hedges sparkled in the light of the gun flashes, the town of Bure stained the white night with a thunderous flame. The British attacked just before dawn, and were thrown back. They went in again, held a few houses, attacked again, and got to the other end of the village.

"There they were cut off. Then their comrades smashed through the snow and ice and the hail of death from the German self-propelled guns, tanks and spandaus to start the battle all over again. So it went on throughout the day. At one time it looked as if those deadly self-propelled guns, shoehorned into the ruins of the once-pleasant wooded village, would win the day. We took a heavy toll of the enemy, but our dead lay there, too many of them, sprawled across the roads or huddled gruesomely in ditches. Our tanks, too, had gone to ground. Flames from their idle hulks added to the fury of the inferno which blotched the silvery hills and valleys of a Christmas-card scene. Fresh troops are now forging forward to consolidate the ground gained and drive the enemy back towards Grupont.

"Two platoons which had been cut off at the eastern end of the village were relieved, but they, too, had casualties. The Germans had turned tanks at the closest range against the houses in which they sheltered. Their gallant resistance alone is described as an epic. But they knew the quality of their comrades, and knew that they were never forsaken. It was the spirit of Arnhem all over again, only this time with the certainty of victory for us. A U.S. officer who came up from the scene of that bloody shambles exclaimed: "You couldn't believe it unless you had seen it, that human beings could fight like these British boys. They are tigers!"

Lieutenant Harry Pollak (Intelligence Officer)

"The futility of war could not be better illustrated than by recalling that during the third night, we were ordered to withdraw at exactly the same time as the Germans were ordered to do likewise. Our chaplain went with some stretcher bearers and with a few lorries under cover of the red cross flag to recover dead and wounded. There they met the chaplain of the Germans on exactly the same mission. They joined in a short prayer and then got on with the job."

Report by Victor Thompson (Herald War Correspondent)

"When they came out of the battle during the weekend they were bearded, ragged, exhausted. But today these men of the 6th Airborne Division are shaven and trim as they file into the little stone church in the ruined hamlet to say prayers for their dead comrades.

"There were many for whom to pray, because the battle of Bure, which these young Britons fought for 3 days and nights was the bloodiest hand to hand fighting that has happened in this campaign, with no quarter given or asked on either side."

On 7th Jan a patrol of the 12th Devons was fired upon as they approached the East end of Bure. They were pinned down for 9 hours in a very exposed position, one man was killed (L/Cpl Gilbey) and several others wounded. An enemy tank was reported as being in action in the village. Next, a second patrol was sent in to extract the first patrol in which they succeeded, but whilst still in Bure the second patrol learned of a wounded Captain in L'Alumnat and in need of urgent medical attention and so a detachment was sent to fetch him. This was the ill fated attempt, mentioned earlier, to collect Captain Milner (RA) that cost the Captain and 4 others their lives after the medics Jeep ran over a mine.[71]

Private G. Coward (12th Devonshire Regiment, 6th Airlanding)

"My memory in some instances is somewhat hazy, but in others very vivid, when for example, at Bure after the Germans had vacated, I passed by the body of a British soldier who looked like a large squashed frog in the snow covered road in his camouflaged smock."

Marie-José Pigeon (Villager)

"The battle came to an end when, at the door talking with an Englishman, a neighbour and Edmond, we saw a German behind a window of the house next door. I was watching the house for fear that the German, seeing us talk with an Englishman, might shoot us. At one point, the German came out on the road. The Englishman saw him and immediately fired at him, killing him. Whether or not a German, it was terrible to see a man killed!"

Felix Despas (Villager)

"A confusing situation between the Germans and the British lasted until January 8th. Quite often some parts of the village changed. Each day, one would expect to find soldiers from one of the two camps. The village was taken and retaken several times. The cellars of the Château still provided the same security. Fortunately, the big buildings were not set on fire, but they did suffer heavy damage from the artillery.

"On the morning of January 8th, it was the most tranquil it had recently been. The Germans were gone and the British appeared to occupy the area. The crowd left the Château and spread out in the streets. Everyone returned to their homes with great apprehension, as many had the misfortune of having their property burned or destroyed.

"On the hill 'de Haurt', we knew that among the dead lying under the snow, there were also the 3 bodies of the Belgian SAS on the hills [South-West of Bure, near the 13th Para Bn assault start line]. There was still great concern that there were mines and we had a morbid fear of these hideous traps. Two intrepid volunteers went out to honour the brave: Auguste and Joseph Hamaide Brilot went to look for the SAS men.

---

[71] This was the Artillery Captain who Felix Despas found wounded under a sheet on 4th Jan and took to the L'Alumnat.

In some places the snow had reached about 50cm deep. They used a small saddle horse with a sleigh and ventured by the pastures and fields, avoiding the paths that we suspected contained mines. With a thousand precautions, they finally placed the bodies on the sled and came back on the tracks they had left.

"Another calamity we faced was that one could see that the contours of the village were entirely mined. Many anti-tank mines and other mines had been laid by the Germans and it was not until the snow melted that we could proceed with the removal of these deadly devices."

Fortunat Zune (Villager)

"After the battle, civilians such as Edward Caussin and Auguste Hamaide collected the bodies and they loaded them on a truck and took them down to the Château.

"In the living room of our house there was still a dead German officer extended, with his head on a pillow. He remained there some time. We didn't dare have a fire because of the risk of having bad smells. Then came Edward Caussin. As the German body was trapped, he tied a rope to the feet and dragged it through the hallway. The corpse was then taken out into the street and laid on the path in front of the large house of Louviaux. But during the day the snow melted from the roofs and the water surrounded the body. Then at night it froze hard and the water turned into ice quickly to form a large ice cube, enclosing the German. But the next day the Germans wanted the body back, they were forced to use a pick to loosen all of ice and then lift up the huge ice block to take it.

"Of course, the battle was over, with other children, we would play left and right in amongst the objects that the battle had left the behind. There were large craters created by the larger artillery shells. Near a haystack in the meadow behind our house, we found the towel that had contained the cakes we had left behind. Of course, they were gone. It is likely that the Germans ate our cakes whilst taking on the English."

Celestine Limet (Villager)

"Finally we returned to our homes and I set about repairing the barn, but the hammering upset my goat, still terrified from the shelling. I cleared the rubble from the pavement, behind which the British machine gunners had been killed. Their bodies had already been removed for burial, but under the snow, I found a pair of boots – with the feet of one of the dead men still inside! I handed these over to Pierre Lardinois, a Red Cross official, who was responsible for burying the dead in our own little cemetery, which was dug near L'Alumnat.

"My brother Camille was one of those who helped collect the bodies of the men killed. Near the homes of Marie Hautot and Auguste Noel [since demolished because of the damage] on the hillside, they found a lot of bodies. In one particular spot were the frozen corpses of 17 'Tommies', lying one behind each other in a line. They must have been killed by a single burst from a machine gun located behind the wall of the Chapel Notre-Dame de Salette."

Guy Jacquemin (Villager)

"The scene was one of destroyed and burned houses. Of dead animals and especially of the soldiers killed and maimed. A leg here, an arm there... Maurice, who had remained with my grandmother across from the Bodart's house, told us the story of Lucien Bodart, he was wounded trying to extinguish the farm on fire. Lucien was taken in a Jeep which hit a mine.

"We were finally released. We ran around the Allied soldiers. The following day, we went around the village. Everywhere was the same. Near the chapel of La Salette, there were 17 British soldiers killed. The sights were the same again on the countryside. There were killed men, weapons and ammunition everywhere. Sometimes we gathered the weapons and played soldiers. There were accidents. Some had fingers torn off by detonators or a hand pierced by a bullet. Luckily, there were no deaths. Many mines were laid around and much worse happened. Marcel Petit was mortally wounded by an explosive device. I can still see his mutilated body when he was back in the village."

Fortunat Zune (Villager)

"We also found the bodies of 17 English killed behind a hedge not far from the home of the Brilot family. [72] In the hedges, there were lots of things. Sometimes with surprises, like the time where we found a bag and pulling it to us we found an arm was still attached. We also came upon bags of various types of ammunition. But we did not touch the grenades. However, having found a little box that didn't look like a grenade. We had fun unscrewing the cap and throwing it. Nothing happened. We then went to pick it up and out of holes a liquid was coming out. It started to smoke at the snow melted. You could see the grass below was beginning to darken. Dad saw us and was angry, calling us dirty kids. He ran and gave the box a big kick. The liquid went on his shoe and he had to be removed quickly because it started to burn. It was phosphorus."

Lieutenant Ellis "Dixie" Dean (MMG Platoon)

"Before we left, the Battalion was now in reserve, badly under strength, having lost the equivalent of one and a half Rifle Companies during the Bure fighting. Several changes in command were made, Captain Desmond "Dizzy" Gethin was now OC 'B' Company, with Maurice Seal recalled from Brigade to be his second-in-command and "Baggy" Allen reverted to his old post as Admin Captain.

"Later that morning there was a minor scare, the convoy leader took the road back to Bure by mistake, but nobody followed and eventually we arrived at Wesselville. While the Battalion rested, Padre Foy returned to the village and all our dead received a Christian burial.

"On the 8th January we relieved the 9th Battalion in Humain where several [enemy] heavy tanks had been destroyed in the village by air strikes. The nights were interrupted by "Buzz" bombs flying overhead en-route for Antwerp.

"One afternoon, we held our own winter sports down a winding lane running from a hill behind the village and finishing at a knocked out Panther tank. Home made sleighs and toboggans were used and not many competitors finished the course without at least one spill."

---

[72] Those 17 frozen bodies of 'B' Company and the Scout Platoon had been left out for a week as no-one could dare venture out into the open.

Above: The graves of the fallen in the field near L'Alumnat (right of photo). The bodies were exhumed and taken to Hotton Cemetery on 21st June 1947.

Below: Location of the field today © Google Map Data and 'Ghost' picture (over).

Rue de Belvaux

Lance Corporal David "Robbie" Robinson (Anti-Tank 'C' Company)

"After Bure we rested in a village and some of 'C' Company were billeted in a single house with a fair frontage and a lean-to on the side. We built a fire outside the front of the house and put iron bars over it. On these bars we put jerry cans of water to heat up so we could have a bath in the lean-to with a tub we'd found.

"The plan was to each fill in turn a jerry can and when hot, top up the water left by the previous bather, have a bath and move on for the next man. This worked fairly well for a while, until O'Neil, being a bit lazy, saw a jerry can already full, claimed it and placed it on the fire. It turned out that this was not water; it was a can of petrol which had been used to start the fire. As it began to swell we realised what had happened and scattered. It exploded and shot flaming petrol all over the front of the house and a sergeant who was in the bath in the open lean-to, had to dive under the water. The petrol was well dispersed out and didn't cause much damage, after all the whole place was under at least a foot of snow!"

Extract from: The Story of the 23rd Hussars 1940-1946

On the 9th ['A' Squadron] were ordered to support the advance of the 12th Devons through Bure to Grupont. The enemy had withdrawn completely by now, leaving an incredible ruin of a place and many dead. Owing to the absence of further opposition, the Squadron moved no further than Bure and returned to Tellin that night. The Devons went on, crossed the river at Grupont and advanced behind the Germans.

Jean-Marie Decontie (Superior of L'Alumnat)

"At last we got deliverance from our incarceration. The Germans finally left the district and the British had re-entered the village. A British Captain asked for me, greeted me courteously and explained that he had a load of books to distribute to the refugees.

"And on that misty morning, a golden haze hovered over the village, and revealed a scene of dreadful desolation, and drew expressions of sympathy for the sufferings of the British soldiers."

'Then & Now'. Typical sights on Rue de Tellin after the 'Tiger' Tank encounters.[73]

---

[73]If you look closely on the 'Now' photograph, the changes in brick colour show where as much as the original wall structures were saved as possible.

Then & Now: Rue de Tellin towards the crossroads

L'Abbe Hubert (Cure of Bure)

"On Wednesday (10th) morning the British arrived in numbers, there was no fighting. The inhabitants of the village had lived for the last fortnight in the cellars, chiefly those of L'Alumnat, where there had been 2 births, Ginette Petit and Marie-Jeanne Rondeau.

"Of the 165 homes, 13 were burnt out, 4 completely destroyed, 42 badly damaged, 47 have considerable damage and only 45 were slightly damaged.

"Two civilians were killed – Lucien Bodart and Louis Laffineur. Many farm animals were killed and the village devastated.

"Later on January 11th Claude Devaux was blown up by a mine and killed."

Even long after the Allied armies had left, the mines continued to be a problem for the villagers, R. P. Charles was blown up by a mine on 4th February and had to have one of his legs amputated.

Plaque at College Alzon:

"IN THE COLLEGE CELLARS

600 INHABITANTS OF BURE

TOOK REFUGE

DURING VON RUNDSTEDT'S OFFENSIVE

DECEMBER 1944 – JANUARY 1945"

Captain David Tibbs MC (RAMC)

"From Bure, the Battalion followed the trail of the retreating Germans, plagued by the mines they had strewn thickly along the way. Every hour or two there was a heavy thump not far off and urgent cries of "Medics!" The RAMC distinguished themselves repeatedly, by going into minefields to pull out casualties. Several were killed or seriously maimed doing this. The mines were usually buried in snow and it was necessary to keep back troops eager to help, and if possible to get in an engineer with mine detectors to clear a way to the wounded man, But often the wait would be unacceptably long for this and then the trick was to tread in the footprints in the snow leading to the man who had been blown up, in the uncertain belief that if a mine were there it would have exploded when the imprint was first made. I have had to enter a minefield in this fashion and found it a very unnerving experience.

"However, my friend Captain Wagstaff, Medical Officer to the 7th Battalion displayed the greatest of courage when he came on a scene where a patrol had three of its men badly injured by 'Shue' mines (small but designed to blow off the foot). First one RAMC man and then another had gone in and each had detonated a mine under his feet. At this stage John Wagstaff came, and after ordering mine detectors to be sent for, instructed that no-one in any circumstances was to follow him until the detectors came. Then, carefully placing his feet in the foot prints of the others, reached the wounded, dressed their wounds, gave them morphine and placed his own coat over one man to provide some warmth. He then knelt behind a man who was still sitting upright to prevent him falling back, possibly onto another mine, and waited. The engineers came after an agonising wait and cleared a way to the group of injured men. Here they found three more active mines, one within 2 feet of John and just where the man he was supporting would have laid down. Truly remarkable courage, but sadly, not rewarded by any medal. It should have been!"

Lieutenant Ellis "Dixie" Dean (MMG Platoon)

"A large party of reinforcements [135 non-jumping, from 33 RHU on 12th Jan] had arrived and were posted to the rifle companies. Whilst we were in Humain and in reserve positions, Private Joseph Butler, a member of the Motor Transport Platoon was killed on 16th January when his 3-Ton vehicle ran over a mine that was buried under the snow. On the 17th, the Battalion settled in Wellin and now we were clear of the 'war zone'. None of the houses were damaged and the Mortars and MMG's occupied the Town Hall, with Battalion HQ and the Officers billeted in a large estaminet across the road. Transport ran into Dinant to the bars and cinema.

"I managed a night in Brussels. There were several little matters requiring attention at various locations in the area. The subalterns drew lots for the privilege and I was the winner. I can remember an endless succession of dancing girls and sultry songstresses and one large beer hall with a band, before tumbling into bed in the early hours.

"The next morning I bought a pair of brown 'Don R' type boots. They were very popular. It was dark when we arrived back in Wellin. The estaminet housing HQ was in darkness and the door closed, as was the platoon billet in the Town Hall. My OC had occupied a billet off the main square, I went across and knocked on the door, and as soon as Madame opened it "Une moment Monsieur" and she bustled back to her kitchen and reappeared with a message scribbled in pencil on part of a cigarette packet – "We have gone to Holland. Follow on. Good luck."

"It was a great disappointment and cause of regret to us all, that the Colonel's courageous and inspiring leadership of the Battalion during the battle of Bure was not recognised and rewarded as it so richly deserved to be. No other battalion of 6th Airborne throughout its existence fought such a prolonged battle against German Panzers, or suffered such heavy causalities – 189 killed, wounded and missing."

The Battle of Bure was an extremely costly 3 days for the 13th (Lancashire) Parachute Battalion: They suffered 65 Killed, 99 wounded and 25 taken prisoner (Total: 189), in short, a third of their strength was taken away. But the full extent of the battle resulted in over 500 casualties in total. The German 2nd Panzer Division, 2nd Fife & Forfar, 23rd Hussars, 8th Rifle Brigade, 12th Para Bn, 2nd Ox & Bucks, 12th Devons, 61st Reccie Regt, 6th Field Regiment (RA), the Belgian SAS, and the people of Bure all paid the price too.

TIGERS?

In more recent times the question has been raised that there could not have been any Tiger activity in Bure. Evidence shows that the Panzer Lehr Division operating had no Tiger tanks at this time and neither did the 2nd Panzer Division who took over the Bure area around the New Year. Tactically Bure was an important rearguard defensive position, from which the withdrawal of the battered 2nd Panzer Division could be covered. Could Tiger tanks have been loaned or assigned to this unit to aid the defence and withdrawal?

Many of the veterans involved in the action state there definitely was a 'Tiger', maybe even two. Officer reports and also the accounts of men from the armoured units of the 29th Armoured Brigade, including the Forward Observation Officers, who you must agree would and should recognise the difference between German armoured vehicles, claim to have seen 'Tiger' activity. Civilian eye-witnesses mention tanks camouflaged with branches and tanks hidden between buildings that could easily be mistaken from distance, especially as the Panther, the King Tiger and Tiger tank have similar profiles, although the Panther is smaller.

Harsh weather conditions consisting of snow showers, glare from the snow, darkness, smoke and dust from burning buildings, constant artillery and mortar fire, not to mention the numerous other stresses of the intense close combat, would all add to the confusion.

Owing to all these factors I myself, am certainly unsure.

Panther Tank

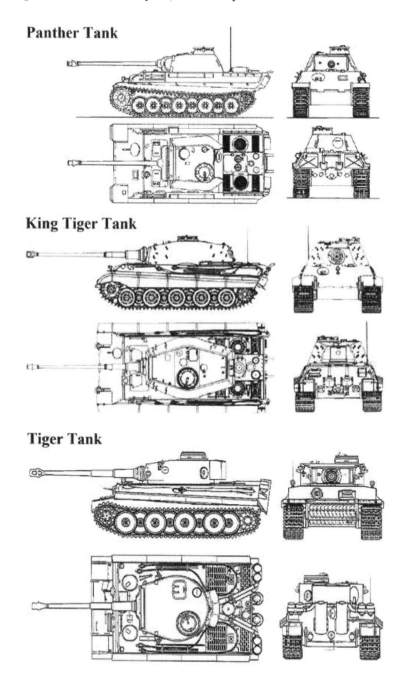

King Tiger Tank

Tiger Tank

ROLL OF HONOUR – BATTLE OF BURE

Sgt	CHADWICK Frank	25	03/01/1945	3655324	Hotton 10-A-5
LCpl	CHARLES Albert F.	22	03/01/1945	6857065	Hotton 5-C-10
LCpl	CLARK Frank	?	03/01/1945	7890546	Hotton 6-D-3
Pte	CLOUGH James	20	03/01/1945	14407304	Hotton 6-D-6
Pte	DAVIS Thomas B.	21	03/01/1945	3663303	Hotton 7-D-3
Pte	EVANS Trevor	28	03/01/1945	14654443	Hotton 8-D-3
Pte	FISHER Leslie T.	23	03/01/1945	5569604	Hotton 7-D-2
Pte	FITTON Alec	19	03/01/1945	1151545	Hotton 7-F-9
Pte	FORTEY Howard J.	?	03/01/1945	4744674	Hotton 7-F-7
Maj	GRANTHAM George K.	26	03/01/1945	99936	Hotton 7-F-6
Sgt	GREENDALE William	33	03/01/1945	791302	Hotton 8-D-12
Pte	HAGGERTY John	24	03/01/1945	3134162	Hotton 7-D-9
Pte	HAIGH Stanley	19	03/01/1945	1151527	Hotton 6-F-5
Pte	HALL William E.	26	03/01/1945	4613176	Hotton 6-F-6
Sgt	HOLLIS Richard E.	20	03/01/1945	14218052	Hotton 10-A-2
Pte	HOLT Thomas	22	03/01/1945	3973592	Hotton 6-D-12
Cpl	JOHNSON Leslie	26	03/01/1945	1514224	Hotton 8-D-6
Pte	JONES Ernest T.	21	03/01/1945	3663311	Hotton 5-F-4
Cpl	JONES Reginald W.	28	03/01/1945	3663368	Hotton 10-A-6
Pte	KENNY Dennis	21	03/01/1945	3663281	Hotton 7-B-1
Pte	KING Vincent P.	19	03/01/1945	14441994	Hotton 8-D-1
Lieut	LAGERGREN Alfred	31	03/01/1945	273624	Hotton 6-D-8
Sgt	McGRATH Arthur H.	28	03/01/1945	14213352	Hotton 7-D-6

Pte	MORRIS Leonard	19	03/01/1945	1151740	Hotton 7-F-11
Pte	MURRAY William C.	25	03/01/1945	3388677	NKG Groesbeek Memorial
Pte	NICHOLL Derek	20	03/01/1945	14719547	Hotton 7-F-3
Pte	O'CONNELL James	27	03/01/1945	1553763	Hotton 7-D-11
Pte	ORME Ronald S.	19	03/01/1945	14726132	Hotton 6-D-5
Pte	PELLING Walter	23	03/01/1945	5499757	Hotton 7-F-2
Pte	REGAN Daniel	19	03/01/1945	14746006	Hotton 6-D-2
LCpl	ROBINSON William	32	03/01/1945	4388132	Hotton 6-D-11
LSgt	SHALES Douglas R.	25	03/01/1945	3655820	Hotton 7-D-12
Pte	SHINGLER Alfred	19	03/01/1945	14713514	Hotton 6-D-7
LCpl	SIMPSON John	22	03/01/1945	7939033	Hotton 5-F-11
Pte	SNELHAM Anslem	23	03/01/1945	14617094	Hotton 7-F-4
Pte	STREETER Percy A.L.	20	03/01/1945	14753184	Hotton 7-D-10
Pte	SUMRAY Hyam	27	03/01/1945	1553884	Hotton 7-D-7
Pte	WADDELL Alexander	19	03/01/1945	14417294	Hotton 5-F-1
Pte	WESTON Edward G.	23	03/01/1945	5260229	Hotton 10-A-3
Pte	WHITE Edward	23	03/01/1945	892678	Hotton 7-B-5
Lieut	WINSER Timothy A.	?	03/01/1945	88411	Hotton 6-D-10
Pte	ASPINALL Joseph	20	04/01/1945	14632790	Hotton 6-D-9
Pte	BELLIS Jesse	24	04/01/1945	3654514	Hotton 10-A-4
Pte	FORD Ronald S.	25	04/01/1945	3135986	Hotton 12-B-11
Pte	HARDY David	22	04/01/1945	14215879	Hotton 6-F-3
Pte	HERMAN Mark P.	19	04/01/1945	14709592	Hotton 10-A-7
Pte	KING Ronald A.	19	04/01/1945	14730162	Hotton 7-F-5

Pte	McANDREW John	26	04/01/1945	5049625	Leopoldsburg 6-E-1
Cpl	McPHERSON George C.V.	35	04/01/1945	1719150	Hotton 7-D-4
Pte	MEYER Thomas McDonald	21	04/01/1945	910777	Hotton 8-D-2
Pte	MORRIS John	21	04/01/1945	14244695	Hotton 8-D-4
WOII	MOSS Percival J.	29	04/01/1945	3383809	Leopoldsburg 6-E-4
Pte	PEARCE Leslie	19	04/01/1945	14431727	Hotton 10-A-8
Pte	POVEY Dennis R.	19	04/01/1945	14723221	Hotton 8-D-7
Cpl	RYAN William	30	04/01/1945	3769872	Hotton 12-B-10
Pte	SCOTT Norman	18	04/01/1945	14732802	Hotton 10-A-4
Pte	SEARS William J.	29	04/01/1945	2613642	Hotton 7-F-1
Pte	TAYLOR Harry	25	04/01/1945	13041707	Hotton 7-F-12
Cpl	WOODS Peter J.	29	04/01/1945	3709705	Hotton 8-D-8
Pte	WOTTON Peter	19	04/01/1945	14701706	Hotton 7-D-8
Pte	BEACH Lawrence F.	18	05/01/1945	14636189	Hotton 12-B-12
Pte	HAYWOOD Vincent	26	05/01/1945	3192784	Hotton 6-D-4
Pte	LOVELL Roger	21	05/01/1945	7948097	Hotton 3-D-8
Pte	SARGEANT William A.	21	05/01/1945	14336476	Hotton 3-D-7
Pte	HUGHES Harold	28	07/01/1945	3769877	Brussels Town Cem X27-37
Pte	BUTLER Joseph W.	28	16/01/1945	3657494	Hotton 5-F-2

The 13th (Lancashire) Parachute Battalion 'Battle of Bure' memorial has now been moved from the original burial ground to the church in the centre of the village.

It wrongly states that 61 Officers and men gave their lives, but this figure only accounts for the 13th Battalion men who were buried in the field originally and does not include 4 others who paid the ultimate price at Bure. Three of those died of wounds (CSM Percival Moss, Private John McAndrew and Private Harold Hughes); the last outstanding casualty has no known grave, Private William Murray, was last seen on 3rd January.

The 66th and final 13 Para casualty of the Ardennes Campaign was Private Joseph Butler, killed as he drove over a mine (16th Jan).

"When I gave him the news, I asked how old he was. "Sixteen" was his reply. I could only express admiration for his discipline and maturity. I would not have wanted to go through the experience of Bure as a 16 year old."

Lieutenant "Dixie" Dean

24.   HOLLAND

Pte Ray "Geordie" Walker (101ˢᵗ British General Hospital, wounded in Bure)

"Everyday was a new experience. I learned that the Heverlee Hospital was originally a convent and had been converted to a 2,500 bed Military hospital.[74] On Sunday afternoons local residents were permitted to visit the wounded to cheer us up. My Canadian friend and I were adopted by a girl called Annie and her sister who lived in Leuven and the day arrived when we were able to call on Annie and her family. They made us most welcome and we overstayed our leave. Annie escorted us back along darkened streets that were not patrolled by the Military police. We entered a back door and through the nuns private quarters. We removed our boots and a nun escorted us back to our beds avoiding the nurses on night duty. The following morning our room-mates were eager to learn of our nocturnal adventures.

"A new admission from Antwerp arrived; this soldier had been in the audience of the Garrison Theatre in Antwerp when it was hit by a V2 Rocket. The explosion killed and wounded several hundred people and his face was pockmarked with shards of glass. We gave him the nickname "Doodlebug".

"In the graveyard were graves of 2 posthumous holders of the Victoria Cross, Flying Officer D.E. Garland and Observer Sergeant T. Gray. They had been shot down in 1940, after having successfully destroyed the bridges at Maastricht and delayed the German advance through the Low Countries."

---

[74] The 101st British General Hospital was situated in Heverlee's "Heilig Hart" Girls School (above).

After the savaging they received at Bure the 13th Battalion was once again busy in the process of being reinforced by the Reserve Company back in England and also from the Army pool.

Lieutenant Peter Downward (Weapons Training Officer 'R' Company)

"I travelled [from the UK to the continent] by another route with what was known as 'R' (Reserve) Company. It was bitterly cold and the last night before we embarked we had to sleep under canvas near the port [Tilbury]. We never seemed to be short of ingenious inventors and one of our number, Geoff Otway (left), produced a form of brazier made from an old petrol can pierced with holes and suspended from a length of cable. By whirling it round in a circle the contents would burn fiercely and give off good heat. The whirling had to be repeated every 15 minutes, so we took it in turns, which meant we didn't get much sleep and the tent was constantly full of smoke.

"We headed for the port of Ostend, which had recently been liberated by the British 21st Army Group. We landed around the 10th January and after a few hours we boarded a train for Namur via Brussels and Ghent. The Belgian train was absolutely packed with British troops as well as many civilians who were all very friendly, particularly the attractive girls who sat on soldier's knees.

"We disembarked at our destination to be met by a staff officer of HQ 5th Para Brigade who briefed us on the latest situation. We already knew that the Battalion had been in action, but we were shattered to hear some of the details. The 13th Battalion had taken a severe battering in a bloody battle in the village of Bure on the edge of the Eifel mountain range. As we learned later, among the killed were Major Bill Grantham, Lt Alf Lagergren and Lt Tim Winser, also CSM Moss and Sgt McGrath.

"The staff officer informed us that although the Germans were withdrawing from the 'bulge', the 6th Airborne Division was now heading northwards to the Belgian/Netherlands border."

Situation map, 29th January 1945

457

Lieutenant Dean returning from his short leave was now following the trail of the Battalion in an attempt to rejoin his MMG Platoon.

Lieutenant Ellis "Dixie" Dean (MMG Platoon)

"I reported to the 'Town Major' in Dinant and he arranged billets tor the night and next morning he pointed us in the right direction for Holland. Within the hour we had picked up the 'Pegasus' signs marking the Divisional axis, and all we had to do was to follow these and before nightfall re-joined the Battalion in the Dutch village of Heldon.

"Holland was not as welcoming as Belgium had been; the Dutch had suffered far greater than their Belgian neighbours. The winter weather also seemed more severe, no sheltered valleys, only vast open stretches of frozen, snow covered farmland. I attended an 'O' Group and the Colonel informed us that we were shortly to move to Kessel and occupy a defensive position. The small town was on the banks of the River Maas, on the far side of which (100 yards away) was in enemy hands. The river was in flood, with water overflowing the tow-path and lapping at the walls of the riverside buildings. My task, with the MG's would be to bring defensive fire down along the stretch of the river.

"I informed the Colonel that the only way in which the Platoon could do this was from an indirect fire position and indicated on the map what I considered a suitable site for the guns. Although this area was part of the 3rd Brigades responsibility, I was given the "go ahead".

"Next day I was looking forward to meeting the 8th Battalions Commander, the best known officer in the Division, Alistair Pearson. I was to be disappointed, Major George Hewittson was in temporary command and I barely had time to explain the reason of my visit, when in walked Brigadier James Hill. Major Hewittson told me to discuss my planned locations with his Intelligence Officer. Whist doing so I couldn't help overhearing the two commanders discussing the employment of MMG Platoons and in particularly the Brigadier's statement to the effect that, "they should really be located back from the river in an indirect fire position, but we don't have dial sights." Minutes later he came across and I introduced myself. Keeping a straight a face as possible, I explained my mission and he wanted to know how we could perform such a task. I had to tell him how we had acquired the sights in Normandy.

"Once dug in, we fired a demonstration shoot into the middle of the river in front of 'C' Company. The river was flat calm and the strike of the bullets clearly visible. As a result of this success, we now established an OP with 'A' Company in Kesselijk, connected to the gun lines by telephone, and began engaging targets on the far side of the river. Ammunition was being stockpiled for the main offensive battles to come and we were rationed to two belts (500 rounds) per gun daily. Perhaps the target didn't always warrant the amount of ammunition expended, but it helped to keep us happy and for once we were able to put our training into practice on a regular basis."

War Diary 30th Jan

Uneventful day and night. Maj McLoughlin assumes command of 'C' Coy vice Maj AR Clark admitted to hospital.

Lance Corporal David "Robbie" Robinson (Anti-Tank 'C' Company)

"Major Clark had begun to suffer blindness as a result of being blown through the window at Bure and had to be evacuated. What could I say about Major Clark? He was a real gentleman and never ordered anyone to do what he wanted; he would just ask you in such a way that you felt that you had to do them. After the war he turned to religion and he travelled to Pakistan, returning to become the Padre of Parkhurst Prison. He then moved to Windsor Castle and became Supernumerary Military Knight. His wife, Violet, once told me that he had so many dress uniforms and robes that she could not get her clothes in their wardrobes."

Major Jack Watson ('A' Company)

"Whilst we kept our part of the line on the River Maas there wasn't any real attacks of sorts, so I spent most of my time writing letters to the families of the men I had lost from my Company in Bure."

Lieutenant Peter Downward (Weapons Training Officer 'R' Company)

"Major Roy Leyland met us and ticked us off for taking so long to catch up with the main body. We had been constantly on the move and without sleep for 36 hours. We quickly moved our kit from the 3-tonners and climbed aboard our respective battalion vehicles. To my horror, I suddenly realised that our truck had recently been used as an emergency ambulance as was apparent by the streaks of dried blood on the floor, and the presence of 4 rolled-up stretchers. We then questioned our 13th Battalion soldiers who had come with the trucks to pick us up, as to who had been killed? Who was wounded? Had anyone been taken prisoner? And a host of other queries relating to the battle in Bure.

"We already knew that 'B' Company under Bill Grantham had taken the worst pounding, and in addition to the 30 plus killed, many more had been wounded. One of these was Arthur Prestt who had joined the Battalion at the same time as myself and I was relieved to know that his wounds were not life threatening.

"Roy Leyland briefed us on the layout of the positions and I was detailed to report to 'B' Company and new Company Commander, Major "Dizzy" Gethin, I took over No.6 Platoon. I found Company HQ in a house over the village bakery and the Dutch family continued to produce a daily quota of bread for the local residents.

"Battalion HQ was situated in quite a prestigious looking house, still occupied by its Dutch owners. I was given about 20 minutes to fit myself into my Platoon and take over the reigns from Sgt O'Brien (below), a little man, but made up for his lack of stature by his strong control of those under his command. I was 20; he was about 28, and an old regular.[75]

"My Platoon HQ was in what was normally a pub, right on the main crossroads. It had suffered a lot of damage in the last few days from mortaring, but at least my men were under cover, except at dark when we manned the slit trenches around the orchard and gardens. Sgt O'Brien explained the arcs of fire, and the general routine of the defence, particularly our counter-attack role if we had to go to the aid of 'A' and 'C' Companies forward of us. My bunk was under the bar counter.

---

[75] Sgt Ernest O'Brien had started the war in Sept 1939 as a Lancashire Fusilier and was evacuated from Dunkirk; he later transferred to the 2nd/4th South Lancs and volunteered for parachuting. He was stick commander of a/c 307 on D-Day.

"The first evening was bitterly cold and on Sgt O'Brien's advice, I rotated the sentries around our defensive position every hour. The sentries were deployed in pairs 30 yards apart and connected by a chord, which acted as a silent alerting system by giving a tug to the chap on the other end. One of the pair would have a second cord tied to his other wrist and this was connected to an NCO on watch in the bakery building. I was tense that night and patrolled around the platoon positions, being challenged and trying to remember the passwords."

Lieutenant Harry Pollak (Intelligence Officer)

"It was a bit like trench warfare. The Germans occupied positions on the opposite river bank. The river at that point was not a 100 yards wide. We had to cross the river by night in dinghies, hide them, do our job and then return to these dinghies with the help of certain navigational aids."

Lieutenant Ellis "Dixie" Dean (MMG Platoon, in 8th Battalion positions)

"It was a bit of a squeeze, with 30 odd men in one house. We were completely self-contained and rations were delivered nightly, by Fred Tiramani himself and one of my regular soldiers, Fred Pengelly, offered his services as cook.

"One night the telephone rang and I heard the river bank OP reporting a small boat approaching. For several tense minutes I listened to the running commentary as the craft approached. It was an anti-climax though, it was a patrol from a neighbouring unit that had been caught in a strong current and had been swept downstream."

Sergeant Len Cox ('C' Company)

"It was all rather eerie on the Maas, made more so by the heavy blanket of snow which covered everything. The river had flooded over the tow path and at night we kept a continual watch on the river from houses alongside the water. On the German side, the land was featureless and the only building was the boathouse at the ferry crossing site. The ground rose gradually for 300 to 400 yards to a low wooded ridge where the defences were sited.

"I went over with a patrol hoping to nab a prisoner for identification purposes. It was quite a job holding the canvas assault boat steady against the current as we

climbed in. In mid stream the current was even stronger, but we made land, more or less where we meant to. There was a problem caused by the river being at flood levels the German barbed wire was now under the water and the boat was caught on it. We had to get out and lift the boat over the wire, the water was freezing.

"You felt very exposed crossing the wide expanse of snow, even when wearing white camouflage suits (left, © IWM B13676). All was quiet as we slowly moved up towards the ridge; at least we had avoided any enemy patrols oil the river bank. We reached the place where we expected to find "Jerry" but the positions were deserted, intelligence must have been faulty. On the way back to the boat we came under heavy machine gun fire but managed to get back to our side of the river without anyone being hit."

Lance Corporal David "Robbie" Robinson (Anti-Tank 'C' Company)

"One patrol I went on, with a squad of men, rode across the river but when across I was left to look after the boat whilst the rest went off for a look around; a very scary period. Whilst alone, I imagined all kinds of shadows and all kinds of noises so that they looked and sounded like Germans were completely surrounding me. 2 hours of this, of nerves on edge, was really scary."

Lieutenant Peter Downward ('B' Company)

"The day after I arrived, I went forward to the forward observation post in 'A' Company's position, there were frequent bursts of the very rapid fire of the MG42 and the much slower rate of fire from our Bren guns. After a crawl behind a low wall and a quick dash across a gap open to the enemy's view, I made it into the barn to find members of the Scout Platoon [Snipers] taking turns in manning the odd slots in the roof. A scoreboard at the bottom of the ladder showed the number of 'kills' and 'probable's'. Sgt Birkhead gave me a panoramic brief on the area in front.

"I could see some vehicle movement about 3 miles back, but could not be certain that it was enemy or civilians. I found it hard to believe that a state of war existed in this area, with cows in the fields, the odd windmill turning, smoke from chimneys and the very occasional appearance of Dutch civilians.

"A German mortar attack had killed a civilian almost outside my 'pub', and I suddenly noticed two small children playing around in the garden outside the bakery. I dashed over to them, gathered them up one under each arm and carried them down to the cellar. As I came up, I heard another series of explosions and was met by a distraught mother looking for her children. I was able to allay her fears, and was to be reminded of this incident many years later in a moving reunion."

Lieutenant Ellis "Dixie" Dean (MMG Platoon)

"One day "Claude" Milman showed me a letter from the War Office department dealing with men missing in action. They were seeking information on the 9 men of my stick that had not made the RV on D-Day. They had not been notified as POW and I now presumed that they were dead.

"On another occasion [at the Colonels daily briefing], I was informed that when the rations had been delivered that night, Private Morton, with all his kit, was to be sent back. The reason being he was under age. I was greatly surprised by this, because of all the young reinforcements after Normandy; he was easily the most impressive physically. A big strong Ulster lad, he revelled in any opportunity to demonstrate his strength. When I gave him the news, I asked how old he was. "Sixteen" was his reply. I could only express admiration for his discipline and maturity. I would not have wanted to go through the experience of Bure as a 16 year old."

Lieutenant Peter Downward ('B' Company)

"One night Major "Dizzy" Gethin did a round of the Company positions to see that sentries were alert. He came to one of my sections, was correctly challenged and then ordered the second sentry to alert Platoon HQ through the pull cord. Nothing happened, whereupon "Dizzy" took hold of the cord and gave it a tremendous yank to alert the NCO inside the 'pub'. There was a crash and a yell from inside and there was the NCO lying on his back clutching at his neck. He had been sitting with his feet up on the table, but in order to leave his hands free to read a book; he had placed the loop of the cord around his neck.

"In many ways we were more at risk from our own troops in the dark than from the enemy. One evening a challenge for some reason went wrong, a shot rang out followed by a yell and a string of oaths in English and then a voice from the dark calmly apologised, "Sorry mate, I thought you was a Jerry!" The response was equally polite, "That's Ok Charlie. You've given me a Blighty!" The recipient had taken a flesh wound through the buttock. I suspect that David Tibbs our Medical Officer, stitched him up and put him back with his platoon.

"David Tibbs was a handsome young doctor who had been one of the very first to land in Normandy. He was badged as Royal Army Medical Corps and it was soon apparent to us all that we had an excellent 'medic' looking after us all. I soon heard from rank and file that he was not only a very professional medic, but also a fearless personality with little regard for his own safety. He was also a good rugger player and more than once his medical skills were called on to cope with minor casualties on the rugger field."

Lieutenant Ellis "Dixie" Dean (MMG Platoon)

"Between Kessel and Waije, there was another small hamlet on the river bank called Kesselijk, 'A' Company moved in, and the following day at briefing, Jack Watson reported that across the river from his position, the Boche was moving about freely in the daytime. His Bren guns were not much use at that range, but there were some tempting targets. Each morning at 'stand to', one of my NCO's with an escort, took up position in Kesselijk, where he had a clear view across the Maas and acted as a fire controller. When a suitable target presented itself, he phoned a map reference to Platoon HQ, we converted this information into a range, angle of sight and deflection left or right of the zero line. Once all this had been set on the sight and it re-zeroed, the order to fire was given.

"Our first target was the best one, 'A' Company had reported the daily queue for the midday meal, so we waited for this to form, before engaging it, causing complete havoc. Twice the Boche came looking for us. On the first occasion, a fighting patrol infiltrated 'A' Company and destroyed the house which they imagined that the guns were firing from.

"One morning I was approached by Private "Rommel" Rodden who announced "Sir, your bath is ready." He had used the farms wash house copper to boil water and filled a big oak tub. The sergeants were next in the pecking order and over the next 3 days the entire Platoon enjoyed a hot bath."

Private Norman Mountney (MMG Platoon)

"We completed our training on the Isle of Wight in late December and were told we would be posted to the 1st Battalion and although I had no preference which Battalion I joined, coming so soon after Arnhem, we all thought it a great honour. Only days later a change of orders and a dozen or so of us were on our way to join the 13th. Arriving at Larkhill we were surprised to find the barracks almost deserted. We were offered the choice of training either as 3" Mortar men or Vickers machine gunners, Albert Steeper [of Scawby, Lincolnshire] and I chose the latter and training began under one of the NCO's, Sergeant Tommy Lathom [wounded in Normandy].

"After only a few weeks in the 13th I went home on 7 days leave but I had only been there 2 days, when the village policeman, who had pushed his bike through 3 miles of deep snow, delivered a telegram recalling me to Larkhill. We were flown out to Brussels and on to a transit camp, where we spent quite a period of time waiting for instructions. Eventually we boarded some trucks and were told at the last minute that we were off to Holland.

"It was bitterly cold and the fields were all deep in snow. For the last part of the journey we travelled without lights, with the final few miles on foot to join the Battalion.

"The next day we joined the Machine Gunners in their own little farm house and realised from the start I was now part of a well trained team, who were very positive about everything they did and I never regretted my decision to be a Vickers gunner. We were kept busy maintaining the weapon pits, manning the guns and 'stand to', night and morning. I once went with one of the NCO's before daylight to a farm building overlooking the river. In one of the out buildings, we removed some tiles in the roof and could now observe the enemy positions on the far bank of the Maas. There was a telephone line back to the gun site, through which we passed the information back to the guns whenever a target appeared. Later we were joined by a sniper who also found a target while we were there."

War Diary 1st Feb

2230   House 807986 received a direct hit by SP. Two men were buried and killed.

CSM "Taffy" Lawley ('C' Company)

"The Battalion suffered mysterious casualties here; a building got mysteriously blown up and although every brick was moved neither the bodies nor the cause of the explosion was discovered."[76]

9 Bermudans joined the 13th as part of 33 RHU from the Bermudan Volunteer Force. "Dixie" Dean many years after the war found the nominal roll of these West Indians, they are: J.S. Alves, W.F. Foreman, F.G.D. Hughes, G.H. Kemp, Pte Maine, A.A. Mederios, Pte Ray, D. Martin, A.E. Smith and E. Spencer. Sadly they had all passed on. Most of these in particular Mederios [who became the Battalion barber] stayed with the 13th until after the war.

On 8th Feb (situation, left) the

---

[76] The casualties were Private's Stanley Powell and Charles Greenough attached from The Queens Royal Regiment, they were 2 of the 135 reinforcements that joined the 13th Battalion on the 12th Jan from 33 Rear Holding Unit. Powell's body must have been recovered sometime later as he is buried in Venray Cemetery. Both men joined up at the same time.

Germans replaced the 606 zbV Division on the opposite bank to the 6th Airborne Division with the newly formed 8th Fallschirmjäger Division and owing to lack of intelligence about this unit; various patrols were sent to capture prisoners to gain vital information.

Lt Peter Downward ('B' Company)

"I was warned by "Dizzy" Gethin that I was to take a fighting patrol across the river with the intention of capturing a prisoner. I was to select 12 men from my Platoon and had 36 hours to rehearse our boat drills and plan for capturing a Jerry, preferably an officer! Blimey! I knew there would be no volunteers, so I detailed the unfortunate individuals with the help of Sgt O'Brien. My rehearsals were supervised by Major Roy Leyland [Battalion 2i/c] who eventually acted as the 'German prisoner'. We also rehearsed the evacuation of any casualties as it was the paramount rule that no-one would be left behind.

"The next day [10th Feb] I surveyed the enemy bank, noting landmarks and possible areas of cover if we came under fire. About an hour before we were due to embark; I had to attend a final briefing from Peter Luard and was told that as we were now carrying any radios, we would have a field telephone connected by 'Don 5' cable to the home bank. My soldiers checked their weapons, primed grenades and were reminded that if captured they would give only number, rank and name – nothing else!

"I did a quick check of my patrol members. To my horror, one chap was completely drunk and smelled of rum. I had to make a quick decision whether or not to take him. Either way, it was going to be unfair on the other soldiers, and if I handed him over, he would certainly face a court martial. I piled him into his assigned position in the other boat.

"I realised immediately that the current was carrying us further down the river than our frantic paddling could counter. The field telephone cable was snaking down stream and tending to swing my boat round. I called the home bank and told them I was going to let the cable go. Every so often a burst of tracer would be fired over our heads in order to keep us orientated to our proposed landing point. My boat got caught up in an underwater barbed wire entanglement and we were filling up with water. Suddenly all hell was let loose as the other boat about 50 yards away came under fire. I signalled by torch to the home bank to put up a red very light indicating 'Abort'. To cap everything, the sky was lit up by flares dropped by an RAF bombing raid near Venlo a few miles away. We landed in the 7th Battalions area and answered a challenge by whistling the first four bars of the Paratrooper's song."

60 lucky men received 48 hours leave to spend in Brussels, they went in two blocks of 30, the first on the 11th February and when they returned the second batch had their turn. Each party stayed at 63 Rue de la Loi (the Wallonia Delegation building today) and was under the command of one officer, who stayed at the relatively new 'Plaza' Hotel.[77] The rest of the men, in groups of 50, attended bathing facilities. These small periods of rest gave soldiers time away from shellfire which helped keep their morale

---

[77] In 1940, during the occupation by the Germans, the hotel was placed under the authority of the military commander for Belgium and the North of France took. The Hotel Le Plaza was made into a booby-trap by the Germans, before the arrival of the Allied Forces. Luckily, only its garden and its stained glass dome were destroyed.

and spirits high. For those remaining behind, shellfire of a different nature began to fall in the area of Kessel.

The 'Plaza' Hotel, Brussels

War Diary 13th Feb

1315   Hostile propaganda leaflets fired on 'B' Coy (specimens attached)
1750   Hostile propaganda leaflets fired on 'C' Coy (specimens attached)

Captain David Tibbs MC (RAMC)

"The weather was bitterly cold with ice flows floating down the river. Nevertheless our patrols brought back prisoners from across the river and in turn they abducted some of our men. I used to walk along the river bank every day visiting company positions. One day as I was doing this there was the characteristic rush of an approaching shell which landed within 3 feet of me with I muffled explosion. I stood dumbfounded and then realised that I was fine but the ground all round me was covered with paper. It was in fact a German propaganda shell full of leaflets calculated to scare us by describing a tank they had which could travel under the water to emerge on our side, together with a lurid picture of this monster coming out of the water to attack."

Lance Corporal David "Robbie" Robinson (Anti-Tank 'C' Company)

"Some of the German shells contained an array of propaganda literature. They ranged from pictures showing GI's latching onto our women to new terror weapons waiting to be unleashed on us, they were supposed to strike fear into us but in reality they provided us with a good laugh and some extra toilet paper."

465

The following propaganda leaflets were fired into the 6th Airborne Division's positions. They are the 'specimens attached' found in the 13th Battalion War Diary for February 1945, National Archives, Kew (WO 171 5138).

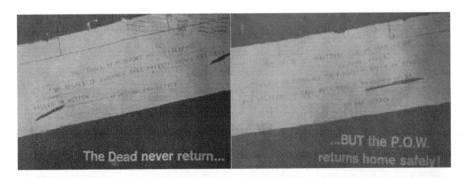

The Dead **never** return... ...BUT the P.O.W. returns home safely!

Winston Churchill told us the truth!

„We can't win the war unless we shall have finished it before the leaves of autumn fall."

Like the waves of a flood lashed by a storm the A.E.F. swept over France. Everything seemed to go according to plan. Nevertheless Mr. Churchill uttered these ominous words:

„I know of terrible things", he said at a time when the newspapers were triumphant and your generals promised an early end of the war.

Now things have turned out as Winston predicted. The Germans having been concentrated within and behind the Siegfried Line for many months have commenced their attack, which you must face now. Weakened by those deadly and senseless battles near Aix-la-Chapelle the Allies are now confronted with the German onrush. Allied Headquarters have to tackle a difficult problem.

The casualties suffered by the American units of the Allied Forces till the beginning of the German offensive amounted to 500 000 men. 36 000 prisoners were brought in during the first week of the offensive. The losses in dead and wounded are by far greater and careful estimates put them down at 150 000 to 180 000 men. As happened before the Americans intended to show off once more by marching up to Berlin on their own in order that their folks at home might celebrate them as the great victors. Now we have broken through their lines and are fighting deep inside Belgium. Instead of working with you in good fellowship they got into a tight corner by their desire to show off. Now you are expected to help them in their efforts to get out of their troubles. You'll certainly realise this when you think of the units transferred from your own sector in order to be sacrificed in this endeavour. Boys, I really feel sorry for you! But you have to resign to your fate and bear in mind that you are at war!

If you should meet the Americans who show off for the merest trifle happening in the USA don't forget to express them your thanks in a suitable manner.

...makes all

Look here gang...

He is one of your friends. — an American!!

He seems to be enjoying himself, at least that's my impression. Those strapping Americans don't know the limit; they simply show off. To those 14 minutes I at least know they are at the wall it's quite a tough job. But, there is another tough job going on over there — Aix-la-Chapelle. These Americans thought themselves fit to tackle this job in a jiffy whistle. Boys, you look at the mess they have made of it. Think of the casualties. God bestows majesty that have suffered so far. And the German ones are three times as you can, I suppose. Now they can't tackle their job ... alone?. Those Americans cannot even try to get them out of their troubles!

Now YOUR help is required!

In this position they don't anyhow their superiority in numbers any more, because from here it all looks THE IN CAVE THEM A PROPER HIDING. But we need soldiers here to help them overcome any?

Boys you can't help thinking that Tommies and Jerry ought to understand each other better. At least much better than you and those American nitwits behind here, it is a thousand pities that you are our ENEMIES!

Peace and a happy return in 1945?

All fellows are longing for peace — well ... (the text is in spite of the strong expectation of your heaven is true, our exterior and industrial professionals, it was impossible for you to devote this way in one of the battle-fields, that are your fighting during those a long years.

Your official actions and your generals foe, hold you that already has the victory in their pockets, but opportunity is to and as easy as all, that?

Millions of troops soldiers are still found, transported across the seas and then lost as the battle-fields, where they go to those.

Rest of you may may well ask now ... What for !? ... Why the bloody business !? ... Why does not bring our superiority on a quick victory ? The *Press-Agency LENTHE* gives you the reason in those details, in the following transcribed despatch.

The London Stock-Exchange dampens the previous, wether it is possible for people to many transactive against a too quick ending of the war. Many business men, and firms are closely interested in a lasting war, because it would be very disadvantageous for their financial position, if the war came to a sudden end. The Business Syndicate schools declared that those who closely this business on account, starved untimely those activities.

A great number of those businesses against a ending war and have already been affected.

Do you understand that ? — No !
Do you really have to die for these profiteers? - No!

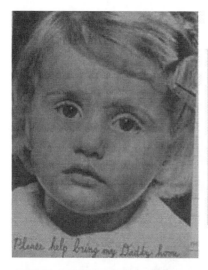

Please help bring my Daddy home

Dear Father in Heaven!
Please help bring my Daddy home.
Mumsy is always so sad and weeps hot tears all day through.
Mumsy says, if Daddy does'nt come soon, Daddy has to stay with that naughty war for ever and ever...

Your name! *when?*

It is'nt necessary that only your fellows are killed in action.
Everybody can and will stumble on it.
YOU TOO!!!

Look at it properly!

That is the latest German amphibian tank having still stronger armour plates than the well-known „Royal Tiger". Its firing capacity surpasses everything known so far. It simply cannot fire.

The funny part about it is that it can swim. It does not bother about the foundations ruined by us.

At any moment it may emerge in front of your positions, but you have to hold out.

Don't think the German offensive was launched in those few places only. That was only the beginning.

We have already advanced a nice bit in Belgium and it has proved an irresistible advance. The fog which undoubtedly favoured us at the outset but rendered operations more difficult later on has disappeared. Ever since we have been making headway.

On the other hand your airmen are again in a position to drop their Teddy carpets in order to plaster our tank spearheads. They are heterilogetic in their endeavours for everything depends upon your efforts.

But their losses are tremendous. It goes without saying that many of our own tanks have been put out of action by allied bombers crashing in great numbers with their bomb loads. One notices at once the reappearance of the Luftwaffe which is of vital importance to our spearheads. You have certainly observed the withdrawal of certain units from comparatively quiet sectors of the front in order to strengthen the fighting forces in the new battle area.

As a result your own positions will be weakened. But you must be prepared to face our attack all the same. Unfortunately you have little or nothing to oppose our assault.

And all this because those Yankees and American fellows meant to reach to Berlin on their own. Now where they are getting a proper licking you have to pay for it and have to come to their aid. Perhaps you will already be there tomorrow? You never know in advance.

It would be better for you to remain where you are now considering that you have established yourself fairly well. And you won't miss anything by remaining where you are because sooner or later you'll be able to see the latest German amphibian tank when it emerges in front of your position.

That will be a nice surprise for you!

Look at it properly!
.... if not to-day, to-morrow.

Dear Jack,

at first a bright new year! You'll certainly have been wondering that you didn't hear from me for such a long time. My wounds seemed to be light when you and Morris brought me to the dressing station. But in addition to that splinter in my left arm there was another one in my knee and a fortnight ago those damned doctors chopped off my left leg. I suppose my left arm will remain stiff too. On the whole a damned shit.

Fortunately my right arm is quite allright so that I can use it for typewriting. Be on your guard that you keep your bones sound. Only after being mutilated as I am now, you know what you have lost.

It's just a few days that New Year's Day will come again, for the sixth time within this damned war. But there is no prospect of the end. Being laid up in hospital I have sufficient time now to think about this rotten business. Where is dear old Chamberlain who meant to finish the war in within three years. Now it's almost double the time. They are foretelling the end again and again but people don't trust them any longer. And our Yankees who intended to defeat the Japanese within 90 days meanwhile have become far more modest. Now they are telling us that another year is necessary to finish off the business in Europe. But how and when is this European war to end? I can't believe yet that those damned Hann will soon have come to the end of their tether. He who vowed to shoot over distances of 300 miles will be able to achieve still greater things.

My own future causes me plenty of trouble. I can't help remembering those poor cripples of the last war whom I saw in the days of my childhood begging and singing in the streets of London. Shall my be treated in the same way? I am eagerly looking forward to the day which will bring the end of that rotten business. I feel uneasy thinking of what may happen if in our race to Berlin the Russians should be first. To-day they have already taken possession of Poland, Hungary, Rumania, Finland, Northern Norway, Esthonia, Latvia, Lithuania and the whole of the Balkans. If in addition to these countries the Soviets should occupy the greater part of Germany — and good old Stalin doesn't seem to have become more modest — they would have amassed a power much stronger than that of the Nazis which has been menacing us.

My stump gives me a lot of pain and on New Year's Eve I am tormented by dreary and melancholy thoughts. You and those already killed in action are always in my mind. Do you remember that long Joe whose wife is now left alone with her four bairns. How is she to bring up her kids?

I realise, dear Jack, this letter will give you little pleasure but sometimes it is necessary to look at the other side of the picture.

Well, think of your old friend now and then and above all take care that you keep up to the mark and that your bones remain intact, for nobody can restore them.

Cheerio old horse and receive the kindest regards from

your

B & B

468

Lieutenant Ellis "Dixie" Dean (MMG Platoon)

"The 8th Battalion positions were taken over by 12th Battalion and one afternoon when we were about to sit down for our tea, in walked Colonel Darling their CO and we all stood up. "Hello Dixie what are you doing here. I thought this was my battalion area?" and before I could answer, he continued "Is that Golden Syrup? It's one of my favourites. I haven't had any since I was a schoolboy, mind if I join you?" He then sat down and tucked into bread and syrup with the rest of us."

Lieutenant Peter Downward ('B' Company)

"Binoculars were constantly trained on the other side, so much so that certain individuals became identifiable to us, and even had nicknames. There was 'Fat Hans' who was obviously in charge of a machine gun. Every morning we would see him put up his gun on the top of his trench and fire a few rounds in our direction, to check his

weapon and then would flog his arms across his chest to get warm before stamping backwards and forwards, occasionally exposing most of the top part of his body. This repetitive behaviour was his undoing, as he presented too good a target for one of our snipers, and he was picked off one morning with a single shot.

"There was also a dog which we used to see at certain times. It would set out from a barn about 600 yards in front of us, and then make its way back around the fields to another building partially hidden by some trees. None of our soldiers would ever dream of firing at it and I trust he (or she) survived the war.

"Another little incident I recall was the sight of a V2 rocket taking off from a site behind cover about a couple of miles away. There was no noise at first as it rose very slowly, it gathered speed and then inclined towards the north west, the sound of its rocket motors at last becoming audible before it disappeared. Our Royal Artillery Forward Observation Officer was quick to react in putting down 2 or 3 salvos onto the area of the launch site. All who saw it wondered where it would land and how many civilians were going to die in about 12 minutes time."

(Photo: RAF Museum)

Account of Patrol night 17/18 Feb

Patrol launched at PRAWN 2115 hrs. They reached shore at 826002 and had to cut first line of wire, which is fully exposed in view of fall of water level in order to beach the boat. NORTH of the road 826001 'S' mines and tripwires were encountered which were either laid during the snow period or rather hurriedly put down. The AP mines are only half submerged and not camouflaged. The tripwires are approx 6-8" off the ground.

Trenches 824999 were found unoccupied and patrol laid up there for 20 min not seeing or hearing any enemy.

At 2230 the patrol commander [Lt Eric Barlow] placed his cover party at 82499 and proceeded along road to crossroads 828998 without encountering any enemy. The road is not mined.

On SOUTHERN end of crossroads a concertina wire is placed across road and as patrol commander could not negotiate it silently he decided to remain this side of it, hoping to hear or see some enemy, to lay up until 0030 hrs without hearing or seeing anything in the area of the road and A/Tk ditch.

Some faint noises came from 829996 which might have been caused by sentries moving on their post. The patrol then returned and landed in area 'CARP' at 0140 hrs without incident.

Lieutenant Ellis "Dixie" Dean (MMG Platoon)

"By the middle of February not only had the general thaw set in, but the Boche had also been driven from the strip of territory lying between the Maas and the Rhine. The Americans [3 Bn 290th Infantry Regiment, US] were moving up from the south and on 20th February arrived to relieve us."

Lieutenant Peter Downward ('B' Company)

"A pretty blonde girl called Christine, who was the object of much banter and flirtation, amazed us all by the fact that she used to take a herd of cows into the pasture right down to the rivers edge. If any soldier had dared to venture out in her tracks, he would have been picked off in a matter of seconds. Christine spoke no English, but I have no doubt she picked up a few good Lancastrian phrases and, hopefully nothing else!

"There was a queue to say goodbye to Christine who was dressed in her Sunday best and seemed sorry to see us go. No doubt the Yanks would be equally friendly to her."

Private Norman Mountney (MMG Platoon)

"I celebrated my 19th birthday while we were in Holland and shortly afterwards the Americans arrived to relieve us. One of them remarked "What's holding you guys back? That little drop of water?" On reflection I reckon I crossed the Rhine before he did."

Lieutenant Ellis "Dixie" Dean (MMG Platoon)

"We marched to Kessel and then on to Helden [in transport] and entrained for Belgium. Early next morning while it was still dark we arrived in a large village and stayed for 24 hours. The following day we moved to an airfield [Nivelles] where the RAF operated a shuttle service, ferrying us back to the UK."[78]

That same day, 21st February, prior to departure Lt-Col Luard presented Major Jack Watson and Captain Rev Foy their Military Crosses and Cpl Bryant, Pte Toogood and L/Cpl Hawthorn their Military Medals. These medals had been awarded for actions during the 'Battle of Bure' on top of which, 3 Belgian Croix de Guerre's were awarded to Davison, Eales and Horton.

---

[78] The remaining reinforcements, consisting of 1 Officer (Lt Rodgers) and 92 other ranks, returned to the reinforcement pool.

By the 23rd February the sea party joined with the 8 Officers and 132 other ranks, who travelled by air, at Newcombe Lines and normal administration and training was resumed.

ROLL OF HONOUR – HOLLAND

Pte	GREENOUGH Charles L.F.	?	01/02/1945	14771027	Reichswald Forest 35-E-2
Pte	POWELL Stanley R.	18	01/02/1945	14771056	Venray 6-B-7

"The spring of 1945 was one of the best I can remember, as the warm sunny days dried the ground so hard, we were banned from playing rugby."

Lieutenant Ellis "Dixie" Dean

26.   REFIT AND RETURN

Lance Corporal David "Robbie" Robinson (Anti-Tank Platoon)

"After returning from Belgium and Holland we were sent on leave at the end of February [28th Feb – 7th March]. Reinforcements had been installed in the barracks when we got back from leave and these mainly consisted of young recruits and the treated wounded from the previous months."

Pte Norman Skeates (MT Platoon)

"I volunteered in December '44. So we did the December fitness test which was at Hardwick Hall. When you finished with it you was A1+. That means you finished with and different tests and route marches and everything to see whether you are fit enough for the route marches and everything so when you passed you go to Ringway which is an airport outside Manchester.

"You had to do 8 jumps to qualify. That was 3 from a balloon – that was a captive balloon – that was two jumps and one night jump. That was war time so you had bonfires in different fields so you knew when you came down. As you came down with the chute you couldn't   see   the   ground   because   it   comes   up   so   dark. Anyway that was three from the captive balloon. Then you had five from a Dakota which was jumping through the door. When you jump out with the chute these lines break and the chute opens and then closes and then opens again and that's the signal to pull your webbing down and you've got control of the silk canopy then and you put your legs together and as you hit the ground you twist together onto your side and that breaks and that's equivalent to a 15ft jump – 15ft from a wall. There's quite a few people break their ankles doing it!

"After that I was stationed at Larkhill, a big military camp and I joined the 13th Battalion as an infantryman."

Lieutenant Ellis "Dixie" Dean MC (MMG Platoon)

"Our overseas excursion only warranted a 7 day period of leave, hence by early march we were back in training. We assembled in the camp hall and Brigadier Poett informed us that we had returned to the UK to prepare for an operation over the Rhine. He couldn't tell us the date or location yet, only that we had little time to absorb the re-inforcements and get ourselves physically fit.

"Even when the existing 'R' Company were distributed, we still lacked a number of NCO's and Privates, but we were up to strength in officers. Eric Barlow and Bill Davison wounded in Bure, were now recovered, Eric rejoined 'A' Company and Bill was now Assistant Adjutant. Leslie Golding too was fit again, taking over 'R' Company. Geoff Otway filled a vacancy in 'A' Company, Alan Daborn likewise in

'C', whist the three newcomers "Nobby" Price, Chris Selwyn and Jack Birkett became 'B' Company Platoon Commanders. During training, "Dick" Burton sprained an ankle and Basil Disley replaced him in 'C'."

Private Alfred Draper ('C' Company)

"The next few weeks were taken up with physical training. Every day started with a run round Stonehenge before breakfast. It was about a 5 mile run and it certainly gave us an appetite for breakfast. The rest of the day was taken up with marches.

"During this time we had to fit in a practice jump. The air currents were very bad and we had a lot of casualties that day through twisting and swinging. Reg Lansdell strained his knee so badly he didn't rejoin us until the following September."

Brigadier Nigel Poett (5th Para Brigade Commander)

"As the waterborne assault was to start early in the morning, there could be no surprise for this vast airborne landing. The whole force of Allied airborne troops was to fly in a single lift. This would consist of 540 US Dakota aircraft carrying 12 Allied battalions of parachute troops flying wing-tip to wing-tip and followed by 1,300 gliders which would land the British and American gliderborne units. The operation would be supported by some 10,000 aircraft."

Lieutenant Peter Downward (Scout Platoon)

"Once I back at Larkhill I was told by Peter Luard I was to take over the Scout Platoon [Snipers] and I was to give them as much practice as I could in the way of field firing and night work. I took my new command down to Cranbourne Chase. I had something like 26 snipers, 2 radio operators and 2 dog handlers, Corporals Walton and Bailey plus Alsatians "Bing" and "Monty". My Platoon Sergeant was Sergeant Birkbeck, a gamekeeper, a good shot and an expert in field craft, camouflage and wildlife.[79]

"We set up in a farm and occupied a barn; there was a village nearby with a good pub, which of course became our evening drinking spot. The snipers worked in pairs and would keep a constant watch through their telescopic sights and record time and place of movement. Only if Sgt Birkbeck or I appeared in the 'killing area' would they fire their blanks. If we spotted them first, it was a 'no kill'."

Pte Ray "Geordie" Walker

[In hospital, wounded in Bure] "The day of departure (1/3/45) arrived and I said "Cheerio" to the inmates of Ward 5. A lorry was parked waiting to take 20 of us to Tournai. Several nurses stood by the door to bade us farewell and wish us "Good Luck". We were handed boiled sweets as our destination was 65 miles away and 2 hours driving time.

"On arrival at Tournai we drove through the main entrance of a barracks and halted outside the guardroom.

---

[79] The dogs had only just returned to the unit as they had been in quarantine for the previous 6 months following their return from France. They had to be quarantined to ensure other war dogs did not pick up any illnesses they could be carrying such as rabies.

Our driver dropped the tailgate and a gust of wind blew our discarded sweet wrappers onto the ground. A very irate Guard Commander yelled "Pick those bloody papers up!" and an equally irate soldier went berserk. "Jock" a burly Glaswegian of the Highland Infantry seized the Guard Commander by the lapels and physically lifted him up, pinned him against the wall and said "You pick them up. These lads have been fighting and been wounded whilst you have had a cushy job miles behind the frontline. If you report this incident, I'll have your guts for garters." The permanent staff gave my intake a wide berth as they wanted no fisticuffs from us.

"In the town centre cafes I learned that my Battalion had suffered more casualties in 3 days fighting at Bure, than it had sustained in 3 months fighting in Normandy. Meanwhile I made good progress and I hoped to rejoined my Battalion and on the 5th March I moved to a transit camp at Ostend to wait for transport back to England. On 9th March after the sea crossing I travelled back to Salisbury by train, then by bus to Larkhill Barracks.

"I was overjoyed to be re-united with the survivors of 'A' Company, as they had recently returned from a week's leave they were busy receiving reinforcements to make good the losses from Belgium and Holland."

Lieutenant Ellis "Dixie" Dean MC (MMG Platoon)

"One evening we were in the bar of the Garrison Theatre, when word got round that the Americans had captured intact, a bridge over the Rhine – The Bridge at Remagen, so we toasted our allies. I was informed of the allocation of aircraft, a very generous 40 Dakotas. What a difference from the days of 1942 when a dozen of old clapped out Whitleys was all that could be mustered. It came as a big surprise on the morning of 19th March, as the barrack square at Larkhill filled up with transport and then it was all systems go."

Lance Corporal David "Robbie" Robinson (Anti-Tank Platoon)

"Mid March saw us all jump from Dakotas on the nearby Netheravon DZ. These were real transport planes with seats for 10 on either side; they were much more comfortable than the old bombers we were used to using."

Private Norman Mountney (MMG Platoon)

"One evening as we were crossing to the NAAFI, we noticed a Dakota flying round and round with a body trailing in the slip stream. Some one said it was a 'Red Cap' and we all laughed. When we came out later, the plane was still flying round but eventually the RAF despatcher floated a loaded kitbag out which the man was able to grasp tightly and he was then hauled back into the plane.

"Before we moved to the transit camp I can remember men who were officially sick, declaring themselves fit. There was a terrific spirit in the Battalion and no one wanted to miss out."

Private Fred Beddows ('B' Company)

"I did my jumps at Ringway at the beginning of March 1945 and then was sent home on 7 days leave, not the 14 days normally given and told when my leave was up to report to the RTO at Waterloo station. This I did with about 150 other newly qualified parachutists and we were put on a train for Bulford. We arrived there mid-afternoon, Monday 19th, where NCOs from the 7, 12 and 13th Battalions were waiting.

As your name was called out you reported to one of the Sergeants and that is how I came to join the Battalion.

"At Larkhill we paraded outside Battalion HQ and were welcomed by Colonel Luard three at a time in his office. I was posted to 'B' Company, where Major Gethin detailed me to join 6 Platoon.

"In the Platoon barrack room, they were all busy checking their kit and weapons, so I asked the bloke in the bunk below me if the Platoon was going on a scheme or something. I'll never forget his reply, "Yes, a bloody big one." I asked what be meant by that, to which his reply was that I would soon find out. Next morning we were off to the Transit Camp."

30 Officers and 555 other ranks set off in 45 trucks destined for Shudy Camps, passing through places such as Reading, Maidenhead, Slough and Hatfield. A further 35 men of the Motor Transport Platoon under the command of the Admin Captain, "Baggy" Allen, would travel in 5 cars and 5 trucks towing trailers forming part of the 'Sea Tail' ("A").

A second 'Sea Tail' ("B") was led by Lt Fred Tiramani and consisted of the OC and 12 men travelling in one car and three 3-tonne trucks. Captain Allen was the overall commander of the entire 6th Airborne Division's Sea Tail.

Sea Party "A" was to begin its journey on the 18th March whilst the smaller Sea Party "B" was to set off the day before the main body travelling by air [D-1]. In order not to disclose that the 6th Airborne Division was about to embark on operations, all red berets were to be hidden and khaki berets worn instead. Badges and flashes were also removed from both vehicles and clothing, airborne Dennison pattern smocks and other airborne clothing and equipment were also hidden.

Private Norman Skeates (Motor Transport Platoon)

"Then the chaps went because they were going to drop over the Rhine on the last offensive up to the Ruhr and up to the Baltic. Being as I could drive a motor car or a lorry I was ordered on to the MT – Motor Transport line – so they took me out of the infantry and put me onto motor transport. With the infantry dropping on the Rhine, transport had to be ready to re-supply them because when they dropped they only had limited ammunition."

Lieutenant John May (44th Squadron, 316th Troop Carrier Group)

"There were many meadows about the area, which the men used for baseball. In the evening there was nothing to do except get settled as comfortably as possible. Enlisted men brought out their radios and rigged them up, then out came the cards and games went on far into the night. The Officers continued with their games of Bridge and Hearts. Operations, Intelligence, and Communications offices were set up temporarily in administrative quarters near the Control Tower. Men in due time found the wash rooms, the shower rooms, and the NAAFI, with its bottled beer. All in all, it was an excellent set-up.

"There was some discomfort however—the 'gentle reminder' of the V bombs. Quite a few men were sitting in the NAAFI drinking brew and bantering a bit around 2045 hours. Suddenly there was a terrific tremor, and in about 15 seconds concussion shook the building. Mouths dropped open—beer was left in the glasses. The bartender shot out the door like a flash—and right behind him in a rat race went the Americans.

He made an abrupt turn to the left, switched off the lights in the corridor, and then sauntered back to the bar. Men piled on each other in the corridor, finally recovered, and grabbed the bartender. He told them the 'noise' was just a V-2, which had hit about 7 or 8 miles away."

Above: Wethersfield Airfield taken on 11th March 1945, Royal Ordinance Survey).

Lieutenant Ellis "Dixie" Dean MC (MMG Platoon)

"The Transit Camp was Shudy in Suffolk, near our airfield of Wethersfield. It took all day driving along country lanes on a bright spring day. The convoy stopped where there was a wide grass verge to stretch our legs, alongside was a neatly trimmed hedge with a field of winter wheat several inches high brilliant emerald green in colour. To one side in a hollow, I could see a red tiled roof of the farmhouse and buildings and a line of washing, fluttering in the breeze."

"Shudy was a Nissen hutted camp in a parkland setting of woods with carpets of violets and primroses. Everything was under cover and the cookhouses run by permanent staff. There was electricity and ablutions with hot water and even beds for us all.

"The first parade was a drive to the airfield to draw and fit chutes. The Dakotas were parked and numbered to match the stick 'chalk' numbers. The 4 planes allocated to the Platoon were all together, with the Mortars waiting adjacent. We were fitting our chutes when a wagon carrying our crew arrived, they introduced themselves and said what a great honour it must be to be carried into battle by such an illustrious squadron [veterans of Normandy, South of France and twice during 'Market Garden']."

Lieutenant Peter Downward (Scout Platoon)

"Most of the Battalion did a practice jump at Netheravon before departing Larkhill for our concentration area. For the next 2 days we were given a series of briefings with aerial photographs and large floor models to help orientate us as we would first see the DZ from the air. The overall operation known as "Varsity" was for an amphibious and ground offensive to cross the Rhine in the early hours of the morning of Saturday 24th March and hopefully after the German counter attack we, the 6th Airborne would start dropping at 1012 hours 15 miles behind the main defences. It was of course, not solely a parachute drop for in addition to 3 Para Brigade and 5 Para Brigade there was the 6 Airlanding Brigade."

Lieutenant John May (44th Squadron, 316th Troop Carrier Group)

"At about 0630 a V2 awoke the Enlisted Men, so they went to breakfast and had eggs. After breakfast men played ball, read, and slept. Departments were set up in more permanent quarters. A tannoy asked men to bring back empty beer bottles to the NAAFI before 1000 hours.

"The set up for Intelligence and all briefing is an entirely original idea for this Squadron. We are to fly in Serial B-4, carrying the 13th Battalion of the 5th British Airborne Brigade of the 6th Airborne Division. Maps were assorted, Field Order No.5 was read, and photographs of the westerly approaches of the DZ were put together.

Navigators and pilots are to be briefed tonight at 2000 hours.

"We were to drop over the Rhine, and effect an airborne landing in an area about 6½ miles east of the Rhine. The course is an excellent one, and the close ground support seems to be the best we've ever had. That and the fighter cover make this mission seem a 'snap'—a 'milk run.' As a rule, the men are a bit leery of the optimism of Group Briefing Officers—this time it is different.

"A Lt. Col. Luard, CO of the British 13th Battalion, whom we are to drop, was the guest briefing officer. This was a combined airborne envelopment with the British dropping to the north, and immediately [southwest?] of this line another Wing [50th and 53rd] would drop the American 17th Airborne Division.

"This was the first time our Squadron hauled the British Troopers into combat. Col. Luard, who is a rather tall chap and as rugged as they come, proved with his contagious humour that we had nothing to be afraid of. He explained the immediate task of his own Battalion and its secondary task in coordination with other Battalions of the 5th Brigade.

"There is a wood, Diersfordter Wald, about 2,500 yards southwest of DZ 'B,' which the 13th Battalion was to enter and fox hunt in, as he called it. They were to reach a clearing on the side to the west of the wood before the 15th Scottish Division, who were to have crossed the Rhine around Bislich at P-6 hours. Battalion honour was at stake in reaching that clearance, because the Scots would never allow them to live that defeat down. The first objective was the Diersfordter Wald; the second objective: wading the 5 ft deep and 30 ft wide Issel Canal and also capturing intact the six bridges in his immediate area. The battle cry of the Battalion was to be 'Tallyho'— and they also meant to make the Volkssturm, a ridiculous reinforcement should Kesselring commit them in that area. He also said there were 30 to 35 German tanks in the immediate vicinity, but they were nothing to get unduly excited about.

"Helmets would not be worn by his men. They were going to put on their Red Berets when they touch the ground. He believes that 'Jerry' bullets go through helmets and berets just as effectively, and anyway, their helmets and 'Jerry's' look too much alike. This was to be a coordinated ground-air attack—the ground phase beginning at P-6, with a continuous artillery barrage with well over 1,800 guns commencing two hours before the land assault across the Rhine would begin.

"The Royal Artillery was going to 'apple pie' the area in the vicinity of the DZ's and the LZ's. "Apple pie"' Col. Luard explained, was a term used by the Royal Artillery for shelling all known flak positions. The shell is so fused that it explodes eight feet before it hits the ground—'worries' the life out of Jerry Ack-Ack crews, but doesn't worry the ground at all. This Colonel was confident of success and full of courage—a good humoured man, a hard taskmaster, a man a fellow would want to follow. He was convinced that this mission was to be a fox hunting do—he intended to catch German fox.

"When the meeting broke up, the Squadron felt convinced that they were going fox hunting, and the enthusiasm and pace of the 'chase' reassured all that the 'humour' of the Colonel's "tallyho" would be felt shortly by the enemy. He showed his hunting horn, a little bronze horn which all Officers in the Brigade carry. He will use it to assemble his Battalion. The last time the Battalion jumped they made a record assembly, taking only 9 minutes. Quite a chap this Red Devil, and quite a show to come."

Lieutenant Ellis "Dixie" Dean MC (MMG Platoon)

"Our first brief was given by the CO himself as we sat on the grass in front of a large scale reproduction of the battle area. Two airborne divisions were to be employed, ourselves and the American 17th, which was going into action for the first time. The airborne commander was to be Major-General Ridgeway and "Windy" Gale his deputy and the overall commander was Field Marshall Montgomery.

478

"The water-borne assault would precede the airborne one and we were to be dropped right on top of our objectives. Doing this would deepen the bridgehead and stop any early counter-attacks, at the same time we would be taking out of the battle a lot of Boche artillery, as we were landing right in the middle of them. Our drop was to be 12 hours after the infantry had crossed by assault craft. The DZ was in flat open country, some 4 miles west of the river and close to Hamminkeln. All necessary features were pointed out."

Lieutenant Peter Downward (Scout Platoon)

"At last we knew the place of the operation, the small town of Hamminkeln a few miles north of Wesel. It was also apparent from the intelligence reports that the Germans were expecting an assault across the Rhine and were holding a strong force some miles to the east, ready to counter our attack. Montgomery's strategy was to get the Germans to commit their counter attack against the surface crossing of the Rhine and then for the 6th Airborne Division to drop well behind them reasonable unopposed.

"Returning to our preparation and briefing, I was told the Scout Platoon would be responsible for taking a farm building which was to be Battalion HQ. I studied the aerial photographs carefully and aligned them with the map; the main landmark I would look for was a tower containing an electric transformer which I would locate from the low level photographs. I made sure all my soldiers knew of its position and the farm building nearby."

Lieutenant Ellis "Dixie" Dean MC (MMG Platoon)

"Two Divisions [51st Highland & 15th Scottish] would start the ground assault and prior to their crossing the town of Wesel would be attacked by heavy bombers of the RAF. The 3rd Brigade of 6th Airborne would drop first onto a single DZ 2 miles beyond the west bank of the river. 5th Brigade would fly over them a couple of miles and would also land on a single DZ. The 6th Airlanding would deepen the bridgehead further and seize crossings over the River Issel and the town of Hamminkeln.

"Of the 3 battalions in the Brigade, 13 would drop first, followed by 12 and then 7th Battalion. We could expect opposition from the moment we landed, but once we made the RV the objectives were only hundreds of yards away. The MG's were to be in 'A' Company positions, covering the Battalions left flank."

Lieutenant John May (44th Squadron, 316th Troop Carrier Group)

"The overall picture showed excellent planning—we would be over enemy terrain about 8 minutes, maybe less, and maybe, if the Scots move far enough, we'll be flying over friendly ground forces all the way. We are to drop at 662 feet indicated at 110mph, make a left turn short of the Reich's Autobahn, and come out at 150mph on deck or in a climb at the discretion of the Serial Leader, Maj. Keiser. High tension wires are in our immediate area, and they are 100 feet high. A turn to the left on deck would bring us under them.

"All in all the pilotage on this mission was perfect. Landmarks were distinct and the weather looks like it will be excellent. Varsity looked like a real 'milk run.' But something always happens on these 'snap' missions."

5th PARACHUTE BRIGADE PLAN

The 7 Para Div was last known to be approximately 3,400 strong but was thought to have been given priority for reinforcement and supplies.

The 84th Infantry Division had been recently mauled during Operation "Veritable" in February and was only around 1550 men strong, 500 of which were newly arrived reinforcements. The 84 Inf Div was so weal that the planners assumed that it would be strengthened by units such as the Volkssturm and the 286 "Ear" battalion, made up entirely of deaf soldiers, which was known to be in the area. ⁸⁰

Communication from these Volkssturm units to the regular troops was expected and that the regulars could be in the area between 30 – 60 minutes later. As the initial contact was to be against Volkssturm troops, high levels of prisoners were expected to be taken in the early stages and so needed to be catered for. Civilians also needed to be considered as the area had not been fully evacuated (estimated 30% remaining).

In accordance with normal military matters, it was reminded that all civilians were to inform the British Army of any firearms, explosives or transmitting devices (including pigeons) in the form of a list pinned to their front door. No help in any way was to be given by civilians to the German Army (including soldiers in civilian clothes). No kind of espionage or attack on the Allies was to be tolerated by the civilian population. Failure to obey these orders was to be punishable by death.

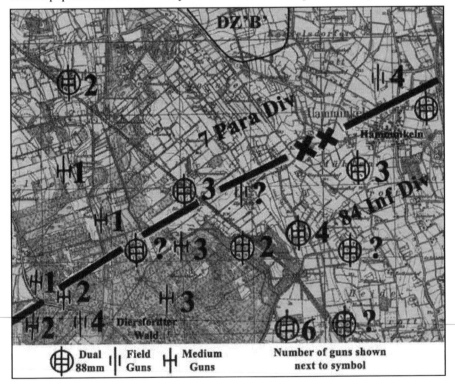

---

⁸⁰ Estimated strength on 12th March and do not include 'B' echelons. Major General Fiebig, Commander of the 84 Inf Div, who was captured later, reckoned he actually had 4,000 by 24th March.

480

Phase I

The 5th Para Brigade was to seize and hold the ground either side of the road from the junction at 197493 to the road junction at 187497. This was to deny the enemy movement of his reserves through the area. The area of the crossroads at 167492 was also to be secured to deny any passage of any enemy reserves from the north.

13 Para was allocated 34 aircraft for the lift as well as 2 Horsa gliders and the aircraft were to come in from the SW of the DZ heading NE. The DZ on which they were to descend, was a very flat area consisting mainly of fields separated by ditches, hedges and fences and to the W/SW was a 3 x 1 mile wood known as the Diersfordter Wald. Other than gun emplacements and trench works, there were no anti-airlanding obstacles to hinder gliders, but there was an electrical power line that runs NW to SE that would need to be avoided (Then & Now maps below © Google Map Data 2012).

To aid forming up at the RV's each unit wore a different visual aid tied to both shoulder straps of the para smock and used a different sound aid. The 13th wore a red scrim and as customary, used hunting horns. Once all units were organised, Phase 2 of the operation would commence.

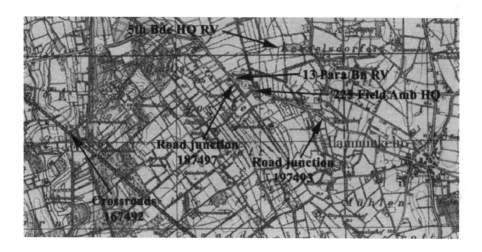

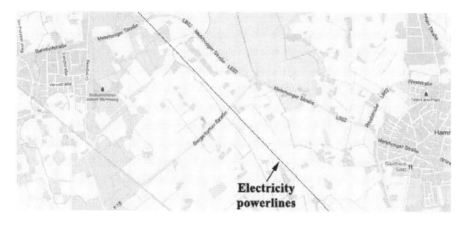

481

Phase II

7 Para Bn with one troop of 4th Airlanding Anti-Tank Battery were to occupy the area of the woods at 193507 and 190507. Protection of the DZ was also to be 7 Para responsibility. They were then to secure the crossroads at 167492 after patrols had reconnoitred the area. A standing patrol was to be located at road junction 167492.

12 Para Bn with two troops of 4th Airlanding Anti-Tank Battery in support was to occupy the area bounded the road junction 196504 to point 198498 to the road junction 197493 to west end of wood 193502. The MMG Platoon of 12 Para was to site their guns to fire, with centre of the arc from 194502 to 183499. A standing patrol was to be located at road junction 193513 and at the farm at 205506. A contact patrol was to meet up with the Airlanding Brigade on the road to Hamminkeln (Then & Now maps below © Google Map Data 2012).

13th PARA BN AREA OF OPERATIONS

13 Para with one 17 pounder troop of 4th Airlanding Anti-Tank Battery were to occupy the area bounded by point 194495 to the road junction 187494 to the road junction 187497 to road and stream junction 186493 to the buildings at 193493. The MMG Platoon of 13 Para was to site their guns to fire, with centre of the arc from 187497 to 193507. A standing patrol was to be located at the area of 183502. 13 Para were also required to send out a patrol to make contact with Divisional HQ at 189479.

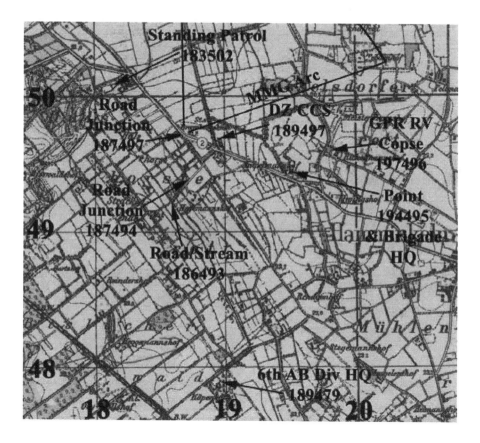

Each parachute battalion had 1 Officer and 3 other ranks from the Forward Observation Unit attached to it and it was their task to call in any artillery support required.

The MDS was to be set up in the farm buildings at 187493 and the Drop Zone Casualty Clearing Station (CCS) was to be located in the buildings at 189497.

The Glider Pilots were to be responsible for the protection of an ammunition dump set up in their RV copse at 197496.

Private Alfred Draper ('C' Company)

"The next few days were taken up looking at models and maps of the area we were to drop in. We were shown where to rendezvous and our objectives and finally told the date, 24th March, the day before my birthday! At the time I didn't think I'd see it."

Private Fred Beddows ('B' Company)

"We had 3 briefings. Firstly the full Battalion was briefed by the CO, next was the Company Commander's turn and finally the really detailed one by my Platoon Officer, Lieutenant Selwyn. I was puzzled by frequent mention of SP's and when the time came for "any questions?" being a keen young soldier I asked in all innocence "What's an SP?" This was a great joke for the old hands but I was made fully aware of the threat that these weapons posed."

Lieutenant John May (44th Squadron, 316th Troop Carrier Group)

[23rd March] "Another fine morning with a V2 reveille. Operations busy getting out paraform reports to Group. This department busy getting individual plane briefcases packed with essential maps, plotters, computers, and escape aids and purses. Radio operators replaced some crew chiefs on guard duty last night, Crew chiefs and pilots meet their British jump masters and help load the para-packs onto the para-racks. British Paratroopers began arriving early in the morning—soon crew chiefs and pilots were chummy and drinking the inevitable tea with the Battalion.

"Major Keiser started the briefing off this afternoon, he could not say at what altitude he would come out of the DZ—it depended upon the flak condition and the small arms fire concentrated in the area during the run in. 20 minutes warning; five minutes red light and green light signals were to be given not so much according to time, but more according to check points on the ground. The red signal will be given at the eastern tip of the Staats Hock Wald, about 4,000 yards from the Rhine. The amber signals from the dome would be flashed by element leaders upon signals from Serial leaders to indicate 20 minute warning. Drops would be made on Maj. Keiser, even if it is known he is off course. It is better to get the men down together."

Lieutenant Peter Downward (Scout Platoon)

"In the final stages as we were snatching a couple of hours rest, Sgt Birkbeck reported to me that one member of the Platoon had accidentally shot himself in the foot whilst testing his weapon. Knowing the individual concerned and the circumstances of the shooting, there was no doubt in my mind that it was self-inflicted. He was duly treated by the medics but there was no question of him being able to jump. Despite his explanation he was later court martialled on a charge of self-inflicted wounding, in other words cowardice."

Lieutenant John May (44th Squadron, 316th Troop Carrier Group)

"Para-forms reveal we are to haul 2 mascots of the 13th Battalion—Alsatians named 'Bing' and 'Monty'. We are also carrying Brigadier Poett, CO of the 5th Brigade, and Lt. Col. Luard, CO of the 13th Battalion. Brigadier Poett is as witty and confident as Col. Luard, and also is quite a chap, must be a fox hunter too—keeps saying 'By Jove' and 'Tallyho!'

"Out on the line, the crew chiefs, who were to guard their planes, were joking with the 'limeys' and a few Canadians. These Red Devils are a wild bunch."

Lieutenant Ellis "Dixie" Dean MC (MMG Platoon)

"The final events of the day were to be an open air Church service in the evening and a Frank Sinatra film in the main dining hall. Before the service I found my men lounging about on the grass in the evening sunshine. They gathered around informally and I said my little piece. Earlier we had received copies of Monty's 'Order of the Day' and I emphasised again how important it was to get to the RV as quickly as possible and how dependant the Battalion was on our supporting fire. I wished them "Good Luck, and I'll see you in Germany." But as I said it, I couldn't help thinking this is the last time I will be speaking to some of them.

"I was approached by Pte Bill Colquhoun, one of the re-inforcements that joined earlier in the week. "This is only an exercise we are going on, isn't it Sir?" As gently as I could I explained that this was the real thing, but there was nothing to worry about, he was with some first rate soldiers. I then spoke to Sgt Fred Drew, his stick commander, asking him to keep an eye on the youngster.

"Next morning as I made my way back from the ablution block, the silence was broken by the roaring overhead of a V1 'Doodle Bug'. Breakfast consisted of porridge, bacon and fried potatoes, bread and marmalade."

Lieutenant John May (44th Squadron, 316th Troop Carrier Group)

"Eggs again for breakfast. Trucks take crew chiefs and radio operators out to their planes. Pilots and navigators assemble in the Group Briefing Room. Weather will be good with SE wind at 8-12 miles per hours at 1,000 feet. Take-off time advanced five minutes to make good time at Marfak because of winds.

"Out in the Dispersal Area, the paratroopers and some crews are having tea (crews say the British put rum in it!!); pilots talking to jumpmasters. Password given as 'Hither-Thither.' Paratroopers were up at 0200 hours checking equipment. Dawn was breaking in the east, and the air was a bit chilly. Some Canadians were kidding the 'limeys' about the Empire and the Commonwealth, and the 'limeys' were reciprocating the banter. Lt. Col. Luard, called the "Enplane" order and all the troopers struggled with their harnesses and lined up for preliminary check by their Jumpmasters. The two dogs, Bing and Monty, had their harnesses put on now, rather than wait until the 5 minute warning. A Subaltern on each plane read a communication from the 21st Army Group Headquarters wishing them 'good hunting' on the other side of the Rhine. This was signed B.L. Montgomery."

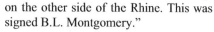

Lt Peter Downward (Scout Platoon)

"Whilst it was still dark, we were driven to our allocated aircraft and on debussing had to wait on the tarmac for about an hour. The only individuals that didn't show any tension was Bing and Monty who were already dressed in their dog harnesses less the chutes (left: model of Bing at the IWM Duxford supplied by Sir Peter Downward himself). Our parachutes were laid out in lines ready for us to pick up. I would be No.1 out the door and not No.13 as had happened on one or two training jumps, certain superstitious individuals would avoid picking up chute 13. At last came the moment to pick up our chutes and fit them. The tension was now very apparent as one could tell from the nervous banter between my chaps.

"As No.1 in the exit from the aircraft, I would be last to embark and standing at the foot of the ladder up to the door, I checked each soldier and his kit on board; something that was being repeated a thousand times by other officers and NCOs on our airfield.

"One young soldier – probably just 18 and with no previous battle experience, suddenly broke down and said he just couldn't go on. He knew he was being a coward and would face a court martial, but he wouldn't jump. I took Private X to one side to talk to him and try and calm him. I explained to him that there were about 8000 other troops dropping and he would undoubtedly come through unscathed. Above all, I explained to him that as a young man he would still have many years of life ahead of him and how he would hate himself if he looked back on this act of cowardice. Also, he had to think of his family, how would they feel to have a son labelled by a court martial as a coward? Whether or not my suggestion to move him forward in the stick changed his mind, I shall never know, but I am happy to report he survived the war. He later thanked me profusely."

Private Ray "Geordie" Walker ('A' Company)

"Reveille was 0245 hours and breakfast at 0330 hours, after which we boarded a fleet of lorries to take us to the airfield. Before leaving Shudy Camp, I was approached by a pal from the Rear Party, Jack Lee of Gateshead who had recently been discharged from Newbury Hospital owing to a foot injury. He asked "How much money have you?" I replied "10 shillings". He then said "Give it to me; you might be dead by dinner time." I gave him the money knowing he would spend it on beer. By 0630 I was seated in a Dakota."

Wethersfield, 24th March 1945 (Lloyd Drake Collection)

ORDER OF BATTLE – 13 PARA BN

OPERATION "VARSITY"

BATTALION HEADQUARTERS

Commanding Officer	Lieutenant Colonel P. J. LUARD DSO
Second-in-Command	Major Roy LEYLAND
Adjutant	Captain "Claude" MILMAN
Quartermaster	Lieutenant Fred TREMLETT
Intelligence Officer	Lieutenant Harry POLLAK
Assistant Adjutant	Lieutenant Bill DAVISON

ATTACHED OFFICERS

Medical Officer (R.A.M.C.)	Captain David TIBBS MC
Padre (R.A.CH.D.)	Capt The Rev Whitfield "Boy" FOY MC
Regimental Serjeant Major	W.O. I. Bob DUXBERRY
Regimental Quartermaster	W.O.II. Jimmy HENSTOCK
A.P.T.C.	W.O.II. Roy PARRISH

HEADQUARTERS COMPANY

Company Commander	Major Andy McLOUGHLIN
Admin Captain	Captain "Baggy" ALLEN
Mortar Officer	Lieutenant Vic WRAIGHT
Scout Platoon Officer	Lieutenant Peter DOWNWARD
Machine Gun Officer	Lieutenant "Dixie" DEAN
Signals Officer	Lieutenant Malcolm TOWN
Transport Officer	Lieutenant Fred TIRAMANI
Company Sergeant Major	W.O.II. Charlie FORD
Company Quartermaster Sergeant	Colour Sergeant Ted HEWITT

"A" COMPANY

Company Commander	Major Jack WATSON MC
Company Second-in-Command	Captain "Joe" HODGSON MC
No.1 Platoon	Lieutenant "Topper" BROWN
No.2 Platoon	Lieutenant Geoff OTWAY
No.3 Platoon	Lieutenant Eric BARLOW
Company Sergeant Major	C.S.M. Bert ALDER
Company Quartermaster Sergeant	C.Q.M.S. Harry WATKINS

"B" COMPANY

Company Commander	Major "Dizzy" GETHIN
Company Second-in-Command	Captain Maurice SEAL
No.4 Platoon	Lieutenant Roy RUDD
No.5 Platoon	Lieutenant "Nobby" PRIOR
No.6 Platoon	Lieutenant Chris SELWYN
Company Sergeant Major	C.S.M. "Duggy" DUGDALE
Company Quartermaster Sergeant	C.Q.M.S. Eric COOKSON

"C" COMPANY

Company Commander	Major Clive PRIDAY
Company Second-in-Command	Captain Fred SKEATE
No.7 Platoon	Lieutenant Frank SUMMERFIELD
No.8 Platoon	Lieutenant Basil DABORN
No.9 Platoon	Lieutenant Alan DISLEY
Company Sergeant Major	C.S.M. "Taffy" LAWLEY
Company Quartermaster Sergeant	C.Q.M.S. Charlie WRIGLEY

"R" Company (IN U.K.)

Captain Leslie GOLDING
Lieutenant "Jock" GRIEVE
Lieutenant Dick BURTON

"The lad in front of me was terrified and he wouldn't go out the door and it took some time to get him out. I was the first one of our stick to make the DZ alive. The first 5 and the lad in front of me, No.6, all got killed; they landed in the forests and were killed by the Germans whilst hanging helpless in the trees."

Private Harry Thomas ('A' Company)

27.   OPERATION "VARSITY"

War Diary 23rd March

0630   Unit took off in 33 DAKOTAS and 2 HORSAS from WHETHERSFIELD airfield and BOREHAM airfield respectively.

Lieutenant Ellis "Dixie" Dean MC (MMG Platoon)

"The door of the plane had been removed, but we required a ladder to get inside and hand the chutes down. Frank Kenny was given a leg-up into the fuselage, on the floor of which were several bundles, which came to life and revealed the crew, one of which said "Gee fellas, what about chow?" and they disappeared across the tarmac in search of breakfast.

"Sgt Cope of the Mortars came across. He had 3 men refusing to fit their chutes [Lt Vic Wraight, the Mortar Officer was going over by glider as a result of an injury caused by playing rugby on the hard ground]. They had been isolated from the rest of the stick and I said that this was a Military operation and refusal to jump would mean a serious Military offence. They all knew what they were doing and were not going to change their minds. By now it was time to board, so they were left for the ALO's to deal with.

"Our crew were still missing as we were sat inside, waiting. All around engines were starting up and eventually a jeep came screeching up, out jumped four bodies and disappeared into the cabin. Within seconds the engines spluttered into life and moments later we rolled along towards the runway."

Lieutenant John May (44th Squadron, 316th Troop Carrier Group)

"Major Keiser resting on his left arm looking desultorily out the window. Someone took his picture—he looked at his watch, and started his engines. Almost simultaneously all the 'geese' were running their engines, and the taxiing began. As plane after plane passed Squadron ground men, there was a mutual thumbs up and good luck—. Planes were lined behind each other waiting for the first Serial to pass over the field.

"At the stroke of 7am a green light winked in the control tower, the American pilots opened the throttles, engines thundered, brakes were released and they were off. Rapidly increasing their speed, the leading echelon tore down the runway, followed 200 yards by the next echelon, and so on."

Lieutenant Peter Downward (Scout Platoon)

"I cannot remember the position of the dogs, but they were probably at the rear of the stick so as to avoid disruption to the soldiers should they decide to throw a wobbly as happened on one of the Normandy sticks. As the engines started up, I realised how the young men of a generation before must have felt whilst awaiting to go 'over the top' on the Somme.

"We took off just as it was getting light and all of us felt a lot better for the fact that we were now committed; there was no turning back. The jump exit was completely open as the door had been removed and we could see the English countryside receding below us. There was a certain amount of circling and change of engine speeds as the various waves of aircraft fitted into the overall formation. Private Porrill produced a mouth organ and played away and Private X was more relaxed."

Private Fred Beddows ('B' Company)

"Take off was at [about] 0700 hours and jumping No.4, I was in a position to look out of the door and watch as the other Dakotas flew around as they gathered into formation for the flight.

"After a time we started to fly over water and there was some argument as to whether it was the Channel or the North Sea. The planes banked a little and I recognised Southend pier and so I was able to settle the matter by announcing the fact and stating that I had lived in Southend for the greater part of 18 years. Someone then suggested I should jump out and take some extra leave."

Private Ray "Geordie" Walker ('A' Company)

"A few miles from the airfield whilst flying over some houses a sergeant shouted, "Look, there's my wife hanging out the washing in the back garden."

A tight box of nine in three 'vics' of three, 25th March 1945 (Lloyd Drake Collection)

Brigadier Nigel Poett (5th Para Brigade Commander)

"It was a beautiful clear day and we had a magnificent view as the formations of our transport aircraft crossed the channel between Folkestone and Cap Gris Nez and linked up just south of Brussels with our American counterpart carrying the 17th US Airborne Division. Then the 450 parachute aircraft passed below the glider stream as they flew on, protected by its fighter cover. This was a sight that none of us who took part will forget."

S/Sgt Mike N. Ingrisano, Jr (36th Tp, 316th TCG)

"Before takeoff the British brewed and drank tea, and, as noted, had a fairly substantial breakfast. That and the anxiety of the upcoming drop had a sad effect on some of the troopers. My plane was on a wing of a 'V'. This required our pilot to fly close to the lead plane. In so doing, often he would have to throttle back or forward to keep a tight formation. This resulted in the plane gyrating up, down, and sideways, and when we got too close, we would catch prop wash. These conditions were not pleasant for any passenger who was prone to airsickness. Just before the red warning light went on, we hit a particularly bad stretch. The door from the cockpit area to the fuselage flew open. I got up to close it and at the same time I looked at our passengers. Those who had experienced airsickness had used their helmets for their debris. When the hook up light came on, these poor fellows had to slap on their full helmets, stand and hook up to the static line. What a helpless feeling!"

Lieutenant Peter Downward (Scout Platoon)

"Those 2 ½ hours whilst approaching the DZ provided time for thought. "How would I face the enemy, when would my family learn of this operation and would I ever see them again?" I drew tremendous strength from some of my soldiers, not solely because of their previous battle experience but, as much as anything, their determination and sense of humour – mainly Scouse."

Fighter cover consisting of Typhoons and Thunderbolts led the massive and awe-inspiring 150 mile long columns of troop carrying aircraft. Swooping down the rocket firing fighters attacked anti-aircraft gun positions and other enemy strong points. The Prime Minister Winston Churchill was one of the lucky people who saw the spectacle.

Alan Moorehead (War Correspondent)

"Churchill stood on Xanten hilltop and looked down across the morning battle mist at the place where the troops [ground forces] were still crossing on boats and rafts. Suddenly the Prime Minister sprang to his feet, and went coursing wildly for a few steps down the hill. "There coming," he shouted, "they're coming!"

"It was the first airborne troops. Indeed it was a wonderful sight. They passed only 200-300 feet above our heads. Here and there one would be hit by Ack-Ack fire."

Prime Minister Winston Churchill

"In the morning Montgomery had arranged for me to witness from a hilltop amid rolling down-land the great fly-in. It was full daylight before the subdued but intense roar and rumbling of swarms of aircraft stole upon us. After that in the course of half an hour, over 2,000 aircraft streamed overhead in their formations. My viewpoint had been well chosen. The light was clear enough to enable one to see where the descent on the enemy took place."

Field Marshal Sir Alan Brooke, Winston Churchill and his assistant, Commander Thompson watch from Xanten Hill, © IWM BU2236.

Lieutenant Ellis "Dixie" Dean MC (MMG Platoon)

"When we first boarded we noticed 4 'flak suits' of body armour, now the jump master came and collected them and returned to the cabin. He then reappeared to announce "Twenty minutes to go." We busied ourselves fitting equipment, kit bags, hooking up and then moving to the door. The next order would come from the jump master, but he was hardly visible, dressed in his 'flak suit' he had gone to the Elsan closet cubicle in the rear and pulled several inflatable dinghies across the doorway so only his face was visible. He then announced "OK you guys. I'll despatch you from here." Frank Kenny, Stick Commander would have none of this and came forward to act as despatcher. I again positioned myself in the doorway.

"A burning farmhouse came into sight "Look at that!" was the cry from behind. I turned my head and No.2 was pointing to the starboard windows. A large group of Dakotas, lower than us flew past in the opposite direction and from one a long orange flame streamed from one engine.

"The airmanship of the Americans was superb; we flew in a tight box of nine in three 'vics' of three. Back and front, left and right, Dakotas rose and fell as the pilots kept formation.

"Surely it's time to descend to the dropping height of 500ft, I thought. We were nearer 100ft. The ground below was covered in discarded chutes as we passed over 3 Brigades DZ, I knew now that there was only 2 miles to go, a minute away.

"We were still flying high and faster than normal dropping speed. Standing in the door, you could watch as the undercarriage was lowered and half-flap applied to reduce speed, but this wasn't happening as we ran in to the DZ. Now we were over the woods and ahead I could see the open farmland, it couldn't be long, my eyes now fixed on the lead aircraft. A blob appeared underneath it, then another and another. On came the "Red" a look down to check we were clear of the trees, then "Green on. Go!" I'm sure we were too high and too fast.

"I released my kitbag but instead of hanging below me, it swung upwards level with my head and oscillated my chute badly. I was in for a backwards landing, something caught my ankles and I was thrown over onto my right shoulder. There was no wind and my chute collapsed slowly around me. I tried to get to my feet and my arm was useless, it just hung by my side. Using my left arm only I got out of my harness, but couldn't unpack my kitbag so I hid it under a bush. In order to do this I had to negotiate a wire and post fence that was responsible for the bad landing I had made. Coming backwards I had caught my heels on the wire."

Lt Peter Downward (Scout Platoon)

"According to our watches there were only a few minutes to go before 'H' hour and this was confirmed as we started to descend to our dropping height. One of our aircrew came back to warn me that we were on the run-in, which meant all of us getting to our feet, checking our static lines and numbering off. There below us was the Rhine though it was difficult to see owing to the thick smoke known as 'Monty's Mist' (pictured, IWM). This had been planned in order to conceal the surface crossing and had been created by a series of smoke generators stretching over several miles along the west bank.

"Gunfire became increasingly apparent below us and then fire started to come up towards us with fusillades of cracks from the German MG42's and increasing airbursts from anti-aircraft fire. I looked back and could see hundreds of aircraft and some ahead. The red light was on over the door and I waited impatiently for the green light, it was exactly 10:12am. I checked that my No.2, still looking terrified, was close behind me and then I was gone. A quick look up to see that the canopy was open and at the same time I could see the remainder of the stick making a rapid exit. What was really incredible was the sight of so many thousands of parachutes in the air.

"There wasn't much time to enjoy the view; I could see that my stick was going to straddle a narrow wood. By now the firing was intense and I was conscious of one big bang close to me shortly before I hit the ground close to a post and wire fence over which my chute draped itself. And then a quick release from the harness and a dash for the nearest cover hoping it wasn't occupied by the enemy.

"Soldiers seemed to be dashing in all directions but above all the din I could hear the 13th Battalion hunting horns being sounded by the company commanders rallying their troops with the morse letter of their respective companies. 'A' Company was "dit dah", 'B' Company "dit, dit, dit, dit" etc. As soon as I had collected up about a dozen of my own chaps (quite a few were the other side of the wood), I set out in search of my objective, the farmhouse which was to be Battalion HQ. One of my NCO's asked me if I was alright as I was bleeding from a cut under my nose. I realised that I had been hit by shrapnel from an airburst on the way down."

Private Fred Beddows ('B' Company)

"While we were standing up waiting for "Action Stations", I saw black puffs of smoke appear among the planes, this was the German welcoming committee. The day we went to draw and fit chutes I had spoken to the pilot who said he would drop us bang on target.

"The American jumpmaster was standing beyond the open door, wearing a flak suit and steel helmet and smoking a big cigar "OK you guys, lets go" were his instructions and we all shuffled forward. I watched as the light turned from red to green and out we all went. I was a long time coming down."

Lance Corporal David "Robbie" Robinson (Anti-Tank Platoon)

"As we were crossing the Rhine we had the call to stand ready to drop. The flak opened up against us and during this period a piece of flak shrapnel came into the plane, hit me in the right cheek, breaking off three teeth, two bottoms and one top. This disorientated me and knocked me about in the plane, but the red light came on so I was hustled forward and thrown out of the plane by my comrades. I was jumping No.2, so if I hadn't been thrown out the rest of the stick of 20 couldn't have jumped."

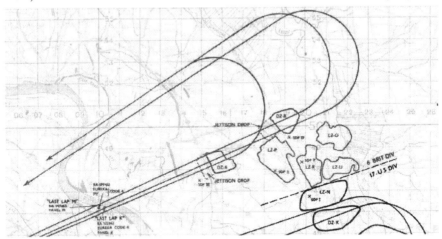

The flight paths and drop zones

Captain David Tibbs MC (RAMC)

"I had had a bad previous night with my fitful slumbers interrupted twice by medical emergencies and felt airsick for much of the way. I was jumping No.2 directly after Sgt Webster of REME (left) who was at the plane's door as No 1. As the warning red light came on I could see the broad glint of the Rhine below. The American planes did not slacken speed. They were arranged in V's of three and I could easily see the planes alongside us and the woods we had to cross below. Sgt Webster and myself had agreed that we should not jump until we had cleared the trees and crossed a line of electric pylons and power cables just beyond the forest. To our horror we saw that the other two planes in our 'V' were dropping their paratroops into the woods and our own American dispatcher was motioning us to go. I thumped Sgt Webster on the shoulder to persuade him to go but he shook his head and pointed ahead. It would, of course, be a court-martial offence to refuse to jump but I realised that Webster was right and waited in mental agony for several long seconds more until, to our relief, the pylons came into view. With Webster jabbing his finger at them and myself responding with a shouted "Yes" we jumped.

"At this stage flak was bursting all round us and one of the other planes had an engine on fire. The usual rush of air and sudden loss of aircraft engine noise was replaced with a new sound - the thump of Ack-Ack shells bursting, but strangely, not fired amongst our blossoming parachutes but at the retreating planes. There was a wonderful view of the flock of planes that had just dropped us diminishing into the distance followed by a cloud of flak. But any relief was short lived because the ground was coming up with a group of 3 or 4 small houses, where a white haired couple were clearly visible in one garden looking up. The man, obviously elderly, turned and ran inside and I thought "supposing he has run in to get a pitch fork and goes for me as I land, do I have to shoot him? Oh, no!" But a cross wind was taking me further over and then to my alarm I saw just at the spot where I was likely to land a battery of three 88mm Ack-Ack guns firing at a new wave of planes coming in. The German gunners were heaving in the shells and firing as fast as they could but fortunately far to pre-occupied to notice me (somebody did fire several shots that passed close to me).

"I landed about 80 yards from the guns and found to my horror I was totally spent and could not find the strength to rise and get moving. Something exploded nearby and I realised that I would die unless I moved away quickly, with that my strength returned and I gathered up my load and strode off to where I hoped the RV was. As I did this 3 paratroopers ran, with that waddling gait of heavily laden men, over to the guns, flung in grenades, and the guns fell silent."

Capt David Tibbs stick had landed safely thanks to Sgt Webster but unbeknown to Captain Tibbs, the aircraft [#42-23931, nose No.17] and its crew were not so lucky…

Lieutenant Merrill J. Jackson (36th Troop, 316th Troop Carrier Group)

"1st Lt. Colvin T. Smith was flying No.3 position in 'B' element and I was flying No.2 position in the same element. When we dropped our troops I fell behind as my troops were very long in leaving the plane. The element leader and Lt. Smith were diving and turning before I had dropped my troops. I was 50 to 75 yards behind as we headed into the 180 degree turn to get out. I was flying right behind my element leader, but lower, and Lt. Smith was ahead of me and about 100 feet above me. I was on the deck. As we straightened out, my element leader and Lt. Smith climbed up to about 600 feet and I stayed on the deck. I flew right over the gun which I think was firing at Lt. Smith. Lt. Smith's ship burst into flames and one parachute came out immediately. I received hits and turned to look and see if I was on fire. As I turned my head another parachute came out at 600 to 700 feet. The plane flew along level and then nosed down in a gentle glide into the ground, exploding on contact, just short of the river. I only saw two men bail out of the plane but there could have been more while I was looking my plane over."

S/Sgt. Wilbur L. Swartz (Radio Op. a/c #42-23931, 36th Tp, 316th TCG)

[In a letter sent home to 36th Troop] "I imagine you will have a hard job reading this, but I wanted to write to let you know that I'm still alive, but pretty much of a wreck. I'm in the hospital here [U.S. Army Hospital Plant 4137], flat on my back. My hands are all bandaged up. I burnt my hands and face and broke my back.

"We got our troops out okay, but on the turn they got us. The plane caught fire. [T/Sgt John J.] Shanta came up and told us and went back and jumped. It didn't take me long to follow him. I don't know whether the pilot or co-pilot got out or not. Could you let me know how they and Shanta made out? Tell me how the rest made it. They told me that I was headed for the States. So I guess I won't be in your squadron any more or for a while at least. Maybe I can join it again sometime. Hope so. I sure thought a lot of the good old 36th."[81]

Lieutenant John May (44th Squadron, 316th Troop Carrier Group)

"The 'geese' were made to fly, turn, and climb as they've never done before. Those who went out as Virgins are no longer so—most of our planes were hit by small arms fire, light and heavy flak. Most of the flak our planes received was 20mm and 40mm, and it was accurate! Six troopers were returned because their lines became fouled. One trooper was hit as he was about to go out the door. His body was pushed out of the plane, so the others could make their jump.

"Five C-47s were seen crashing, burning, or flying out of control. They seemed to be from the Serial [B-3] which dropped on DZ 'A.' Five chutes were seen coming out of one burning plane, which was possibly from the 36th Squadron.

"During the turn from the DZ, many crew chiefs were having a tough time pulling the stringers [static cords] in. The British stringer is longer than ours: 12 feet outside the plane, 9 feet inside, and that weighty cover at the end. Most planes had the navigator, radio operator and crew chief tugging them in, while Hell was breaking loose. Real team work!"

S/Sgt Mike N. Ingrisano, Jr (36th Troop, 316th Troop Carrier Group)

"The 36th Squadron planes met with heavy and accurate flak and small arms fire causing them to break formation. Two aircraft, nose No.5 and 17, went down in flames in the Hochwald area near the Rhine. The crew of No.5 all bailed out.

"14 aircraft returned to Cottesmore. Two of these were badly shot up but none of the crews was injured. Four aircraft (nose No.2, 8, 11, and 19) made emergency landings at airfields in the Eindhoven area. None of these crews suffered any injury. Crew members of nose No.17 were reported missing in action.[82]"

Private Dave Beedham ('B' Company)

"Our plane must have been flying 1,000ft up, rather than the 500 we were supposed to drop from, because I was a long time in the air and there were those 20mm flak

---

[81] T/Sgt John J. Shanta, 1st Lt Colvin T. Smith & 2nd Lt Gerald W. Smith all lost their lives during Operation Varsity.
[82] The a/c previously mentioned by Merrill & Swartz.

guns blazing away at us. There was a small wood near where I landed and some of the lads were hung up in the trees. I dropped in the open in an area of post and wire fences just like in England, but it was quite a job having to keep climbing over them before I could reach any cover. The first thing I can remember seeing was a German farmer standing in a two wheeled cart lashing the horse with a whip to get away from us."

Private Norman Mountney (MMG Platoon)

"I was jumping with a kit bag carrying 2 liners of ammunition (500 rounds of Mark VIIIZ). Before take off the pilot said he was going to drop us as low as possible and as slow as possible. But his god intentions were forgotten when waiting for the "green", we were hit by flak and he climbed increasing speed as he did so.

"I made a good exit there were chutes all round and I noticed two Dakotas on fire but I couldn't see the ground for smoke or dust. I hit it hard and rolled into a hollow as a mortar bomb exploded nearby. There was also sporadic machine gun fire. A short distance away I saw some men hung up in the trees, but when I got closer, I could see they had all been shot, still in their harness. I linked up with my Platoon Commander Lieutenant Dean and as we neared the RV a glider still trailing the tow rope nearly caught us."

Lieutenant Ellis "Dixie" Dean MC (MMG Platoon)

"Facing the line of the fly-in and looking left, I tried to locate the tower of an electricity sub-station. I couldn't make it out as the area was covered in a cloud of smoke. I moved back along the line of fly-in and collected those who had dropped nearby. The 12th Battalion were now landing and as one figure came trotting us, I called "Good morning Sir, enjoy the jump?" to their CO. "Yes. Yes. Have you seen my Battalion?" Which I thought was a silly question, since they were landing all around us.

"At last the Boche came to life and spandaus opened up from our right and battles started to fly. The visibility was so poor; I don't think we made a clear target and some of the men around me must have been re-inforcements as they all dived to the ground. A couple of calls "On your feet, let's get off this DZ" and we were moving again.

"The Battalion were funnelling to woods, where the road dog-legged. Some must have landed close and had already flushed out parties of the Boche. Arthur Higgins was in charge of one such party and was disarming and searching a sizable group. As I approached and greeted him, he asked me whether I would like a Schmeisser or a Luger, I settled for a very fine pair of artillery binoculars with a magnification of 10x50, far superior to the Army issue ones."

CSM "Taffy" Lawley ('C' Company)

"This time I was jumping as No.1 of the stick. On nearing the DZ we got the signal "Action stations" and I took up my position in the door, there was much flak bursting around and while I was watching for the signal to "Go", a burst of flak exploded a short distance from me and but for the fact that my hands was gripping the outside of the door, I would most probably have been blown through the other side of the fuselage. The next second the green light came on and I was away.

"It seemed a very long time before I landed, in an open field near some buildings. I was soon out of my chute and made for the buildings, where I found a number of my Company and learned that the Company 2i/c [Captain Freddie Skeate] was wounded. I obtained his hunting horn and blew the Company call, thereby mustering nearly the whole of the Company. Whilst this was happening a truck load of Jerries drove around the corner of a wood not more than 200 yards away. We soon took care of them. I then took my Company back to the RV some distance away and found our OC Major Priday."

Private Harry Thomas ('A' Company)

"I was in 3 Platoon 'A' Company. The plane that was booked for the Mortar Platoon was out of action, so they gave them our plane because the substitute plane had a very small door, not very suitable for 3" mortars. Because of the change I was no longer jumping 19, I became No.7.

"When we came to the crossing the light came on and out we started to go. The lad in front of me was terrified and he wouldn't go out the door and it took some time to get him out. I was the first one of our stick to make the DZ alive. The first 5 and the

lad in front of me, No.6, all got killed; they landed in the forests and were killed by the Germans whilst hanging helpless in the trees. If he hadn't taken time in jumping, the rest of us would have been dead as well, he saved our lives... When I landed and looked back towards the trees, there seemed to be hundreds hanging up in the trees, all dead..."

The planes took heavy casualties. Private John "Jack" Wray (pictured left) from Everton, enlisted as a boy soldier in 1935 and joined the 13th in August 1943, was one of 19 paratroopers to exit from his C-47 before the Dakota was shot down over the DZ.

Private Ray "Geordie" Walker ('A' Company)

"At 1010 hours I was parachuting down into a field. On landing and discarding my parachute I was joined by two young lads in action for the first time. Having survived the fighting in Normandy and the Ardennes, I was an 'old' soldier at 19, so they decided that their best chance of survival was to stay close to the veteran.

"Now I had to locate the rest of my Platoon [No.2 Platoon], but where were they? Above the noise of battle I hear our call sign, being played on a Hunting horn. I told my companions to follow me and to run as we were now coming under enemy machine gun fire. We arrived at the RV breathless, but fortunately we were not hit by an unseen gunner. We remained at the RV for a few moments hoping that more men would join us. Unable to wait any longer we set off to link up with our Company Commander, Major Jack Watson and prepare defensive positions in anticipation of a German counter-attack."

Major Jack Watson ('A' Company)

"I hit the DZ with no problems at all and with my hunting horn I tried to rally my Company. There were Americans dropping all around me, so for a short while I had them in my Company. The most encouraging thing was the amount of men around me; the whole Brigade had landed in the space of 15 minutes and had quickly formed up.

"We carried our Sten guns made up in our webbing, unlike in Normandy when we had to assemble them after landing, so that we were ready for battle as soon as we landed since we were landing on top of our objectives. The first thing we did after landing was to remove our helmets and put on our red berets.

"We attacked our objective, the Schänzer-Weyers Farm (below, © Google Map Data 2012) without any difficulties and then secured the area. Whilst I was in the farmhouse, my Battalion Commander, Peter Luard, with Brigadier Poett walked in. I invited them to sit down for breakfast and my batman cooked us eggs and ham."

Painting by Lieutenant Geoff Otway depicting Major Watson rallying his troops on the DZ using his hunting horn (courtesy, Major Jack Watson).

Lieutenant Peter Downward (Scout Platoon)

"At last I spotted the transformer tower and there was the farmhouse (below, © Google Map Data 2012). We started to move along a ditch checking our progress periodically by peering over the top, suddenly a figure appeared above us on a cart-horse with no reigns or saddle; I was amazed to see Peter Luard with a hunting horn in one hand and a carbine in the other. "For God's sake, Downward, there's your objective. Take it!" I needed no further encouragement and I, with my party of 12 chaps, made a dash for the barn about 100 yards away. We arrived panting, just in time to find some of the Machine gun Platoon already in possession."

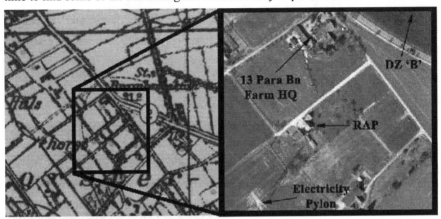

Private Fred Wilcock ('A' Company)

"I jumped from a Dakota in Sergeant Alan Badel's stick. After the war he went on to be a successful actor. I also was jumping with my best mate Roy Parr, who was later became my best man (photo: Roy and Fred a month earlier in Larkhill). After landing I got together with Roy and he asked me to follow him, but I refused and went off the other way. I was lucky because Roy was later taken prisoner. Not long later I let out a burst from my Bren gun not realising it was Alan Badel I was actually shooting at."

Lance Corporal David "Robbie" Robinson (Anti-Tank Platoon)

"I came down in a wooded area and landed amongst the trees. My chute was up one tree and my kit bag, which had been strapped to my leg was in another tree. I was suspended between the two trees feeling very sorry for myself, all dazed because of the flak that had hit me in the cheek and mouth, confused and feeling that I might be dying.

"A chap named Gibbons, who had previously been in the 156th battalion and had joined us for this particular drop, was the man who has pulled me down from the trees. When he got me down as I lay on the floor moaning and groaning and feeling sorry for myself, he gave me a kick and said, "get up you silly bugger you're not hurt." Believe it or not this did the trick, although I didn't feel very well and I subsequently suffered through the broken teeth, black eyes and swollen face. I didn't feel too bad and then happily emptied my kit bag, got the PIAT and what not out, and away we went.

"We came out of the woods and we were just, I suppose it would have been east of the RV. Here on the landing ground the Battalion formed up. I remember seeing a lot of gliders and a lot of planes getting hit and set on fire and plenty of shooting and shouting going on."

Private Alfred Draper ('C' Company)

"The anti-aircraft fire was heavy and I was jumping No.18. Going through the door with all the bangs and flashes outside was frightening but I was more afraid of showing my mates that I was a coward. This applied to most of us I think. There was one poor lad sat on the seat near the entrance crying his eyes out – his nerve had broken with all the noise and the fear. It was something that could have happened to any of us.

"My landing was very good. I could see a hedge coming toward me and I just pulled my rigging lines, sailed over the top of it and landed easily on the other side. I lay there for a few seconds to take in the sight of the parachutes and the planes.

"It was a long run to the RV and they say the amount of adrenaline released during a parachute jump is enormous and lasts several hours. It was certainly so that day!"

Private Peter Maynard ('B' Company)

"All I can remember is, as I jumped out the plane I somersaulted and my chute deployed with my leg court in the risers. Soon as I untangled myself I smacked the ground and that was it. I woke up 3 days later in a hospital with my legs and arms in plaster and my back in a brace."

Private William "Paddy" O'Rourke (2 Platoon 'A' Company)

"Now it was my turn, and I took a grant step through the door. For a moment I was held up in the slipstream, but then began to drop. A lot of fire was coming up from the ground.

"I landed at the side of the road, and as we got rid of our parachutes and prepared to move to our RV, there was a shout of "Down, down! Get your heads down!" Along the road came a motorcycle combination, with two men on the bike and one in the sidecar with a machine gun. We all began firing at the motorcycle, but it just sailed past. We then got up and headed off to the RV, where we dug in."

Private Harry Trew ('A' Company)

"I landed in the correct zone, but couldn't avoid some trees. Fortunately, unwounded, I found my way to my Company RV by the sound of the hunting horns. We headed to our objective, a fork in the road north of a farm [Bovenkerk-Amerkamp Farm, below © Google Map Data 2012]. I moved up to the fork and waved my comrades to follow while I covered them and there several of us hid behind some bushes. Suddenly from the left I saw a number of German motorbike and sidecar combinations heading our way. The sidecars had machine-guns mounted on them and I began to feel the fear in my limbs. It was the first time I had seen Germans and I was only 19 years old.

"I ducked back behind the bushes and warned my mates about the danger. As they approached my corner we all jumped up screaming "Hands up!" and pointing our weapons at them. The Germans were at first reluctant, but eventually threw down their weapons and dismounted from their motorbikes."

Lieutenant Peter Downward (Scout Platoon)

"Very soon, at about 1030 hours, the glider force started to arrive with waves of Horsa descending steeply onto the areas now littered with discarded parachutes. It was obvious from the amount of ground fire, particularly the German 20mm, that the gliders were suffering quite a few hits. This resulted in some bad crash landings. Pilots did their best to land in such confined spaces through trees, over ditches and walls. Wings and tails were ripped off but nevertheless, men and vehicles emerged from shattered fuselages, except in one case where a Horsa crashed almost vertically from about 400ft near the railway line. The 28 men inside didn't stand a chance. Equally sickening was the sight of the odd tug aircraft spewing out smoke and flames in a long shallow dive into the ground about a mile ahead.

"Next came the Hamilcar gliders carrying light tanks known as Tetrarchs. The Hamilcar was an enormous glider and once they had come to a standstill, the nose would lift up and the tank would drive out. The pilots were left to fend for themselves."

Lt Peter Downward (Scout Platoon)

"At last we started to gather up German prisoners and herd them into an area in the yard alongside Battalion HQ. They then became the responsibility of the Provost Sergeant after the Intelligence Officer [codename Acorn, but otherwise Harry Pollak] had given them a quick interrogation in German. They all looked very young and in many cases were only about 17, but likewise some of my chaps were also only 17 as I was to be painfully reminded later in the day."

Citation: Lieutenant Harold Max Pollak ('C' Company)

Award: Military Cross

Lieutenant H.M. Pollak dropped on 6th June 1944 with the 13th Battalion (Lancashire) the Parachute Regiment. He was leading the first platoon to clear the village of Ranville on landing. He personally killed several Germans, while leading his platoon, regardless of personal danger. Constantly alert and thinking always of his men he was wounded severely in the arm and leg, some days later from shellfire, while visiting sentries.

Through sheer will power he made himself get over his wounds and returned to the Battalion, this time as Intelligence Officer. In the Battle of Bure in Belgium on 2nd, 3rd and 4th January 1945, he was untiring in his duty. He constantly volunteered during the heaviest possible fire to go forward on reconnaissance. The information he obtained was of the highest value. He was again wounded be shellfire at Battalion Headquarters on the Maas in February.

Although not fully recovered from this wound, he nevertheless jumped with the Battalion over the Rhine on 24th March. Disregarding enemy fire he was the first man to the Battalion rendezvous, personally taking 40 prisoners, after a short engagement. From then until the end of the campaign his courage, example and endurance has been beyond praise.

Lieutenant Ellis "Dixie" Dean MC (MMG Platoon)

"The scene [at the RV] was rather chaotic, with a 100 or more men milling around, and officers and NCO's trying to sort out companies and platoons. The Boche gave up and showed no fight at all. Men continued to arrive from all directions, someone called "There's a Jeep coming." We all took up positions covering the road, ready to open fire, then another shout "Don't shoot, it's Sergeant Webster" and indeed it was. Somehow or other he had convinced a German Medical Officer to hand it over."

Private Tom Backshell (RAMC)

"While many of the Medics dropped off the mark and had colourful times hiding in woods, fighting for their lives or being taken prisoner, others like myself had a very ordinary time with the crowd. My first memory is of my neighbour in the plane stuffing an orange into my kit bag as we stood in the door. My next, is of hovering over a pylon, but finally landing a considerable distance away. As I emptied my kit bag I wasted no time groping for the orange.

"I was another one who, unable to locate my position, followed the herd into the woods. There, catching sight of our Red Cross armbands, someone delivered into our hands a batch of Jerry Medics, complete with MO and Padre. Our feeling of importance was short lived however as with the next event we forgot our prisoners.

"This was the approach of a Jeep up the road and the turning out of an indignant Jerry doctor by our tough, little REME Sgt and taking it over for casualties. Some how we found the way to the RV where we arrived with nothing more than one sprained ankle. We found a handful of our chaps showing concern over the question of reinforcements as they stood guard over 60 prisoners and civilians."

Sergeant Bill Webster (REME)

"I landed close to a cottage alongside the road and standing outside watching the drop were all elderly couple. I could hear a vehicle approaching so I motioned with my Sten for them to get inside in case there was going to be any shooting. Hearing the vehicle stop, I swung round with my weapon pointing towards it. "You can't shoot me" the officer standing up in the front scat of a Jeep called, "I'm a doctor". The others with him must have been medics too because they made no attempt to fight.

503

Despite the angry protests of the doctor, I commandeered the vehicle and drove on along the road until I came to the wood where the Battalion were gathering. Later I drove the CO and Captain Skeate, who was wounded, to where we had been briefed to dig in."

Captain David Tibbs MC (RAMC)

"We had been dropped ¼ mile to the east of the intended area and our rendezvous was nowhere to be seen. By some fortunate instinct, aided by hunting horns, about 300 men made for a solitary farmhouse. A dangerous congregation of men if those guns had still been active! A grinning Sgt Webster appeared driving a Jeep (itself a USA one from the Ardennes) he had captured. I loaded our Mortar officer (Freddy Skeate, who had been concussed, onto this and we moved off, skirmishing with some Germans firing from the trees nearby as we went."

Many of the US 513th PIR had landed on the British DZ. Lt-Col Miller (2nd Bn) soon realised that he was on the wrong DZ when he noticed the electricity wires and pylons far away to the east. Using his map he soon figured out that he was almost 2 miles north from DZ 'X'. Next he began to gather as many of his own troops so they could and follow the HT lines south towards his own objectives. Luckily his troops had dropped close together so he soon gathered 200-300 of his men.

Sergeant Arthur Laycock (Intelligence Section)

"As I came down I planned to land in the western part of the DZ, my plan did not quite come off and I landed in a tree, which was taking me some effort to get out of. Because of the time it was taking me to get down, I was obviously a very good target for German snipers and I got shot in the leg. I managed to get down and dragged myself across the meadows and fields until I reached a street [Mehrhooger Straße]. I reached a farm [Brambergskath, Battalion HQ] and was glad to meet my fellow paras and was also glad to see that an RAP had been set up."

Private Jack "Clem" Clements (9 Platoon 'C' Company)

"I joined 9 Platoon, 'C' Company in time for the drop over the Rhine. My Platoon Officer was Mr Disley and Bill Railton was the Platoon Sgt. From where I landed I could see some Ack-Ack guns to my left and headed for the nearby pine trees after getting out of my harness. There I met a corporal of the medics. We worked our way to the front of the trees and I set up the Bren and started firing at the German gun emplacement. I felt a thump in my chest and thought "Who on earth is throwing stones at me?" The medic said, "You've been hit." I opened my blouse and found a bullet had gone through both my wallet and pay book. Some one took the Bren off me and I was sent to the RAP in a farm, along with some more wounded. From there I was sent back aboard a DUKW across the Rhine to the British 111 Field Hospital, where the surgeon removed the bullet from my chest."

1010   H hour. 5 Para Bde landed successfully on DZ 'B' area 1850 and formed up as per attached trace. Opposition encountered was slight and the majority of casualties suffered by Unit was due to rather heavy enemy AA fire and airbursts brought down on DZ. In view of bad visibility the majority of the Unit landed slightly EAST of actual DZ thereby causing a certain amount of delay in forming up. One HORSA Glider containing one Mortar section failed to arrive and is considered lost.

Captain David Tibbs MC (RAMC)

"Soon after we had reached our intended positions the gliders came. Sadly the battle was far from over and many active German gun positions with multiple 40mm guns opened up on the slowly wheeling gliders as they came in and created devastating losses. Gliders were on fire in the air, crashing to the ground or being raked with fire as soon as they had landed. It was a depressing sight and nearly one third of the glider force perished in that landing, over 900 men died in a few minutes. Nevertheless many did reach the ground unscathed bringing men and artillery, and moved off quickly to deploy their weapons vigorously."

Brigadier Nigel Poett (5th Para Brigade Commander)

"Just as the parachutists were reaching their RV's the glider element of the Brigade Group began to land in front of us and others to the south. These landings caused a considerable diversion of the fire away from us, but it was a tragic sight for us to see our gliders being hit and often blown up. The losses among the gliders were very heavy and only a small proportion of the anti-tank guns and vehicles carrying machine guns reached us. If a strong enemy counter-attack had come that afternoon we should have had a difficult time."

The American troops of 513th PIR also witnessed the terrible sight of the gliders coming in. Private Sarrell witnessed a Horsa crash right through a farmhouse, dragging a wire fence complete with posts with it. Others saw one Horsa hit another building, stopping the glider and "those Brits came out like popcorn." He recalled incidents like gliderborne troops being cut down by MG fire as they attempted to flee their glider. Private Cobb saw one glider hit by an 88mm, he watched it fall apart and, the Jeep and field gun it was carrying fell to the earth. He also saw a glider pilot's body with both arms and legs burned off.

Soldiers of the US 17th Airborne Division, 513th PIR on DZ 'B' watch the British gliders come in (Cornell Capa Magnum Photos).

Private Derek Kenyon (Unknown Company)

"We met in a yard on a street [Brambergskath] and there had already been a Medical Aid Post set up. We were waiting in the yard for further instructions when a large Hamilcar glider quietly but suddenly came hurtling at us. As quick as lightning we were able to dive out of the way round the back of a house. The glider came to down into the yard and crashed into a barn at the end of the yard. On the right side of the yard there had stood some small apple trees, the glider had chopped them down. Some of my mates said that 2 or 3 men had also suffered the same fate as they saw the glider too late and couldn't get out of the way.

"Still shocked we stood and watched as the pilots jumped down from the cockpit and never spoke a word. The fuselage opened up, and a small tank drove out and past us, it disappeared off and still not a single word had been spoken. I still cannot get over the lack of talk by everyone there."

Ernst Krelwing (Owner of the Brambergskath Farm)

"My yard had about 50 German soldiers before the invasion and when they began firing the artillery at the English, the soldiers and civilians stayed in the cellar most of

the time. Early in the morning an Italian horse and cart came up the street and because of the artillery fire they also stayed with us, the horse was put in the barn. When the landings began the soldiers headed into the cellar of the house and they offered no resistance and they all ended up in captivity. The glider that crashed into the barn killed the horse that was left in there and the civilians that remained in the cellar, stayed in there for 3 days."

Lieutenant Ellis "Dixie" Dean MC (MMG Platoon)

"Order was gradually being restored and the RSM [Bob Duxbury] was left to do the tidying up as the CO took his 'O' Group to a nearby cottage. It was unoccupied and CO gave orders to move from the impromptu RV and the seizing of the objective. After we had finished I asked Dr Tibbs MC to have a look at my useless right shoulder. "You've dislocated it" he said. Private Bert Roe MM was there and he cut me out of my smock, removed my battle dress blouse and shirt, before resetting my shoulder. It was then strapped in position and put in a sling. They re-dressed me, fastened my equipment about me, slung the Sten over my shoulder and we moved back towards the woods.

"I joined the gunners and Sgt Egleton reported that 9 men, 2 guns and tripods were missing. The Airlanding Brigade gliders were coming in thick and fast and were sitting ducks coming in to land. Very few landed completely intact. There was no opposition on the ground and we took up pre-briefed positions. One of the missing gun teams awaited us; Jack Carr and Tommy Howell had landed almost on top of their planned position and had set up their gun firing across the DZ, before the gliders had started to arrive. A Hamilcar glider came diving straight at them and they had to get out of the way pretty dammed quick. The glider caught the gun, knocked it over and then smashed into a large wooden farm building."

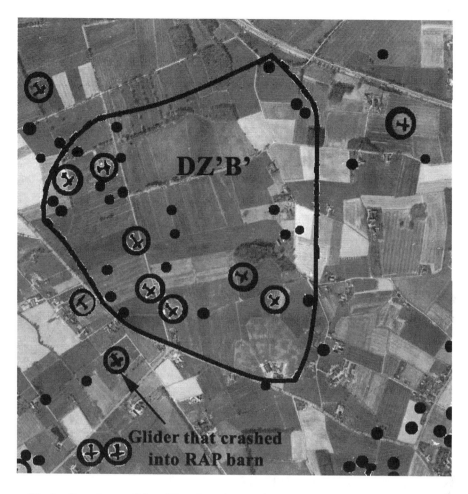

The landing places of the gliders in and around 13 Para's area (Hamilcars circled)
Created using Google Map Data © 2013

Lieutenant Peter Downward (Scout Platoon)

"The gliders continued to arrive as we gradually cleared the enemy from positions dominating the LZ. One particular glider, a Hamilcar came hurtling across the field towards us scattering the German POW's and crashed into the barn alongside Battalion HQ. I saw one of our Vickers MG sections disappear under the wreckage.

"There was no hope for the two glider pilots, nor was there much hope for the tank crew inside that devastation. Many soldiers including some POW's set about clearing the wreckage, lifting the heavy roof beams of the barn and doing their best to get to the chaps inside. Suddenly, to our amazement we heard an engine revving up inside this pile of rubble and after two or three grinding's and pushing's, the tank emerged and stopped a few yards away on some open ground. The main armament was bent and out of action, but amazingly the crew were all intact, though somewhat shaken. They got out and chatted away with us checking their maps and photographs, and even established radio contact with their HQ. The German POW's could not believe what they had just witnessed!"

507

A large Hamilcar glider hit Pte "Bill" Sanders (left). He was knocked out by one of the large wheels. His mate Pte GA Booth (right) was not so lucky; he was killed by the same aircraft as it crash landed. Bill's memory is somewhat sketchy, but he remembers that the glider carried a small Tetrarch tank.

Crashed and burned-out Horsa near Hamminkeln (IWM, Duxford)

Captain David Tibbs MC (RAMC)

"To my surprise I saw a tall, distinguished looking German officer striding through all the shot and shell with several men following him. As they approached I could see that this was a medical officer with his medics making for the Red Crosses on the house I had taken over for my RAP. He saluted me smartly and wished me good morning, and said "Vy have you been so long? Ve have been up all night vaiting for you!" He went on to explain that they were expecting us to come during the night but just as they were about to stand down this extraordinary air armada appeared.

"We worked in amicable fashion and he left as soon as the main battle had subsided. In these circumstances the German Army Medical Corps of the Wehrmacht seemed similar to our own RAMC."

Lieutenant Peter Downward (Scout Platoon)

"Captain David Tibbs [codename Starlight] set up his RAP in another of the barns as part of the HQ complex. In addition to our own casualties were several young Germans who had been wounded and were being tended by a German officer with a Red Cross armband. He also spoke English which helped our medics. In the entrance

508

of the barn were several stretcher cases awaiting evacuation but this wasn't going to be possible until the ground force linked up with us. I suddenly recognised one body on a stretcher as Lieutenant Austin Delaney (a Canloan officer serving with the 12th) and remarked to someone how sorry I was to see that Austin had been killed. There was a quick response from the prone figure. "I'm not dead, I've been hit and I can't bloody well move!" I was glad to learn later that he survived."

Lieutenant Ellis "Dixie" Dean MC (MMG Platoon)

"Digging in though essential, was always a bit of a bind, but there was the local volunteer diggers. Well I say they volunteered, we marked out what was to be dug, then handed our picks and shovels to our Boche POW's. They were still hard at work when the re-supply arrived.

"It was heralded by the growing roar of engines; the crescendo came from the rear and was overhead. A long line of 4 engine Liberators flashed over and immediately the sky was filled with multi-coloured chutes, floating gently to earth. Suddenly one of the planes rose almost vertically skywards, hung there for a moment, then plunged to the ground, exploding in a mass of flame and black smoke."

Private Ray "Geordie" Walker ('A' Company)

"We could hear the distant roar of four-engine bombers heading towards us, as they approached over the horizon we frantically waved our yellow triangle recognition neckerchiefs. A container landed at our feet and I said "Let's hope it contains rations, chocolate and cigarettes and not ammo."

Captain David Tibbs MC (RAMC)

"Some captured Germans troops whom we had put on to digging slit trenches were shot to bits by their own guns and I could not help feeling that it was deliberate. At that stage of the battle there were no set position and several times we had clear views of German hurriedly setting up guns a few hundred yards away perhaps not realising how close we were. During this phase one of our own artillery observation officers came into my RAP and unnoticed went to an upstairs window. I reminded him rather half heartedly that this was a building protected by a Red Cross flag and he replied with great charm "Good of you to let me in, Doc. Come and watch!" The invitation was irresistible and we watched a group of Germans heaving a gun put into position a few hundred yards away and putting branches as camouflage around it. He gave a brief order over his radio and 20 seconds later the area irrupted with shell fire and all activity ceased. It was not always easy to observe strictly the Geneva Convention and I was relieved when he left almost at once saying "Thanks, Doc"."

Sergeant Bill Webster (REME)

"We were dug in around Battalion HQ and I heard them talking about some members of the Battalion who were still missing after the drop. I went and reported that while standing in the door, I had seen some of the planes dropping men short of the DZ and while we were still flying over the woods. The CO questioned me and then I was sent back along the line of the fly in to see it I could find any of them.

"We drove off in the Jeep and soon were able to see chutes hanging in the trees. When we got closer we saw dead bodies on the ground too, they were all still in their harnesses. They never had a chance; they had come down right on top of a well prepared and camouflaged German Command Post. The bunkers and dugouts were some of the best constructed I ever saw and clearly the enemy had been expected to fight it out but there was no sign of them. To make sure, we dropped grenades inside before we entered they were empty."

Lance Corporal David "Robbie" Robinson (Anti-Tank Platoon)

"There were some nasty sights. Paratroops had been shot as they hung in the trees. It was sad for me to find the body of our young Colour Serjeant Charlie Wrigley, a great friend of mine and a South Lancs original. He had landed in a wood and been shot in the back."

Lieutenant Ellis "Dixie" Dean MC (MMG Platoon)

"Whist the positions were being dug I took the opportunity to ask around about the missing MMG Platoon members, and learned that they had definitely been killed attacking an Ack-Ack position at the bottom of the DZ.

"Corporal Anthony Cabrera (affectionately known as "Cab") was a MG No.1 [man who carried the tripod and fired the gun]. He joined the Platoon on our return from Normandy and was a well educated public schoolboy, a born leader and of Spanish descent. In the early days of the war he had been commissioned and sent out to West Africa, where he got into serious trouble and lost his commission, and had to re-join as a Private. He was determined to redeem himself and in my opinion did so. His aircraft was one of several which gave the signal to jump before they reached the drop zone, which resulted in the early numbers landing in enemy occupied posts. Lt Eric Barlow ['A' Company] collected such men and led them through to join the main body. Cpl "Cab" with the MMG tripod over his shoulders was an obvious target for snipers and was advised to drop the tripod; he refused to do so and paid the price for his self discipline and devotion to duty.

"L/Cpl Benjamin Langton, called "Ginger" because of his red hair was a Geordie and the finest type of young soldier – ever smart, aggressive and a quick learner. He was No.2 to "Cab" with the Vickers gun in his kitbag. He too joined up with Eric Barlow and also ignored the advice to leave the gun behind. He was killed by a sniper.

"Sergeant Fred Drew – The finest example of the professional regular soldier, whom I admired and respected, had many years of overseas service with the Kings Shropshire Light Infantry in Africa and Italy. In 1943 he, then a CSM, was given the opportunity to return home [Operation "Python"]. For some reason he over stayed his leave and was court martialled and reduced to the rank of Corporal. He joined the MMG's after Normandy and was by far the most 'battle hardened' man of us all, but he served under the 10 years younger Sergeants without a murmur of complaint. It was he who I asked to take Pte Colquhoun under his wing. They were both killed by small arms fire attacking a battery of 88mm guns.

"Private Joe "Taffy" Price was quiet and unassuming, but a brave, determined and a hard working member of the Platoon. He was wounded at the "Brickworks" in Normandy and re-joined in time for the Ardennes campaign. He too was killed by small arms fire attacking the 88's."

Lieutenant Peter Downward (Scout Platoon)

"About midday, Peter Luard ordered the Scout Platoon to go and help 'A' Company under Major Jack Watson about 400 yards away, as there was a wooded area nearby from which the enemy were sporadically firing with a 20mm 4 barrel anti-aircraft gun. It had already caused a few casualties and had to be eliminated. I closed in on Lt Eric Barlow's [No.3] Platoon to get a few pointers as to where the troublesome gun was. We moved forward through his position and dropped into a large ditch about 2 feet deep in water and started to leap frog forward, with one group observing whilst the other group went ahead. Above us there were bushes along the edge of the field, suddenly a series of machine gun bursts made it clear the enemy knew where we were. More was to follow, with that blessed 20mm gun blasting away at us with its explosive shells bursting above us. Earth and saplings were flying everywhere and we responded with a few shots in the enemy's general direction about 100 yards away. Fire was also coming from 'A' Company in support. One of my chaps pointed out that we had a casualty; I sloshed through the water to the crumpled figure lying in the water to find Pte Porrill, one of my youngest soldiers, still alive, but struggling for breath. With the help of a couple of others we dragged him part way up the bank so I could examine him properly and then realised he had been hit in the chest. I quickly unzipped his smock to uncover the wound, and out fell the mouth organ which he had been playing on the flight from England. Porrill was unconscious and losing a lot of blood which we tried to stem with field dressings. In a matter of seconds he was gone.

"There was no point in trying to bring the body back with us as we could suffer further casualties and already we were in difficulty as the Germans systematically raked the area above our heads. If they managed to get into an enfilade position at the far end of the ditch they would kill us all. I signalled to 'A' Company we were pulling back into their line and they intensified their covering fire, but we still had 30 yards to run to cover once we emerged from the ditch. I threw a smoke grenade to give us cover from view but it was not enough. From somewhere a 2" mortar smoke bomb landed a short distance away and then another, but neither gave us the cover we needed. Suddenly, to my amazement I saw one of 'A' Company's soldiers run forward under cover of the smoke generated, pick up the bombs and hurl them another 20 yards in our direction. We needed no further encouragement, we charged through the smoke and crashed down in the orchard amongst Eric Barlow's Platoon, followed by a fusillade of shots from the enemy into the smoke."

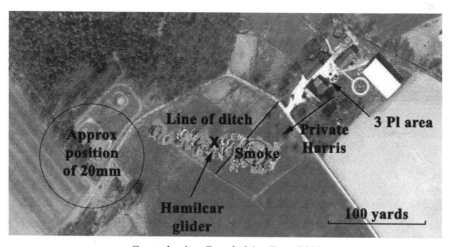

Created using Google Map Data 2012

Citation: Private Stephen "Taffy" Harris ('A' Company)

Award: Military Medal

On Saturday 24th March, 3 Pl 'A' Coy, 13th Bn. Parachute Regiment was detailed as a standing patrol on the extreme of the Brigade and Battalion's flank. In this position it was very strongly attacked by SP guns and infantry. Pte Harris during one enemy attack noticed that the Platoon flank was being threatened. He immediately dashed forward from the cover of his slit trench firing his Sten, and heedless of point blank 20mm and Spandau fire. The enemy surprised by the suddenness of his action retreated, leaving many dead. Later, when some Bn snipers were in difficulty, Pte Harris realising their danger went forward at once with a 2" mortar. In order to shorten his range, although himself exposed in the open and completely disregarding the enemy fire, he gave the snipers smoke cover to withdraw.

Throughout Pte Harris showed initiative and personal bravery of a very high order, and complete contempt for the enemy.

Lieutenant John May (44th Squadron, 316th Troop Carrier Group)

"At 12:30 we began coming in [to land back in Britain]—scattered, ragged remnants of a formation. Col. Lewis' Serial in the pattern preparing to land. B-4 Serial came over, and the pattern became a nightmare. There was gulping tenseness in the faces of ground men, as their eyes strained to count their planes. They began to land. Red flares were shot. Some planes began to taxi to the control tower. Ambulances throttled their engines. Men on the ground knew instinctively from the ragged formation in the air that something had gone wrong, that it wasn't a 'milk run.'

"In about 20 minutes all 20 of our planes had come back and no-one was wounded. Lucky 44th!! Some others were not so fortunate! In the 45th, two aircraft were reported missing in action."

1500   'A' Company outpost counter-attacked strength one company. 35 enemy killed and attack beaten off. By last light situation was quiet and apart from spasmodic shelling enemy made no attempt to counter attack during the night. Total PW captured during day 353.

Private Ray "Geordie" Walker ('A' Company)

"We now occupied and held a position on the west side of the Diersfordter Wald to protect the main road into Hamminkeln. This we held and repulsed an attack and suffered no casualties. During a lull in the fighting it was a pleasure to meet my pals, including Sergeant Braddock, Private's "Yanto" Evans, "Jock" Patton, "Paddy" O'Rourke and "Smudger" Smith. Sergeant Braddock was a first class battle experienced soldier who had fought in Europe, Algeria and Tunisia. We felt confident that we would survive the war under his leadership."

Private Dave Beedham ('B' Company)

"We finally dug in as briefed, close to a farm which the Germans must also have used because "Flash" Walker found one of their horse drawn cooking stoves. There were also chickens about and he caught, killed, plucked and dressed enough of them to fill the big copper boiler of the stove. There was more than enough for the whole Platoon and we all got a big mess tin full of really tasty chicken broth it beat the meat cubes of the 24 hour ration pack, I can tell you."

Lieutenant Peter Downward (Scout Platoon)

"It soon became apparent that the enemy fire was less intensive, and we learned that our ground forces were only a few miles away. There was intensive air support in the form of Typhoon fighters equipped with rockets. They wheeled around at 8,000 feet in what were termed 'cab ranks' and would break off and dive towards a target. One RAF pilot had to bail out, but was fortunate enough to land in our area. I believe one of our soldiers presented him with a pair of para wings.

"With the approach of nightfall, everyone became more anxious whilst awaiting the ground force to break through to us. Under the cover of darkness we recovered Porrill's body from the ditch. Other bodies were also being recovered and brought back to a central point for temporary burial by Padre Foy."

Private William "Paddy" O'Rourke (2 Platoon 'A' Company)

"Luard came down the line and said, "Get a patrol out to get those men out of the trees." I was chosen, and we set off for the woods. When we got there, Luard looked up into the trees and said, "Christ, no, it can't be. No, it can't be!" Then he said, "Cut those men down! Cut them down!" We did this quickly, and then I saw him looking at one of the bodies. It was that of a chap named Morrison. He wasn't nineteen, so he wasn't allowed to jump. He'd been to see Luard to ask permission. Luard had said, "It's the end of the war. There won't be much resistance, so I'll grant you permission." Morrison came back, cock-a-hoop." I remember Luard's face in the woods. I'd never seen tears in a man's eyes before. He said, "If I hadn't given him permission to jump, he'd still be alive."[83]

Captain David Tibbs MC (RAMC)

"As was my custom after a battle I walked widely over the area to make sure that all casualties had been gathered in. In the wood into which I had seen our men dropping at the initial assault, I found, to my distress, about 25 dead parachutists who had been caught in the trees, and whilst struggling to free themselves had been shot by Germans who had been gathered there in large numbers. Most of the parachutists were still hanging in their harnesses but some had reached the ground and one young officer, Selwyn, son of the Dean of Winchester, still had an automatic in his hand but with the side of his face blown away by a grenade. They were all from our Battalion and many I knew well. It was then I realised how fortunate we had been that Sergeant Webster had held off jumping until we had cleared the trees.

"In the 6th Airborne Division many RAMC Officers carried a revolver and so did a few Padres. The justification for this was to be able to defend the casualties under their care. I believe this was permissible under the Geneva Convention provided action of this sort was strictly limited. However, there was an element of fashion-ware in wearing a side arm. Also, I must confess that I used to carry a German Schmeisser

---

[83] Account from "The Last Drop" by Steve Wright.

9mm submachine gun to resist being taken prisoner when I was walking alone between widely separated Company positions. Probably, this put me in far greater danger even though I was competent in using it.

"I continued my walk across the open area and came across, perhaps 8 gliders that had attempted to land in full view of German Ack-Ack guns. Each was a tangled wreckage, some burnt out, and all surrounded by dead men, everyone in the glider, 30 in each case. It was deeply upsetting to know that these men had died without any opportunity to fight back and without any chance of surviving, but such is the penalty for being the attacking force with no element of surprise. Gliders, so marvellously successful with a silent approach at night, were totally vulnerable in an opposed landing by day."

Lieutenant Ellis "Dixie" Dean MC (MMG Platoon)

"Evidence of the violent reaction by some Ack-Ack guns lay all-around. In the next field to us, an American 'Curtis Commando' had forced landed. The GI's were uninjured and for a time stiffened our defences. Broken gliders littered the fields and a Hamilcar to our rear was loaded with spare Brens and ammunition. One Vickers was missing and one was damaged, so to boost the fire power of the Platoon everyone except the gun numbers acquired a Bren. CQMS Harry Watkins came round next morning and had orders to confiscate all such acquisitions, since there was a genuine need for them elsewhere. I accused him of being a spoil sport."

Corporal Doug Kelly (Battalion HQ)

"At 1600 hours everything was quiet in our sector. I had taken off my equipment and put it down in the barn. Being but a humble clerk with nothing to do I was approached by the Provost Sergeant and the next thing I knew I was guarding 40 prisoners. I was relieved about 2000 hours and my first thought was for 40 winks. Stumbling about in the dark I eventually found my equipment and got my head down.

"A few moments later I felt a gentle touch on my shoulder and a kindly voice asked me if I was warm enough. I replied in the positive but he insisted in putting more straw on me to keep me warm. I thanked him and thought to myself, "By Jove, he's a decent chap". Next morning I awoke, to find myself surrounded by wounded comrades and only then did I realise that they had made the Headquarters' barn into the sick bay."

Sergeant Arthur Laycock (Intelligence Section)

"The medics saw to my leg and I sat for some time on a chair in the kitchen. All the time more wounded came in and I had to make way for them. I was told to head for the main MDS [Hegemann-Hülshorst]. On my way, it started to become dark and I began to feel weak and miserable. I drove myself on slowly and finally I reached the farm. It felt as though I had travelled several miles, but on returning to the battlefield many years later, I was surprised to find that it was only about 500-600 yards.

"At the MDS, several orderlies were dealing with British, American and German wounded. I, myself was treated by a German doctor. I was left to lay with the others with a rolled up piece of parachute for a pillow. The next day I was put on a plane and flown back to England, where I was to spend the next 15 months in various hospitals."

Private Harry Trew ('A' Company)

"Later we marched through a number of gardens towards our aid station. Along side a hedge I saw a dead English soldier, this was the first time I'd seen a dead comrade. My Lieutenant [Lt Eric Barlow] didn't allow us the time to reflect and led us on. We had to defend the RAP garden through the evening and night in case of possible German attacks. I dug my foxhole with my mates under the kitchen window and from time to time the window was opened and a dead German or Englishman was passed out on a stretcher and placed under the window. After a long night they were all buried in the garden under the kitchen window the next day."

Private Derek Kenyon (Unknown Company)

"Late in the evening, when it was dark, I got the task of delivering a message about our situation to Brigade HQ. With my Lieutenant, we ran down the left side of the street, here there and everywhere we could hear shots being fired. In the darkness we were nervous about running into a German ambush and I don't mind admitting that I was very happy to reach the HQ. The return journey was much the same, again I was glad to reach my comrades once again and settle in my foxhole."

A – 13 Para Bn HQ   B – 5th Brigade HQ © Google Map Data

Private Ray "Geordie" Walker ('A' Company)

"By evening the Battalion had lost many Officers and men, including 7 men of my Platoon. Many men were wounded and several reported 'missing' eventually turned up. Captain "Joe" Hodgson [2i/c 'A' Company] was wounded and taken prisoner. A very close friend, Pte Eric Sell (left) of Canton, Cardiff was first reported missing and then presumed dead. Eric lived near of Shirley Bassey and claimed that she was 'coarse' and knew every English and Welsh swear word. I'd flown in the same Dakota and was saddened by his loss."

Eric Sell was only 19 when he was killed. Two years previous he had passed Ringway course 92 as a "Well disciplined, very satisfactory jumper." Eric and Ray Walker had become friends on the same jump course at Ringway and fought together in Normandy and the Ardennes.

Private Dave Beedham ('B' Company)

"That night in brilliant moonlight our section led by Sergeant Roughead were sent out onto the DZ as a listening patrol. We moved forward among the gliders and went to ground under the wing of a Hamilcar, because we could see German patrols moving about just ahead of us. We lay watching them all tensed up, because they were stronger in numbers than us, eventually they moved away and we were then able to continue to the wood where we had to wait and listen. However, short of our objective we could bear the Germans exchanging whistle signals from inside the wood, a better method than our 38 sets which were often useless. We had one on the patrol and the operator was next to me and all he could get was the American Forces Network."

Lieutenant Ellis "Dixie" Dean MC (MMG Platoon)

"The CO, seeing my arm in a sling, called for my batman [Jock Sloane] to put me to bed. He laid a parachute in the bottom of my slit trench and I wrapped up and settled down. I didn't wake until morning, so it must have been an uneventful night."

Lance Corporal David "Robbie" Robinson (Anti-Tank, 'C' Company)

"We eventually consolidated the area and for the night I was dug in on the German side of a railway line which ran through the landing area. During the night I was in a trench, a two man slit trench, with a chap who had just joined us. I was considered by now to be one of the old men of the Battalion, I was 21. This chap was a young lad of 18 named Hunter.

"Sometime in the early morning before light some Germans that had been captured escaped. One came over the railway lines and across from behind us almost jumping over our slit trench. I was armed with a pistol at this time as my weapon, with carrying the PIAT you couldn't carry a rifle. I pulled the trigger to shoot this Jerry and misfired. I yelled for him to stop and at the same time yelled at Hunter to shoot. He did shoot and shot the German. I went out the couple of hundred yards to the German and found that he'd been shot dead. Coming back to the slit trench I got in with Hunter again and all night long he kept saying to me, "Corporal I did right, didn't I? I shot him in the back you know, he wasn't armed you know. I did right, didn't I corporal?" This went on all night. Him being very nervous and wasn't sure whether he was being very soldierly by shooting an unarmed soldier in the back. Of course, he was reaffirmed that he had made the correct decision by a lot more people than me the following day."

Citation: Brigadier J.H.N. Poett (Commander 5th Parachute Brigade)

Award: Bar to DSO

On the 24th March 1945 Brigadier Poett dropped with his Brigade East of the Rhine with the task of clearing and holding the northern face of the divisional area. The dropping zone was strongly defended by infantry and flak guns. It was a case of every man for himself during the first few minutes, and it was here that Brigadier Poett, by personal example, inspired those around him with a fierce determination to get in amongst the enemy. It was in no small measure due to their leaders own complete disregard for his personal safety that the dropping zone was quickly cleared to enable units to rally. During the rally Brigadier Poett was constantly exposing himself in order to organise *his men for the assault on the Brigade objectives. These were taken in a remarkably short time. Throughout the day he put up a remarkable personal effort of sheer courage and determined leadership which infused his whole Brigade with tremendous enthusiasm.*

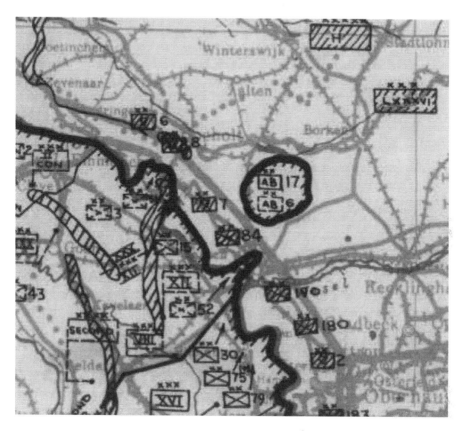

Above: Situation at 2400 hours, 24th March

ROLL OF HONOUR – OPERATION "VARSITY"

Pte	BOLTON John R.	24	24/03/1945	1680211	Reichswald Forest 41-B-2
Pte	BOOTH George A.	20	24/03/1945	14984669	Reichswald Forest 41-B-1
Pte	BOWERS Leslie T.	19	24/03/1945	14437811	N.K.G. Groesbeek Memorial
Pte	BOYES Harold W.	23	24/03/1945	1794779	N.K.G. Groesbeek Memorial
Cpl	CABRERA Anthony W.J.	24	24/03/1945	14711039	Reichswald Forest 41-A-10
Pte	COLQUHOUN William	18	24/03/1945	14851384	Reichswald Forest 41-D-10
Sgt	DREW Frederick A.	33	24/03/1945	4031235	Reichswald Forest 42-C-4
Pte	GRAVES Sidney	18	24/03/1945	14782076	Reichswald Forest 42-B-3
Pte	HALLIGAN Thomas	19	24/03/1945	14837591	Reichswald Forest 33-E-7
Pte	HILLS Dennis J.	21	24/03/1945	14992450	Reichswald Forest 41-A-7
L/Cpl	LANGTON Benjamin	20	24/03/1945	14733934	Reichswald Forest 41-C-5
Pte	McNICHOLS Thomas	18	24/03/1945	14995825	Reichswald Forest 41-B-7
Cpl	NEWTON John D.	29	24/03/1945	4269631	Reichswald Forest 42-C-10
Pte	PORRILL William	18	24/03/1945	14799062	Reichswald Forest 42-D-4
Pte	POULTER William J.	21	24/03/1945	14204468	Reichswald Forest 41-A-9
Pte	PRICE Joseph H.	25	24/03/1945	985515	Reichswald Forest 41-B-1
Pte	SELL Eric	19	24/03/1945	14635787	N.K.G. Groesbeek Memorial
Lieut	SELWYN Christopher A.		24/03/1945	94130	Reichswald Forest 42-D-2
Pte	SMIRKE Alfred T.J.	20	24/03/1945	14551845	Reichswald Forest 41-B-9
Pte	SMITH Marshall B.	31	24/03/1945	14363561	Reichswald Forest 42-A-9
L/Cpl	STRACHAN Thomas		24/03/1945	1132613	Reichswald Forest 42-E-3
Pte	THOMPSON Harold R.	18	24/03/1945	14433912	Reichswald Forest 42-D-1

Pte	THORNBORROW Kenneth	18	24/03/1945	14838809	Reichswald Forest 42-A-10
Pte	WALKER Godfrey E.	19	24/03/1945	14823878	Reichswald Forest 42-D-11
Pte	WARD Enoch J.	19	24/03/1945	14496425	Reichswald Forest 41-C-2
CSgt	WRIGLEY Charles A.	26	24/03/1945	3655942	Reichswald Forest 41-A-6

One name missing from the 13th Battalion Roll of Honour is that of Lieutenant-Colonel Gerald Henry Dearlove Ford MC. The former 13 Para second-in-command was killed during the day when his Divisional HQ was attacked by a force of German infantry. He personally led a counter-attack and was killed in the process.

Whilst serving with the 13th Battalion throughout Normandy, he had earned his Military Cross for his role in the actions at Putot-en-Auge and Pont L'Évêque before his promotion to Lieutenant-Colonel and transfer to Divisional HQ.

"The first sight of the inmates was unbelievable as they lined the inside of the fences looking out. They looked like living skeletons in striped prison uniforms, shaven heads, sunken eyes and all standing or supporting themselves against the wooden posts in absolute silence."

Sir Peter Downward

28.   MARCH TO THE BALTIC (25th March – 9th May 1945)

Lieutenant Peter Downward (Scout Platoon)

"Next morning, the tanks broke through and most impressive were the large canvas hulls now folded down to the level of the main body. There was a lot of chat between the Airborne and the Tank men recounting their experiences of the last 36 hours. Suddenly, there was an explosion on one stationary tank, hit by a German 88mm gun from several hundred yards away. The crew escaped and once again the Typhoons dived down out of the morning sky, whether they got the 88, we never found out."

Pte Ray "Geordie" Walker ('A' Coy)

"We now had some 350 prisoners and we found their presence a hindrance. Soon their numbers would be greater than our own. We were only too pleased to get rid of them by passing them onto other infantry regiments behind the frontline.

"Before leaving Hamminkeln we handed in our steel helmets and from this moment we wore our Red Berets. The sight of which would put the fear of God into German hearts and minds."

Photo: © IWM BU 2399

Lieutenant David Clark (225 Field Ambulance)

"I had started out in the plane with a staff sergeant, a corporal, 2 lance corporals and 15 men. By the end of the day the corporal and 2 men were dead, the staff sergeant and one lance corporal and 2 other men wounded.

"The unit [225 Field Amb] moved into a house in Hamminkeln and reinforcements joined us. A new staff sergeant and corporal were posted to my section and we began to put our equipment together again and to get to know one another. We also began to learn about our new position as a conquering army. Up till now, in France, Belgium and Holland we had been liberators - welcomed, providing medical (and other) services for the villages we were in, making happy friendships. Now we were among the Germans, our enemies.

"The flat fields, the solid farmhouses, seemed very like Holland and Belgium. The main difference was the plump prosperity, fields full of cows, barns full of corn, cellars full of preserves, hams and sausages, well fed women and children, in marked contrast to the starved Dutch and Belgians we had seen only 2 months earlier.

"The Germans' attitude to us, their conquerors, was not what we expected. They showed very little resentment or hostility. Some scowled but many smiled. All were deferential and keen to obey orders; many wished to be cooperative. All seemed delighted that "For us the war is over". The soldiers we captured on the battlefields turned willingly to necessary tasks such as digging graves and clearing rubbish. The villagers asked for orders and directions. Most of them seemed to welcome authority."

Lieutenant Ellis "Dixie" Dean (MMG Platoon)

"Major Jack Watson (below) was now standing in for Roy Leyland as second-in-command. Roy had been called to help out at Brigade as both Brigade Major [Mike  Brennan] and Ted Lough were wounded. Lt "Joe" Hodgson was missing[84] and Freddie Skeate was walking wounded, the only officer known to be killed was Chris Selwyn.

"There were letters to be written to the next of kin of the killed Platoon members. I sat at the table in a nearby farmhouse and practiced writing with my left hand.[85] I laboriously finished and then had the much more pleasing task of promoting Cyril Andrews to L/Sergeant.

"Later in the day we were on the move, passing Hamminkeln railway yard was a scene of indescribable chaos. Several Horsas of the Ox & Bucks had hit the tall trees. However they succeeded in their task of seizing the bridge over the River Issel. Over the bridge we passed a knocked out Panther, hit by a 6 Pounder and slewed off the road into a ditch."

Above: Hamminkeln Railway Station 25th March 1945 (IWM, Duxford)

---

[84] Lieutenant Hodgson was wounded and captured during the drop.
[85] Injured his right shoulder on landing.

Lieutenant Ellis "Dixie" Dean (MMG Platoon)

"March 26th was a frustrating day of stops and starts; it was cold, with drizzly rain from time to time. The 7th were in the lead and our move forward was interrupted several times by minor skirmishes. Even after dark the frequent rattle of MG42's and Bren's could be clearly heard."

The Scout Platoon were often in the lead and at one point "Bing" was sent to investigate a house, nearing the house he froze indicating German presence to his handler and at this point 2 German dogs ran towards him, wanting to play. One of the Scout platoon spoke German and quickly took command of the dogs. The building was promptly surrounded and many prisoners were taken.

Lieutenant Peter Downward (Scout Platoon)

"Very soon we were on the move. Our route was towards Graven, a small town where we anticipated there might be some stiff resistance. As we crossed the railway line running northwards from Hamminkeln, I could see some aircraft wreckage in the trees about 200 yards to our left and sent a small party of my chaps to investigate. It was the Horsa glider we had seen plummet into the ground 2 days earlier. Of the 20 or so [Royal Ulster Riflemen] bodies still trapped inside, 3 were still alive. One of the three was reasonably 'compos mentis' and whist waiting for the medics to take over he gave a brief account of what happened. The two pilots had both been hit and the glider had simply gone out of control. We weren't allowed to linger as Luard was urging me to push on.

"In the ditches odd bits of German infantry equipment and weapons could be seen, then a knocked out halftrack with twisted bodies lying around it. By this stage I was becoming immune to the sight of death, which would evoke remarks from the soldiers. Lt-Col Luard enforced rigidly, "No looting". We all knew this would be a court martial offence and it was up to the officers to enforce."

Lance Corporal David "Robbie" Robinson (Anti-Tank 'C' Company)

"In all my time in the army, the most horrific sight I remember was that of the burned out gliders – with charred bodies still sat in their seats. The pilots still held onto their controls and were literally cooked alive."

Lieutenant Harry Pollak (Intelligence Officer)

"From then onwards we made rapid progress. Our job was to lead the British 2nd Army to the Baltic, and on our way to liberate as many prisoner of war camps as we could; further to meet the Russians as far east as we could and to prevent them from getting too far into the west of Germany."

War Diary 27th March

1045   Advance resumed with ERLE 398503 being objective of 5 Para Bde. Order of march 7th Bn - 12th Bn - 13th Bn. Route BRUNEN 4827 - X Tracks 279486, STEERGERMANT.

1400   Advance temporarily halted owing to bridge River ISSEL at 304483 and 306486 being blown.

Brigadier Nigel Poett (5th Para Brigade Commander)

"We received orders to advance at once on the town of Erle. As we moved forward the German resistance stiffened. We made our advance into the town by night and attacked it from the rear.

"This type of encirclement operation became a pattern for most for our operations and was highly successful. The important thing was to keep up the momentum of our advance and not allow the Germans time to withdraw in an orderly manner and reform. At this stage all movement was on foot."

2300   7th Bn encountered heavy opposition from light 20 mm AA guns and were delayed in their advance at MR 309484. Consequently 13th Bn were ordered to outflank enemy positions and to seize and hold SOUTH WESTERN outskirts of ERLE.

Lieutenant Peter Downward (Scout Platoon)

"We could see 2 villages on fire ahead of us to the right and left of our axis, and understood that the 7th and 12th Battalions were already in action. We had to advance between them and take the village of Erle. I was given the task of leading the Battalion almost in single file. I was aware that I was very vulnerable, with a map in one hand and a torch I could only use sporadically for fear of showing up my position.

"Pte Kirkbride, a Liverpool docker, who was a couple of paces in front of me, acted as my ears and eyes in the dark, suddenly heard a weapon being cocked about 50 yards ahead and then a subdued voice issuing a challenge. We froze and gave a convincing reply to be rewarded by a clear English command "Advance!" We found it was a company of the 7th Battalion. They told us the enemy was not far ahead and undoubtedly in the village of Erle, half a mile ahead. There was no time to hang about as I kept on getting calls over the radio from Peter Luard to get a move on. I was far more afraid of him than I was of the enemy."

Lieutenant Peter Downward (Scout Platoon)

"Soon we found ourselves on an elevated road with steep banks either side down the fields and then a stream under the road, which according to my map showed that we were close to the village. Suddenly a burst of MG42 fire was directed at us and then rifle fire confirmed we were in contact. I shouted "Go left!" to get behind the high shoulder of the road as most of the fire was coming from the right. There followed a long exchange of fire, flares going up and after about 10 minutes a series of friendly artillery salvoes which at first were too close for comfort. More exchanges over the radio and I was told to stay where I was and continue firing whilst 'C' Company moved round to our left. The best we could do was to fire in the enemy's direction as it was pitch dark and engage the numerous flashes. One particular MG was obviously on fixed lines and the constant firing of this belt-fed gun was good enough to pinpoint its position and a concentrated burst from two of my Brens, firing a full magazine of 28 rounds apiece seemed to do the trick. My LMGs were red hot as the recognised practice was to fire bursts of 3 or 4 rounds.

"Eventually the enemy fire diminished as 'C' Company closed in on them with grenades and close quarter fire from the Stens. There were a few casualties but no one was killed. The enemy however had suffered 2 killed and there were 4 or 5 young prisoners being passed back who seemed only too ready to give up.

"Next morning to our concern, there were 2 cows that had been caught in the fire fight. Peter Luard inspected them and the most badly wounded one was put down with a high velocity shot in the middle of the forehead. He then ordered as many young officers that could be spared to come forward to the main farmhouse as he had a job for them. About 10 of us reported and were asked by Peter if any of us knew how to milk a cow. There was silence, whereupon we were given a demonstration, then allocated 2 or 3 cows that were bursting with milk. There was no question of saving the milk; it was merely to make the cows more comfortable. I think the German farmer was grateful and he was assured that the war had gone past him."

War Diary 28th March

0845   Advance resumed objective COESFELD 5969. Route ERLE 398503 - RHADA 443506 - HOFE 447523 - MR 457527 - 508597 - 515598 - Road junction 552675. Unit halted at 590696 and received orders to pass through 12th Bn who had led the advance up to then and to secure and hold bridge and road area 590714 supported by two troops of CHURCHILLS of 4 Bn GRENS.

Brigadier Nigel Poett (5th Para Brigade Commander)

"Morale was high and long distances were covered, knowing that in this way, casualties could be kept to a minimum. Fifty miles were covered on foot during the first three days. This included two night attacks and almost continuous fighting or marching. It was a tremendous achievement and the troops had every reason to be proud of themselves."

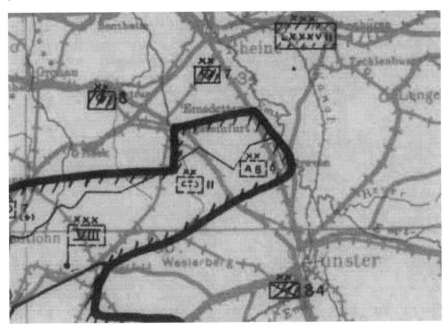

Sergeant Len Cox ('C' Company)

"After a week of almost non-stop marching the advance was held up at Greven, where we had to wait for the Sappers to bridge the river. No.3 Commando was also in the vicinity and I got permission from the CO to visit them. I was re-united with CSM Maurice Bennett who had escaped with me in Normandy. The Commandos had liberated a barrel of beer, so we had a good booze up together."

War Diary 31st March

0845 *Move continued without opposition to road junction 874886 where Unit suffered slight casualties from enemy air bursts at 1010 hrs.*[86]

1230 *AARR reported that 3 Para Bde were in possession of GREVEN and preparing to continue advance.*

1300 *Unit was ordered to move into GREVEN on foot as bridges were blown, and to secure and hold the WESTERN side of GREVEN, which was completed by 1500 hrs. Throughout the afternoon enemy airbursts came down over the Bde area.*

Lieutenant Peter Downward (Scout Platoon)

"We moved through Coedfeld on 30th March without too much resistance and next day as we approached Greven there was strong resistance around the outside of the town and the Scout Platoon came into its own with my snipers notching up some 'kills'. Our supporting tanks helped clear the way and we soon entered the deserted town. We searched the houses, expecting booby traps or 'stay behind' parties intent on dying for the Fuehrer, but we found no-one. One house I entered was obviously occupied as we could tell by the hot kettle on the stove. After shouts of "Kommen sie hier!" and "Handes hock!" we heard a noise in the cellar, like an automatic weapon being cocked. Two of my members Pte Kelly and Pte Webb drew pins from their grenades and were about to bowl them down the stairs when I heard a female voice in the dark below. They replaced the pins and we ordered those in the cellar to come up. To my amazement and horror it was an elderly German frau and her daughter and five grandchildren. What could have happened, I hate to think.

"Another incident that occurred in Greven was an attempted rape of a German fraulein by one of my soldiers. I remember his name well, but will refer to him as Pte X. Somehow the girl's complaint had come to the notice of Sergeant Major Batho MM and a Field Court Martial was convened in Graven. Pte X was given something like 56 days "field punishment". The court was comprised of Major McLoughlin, myself and Sgt Major Batho. The translation between the German girl and us was done by Harry Pollak [Intelligence Officer].

"Greven had practically no war damage and soldiers were able to sleep in beds, cook in kitchens and stroll down the streets looking at shops (all closed) and even chat to the occasional German civilian. We came across a young German girl (about 18 or 19) who not only spoke good English, but was an ardent member of the Hitler Youth movement. She assured us that the Fuehrer would retake this area and we would all be punished. My Liverpool soldiers could not think up a suitable German equivalent of "Get stuffed" and she was promptly handed over to the Intelligence Section."

---

[86] Private Wilfred Gardner was the only listed casualty on the Roll of Honour for 31st March.

Lieutenant Ellis "Dixie" Dean (MMG Platoon)

"On a rest day for the Battalion I was sent by David Tibbs to the ADS for my shoulder to be inspected. The ADS was in a pleasant villa on the outskirts of Hamminkeln (185495) and after speaking to an NCO, who was calling out names, I found out that everyone there was "an evacuation casualty". I didn't like the sound of that. The windows in the room were large and wide open, I recognised a Jeep from 225 Field Ambulance, out the window I went and I climbed aboard and was driven back to the Battalion, reporting that nothing further needed doing.

"For the next few days we saw for the first time DP's [Displaced Persons] who were slave labourers of the Reich, forced from their homes in astern Europe and made to work. They were close to starvation and the thin striped uniform they wore could hardly hide their thin bodies.

"One sighting in particular sticks in my mind. Moving along a road through a Pine forest as we approached the river Elbe, a (German army horse drawn supply column had been strafed by the RAF, killing the animals. These, by the time we passed were just skeletons, every last strip of flesh having been removed by the scavenging, starving workers."

Captain David Tibbs MC (RAMC)

"As MO I joined in and from time to time relieved a man who was having difficulty in carrying a heavy load (such as a machine gun barrel or mortar base plate), and had to admit that it was very tough going! The British paratrooper was renowned for his ability to march and had had very hard training in this. The American paratroops, which were still with us, were quite unused to marching but stuck it out very well. I had to give their feet repeated attention for blisters, they showed great spirit and we were sorry to see them go a few days later."

Alan Moorehead (War Correspondent)

"The farms were rich, pigs and horses running everywhere. One could turn into any house at random and find a cellar lined with preserved vegetables and fruits. It was nothing unusual to come on many sides of bacon. Silk stockings were common place, and there was always a variety of electrical gadgets like radio sets, cookers and vacuum cleaners. On the walls no signs of Nazi flags or pictures of Hitler; these had been snatched down at the last minute, you would always find a discoloured patch of wallpaper."

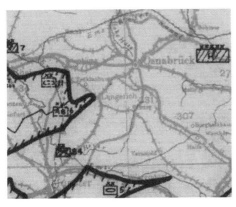

Lt Ellis "Dixie" Dean (MMG's)

"Platoon HQ occupied a DIY shop and behind it was a large wooden building housing a Wehrmacht clothing store. Hanging in the cupboard was a brand new greatcoat, lined with Astrakhan fur. It fitted me perfectly, but I had no way of transporting it, so it remained behind.

"The next day was Easter Sunday [1st April] and Padre Foy held a service in the cinema. Colour Sergeant Ted

Hewitt complained that no-one was turning up for meals, we were all "living off the land" – every house was well stocked with eggs, ham and rows and rows of bottled fruit in the cellars."

Brig Poett (5th Para Bde Commander)

"At this stage a squadron of Grenadiers from Lt-Col Charlie Tryon's Armoured Regiment joined us. It was a great help. We also began to get some lorries which speeded up our movement. And thus the advance went on; Osnabruck became our next objective, always using the same tactics, which were proving so successful."

War Diary 2nd April

0915   *S.P. MR 908883 crossed and advance continued in TCV with the objective of road to OSNABRUCK and high ground EAST of LENGERICH 082965.*

1000   *Owing to congestion of bridge of DORTMUND EMS CANAL 978892 Unit halted area 937885.*

1645   *Canal crossed and outskirts of LENGERICH 0896 reached.*

2200   *Advance resumed with objective High Ground dominating OSNABRUCK extending from MR 146035 - 179023.*

2300   *Enemy LMG fire caused two casualties. At the same time 12th Bn came up against serious opposition on high ground 1201. They were given the task to mop up the area by first light and this Unit consolidated in area 123011 with orders to resume advance at 0200 hrs. Patrols detailed to secure the flanks captured 8 PW and wounded the enemy NCO.*

Private Ray "Geordie" Walker ('A' Company)

"Our daily progress was measured by forced marches of 25 to 35 miles, punctuated with spells of fighting. These marches wrought havoc on my feet as they were now blistered and bleeding after marching in new boots and after having recently lain in a hospital bed, the soles of my feet were as soft as a baby's. My feet looked like plates of raw meat. I 'acquired' a bicycle and rode it until punctures made further use hopeless. I threw the cycle into a ditch and sat on the grass verge. The Battalion moved on, leaving me to fend for myself.

"Good luck attended me by way of a Churchill tank of the Grenadier Guards. The lead tank stopped and the Commander asked what my problem was. On my reply he said, "Come aboard" and I sat with my back against the gun turret. After a few miles we stopped at a farmstead for an overnight halt. They gave me a meal and I bedded down on some straw in a barn after having my feet attended to by their medics.

"After a good night's rest we moved off and soon caught up with my battalion. I thanked the Commander for the hospitality and medical treatment and wished each other "Good Luck."

"I had to withstand many jocular comments regarding my absence. However, it was good to be back amongst friends. We advanced on Osnabruck and our casualties were few and we took more prisoners everyday, they were delighted to be free from the horrors of war."

Lieutenant Colonel Peter Luard DSO (Commanding Officer)

"Then a short MT move followed by the wonderful sight of the 13th supported by an armoured Squadron of the Grenadier Guards, advancing 2 companies up and refusing to pause, no matter what the enemy might do, over running all opposition for 8 miles on the road to Osnabruck. Success was due to the vigorous attacks put in by the leading companies each supported by a troop of tanks."

Lieutenant Ellis "Dixie" Dean (MMG Platoon)

"The Germans were determined to delay us as much as possible and there followed many minor skirmishes. The night was punctuated by a series of bursts of MG fire and the occasional Verey light arcing into the sky. Each time this happened we went to ground on the rain sodden pastures and before long we got wetter and wetter. I became very miserable indeed. At one stage there was a feeble attempt to ambush the rear of our column, resulting in 2 casualties, one of which was the RSM (Duxbury, left); he went back off to hospital.[87]

"The CO called an 'O' Group in a cottage and as we were inspecting the maps by torchlight, in walked the Brigadier. He said he was calling a halt to the advance and in the morning we were to pass through the 12th and would form the vanguard. We were to get a good night's sleep and be ready to move at dawn. A "good night's sleep" would be all of 3 hours."

"Breakfast arrived in the dark and it was a scramble to get everyone served, as a result men marched to war, mess tins in hand. Shortly after setting off a squadron of Churchill tanks caught up with us. The Boche was still trying to delay the advance and the Churchill's responded with HE and machine guns. As the houses were set ablaze, out came tumbling the prisoners.

"A low wall ran from a farmhouse to a barn and I crouched behind it searching the middle distance with my binoculars. I was aware that a Churchill had manoeuvred behind me into a gap, but the firing of its main armament took me by surprise. There were only 3 yards between us and the gunner let fly. The sound was deafening and the blast threw me against the wall of the house, leaving my head ringing. No apologies the tank rolled forward, firing as it went. It must have been fun for an armoured unit when there were no anti-tank guns about."

Panoramic view of Osnabruck, early 20th Century

---

[87] A report on this incident states the capture of 10 POW armed with MG's and a Panzerfaust. CSM Roy Parrish (APTC) was installed as the acting RSM.

War Diary 3rd April

0830   Advance continued with 'C' Coy on left and 'B' Coy on right of road and 'A' Coy in position. One troop of CHURCHILLS supported each forward Coy and one troop and SP anti-tank remained in position. The terrain was well suited for defence and 'B' Coy soon came up against strong dug-in positions in the hilly and wooded features. After a determined attack by 'B' Coy the enemy was over-run and 70 PW including a Lt-Col were taken.

Lieutenant Peter Downward (Scout Platoon)

"The battle for Osnabruck was expected to be quite a big operation and the whole of 5 Para Brigade was assigned to it. Initially 13 Para were leading and as we crossed the railway line on the south-west of the town 'B' Company came under heavy fire from some 88's and MG's. Our supporting tanks were well forward and were putting down some heavy fire. Through my binoculars I could see some 'B' Company casualties prone in the middle of some open ground; one of them I could see was Pte [Leslie] Clissold who had been with me in Holland when I was commanding No.6 Platoon. As we moved forward up a slope to the outskirts of the town we found an electric tram abandoned at the end of the line which sloped away into the centre of the built up area. There was a lot of small arms fire being directed at us from various houses and it was obvious that the enemy was going to fight it out. For the Scout Platoon this was going to be a real sniper operation, or at least counter-sniper."

1100   A further strong enemy pocket of resistance was encountered on the left of the road in area of railway line MR. For the loss of 6 men 'C' Coy captured and killed 48 enemy.

1540   'B' Coy reached the outskirts of OSNABRUCK followed by 'C' and 'A' Coys and BHQ. An enemy counter attack by LMG fire was disposed of by fire from AP anti tanks. Enemy sniping continued throughout the rest of the day and was successfully dealt with by the Scout Platoon who killed 8 enemy snipers. The success of the day was mainly due to the vigorous attacks put in by the forward Coys and the excellent support given by 4 GRENS.
Total PW taken 143.[88]

Sergeant Len Cox ('C' Company)

"After a couple of hours sleep we were on the move again, passing through the 12th and were soon joined by the Churchill's of the Armoured Guards. Several small villages were cleared with the help of the tanks without any slowing of the advance. We crossed a railway line and could see a low ridge some distance ahead. When we were right out in the open the Company were caught in heavy machine gun fire, suffering a number of casualties. We took what cover we could until an artillery barrage was brought down on the enemy positions and we could move forward once again with the tanks in support. The action ended with the a platoon bayonet charge into the woods, led by Lieutenant Basil Disley [No.8 Platoon] and where we took quite a bag of prisoners."

---

[88] For the loss of privates: John Broadbent, Leslie Clissold, Gwilym Griffiths, Thomas Harmer, Robert Irvin, Jack Lawes*, William Morse*, Leslie Rodgers and Lawrence Whitlock.
* Both attached from the Royal Scots.

Osnabruck displays its battle scars in April 1945

Lieutenant Ellis "Dixie" Dean (MMG Platoon)

"I had been given the task of consolidating the road junction defensive position. I decided to have a closer look at the building that Colonel Luard had chosen for his HQ. It was easily the most distinctive property in the neighbourhood, standing on a hillock, with a commanding view back along the line of the advance. It was constructed in a golden stone. The gardens were well tended and there was no front door. "Jock" Sloane and myself walked its full length and eventually found the entrance, inside, piled high was cardboard coffins containing charred bodies, victims of a recent air-raid. It was the city crematorium.

"Around the corner came Jack Birkbeck (left) of the Scouts and a real character. "Excuse me Sir; I think I've been hit." I laughed and said "Come on now Sergeant, you've seen enough action to know if you've been hit." He raised his trousers to his knee and surely enough a bullet had passed clean through the fleshy calf muscle without causing bleeding.

"The rifle companies, judging by the sounds of battle, were heavily engaged in the city. I wasn't sorry not to be involved in the street fighting. Urban areas were not the place to use the Vickers, as we had learned to our cost in Pont L'Eveque and Bure.

"The forward companies reported over the air that they were running short of ammunition and Bill Webster the REME fitter, impossible to keep away from the fighting, volunteered to take a Jeep and trailer and drove off into the city. The exact location of the leading troops was not known, since they reported to HQ that a Jeep and trailer had driven through their positions and crashed after being shot up."

Sergeant Bill Webster (REME)

"I know I should not have been there but I was up with Battalion HQ when word came that the leading Platoon of 'C' Company were held up by machine guns on the right. I collected a couple of the lads and we started to work our way forward on the left through some rough ground near the graveyard so we could get within grenade throwing range.

"We were not spotted until we flushed out a single German soldier from behind a bush. He jumped up and started to run away. We opened fire, hitting him and he fell to the ground yelling blue murder. Then we crawled forward to where he was lying and he screamed louder than ever, thinking we were going to kill him. I knelt up on one knee to treat his wounds, when another MG on the other flank, which up to now had not fired, opened up and I caught a burst in the neck and side which threw me over backwards. I couldn't move but was able to speak and I told the other lads to go and fetch the Medics. As I waited for them to come two German civilians waving a white flag and carrying a stretcher appeared. The woman could speak English and she said they would take the wounded German and then come back for me. Which they did and I think it must have been their own house they carried me to and where I waited until four stretcher bearers arrived to carry me to their first aid post.

"From here I was moved to a convent at Haste outside Osnabruck to the east, where I was prepared for an operation. They came to put the mask over my face and I tried to stop them, so a young nun said "Don't worry we will not harm you.""

Captain David Tibbs MC (RAMC)

"We moved on to Osnabruck. A German woman came up and begged me not to allow my soldiers to rape her daughter, to which I replied "Madam, these are British soldiers" much to the amusement of my men. It was here that Sgt Bill Webster went to the assistance of a wounded German only to be shot in the neck and seriously injured. The Germans realised that they had made a mistake and took him to a Hospital on the other side of Osnabruck. Word reached us (by the German medics) that this was so and the Padre and myself, plus a driver, set off in a jeep with a large Red Cross flag to make sure that Bill was being well looked after.

"It was an extraordinary journey, driving with headlights on and horn blaring at crowds of civilians milling about in the roads, uncertain where to go. The centre of Osnabruck was a scene of utter desolation, with a mass of burnt out ruins amongst which many unexploded hexagonal (British) incendiary bombs could be seen. Surprisingly, we found the hospital undamaged on the outskirts of Osnabruck. It was run by Nuns, largely filled with German wounded and a few British soldiers. We were greeted in a correct but helpful fashion by the Medical Colonel in charge and the Mother Superior. Yes, Sgt Webster was here. The bullet had passed close to his cervical spinal cord and caused total paralysis. The surgeon had removed the bullet and believed that recovery was possible.

"We were taken to see him and found him in his usual irrepressible good spirits although now tinged with apprehension. He was, of course, enormously pleased to see us and said how well the Germans had looked after him and had apologised for shooting him whilst helping one of their men.

"There were several British soldiers in the same ward and the Colonel could not resist telling us that they had been wounded by our own artillery. Whilst talking, there was a series of heavy explosions and columns of smoke not far away, and we were told that these were ammunition dumps being blown up to prevent them from falling in to our hands. Our contact with the Colonel and Mother superior had become quite cordial and before we left we joined them in a glass of schnapps, drinking to an early end to the war. We drove back as we had come with a charmed passage by the Red Cross flag, and saw again the confused masses of civilians that parted before us like the Red Sea for Moses."

Sergeant Bill Webster (REME)

"Doctor Schmidt a German civilian doctor operated on me and although I was completely paralysed at the time, he assured me I would eventually be all right. Doc Tibbs and the Padre came through the German positions to visit me and agreed with Doctor Schmidt that I should not be moved for the time being. The Germans even provided me with a Yankee orderly he had spent most of his life since early childhood in the States, but was visiting his parents in Germany in 1939 and since he had not become an American citizen was called up for military service."

Lieutenant Peter Downward (Scout Platoon)

"We moved in pairs and I acquired a sniper rifle from someone in the platoon so that I could have a go; normally I carried a Sten. Kirkbride acted as my No.2 as we spotted for each other, looking for targets. We climbed into a fairly high building from the back of which we could see some open ground and what appeared to be allotments in the centre of which was a mound possibly concealing an air raid shelter. There was no doubt there were numerous weapons in the area as we kept hearing the crack and thump of single rounds coming in our direction.

"The approach into the town was becoming a real 'sniper's alley' and the Scout Platoon was kept busy as we spotted and fired from inside the buildings, far back from the open windows. Sgt Birkbeck and his team were looking after the street and buildings opposite; I with my team was watching the open ground at the back, though all of us were in separate rooms and buildings.

"Kirkbride and I pulled a large cupboard into the centre of what was somebody's bedroom, placed some pillows on top and then took up firing positions about 6 feet back from the window. Kirkbride was scanning the area through his scope and drew my attention to the air-raid shelter 300 yards away. "Someone has just fired from the top of that mound and is moving to the left" he explained. "Go left to the telegraph pole at the end of the shelter. I think he is making his way to another fire position. Yes, I can see the top of his helmet." I followed along the top of the shelter through my telescopic sight and there was the German helmet very slowly turning as the sniper scanned his area of fire through his scope. I had his head spot in the middle of my telescopic sight, my safety catch off, but couldn't press the trigger. I realised that I had a young mans life in my hands and for the cost of one round, could wipe out his 18 or 19 years of life. Kirkbride suddenly shouted, "Go on Sir. Shoot the bastard! He's going to fire again." I pulled the trigger and saw the helmet jerk back. I had obviously got him and I felt completely drained. What had I done? Despite Kirkbride's congratulations I could not help thinking of the events that were to follow. The identification and registration of the German casualty, the telegram to his parents and then the grieving. Although I had caused casualties before, but never before in such cold blood. Like the rest of my chaps in the Scout Platoon, I could be identified as a sniper; nearly all of us bore the bruise and cut over the right eye having been too close to the sight as we fired."

The Lee Enfield No.4 (T) Sniper Rifle with No.32 Scope

"As the enemy retreated into the town and our tanks came forward, one of my soldiers decided to release the brakes on the electric tram and it careered down the hill and round the bend into 'A' Company's area. I could hear various exchanges over the Battalion net that a No.9 tram had come round the corner and was being investigated. I didn't admit that it was a bit of Scout platoon horseplay, but the incident passed. I retraced the area 35 years later and found the tramlines had disappeared as had my unobstructed view of the allotments and the air raid shelter had gone.

"Before resuming the line of our march, my soldiers were intent on finding their kills. Mine was exactly where I had hit him. He was a young man probably around 18 or 19 and I had got him just forward of his left ear, his helmet, still on his head, had been knocked backwards and his rifle was under his body. I was horrified at the callous way my chaps went through his pockets, looking for items of intelligence value and then rolling him down the side of the mound into the allotment below. How ghastly war could be. The RAF could kill hundreds and never see their victims, but sniping was almost like a personal duel; it was you or the other chap and a case of who fired first."

Lieutenant Ellis "Dixie" Dean (MMG Platoon)

"Later in the day units of the Commando Brigade passed through and took on the task of clearing the city. We had a quiet night and next morning all was peaceful and I was in my CP making a leisurely survey of the broad valley before me. I caught sight of a Jeep moving along to another part of Osnabruck. I was watching its progress with binoculars, when suddenly a Panzerfaust was fired in its direction I could clearly note where it was fired from and had the nearest guns engaging the area for 5 minutes.

"For the next week we rolled on relentlessly, moving in transport most of the time. The RAF had established complete mastery of the skies and since there was a series of water obstacles to be crossed the sappers worked non-stop. There were inevitable delays and huge quantities of vehicles, standing nose to tail frequently built up and would have been an easy target for Focke-Wolfs, but they never appeared."

Private Ray "Geordie" Walker ('A' Company)

"Somewhere along the road between Osnabruck and Hannover, I had a pleasant surprise; I met my old pal Jack Lee (who I had given 10 shillings before we emplaned). Learning of our exploits in the press he decided to come and join us. This involved deserting the Royal Ordnance Depot at Didcot, from where he had been posted after leaving us at Shudy Camp. After many adventures he had been able to hitch hike to Dover, caught a ferry to Calais and then across North West Europe on the back of various lorries moving up to the frontline. Being resourceful he completed his journey without too many problems. The charge of desertion was dropped on the grounds that a soldier could not be charged with this offence whilst fighting in the frontline. Everyone was happy when his situation was finally and satisfactorily resolved."

Photo taken in Osnabruck, April 1945 and some years later given to David Robinson: "I have forgotten who gave it to me. But, he did say that I was the one standing on the left, but I don't recall the incident."

Lieutenant Peter Downward (Scout Platoon)

"Early morning 6th April, we were on the march again. It was very hot and the troops were becoming extremely thirsty. We halted in a village for 10 minutes rest having covered 10 miles. Thirsts were quenched and water bottles refilled from a

pump in a nearby garden. Everyone readjusted their kits and we were ready to move on, only to find we were one member of the platoon short; Alsatian Bing (pictured with Cpl Aaron "Jack" Walton of the Scout Platoon, IWM Duxford) was missing. After a frantic search we found a barn door with a clearance from the ground of about 12" and there was Bing, who had found a large basin of clear liquid and had obviously slaked his thirst in it. It was a drip tray under a huge wine butt and I suddenly realised that we had an intoxicated war dog on our hands. He was bundled into the back of a Jeep together with his handler and we set forth."

Lieutenant Ellis "Dixie" Dean (MMG Platoon)

"By late morning [7th April] we had advanced a fair way towards our objective [the River Leine Bridge at Neustadt] before it was destroyed. Ahead of us MG42's opened up on 7 Para still in their trucks, we later heard. Immediately we were out of our transport and dispersed about the fields. The battle was for the Wunstorf airfield."

Lieutenant Colonel Geoffrey Pine-Coffin (CO 7th Battalion)

"After passing Wunstorf the road swings due north and passes over an airfield; at about 154303 there was a bit of badly churned up mud and after crossing it myself, I slowed up considerably to see if the 3-tonners could get over it all right.

"When I saw that they could I sped up again and had myself just reached the edge of the wood at 155308 when I spotted 2 Germans at the side of the road about 50 yards in front of me. They were not behaving like the other Germans we had met and could be seen to jump into a slit trench. The scout car unhappily, did not mount a Bren gun and all the occupants of it were pistol armed. Expecting a burst of MG fire at any moment, I stopped the car and ordered everyone out of it, this was accelerated by the expected burst of MG fire and then by a loud explosion close to the car. This latter was a Panzerfaust which passed just in the rear of the car and was clearly seen in the air by the 2i/c [Maj Taylor MC] who had been travelling just behind my car in his jeep, and had run up to see why the scout car had stopped. A ditch beside the scout car provided cover for the whole party.

"All this happened very quickly and while it was happening the leading 4 trucks of 'B' Coy were all on the stretch of road between the muddy patch and the scout car and had come under fire from both flanks (afterwards found to be from 2 MG's, one on each side of the road, and a flak gun somewhere on the right, or east, of it). Their casualties amounted to six killed and eleven wounded with the leading platoon commander (Lt Pape) amongst the killed."

War Diary 7th April

1500   *ALTENHAGEN 0927 was reached at 1500 hrs and the Bn was ordered to seize GROSBENHEIDEN 1230.*
1600   *STEINHUDE 1029 was reached by forward Coys. Slight enemy resistance was soon broken up.*
1700   *Bn reached 131300 the only enemy resistance consisting of AA guns firing airbursts from WUNSDORF airfield at 163304. 8 platoon of 'C' Coy captured enemy gun position intact, killing 3 and wounding 4. They took 30 PW at 117282.*
1830   *'C' Coy then cleared WUNSDORF Airfield and made contact with 7th Para Bn in area 1530.*

Private Alfred Draper ('C' Company)

"We stopped outside the perimeter and could see the Germans working in the distance about a mile away. The Platoon Sergeant, Chris Hornsey, asked for volunteers to go with him to see who they were. Nobody stepped forward and I felt sorry for him and volunteered. Bob Giles immediately joined me and then another lad came.

"We set off towards them up a slight hill and in full view of them the whole way. When we were in talking distance, Chris shouted to them to put their hands up. They turned around in surprise and jumped in their trenches they were digging. Nearby was an anti-aircraft cannon and it swung round towards us and fired. When we saw it move we dropped to the ground. Luckily we were in dead ground and the gun couldn't depress low enough and the shells went over our heads. Unfortunately they went towards the rest of the Platoon and several of the lads were wounded."

Lieutenant Peter Downward (Scout Platoon)

"We advanced towards a large Luftwaffe airfield called Wunstorf which was obviously still active and certainly defended by the Germans. Small arms fire greeted us as we got nearer and there were some casualties in the forward platoons. I could see through my binoculars one casualty out in the open but obviously still alive as he was trying to crawl into some cover. Suddenly we saw one of our medics, Sgt Scott who had been at Belsen 2 days before, charge across the open space on a motorcycle to go to the wounded man's help. He didn't make it as he was brought down by a burst of machine gun fire from the airfield defences and must have died instantly.

"One person who was extremely lucky in this contact was Alan Daborn who received a bullet through his beret and no more than a scratch to the scalp to prove it."

Private Dave Beedham ('B' Company)

"The Company advanced in extended order cross the open stretches of the airfield with those dreaded 4 barrelled 20mm. flak guns firing directly at us, but we held out line and when close enough charged with fixed bayonets. They didn't like that and they just packed in. We look a lot of prisoners but lost another very brave man when the Medic, Sergeant Scott was killed."

Captain David Tibbs MC (RAMC)

"German Hitler youth, between 15 and 17 years old, manning multiple barrelled 20mm, rapid fire, anti-aircraft guns, attempted a last ditch defence and wounded several of our men. My beloved Sgt. Scott fearless as ever, rode up to them on a light motor cycle with a Red Cross clearly displayed but regardless of this the Hitler youth opened up and Sgt Scott died instantly.

"When I reached him I found his head was completely shattered. A wounded man he had gone to help was lying close by with a severe leg wound. He looked at me with a strange intensity and said in a low, urgent voice, "Doc, please remove Sergeant Scott's brains from my tunic." Aghast, with great care I cupped my hands and lifted the still warm tissue across to Sgt Scott's body. It seemed as though I was holding the very essence of this man in my hands. A man admired and respected by all, who had been awarded the Military Medal for his courage in repeatedly retrieving so many wounded from dangerous positions whether they were British or Germans, and always an inspiration by his cheerful acceptance of arduous conditions. We had been comrades through many formidable times together and his loss left a huge void, To this day many memories come back to me but none so vivid as this. Such memories do not now unduly distress me but I allow them to float through my thoughts rather than to attempt to suppress them. They happened and I cannot change them. Such is the cruelty of war!

"This was an exceptional and distressing episode committed by youths thoroughly imbued with the Nazi creed and no doubt who felt they were defending their country. The Hitler Youth were well known for their atrocious behaviour."

Sergeant Robert Scott, MM and Padre Bristoe. Captain David Tibbs only took this photograph days before Sergeant Scott was killed.

Lance Corporal David "Robbie" Robinson (Anti-Tank, 'C' Company)

"I had Gibbons with me and we had the PIAT aimed at an anti-aircraft gun position with an accommodation hut next to it. A section of 'C' Company was despatched to attack this hut and during the scuffle one of the lads, McDermott, fired his rifle at a German, but had forgotten in the heat of the moment that he had a pull through stick in the barrel. This split the barrel and flew at the German severing most of the Germans right hand, all except the thumb. I had to escort the German later to the First Aid Post.

"We lost on this aerodrome a chap named Chitty who I joined the paras with, he lost his leg, he's still alive today and I communicate with him still. Our losses had not been as great on this episode as the rest but they were still fairly substantial. I think this was a very worrying part of the war for me. It was noticeable from the distance we were travelling and the amount of Germans that were giving themselves up that the war would soon be over and the worry was that after all that had already gone

537

before one could still get hit, hurt or killed during the last few phases of the war. "It also brought it home to you when close to the end that people like the medic Sergeant Scott could get killed and Chitty could have his leg blown off and others shot or maimed through little incidents by a few fanatical Germans or even by the German home guard, the Volkssturm, I think they were called, because even these who didn't fight much could point a rifle or a gun in your direction and still finish the job off."

Citation: Private Leroy Forter

Award: Military Medal

On Saturday 7th April 45, 8 Pl, 'C' Company, 13th Bn, Parachute Regiment were engaged in a right flanking movement to cut off the enemy rear during the advance from the WESER to POGGENHAGEN.

During this movement the Pl became engaged with concealed and dug in flak batteries. A withering fire was brought to bear on them. The Pl was in the open, extended. Pte FORTER noticed that another man had been wounded and lost a foot, and was completely exposed. Without hesitation and with amazing coolness he went to his assistance. Shells from the flak guns were bursting all around him and he was himself wounded in the leg. He completely disregarded the enemy fire and bandaged up the wounded man, giving him morphia. He was himself unable to walk and crawled to cover taking the wounded man. He then continued to fire his rifle until the flak guns were silenced and he was evacuated.

His great courage and coolness was a splendid example to all at a particularly dangerous time.

Captain David Tibbs MC (RAMC)

"I watched as a platoon officer [Lt Prior No.5 Platoon] walked over to them with his men holding their weapons at the slant to show that they were not going to shoot and the youth then surrendered, I marvelled at the cool courage of the British officer and his men when they knew how irresponsible the Hitler Youth had shown themselves to be, Lt Prior said to me afterwards "l couldn't shoot them, they are only kids." There was no hint of recrimination against them but I fear this generous attitude was wasted because when I tried to treat one Hitler youth who was slightly wounded, he hurled abuse at me. I imagine they felt they were doing their duty for their country and were too young to have worked out that we were all that stood between them and the Russians who might be much less merciful than ourselves."

Lt Peter Downward (Scout Platoon)

"After a lot of mortaring, artillery and tank fire we gradually moved into the built up complex of the airfield where we could see hangers, the control tower, barrack blocks and numerous other buildings, even aircraft which had been raked with machine gun fire by our chaps in the hope of producing a fire ball (left, IWM Duxford). There was plenty of opportunity for my snipers to engage targets as it was soon obvious that the Germans were falling back and could be seen running between buildings and hangars.

"To our right 7th Battalion was busy clearing the nearby village. After a series of dashes and volleys of covering fire we were into the buildings, quickly searching rooms and corridors with muffled bangs coming up from the cellars as we lobbed grenades into the basements. Finally the Scout Platoon, together with our leading company, converged on what was the Officers Mess. One could see that it had been the scene of a hurried evacuation only an hour or so before."

Above: Another shot up aircraft at Wunstorf Airfield.

2359   Total PW taken during day 344.

Pte Ray "Geordie" Walker ('A' Coy)

"Much to our surprise the Germans taken prisoner were mainly members of the Volkssturm and included young boys and old men, some of whom had wooden legs. We then cleared the airfield of the wounded and the dead. Sgt Stan Braddock (left) and I ordered two surly and arrogant prisoners to place the body of one of our comrades into a groundsheet [most probably one of the 6 men killed from 7 Para] and carry it to the main buildings. On two occasions they dropped the body on the runway. This infuriated Stan and he thrust his Sten gun into the stomach of the nearest prisoner and said, "Do that once more and I'll bloody well shoot you." Needless to say, we had no further trouble from them."

Private Dave Beedham ('B' Company)

"We occupied the modern barrack block on the base and there was talk of a brothel in the camp, provided for the Luftwaffe aircrews. If there was, we in 5 Platoon didn't even see it, never mind enjoy its delights."

Private Alfred Draper ('C' Company)

"There were several 3 storey barrack blocks and on the edge of the airfield there was a single storey building with young women lounging outside. This turned out to be a brothel and by lunchtime the next day, half the Battalion was there! Bob and I had gone exploring (looking for loot) and had not been involved. The CO had seen what was going on and ordered the place to be closed down and a guard put on to stop anyone going in. Bob and I got the job because we hadn't been involved.

"It was a hot sunny afternoon, the girls were lying on the ground, flaunting themselves and several of the lads were trying to bribe their way past us."

Lieutenant Ellis "Dixie" Dean (MMG Platoon)

"Eventually the Boche was sorted out and we continued on foot, afterwards coming to the spot where 7 Para had been shot up in their transport, a number of TCV's all with flat tyres, shattered window screens and numerous bullet holes, stood abandoned on the road. 7 Para were now in Neustadt waiting for dark before attempting to capture the bridge. The explosion of the demolition charges broke the nights silence and we later heard that the assault force were actually on the bridge when it was blown."

Lieutenant Colonel Geoffrey Pine-Coffin (CO 7th Battalion)

"Meanwhile, 'B' Company had been working up the river and were able to hear German voices on the bridge - they heard Lloyd and his escort being challenged at one or quite clearly. When within 400 yards of their objective, they were forced to swing westwards and follow the bank of a loop canal as this was a considerable obstacle in itself. This deviation took them onto the main east-west road through Neustadt and left them with two bridges to deal with instead of one, i.e. one over the loop canal and the main one, the two bridges were 100 yards apart. A civilian was encountered soon after coming on to the road and Maj Reid, who speaks German, questioned him about the bridge and garrison. The civilian said the bridge was prepared for demolition and stressed the need for speed if it was to be captured intact. This confirmed Maj Reid's original plan which was to rush the bridge and trust to getting across in time to prevent it going up.

"He therefore ordered his men to charge and the two leading platoons under Lt Gush and Sgt McIver (Lt Pape's platoon) and led by the Company 2i/c Capt Woodman had crossed both bridges when the first arch of the main road was blown behind them at approx 0015 hrs 8th April. Heavy and severe casualties were suffered by the troops on both sides of the explosion but the small party that got across completely routed the garrison there and held their small bridgehead all night."[89]

---

[89] Capt Woodman kicked several explosives off the bridge as he ran across it, this almost certainly saved the rest of the platoon. 22 men were killed in the explosion and a further 19 were wounded.

Above: Photo taken by Lt Col RG Pine-Coffin on 8th April 1945. The damage done to the first arch can be seen. A Bailey bridge was used to enable the use of the bridge. The trees to the left of the picture highlight the force of the blast.

Below: Neustadt Bridge as it is today. Note the repair work on first arch.

Lieutenant Peter Downward (Scout Platoon)

"As we prepared to move on beyond the airfield there was a sudden muffled explosion from one of the blocks we had cleared. It was an aircraft bomb which had been placed there by the retreating Germans and detonated by a timing device. Immediately there was a quick search of the other basements and sure enough there were other devices, all in their wooden crates. A party of sappers carried out the defusing without further incident.

"We were being pushed forward rapidly up to the line of a canal or a small river about 4 miles away. 7th Battalion were still in contact with the enemy and we had to capture a couple of bridges vital to the advance. This was the only time I ever rode on the back of a tank together with the rest of my platoon hanging onto the back of Comets. We stopped close to the first bridge where it was apparent 7 Para had been in contact as there were 3 or 4 British dead lying on the bridge. We rushed across under cover from our tanks, but met no resistance and occupied some buildings 1000 yards further on, where we stayed throughout the night, expecting a counter attack by the enemy intent on retaking the airfield. That evening, talking to one of 7 Para's officers, I learned that one of the dead on the bridge was a boy from Isle of Man whom I knew well called Laurie Kewley.

"The next day, 10th April (my 21st birthday), we were pulled back onto the airfield, where we did a certain amount of tidying up. That evening we put on a dinner of some sorts for about 10 officers in the main dining room. Cutlery, plates and glasses had been produced, even a table cloth and most enjoyable, some German wine. There were no speeches but Peter Luard toasted The King and then my 21st birthday. As we were sitting round the table, I heard a noise in the ceiling and one of the enormous wrought iron chandeliers each bearing about 20 electric bulbs (unlit, as there was no electricity) came rattling down to a few inches above our heads where it stopped with a jerk. A member of the Signal Platoon exploring the loft area had released a ratchet and the chandelier responded to the laws of gravity."

Lieutenant Ellis "Dixie" Dean (MMG Platoon)

"Forewarned of movement into reserve, the CO had sent a company to occupy Wunstorf and the rest of the Battalion joined them. Clearly, just as the RAF returned to their home comforts, so did the Luftwaffe. Wunstorf had a modern brick built barracks with far superior kitchens to any British Army ones. There was also the addition of a regimental brothel! The Officers Mess had the luxury of a top class hotel; we slept between clean sheets, with running water in our bedrooms. Unfortunately the bar stock of wines and spirits had been cleared, but there was still draught beer in the barrels.

"In the ante-room were several table lamps. One of these consisted of a handsome brass stand and a large parchment shade, which was covered with signatures. Myself, Peter Downward and Basil Disley added our own. A day or so later the lamp disappeared and enquiries revealed that a number of senior officers from Divisional

HQ had called and one had shown an interest in the lamp. Among the signatures he found those of Herman Goering, head of the Luftwaffe and Willie Messerschmitt, famed aircraft designer and without further ado he liberated it. I know that anyone who was anyone in the Luftwaffe had signed that shade, including Adolf Galland, their leading fighter ace and Hannah Reiss, Hitler's personal woman pilot.

"As far as I'm aware, this priceless war trophy is still the property of LT-Col Bill Taylor, who in 1945 was the senior RASC Officer of the 6th AB Div."

Left: 'The Wunstorf Lamp' (Courtesy 'Dixie' Dean).

Brigadier Nigel Poett (5th Para Brigade Commander)

"At this stage the 6th Airborne Division was ordered, to their great disappointment, to halt and allow the 15th Scottish Division to pass through. We regarded this as quite unnecessary; we were fit and anxious to go on. A delay of 3 or 4 days was involved in passing the 15th Scottish through. This slowed up the whole advance and resulted in considerable casualties to their Division. The momentum of the advance having been lost, the 15th Scottish were again held up on the River Elbe and we passed through them there."

Captain David Tibbs MC (RAMC)

"3 miles outside Celle we picked up the familiar stench of dead bodies, increasingly strong as we approached. This was due to a railway train of cattle wagons, on a raised embankment, that had been laden with civilian 'prisoners' on their way to Belsen concentration camp nearby. Apparently, it had been strafed by RAF mosquitoes about 2 weeks before and many carriages burst open. Rather than allowing any to escape, the German guards had shot all survivors so that hundreds lay dead alongside the train and no attempt had been made to bury them."

Photo: The dead 'prisoners' shot on the embankment, taken by Captain Tibbs himself (Courtesy David Tibbs).

Lieutenant Ellis "Dixie" Dean (MMG Platoon)

"We rested for a few days then moved to the town of Celle. 5th Brigade were put on standby for an operation in support of the assault crossing of the River Elbe and this put me in a dilemma, as it was to be a rifle company only drop. Having fought all the way from Normandy and never missed any of the action, I wasn't going to be side-lined now. But it would mean leaving my beloved gunners. In the end my selfishness won and I set about getting on the operation.

"Andy McLoughlin was now commanding 'B' Company, where 6 Platoon was commanded by a Sergeant. In 'B' Company were a lot of young soldiers and NCO's with not many experienced old hands to guide them as they had suffered heavy casualties in Bure. I discussed my plan with Major McLoughlin and he was in agreement with my proposals. Exactly what he said to the CO, I don't know but the plan worked and I took over 6 Platoon. This had been my first command when I joined the Battalion back in September '43 and a lot had happened since then – there wasn't a single member of my original platoon still serving with them.

"The first opportunity to see how my new command could function came, a couple of nights later. We were sent to investigate the ambushing of a despatch rider by "Werewolves". Our investigation of the whereabouts of these underground fighters failed to find any trace, so we returned to billets untested."

Lieutenant Peter Downward (Scout Platoon)

"We soon realised that there was a concentration camp nearby called Belsen where these poor devils were destined. Word came down from Battalion HQ for any medics who could be spared to go to Belsen as there was a crisis. David Tibbs mustered his RAMC chaps together, plus Padre Foy and myself, and we set off in 4 Jeeps. We soon realised there was a major medical crisis ahead as one could deduce from the large number of Army vehicles with red crosses all heading in the same direction."

"We were directed off the main road towards a large camp surrounded by high barbed wire fencing interspersed with look-out posts. There was also a barracks outside the camp and numerous German soldiers unarmed being directed by groups of Scottish soldiers from the 15th division.

"The first sight of the inmates was unbelievable as they lined the inside of the fences looking out. They looked like living skeletons in striped prison uniforms, shaven heads, sunken eyes and all standing or supporting themselves against the wooden posts in absolute silence. Worst was to come, going further into the camp, one could see bodies piled up by German soldiers under strict control of our troops. In an effort to counter the further spread of infection one was conscious of the strong smell of chloride of lime being put down in the area of the piles of skeletal bodies waiting burial. As the piles grew, our soldiers became more and more intolerant of their SS charges.

"I saw the large mass graves of the thousands of Jews buried there and the stark reminder of the disposal of so many others in the crematoria ovens. Well before dark I left that grisly site and drove back to Celle, to report to Peter Luard. David Tibbs and his medics stayed on until some hours later."

One of the mass graves. Photo taken by David Tibbs himself at Belsen.

Captain David Tibbs MC (RAMC)

"It was exactly as described and I have yet to see any description that exaggerates the appalling conditions there. A number of large pits had been scooped out by bulldozers into which German guards, with armed British Tommies behind them, were throwing emaciated bodies. These people had starved to death in their thousands, often hastened by tuberculosis or the louse-borne disease, typhus. Many of the huts had been cleared and burnt down but others were still being cleared of dead, amongst whom surprisingly, a few still survived in a pitiful state. Elsewhere, in a barracks nearby, gas decontamination chambers were being used to rescue as many as possible of the gaunt, surviving victims, still crawling with lice, by washing and shaving them completely, and dusting with DDT to exterminate any remaining lice."

Lieutenant Peter Downward (Scout Platoon)

"We occupied a fairly important looking office building which, in fact was a college but completely unoccupied. There was signs of a hurried evacuation but all seemed to be in good order, there was running water and we were in reserve so my chaps took advantage of the showers, the first proper body wash they had enjoyed since we left England. Also about this time arrived our first delivery of mail. I read out the names and handed the letters to the individuals. I was glad to see that I had one from my mother, but saddened to find one for Pte Porrill [KIA 24th March] which I knew must have been written by his parents. I opened my letter written on 25th March saying she had just learned of the 6th Airborne's big offensive into Germany and was glad I was in the 13th as she would have been very worried indeed. This was certainly a case of ignorance being bliss; she had obviously forgotten my final words to her when I was on leave!

"With the arrival of the mail, the showers and the discovery of some bottles of German wine, there was a relaxed atmosphere and someone tried his hand in the kitchen; I was handed a large mug of tea and a couple of boiled eggs. I was horrified to find each of them had a small pin-hole in the end and realised they had probably been used for scientific research. On cracking them open there was no doubt that they were not fresh and as a result of my enquiries told everyone to leave them alone, they were from the college's Science Department."

Lieutenant Ellis "Dixie" Dean (Now 6 Platoon 'B' Company)

"We marched into Wieren one morning [17th April] and 6 Platoon's responsibility was the only road entering the place from the east. We dug our slits on the fringes of a worked out quarry, slightly east of the main built up area. After stand down I checked the sentries and then retired to the farmhouse to get my head down for the first half of the night as it was my turn to rest first. I was hardly asleep before Sgt Adams was shaking my shoulder, "there's something coming up the road."

"I joined the section covering the road. Whatever it was halted at the roadblock of 2 turned over carts. I led 2 men down the roadside ditch and with cries of "Hands Up" and "Hande Hoch", surrounded a horse and cart and a body of men. We separated bodies and transport, although a girl on the cart was permitted to stay there. Someone seized the head collar and guided the cart through the road block.

"I thought it was a ruse to put us off our guard, the men was searched for weapons, but we found nothing suspicious. Inside the house, I decided to see the men one at a time. The first one came in and I noticed he was wearing an old battle dress so I asked who he was. Standing smartly to attention, he gave number, rank, name and then added his Scottish regiment. I wanted to know why he was in that part of Germany and he explained that he was captured in France in 1940 and since had done farm work under guard, but their guards had disappeared and he and his companions had set out to find friendly forces in the west. "And the girl?" I asked. She was a slave labourer of Eastern Europe, the girlfriend of the Frenchman and she was pregnant.

"The story seemed plausible; I didn't think any German could imitate a broad Scottish accent. I interviewed the rest and was convinced they were genuine ex-POW.

I talked to them about their experiences and brought them up-to-date. They all seemed to look at my head whilst I was talking to them, "What mob are you then Sir?" It was my head-dress, forced to surrender at St Valery in 1940 and spent 4 years in captivity; they had never heard of the Parachute regiment and had never seen a soldier wearing the 'Red Beret' before.

"I escorted the group to the big house up the road that was Company HQ and was told to settle them in the out buildings for the night. I was then told to take the pregnant girl and her French lover to one of the bedrooms. I indicated with my torch the room with the double bed and I will never forget the beautiful smile of thanks that simple peasant girl gave, this was a luxury undreamed of for her.

"Our next move was to Kahlstorf and I was to receive news that I was to become Brigade Liaison Officer, later Divisional Liaison Officer."

Lance Corporal David "Robbie" Robinson (Anti-Tank 'C' Company)

"I was ordered to fire my PIAT at a house that firing had been seen around this time, and in a forgetful mood, I fired the PIAT and didn't get out of the way. The much troublesome and every PIAT mans enemy, the brass primer cap from the tail fin of the bomb, came flying back at me and smacked me in the face under my right eye. There was much blood and another black eye, I still have the scar but my wrinkles cover it now!"

Private Ray "Geordie" Walker ('A' Company)

"It was now late April and I could sense the end of the war. German troops were surrendering in their thousands as they made their escape from the Russians. German troops passed us by on the same road; the adjacent fields were now occupied by German armour. Tanks, self-propelled guns and armoured cars drove west and would only halt when they ran out of fuel. With their combined firepower they could have blasted us off the face of the earth."

Captain Wilfred "Bill" Davison (Adjutant, HQ Company)

"The memorable thing for me was the fact that we were able to drive at about 40 mph for hours on end without opposition. It was amazing how suddenly the German Army seemed to collapse and the majority of prisoners had no spirit left in them."

Most of the German officers wanted the British to join forces against the Russians, claiming that the Russians had almost run out of food, petrol and ammunition. They also spoke about the atrocities that the advancing Red Army was inflicting on German soldiers and civilians, but the men of the 6th Airborne Division were not so forgiving as the sights they had recently witnessed in Belsen were still etched on their minds."

Captain David Tibbs MC (RAMC)

"We came face to face with a full regiment of Waffen SS troops all with the skull emblem on their caps. At that time we were way ahead of any support but Colonel Luard stood on a lorry, fired a shot into the air and shouted in German "Lay down your weapons and march to the West or I shall call up British artillery and Typhoon rocket [firing] planes to destroy you." This was a complete bluff but after a few minutes a ripple ran down their long, well armed column and they all started to drop their weapons and walk westwards!

"They came through us laughing and shouting, obviously happy to surrender to us rather than stay for the Russians. For them the war was over. Many thought it was a huge joke to throw their side arms (often Luger pistols) into my ambulance which visibly sank down on its springs with the weight of them. They could have obliterated us if they chose so we were relieved to press on fast before they discovered our deception. It is possible that their officers told them that they would be regrouped and fight alongside the Allies to stop the Russians. This story circulated widely amongst the Germans, sometimes encouraged by us, to persuade their troops to surrender but most knew the war was lost and wished only to get away from the Russians.

"At Schwerin, on the railway line alongside a large lake, two long German ambulance trains, with large Red Crosses on each carriage and full of wounded German troops, pulled in from the Russian front. They were desperate to get away from the Russians but had now run out of fuel. On one of them, our men had found, and showed me, several large trunks full of jewellery probably from concentration camp victims.

"The news of Hitler's death came through soon after this so I returned to the ambulance train and said to the Train Commandant, a medical colonel, "Hitler has died from a stroke" although no details had come through as yet, He drew himself up to full height and angrily said "Nein, nein! He died a hero's death!" Against my instructions the wounded from these trains were dispersed over the countryside, so great was their fear of the approaching Russians. The Train Commandant gave as his reason for doing this was that when the Russians came they would burn the train from end to end, with everybody, including nurses, on it as they had done on many occasions on the Russian steps, and added contemptuously "and you could not stop them!" I did not doubt his assessment."

Private Alfred Draper ('C' Company)

"One night back at the billets some of the others had found a goods train in one of the sidings that was full of loot. It was full of watches, rings, paintings, furniture etc that had been stolen from the Jews before they were sent to the concentration camps. The lads were absolutely loaded with watches and rings – the easily portable stuff. We went back the next morning, but found it had been stripped bare. Some foreign forced labourers had found it!"

Pte Ray "Geordie" Walker ('A' Coy)

"Evermore Germans were spilling out of fields to surrender. Three men came up to me; two were Officers accompanied by a civilian who proved to be a member of their Consular Service. They all spoke excellent English and the Officers were dressed in their best uniforms and greatcoats. I noticed that one was wearing a brand new army watch and I asked if I could have it as a souvenir, as it would be of little use to him in a prison camp. He gave it to me without malice and I instructed them to follow the line of prisoners and keep walking west."

Lieutenant Peter Downward (Scout Platoon)

"Somewhere near the Elbe we came across a camp surrounded by barbed wire and we thought it might be another concentration camp. It became a joyous moment for us all, as well as the inmates, as it turned out to be a POW camp holding several hundred British prisoners, mainly Army but also some RAF aircrew.

"The River Elbe was to see the last serious battle on our part of the front. The pontoon bridge across the Elbe was crossed on foot. Briefings coming down from higher command told us that at any moment in the next day or two we would meet up with the Russians and we were warned to be on our best behaviour and properly turned out, berets on straight and where necessary, replaced, boots to be cleaned, everyone shaved and no smoking on the line of march. We were also warned to lookout for members of the SS amongst the German POW's as many were wanted men. To avoid detection they had removed badges and black uniforms, trying to keep a low profile. The soldiers had their own ideas on how to deal with them.

"At last we could see through our binoculars a couple of Russians heading towards us on a horse drawn cart. They seemed to be more pre-occupied in looting some buildings, all of which had white flags hanging from the upstairs windows. There was no embracing and only a few guttural exchanges including a burst in the air from one of their 'burp guns'. In the cart amongst bits of loot were two drunken uniformed figures. We were disappointed to say the least, as it soon became apparent that these were Mongolian soldiers serving in the Red Army."

Private Norman Mountney (MMG Platoon)

"We seemed to march most of the way after the drop, several times moving by night across country in order to get behind the German defences. Then came the final days march after crossing the Elbe when we took more than our share of prisoners, there were fields full of disarmed German soldiers. The Battalion had advanced too far and we had to pull back. A time had been agreed with the Russians but they arrived 2 hours early and by the time we left the farm had been stripped completely. There was a German farmer who passed through our position each morning with a horse and cart and he always left us milk. That morning he came on his own the Russians had taken all his cows, also his horse and cart."

Lt Peter Downward (Scout's)

"We found some real Russians, including a couple of women soldiers, one of whom spoke a bit of English. The vodka started to flow, even our most hardened drinkers could not cope with the Russian toasting, knocking back the contents of a glass in one, followed by a shout of "Nostrovia!" ["Cheers!"]. It didn't seem to worry the Russian officers as to how drunk their troops became, I saw one Captain deliver a tremendous blow to the jaw of one individual who went sprawling backwards, to be picked up by his comrades and thrown into the back of a truck."

Private Fred Wilcock ('A' Company)

"I believe that we were one of the first lots of troops to meet up with the Russians. I remember seeing one tank commander, it was a woman and she was the most beautiful woman I think I ever saw."

Lt Peter Downward (Scout Platoon)

"A German officer reported that his General and his staff were in their vehicles a short distance away and he wished to make a formal surrender. Peter Luard sent me with my platoon to bring him in. The General in typical peaked cap and leather overcoat saluted me and handed over his Luger as the first indication of his surrender. He was in a large grey Mercedes open car (above, courtesy Sir Peter Downward) with 3 others including the driver in the other seats. Behind him followed a German equivalent of a Jeep and a couple of Zundatt motorcycle side cars. I headed the column in my Jeep with RSM Duxbury bringing up the rear in his Jeep. I ordered my Scout Platoon members to keep their weapons trained on the surrendered party. Particularly the General's escort of motorcycle side cars. We drove into Battalion HQ, a school building, to be met by the Adjutant [Captain "Claude" Milman], Bill Davidson and Roy Leyland. The party debussed and were deliberately kept waiting by Peter Luard as he watched from an upstairs window.

"I wasn't present at the act of surrender. I gather that the General laid out his map and explained the composition of his Division (6-7000 troops). It seemed he was ready to turn his forces about and so take up defences with the 6th Airborne Division facing eastwards as he was sure the Russians would keep on advancing! This was turned down and I had to take him to Brigadier Poett, but not in his Mercedes, it remained under Peter Luards window."

Captain David Clark (225 Field Ambulance)

"Our ambulances were in a long line of British army vehicles pushing steadily north. Down the other side of the road moved an endless column of German soldiers walking thankfully towards British imprisonment, away from the dreaded Russians. Every unit of the German army was there, field grey jackets, air force blue, black tank overalls, fit young men, bandaged limping old men with WWI medal ribbons, women auxiliaries in shapeless grey uniforms, even an SS colonel striding along in his black overcoat - an endless stream."

Captain David Tibbs MC (RAMC)

"A complete German infantry division, fleeing before the Russians, surrendered to us and on our instructions dropped all their weapons and then marched in their thousands towards the West, deep into British held territory, They were very happy men but still half expecting that they would regroup and join with us in keeping the Russians out. The amount of military equipment they left behind was prodigious, from automatic rifles to armoured troop carriers, and whole regiments of artillery. I saw a splendid Zundapp motorcycle (pictured) combination and ordered the crew to leave it and walk west. They did this reluctantly saying they had been to Moscow and back on this machine.

"As soon as they had gone I tried driving this monster but found driving a heavy combination unexpectedly difficult and went into a ditch! With practice I tamed the brute but decided it would be more fun as a solo machine and so I unbolted the sidecar and found it was excellent to drive. Eventually I managed to get this home and drove on the Isle of Wight for a while. I nearly tried driving an armoured troop carrier but decided not to when a refugee civilian, who was making his way back to Latvia, warned me that it was probably booby trapped and would blow up if I tried to start it! The possibly of booby trapped equipment stayed in my mind and I was much more cautious about abandoned weapons from then onwards."

Lieutenant Peter Downward (Scout Platoon)

"It was fascinating to see the German military machine carrying out the orders for the disbandment. The officers kept together in groups away from the soldiers who were busy stocking up piles of weapons. Rifles and MG42s were fairly well known to us, as were Schmeisser sub-machine guns and 9mm Lugers, but something I hadn't seen before was the Panzerfaust anti-tank rocket launcher. One German sergeant's parting remarks were "Thank Gott we are surrendering to you and not the Russians!" The date was 4th May 1945.

"Next day we advanced another couple of miles or so and eventually came to a very impressive German schloss at a place called Maltow, 15 miles south of the German port of Wismar. The owner was a Prussian Count who had served as a General in the Wehrmacht in the 1914-18 War, an educated man with a good knowledge of English. The interior was truly magnificent with oil paintings, glass chandeliers, Prussian Army uniforms and some medals in glass cases in the hallway. Peter Luard made it clear that the family and their possessions would be respected. We all admired the Count; he was dignified and did not seem to show any hatred of us, the enemy.

"The Count had to hand over any firearms and he opened up his gun room, which contained quite an armoury of sporting rifles, shot guns, small bore rifles an a couple of pistols. Peter Luard insisted on him handing over his Manlicher rifles and the two pistols, but allowed him to keep his shot guns. Peter knew how he valued his guns as they were valuable and had been handed down through the family.

"We stayed in the schloss for two days during which we learned that the war in Europe was virtually over as the Russians were in Berlin. Some agreement was drawn up and the line was to be straightened; we were to pull back due south from Wismar. We would be on one side of the road, the Russians the other. Knowing that we were leaving the schloss for the Russians to take over, the Count asked if he could have one of his pistols back and a couple of rounds of ammunition. His wish was granted!"

Captain Wilfred "Bill" Davison (Adjutant, HQ Company)

"Early one morning whilst out riding alone, I met a Russian convoy of horse drawn vehicles headed by a single, battered US truck. They all looked untidy, cold and miserable. I noticed a few women huddled up on some carts and they appeared to be in some sort of uniform.

"My batman told me a Russian soldier stole my horse from the farm we were staying at. I chased him in my car and eventually caught him. He pretended to not understand so I pulled out my pistol and made him dismount... It's not very easy to drive a car whilst leading a horse!"

Lt Peter Downward (Scout's)

"We took over a farmhouse near a small lake called Bad Kleinen, with stables and horses complete with saddles. I found a 220v petrol generator and connected it to the main terminal box in the kitchen.

"For the next 24 hours we got reports of small groups of German soldiers hiding in the woods nearby who, it seemed, were not prepared to pack in to the Russians and were awaiting the right moment to surrender to the Brits. I was sent out with the Scout Platoon to search a wood on our side. We spotted them 200 yards away on the edge of the wood, and it was obvious that they were unaware of our presence until a shot rang out from another company area, and they ran in our direction. They quickly gave themselves up and surrendered their weapons. One of the three kept silencing the other two to any answers they might give. Our conclusion was that he was an ardent Nazi and should be separated from the other two. I searched their pockets and found some photographs.

"Our Nazi friend was placed in the care of Sgt "Buck" Jones who was quite prepared to subject him to one or two APTC arrest techniques if he stepped out of line. The last I saw of this Hitler fanatic was his admission to the cellar under Battalion HQ. He happened to make some derogatory remark to Buck like calling him a 'Dummkopf' and was promptly rewarded by a push in the back catapulting him to the bottom of the steps."

Above right: Peter Downward and Bill Davidson on Bad Kleinen (Courtesy Sir Peter Downward).

Left: The two young POW's who surrendered to the Scout Platoon. The photograph was found on the POW on the right (Courtesy Sir Peter Downward).

Private Dave Beedham ('B' Company)

"After crossing the River Elbe we advanced towards the Baltic Sea and met the Russians on the outskirts of Wismar. They were encamped in the woods and had their own women camp followers. I went with the Company 2i/c into a village looking for billets. There was a terrible shouting and screaming coming from one of the houses and we ran across the road and into the room from where the noise was coming. On the floor in the middle of the room, a big Russian was raping a little girl of no more than 12 years old, while her mother stood helpless, yelling her head off. The Russian jumped up leaving the little girl in a nasty, bloody mess. Without any hesitation, Captain Seal lowered his Schmeisser and shot the man dead."

Major Jack Watson (OC 'A' Company)

"We reached Wismar and were told to find our own digs. I found a beautiful farmhouse and bedded my men into the barns and outhouses. That's where we stayed for a while. I had a very good butcher in my company and as you can imagine we ate some very good meals while we waited for our next move.

"We had constant visits from the Russians who I didn't like very much. They were arrogant and wanted to pilfer everything from the house. It took a tremendous effort to keep them out, otherwise the furniture, the bedding and the lot would've been taken. They were very scruffy and had to be forcefully made to leave. The family of the house were in fact still there, so we felt that it was our responsibility to protect them."

Lance Corporal David "Robbie Robinson (Anti-Tank 'C' Company)

"Through this period our contact with any of the German civilians was minimal. If I spoke to a dozen civilians during this period, that was all. It seemed that as forward troops wherever we went the civilians evacuated or hid. It was only the rear troops that then met with the civilians after the battle areas had gone forward. So of the civilians I can tell you very, very little."

Captain David Tibbs MC (RAMC)

"An attractive German school mistress with mild diphtheria came to me as a patient and to my surprise wept with gratitude that we had come. This was because she was due to go to a 'Joy camp' for German soldiers to give them pleasure and to bear a child for Nazi Germany. Looking back it was hard to escape the evidence that not only had huge concentration camps existed, that slave labour bringing workers, both men and women from all over Europe, had been practised on a vast scale, and that the Nazis had expected sacrifices from their own citizens that we found hard to believe. Yes, it was war but I am happy to say that the Allied never descended to such deliberate acts of cruelty. In my experience the British Army acted, as far as war would allow, with honour and never tolerated rape or other acts of barbarism. I felt very proud of the way in which we handled prisoners, looked after wounded Germans and particularly the efficiency with which such disasters as the Belsen concentration camp were dealt with. Here the role of the RAMC was outstanding."

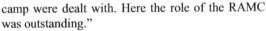

Photo: Corporal Aaron Walton and Bing (IWM Duxford).

Private Ray "Geordie" Walker ('A' Coy)

"After having marched nearly 350 miles from the Rhine to the Baltic we were due a period of rest and relaxation. As soon as possible I took the opportunity to go for a swim, although the Baltic was cold, I enjoyed the freedom of being out of uniform after not having bathed for 8 weeks. Horse riding proved popular thanks to a defeated German Army. They turned loose all their cavalry and draught horses, consequently most of us acquired a

552

horse and a race meeting was organised. One of the lads had been a bookmaker in civil life and he opened a book and took on bets on the races. Race day had its hilarious moments as several lads fell from their mounts, most rode bareback."

Lieutenant Ellis "Dixie" Dean (6th AB Division Liaison Officer)

"After the war I learned that on 28th April, Allied Intelligence had learned that the Russians intended to occupy Denmark. The information was gained by reading intercepted Russian signals. I knew of the 'Enigma' and reading German signals, but never of reading Russian messages. These signals revealed the Russian armoured formations under Marshal Rokossovsky were to drive via Wismar to Kiel and Flensburg, providing Russia with an outlet into the North Sea and the Atlantic.

"As the nearest Allied Division to Wismar, the 6th Airborne were given the task in preventing "Uncle Joe" achieving his ambitions. On 29th April, General Bols was given his orders. Halt the Russians and avoid any clash of arms with them, as the retreating German Army hoped and expected. At this time the 6th Airborne Division was still on the west bank of the River Elbe, 60 miles away from Wismar. The orders from there had been to advance as rapidly as possible, ignoring all dangers and occupy Wismar. Advancing past Gadesbuch Wismar was reached only hours before the Russians who demanded to be allowed to continue, until General Bols threatened to call in the Rocket firing Typhoons if they did."

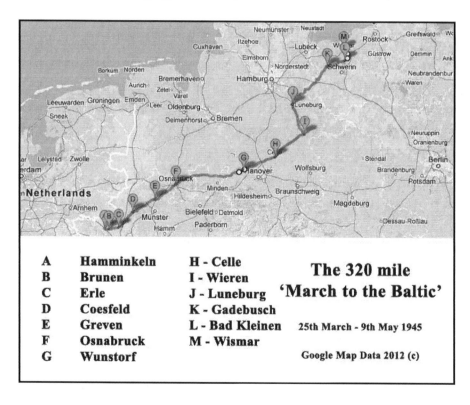

A	Hamminkeln	H - Celle		
B	Brunen	I - Wieren	**The 320 mile**	
C	Erle	J - Luneburg	**'March to the Baltic'**	
D	Coesfeld	K - Gadebusch		
E	Greven	L - Bad Kleinen	25th March - 9th May 1945	
F	Osnabruck	M - Wismar		
G	Wunstorf		Google Map Data 2012 (c)	

Citation – Major-Gen Eric Bols (Commander, 6th AB Division)

Award – Bar to DSO

General BOLS landed with the 6th Airborne Division on the East side of the RHINE on the 24th March 1945.

As a result of the extremely heavy close range artillery and small arms fire met on the landing by paratroopers and gliderborne troops alike, the handling of the situation required the utmost coolness and powers of leadership. In these hazardous conditions General BOLS led his division with great skill and daring.

His presence among the troops and his courageous bearing under heavy fire set the highest example to all ranks under his command and his inspiring leadership at this most vital time played a decisive part in securing the RHINE crossing, opening up the way for the advance of Second Army into Central Germany.

Lance Corporal David "Robbie Robinson (Anti-Tank 'C' Company)

"When the war ended we were at Wismar, some 3 of 4 days before the war was proclaimed over. There we made an approximate line across Germany with the Russians some 200-300 yards away from us. We kept ourselves separate although we did meet the Russians occasionally.

"A job during those few days was to keep taking in any Germans that came across from the Russian side, if they managed to get past the Russians because they didn't want to get captured by the Russians. So mainly we looked after German prisoners which had given themselves up previously and keep a patrol, I suppose on our boundary lines."

Lieutenant David Clark (225 Field Ambulance)

"In Wismar there was a large well equipped hospital, built for the Luftwaffe. 225 Field Ambulance took it over. It was empty when we arrived, but next day several hospital trains steamed in from the east, packed with wounded, doctors, nurses and refugees of every kind. Many of the wounded were in a pitiable state; they had major wounds dressed with paper bandages and they had been lying for days on stretchers in their own pus and faeces. We organised the nurses to get them out and into the wards, to get them cleaned and fed. Our surgeons started operating on the urgent cases. Soon we had a fine hospital running well. I was put in charge of a convalescent ward, containing Germans from the eastern front, airborne wounded and some Russians.

"We had started to meet our 'Gallant Russian Allies', the soldiers of the Red Army, and this was a shock for many of us. Roaming the streets of Wismar were Russians with tommy guns, festooned with watches and outrageously drunk, shooting at anything that caught their eyes. Everyday German women came into the clinics saying they had been raped repeatedly by Russians."

Lieutenant Ellis "Dixie" Dean (6th AB Division Liaison Officer)

"L/Corporal Samuel Fell was one of our Regimental police and on 4th May he was accidently killed by a fellow RP whilst weapon cleaning. He had dropped on D-Day as part of 9 Platoon 'C' Company in Dakota 325 [see 'The Missing' chapter]. Fell eventually made his way back to the Battalion and served right through the war only to be killed so near the end. His body was initially buried in Wismar, but at the 'Yalta Conference' it had been agreed that the Wismar area was to be in the Russian zone and consequently we withdrew. The Russian authorities refused to allow the CWGC access to the military graves and so Sam Fell, along with others was moved to the Berlin War Cemetery.

"Divisional HQ was set up under the trees around a square in the suburbs of the town, and someone decided we needed smartening up, and arranged the services of a German barber, who came and set up his chair under the trees. A queue stated to form, so army issue benches accommodated for those waiting. Colonel Luard and Roy Leyland had come visiting, and seeing the barber at work, decided to avail themselves of his services, and so joined the queue.

"I was summonsed from the Information Room, where I normally worked, to the Operations Caravan, where I was handed a 'Top Secret' message of 'Immediate Priority' to be handed personally to Brigadier Poett. Now Brigadier Poett had earlier that morning called at the 'Information Room' for the latest up-date on the Russian positions, as he was on his way to meet his Russian counterpart. This I explained to Major Wrightson the Staff Officer I worked under, and added as an after-thought, that "Colonel Luard of the 13th was visiting HQ and would he be a suitable person to receive the message?" I was then requested to ask the CO to speak to Major Wrightson, on a matter of some urgency. The Colonel was only in the caravan a few minutes, before he emerged, and calling for Roy Leyland and his driver, departed at high speed.

"It was only when the file copy of the signal arrived, that I knew the cause of the urgency. The message was from "SHAEF SUPREME, HQ, ALLIED EXPEDTTIONARY FORCE", calling for an armed escort to be provided for the American General Dewing, who was flying into Copenhagen to accept the surrender of all German Armed Forces in Denmark."

Alan Moorehead (War Correspondent)

"On Saturday, May 5th, the morning after Montgomery's armistice, a little group of men gathered round the transport aircraft on Lüneburg airfield: a company of airborne troops in their red berets and curious lizard-coloured camouflage jackets; a General and an Admiral and correspondents.

"Young officers ran about ticking off names and while the cease-fire was only a few hours old the machines took off – a dozen Dakotas, the fighter escort ranging high and wide on either side. German ships seeing us coming ran up the white flag and turned apprehensively away. Then, one after another, the green Danish islands. Every house flew the national flag, the white cross on a red background and from the air the effect was if one were looking down on endless fields strewn with poppies.

"One after another the Dakotas slid into a landing between the stationary German aircraft and drew up in a line before the airport buildings. The airborne troops jumped down, and with their guns ready advanced upon the hangars. The scene did for a moment look slightly ominous. Armed German guards were spaced along the runways. Two German officers stood stiffly in front of the central office and began to advance towards the landing aircraft. General Dewing met them halfway and in 2 minutes it was clear: we would have no trouble in Denmark.

"At that moment the Danish crowd burst on to the field, and from then onward I doubt that any of us had a coherent memory of the next 2 days. The Danes threw flowers at the airborne troops and sang 'Tipperary' and the Germans were forgotten. A long line of young Danish soldiers were drawn up for Dewing to inspect and whilst all this was going on the 2 German officer's staff car was stolen and the last I saw of them they were trudging unhappily away from the airfield.

"A column of some 20-30 cars led by Dewing headed for the 'Hotel Angleterre' which he intended to make his HQ. Roaming up and down the corridors of the hotel was a German Admiral looking for someone to surrender the cruisers *'Nürnberg'* and *'Prinz Eugen'* and their attendant destroyers lying in the bay."

It was Lieutenant Piers Raymond Gerard Rault who had taken over from Lieutenant Dean as OC 6 Platoon 'B' Company, the Company which had been chosen to be the protection of the mission. Lt Rault was a reinforcement officer arriving after the Ardennes and a Normandy veteran who dropped with the Military Police on D-Day.

Private Dave Beedham (6 Platoon 'B' Company)

"The Company [6 Platoon, 'B' Company] were detailed to fly to Copenhagen to protect an American General. There was no knowing what the situation might be when we landed so we went prepared to fight, but as soon as we climbed out of the Dakotas we were mobbed by the Danes who carried us off to their homes to celebrate and it was 2 days before the full company were rounded up and then were billeted in a girls school."

The 13th Para Bn, centre photo, arrive in Copenhagen 5th May 1945

Lieutenant Ellis "Dixie" Dean (6th AB Division Liaison Officer)

"The biggest event of all occurred on the 7th May, when Field-Marshal Montgomery met Marshal Rokossovsky at Divisional HQ and we all turned out for this historic meeting. "Monty" arrived first and awaited his Russian counterpart.[90] The Russian was greeted with a salute of 19 guns (below, IWM Duxford). "Monty" through an interpreter said "Tell the Marshal, that I have taken the surrender of all German forces in the West."

"That was it then, the war was over and I heard the announcement from the great man himself."

Lieutenant Peter Downward (Scout Platoon)

"On 8th May we were given the news that the war in Germany was officially over and that Hitler was dead having committed suicide together with Eva Braun, his wife of one day on 30th April. We had our celebrations in the various company areas with a few Russian officers coming over the road to share in the jubilations. That evening we had a bonfire in the farmyard which left the farmer's stocks of straw and wooden fencing somewhat depleted. Verey lights and 2" mortar flares lit up the sky and more alcohol was consumed. I was drunk and must confess that I nearly came a cropper by falling into the bonfire."

Lance Corporal David "Robbie Robinson (Anti-Tank 'C' Company)

"I shot a deer in the early morning's dawn and this went straight to the cook house for our first fresh meat for quite some time. We ate this deer as part of our celebrations. There was a parade in Wismar which I wasn't on; I was probably on duty somewhere."

---

[90] Konstantin Rokossovsky after the war claimed that Bols' 6th Airborne Division had manoeuvred behind Soviet troops advancing towards Lübeck, and Russian troops were all set to open fire on the airborne troops until they recognized the British uniforms.

Private Ray "Geordie" Walker ('A' Company)

"During the afternoon we relaxed in preparation of the evenings celebrations. The only thing we lacked was liquor. Fortunately the Russians had ample supplies of vodka and we hoped to barter a few tins of Players cigarettes for a bottle or two. I, along with two pals saddled up our horses and rode over to the Russian lines; they had gathered around a camp fire and were singing and dancing to an accordionist. Soon we too got into the spirit of the party, thanks to a liberal supply of vodka.

"As the evening wore on the party got wilder, with Russians firing their rifles and tommy-guns in all directions. Not wishing to get killed, we decided to return to our own lines. We bade farewell and clutching our bottles of vodka, rode off into the night. On reaching the crest of a hill, we stopped and admired the view. By now the whole of North Germany was aglow from the flames of bonfires, stretching all along the Baltic coast from Wismar to Lubeck. This was a day to be remembered."

Photo by R. H. Zachary, US Army Signal Corps "Officers & men of 6th AB Div at Nikolaikirche in Wismar for Divine services, the first of its kind since D-Day, 8th May 1945".

The beautiful altar of Wismar's Nikolaikirche built in 1774.

Lt Peter Downward (Scout Platoon)

"Next day, with quite a hangover, I along with Lt Geoff Otway and a sergeant, saddled up 3 horses and set off for the schloss at Maltow about 2 miles away to see if the Count was alright. What we found was heartbreaking. The place had been looted and vandalised. There was no sign of the Count or his wife and the 2 or 3 Russians about the place seemed completely indifferent to our presence. All the pictures had been ripped off the walls; the chandeliers were in fragments on the floor and personal possessions strewn all over the place."

Captain David Tibbs MC (RAMC)

"Luard had told him [the Count] to load up a horse and cart and flee the area together with his wife and staff. The last we saw of him was the cart disappearing over the horizon into the setting sun."

Lt Harry Pollak (Intelligence Officer)

"It was an important part of our celebrations, so we were told, to make friends with the Russians. This was not easy. They were friendly enough but our troops strongly resented their attitude and behaviour. They were some Mongolian unit and to say the least they were more than rough. To give an example, we occupied a village and they were encamped in open country. During our first night in that village a Russian truck with a few soldiers aboard asked to cross our lines. They were allowed into the village and then went and rounded up every female regardless of age, took them back to their own lines where they were publicly raped. Our troops waited for them to return the following night and when they did, beat them up mercilessly and then sent them packing. This incident nearly caused a major diplomatic row. A couple of other officers and I were sent to the Russian Commanding Officer to make the peace, but through an interpreter we had to explain that our troops just would not stomach this kind of thing. We pleaded with him to prevent a recurrence. I have no idea what the interpreter told him but a bottle was produced and passed round for us to drink out of. The effect was indescribable. It was supposed to be vodka but I am sure it was aviation spirit. Whilst we coughed and spluttered, they seemed to enjoy drinking it. At any rate, it made them feel vastly superior."

Major Jack Watson (OC 'A' Company)

"My brigadier, the CO, and some others were invited to meet the Russian commander. So off we went in a German car we'd picked up. Along the way I noticed something that was disturbing and pointed out to Peter Luard that every garden seemed to have a mortar or artillery piece well dug in and Russia soldiers manning them. To me this was the beginning of the cold war, although I didn't know it then. There we were recuperating, with fresh clothes; almost like we were on holiday and not far away, the Russians had dug their defences with their guns pointing towards us.

"The party was, I thought anyway, was a bit rough. The food was just plonked on the table and we ate with our fingers, I remember thinking "is this how they do things in Russia?" I was quite glad to get out, especially after receiving a full blooded kiss on the lips from the Russian General. I can still taste the awful taste now."

Private Dave Beedham ('B' Company)

"Next night I was on guard outside Company HQ, the war was over and lights were on inside. I saw Colonel Luard approaching and stood to attention. The CO stopped in front of me, grabbed hold of me and lifted me off the ground, but I won't tell you what he called me for not challenging him. But that was the end of the matter and I wasn't put on a charge."

Lieutenant Ellis "Dixie" Dean (6th AB Division Liaison Officer)

"Private Alan Blake, another of the young soldiers who only joined us on 19th March, was a well built strong lad who quickly became a member of my MMG Platoon went missing after a bathing trip in the Baltic on 14th May. He was presumed drowned and his body was never recovered.

"By the middle of May we knew we were to return home, prior to the Division joining the Far East Land Forces – how right the 'wags' had been, who interpreted the initials of our European postal address, BLA, as 'Burma Lies Ahead'.

"I was eager to get back to the 13th and arrived as they were about to eat supper. The Colonel asked me to join them and I sat with my old colleagues. My evening was really made, when the CO told me that he had already had the Brigadier's consent to my posting back to the 13th immediately on returning to Salisbury Plain."

One more award was added to the 13th Battalion's total, Lieutenant Dean, after his return to Britain became the recipient of the Military Cross.

Citation: Lieutenant Ellis Dean

Award: Military Cross

Lieut Dean jumped into Normandy on 6th June 44, as Machine Gun Officer, 13th Battalion (Lancashire) The Parachute Regiment.

Throughout the campaign in Normandy he commanded his platoon with outstanding skill, courage and devotion to duty.

In the battle of Bure in Belgium on 3rd January, a German Royal Tiger Tank with infantry escorting, was advancing down the village street covered by the guns of Lt Dean's Platoon. A gun team was hit and all killed or wounded. At point blank range, Lt Dean crossed the street. He carried the only survivor to safety, then, in spite of heavy fire from the tank not 100 yards away he returned for the gun. He returned to continue to command his platoon as imperturbable as ever.

He again jumped with his Machine Guns into Germany over the Rhine on 24th March. During this campaign his conduct, cheerfulness, and leadership have been beyond praise, and a wonderful example to all ranks.

There were also 4 Mention In Despatches awarded to 13th (Lancashire) Parachute Battalion men for their rolls in Operation Varsity and the subsequent 'March to the

Baltic'. The recipients were: Captain Claude Milman, Lieutenant Malcolm Town, CSM "Taffy" Lawley[91] and L/Sergeant Ben Shelton.[92]

Lieutenant Peter Downward (Scout Platoon)

"After a couple of days we were given the news that we would be going back to the UK. Before we left there was a large Russian stage party at Wismar. The Cossack dancing was absolutely amazing and very exhilarating, particularly with so many pretty girls pirouetting around the stage in Russian folk dances."

Lieutenant David Clark (225 Field Ambulance)

"We also had a special divisional concert. Marshal Rokossovsky sent his army concert party to entertain us. The opera house in Wismar was filled with paratroopers. The concert party were all lighting soldiers, but brilliant performers. There were of course massed male voice choirs, singing rousing songs of the Red Army and also Cossack dancers and sword dancers, but best of all were girls dancing the national dances of many Russian races. Most popular was a dark eyed Uzbeck beauty who danced a variant of the dance of seven veils - to tumultuous applause. We were told she was a corporal telephone operator!"

Private Alfred Draper ('C' Company)

"One of the highlights of our stay was an invitation to the Red Army Choir. It was held in a theatre in Wismar and was a wonderful show. Everybody enjoyed it and we felt honoured to have been invited."

Lance Corporal David "Robbie Robinson (Anti-Tank 'C' Company)

"Around 12th or 13th May we were transported back to Belgium to Brussels airport and we were flown home from there. I remember we stopped one night at Brussels. There was some dispute as to whether we should have priority on the aircraft as against a lot of prisoners of war that had been released in Germany and were trying to get back home. I don't know how this dispute was settled and how it was finalised but we stopped one night on Brussels aerodrome, most of us sleeping on the ground on the aerodrome or scattered around in hangers and buildings. This was no hardship to us having been out in slit trenches etc with no worries of getting shot at. It was easy to get down and sleep no matter where we were.

"Some of us went into Brussels for the night but there was nothing doing, the place had no real life in it at that stage. There was little to do, no places open, it was just a matter of walking round and back to the aerodrome for a kip. The civilians in Brussels if they had celebrated earlier on the 8th or 9th or so, they'd celebrated so much that they certainly weren't about any more by the time that we went there. They'd probably all got one hell of a hang over from previous nights. We didn't see any, not even girls."

---

[91] CSM Lawley was also awarded the Military Medal after the war for his part that he played in helping POW's escape when he, himself, was interned in an Italian POW camp in 1942-3.

[92] L/Sgt Shelton fought in every campaign with the 13th and after the war continued his Army career by fighting in the Korean War finishing with the rank of WO2.

13th Para Bn Scout Platoon prepare to move out of Germany (IWM Duxford).

Corporal Dennis Boardman (Signaller)

"One of the dogs had been killed on the jump over the Rhine and 2 days after the jump, 'Bing' sniffed out 2 German Army Alsatians and they became good friends and joined the Battalion. They had stayed with us from Hamminkeln right up to the Baltic and we knew that the dogs would cause us problems with quarantine rules. The lads were desperate to keep the dogs and found a solution."

Private Alf John (Signal Platoon)

"As I remember it, the bulk of the Battalion flew back to Larkhill, but the MT Section, had to drive back with a lot of the Battalions heavy equipment. Although I wasn't in the MT, I was detailed to be one of the parties travelling by road (this took a week, 4 days on the road from Wismar to Ostend, a day to load onto LST, a days Channel crossing, and finally unloading and driving to Larkhill).

"In Wismar, Capt Davison's dog was very popular and very brave, and I often wondered how it managed the transition from German to English, but it seemed to understand our commands easily enough. Ken Bailey had more than one. Ken told me that he hoped to set up a breeding centre, using the German dogs as the basic stock.

"The rear party was a mixed bag, a cook, a Medic, the MT drivers (under Lt Fred Tiramani), and various others. Driving across Germany was a real eye opener. We saw enough of the destruction while we were in action, but that in reality was a tunnel vision view of the destruction. Now on the drive, we could see the enormous amount of damage caused by the RAF and the American bomber forces. Every mile we drove, we encountered displaced civilians, walking back to their own countries. There were thousands of them, simply marching home. There were make-shift camps holding the tens of thousands of German POW. Outside the wire, German women were gathered, and as we drove past, we received dirty looks or uncomplimentary gestures. Nazism was still very much alive.

"We camped several night's during the journey, and even before we reached the embarkation port, we were discussing what sort of reception the dogs would get when we landed. This was still unresolved when we set sail for home.

"The voyage itself was uneventful, but en-route we were informed that the port of disembarkation would be either Tilbury on the Essex side of the Thames or Gravesend on the Kent side. Later it was confirmed that we would dock at Tilbury, and that Customs officials would be waiting to speak to us. I suspect that the vehicles contained more than simply Battalion stores. But the main worry was undoubtedly the dogs, and a plan was thought up. The dogs would be put at the front end of a truck, and then given a jab of morphine, using the ampoules we all were issued with. Crates and boxes were then piled around the animals, to conceal them from a casual inspection of the vehicle. Hopefully the doped dogs would make no noise and remain undiscovered.

"I don't know if the plan was even put into operation, since at the last minute we learnt that we would now be docking at Gravesend, and the Customs would try to meet us there. The question was could we dock and disembark at Gravesend before the Customs got there? Happily we did, and were driving away before the Officials turned up. I remember our driving was somewhat disorderly, because we were anxious to put distance between us and Gravesend as quickly as possible, and also because we left the docks on the wrong side of the road. We had driven on the continent for so long. What a way to end your war in Europe… Smuggling dogs back to Britain!"

Members of Scout Platoon near Wismar 1945, (IWM, Duxford).

Lieutenant Ellis "Dixie" Dean MC (6ᵗʰ AB Division Liaison Officer)

"Others that I know who also brought dogs back with them include Ken Bailey (Scout Platoon) and Roy Leyland, 2i/c of the Battalion. One of Ken's dogs, a very fine looking Alsatian bitch, produced several litters, which he was able to sell at a fair profit. Roy was not so fortunate, because the pretty long haired Dachshund bitch he brought with him, produced a litter of pups, while still in quarantine, leaving him a rather large bill."

Claude Milman (left) and Freddie Tremlett, May 1945 (Sir Peter Downward)

Lieutenant Peter Downward (Scout Platoon)

"We were flown back to RAF Lyneham and the sight of the English countryside as we landed was unforgettable and something which will always be in my mind as we drove over from Lyneham airfield towards Swindon was the sight of two Land Army girls on bicycles looking very attractive. They evoked lots of cheers and whistles from the backs of our 3-tonners."

Unknown members (except Jim Beasant 2nd left) of the 13th Battalion proudly showing off their medals after returning home after the war (IWM, Duxford).

ROLL OF HONOUR – 'MARCH TO THE BALTIC'

Pte	GARDNER Wilfred	19	31/03/1945	14852129	Reichswald Forest 32-A-1
Pte	BROADBENT John		03/04/1945	14849337	Reichswald Forest 33-A-2
Pte	CLISSOLD Leslie		03/04/1945	5733947	Reichswald Forest 33-A-3
Pte	GRIFFITHS Gwilym D.	23	03/04/1945	4042824	Reichswald Forest 33-B-4
Pte	HARMER Thomas	18	03/04/1945	14827912	Reichswald Forest 33-C-8
Pte	IRVIN Robert	28	03/04/1945	2754848	Reichswald Forest 33-A-4
Pte	LAWES Jack E.		03/04/1945	2064310	Reichswald Forest 33-A-5
Pte	MORSE William C.		03/04/1945	2067256	Reichswald Forest 33-A-6
Pte	RODGERS Leslie	19	03/04/1945	14719561	Rheinberg 13-B-8
Pte	WHITLOCK Lawrence	19	03/04/1945	14794329	Reichswald Forest 33-A-7
Sgt	SCOTT Robert		07/04/1945	7262166	Hanover War Cemetery
LCpl	FELL Samuel	22	04/05/1945	14203051	Berlin 10-K-16
Pte	BLAKE Alan	20	14/05/1945	14850952	NKG Groesbeek Memorial

One more member of the 13th (Lancashire) Parachute Battalion was to receive recognition for his bravery in the face of the enemy.

Cpl Dennis Boardman (Signaller)

"With the war finished, the lady who had owned Bing [Betty Fetch] was approached by the War Office, requesting to keep the dog for further duties. She refused saying he had done enough in the war. 3 weeks later, she had a telephone call from the local Stationmaster, saying a crate had been taken off the train with a dog in it. For 3 or 4 weeks, Bing acted very strange and she was thinking of returning him to the Army. Then one morning he had completely changed, he was back to knowing her.

"Bing was awarded a medal, equivalent to the Victoria Cross; the 'Dickin Medal' (pictured receiving the medal, IWM, Duxford).

565

The medal was eventually auctioned on 22nd September 2006 for £13,000! An American and a Canadian were the final bidders, fortunately the Canadian won. The American was going to melt the medals down to make a necklace for his wife."

Bing passed away on 26th October 1955 aged 13 and is buried in Ilford PDSA Animal Cemetery.

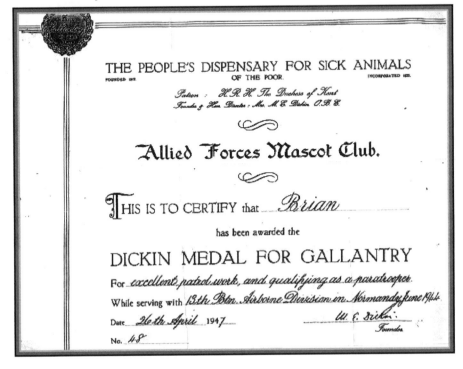

"It was about this time that 'Dear John' letters began to arrive. Many women back home had had extra-marital relationships and wanted divorce."

CQMS Ray "Geordie" Walker (HQ Company)

29. THE FAR EAST

Brigadier Nigel Poett (5th Para Brigade Commander)

"I was enjoying my leave fishing on the Tweed when a telephone message came from the house asking that a car be sent to meet a light aircraft which would be landing shortly in a field nearby. It would bring a letter for me. The aircraft touched down and out got John Wrightson of the Divisional staff. The letter said that I was to return immediately to Bulford. My Brigade was under orders for South-East Asia. We were to play our part in the war against Japan. It was sad for our wives and families that we should be leaving again so soon, but that is the life of a soldier.

"I was to leave as soon as possible, by flying-boat. General Bols, the Divisional Commander, and two of his staff would come with us. We were to go first to Kandy in Ceylon, the HQ of the Supreme Allied Commander, Admiral Mountbatten."

Private Ray "Geordie" Walker ('A' Company)

"Life in the barracks was always hectic and the arrival of reinforcements brought us up to operational strength. The 3rd Brigade was to go to Palestine and our 5th Brigade to India. We were told by an Aussie Air-force Officer how to survive in the jungle, where to find water and what wild animals could be eaten."

Lance Corporal L Edwards ('C' Company Clerk)

"I reported to the 13th Battalion and was posted to 'C' Company as company clerk. For all its reputation, I didn't like this battalion. I did, however like my Company Commander, Major Krell and his second-in-command, Captain Barlow. Major Krell was a small modest looking man with a moustache, had served in Burma and was a recent arrival. Captain Barlow was a big man with a black, curly moustache which he spent all his time curling with his fingers. None of the ["C" Company] platoon officers had been abroad prior to coming, except one, Lieutenant Whorton, who had landed in a tank during the Dieppe raid in 1942.

"Many members of the Battalion were very young reinforcements and the Battalion was a shadow of the one that fought in Normandy. The Battalion was a Lancashire one and perhaps this was why I never felt at home in it."

Private Alfred Draper ('C' Company)

"We came back from leave and started re-equipping for our posting to the Far East. All our kit was a new design for fighting in the jungle, it was lightweight and green, even our underpants and toilet paper. Our rifles were lighter and shorter but when we fired them on the range, we found they had a kick like a mule."

Corporal Ray "Geordie" Walker ('A' Company)

"Typical Army planning – instead of taking a 30 minute drive to Southampton we had to take a 435 mile journey to Scotland."

L/Cpl L Edwards ('C' Coy Clerk)

"We boarded a train and dawdled all day and at last we reached the River Clyde. Out in the river I saw a grey painted ship, which turned out to be the P&O liner 'Corfu' (below). Small boats ferried us out in batches. We sailed that evening and I soon felt the roll of the ship as it reached the sea. I endured 3 days of acute sea sickness and then thought "This is ridiculous, I must eat." I then had a breakfast and never felt sick again.

"As the German war was over, our route took us through the Mediterranean Sea. I saw Gibraltar through the heat haze and the white houses of Tangier. The ship entered the Suez Canal and proceeded slowly past the palm trees. It parked up again and

everyone crowded in order to see the ATS girls clad in swim suits lounging around a swimming pool under large umbrellas. Cat calls and wolf whistles were directed at them and they battered no eyelid, having experienced this before many times.

"We passed another troopship crowded with Burma veterans who jeered at us and held up 5 fingers, indicating 5 years out in the Far East. They got an earful back."

Corporal Ray "Geordie" Walker ('A' Company)

"Steaming along the Algerian and Tunisian coasts brought back memories for my Sergeant, Stan Braddock. He had fought there with from the 8th November 1942 to 13th May 1943 with the Lancashire Fusiliers. Now he could relax and enjoy a peaceful Mediterranean cruise."

Private Alfred Draper ('C' Company)

"We sailed on the 31st July and 6 weeks later arrived in Bombay. We had passed through the Suez Canal and had our first taste of the east with street traders coming on board to sell their goods. A lot of the lads bought 'gold' rings that turned their fingers green after 3 days at sea."

The advance party travelled 10 days earlier by Dakota, hopping across Sardinia, Libya, Palestine, Habbaniya, Bahrein and to Karachi in India. From there they travelled by train.

Lieutenant Peter Downward (Signal Platoon)

"On arrival at Victoria Station, Bombay [Mumbai], we finished up in Kalyan Military Camp about 12 miles away. This was to be base for 5th Para Brigade for the immediate future whilst we trained up for some undisclosed operation. The main party would arrive in a few days time having travelled by troopship."

Lance Corporal L Edwards ('C' Company Clerk)

"We boarded a train with no glass in the windows and one besieged with beggars and salesmen trying to sell trashy jewellery to us. A man in our carriage who wore the pre-war Indian Service Medal ribbon calmly put his foot on the stomach of a man selling rings and pushed him off the carriage onto the track."

Captain Harry Pollak (Intelligence Section)

"Between the end of July and beginning of August 1945 the Americans dropped countless leaflets on Japanese cities warning them that unless the Japanese government co-operated by surrender, incalculable bloodshed and ruin to their cities would result. They also announced that just to demonstrate that the Allies could reach the Japanese mainland without difficulty they would drop a token number of bombs on 10 Japanese cities. There was no response. The final warning was given on 5th August 1945, the Americans dropping 1½ million leaflets primarily on Hiroshima and Nagasaki. Again there was no response. On August 6th 1945 an atomic bomb was dropped on Hiroshima and since there was no reaction from the Japanese government a further atomic bomb was dropped on Nagasaki on the 9th August. 5 days later on August 14th the Japanese government accepted the allied ultimatum and surrendered. Nevertheless fears were confirmed that their troops scattered over vast areas of South East Asia would be ignorant of their government's surrender and fight on. Hence the allied command put into operation the plan for rapid re-occupation of all Japanese-held territories. It became our task to land on the coast of Malaya near Port Sweatenham."

Brigadier Nigel Poett (5th Para Brigade Commander)

"In mid-August, just as were about to embark, the atom bomb was dropped. 'Zipper', as planned, was cancelled. Nonetheless we embarked on our troopship and set sail for Malaya. The revised plan involved a landing, from landing craft, on the Morib beaches in Malaya."

Private Alfred Draper ('C' Company)

"After about 3 weeks the rumour came round that an atom bomb had been dropped on Japan and the war was over. Nobody believed it at first but it finally came through officially and we were over the moon. We had been given rough details of our operation and nobody was happy about it. The casualties were estimated to be 50%. The 14th Army was already attacking Malaya from Burma and we were to land from the sea. When we had captured the airfield, planes would come in, take us to Singapore and drop one battalion on the mainland, one on the causeway and one on the island. At the same time a seaborne landing would be landing in front of the island. In all 120,000 men would be taking part."

Lieutenant Peter Downward (Signal Platoon)

"It was not until the second weapon had been dropped that we learned that the Japanese had capitulated. It was so sudden and unexpected and quickly gave way to hopeful belief that we would be home by Christmas. There was great celebration in the messes and canteens, and I remember poor David Tibbs and his medics having to treat quite a few alcoholic casualties."

Captain Harry Pollak (Intelligence Section)

"On 9th September we were to land as originally planned. The Japanese did not put up much resistance; nevertheless the landing was like a nightmare. The mud in the shallow waters became a very formidable obstacle. We had been transferred from the

Orontes into assault landing craft which lowered ramps about 200 yards offshore for us to disembark into water chest high and into mud which sucked our legs down. All those of us on foot made some progress, laborious though it was, whilst many lorries and tanks were stuck and later had to be winched ashore. It was a great blessing that there was virtually no opposition.

"When we had re-formed, wet to the skin and covered in mud, we moved a few miles inland and spent the night in an orange grove only to be told in the morning to return to the beach and get back on board the troopship. So once more into the water and the mud, except this time the landing craft came close inshore. By the end of the day we were all back aboard.

"Within hours of getting aboard I was given orders to go to Singapore on a Motor Torpedo Boat with a few men to re-occupy the police depot in Thompson Road Singapore. My orders were to gather as many policemen loyal to Britain as possible. I was also ordered to install myself in one of the villas above the depot which had originally been occupied by British officers and their families, later by the Japanese. I was authorised to immediately engage some Chinese servants and set up a household which would impress the local population. Next, I met an Australian officer who had been imprisoned in Changi jail throughout the war. He was so emaciated he could hardly walk but enjoyed telling me how to go about gaining the confidence of policemen to get them to rejoin and how to conduct myself to gain 'face' amongst them. Obviously Britain's image had sunk to a very low ebb during the occupation."

Lieutenant Peter Downward (Signal Platoon)

"It was a historic moment for us all as we came alongside Singapore on 11th September. We had seen the photographs of this famous port in the newspapers 4 years earlier when it fell to the Japanese. For some reason soon after it became dark, there was a sudden halt to the off loading by the crane operators and it became apparent it was a form of dispute. Two or three of the 13th Battalion soldiers who had been Liverpool dockers volunteered to take over the cranes and I joined them. What had been a fairly minor dispute became a shouting match. I was ordered by the 2/ic, Roy Leyland to "Pack it in!" as we were aggravating a trade union problem."

Corporal Ray "Geordie" Walker ('A' Company)

"After marching for 1½ hours we arrived at Raffles College. Before making our new billets comfortable we had to clear all the classrooms of furniture and organise our bedding. We had electric lights, ceiling fans and could tune into Radio Singapore.

"I found peacetime soldiering irksome, too much spit and polish. We had visits and had to look immaculate in our jungle greens and white belts."

Private Norman Skeates (Motor Transport Platoon)

"On arriving at Raffles College, whose buildings formed our first billets in Singapore I was serving 7 days 'confined to barracks' for jumping ship in Bombay docks whilst the MT Platoon were waterproofing vehicles. As I was not allowed out of camp I took a self-guided tour of the buildings. I found an unoccupied room containing a wooded chest. I prized off the lid and found wood shavings and beneath them were white crystal like pebbles. I was disappointed with my find so replaced the lid and thought no more about it.

"Thinking back, I have often wondered if they were un-cut diamonds!"

Lieutenant Peter Downward (Signal Platoon)

"Life became more relaxed, but at the same time more formal with regimented parades for high-ranking officers such as Admiral Mountbatten and General Slim. We also had to provide a guard for Government House, which required much 'spit and polish' and 'square bashing' in rehearsal for the daily Guard Mount. This commitment was left very much to the rifle companies; consequently my signallers were not involved."

Corporal Ray "Geordie" Walker ('A' Company)

"We assembled in the college quadrangle to hear General Slims address. As we had fought in Europe we appreciated his kind comments. My thoughts turned to "Spit" McCrudden my pal who was killed in Normandy. Later I was detailed to guard the entrance of the Hong Kong & Shanghai Bank in the city centre."

13th Bren gun position in Far East (IWM Duxford)

Private Dave Beedham ('B' Company)

"I was in 'B' Company and most of our time was spent on guard duties at Government House where Louis Mountbatten lived. 'A' and 'C' Companies did guard duties on various warehouses which were filled with food and other things. I did hear of some of our own men making a few pounds by selling to the Chinese.

"We ['B' Company] were guarding in platoon strength and we guarded one day on then two days off [No.4, 5 & 6 Platoon rotating]. There was a lot of blancoing and such, but that was to be expected now the war was over. With all the time off we looked around Singapore itself and the Chinese soon got things organised, shops opened and girls became available. Then came BMA with the MP's and made lots of streets out of bounds. There were places like 'Happy World' which you could compare with Blackpool. We made our own 'Pegasus Club' on Beach Road and I suppose when we left some other branch of the services would've taken it over."

Lieutenant Peter Downward (Signal Platoon)

"Whilst at Raffles College we had an ENSA concert staged in an open courtyard; the Signal Platoon was tasked with setting up a wooden stage and arranging some floodlighting. It had to be delayed because of a heavy downpour, but at 5pm the various artists including a dance troop of 6 girls started their rehearsal. The floodlights were switched on and the girls pranced onto the damp stage in sort of a can-can dance. Suddenly the dance broke up as the girls leapt off the stage with shouts and yells, at first we thought it was part of the act, but not so... it transpired that the wet stage was carrying an electric shock. The fault was rectified and they resumed dancing.

"We had to vacate the college and move to a military establishment near Changi Gaol. As part of the advance party I took my soldiers into Selorang Barracks."

The barracks had been taken over by the Japanese air-force during the invasion of Singapore and was piled high with aircraft components, engines, propellers and other equipment. On the grass outside there was several Japanese Zero fighter planes and piles of aerial bombs.

The buildings were cleared and turned into sleeping quarters, telephone wires were laid and the water supply needed to be reconnected. The pumping station was in a state of disrepair and required manual labour supplied by Japanese POW's.

It was at this time that a German U-Boat Commander and his crew surrendered to the 13th Battalion. The Commander spoke perfect English as he had been educated at Lancing School.

Lieutenant Peter Downward (Signal Platoon)

"I was able to put him to the test very quickly as Lieutenant Geoff Otway (left and below, courtesy Bingham Collection) was an old Lancing boy and there was a good chance they might have overlapped school days. Sure enough they recognised each other, but they were in different houses and forms. More importantly he was prepared to put his crew at our disposal in getting the water supply going."

Naval Intelligence discovered that the U-Boat was carrying a load of atomic material for the Japanese atomic weapon programme.

Lieutenant Peter Downward (Signal Platoon)

"The Germans took over in true naval style. Spanners, hammers, wrenches and numerous other tools appeared and the pump-house became a hive of activity. Electric motors and pumps were stripped and electric circuits rewired, valves were cleaned and tested, the whole system was overhauled. At the end of the third day the Commander informed me that they were "ready to dive". The crew stood to attention at various points around the pump-house and even one at the top of the tower. One could imagine them in their action-station positions in their U-Boat. Switches were thrown and the motors hummed, driving the two large pumps. The gauges showed that water was being drawn up.

"We let the pumps run for half an hour to wash the tank out and then the Jap prisoners were sent up to the tank to scrub it out. But the inevitable happened, the pumps suddenly started up again and there was chaos in the water tank. The Japs were being soaked by a powerful jet of water spraying in all directions. By coincidence the ladder had been removed and after a lot of yelling the water was turned off, and the Japs allowed to escape like a lot of bedraggled wet dogs. I suspect some of my signallers were at the root of this prank with the full connivance of the submarine crew.

"An incident I recall in the cleaning up of Selorang Barracks was during the cutting back of the grass around the camp. Parties of Jap prisoners, 4 or 5 strong under the supervision of one of our soldiers, were working away when suddenly one soldier went berserk, hitting them with his rifle butt and verbally abusing them. It turned out the party had left a patch of long grass and when the soldier investigated he found the remains of an allied soldier, probably an Australian. It had obviously been there a very long time and difficult to identify.

"Eventually 13 Parachute Battalion was able to move into the restored barracks and the Union Jack flew proudly over Battalion HQ, and the gateway displayed the full title of the Battalion."

13 Para at the "Halfway House" (IWM Duxford)

Private Alfred Draper ('C' Company)

"A German submarine had been in the harbour when the war ended and the crew were living in our camp waiting to go home. They had no pay and would do anything for money. Some played in an orchestra and some made whiskey from cookhouse left over's. They were a good bunch and it was hard to believe they had once been our enemies.

"Tea making was an art. We put ten five gallon containers on the fire and when they boiled, three handfuls of tea were thrown in then three scoops of sugar followed by two tins of evaporated milk.

"Bob Giles and Bob Wilky found they had had enough 'bullshit' from the new RSM and joined me in the cookhouse as cooks. They willingly gave up their stripes to get away from it all.

"I started buying revolvers from the lads who 'found' them and sold them to a detachment of Americans."

Corporal Ray "Geordie" Walker ('A' Company)

"As demobilisation of the Armed Forces had begun in June it was now affecting the Battalion. Our "old" soldiers who were the most experienced would soon be departing for the UK and home. Younger NCO's could expect early promotions and by mid-November I was no longer in 'A' Company, but serving in HQ Company as a clerk in the Quartermasters office."

Private Alfred Draper ('C' Company)

"Just before Christmas, we sailed to Batavia [Djakarta], the capital of Java. We hated this because it was to help the Dutch retain their rule. Our sympathies were with the people and we did more fighting with the Dutch than the rebels.

"We sailed to Semarang; this was a small town on the coast. The Japanese were still in charge and we rearmed them to stop terrorists trying to take over the town.

"I had a brush with the Sergeant-Major. He insisted that the other 3 cooks did parades on their day off and I thought this unfair. I went to the Company Commander and asked to be transferred back to my own company and told him why. I got my transfer and the parades were stopped."

Photo of Inter Divisional football match, courtesy Norman Skeates (2nd on left, Townrow and Scofield either side of him).

Private Dave Beedham ('B' Company)

"It had been said there wasn't many Japs on the island and that most were in Malaya. When we arrived we found more of the enemy than was thought. Not that it mattered because they all surrendered.

"We were in some barracks at Changi. There were a lot of POW's of all nationalities, I have read lots of different books on how our POW's were treated and what we saw was terrible. Eventually these POW's were sent home and the battalion settled down to normal duties. We started football games with the locals, Colonel Luard had gone home and the new CO [Roy Leyland] was a very keen rugby and football fanatic."

Lance Corporal L Edwards ('C' Company Clerk)

"It was around this time that I met a released Australian POW clad in his bush hat and a minute Japanese loin cloth, swearing bitterly as he walked along. "What's the matter, digger?" I asked. He proceeded to tell me how, prior to the surrender in 1942, he had buried a cache of ill gotten gains, jewellery and such like, in the Botanical Gardens. He had just been to retrieve his loot only to find that the Japanese had constructed a concrete pillbox on the very spot.

"I never really liked serving in the 13th Battalion, the RSM was a large, unpleasant person and best avoided. There was also an unpleasant suggestion coming from Battalion HQ, that now the war was over, real peacetime soldiering would begin again."

Lieutenant Peter Downward (Signal Platoon)

"Peter Luard decided that the young officers should learn to play polo and over the next few days brought in ponies, Japanese army horses, race horses and even the odd dray. Stables were set up and a pitch mapped out on the airstrip. Peter was an excellent horseman; I can still hear his cries of "Downward, I can see daylight between you and your saddle! Get your heels down! Hands closer together as though you are reading a book. You are not riding a bloody bicycle!" The poor ponies suffered more than us as they received whacks from misdirected swings.

"Less happy things were happening in Singapore as war crimes were being investigated. One of our members Arthur Prestt destined to become a High Court Judge in later years, was in the team of judges after recuperation from wounds received in Bure. We learned about the crimes committed by the Japanese and not surprisingly the death sentence was passed. It was reported that 7th Para Battalion who were looking after Changi Gaol, were asked if anyone had experience of delivering capital punishment; if so step forward. Apparently the whole Battalion stepped forward, but it was eventually decided no servicemen would be involved."

Trouble started in Java during December 1945, where Indonesians were resisting the attempts by colonials; mainly Dutch to take back the Dutch East Indies after the Japanese had surrendered.

Lance Corporal L Edwards ('C' Company Clerk)

"During December, our brigade was ordered to Java and after Christmas, orders came for us to move once again. We embarked on an ancient liner called the 'Otranto' and after 2 days anchored at Semarang."

Company Quartermaster Sergeant Ray "Geordie" Walker (HQ Company)

"We adopted 3 youngsters, 2 sisters aged 3 & 4 and a boy aged 5, we'd found them sleeping in an old shed full of rats. They were weak and could barely hold a cup of tea. We made dresses out of velvet curtains and fed them up.

"It was about this time that 'Dear John' letters began to arrive. Many women back home had had extra-marital relationships and wanted divorce. One friend received a letter that simply said "Tired of waiting. Have married Joe... Jean." Another comrade's wife died during childbirth and he was refused compassionate leave. Needless to say he was heartbroken and un-consolable."

Lieutenant Peter Downward (Signal Platoon)

"February 1946, Peter Luard came to the end of his distinguished period of command and handed over to Roy Leyland. As I was due to attend a War Office Selection Board in Singapore with a view to going for a regular commission, I flew back in the same aircraft as Peter."

Company Quartermaster Sergeant Ray "Geordie" Walker (HQ Company)

"We bade farewell to Colonel Luard from an RAF airfield and a week later Brigadier Poett flew back to the UK, he was replaced by Brigadier K. T. Darling and his initials gave him the nickname "Katie".

"Demobilisation continued to reduce our ranks and the youngsters were to soldier on for another 2 years and I wondered if I would ever see home again."

"I just cannot see the men who had endured the streets of Bure objecting to a bit of blancoing. I myself know what was the easiest to do."

Private Dave Beedham ('B' Company)

30.   'MUTINY'

Lance Corporal L Edwards ('C' Company Clerk)

"Our Brigade was ordered to hand over our positions to the Dutch and return to Singapore. We had adopted a small orphan boy, an Indonesian, and his future had to be secured. He accompanied us every where dressed in shorts and red beret. Being Indonesian he couldn't come to Singapore so we had a whip round and enough money was raised for him to be looked after and educated by nuns of a new convent.

"A 2 day voyage brought us to Malaya and we embussed on 3-tonners and drove through Singapore towards our next destination. We arrived at a small town called Muar on the west coast south of Malacca. The Battalion was quartered in tents and there were a few bungalows built on stilts and these were occupied by the various Company HQ's and by Battalion HQ.

"It was a very different Battalion from the one that arrived in India a year before. Demobilisation, whilst it had been gradual had caused our numbers to almost halve. The strength of the companies was down to 60-70 men each, yet duties had not been reduced. We had no clothing issue since first arriving in India and the climate had played havoc with it."

Photo: Believed to be Muar camp's bungalows (K.G. Davison Photo Collection)

Company Quartermaster Sergeant Ray "Geordie" Walker (HQ Company)

"I bedded down in a sea-side bungalow. It was built on stilts and adjacent to the seawall and my room had a dual role of being the Quartermaster's office. I shared with 4 others, not to mention the lizards and mosquitoes.

"As 90% of the men lived in tents, life for them was miserable especially when the tide came in and flooded the town's drainage system."

Private Alfred Draper ('C' Company)

"The old RSM had been demobbed and the new one was an upstart who had been promoted too quickly (he was the one I had brushed with in 'C' Company). The CO left the running of the battalion to him, he was more interested in playing rugby, and it went to the RSM's head."

Lieutenant Peter Downward (Signal Platoon)

"Back in early April we were informed that we would have a Brigadier's inspection in 2 months time and every effort would be made to ensure everything was up to the highest standard. Every item of equipment, clothing, records of service and more had to be ready for scrutiny. Extra attention was needed for the soldiers accommodation, the tents had to be properly lined up and the guide ropes whitened, personal kit had to be arranged on the beds and sometime in the second week in May, there was a very high tide, which overflowed the seawall and into the tented area of the rifle companies.

"All the good work of preparing for the inspection was undone, and there were many disgruntled soldiers some of whom were awaiting early demobilisation."

Private Dave Beedham ('B' Company)

"Now was the time when some of the men went home on demob. I myself was thinking of signing on for a few more years as a regular, so I stayed. This is the time I think we had some reinforcements; they came from a para unit that hadn't seen any wartime action. Most of our senior NCO's had gone home and their replacements came from this para unit.

"I know they were very keen on discipline, but nothing a good soldier couldn't manage. A lot of privates came along with them as well and it wasn't the same old 13th. I was fortunate, along with about a dozen others, we were granted a weeks leave around this time."

Company Quartermaster Sergeant Ray "Geordie" Walker (HQ Company)

"Although our ranks were being depleted by demobilisation we took two intakes of reinforcements. One group of 70 men had been in hospital suffering from minor ailments and the second group was 50 fresh faced young recruits from England. They were all shocked to see their living conditions. In moving about the camp I learned that the men were constantly complaining about their living conditions and no-one took notice of their plight."

Private Alfred Draper ('C' Company)

"It all started at the end of the European War. All the older men with a low demob number were transferred to the Depot to await demobilisation. The 1st Division was disbanded and most of the men sent to our Division to replace them. There was then a shortage of senior NCO's and they had to be replaced. RSM Railton had signed on for a further 7 years so his promotion was very rapid. He was promoted to Company Sergeant Major in 'C' Company in Java. I had a brush with him over making the cooks do parades on their day off when I was in charge of 'C' Company cookhouse. Shortly after that he was promoted to RSM.

"Now the RSM is the most powerful man in the battalion after the CO. Our CO was more interested in rugby than running the battalion so nothing was done about his excesses. Conditions were bad but that was nothing new. A lot of the men had never seen action and didn't know how to handle the situation. 5 men who were the ringleaders inflamed them. Very few if any of the old lads of the battalion took part in the strike; they had mostly got themselves 'cushy numbers'.

"The sergeants and warrant officers had their own mess at HQ and also slept there. When he was CSM of 'C' Company he and several others had women sleeping with them. When he became RSM he put them on a charge for the offence.

"He had a mania for drill parades and insisted on having one every day. Anyone who was not properly dressed was put on a charge. There was one instance when we were in Malaya under canvas we paraded on the road. All the ground was dusty or muddy due to the weather. Consequently our boots were always dusty or muddy when we reached the road. When he saw us he raved and shouted like a maniac and put the worst of us on a charge."

Lance Corporal L Edwards ('C' Company Clerk)

"One of the first instructions was "back to peacetime soldiering". This really was nonsensical. Leyland, the new CO who I never cared for, took great pride in insisting

that the half-strength unit should still maintain its full quota of duties. This meant that no respite at all was given to a unit which had quite a hard time in Java. On top of this "peacetime standard" was interpreted by the new RSM [Railton, left] as a harsh form of discipline. Railton had been the CSM of my company and quite a decent, reasonable man. However, I suppose that his promotion may have affected him and felt that he had to implement the CO's orders. Leyland issued an order that NCO's should not associate with private soldiers and this order was strictly enforced. He thus separated wartime comrades and friends from each other. There was really no need to do this and it really increased the bad feeling which was growing in the battalion.

"Even so, the ensuing trouble wouldn't occurred but for 2 things. One, demobilisation was painfully slow. It really was wrong that more than a year after the end of the war, men called up for hostilities only should see no end to their army service. This was the Labour Government's fault. Secondly, we did actually receive a reinforcement of about 50 men from England whilst we were at Muar and I am sure that this draft included one, or perhaps more, Communist agitators. After the arrival of this draft mysterious meetings occurred in the canteen. Lights would go out and remarks, such as "Are you with us?" shouted out. Thus in the dark no-one could be identified."

Private Alfred Draper ('C' Company)

"There were 5 hotheads in the battalion and they started stirring up trouble. Finally one morning when I came off guard everybody was on strike. I was asked if I was joining, luckily I said no."

Company Quartermaster Sergeant Ray "Geordie" Walker (HQ Company)

"May 14th 1946 was a day never to be forgotten: it was the day when the Battalion commenced its long march into oblivion. The day begun with reveille and after which the men refused to parade for PT. Instead they wore their day clothes and sat on the seawall. All orders from sergeant-majors and officers were met by a stony silence. This lasted for some time until a deluge of rain forced the men to run and seek shelter in the canteen. Here they barricaded doors and awaited the arrival of Colonel Leyland. Despite his orders to return to duty the men refused.

"Breakfast and mid-day meal was forfeited and then at 1500 hours they had an unexpected visit from Major-General Arkwright. He read them the riot act and that they had 2 options. Open or close arrest."

Major DE Rendell OC 'A' Company noticed that not many men were in his company area and then CSM O'Brien reported that only 2 men had turned up to draw rifles Major Rendell then went to the canteen to where the men were now sheltering and spoke to them about their actions.

Private Dave Beedham ('B' Company)

"After our weeks leave I came back to the battalion to find a lot the privates had been taken away. Apparently one night in the canteen someone put the light out and a spokesperson got the men to go on strike over the conditions. They had objected to the new discipline of blancoing equipment. I to this day still don't know who the ringleader was, but my opinion for what it is worth is I don't think it was anybody from the original 13th.

"I just cannot see the men who had endured the streets of Bure objecting to a bit of blancoing. I myself know what was the easiest to do."

Lance Corporal L Edwards ('C' Company Clerk)

"I looked out from the window of the Company HQ and saw a mob of private soldiers gathered on the sea front. Our CSM, a Devon man, spoke to them, then an officer or two and they ascertained that they would not parade. They gave no reason for their behaviour at all. No NCO's were among them or any long serving privates especially those whose demobilisation was near. Leyland quickly took action; we entered all the tents and gathered up the rifles. Armed guards were put on all the cookhouses and food only given to the people not involved.

"A battalion of the Devonshire Regiments arrived. We NCO's had been ordered to forma cordon around the mob, which we did. The Devons then formed a cordon behind us. We then withdrew to our Company HQ's. The mob was then shepherded into waiting 3-tonners and driven away."

Report by Brigadier Darling to Field Martial Montgomery (24ᵗʰ May 1946)

Men involved

a) The bulk of the men involved (80% or more) are between the ages of 18 and 21 years, of these 45% are men who have seen no active service whatsoever. If these men who joined this Bn during the fighting in Germany, when all was over bar the shouting, are added, this becomes nearer 60%.

b) In the above numbers are included 47 out of 50 men of a draft, ex UK, which have been under one week with the Bn. I interviewed one of the 3 men not involved who spoke in a very straight forward manner. He stated that he did not join the mutiny because he thought it was extremely foolish. He said that the men of his draft had been involved in a mutiny at the ASC ITC, which took the form of a "go slow" movement as a protest against doing drill. He also stated that the draft had been involved in a scene at Kalyan Transit Camp, in which the men on parade addressed officers and NCO's in an insubordinate manner.

Opinions of NCO's and men NOT involved in the mutiny

a) Whilst inspecting the Bn area I spoke to a large number of these men. I was very much struck by the men's disgust with the whole affair.

b) Although it hardly seems credible, from what NCO's said, that not many had any inkling of the outlay. In fact it appears that the mutineers deliberately refused to allow the NCO's to gain any knowledge of it.

c) Some NCO's had heard chance remarks in the meal queue or in the canteen about a 'strike'.

Grievances

a) The feeling was that with the end of the war men were now serving as civilians in uniform.

b) They did not regard it as a mutiny but a 'strike'.

c) They did not agree with the training due to the end of the war.

d) There were too many charges for minor breaches of discipline and that the RSM was unreasonable. I examined the punishment books and do NOT consider that the number was excessive. The RSM had been in the Bn for some time, but had only held the position for 2 months. I have complete confidence in him.

e) The men complained about the lack of games. I am satisfied that the allotment of grounds was fully used.

f) It was felt that the accommodation was bad, particularly the sleeping tents which as a result of 3 night's rain combined with high tides, were under water. It was felt unreasonable to expect a high standard of turnout and unnecessary to blanco equipment. I dare say that it must be very irksome for some men to wake up and find their equipment soaked, particularly as this Bn has always had an outstanding standard of turnout.

g) Objection was taken to the order that NCO's should NOT walk out with the men and to its enforcement by the RSM.

Conclusions

I have complete confidence in Lt-Col Leyland, who is well known to the men. In my opinion, the officers holding the key positions of QM, MO and Padre, all are very close to the men, are outstanding. Furthermore, when I last saw the Bn nearly 3 weeks before the mutiny, they were in the best possible shape and heart.

A large number of men merely followed the crowd without reason, other than they felt loyal to their "mates" and would be victimised if they did not mutiny. There are many instances of batmen, clerks etc who joined without knowing what it was about. There are some cases of being intimidated to join the mutiny. These men, because of these employments, could not possibly have had the grievances stated above.

Signed:

Brigadier K.T. Darling

Lance Corporal L Edwards ('C' Company Clerk)

"This was a disgraceful episode and I have always been reluctant to admit I was in the 13th Battalion because of this. I have never understood why those idiots allowed themselves to be fooled into taking this action, nor what they expected to achieve by it.

"About 6 of us were posted to Kluang. It was where the mutineers of the 13th Battalion were being held. We were to do administration for the Provost Company who was guarding them. They were held in a tented enclosure, it had been used for holding Japanese war criminals, some of which were still held in screened enclosures. At least one Japanese Warrant Officer of the notorious secret police [Kempeitai] hanged himself whilst I was there by winding barbed wire around his neck and leaning forward until he died.

"The main camp was on one side of a concrete airstrip and our little camp was on the other. At the far end of the strip was a collection of derelict Japanese aircraft and a camp of Japanese Air Force personnel waiting repatriation. The whole area was surrounded by jungle covered hills.

"In command was an officer of the 42nd Highlanders, Lieutenant Hewett, who wore a gold rimmed monocle."

Private Dave Beedham ('B' Company)

"They had been taken to an old Jap airstrip and put under close arrest accused of mutiny. No NCO's were involved and I was sent there to assist in the cookhouse. The guards at the camp were from a Sikh Regiment and commanded by an officer wearing a Black Watch uniform, kilt and all.

"He was a bit of a character, born in India of British parents and he roamed around with 2 US .45 Colts around his waist. Sometimes at night he would get two searchlights, one at each end of the runway and make the men run in between the beams, now and again firing his guns in the air.

"The men slept in bell tents and paraded each day to the hangar for the court martial. Each man had his own large number [a crimson armband with a number in white canvas stitched on]."

Private Pat Schofield

"Actually, I didn't wear it for long, when the Judge-Advocate saw them on our arms he was livid and bellowed "Take them off these men. They are not war criminals." It was a nice gesture, but he was wrong in one sense. We were treated worse than war criminals.

"Like most soldiers we had put up with practically anything when it was necessary. But when we moved into the camp in Malaya, we were told that it was a rest camp. That was really a sick joke.

"Apart from the monsoon rains, the sea kept coming over the harbour wall to flood us out even more. In those conditions how could we possibly turn out on parade spick and span? Mutiny is a very serious offence, but as far as we were concerned we never mutinied, we went on strike. That cut no ice with anybody.

"I was sentenced to 5 years hard labour. Our action wasn't a careless, thoughtless gesture. We decided after a lot of heart-searching. For instance, I had formally complained about the conditions, but ended up being placed on a charge.

"We were rounded up at bayonet point by British soldiers and handcuffed. I was one who was put into what was called an atrocity house – a place where several nurses had been butchered by the Japs. Even our letters were stopped.

"Outside we could see the Japs strutting around quite cockily and with no kind of restraint. We didn't even have any soap or water, when we did it was slipped to us by Indian troops.

"None of us ever imagined the sentences would be so harsh. I almost wept when I saw men rip off their medal ribbons and throw them away in disgust.

"I was put into the Royal West Kents. It was rather amusing really, because I was asked to stay as a regular soldier. I remember being inspected sometime later by Field Martial Montgomery. He stopped and asked me where I had come from, I said the 13th Paratroop Battalion and I was still very proud of what we had done in action, even if I wasn't proud of the 'strike'. But Monty could not forget. He turned and walked away."

Two more names were added to the Battalion Roll of Honour. 12th May 1946 saw the death of 'B' Company's Lieutenant Robert Warren; he was killed in a road accident after only just joining the Battalion prior to sailing for India. He is buried in the Kuala Lumpur War Cemetery.

On the 19th June 1946 Major Maurice Seal OC 'B' Company died in Singapore Hospital. After first becoming ill in Semarang, with anaemia which Captain Tibbs thought might be caused by a duodenal ulcer but, on referring him to the hospital there, it was eventually diagnosed as leukaemia. He was sent back to Singapore where he died.

Captain Ellis "Dixie" Dean ('B' Company)

"Major Maurice Seal was an outstanding officer and I am certain the Company would've followed him anywhere. He joined us after Normandy, and following the heavy casualties in Bure he became 2i/c 'B' Company and dropped over the Rhine. For the deployment to India he became OC of the company and I became his second-in-command. From then on I realised what a sound knowledge he had of tactics and man-management.

"When the Company arrived in Java he was left behind in Singapore – he had been admitted to hospital, and I assumed command of the Company. He did return for a short while – about a fortnight, before being flown back to hospital in Singapore.

"Whilst in Malaya in early May, I learned that he was still in hospital several hours drive away. As soon as possible I drove down to see him and was shocked – he was heavily sedated and hardly able to speak. Within weeks I was attending his funeral at Kranji War Cemetery. Why he was not invalided home to his family has me lost for words."

"It is very sad to think of all the good chaps being dispersed because of the senseless behaviour of an irresponsible and gutless few."

Lieutenant-Colonel Peter Luard, DSO.

31.   THE TRIAL

Some of the accused 13 Para men are marched to the trial (courtesy Harry Thomas).

Captain J. F. Reilly was the Officer chosen to defend the troops for the trial and he explained the troop's grievances. 13th May 1946 in Muar, living under canvas, the main body were waiting patiently to return home to Blighty and their families.

In the Muar camp the mud had been at times ankle deep and the men were never dry. There were no washing facilities, save 4 taps and one of those was for the sergeants. The men had to eat next to drains and the food was described as atrocious. But the demands to turn out on parade every morning were still there. Every piece of clothing and equipment had to be blancoed and all brasses and boots had to be polished. Anyone not up to standard was immediately placed on a charge.

The evening before the 'mutiny' a meeting was called and the lights turned out in the canteen so that the instigators could hide their identities. "We're going out tomorrow. Are you with me?"

5 men did not attend the trial. 4 were in hospital for various ailments, but the fifth was "Flash" Walker, who was mysteriously removed from the detention camp the night before the trial. It is rumoured that the voice heard in the canteen when the lights were turned out belonged to "Flash".

When asked why Walker was not in court, the Judge Advocate replied that he had not been charged so he was rightfully not in court. It was never explained further and Private Walker was never seen in the Battalion again. Further rumours alleged that he was a member of the Communist Party and had been taken by Special Branch for interrogation.

They were kept under armed guard and rationed to 7 cigarettes a day whilst the Japanese POW's could roam unguarded and were allowed to smoke as often as they wanted. Several men broke out after a long period and obtained food from a nearby town. They were caught, handcuffed and returned at bayonet point to the court martial.

Lieutenant-Colonel Roy Leyland was asked weather he had been informed about any complaints and what action he had taken. He answered that, 4 days before the 'strike' he had written to the Divisional HQ about the camp conditions.

Lieutenant-Colonel Roy Leyland (CO, 13th Para Bn)

[Letter to HQ] "Although British and Ghurkha troops have been in occupation of the camp since September, it is in disgraceful condition. There are no ablutions of any sort, other than a few taps. The one improvised cookhouse is totally inadequate, being a dilapidated outhouse without sidewalls and with a leaky roof. There are no facilities for storing food."

Unsavoury evidence began to come out, including Company Commander, Major Masterton admitting that he published an order which listed the names of men that refused to contribute for a watch that was given to Colonel Luard as a farewell gift. The notice stated 'I append below the list of names of men who have refused to donate. I know the feelings of the rest of the company towards these men and to prevent disclosures of their disloyalty, the donations which the men would usually give will be found from other sources.'

Men spoke of how they were interrogated by the SIB and some spoke of how they were told that they could get between 3 to 10 years and some could even be shot.

Company Quartermaster Sergeant Ray "Geordie" Walker (HQ Company)

"The Daily Express reported on 21st August that CSM E. O'Brien who gave evidence was in Malacca Hospital after having been found injured and was unable to give further evidence. As his injury was a fractured skull he could no longer participate in the trial. Perhaps an 'old score' had been settled by an unknown assailant? I felt sad because I had fought alongside him from Normandy to the Baltic with him in 'A' Company."

Ernest O'Brien had been a veteran of Dunkirk, Normandy, The Ardennes and Germany. After recovering from the injuries, he became RSM of the 13th Battalion taking over from Railton. He then continued his Army career with the Manchester Regiment when the 13th was disbanded.

Private Dave Beedham ('B' Company)

"It was said that some men tried to get out of the camp and these were manacled to the centre tent pole by their ankle. The defending officer said that there were too many irregularities in the camp. It was said that some men were bribed by a certain Special Investigation Branch officer, that if they told who was the man that had stood up in the canteen, they would be given an immediate demob and 3 months leave."

Captain J. F. Reilly (Officer Defending)

[Summarising his defence] "Field Martial Montgomery has said the British soldier is a reasonable man and if he is told the necessity for any deprivations he will willingly and readily put up with them.

"This is an occasion on which the court can well afford to be generous in the knowledge that any generosity shown to these men will pay large dividends. The court can by its generosity in limiting the severity of the sentences, perhaps by recommending mercy, ensure that 255 well trained, hand picked men can return to the service of the King, allegiance to whom they have for one moment denied."

Only 12 of the 255 men were found to be not guilty, 8 were sentenced to 5 years hard labour and the remaining 235 received 3 years hard labour. They all lost their coveted 'wings'. Many people of Britain could not quite understand why 486 years of hard labour had been sentenced on 243 paratroopers. Only a few years previously the unit had fought gallantly across Europe and help free the world of the Nazis. Led by the press, the people wanted an answer.

Millions of signatures began to appear on petitions and the press kept up the story until the politicians had to do something about the affair.

Unaware of the support back home in England the paras were held in Kluang prison camp. Newspapers such as the Mirror, The Star and the London Evening Standard led the support, 100 back benchers supported the paratroops, every town and football match held a petition. The government was eventually forced into reviewing the case to determine why the soldiers would take such actions; someone or something must have made them do it.

Mr Garry Allighan (House of Commons)

"Mr. Speaker, I have here two Petitions, one signed by nearly 10,000 residents in Gravesend in respect of two men of Gravesend, and one signed by 1,614 people, being the total population of the village of Cuxton, in respect of one Cuxton man in the Paratroop corps, protesting against the sentences and humbly petitioning a revision and reduction in the sentences. I beg to present the Petitions."

Mr Frederick Lee (House of Commons)

"I beg the House to receive a Petition signed by 35,000 people. The Petition asks for sympathetic reconsideration of the sentences passed on 243 British paratroops now held in Malaya."

Mr Francis Bowles (House of Commons)

"I beg leave to present a Petition on behalf of nearly 8,000 of my constituents in reference to the sentence on Private Stafford and other Paratroop prisoners sentenced recently."

Mr Ernest Davies (House of Commons)

"I beg leave to present a Petition on behalf of 2,500 residents of Enfield who humbly pray that the sentences on the 243 Paratroopers, now held in Malaya, be remitted."

Mr Ivor Owen Thomas (House of Commons)

"I beg leave to present a Petition signed by 2,032 people in my constituency protesting against the sentences passed by court martial on the 243 men of the 13th Parachute Battalion, South East Asia Command, in Malaya, including Private E. Poulter (pictured), of Hadley, Shropshire, and requesting that the sentences be quashed."

Mr Victor Yates (House of Commons debate, 8th October 1946)

"To ask the Secretary of State For War if he is aware that in the case of the 243 Paratroopers in Malaya recently court-martialled, some have complained that whilst walking in 4" of mud working conditions have become unbearable, while one soldier has complained, particulars of which have been sent to him, that he was only able to have one bath in 11 months; and if he will review the sentences in the light of these complaints and report to this House upon the steps he proposes to take to prevent a repetition of such working conditions being imposed upon any section of His Majesty's Forces."

Mr Frederick Bellenger (The Secretary of State of War, 8th Oct 1946)

"The trial commenced on 12th August and was completed on 19th September. Of the 258 men charged 3 were acquitted and all the remainder were convicted. Of these, 8 were sentenced to 5 years' penal servitude and to be discharged with ignominy. The General to 3 years penal servitude and to be discharged with ignominy. The General Officer Commanding-in-Chief as Confirming Officer did not confirm the proceedings in the case of 12 accused who were accordingly released, and in the remaining 243 cases commuted all the sentences to 2 years imprisonment with hard labour and to be discharged with ignominy.

"There can be no shadow of doubt that these men were rightly charged with mutiny. The law regards mutiny as a most serious military offence and provides death as the maximum penalty. Mutiny may be described as the act of two or more soldiers who join together, whether actively or passively, in resistance to, or disobedience of, lawful authority. The obedience of lawful orders is vital in any fighting Service, and it is obvious that in the Armed Forces any form of resistance to lawful authority, whether active or passive, cannot and will not be tolerated. I am waiting the advice of the Judge Advocate-General on the legality of the proceedings and I will make a further statement when I have received it. The proceedings of the trial arrived in this country only a week ago and it has not yet been possible, owing to their great length, to complete a full review."

Two days later Mr Bellenger received the advice of the Judge Advocate-General and once again addressed the House of Commons.

Mr Frederick Bellenger (Bassetlaw)

"The advice I have received from the Judge Advocate-General with regard to this particular trial is that there was a number of irregularities of a substantial nature which may well have prejudiced the accused individually. These irregularities in his opinion rendered the trial as a whole so unsatisfactory that the convictions ought not to be allowed to stand. In the circumstances I feel bound to quash all the convictions on the charge of mutiny, and to relieve each of the accused of the consequences of his trial. Orders to this effect and for their release from imprisonment are being issued forthwith.

"I would like to stress that I have followed this course of action entirely on legal grounds, and I am still satisfied that there was sufficient prima facie evidence to justify a charge of mutiny being preferred. Although it will be a matter for relief in many quarters that the men who were convicted should be relieved from the consequences of their trial, I must emphasise that there are proper means of representing grievances in the Army which must be followed if discipline is to be maintained.

"Finally, I think the House will agree with me when I say that this case is an outstanding example of the way in which the processes of military law can operate quickly to safeguard the interests of justice."

Mr Winston Churchill (Woodford)

"Can the right honourable gentleman explain how it was that the Judge Advocate-General was not consulted and made acquainted with this procedure at an earlier period? The mutiny or what is called a mutiny, although it seemed a very mild form of mutiny compared with some we have seen in our own time, occurred in May. All June passed. Am I not right in presuming that in June convening orders were given, or the question of bringing these men to trial, either individually or collectively, was discussed? Was not the Judge Advocate-General consulted at that time? What happened in June? What happened in July, when this matter was going on? What happened in August, when these men were still confined under the severe conditions of a tropical land? Why is it only now, when a great storm has been raised in the Press and Parliament, that the Judge Advocate-General is suddenly consulted, and the right honourable Gentleman has to defer to his legal opinion and say that the whole procedure from beginning to end is quashed for the ringleaders as well as the rank and file—all their trials are quashed? How is it that for 5 long months the Government, with the advice of the Judge Advocate-General always available at their disposal, have permitted this matter to drag itself out to the general suffering of individuals and the impairment of discipline in the Army?"

Mr Frederick Bellenger (Bassetlaw)

"The right honourable gentleman himself has held the office which I now hold, and he is very well acquainted with the machinery of courts-martial procedure. He will know that even in an individual case there has to be a considerable time in taking a summary of evidence before the accused can be brought to trial. In this case there were 258 men and more—cases in which individual investigations had to be made and their defending officer instructed. I do not think, looking back, that any delay was made in bringing these men to trial. The mutiny occurred on 14th May, and the trial commenced on 12th August. In the circumstances, I think, with the large numbers of accused, that that was not an unreasonable delay. In regard to the Judge Advocate-General, his deputy was there in Malaya, and he had full powers to advise the Commander-in-Chief and also the court. In view of the position of the Judge Advocate-General as the final reviewing authority on matters of law, I think that it would have been very improper if he had interfered at any stage in the proceedings."

Mr Winston Churchill (Woodford)

"Are we to understand then that the then Secretary of State for War was officially apprised of the fact that action was to be taken against 258 men on a charge of mutiny—a collective trial as it were—and he never had any idea of asking "Is this legal? What precedents are there for this?" Are we to understand that he never asked the Judge Advocate-General, "Is this all right? Is this a legal and proper way of doing it? and that no member of the Government or of the Army Council promoted inquiries of that kind?"

Mr Reginald Manningham-Buller (Daventry)

"Could we not be given some indication of what these irregularities were, so that the House may be fully acquainted of the grounds on which the right honourable Gentleman has come to his decision? Further, is it not the case that the official to whom the right hon. Gentleman referred in his statement serves under the Judge Advocate-General in this country?"

Mr Frederick Bellenger (Bassetlaw)

"I am not quite sure as to the precise implication of the latter part of the honourable and learned Gentleman's supplementary question. With regard to the reasons for the Judge Advocate-General's advice to me, I am not prepared to offer them to the House in detail. I am satisfied that the statement I have made this afternoon, that the Judge Advocate-General considered that there were a number of irregularities of a substantial nature, which may well have prejudiced the accused individually, gives sufficient indication of the grounds on which he has based his advice."

Mr. H. D. Hughes

"Will my right honourable friend assure the House that adequate inquiries will be made, and disciplinary action taken, if necessary, in regard to those responsible for the conditions in the camp, and responsible for the irregularities in the procedure which have caused so much suffering to so many people?"

Mr Frederick Bellenger (Bassetlaw)

"The House will understand that these irregularities are not only military irregularities. Now and again they occur in civil proceedings. Two courts of inquiry have already been held into the conditions in this camp, and, already, certain action has been taken against those who we think were mainly responsible for not rectifying those conditions."

Mr Winston Churchill (Woodford)

"Is there any reason why the irregularities which the Judge Advocate-General has now considered were such as to vitiate the trial should not be stated? I do not mean at this moment, but why should they not be made public? Surely it would be of great advantage to the future to know what are the principles on which we are proceeding. Since when has it been held to be disadvantageous to the cause of justice for the principles on which judicial authorities give their decisions to be made known? If that is not so, how are others to regulate their conduct? Was the question of the mass trial one of the causes of the irregularity? In any case, will not a full statement be made of the legal grounds which have led to the quashing of these sentences?"

Mr Frederick Bellenger (Bassetlaw)

"I am prepared to consider whether it would be possible to give a more extensive explanation of the reasons which the Judge Advocate-General has given to me and which led him to believe that these convictions could not stand."

Mr Winston Churchill (Woodford)

"That, I am sure, would be advantageous from every point of view. The quashing of a trial is a very serious matter. People ought to know why."

Sir Arthur Harvey (Macclesfield)

"Will the right honourable gentleman give an indication as to what the future of these men is to be? Are they to be given a chance to serve in another command, and not in the present command?"

Mr Frederick Bellenger (Bassetlaw)

"Would hope that the future of these men is the future of all good soldiers—that they will be good soldiers and serve their time in the Army and come out with an honourable discharge."

Many Ministers still wished to know full particulars of the irregularities which invalidated the proceedings of the court-martial and on 15th October 1946 the Secretary of the State of War gave the answer.

Mr Frederick Bellenger (Bassetlaw)

"There is nothing irregular in the holding of a joint trial as such, in the case of mutiny or any other offence the essence of which is combination between the accused. In a case of mutiny it would generally be convenient for a joint trial to be held, but where the number of accused is very large and where several incidents are involved it must be ensured that injustice does not result from such mass trial. Great care has necessarily to be taken that the trial is so conducted as properly to safeguard the interests of individual accused both as to the manner in which evidence is given and as to the guidance afforded to the court on the extent to which the evidence of one accused may be taken to incriminate or exculpate co-accused.

"It was in the following respects that serious irregularities occurred in the course of the trial in Malaya:

"In the first place, evidence in the majority of cases was allowed to be taken from spokesmen of groups, a method not in accordance with the Rules of Evidence.

"Secondly, the Judge Advocate acting at the trial misdirected the court in law as to the bearing of the evidence in its application to each individual case.

"Thirdly, he failed to deal with the case of each accused individually on its own facts.

"In short, the evidence was neither elicited nor applied in such a way as to establish either the guilt of those who were really guilty or the innocence of all those who were really innocent. There was thus no assurance that justice had been done, and in view of the legal opinion I had received that the convictions ought not to be allowed to stand, I felt it my duty to quash the proceedings."

Each of the freed paras received £10 back pay and in November they sailed home. There was a collection for the defence team and this time everyone contributed. Several watches engraved with 'Remember Kluang' were given out.

Company Quartermaster Sergeant Ray "Geordie" Walker (HQ Company)

"During the trial that lasted months we moved on to the Middle East. 23rd October saw us embark on a troopship and we set sail. We arrived at Port Said on 6th November. Our new home was Camp 12 and the next morning I enjoyed a cup of tea served by a German POW working in the cookhouse before assembling on the Parade Square. The CO informed us that the 6th Airborne Division in Palestine had its full compliment of men, therefore 13th Para were "surplus to requirements" and we would be posted to Infantry Regiments.

"From now on we had to bear the scars of being branded 'mutineers' although completely innocent."

"Everyday men departed for foreign parts and within 8 days of arriving in Egypt, 13th Para ceased to exist, on 14th November 1946. in all probability Peter Collins, Orderly Room Sergeant and I were the last to leave Camp 12; that was a date I shall never forget. I still have my 3rd class rail ticket No.00268 from Kassassino to El Hallah. Eventually a truck arrived and took me to my new unit the 2nd Bn East Yorkshire Regiment."

Private Dave Beedham ('B' Company)

"The Battalion was split up and the men went in two's and three's to various other regiments, but not Parachute Regiments. Even though I was not involved in the mutiny I was also posted to another regiment and I never did settle down in it.

"After all these years I still feel very bitter about what happened and I still think in my own opinion the new people that joined us were to blame for what happened. I still remember the 13th Battalion for what we did all through Europe and remember with great affection Colonel Luard and many good men who are not with us now."

Pat Caveney had joined the Lancashire Parachute Battalion in February 1945 and jumped over the Rhine a month later. He quickly rose through the ranks and by the time of the mutiny he was a Sergeant and so did not take part in the escapade. But he too was a victim and ended up back with his parent unit, the Highland Light Infantry. He tried unsuccessfully to rejoin the Airborne Forces, disgusted he wrote to Lt-Col Luard hoping his good word would aid his cause.

Letter from Lt-Col P.J. Luard DSO, OBE

9th December, 1946

Dear Caveney,

I have your letter of the 13th November and am so sorry to hear that you are no longer in the regiment.

I find that there is little that I can do directly. If, however, you apply officially through your Commanding Officer, to go back to the Parachute Regiment you can certainly use my name as being very pleased to have you back under my command, and also as a recommendation for your service in the Regiment.

It is very sad to think of all the good chaps being dispersed because of the senseless behaviour of an irresponsible and gutless few.

With every good wish and for good luck in your effort to return.

Yours

P.J. Luard

Lieutenant-Colonel Luard, who led the 13th (Lancashire) Parachute Battalion during their preparations for the second front and on the airborne assault on D-Day. Then he stood firm with his men through the constant bombardments in Ranville, the first French settlement to be liberated, and during the mosquito infested woods of Le Bois de Bavent. The man who saw first hand as his troops fell storming the heights at Putot-en-Auge and again during the street fighting in the inferno called Pont L'Évêque. He endured the cold and shared darkest days of the Battalions history in Bure, before jumping over the Rhine and marching across Germany. He had sent his men to receive the surrender of Denmark and then planned for the defeat of the Japanese in the Far East. In his letter he clearly shows his disgust of the men who tarnished his once proud unit.

I have decided myself, that I will not pass judgement either way on this very two-sided affair. I have merely put together pieces of evidence that try to portray what happened to this very proud and gallant battalion.

It must be remembered that the men in the 13th Parachute Battalion during 1946 was not a true reflection of those who had served in orchards of Normandy, froze and died in the Ardennes and marched across Germany. There had been mass reinforcing due to constant demobilisation. Most of those that had remained had been promoted and were therefore not involved.

There was to be one final entry in the Battalion Roll of Honour, that of Private Thomas Martin. His date of death is 16th February 1947 and given that the 13th Parachute Battalion was disbanded 3 months previous, I am still puzzled by this one. His service number is 14991470, which would indicate he was a late reinforcement, most probably after the war in Europe. He is buried in Bentley-with-Arksey Cemetery and I can only surmise that he died due to illness and was returned home…

ROLL OF HONOUR – THE FAR EAST

Lieut	WARREN Robert	20	12/05/1946	335192	Kuala Lumpur 877
Maj	SEAL Maurice T.F.		19/06/1946	164935	Kranji 27-B-18
Pte	MARTIN Thomas R.	23	16/02/1947	14991470	Bentley-with-Arksey Cemetery

Ex 13th Battalion and World Champion wrestler George Condliffe, AKA "Count Bartelli" visits Major Seal's grave in Kranji Cemetery.

K.G. Davison Photo Collection of Far East

32.   RE-FORMATION

In 1947 when the Territorial Army was being restructured, a new 13th (Lancashire) Parachute Battalion (TA) was formed and the 13th Para Bn (TA) became part of the 44th Independent Parachute Brigade Group (TA) alongside the 10th (City of London) Parachute Battalion, 12th (Yorkshire) Parachute Battalion, 15th (Scottish) Parachute Battalion and the 17th (Durham Light Infantry) Parachute Battalion.

The new 13 Para Commanding Officer was Lieutenant-Colonel D.R. Hunter, MC from 1947 until 1952. Taking over from Hunter was Lt-Col Cleasby-Thompson, MBE, MC of 1st Airborne Division fame. He took part in the first major demonstration of British Airborne Forces, capturing Crown Prince Olaf's car in 1940. He fought with the BEF in France, across North Africa, Italy and Sicily, eventually becoming Commander 1st AB Div when Alistair Pearson was ill.

During Cleasby-Thompson's spell, 13 Para (TA) received their colours. Presented by Field Marshal Montgomery in October 1953, the 13th (Lancashire) Battalion The Parachute Regiment received their colours outside St George's Hall in Liverpool (below, IWM, Duxford).

Lieutenant-Colonel Richard Crawshaw (later Lord of Aintree), OBE was the unit's final Commander, taking charge between 1954 and 1956.

Due to defence cuts in October 1956, the 13th Battalion was reunited and combined with their old companions from the 5th Parachute Brigade – the 12th Battalion, to form 12/13 Para (TA).

596

For 10 years they remained 12/13 Para (TA) until becoming the 4th Battalion in 1967, after the 12/13 Battalion was merged with the 17th Battalion. The 4th Battalion The Parachute Regiment still exists to this date and still has ties in Lancashire (below, the 13th TA after receiving their colours IWM Duxford).

By the time the 13th (Lancashire) Parachute Battalion had disbanded, 219 Officers and Men had given their lives for World freedom.

**They shall grow not old, as we that are left grow old:
Age shall not weary them, nor the years contemn.
At the going down of the sun and in the morning
We will remember them.**

Laurence Binyon, 1914

Not forgetting the 1000 – 2000 that was left with the scars – both mentally and physically...

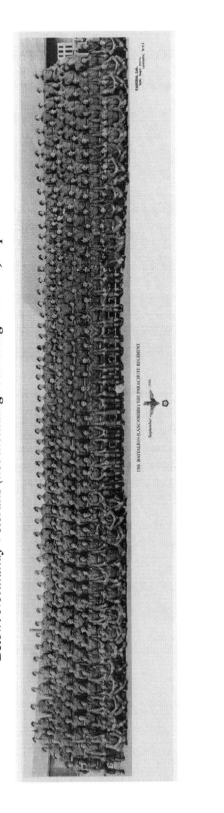

Above: 13th (Lancashire) Parachute Battalion at Larkhill Barracks in December 1943.
Below: Normandy Veterans (not including recovering wounded) September 1944.

No.1 Platoon 'A' Company 13th Parachute Battalion, October 1943 Salisbury Cathedral.

Back: Cpl Greaves, Unknown, Unknown, Unknown, Unknown, Unknown, L/Cpl Thomas Thresher, Unknown, Sgt Russell, Unknown, L/Cpl Birchall.
Unknown, Pte Tarry, Unknown, Pte Alan Gregory, Unknown, Unknown, Unknown, Pte Anselm Snelham, Unknown, Unknown, Pte Bernard D'Oyly.
Front: Unknown, Sgt Ernest O'Brien, Sgt Frank Chadwick, Lieutenant Gordon Harry O'Brien-Hitching, Sgt William Greendale, Sgt McGrath, Cpl Stan Braddock

No.2 Platoon 'A' Company 13th Parachute Battalion, October 1943 Salisbury Cathedral.

Back row: Sgt S Alder, Ptes C Darby and R Batten, L/Cpl R W Jones, Ptes C Sweeney, J Leggett, E Sawers and F Beach, Cpl G H Tomlin, Pte C Darby and Sgt E Chadwick.
Middle row: Privates J Bayley, N Ritchie, R Walker, E Sell, J D Morris, Solley and H Partington, L/Cpl R G Sutton, Corporal Quirk and Private A Forrester.
Front row: Privates F Duggan, W Poulter and K Evans, Sergeant F A Bradley, Lieutenant W F Hodgson, Sergeant Llewellyn, Private E V Smith and Corporal H Williams.

No.3 Platoon 'A' Company 13th Parachute Battalion, October 1943 Salisbury Cathedral.

No.4 Platoon 'B' Company 13th Parachute Battalion, October 1943 Salisbury Cathedral.

Privates C Glover, E Jones, D Kenny, Parlby, S McConnell, H Annal, P Maynard, J Gustafson, T Hogan, T Darbyshire, A Brown, G Irwin and J Aspinall. L/Cpl S Ware, Corporals D Shales and J Haydock, Sergeants Tickell, T Hindle, G Read and T Atkinson, Corporal A Cross, L/Cpl A Lyons and Private T Holt. Privates B Davis, A Burn, T Harries and S Westhead, Lieutenant B S Arnold, Privates V Lightfoot, F Boulger, W Hankin and G Dingley.

No.6 Platoon 'B' Company 13th Parachute Battalion, October 1943 Salisbury Cathedral.

No.8 Platoon 'C' Company 13th Parachute Battalion, October 1943 Salisbury Cathedral

Back: C/Sgt Dougdale, Ptes C Kingett, J Liversedge, G Rhodes, L/Cpl T Walton, Ptes L Neale, J Turner, H Brown, J Kirkby, R Rhodes, W Clouston, A Blazard
Middle: Ptes E Davies, R Swindell, N Prince, J Thomas, Cpl C Dunbar, Ptes W Dickenson, G Ewen, S Adcotts, A Orrel, J Gregory, Cpl Ingram (standing)
Front: Ptes T Docherty, Pte Harrigan, M Frodsham, Sgt W C Collier, Lt J B Sharples, Sgt E Walsh, Ptes A Hamnett, R Wilkinson, G Moyers

Officers of the 13th Parachute Battalion, September 1944.

Back: Lts Alf Lagergren, Dick Burton, Geoff Otway, Unknown, Dixie Dean, Major Nobby Clarke, Lt-Col Peter Luard, Capt Claude Milman, Majors John Cramphorn, Gerald Ford, and Bill Grantham.

Front: Padre Whitfield Foy, Lts Joe Hodgson, Ken Walton (kneeling above the rest), Capt Leslie Golding, Lts Malcolm Town, Harry Pollak, and Capt Jack Watson.

NCO's of the 13th Parachute Battalion, September 1944

Warrant Officer's and Sergeant's Mess, 13th Parachute Battalion, February 1945

(Note: not all are present as some men were on leave and others recovering from wounds obtained in the Ardennes)

Back: Unknown, Sgt Weaver, Unknown, Sgt Holland, Unknown, Sgt Edmundson, Clarke, Cahill, Farrell, Brimmicombe, Webb, Roberts, Pritchard, Unknown, and Badel.

Fourth: Sgt Unwin, Sullivan, Ferguson, Scott (RAMC), Stubbs, J Smith, Unknown, O'Brien, Copie, Hewitt, Snow, Muir, Webster, Innes, Unknown, Sgt Runacres, & Lewis.

Third: Sgts Braddock, Railton, Hobday, Brady, Eggleton, Boys, T Smith, Cox, Higgins, Hilton, Russell, and Neat.

Second row: Sgt Butler, Hornsby & O'Connor, C/Sgt Wrigley, S/Sgt Cookson, C/Sgt Watkins, Sgt Ford, C/Sgt Meechin, Sgt Jones, McPhail & Morris, T English.

Front row: Sgt Chadwick, CSM Batho MM, CSM Dugdale, RSM Duxbury, Lt-Col Luard, Capt Milman, CSM Moreland, CSMI Parrish, and CSM Lawley.

Group photo of 'A' Company, 13th Parachute Battalion Officers and NCO's, February 1945

Rear: Unknown, Sgt Cook, Sgt A F Badel, Unknown, Unknown, Sgt F Braddock, Unknown, Unknown, Sgt S Smith.
Front: Sgt S Farrell, C/Sgt H Watkins (CQMS), Lt E Barlow, Maj J B R Watson MC, WOII S Alder (CSM), Lt K W Brown, Sgt R Scott MM (RAMC).

Officers of the 13th Parachute Battalion February 1945

Signal Platoon 13th Parachute Battalion February 1945

Buckingham Palace 28th June 1945

Left to Right: Captain David Tibbs MC, Captain Reverend Whitfield Foy MC, Private Steve Harris MM, Sergeant Bernard Batho MM, Major Reeves Clark MC, Lieutenant Colonel Peter Luard DSO, Private Bert Roe MM, Major Jack Watson MC.

BIBLIOGRAPHY & RESEARCH

Interviews in person, by letter, telephone and email with veterans and eye witnesses

Veteran accounts

Imperial War Museum

Airborne Assault (IWM Duxford)

D-Day Museum, Portsmouth

www.pegasusarchive.org

www.ww2talk.com

National Archives, Kew

The Library of Congress, USA

Ohio University, USA

13th Parachute Battalion Newsletters

BOOKS

The Red Beret – Hilary Saunders
With the 6th Airborne Division in Normandy – Richard Gale
Pure Poett – Nigel Poett
The Day the Devils Dropped in – Neil Barber
The Pegasus and Orne Bridges – Neil Barber
The Last Drop – Steve Wright
Gale's Eyes – Carl Rymen
The D-Day Landings – Philip Warner
Deceivers Ever – Steven Sykes
The Story of the 23rd Hussars – 23rd Hussar Regiment
The Unknown Dead – Peter Schrijivers
Old Yourself One Day – Sir Peter Downward
GO TO IT! The Illustrated History of the 6th Airborne Division – Peter Harclerode
The War Illustrated

Made in the USA
Lexington, KY
08 March 2015